Horror Literature
A Reader's Guide

Garland Reference Library of the Humanities
(Vol. 1220)

Horror Literature

A Reader's Guide

EDITED BY Neil Barron

Garland Publishing, Inc.
NEW YORK & LONDON 1990

Library of Congress Cataloging-in-Publication Data

Horror literature : a reader's guide / edited by Neil Barron.
p. cm. — (Garland reference library of the humanities : vol. 1220)
ISBN 0-8240-4347-2 (alk. paper)
1. Horror tales—Bibliography. 2. Horror tales—History and criticism. I. Barron, Neil. 1934- . II. Series.
Z5917.H65H67 1990
[PN3435]
016.80883'8738—dc20 89-27454
CIP

Printed on acid-free, 250-year-life paper

MANUFACTURED IN THE UNITED STATES OF AMERICA

To Carolyn

On me your voice falls as they say
    love should
Like an enormous yes.

—PHILIP LARKIN

Contents

Preface

Neil Barron

Fantasy Literature: A Reader's Guide and its companion, *Horror Literature: A Reader's Guide*, provide the most comprehensive critical introductions to two literatures whose best works deserve far more critical attention than they have heretofore received. The popularity of fantasy's secondary worlds was stimulated by the publication of Tolkien's *Lord of the Rings* [F3-340], particularly the paperback reprints in the mid-1960s. Although individual works of horror fiction, such as *Dracula* [H3-386], have achieved widespread popularity, by far the most popular writer of horror fiction in history is Stephen King who, like Tolkien, has become somewhat of a cottage industry. They have spawned legions of imitators, but more importantly they have given greater legitimacy to two types of popular literature often scorned by literary critics who find anything popular automatically suspect.

These guides are companions to *Anatomy of Wonder: A Critical Guide to Science Fiction* (Bowker, 3rd ed., 1987), the standard in its field, and have a similar format. Like the science fiction guide, they are designed as collection development and evaluation and reader's advisory tools for librarians and as guides for any interested reader. Distinctions between popular literary genres are often artificial, and the distinctions between fantasy and horror are still more blurred, with some critics referring to horror as dark fantasy. One distinction suggested by some critics is in the type of emotion generated by the work: science fiction arouses interest, fantasy arouses wonder, horror fiction arouses fear, terror or revulsion. Many works blend elements: the film *Alien* is a good example. Because of the blurred distinctions between the two genres, there is some overlap in the coverage of these two guides. The chapters on the secondary literature ("Research Aids") are the same in both volumes except for those chapters devoted to history and criticism, to author studies and to films.

When it was judged necessary to split an author between the two guides, a generic cross-reference is used: [For other works of this author, see the companion guide to fantasy/horror.]. Approximately eighty authors appear in both volumes. Some authors could be placed equally well in either volume for reasons explained by Brian Stableford in his chapter 3 of the fantasy guide. The works of some authors are discussed in two chapters of the same guide. Consult the index or the adjacent chapter if you suspect this may be the case.

The scope of these guides is largely limited to prose works published in or translated into English. A small amount of poetry and some dramatic works were included. Readers interested in poetry may wish to consult the relatively comprehensive treatment in Steve Eng's "Supernatural Verse in English," a chapter in Tymn's *Horror Literature* [6-33].

The contributors were selected because of their expertise, briefly summarized in the notes on contributors. Outside readers also assisted in ensuring comprehensive coverage and balance in the selections. Preliminary lists of books to be annotated were circulated among contributors and later among the outside readers to ensure that no significant titles were overlooked. Although every attempt was made to limit choices to the best, better or historically or commercially important books, a strong element of personal judgment is unavoidable.

Each chapter provides a historical, analytical and critical introduction, followed by a critically annotated bibliography, in which many of the books mentioned briefly in the introduction are discussed more fully. The introductions collectively provide a relatively detailed history of fantasy and horror literature, although they are not meant as a substitute for the more comprehensive histories discussed in chapter 7. Coverage is through late 1988, with some editorial revisions added as late as summer 1989.

The bibliographies are usually arranged alphabetically by author of novel or collection, by author or editor of nonfiction works and by title of anthologies. In chapter 4, anthologies are listed separately, following novels and collections. Each annotation consists of these elements:

Entry number, assigned according to each chapter and used in the indexes and for cross-referencing within the text. Most cross-references refer to the same volume, but some refer to the companion volume. In the latter case the entry number is preceded by a letter: F3-340 refers to the fantasy volume, H3-340 to the horror volume.

Author. The most common form of an author's name is shown, with the less common portions in parentheses, e.g., James, M(ontague) R(hodes). In most cases the author's real name is used as the standard name. If the book was published under a pseudonym, this is indicated, e.g., King, Stephen (as by Richard Bachman), and cross-references are included in the author index.

Country of nationality of author or editor, if known and if other than the United States. Years of birth and death are shown when known.

Supplemental information. In order to make this guide as useful as possible to its various audiences, references to other sources of biocritical information on authors of novels and collections have been included. All sources except *Contemporary Authors* are annotated in chapter 6. The abbreviations in the list below follow the word "About:" on the line below the author's name. These supplemental sources include:

WW	Ashley, Mike. *Who's Who in Horror and Fantasy Fiction* [6-18]
GSF	Bleiler, E. F. *The Guide to Supernatural Fiction* [6-19]
SFW	Bleiler, E. F. *Supernatural Fiction Writers* [6-20]

F	Cawthorn, James, and Michael Moorcock. *Fantasy: The 100 Best Books* [6-21]
CA	*Contemporary Authors.* Gale Research [serial]
TCA	Cowart, David, and Thomas L. Wymer, eds. *Twentieth-Century American Science-Fiction Writers* [6-25]
FG	Frank, Frederick. *The First Gothics* [6-14]
NE	Gunn, James, ed. *The New Encyclopedia of Science Fiction* [6-26]
H	Jones, Stephen, and Kim Newman, eds. *Horror: 100 Best Books* [6-22]
SMFL	Magill, Frank N., ed. *Survey of Modern Fantasy Literature* [6-24]
SFE	Nicholls, Peter, gen. ed. *The Science Fiction Encyclopedia* [6-27]
MF	Pringle, David. *Modern Fantasy: The Hundred Best Novels* [6-23]
SFFL	Reginald, R. *Science Fiction and Fantasy Literature,* vol. 2 [6-3]
RG	Searles, Baird, et al. *A Reader's Guide to Fantasy* [6-29]
TCSF	Smith, Curtis C., ed. *Twentieth-Century Science-Fiction Writers* [6-30]
PE	Sullivan, Jack, ed. *The Penguin Encyclopedia of Horror and the Supernatural* [6-31]
ESF	Tuck, Donald H. *The Encyclopedia of Science Fiction and Fantasy through 1968* [6-4]
FL	Tymn, Marshall B., et al. *Fantasy Literature* [6-32]
HF	Waggoner, Diana. *The Hills of Faraway* [6-34]
FF	Winter, Douglas. *Faces of Fear* [H8-112]

Book-length works annotated in chapters 7 and 8 supplement these general reference sources, and they are indexed under the name of the subject. The reference works by Cowart, Gunn, Nicholls and Smith include many entries for writers of fantasy as well as science fiction. The entries emphasize the SF but do not usually exclude discussion of the fantasy fiction. *Contemporary Authors* is included because of its wide availability in all types of libraries, many of which will not own most of the more specialized reference works listed. A check of the cumulative index in the latest volume of CA will lead not only to entries in CA proper but also to other related Gale series, such as the *Dictionary of Literary Biography, Contemporary Literary Criticism,* etc.

Title. The title and subtitle, if any, are transcribed from the title page. Variant titles are common, especially for American and British editions, and these are usually listed, along with any note indicating significant differences in content.

Publisher. A shortened form of the publisher's name is used for most books, e.g., Knopf rather than Alfred A. Knopf. City of publication is included for books published in the nineteenth century and earlier and addresses are given for small specialty publishers for which such information is sometimes difficult to locate. See also the list of specialty publishers in chapter 5.

Translator. Every attempt was made to select the best books translated into English, and translators are credited when known. The original title and year of publication are also shown for translations.

Recommended editions. In most cases any complete edition of the text is satisfactory. Only the first edition is listed, relying on the bibliographies by Currey [6-2], Reginald [6-3], Bleiler [6-1] and Brown and Contento [6-6]. However, the collector should rely on detailed descriptive bibliographies such as Currey for the points necessary to identify true first editions. Specific editions are recommended when the text is more reliable, there is an introduction by the author or an editor or the text is annotated in some manner. Recommended editions are most common for books that have appeared in many editions, such as *Frankenstein* or *Dracula*.

Sequels; series. Many books, especially mass-market paperbacks of recent years, have been followed by sequels or been part of series. In most instances the first book in the series is used for the entry, with sequels or later books discussed in the body of the annotation. In other instances the individual books are annotated separately. Because readers are often interested in other books in a series, a relatively comprehensive list of series and sequels is included in chapter 13.

Collections. Short fiction is common in both fantasy and horror fiction, and some authors have distinguished themselves more at this length than in novels. The collections chosen contain the best or representative works of such authors, with other collections often discussed in the body of the annotations.

Annotations. The annotation in all cases is genuinely critical, assessing the book's merits and weaknesses. Although some plot summary is provided for novels and some collections to suggest what the book is "about," the emphasis throughout is on critical evaluation. Given the large number of books annotated and the need for terseness, we may occasionally somewhat alter or distort a book's central concept. We recognize that no work of art can be reduced to its paraphrasable content. Crucial plot elements or surprises are not revealed in the annotations. Significant awards are mentioned; see chapter 13 for a comprehensive list of awards. Many annotations conclude with a compare/contrast statement, in which the annotated book is linked to books having similar themes or structure.

First-purchase titles. Indicated by an asterisk preceding the entry number, these titles were selected on the basis of one or more of these characteristics: awards received (see chapter 13), influence of the work, outstanding or unique treatment of a theme, critical and/or popular acceptance, importance of the work in the author's total output, historical importance, especially for early works. Nonfiction works were judged by the usual criteria of scope, accuracy, currency, ease of use, critical acumen, balance and so on. Unstarred titles are those judged relatively less important, but include many works of distinction. Some books were selected as representative of their type; other, equally good works could have been selected. With few exceptions, all annotated books are recommended.

Young adult books. This is a marketing category for publishers and a useful category for librarians selecting books whose primary appeal is to teenage readers, although the precise age limits of YA books are hard to specify. Most YA books feature a teenage protagonist with whom the reader can identify, but in most other respects they are indistinguishable from nominally adult books. Many of the finest works of fantasy are nominally written for a younger audience, and any adult who overlooks such books will miss many riches. Horror fiction is much less common than fantasy for younger readers, perhaps because publishers or librarians feel that graphic horror is unsuitable for younger readers. As a matter of convenience, both fantasy and horror fiction are discussed in chapter 4B. The suggested age range in years is shown following all YA titles in chapter 4B. Contributors of other chapters were asked to identify those books they felt would have appeal to younger readers, and such books are cross-referenced in chapter 4B, which is included only in the fantasy guide.

In addition to the contributors who have shared their knowledge and enthusiasm, I wish to thank the following outside readers who have assisted in making this guide more reliable and useful: Sam Moskowitz, one of fantastic fiction's most prominent historians and a Pilgrim winner for 1981; Lloyd Currey, an antiquarian bookman specializing in fantastic literature (see chapter 5); Diana Waggoner, author of *The Hills of Faraway* [6-34]; David G. Hartwell, one of fantastic fiction's most knowledgeable editors and critics; R. Reginald, a catalog librarian and one of the field's principal bibliographers [6-3].

Thanks also to these people who assisted with specific topics: Milton Subotsky (film); Ruth N. Lynn (young adult fiction). Readers of these guides owe thanks to Garland's copy editor, Barbara Bergeron, whose careful checking and comments led to a much more accurate guide. I suspect she shares my goal: to strive for infallibility without pretending to it.

Special thanks are due the Atlanta Worldcon, Inc. committee, who generously provided a $5,000 grant from the surplus from the 1986 world SF convention. This grant was paid to the contributors to supplement the inadequate share of the royalties I could afford to distribute.

Although these guides are much better for my having edited three editions of *Anatomy of Wonder*, there are unavoidably errors and omissions, which will be corrected in future editions. I hope that conscientious readers will take the time to write me (see list of contributors) with suggestions for improving future editions.

Contributors

Neil Barron. A former academic librarian and sometime fan of fantastic literature, he has edited three editions of the standard critical guide to science fiction, *Anatomy of Wonder* (1976, 1981, 1987). The second and third editions were Hugo Award nominees. Address: 1149 Lime Place, Vista, CA 92083 (letters welcome).

Walter Albert. A professor of French and Italian literature at the University of Pittsburgh, a bibliographer of detective fiction and a longtime reader of horror fiction, with a particular interest in the vampire, his interest in the visual arts dates back to an early obsession with horror and fantasy films.

Mike Ashley. One of the leading bibliographers of fantastic literature, author/editor of more than twenty books and 250 articles and reviews, his *Science Fiction, Fantasy, and Weird Fiction Magazines* [11-54] is the standard study.

Michael Bishop. He has written fantasy and horror fiction, but is best known for his science fiction (*No Enemy but Time* won the 1982 Nebula Award). Each book he has written is significantly different from its predecessors, a praiseworthy practice which has led more to critical than to popular acclaim.

Frederick S. Frank. National Endowment for the Humanities Research Professor of English at Allegheny College, Pennsylvania, he has a long-standing interest in Gothic fiction and has published extensively in this area (see chapters 6 and 7).

Michael Klossner. A librarian at the Arkansas State Library, Little Rock, he has an extensive knowledge of fantastic cinema and has reviewed film books for specialty journals.

Bentley Little, who contributed to chapter 4, has published more than 40 horror stories in magazines and anthologies. His first novel, *The Revelation,* was published by St. Martin's in late 1969.

Michael A. Morrison. A professor of physics and astronomy and an adjunct professor of English at the University of Oklahoma, he has reviewed SF and horror fiction for fanzines and the *Washington Post Book World,* and has written critical essays on contemporary horror fiction writers.

Keith Neilson. Project director for and contributor to *Survey of Modern Fantasy Literature* [6-24] and *Survey of Science Fiction Literature* (1979), he has contributed to several other Salem Press publications. At California State University, Fullerton, he teaches courses on horror and popular literature.

Randall W. Scott. A longtime reader of fantasy and horror, he is a cataloger for the Russel B. Nye Popular Culture Collection of Michigan State University Libraries [12-13]. He contributes a chapter, "Research Libraries of Interest to Fandom," to the annual *Fandom Directory*.

Brian Stableford. The author of many works of science fiction, he is also well known for his many critical and historical studies of fantastic literature. In 1987 he received the Distinguished Scholarship award of the International Association for the Fantastic in the Arts.

Children Who Survive:

AN AUTOBIOGRAPHICAL MEDITATION ON HORROR AND FANTASY

Michael Bishop

Many of my most vivid, and hence lasting, childhood memories are of terrifying or awe-inspiring scenes from storybooks, films, daydreams, nightmares.

By consensus definition, these genres all lack palpable reality. Oh, they exist, all right. Books we can find in bookstores and libraries; films we can see at movie theaters or on our state-of-the-art VCRs; daydreams are often real enough to lower our productivity at work; and nightmares have probably always sent us scurrying from the menace of their chaotic imagery to the real-life comfort of a loved one's arms.

No one disputes the *existence* of storybooks, films, daydreams, nightmares. What we doubt is their *seriousness*—their underlying redemptive significance. In fact, many of us seem to have been programmed by the imperatives of the workaday world to write off their images not only as unreal but also as totally irrelevant to the more crucial transactions of our waking lives:

"Don't worry about that, hon—it was only a dream." "For God's sake, Charlie, it was just a stupid story." "You're not letting an asinine old horror movie keep you awake, are you, Kit?"

But, such facile reassurances aside, our bravest longings and our deepest fears persist. We suspect—with Freud, with Jung, with Bettelheim, with the dream merchants themselves—that maybe these startling imaginings do have a deeper seriousness; that maybe they mean significantly *more* than, say, an everyday act like cashing in a certificate of deposit or trying to climb yet another rung on the corporate ladder.

And, of course, we suspect correctly. If we didn't, I wouldn't be writing these words.

Eisenhower is president. I am seven or eight years old. One Saturday afternoon I am walking with my mother and my stepdad-to-be along a busy street in Wichita, Kansas. We pass the open front of a movie theater. On the marquee above us, and also on the posters bookending the lobby, are garish invitations to come inside and see Vincent Price, Carolyn Jones and somebody named Charles Buchinsky (later Bronson) in a 3-D horror flick called *House of Wax*.

My mother's escort, Charles Edwin Willis, a captain in the Air Force, is the owner of a Distinguished Flying Cross. (During World War II, he nursed his B-17 back to England after it had taken some crippling anti-aircraft fire over Germany.) Today, Captain Willis has a keen peacetime fondness for pulp sci-fi and B-grade monster movies. He asks me if I'm game to see *House of Wax*.

"It's going to be spooky," he cautions, but there's an amiable dare in this warning. He also notes that it'll be expensive—not to mention disappointing to my mom and him—if the movie so badly scares me that I beg to be taken back out into the anxiety-allaying Kansas sunlight.

"I *want* to see it," I insist.

The two adults are skeptical. Says Mom, "Are you sure?"

Well, of course. *House of Wax* is something new, a 3-D movie. Every paying customer gets a pair of cardboard glasses with lenses of blue and red cellophane; these give the blurred images from the projector definition and impart an astonishing three-dimensionality to every actor and prop.

My stepdad-to-be buys us tickets. We go inside. We put on our glasses. The movie proves remarkably intense. The bearded fellow with the bolo paddle at the beginning isn't bad (in fact, snapping my head back to avoid getting bopped by the ball is sort of neat), but Price's tendency to hurl screaming, half-clad young women into vats of molten wax sabotages my equanimity. I melt into gibbering terror, utterly disgracing myself.

Even good old Wichita sunlight doesn't wholly restore my peace of mind, and for the next two weeks I go to bed with a night-light, irrationally persuaded that a berserk waxman is stalking Mulvane, Kansas, my hometown. Unless I'm vigilant, I'm doomed to awaken—*if* I awaken—sarcophagused from head to toe in paraffin. A worse fate I can't imagine, and the disappointed tut-tutting of my mother has no power to convince me that I can make it to adulthood without my "babyish" night-light.

Let her coax, let her chide, let her frown. Can't she see that my very life is at stake?

Later, or perhaps earlier, I find other unrealities—literary, filmic, psychological—to awe or terrify me. They bob in the sea of my memory like buoys, markers enabling me to strike out toward that ill-defined shore upon which, for better or worse, I must one day crawl and stagger to my feet.

A tableau from *The Odyssey* wavers on that shore. Polyphemus, the Cyclops, holds Odysseus and his men captive in his cave. In order to free themselves, the brave Greek traveler and his cohorts must blind this one-eyed giant with a flaming stake. Their escape, with the Cyclops raging at their backs, is such a dicey affair that I shudder to recall how close they come to *not* making it, to having to endure further imprisonment and the sanity-fragmenting threat of becoming, at any moment, Purina Cyclops Chow.

(A holdup on Main Street—especially if reported secondhand—could not have been more horripilating. I'd've faced a puny human villain over Polyphemus, any day.)

Every Easter on TV, long before I've read L. Frank Baum's book, *The Wizard of Oz* rolls out its yellow brick road in Motorola black-and-white. I tremble—hands clammy, eyes a-bulge, gut knotted—as the Wicked Witch of the West cackles like a crazy hen. Meanwhile, her herky-jerky flying monkeys afflict the opalescent MGM sky like a hideous simian plague. Dorothy and her companions are in mortal peril. The jig is almost up.

(A trip to Mulvane's dentist—in that boxy little office with a drill boom made in 1904—could not have bathed me in a funk-sweat any more copious or pungent.)

On *The Wonderful World of Disney*, an episode from the animated classic *Fantasia* plunges me into a similar kind of fretful dread. Mickey Mouse, as the sorcerer's apprentice, struggles mousefully to bail out of the troubles he has brought upon himself by commanding a broom to carry water. The broom won't desist, however, and when Mickey chops it to pieces in frustration, the splinters sprout arms and join the nightmarish bucket brigade.

(A pop spelling test for which I'm totally unprepared couldn't unsettle me more.)

One spring night, I dream. At my bedside, when I open my eyes, perches a solicitous skeleton—female. How do I know this upright assemblage of bones is female? Well, she's wearing a short-sleeved sweater, and although her arm bones and grinning skull emerge from its sleeves and neck as bald as ivory, my visitor has bosoms. This is the Lana Turner of skeletons, her inappropriate but well-shaped breasts caught within a sweaterly hammock of pink alpaca. I don't know whether to scuttle away from or to hug her—but, at her back, a male figure in cowboy garb hurtles through my bedroom window to safety.

(I couldn't've been more scared or confused if J. Edgar Hoover had strolled into my elementary school with a dozen federal agents and a warrant for my arrest.)

Lewis Carroll's Alice sidles into my ken, out of the pages of her *Adventures in Wonderland*. Beside her, huffing and puffing, the Queen of Hearts holds a flamingo under her flabby arm as a croquet mallet. She shouts, "Off with his head!" or "Off with her head!" and the playing-card soldiers doing double duty as wickets haul off her victims under unappealable sentence of execution. I'm appalled by the Queen's behavior—horror-struck, in fact—but I'm admiringly gape-mouthed at Alice's dauntlessness. Why can't I be as brave as this blonde little girl?

(Damn! An off-center look from one of my grandmother's friends *still* triggers in me a fluttery dyspepsia.)

At least I'm not as small—relatively speaking—as Gulliver in the kingdom of Brobdingnag, about which I read while recuperating from a groin injury sustained trying out, as a thirteen year old, for a football team in Tulsa, Oklahoma. (Scarcely over five feet tall and weighing maybe eighty-five pounds, I was an idiot to get involved. Most of the other boys towered over me like . . . well, teen-aged Brobdingnagians.) One day, a monkey seizes the minuscule Gulliver, climbs to the ridge of a building, feeds him by cramming disgorged food into his mouth, squeezes his sides and threatens to drop him to his death. And other incidents equally traumatic—to me as well as to Swift's hero—occur to Gulliver on his voyages to unmapped parts of the globe.

(Now, my own world seems less spooky—so long as I don't start diminishing to nothing like that joker in *The Incredible Shrinking Man,* another flick that scared the bejabbers out of me.)

And then I encounter Edgar Allan Poe. "The Fall of the House of Usher." "The Bells." "The Pit and the Pendulum." "Hop-Frog." "The Murders in the Rue Morgue." "Ligeia." "The Raven." "The Masque of the Red Death." "The Cask of Amontillado." "The Oval Portrait." Gloom, and dank, and November decay. Romantic loss and alliteration. Onomatopoeia and more lugubrious long vowels than a locomotive's dopplering wail.

Eventually, Poe mutates into Ray Bradbury, via the Brothers Grimm, Hans Christian Andersen, old Flash Gordon serials, Charles Dickens, H. G. Wells and a host of others; and, depending on your values, either I'm ruined forever or I'm willy-nilly rescued from the grinding humdrum of unadulterated reality. In the ninth grade, I compose a long, ambitious, very clumsy Poe-esque story—a *horror* story, you'd have to call it—portentously entitled "Of a Dying God," and my fate is sealed.

What is it, as children, that we most fear? Abandonment. The dark. Helplessness (as in being assigned a task that defeats our childish capabilities). Pain (particularly if, like violent abuse at the hands of adults, it's senseless). Betrayal. Mockery. And, yes, even death, the annihilation of our developing egos.

Monsters may figure vaguely in these fears—rampaging zombies, wrathful bears, hungry tyrannosaurs—but children's most elemental fears are of backassward relationships and the numbing indifference of those whose love they need. Monsters and impossible tasks are proxies for these fears; they structure a kid's fantasy life in the same way a wire armature supports a papier-mâché mask. By donning these fears, by wearing them in the thought-experiment realm of the imagination, children—hell, all of us—find a way to look through and to overcome them.

Grownups, then, are survivors.

In "Why Are Americans Afraid of Dragons?" [see F7-28]—an important essay on the necessity of fantasy and, by extension, of *honest* tales of horror—Ursula K. Le Guin writes, "I believe that maturity is not an outgrowing, but a growing up: that an adult is not a dead child, but a child who survived." Le Guin insists that the free but disciplined play of the imagination is a key to healthy survival. She argues that repressing such play as frivolous, or immoral, or false, is the surest way of murdering the child in us—indeed, the surest way that the tyrants of mediocrity and the status quo could ever devise.

Why, however, would they want to murder that child? Because, fearing the chaotic powers of the imagination, they truly believe that sterility is better than fecundity; that a comforting cliché is preferable to an upsetting original truth; that a lived-with bias is better than an impromptu openness. They are dead children, who must sweep their own graves clean of the far-flying seeds of creativity. In Le Guin's estimation, they aren't real adults at all, for they've stifled a part of themselves that they should have nurtured.

Meanwhile, resourceful kids (or kids whose adult guardians *want* them to survive) fear the very same things that all other children fear, but they take (or they're given) the chance to confront their fears in wonderfully unthreatening guises. Namely, in celluloid or phosphor-dot fantasies; in fairy tales, horror stories and science fiction; in seemingly aimless woolgathering; and (least welcome of all but endurable if a sympathetic adult or sibling is nearby) even in grisly nightmares.

How much better to watch the Shrinking Man battle a spider than to go *mano a mano* with some living Goliath. To read about Rapunzel than to be locked in an honest-to-God tower. To daydream a journey down the Amazon than to get fanged by a real piranha. To nightview your own murder than to experience it in irreversible fact. Which is *one* of the reasons—along with our innate curiosity about every aspect of being human—that both children and adult survivors find fictive narratives so fascinating. Sometimes, it seems, we *do* like what is good for us.

Maybe the most insightful book ever written on the existential significance—the essential integrating function—of fairy tales is Bruno Bettelheim's *The Uses of Enchantment* (1976) [F7-3]. I believe that Le Guin would second most of Bettelheim's conclusions; I believe, too, that his conclusions have legitimate application to the fields of fantasy writing and of adult horror fiction. Argues Bettelheim in his introduction:

> An understanding of the meaning of one's life is not suddenly acquired at a particular age, not even when one has reached chronological maturity. On the contrary, gaining a secure understanding of what the meaning of one's life may or ought to be—this is what constitutes having attained psychological maturity. And this achievement is the end result of a long development: at each age we seek, and must be able to find, some modicum of meaning congruent with how our minds and understanding have already developed.

And a little later:

> In child or adult, the unconscious is a powerful determinant of behavior. When the unconscious is repressed and its content denied entrance into awareness, then eventually the person's conscious mind will be partially overwhelmed by derivatives of these unconscious elements, or else he is forced to keep such rigid, compulsive control over them that his personality may become severely crippled. But when unconscious material *is* to

> some degree permitted to come to awareness and worked through in imagination, its potential for causing harm—to ourselves or others—is much reduced; some of its forces can then be made to serve positive purposes.

Thus, I would contend that the contemporary horror novel—when well and truly done, as it is by such latter-day practitioners as Stephen King, Peter Straub, Anne Rice, Thomas Tessier, Robert R. McCammon and others—is the new adult equivalent of the folkloric stories of the Brothers Grimm and of the "literary" fairy tales of Hans Christian Andersen. Maybe, in fact, novel-length fantasies of ghosts, golems, vampires, werewolves, mad killers, hostile aliens and/or phantasmagoric after-Armageddon quests play the same sort of integrative psychological role for twentieth-century adults that "Hansel and Gretel," "The Ugly Duckling" and "Snow White" played for children a century ago and, of course, still play for children lucky enough to encounter them today.

Stephen King implies as much about modern horror writing when he declares, "[As] this mad century races toward its conclusion—a conclusion which seems ever more ominous and ever more absurd—it may be the most important and useful form of fiction which the moral writer may command."

Why, though, do we *like* stories that scare the living piss out of us? And what good does it do us to place ourselves, again and again, in situations—whether a theater seat at another sequel to *Halloween* or a wingback with the latest Clive Barker or K. W. Jeter opus—that produce these goosebump-lifting and/or bladder-draining sensations? Are all of us who enjoy this kind of "entertainment" already past hope of psychological reclamation? Have we bartered our twisted souls to Satan?

Absolutely not. Fear is not only a guilty pleasure—at least under circumstances where the threat is fictively distanced—it is also a psychological necessity. People who are literally fearless are people whom the rest of us regard as appallingly inhuman, and in *The Uses of Enchantment,* Bettelheim points out that many fairy tales dramatize the need to be able to experience fear. (Fear, after all, is an evolutionary adaptation. If you don't run from the hungry leopard, you get eaten.) The best example of this sort of story goes by such titles as "The Story of One Who Set Out to Study [or Learn] Fear" and "The Youth Who Could Not Shudder." It concerns a younger brother who wonders what he must do, in Lore Segal's amusing translation, "to make my flesh creep," for no task that his father assigns—even tiptoeing through a churchyard at midnight—has any power to make him tremble and he correctly feels that he's missing something.

The hero of this bizarre tale is a prodigy of courage. Better, a *monster* of courage. No "normal"—i.e., sane—human being could face the same daunting challenges with either the calmness or the confidence that our hero invariably summons. Seven hanged corpses don't in the least discomfit him; he cuts them down, places them around his fire to warm them and, when their rags ignite because he has put them too near the fire pit, disgustedly strings them up again. In a haunted castle, he lies down on a bed that begins to gallop him from room to room, but, rather than leap for safety, he commands the bed to go faster. One night later, he plays ninepins with a team of halved corpses that reassemble themselves before him and challenge him to a bowling match. Altogether matter-of-factly, our Grimm hero uses a lathed skull for a bowling ball.

Strangely, none of these adventures has caused the young man to shudder; and even after he has married a beautiful princess—whose hand he has won by disenchanting the castle—his daily complaint is that he still doesn't know what it means for his "flesh to creep." At last, his new bride, fed up with this refrain, goes to a nearby brook, dips out a bucketful of icy water and squirmy minnows, pulls the blankets off her sleeping husband and dumps the cold water and its fishy contents all over him. Our hero, simultaneously shocked and delighted, cries, "Something is making my flesh creep! Dear wife, how my flesh is creeping! Ah, now I know what it's like when one's flesh creeps." Presumably, he and his ingenious bride live happily ever after.

Bettelheim identifies the young man's inability to shudder as the consequence of sexual repression, sexual anxiety. Readers out of sympathy with the Freudian approach may cry, "Bullshit!" After all, isn't it possible that the tale-teller who ended this narrative with a singularly unorthodox instance of the bedroom shivers just wanted to amuse us? And isn't a bed full of wriggling gudgeons as funny a climax as we are likely to imagine? Well, sure. Even so, Bettelheim *has* hit on something here.

"There is a subtlety in this story that is easy to overlook consciously," he points out, "although it does not fail to make an unconscious impression." He adds, "Whether or not the hearer of this story recognizes that it was sexual anxiety that led to the hero's inability to shudder, that which finally makes him shudder suggests the irrational nature of some of our most pervasive anxieties. Because it is a fear of which only his wife is able to cure him at night in bed, this is a sufficient hint of the underlying nature of the anxiety."

Bettelheim further explains that this story teaches the child that those who brag about their fearlessness may harbor immature fears that they are actively denying. It also hints that marital happiness requires both partners to acknowledge feelings that they have heretofore concealed. Another of the tale's messages is that "it is the female partner"—as in "The Beauty and the Beast"—"who finally brings out the humanity in the male. . . . [In] the last transition needed for achieving mature humanity, repressions must be undone."

That's a heavy lesson for a fairy tale to teach, but the point is that fairy tales—without sacrificing an iota of their cleverly disguised seriousness—teach such lessons lightly. They work on the unconscious, and they do this work through the attention-fixing enticements of narrative. "What's going to happen?" my children used to plead when I read to them from Grimm. "Daddy, what's going to happen?"

And horror novels like King's *The Shining* [H4-173], Straub's *Ghost Story* [H4-289], Rice's *Interview with the Vampire* [H4-250], Tessier's *The Nightwalker* [H4-297], McCammon's *Baal* (1978) and Thomas Harris's bloodcurdling study of the workings of a sociopathic killer's mind, *Red Dragon* [H4-135], are legitimate, sophisticated, set-your-flesh-to-creeping fairy tales for adults.

Wait a minute, I can hear a skeptic saying. Why must an adult, specifically a twentieth-century adult, go to such extremes to find something shudder-provoking? And aren't adults too far along in their psychological evolution to learn anything substantive from a mere horror novel? After all, we've got the H-bomb to worry about, and international terrorism, and Star Wars, and acid rain, and the greenhouse effect, and cancer, and heart disease, and, if we're of a religious turn of mind, even eternal damnation. Why flail around *inventing* stuff to fear, and why then claim that reading about our invented horrors—specters, zombies, bug-eyed aliens—is a viable means of achieving mental and emotional equilibrium?

In the introduction to his landmark anthology of contemporary horror tales, *The Dark Descent* [H4-345], editor David Hartwell writes, "A strong extra-literary appeal of such fiction"—he means here the stream of supernatural horror— ". . . is to jump-start the readers' deadened emotional sensitivities." Hartwell divides contemporary horror writing into three streams (the other two being metaphorical psychological horror and stories taking their peculiar frisson from a disturbing ambiguity about the reality of depicted events). "At the end of a horror story," he tells us, "the reader is left with a new perception of the nature of reality."

I agree with this last statement (about all three streams), and believe that both supernatural and psychological horror may serve "to jump-start . . . deadened emotional sensitivities"; that, in fact, doing so is not only an appeal of these types of horror, but also one of their primary goals.

Our sensitivities are deadened, of course, because the media—newspapers, TV, magazines—daily bombard us with horrific images. Moreover, we encounter these images in such brief, impersonal or clinical contexts (during the Vietnam War, for instance, as little more than jumpy frames of film on the six o'clock news) that it is difficult to *feel* about them. The threat of nuclear attack or the widening hole in the ozone layer, meanwhile, are such vast, complex problems that when we try to grapple with them, they self-destruct like taped *Mission: Impossible* assignments, again depriving us of a human-scale yardstick by which to measure them. Horror fiction and horror films, however, usually restore a tangible human context to the nightmares structuring them, enabling us, once again, to *care*—to cheer for those struggling to dispel the nightmare, to quake in terror when they seem to be failing, to hate the pernicious forces opposing them, and to find ourselves, because of this involvement, gratifyingly *alive*. And, of course, we undoubtedly take a certain guilty satisfaction in our awareness that the real danger is not to us, but to the imaginary characters battling the evil powers whose actions alternately thrill and repulse us.

King has written that horror is "the most important and useful form of fiction which the moral writer may command." Others have argued that because of its vivid provocativeness, it is dangerous; that it can corrupt. I would argue (on gut instinct rather than on statistics) that those adult readers most likely to be corrupted by horror fiction are precisely those who had no chance to internalize the tales of Grimm and Andersen as children. Those adults, in other words, who outgrew fantasy or who never discovered it at all. "Dead children," in Le Guin's canny formulation, rather than "children who survived"; children who've grown into adult monsters as a partial result of their deprivation.

The ideal reader of adult horror, then, is Le Guin's "child who survived." It is this reader who is most likely to appreciate it, most capable of recognizing the psychological validity of the grim archetypes at play in it, and most open to the healing catharsis of its violent images and apocalyptic resolutions. Which is not for a minute to deny with highfalutin' theory the simple fact that horror—a bang-up scare expertly administered—is great good fun, and all the more fun for our underlying awareness that the "danger" we are in is delectably hypothetical.

No, my point is that horror tales have a hidden, and important, function beyond entertaining us, and that the resurgence of their popularity in technological Western culture—a resurgence dating from the publication of Ira Levin's *Rosemary's Baby* [H4-206] in 1967 and building through the appearances of Thomas Tryon's *The Other* [H4-306] and William Peter Blatty's *The Exorcist* [H4-42], both in 1971—is a result of the ramifying anxieties attendant on the proliferating political, economic and ecological crises of the final quarter of our "mad" twentieth century.

It's reassuring to suffer a solid fright and to survive. It's also healthily edifying to our subconsciouses. For if we can find the psychological coin to get past a fictional slasher assault, or vampire invasion, or alien body-snatching expedition, or insidious satanic possession (pick one, and only one), then perhaps we also have the resourcefulness to deal with the real-world problems that seem, individually and collectively, so overwhelming and impervious to solution. We may or may not actually have this resourcefulness, of course, but I would argue that we need to believe we do and that horror fiction is finally, if paradoxically, a literature of hope, a literature of affirmation.

What did I learn as a well-loved but occasionally insecure kid from my most terrifying or awe-inspiring fantasy experiences? From the villain in *House of Wax*, from Polyphemus, from the Wicked Witch of the West and her ugly flying monkeys, from Mickey Mouse as the sorcerer's apprentice, from the skeletal pin-up girl leaning over my bed, from the Queen of Hearts, from the pint-sized Gulliver, and from the flamboyant writings of Poe and others?

Chiefly, I think, I learned not that horror fiction is at base affirmative (a conclusion that would have struck me as dumb, if not so abstruse as to be incomprehensible), but that, to rephrase David Hartwell's notion of horror's defining impact, reality isn't always what it appears to be. Wonder sometimes breaks in. Magic, black and white, can transform the two-dimensional outlines of life into dauntingly solid arabesques. Beneath the placid surfaces of habit, regimentation and order, fearful krakens lurk. The world is both more exciting and more terrible than we think, and fantasy—whether cinematic, literary or dream-triggered—is a surefire open-sesame to its secret awesomeness.

In October 1988, I was in Atlanta to do a reading at Georgia State University and to conduct a pair of seminars for advanced writing students. On the way to Georgia State's urban campus one morning, my host, Dr. Tom McHaney, took me to McGuire's Bookshop on Ponce de Leon Avenue, where the owner, Frank McGuire, told me of a recent horror novel called *Deliver Us from Evil* (1988) by a new Atlanta-based writer, Allen Lee Harris. "Bantam did it as an original paperback," Frank said, "and it sold pretty well for us. I don't have a copy in the store right now, but I'll send you one if you're interested." I was, and Frank did.

Deliver Us from Evil strikes me both as a strong, well-crafted representative of the contemporary horror novel and as a promising debut. Released in March 1988, it proves that the trend in horror writing inaugurated in the late 1960s/early

1970s, a trend given direction and impetus by the conspicuous successes of Stephen King, has by no means exhausted itself. Talented new writers can still find untilled territory within the field to stake out and claim as their own, and they can contour these parcels with as much élan and originality as their private visions allow. Meanwhile, they do this work within a tradition giving it additional resonance and simultaneously demanding structural and thematic innovations to keep it fresh.

Harris's *Deliver Us from Evil* is traditional horror, with many of the anticipated hackneyed trappings—from an evil-beset southern small town, to a Good Sheriff protagonist, to a ubiquitous Village Idiot, to a Mysterious Interloper, to an All-American Kid Who Saves the Entire Community—but the author, who began college at fourteen, got his degree at nineteen, attended Harvard Divinity School and later took a Masters in Philosophy at the University of Toronto, transfigures these weary plot elements with the power of his vision, the simple clarity of his writing, and the forcefulness of his intellection. As a result, his novel possesses exactly the sort of compassionate, existential dimension to qualify it as a mature adult fairy tale. Harris knows what a good horror story should demonstrate, and he also understands the sort of healthy psychological integration that this demonstration should work in us.

Jerry Robins, a character who describes himself as a "lapsed nihilist" (i.e., someone for whom the cynical belief in nothing has failed), relates for the novel's Good Sheriff, Charlie McAlister, why his grandfather used to like to tell, and subsequently gloss, the Old Testament story of Jacob's Ladder:

> "[What my grandfather] always dwelled upon was Jacob's terror at his vision. A terror that came out of the realization that the world around him, the everyday world he was so comfortable in, was not the only world. That there was another one, alien and awful, unyielding and incomprehensible. But even that wasn't the worst part of it. The worst part wasn't his vision of the other world but his vision of the ladder. Because, from then on, Jacob knew that this other world could erupt at any moment into his own world and that the two worlds were invisibly intertwined."

(Hartwell again: "At the end of a horror story, the reader is left with a new perception of reality.")

Although *Deliver Us from Evil* contains a lot of the requisite jeepery-creepery of the post-*Rosemary's Baby*, post-*The Other*, post-*The Exorcist* commercial horror novel (innocent characters groping about in the dark or facing bleak personifications of the forces of eternal night), several of its scenes actually managed to make my flesh crawl; they did so by brilliantly dramatizing the eruption of Robins's grandfather's "other world" into this one. And Harris, a fellow Georgian whom I have never met, corresponded with or talked to on the phone, redeems even his less sterling jeepery-creepery by visiting it upon unfailingly sympathetic characters and by giving his entire novel a hopeful, affirmative shape.

At the end of the book, Robins is lost in thought: "The wonder is not that there's so much darkness, his grandfather had told him. The wonder is there's any light at all."

I didn't understand that when I was yelling to get out of that theater in Wichita showing *House of Wax*, or when I edged away from the bony *femme fatale* at my bedside in Mulvane, Kansas, or when I eagerly imbibed the seemingly poisonous concoctions of Edgar Allan Poe's pen in Tulsa, Oklahoma—but, having made it to adulthood with my inner child intact, I do understand it now: "*The wonder is there's any light at all.*"

Horror fiction teaches this essential lesson again and again, a lesson that bears repeating, preferably in new and more compelling guises, because the times are such that we can too easily surrender to the vitiating suspicion that the darkness is everywhere and the light is merely illusory. It may seem tautological to say so, but children who have survived are more likely than snuffed children—those stranded among us in the corpses of spiritually impoverished adults—to believe in, and work for, everyone's survival.

Thank you, *House of Wax*. Thank you, Polyphemus. Thank you, L. Frank Baum. Thank you, Mickey Mouse, Jonathan Swift, Edgar Allan Poe, Ray Bradbury, Stephen King, Peter Straub and, latterly, Allen Lee Harris. Thank you, thank you, one and all. . . .

Horror Literature
A Readers' Guide

1

The Early Gothic, 1762–1824

Frederick S. Frank

Denounced by reviewers and devoured by readers when it spewed from the presses in enormous quantities at the end of the eighteenth century, the Gothic novel established itself as the most dominant force in English fiction between Horace Walpole's first Gothic, *The Castle of Otranto* [1-108] in 1764 and Charles Robert Maturin's novel of terror, *Melmoth the Wanderer* [1-64] in 1820. These six decades in literary history are the Gothic years when hordes of authors gratified the supernatural and irrational cravings of thousands of readers in a profusion of Gothic horror and terror. From its beginnings Gothic fiction subverted the norms of polite and rational literature and appealed directly to the timeless human need for inhuman things, a need not well served by the sane and decorous literature of the Age of Reason. The inventor of the Gothic, Horace Walpole, was responding to such a deprivation of the imagination when he informed his readers in the preface to his Gothic novel that "the great resources of fancy have been dammed up by a strict adherence to common life." In the very midst of the Age of Reason with its emphasis in the arts on symmetry, control, aesthetic order and classical restraint, Walpole proposed a literary countergenre designed to gratify the darker and ignored yearnings of the human mind. Horror, terror, psychic and social disorder and the very existence of a universe controlled by supernatural law had been unconditionally denied to the imagination by the neoclassic value system. Pleasure in ruins, admiration for decay, disorder and spectacular death, and the enjoyment of fear were all symptoms of the emotional starvation which provoked the Gothic eruption. The Gothic was a well-defined literary genre, but it was also from its beginnings a mode of perception or way of seeing the other universe which had lain buried for too long beneath the rationalism of the age. The motives which called the Gothic into existence in the eighteenth century remain active today and explain the enduring popularity of the Gothic impulse in contemporary art.

The reader who approaches the classic or early period of Gothic literature for the first time will naturally wish to know the answers to four critical and historical questions often raised about the development of the Gothic novel and its far-reaching influence. What were the origins and the distinguishable types of early Gothic fiction? What are the formal characteristics or technical requirements of a successful Gothic novel in any literary period? How have critical attitudes toward Gothicism shifted since the nearly universal ire and hostility of the early reviewers? And finally, what is the reason for the survival of the Gothic as an unbroken and vigorous tradition from the work of the eighteenth-century Gothic novelists to the masters of modern horror? The answers to several of these questions are still being sought by researchers applying a variety of sophisticated methodologies. Today, structuralists, Marxist critics, psychoanalytic critics, semiologists, traditionalists, historicists and feminists in ever-increasing numbers are studying the Gothic phenomenon from many perspectives in order to explain the content and intent of Gothic fiction and to define exactly what the Gothic communicates about the problems of self and culture.

The first author to apply the bizarre adjective, "Gothic," to a novel was Horace Walpole. In the middle of the eighteenth century, the term would have had disapproving or contemptuous implications and had often been used by neoclassic artists to discredit works which they deemed barbarous, unpleasingly grotesque and coarse, crude, formless, tasteless, primitive and ignorant. By describing his *Castle of Otranto* as "A Gothic Story," Walpole intended to elevate the status of the adjective to something thrilling, Romantic and sublime. If frequency of usage is any test of its utility, Walpole's choice of "Gothic" for his novel was both brilliant and apt, for it captured the quintessence of the form in a single word. Walpole's Gothic Story was "Gothic" in three senses. First, the Gothic carried associations of spatial and temporal remoteness in the setting and atmosphere. A Gothic novel would locate itself in a strange and often a fallen world in which the reader could feel as lost and disoriented as the characters. Second, the "engine" or driving mechanism of the novel would be its inlaid system of terror devices and props. Indeed, from *The Castle of Otranto* to present-day Gothic novels, Gothic has become almost synonymous with certain standard contraptions of fear, flight and supernatural danger. Third, Walpole equated "Gothic" with containment or entrapment by insular space and animated architecture. In fact, it was not unusual for the Gothic building to possess more mobility and mentality than the human beings imprisoned within its intricate interior. The movement of the human characters was highly restrained and usually limited to the subterranean and labyrinthine sections of the ghastly building, typically a haunted castle in the earliest stages of the form. Walpole's Gothic was a coalescence of supernatural properties and lethal emotions with the Gothic castle itself behaving organically and assuming insidious traits of character.

Throughout Walpole's strange novel, we see an uninhibited convergence of certain forbidden feelings and drives that would later shake the Age of Reason to its core. Walpole was the first Gothic novelist, but he was by no means the first Gothic voice to be heard in the literature of the eighteenth century. In the 1740s, a group of poets had vented their morbid fantasies and discontent with the primacy of reason and order in a dark torrent of poems called "Graveyard" verse. Parnell, Akenside, Edward Young, Robert Blair, the Brothers Warton and Walpole's close friend, Thomas Gray, had anticipated Gothic moods and passions by brooding grandiloquently on the pleasures of the grave and by exploring the connection between horror and ecstasy. A compulsory moment in the lines of the Graveyard poets was the spectral encounter, the dreadful and yet pleasing experience of being confronted by a shape or shade from the other side which would not be denied. Wandering alone through a gloomy corridor, a self-entombed character in one of the Graveyard poems (Thomas Warton's "The Pleasures of Melancholy," 1746) has just such a primal Gothic experience as he "watches the flame of taper dim, while airy voices talk along the glimmering walls, or ghostly shape at distance seen, invites with beckoning hand, [his] lonesome steps through far winding vaults." Only a few additional steps are required to cross the threshold of the irrational and descend into the darkness of Walpole's haunted castle.

Several other unmistakable signals in the arts of the period presage a Gothic outbreak of great magnitude. A group of philosophers who were interested in the psychodynamics of artistic response had begun to debate and analyze the aesthetic possibilities of fear, terror and horror. Could a sublime artistic experience be simultaneously gruesome and beautiful, and could an object's beauty or sublimity actually be heightened by its very gruesomeness and grotesqueness? Considering these paradoxes in the treatise *A Philosophical Enquiry into the Origin of Our Ideas of the Sublime and Beautiful* (1756), Edmund Burke postulated a Gothic aesthetic soon to be adapted by the Gothic novelists to generate the aesthetically satisfying terror and horror of the castle interior. Without using the adjective "Gothic," Burke nevertheless stated the pleasure principle of all Gothic literature. According to Burke, dreadful pleasure occurred when fear displaced reason in the face of awesome and awful objects and events. The optimum of such dreadful pleasure was the consequence of supernatural fear, terror of the unknown and the unknowable. "The mind," he wrote, "is so entirely filled with its object that it cannot entertain any other, nor by consequence reason on that object which employs it. Hence arises the great power of the sublime that hurries us on by an irresistible force." In its intensity, such supernatural horror was the psychological equivalent of religious awe and could transfix an observer in a manner similar to visionary or transcendental experience. Setting the pattern for all future Gothic novels, Walpole's *Castle of Otranto* validated Burkean theory by conducting its readers through a "long labyrinth of darkness" to a secret and sealed door. What lay beyond? Some would say the subconscious of an entire century.

The second indication in the arts of a coming Gothic upheaval may be seen in the polarization of character in the Gothic novel's precursor and close relative, the sentimental novel or novel of tearful sensibility. The characters of Walpole and of nearly every Gothic novelist to follow derive their emotional natures from the persecuted maiden and the amatory villain of the first English novelist, Samuel Richardson. His *Clarissa; or, The History of a Young Lady* (1747–48) furnished the primal maiden-villain conflict of the novel of terror. Richardson's rapist villain, Robert Lovelace, is an early version of the satanic or Gothic hero-villain, a mysterious and powerful creature who risks all for evil and ruthlessly pursues and torments the maiden. Driven by violent impulses which he knows to be evil but cannot control, the Lovelace figure is not pure evil but a fallen angel like the Gothic villains who succeeded him. Richardson's tearful and sensitive heroine, Clarissa Harlowe, is the prototype for countless menaced maidens who are forced to occupy the castles and abbeys of Gothic fiction. In Richardson's sexological melodrama, man and woman are exaggerated into victimizer and victim, predator and prey, precisely the relationship of the villain to the hysterical maiden of the typical Gothic novel. By cleverly supernaturalizing and medievalizing Richardson's tense episodes and neurotic characters, and by eliminating his tedious moral formula of "virtue rewarded," Walpole transformed the novel of sentiment into a first Gothic novel. Following Walpole's ingenious example, the Gothic novelists would immerse their readers in what Walpole called "a constant vicissitude of interesting passions," and then proceed to dry their tears, not with promises of salvation and virtue rewarded, but with hell-fire.

The impact of *The Castle of Otranto* shaped Gothic fiction well into the 1770s and 1780s. As the genre emerged, it defined itself along two lines of development, one conservative, domestic and didactic, and the other an extension of the spirit of Walpole's outrageous, amoral fantasy. In 1777, Clara Reeve brought out a subdued and domesticated historical tale, *The Old English Baron* [1-88], which contained a single Gothic situation, the night vigil within the apartment haunted by the ghost of a murdered relative. In toning down her Gothic and giving it moral respectability, Reeve was reacting to the supernatural excesses of Walpole, but she also contributed to the recipe for the many victim-centered family Gothics to come. Her terrors were real, but moderate and subordinate to the moral ends of her story. In 1786, the eccentric dilettante William Beckford responded to Reeve's conservative and timid Gothicism with his *Vathek* [1-6], a tale of demonic quest which probed the absolute limits of sadomasochistic fantasy and conveyed its sensual hero to a hell of no return. Rather than edifying the reader with a vision of restored order and a victory for the forces of goodness, Beckford's Gothic sought to electrify the reader by projecting an irrational demonic world where Satan was ever in control and where evil was mightier than goodness. Both Reeve and Beckford had made important, if opposite, additions to Walpole's haunted castle and had enlarged the Gothic model in the process.

In the 1790s the contradictory influences of Reeve and Beckford asserted themselves in the divergent Gothics of the two greatest figures of the Gothic school, Mrs. Ann Radcliffe and Matthew Gregory "Monk" Lewis. Prior to the work of Radcliffe and Lewis, terror (i.e., anticipation of the dreadful) and horror (realization of the hideous) had been separate but compatible responses in a Gothic work. Now the two Gothic attitudes begin to break down into antithetical effects yielding separate Gothic types, the novel of terror and its opposite, the Gothic novel of horror. Radcliffean Gothic is always maiden-centered and the terrors experienced by her heroines are hallucinatory by-products of their disturbed imaginations. There are real dangers in Mrs. Radcliffe's Gothic novels, but none of them is supernatural in character. In her feminization of the Gothic, Mrs. Radcliffe projected the awful events from the menaced maiden's point of view, then finally allowed her heroine to return to a world of moral safety and rational security after her confinement within the castle or abbey. Basically an illusory and explained Gothic of gruesome terrors rather than of nauseous horrors, Mrs. Radcliffe's vision of the Gothic retained the technology of Walpole's original castle, but rejected the audacious supernaturalism and blatant horror of the early Gothic.

If Mrs. Radcliffe's Gothic resembles the delicacy of Clara Reeve, Monk Lewis's Gothic resembles the bold and sadistic supernaturalism of Beckford. His book *The Monk* [1-58] became the authoritative model for the high Gothic novel of unmitigated hideousness and extravagant supernaturalism. Scorning Mrs. Radcliffe's vague thrill scenes and gloomy shadow pictures, Lewis offered the Gothic audience a sickening extravaganza of horrid shock while abandoning both his good and wicked characters to the powers of darkness. His rendition of the haunted castle permits no exit for both sufferers and sinners alike and his treatment of the diabolic supernatural carries no apologies or explanations. With Lewis, the Gothic novel reached a new horizon of ruthlessness and began to dedicate itself to the revelation of the unthinkable horror of horrors, a malign cosmos where the devil, not God, is the only authority and prime mover. The rival Gothic conceptions of Mrs. Radcliffe and Monk Lewis that were so prevalent throughout the 1790s show conclusively that far from being variant aspects of the same response, terror and horror were mutually exclusive responses, just as Mrs. Radcliffe later maintained in her essay "On the Supernatural in Poetry" (*The New Monthly Magazine*, 1826).

Many advocates of unremitting supernatural horror expressed their approval of Lewis's mode of Gothic in the flood of bluebooks and chapbooks which glutted the Gothic marketplace in the late 1790s and early 1800s. These short Gothics ran from thirty-six to seventy-two pages and often proved to be plagiarized abridgments of *The Monk* or even just a single sensational episode extracted from Lewis's horror novel. Luridly illustrated and cheaply bound in paper wrappers, these hundreds of shilling shockers brought their characters along a corridor of blood to the altar or the grave within the prescribed quota of pages. Glancing at their phantasmic titles, which shrilly proclaimed their hardware of horrors, it is easy to understand why the Gothic became vulnerable to parody or why serious Romantics such as Wordsworth disclaimed the Gothic as mere trash literature whose sole purpose was "the degrading thirst after outrageous stimulation."

Yet the Gothic chapbooks, no less than the lengthy triple-deckers or four-volume Gothic romances so common in the period, were tangible evidence of the Romantic revolt against reason and rigid social structure. Like the more luminous forms of Romanticism, Gothic Romanticism was yet another expression of the "spontaneous overflow of powerful feelings," Wordsworth's famous definition of poetry. As a counterpoint to the crudity of the Gothic chapbooks and the shoddy commercialization of horror and terror, the Gothic also received sophisticated and intellectual development from some writers of tragic vision and profundity of imagination, even as the rage for things Gothic abated. Three late masterpieces of the Gothic school were published during the decadent and moribund phase of the Gothic movement. Mary Shelley's *Frankenstein; or, The Modern Prometheus* (1818) [1-97], Charles Robert Maturin's *Melmoth the Wanderer* (1820) [1-64] and James Hogg's *Private Memoirs and Confessions of a Justified Sinner* (1824) [1-41] all demonstrate the tragic potential of the Gothic novel for accommodating the grandest of metaphysical themes. The psychological depth and symbolic richness of these last Gothic novels foreshadow the metaphoric role that Gothicism would later play throughout the nineteenth century in energizing the darkest dreams of many great writers. In English literature alone, the three Brontë sisters, Dickens, Hardy, Conrad and Wells reflect a considerable artistic obligation to the early Gothic novel. Commencing with the nightmares of Charles Brockden Brown's *Wieland* (1798) [1-9], a new strain of American Gothic emerged as a powerful tributary of English Gothicism and flourishes today in the refinements of Poe, Hawthorne and Henry James and in the rural Gothic of Flannery O'Connor, the urban terrors of Joyce Carol Oates and the disintegrative cultural themes of the masters of Southern Gothic, William Faulkner and Truman Capote.

From Walpole to Faulkner and the modern masters of the Gothic, the dark energy centers and spectral motifs of the Gothic tale or novel have remained remarkably unchanged and cohesive. In terms of its psychodynamics, the most effective Gothic novel in any period can be defined as a fantasy of the multiple self in which various hypothetical personalities or repressed and undesired identities are projected into an architectural dream collage where anything might happen and normally does. Whether contemporary Gothic writers are historically aware of the fact or not, every twentieth-century Gothic tale owes some technical and thematic debt to the classic Gothic novelists of the early period. In its purest state, the high Gothic novel of the eighteenth century evinces ten elements which are indispensable to a good Gothic. The more of these elements in an individual work, the purer its Gothicism. The elements are:

1. **Claustrophobic confinement and threatening architecture**. Gothic characters must feel enclosed by menacing buildings and by other circumstances of enclosure within the Gothic structure. In its earliest stages, the sequestration was within a ruined castle or abbey; many variations followed as the Gothic evolved. Claustrophobic confinement is the psychic imperative of all Gothic fiction.

2. **Underground pursuit and subterranean sexual peril**. The commonest plot pattern in Gothic fiction is the stalking of an angelic maiden by a satanic villain through a charnel setting initially described by Walpole as "vaults totally dark." When characters enter the underground maze, they are "amazed" by their contact with the supernatural world.

3. **Supernatural encounters and encroachments**. Specters, phantoms, apparitions, shades, demons and other supernatural personages constantly intrude upon the natural characters or disrupt natural law. Their reality cannot be denied as these creatures confront the human characters and demand immediate attention. Probably the commonest Gothic ghost is the wronged or murdered ancestor and the commonest shape of the specter is the mobile skeleton or bleeding nun.

4. **Sentience of architecture and organicity of art**. Inside the Gothic world, inanimate or inorganic matter exhibits a peculiar and powerful aliveness. Walls, turrets, compartments, corridors, statues, portraits, tapestries and entrances are alive and display minds and wills of their own, often perverse. Even windows and mirrors have optical abilities and occasionally a vile intelligence that is superior to that of the entrapped human characters.

5. **Extraordinary positions and lethal predicaments**. Death by lightning or spontaneous combustion, by the crushing impact of a falling helmet, by live burial when walls or floors collapse, by being hurled from a cliff, tower or from a great height by a demonic being are all instances of what Walpole called "extraordinary positions" in the Gothic. Fatal occupancy of a pit, a whirlpool or other

sorts of diminishing space sometimes has the effect of placing the characters in extraordinary positions of mind as well as body.

6. **Suspension of rationality and morality**. Anxiety or dread caused by a sense of rational helplessness and hopelessness in the face of chaotic forces which threaten pain, insanity and horrible death is a primal condition of the high Gothic. Moral laws prove weak or meaningless, and a character's own high morality is no defense against dark powers which often exert themselves through political or religious institutions.

7. **Spectral and demonic machinery**. The high Gothic relies strongly on props and devices installed to startle, thrill and shock the prisoners of the castle, abbey, mansion or house. Such apparatus is both literal and symbolic in nature, and a novel is not truly Gothic unless it contains some of the machinery in some recognizable form such as Gothic acoustics and other audiovisual effects. Among the most familiar pieces of Gothic equipment, we find certain mechanisms in abundance: the picture that walks or talks; the door or portal which opens or closes independently and inopportunely in the path of the fleeing maiden; secret manuscripts and cabalistic documents frequently delivered by specters; bleeding statues; sighing black veils; passageways that contract without warning; vaults, cells or rooms to which entrance has been strictly forbidden.

8. **Atmospheric superiority of evil**. One way that the Gothic horrifies and terrifies is by creating the possibility that evil will triumph over good. A high Gothic often terminates with evil forces in control. Although it need not actually occur, the appalling prospect that evil might defeat good is integral to the atmosphere of fear and dread.

9. **Psychopathic and destructive emotions**. Acute passions bordering on madness must drive the characters to extremes of homicidal and suicidal behavior. Gothic emotions can motivate the supernatural figures as well as the maiden and villain. The emotional context of the Gothic tale is characterized by a chronic sense of apprehension and premonitions of impending but unidentified catastrophe. The passions threaten to overwhelm, thus precipitating ruin and damnation. The emotional climate of the Gothic was delineated by Walpole in his phrase "a constant vicissitude of interesting passions."

10. **Genealogical complications, jeopardy and mysteries**. Paternal, maternal and avuncular villainy are regular sources of evil in Gothic fiction. Although she does not know it, the maiden has much to fear from close relatives who hide their identities from her and plot her death or disinheritance. Many Gothics are parables of the missing or mistaken parent, with the maiden's sojourn within the haunted castle serving as an ordeal of self-disclosure in her struggle for identity. The quest for one's origins or the heroic unraveling of a complex genealogical problem, climaxed by the moment of discovery or reunion, functions as a Gothic archetype and can sometimes be interpreted as a relocation of the self.

About the Bibliography

The bibliography presents annotated specimens of the various types of Gothic fiction that typify Gothicism's major phase in England, America and Europe from 1762 to 1824. The user should realize that thousands of Gothic titles crammed the circulating libraries during the Gothic period and that the present listing is only a minute sampling of such intense Gothic activity. An educated estimate of the number of Gothics mass-produced between Walpole's *Castle of Otranto* and Maturin's *Melmoth the Wanderer* might reasonably be in excess of 5,000 novels of the Gothic variety, but it should be stressed that no final and complete bibliographical census is possible. The outstanding Gothic collection in the world of letters, the famous Sadleir-Black Collection housed in the Alderman Library of the University of Virginia [12-30], offers the researcher 1,200 titles, but is itself selective and partial, thus hinting at the vast dimensions of the Gothic movement as a whole. Many of the rare Gothic titles contained in the Sadleir-Black Collection have recently been made available to scholars and general readers in modern editions. The availability of these once inaccessible Gothics together with contemporary reprintings of Gothic drama and shorter tales of terror becomes the major criterion of inclusion in compiling the present bibliography. Of the 112 Gothic titles cited, the user will find 86 titles currently available in modern editions. This bibliography is even more rigorously selective in its representation of the seven categories of early Gothic fiction and limits itself to single examples of some of the various Gothic types which multiplied at the height of the international Gothic mania. Allowing for some interfusion of types, the early Gothic breaks down into the following classifications:

1. The Pure or High Gothic Romance

Study examples: Ireland, *The Abbess* [1-44]; Warner, *Netley Abbey; A Gothic Story* [1-110].

Probably the most durable category of Gothic novel, the high Gothic novel aims to terrify, horrify, startle, shock and thrill the reader beyond recall. The type may be divided into several subcategories such as the monastic shocker, the romance of the ruin, tower and turret Gothic, and infernal voyage Gothic. The supernatural in the high Gothic is generally malign and real, or at least seems so to the anxious characters for most of the narrative.

2. The Gothic Chapbook and Bluebook

Study examples: *The Monk of Horror; or, The Conclave of Corpses* [1-71]; *Spectre Mother; or, The Haunted Tower* [1-106].

Garishly illustrated and cheaply bound shilling shockers, varying in length from thirty-six to seventy-two pages, comprised the chapbook industry. These small Gothics, the ancestors of penny dreadfuls and throwaway dime novels, vary greatly in artistic quality and inevitably turn out to be plagiarized abridgments of long Gothic novels or single sensational episodes expropriated from legitimate Gothics. Almost always anonymous, the chapbooks have cacophonous titles and horrendous engravings. In physical quality, they were primitive paperbacks, meant to be thrown away or literally "read to pieces."

3. The Polemic Gothic and Philosophic Gothic

Study examples: Fenwick, *Secresy; or, The Ruin on the Rock* [1-29]; Godwin, *Things as They Are; or, The Adventures of Caleb Williams* [1-32].

Some serious novelists adapted the conditions of the novel of terror to symbolize in protesting terms certain social or political horrors such as the wretched situation of women. The objective of polemic Gothic was revolutionary and didactic in that it sought to edify as well as electrify the audience by fusing

Gothic horror with radical ideology and the concerns of the social conscience. Philosophic Gothic did have shudders to offer the reader, but its primary goal was to ignite moral indignation and change readers' minds about "things as they are" (Godwin's phrase). In philosophic Gothic forms, the entrapment of the haunted castle is converted into the injustice of the haunted society which denies the individual both freedom and identity.

4. The Gothic Play

Study examples: Lewis, *The Castle Spectre* [1-59]; Walpole, *The Mysterious Mother* [1-109].

Many Gothic dramas were condensed adaptations of the novels, especially the works of Mrs. Radcliffe. Sensational scenery and stagecraft, fabricated storms and spectacular dramaturgy, mechanically reproduced melodramatic effects and operatic dialogue gave the Gothic plays of the period a fashionable popularity and audiovisual appeal on a par with the Gothic novels.

5. The Anti-Gothic Parody

Study examples: Lawler, *The Earls of Hammersmith; or, The Cellar Spectre* [1-55]; R. S., *The New Monk* [1-91].

The absurdities and excesses of the Gothic stimulated two kinds of parody or satire: corrective and critical parody, which accepted the Gothic but wished to elevate its artistic standards; and destructive satire, which sought to eradicate the Gothic and replace it with realistic and sensible fiction. The Gothic was satirized in both novel and dramatic form.

6. The French Gothic Novel (*Roman noir*)

Study examples: Ducray-Duminil, *Victor; or, The Child of the Forest* [1-26]; Sade, *Justine* [1-92].

The French *frénétique romance* or dark novel often contained religious, political and sexual horrors appropriate to the Reign of Terror during the French Revolution. *Romans noirs* were sometimes rapid translations of imported English Gothic works or sentimental romances given a gloomy and morbid component or a supernatural air.

7. The German Gothic Novel (*Schauerroman*)

Study examples: Hoffman, *The Devil's Elixirs* [1-39]; Schiller, *The Ghostseer* [1-94].

The *Schauerroman* or "shudder novel" influenced the English novel of horror by its extreme supernaturalism and excessive, if not outrageous, horrors. Gore-clotted ghosts, ambulatory corpses and interviews with demons were normal events in the *Schauerroman*. The impact of *Schauerromantik* or Germanic Gothicism is highly visible in *The Monk* and becomes the standard ingredient of many Gothic chapbooks.

List of Essential References and Study Aids

In conjunction with this introduction and the primary bibliography, the reader is urged to explore the books, articles and chapters on the history of Gothicism listed below. For individual author studies and reference guides on Gothic fiction and criticism, see chapters 6, 7 and 8, in which a number of these books are fully annotated.

Anderson, Howard. "Gothic Heroes," in *The English Hero, 1660–1800*, ed. by Robert Folkenflik. Newark: Delaware Univ. Press, 1982, pp. 205–221.

Benton, Richard. "The Problems of Literary Gothicism," *ESQ: A Journal of the American Renaissance*, 18 (1972): 5–9.

Birkhead, Edith. *The Tale of Terror: A Study of the Gothic Romance*. London: Constable, 1921; repr., 1963. [7-2]

Brown, Marshall. "A Philosophical View of the Gothic Novel," *Studies in Romanticism*, 26 (1987): 275–301.

Carter, Margaret L. *Spectre or Delusion? The Supernatural in Gothic Fiction*. Ann Arbor: UMI Research Press, 1987. [7-23]

Coad, Oral. "The Gothic Element in American Literature before 1835," *Journal of English and Germanic Philology*, 24 (1925): 72–93.

Coleman, William Emmet. *On the Discrimination of Gothicisms*. New York: Arno Press, 1980. [7-24]

Cooke, Arthur. "Some Side-Lights on the Theory of Gothic Romance," *Modern Language Quarterly*, 12 (1951): 429–436.

Day, William Patrick. *In the Circles of Fear and Desire: A Study of Gothic Fantasy*. Chicago: Univ. of Chicago Press, 1985. [7-17]

Engel, Leonard. "The Role of the Enclosure in the English and American Gothic Romance," *Essays in Arts & Sciences*, 11 (1982): 59–68.

Evans, Bertrand. *Gothic Drama from Walpole to Shelley*. Berkeley and Los Angeles: Univ. of California Press, 1947.

Fiedler, Leslie. *Love and Death in the American Novel*. New York: Criterion, 1960; repr., 1966. [7-36]

Frank, Frederick S. "The Gothic Romance: 1762–1820," in *Horror Literature: A Core Collection and Reference Guide*, ed. by Marshall B. Tymn. New York: R. R. Bowker, 1981, pp. 3–175. [6-33]

Garber, Frederick. "Meaning and Mode in Gothic Fiction," in *Racism in the Eighteenth Century*. Cleveland: Case Western Reserve Univ. Press, 1973, pp. 155–169.

Garrett, John. "The Eternal Appeal of the Gothic," *The Sphinx: A Magazine of Literature and Society*, 2, iv (1977): 1–7.

Harwell, Thomas Meade. "Toward a Gothic Metaphysic: Gothic Parts," *Publications of the Arkansas Philological Association*, 12, ii (1986): 33–43.

———. ed. *The English Gothic Novel: A Miscellany*. 4 vols. Salzburg, Austria: Universität Salzburg, 1986. [7-26]

Heller, Terry. *The Delights of Terror: An Aesthetics of the Tale of Terror*. Urbana: Univ. of Illinois Press, 1987. [7-71]

Hennessy, Brendan. "The Gothic Novel," in *British Writers*, ed. by Ian Scott-Kilvert. New York: Charles Scribner's, 1980, III: 324–346.

Howells, Coral Ann. *Love, Mystery, and Misery: Feeling in Gothic Fiction*. Atlantic Highlands, NJ: Humanities Press, 1978. [7-27]

Hume, Robert D. "Gothic versus Romantic: A Revaluation of the Gothic Novel," *Publications of the Modern Language Association*, 84 (1969): 282–290.

Jarrett, David. *The Gothic Form in Fiction and Its Relation to History*. Winchester, U.K.: King Alfred's College, 1980. [7-28]

Keech, James M. "Survival of the Gothic Response," *Studies in the Novel*, 6 (1974): 130–144.

Lévy, Maurice. *Le Roman "gothique" anglais, 1764–1824.* Toulouse, France: Association des Publications de la Faculté des Lettres et Sciences Humaines de Toulouse, 1968.

Lewis, Paul. "Mysterious Laughter: Humor and Fear in Gothic Fiction," *Genre,* 14 (1981): 309–327.

Lovecraft, Howard Phillips. *Supernatural Horror in Literature.* New York: Ben Abramson, 1945; repr., 1973. [7-7]

MacAndrew, Elizabeth. *The Gothic Tradition in Fiction.* New York: Columbia Univ. Press, 1979. [7-18]

Malin, Irving. *New American Gothic.* Carbondale: Southern Illinois Univ. Press, 1962. [7-42]

Napier, Elizabeth R. *The Failure of the Gothic: Problems of Disjunction in an Eighteenth-Century Literary Form.* New York: Oxford Univ. Press, 1987. [7-31]

Nelson, Lowry, Jr. "Night Thoughts on the Gothic Novel," *Yale Review,* 52 (1963): 236–257.

Nochimson, Martha. "Gothic Novel," in *Critical Survey of Long Fiction,* ed. by Frank Magill. Englewood Cliffs, NJ: Salem Press, 1983, III: 3121–3131.

Punter, David. *The Literature of Terror: A History of Gothic Fiction from 1765 to the Present Day.* London and New York: Longman, 1980. [7-10]

Railo, Eino. *The Haunted Castle: A Study of the Elements of English Romanticism.* London: E. P. Dutton, 1927; repr., 1964. [7-32]

Ringe, Donald A. *American Gothic: Imagination and Reason in Nineteenth-Century Fiction.* Lexington: Univ. Press of Kentucky, 1982. [7-44]

Scarborough, Dorothy. *The Supernatural in Modern English Fiction.* New York: G. P. Putnam's Sons, 1917; repr., 1967. [7-12]

Summers, Montague. *The Gothic Quest: A History of the Gothic Novel.* London: Fortune Press, 1938; repr., 1964. [7-33]

Thompson, G. R. "Gothic Fiction of the Romantic Age: Context and Mode," in *Romantic Gothic Tales 1790–1840.* New York: Harper & Row, 1979, pp. 1–54. [7-21]

Varma, Devendra P. *The Gothic Flame; Being a History of the Gothic Novel in England: Its Origins, Efflorescence, Disintegration and Residuary Influences.* London: A. Barker, 1957; repr., 1966. [7-34]

Varnado, S. L. *Haunted Presence: The Numinous in Gothic Fiction.* Tuscaloosa: Univ. of Alabama Press, 1987. [7-22]

Watt, William Whyte. *Shilling Shockers of the Gothic School: A Study of the Chapbook Gothic Romances.* Cambridge, MA: Harvard Univ. Press, 1932; repr., 1967. [7-35]

Bibliography

Entries in this bibliography are arranged by author or by title when the author is anonymous. Anonymous works are shown as ***. Titles by the same author are listed chronologically. Recommended modern editions and reprintings, where available, are indicated. Many early Gothics republished in the three Arno Press series (1972, 1974, 1977) are currently available from the Ayer Company, Box 958, Salem, NH 03079.

***

1-1. Adventures in a Castle, An Original Story Written by a Citizen of Philadelphia. Harrisburg, PA: J. Elder, 1806.
This typical early American Gothic novel of horror reflects the sensational supernaturalism of the English Gothic chapbooks. The struggle between good and evil relatives for ownership of the castle, which is finally settled by the intervention of supernatural forces in favor of the virtuous characters, is a familiar pattern of action. The two upright brothers, Louis and Henri Boileau, are victimized by their uncle, Count Vauban, who schemes to deprive them of their legacy. The Count's castle offers numerous Gothic dangers, including the sealed chamber from which Henri disappears for much of the narrative, and a maiden in need of rescue, Antoinette de Alençon. A fiery climax finally disposes of the villain and his plans for power. Formulaic Gothic imports of this type indulged in supernatural sensationalism for its own sake without any concession to a moral theme.

Austen, Jane (U.K.), 1775–1817.
About: FG, H, SMFL

***1-2. Northanger Abbey**. London: John Murray, 1818. Recommended edition: ed. by Anne H. Ehrenpreis. Penguin Books.
Austen's parody of Gothic tastes was written in the 1790s at the zenith of the Gothic mania, but was not published until 1818. The satire is directed more against how Gothic fiction was read than against specific Gothic writers. The story deals with the delusions of Catherine Morland, a plain young woman who envisions horrific roles for herself after being exposed to the Gothic virus through a reading list of shockers. Catherine accompanies the Tilney family from Bath to their country seat of Northanger Abbey, where she hopes to become the heroine in a Radcliffean fantasy of thrills and shudders. She converts her host, General Tilney, into a wife murderer and finds a mysterious manuscript which sends her into a Gothic panic. The book criticizes overimaginative novel readers of the day, whose folly lay not so much in the Gothic books they chose to read, but in the manner in which they read them. Chapter 6 contains the famous "Northanger Septet," seven Gothic titles recommended as essential reading to Catherine Morland by Miss Thorpe.

Baculard d'Arnaud, François de (France), 1716–1805.
ABOUT: WW

1-3. Euphémie; ou, Le Triomphe de la réligion [*Euphémie; or, The Triumph of Religion*]. Paris: Lejay, 1768.
The novels and dramas of Baculard d'Arnaud "had a great influence on the development of Gothic romance," according to Montague Summers. The traits of the French Gothic novel or *roman noir* can be seen in *Euphémie* and in its predecessor, *Les Amants malheureux; ou, Le Comte de Comminge* (*The Unfortunate Lovers; or, The Count of Comminge*; 1764). Both works feature cryptic scenery, monastic horrors, fiendish underground settings and fetid burial vaults. Anticlerical horror and the persecution of maidens like Euphémie amid charnel surroundings anticipate the Catholic horrors soon to become a major feature of the English Gothic tradition.

Barbauld, Anne Letitia Aiken (U.K.), 1743–1825.
ABOUT: GSF, FG

1-4. Sir Bertrand; A Fragment. London: J. Johnson, 1792. Recommended edition: in *Gothic Tales of Terror*, ed. by Peter Haining. Taplinger, 1972.
Barbauld's model tale of terror, the *Sir Bertrand Fragment*, was introduced by the essay "On the Pleasure Derived from Objects of Terror." The goal of the Gothic is "to feed the appetite for wonder by a quick succession of marvellous events to raise in the mind that thrilling, mysterious terror which has for its object 'the powers unseen and mightier than we.'" Sir Bertrand follows the toll of a solemn bell as it summons him to an "antique mansion" which looms like a Grail castle. An invisible host welcomes him by "thrusting forward the bloody stump of an arm," and a blue light illuminates his way to an inner sanctum where a shrouded lady stirs hopefully in her sarcophagus at Sir Bertrand's approach. When she bestows her kiss upon him, the scene dissolves and the quester is transported to a wonderful feast where he is welcomed once more by the lovely lady, now restored to life. The *Fragment* aborts at that point, at which Mrs. Barbauld hoped a maximum peak of astonishment had been attained.

Barrett, Eaton Stannard (U.K.), 1786–1820.
ABOUT: FG

1-5. The Heroine; or, The Adventures of a Fair Romance Reader. London: Henry Colburn, 1813. Recommended edition: ed. by Michael Sadleir. Matthews & Marrot, 1927.
Barrett's burlesque stands in contrast to the milder ridicule of Gothic fashions in Jane Austen's *Northanger Abbey* [1-2]. His lampoon tries to laugh the Gothic off the literary stage and to forestall future Gothic nonsense. The Gothic novel had become "so seductive that it tends to incapacitate us from the turmoils of active life." Hence, he sought the extermination of the genre itself. The heroine is Cherry Wilkinson, who changes her name to Cherubina de Willoughby to pursue a Gothic career for herself. She responds to thunder when it rolls in "an Ossianly manner" and peers into each male face hoping to behold "the quivering lip and

Schedoniac contour." The Gothic drama of her life takes her to the prerequisite confinement at Moncton Castle where she imitates the "tripping, gliding, flitting, and tottering" movements of all of the hysterical heroines she has read about. Barrett's scorn for the excesses of the Gothic approaches the limits of parody where the satiric can barely be distinguished from authentic Gothic narrative.

Beckford, William (U.K.), 1760–1844.

About: WW, GSF, SFW, F, FG, SMFL, PE, ESF

***1-6. Vathek; An Arabian Tale from an Unpublished Manuscript, with Notes Critical and Explanatory**. London: J. Johnson, 1786. Recommended edition: in *Three Gothic Novels*, ed. by E. F. Bleiler. Dover, 1966.
An orientalized Gothic and a subterranean quest romance, *Vathek* signaled a move in Gothic fiction toward a demonic vision of human existence. Satan (or Eblis) presides over the universe of *Vathek*, a cosmos in which disorder is far more likely than order. Only damnation itself can gratify the Caliph Vathek, who leaves his capital of Sammarah to undertake a perverse pilgrimage which brings him to the Halls of Eblis. Vathek's passion for absolutes is symbolized by his lethal eye, which can maim or slay. Renouncing Allah, he follows his desires to their infernal limits by descending through forbidden portals to the dark center of the Earth; as he descends ever deeper into the Earth, he descends by extension ever deeper into zones of subconscious desire. Few scenes in Gothic literature can match the horror of the subterranean climax of *Vathek* in which the Gothic hero sees Eblis and watches his heart become transparent with hell-flame. Damned to wander eternally through the corridors of desire, the hero is doomed in the end to a condition of everlasting torment. The work's subterranean climax influenced many later writers including H. P. Lovecraft, whose "Rats in the Walls" [see 3-132] is a Beckfordian Gothic fantasy. Also annotated as [F1-8].

Boaden, James (U.K.), 1762–1839.

1-7. The Italian Monk; A Play in Three Acts. London: G. G. & J. Robinson, 1797. Recommended edition: in *The Plays of James Boaden*. Garland, 1978.
The playwright of terror James Boaden was acclaimed as an adapter of Gothic novels. *The Italian Monk* is a dramatization of Mrs. Radcliffe's *The Italian* [1-84]. Boaden kept the gloomy scenery, but intensified the melodrama of Father Schedoni's stalking of Ellena di Rosalba. Adding thrill to the normally slow Radcliffean plot, he omitted long sections of the novel's journeys in order to bring the maiden under the villain's dagger without delay. Boaden was careful to render all terror as authentic, in order to leave these effects unexplained. In eliminating the rational dénouements of Mrs. Radcliffe, he did more than simply adapt her best Gothic work for the London stage. "His decision was to omit not Mrs. Radcliffe's excesses, but her natural explanations of the supernatural. For the first time, a playwright undertook to out-Gothicize a novelist," noted Bertrand Evans in *Gothic Drama from Walpole to Shelley*.

Boutet de Monvel, Jacques-Marie (France), 1745-1812.

1-8. Les Victims cloîtrées [*The Victims of the Cloister*]. Paris: Lepetit, 1792. Recommended edition: in *Three Centuries of French Drama.* Falls City Press, 1959.
The criminal monk appears as a fully drawn Gothic villain in the person of Father Laurent, a model for Lewis's Father Ambrosio in *The Monk* [1-58]. Catholic horrors, monkish secrecy and the victimization of women furnished the ardent revolutionary Boutet de Monvel with powerful propaganda for his assault on the class privilege of the *ancien régime*. With Diderot's *La Réligieuse* [1-24], this drama influenced the moods of religious terror to be found in so much English Gothic fiction of the late 1790s with its scenes of monastic rape and abuse of religious power to gratify the lusts of the flesh.

Brown, Charles Brockden, 1771-1810.

ABOUT: WW, SMFL, PE, ESF

***1-9. Wieland; or, The Transformation**. New York: H. Caritat, 1798. Recommended edition: ed. by Fred Lewis Patee. Hafner, 1960.
Wieland is a dark fable of moral horror and mental terror whose Gothic content questions the assumptions of innocence underlying the American experience and character. The novel takes the form of a family history recounted by Clara Wieland who draws her strange and terrible data from the dark pool of memory. The Wielands are an accursed family living in the family mansion on the shore of the Schuylkill River outside Philadelphia. A malady hangs over the House of Wieland and causes the death of Clara's father by spontaneous combustion and the homicidal madness of her brother, Theodore, who believes that the voice of God has commanded him to take the lives of his wife and children. Entrapped within the castle of self, Clara Wieland is the first American Gothic heroine to understand that there is a stain of evil on the American oversoul. The book's most conventional Gothic character is the ventriloquist, Carwin, who uses his voice to usurp the function of the Almighty and to animate the evil that exists in the Wieland family. Carwin is a Gothic superman who exercises his peculiar power to damn some characters and to save others, finally saving Clara from homicidal assault by her brother. These characters predict the future shape of a morally serious American Gothic mode that would emerge in Hawthorne's *The House of the Seven Gables* and later in the dark family sagas of Faulkner's *Absalom, Absalom!* and Jackson's *The Haunting of Hill House* [4-155]. In its terrifying thesis concerning a lower or Gothic self which can seize control without warning, *Wieland* anticipates the central themes of the American Gothic experience. Also annotated as [F1-11].

1-10. Arthur Mervyn; or, The Memoirs of the Year 1793. Philadelphia and New York: H. Maxwell, 1799-1800. Recommended edition: ed. by Warner Berthoff. Holt, Rinehart, 1962.
An urbanized Gothic, wherein the city streets replace the castle maze, appears in *Arthur Mervyn*. The site of terror is Philadelphia during the 1793 epidemic of yellow fever. The public burial teams, the stench of death, the disintegration of civic order and the entrapment of young Mervyn give the novel its unique Gothic texture. In his search for a missing man named Wallace, Mervyn becomes in-

volved with a master criminal, Welbeck, a Yankee version of the traditional Gothic villain. Manipulated by Welbeck, young Arthur is forced to help in the interment of a murdered man and is subjected to the nightmare of the pit. While his dream is in progress, his unconscious body is loaded into a coffin by one of the public burial teams. Through such Gothic experiences, Brown foreshadows the deeper character of the American Gothic mode. The haunted city of *Arthur Mervyn* exposed a rich vein of American Gothic horror that would descend to even greater depths in later tales of the Gothic city such as Hawthorne's "My Kinsman, Major Molineux" and the urban horrors of Richard Wright and Joyce Carol Oates.

1-11. Ormond; or, The Secret Witness. New York: H. Caritat, 1799. Recommended edition: ed. by Sidney J. Krause and S. W. Reid. Kent State Univ. Press, 1981. The most compelling Gothic condition in this dark political fable is the yellow fever pestilence which creates an atmosphere of sickness, death and fear. Through the infected air stalks the blighted figure of Ormond, a personification of the plague itself. He maintains ties with the secret society of the Illuminati and demonstrates the other traits of the traditional Gothic villain. Ormond schemes to break the will of Constantia Dudley by imprisoning her in "a solitary and darksome abode" where he terrifies her with a corpse and threatens her with necrophiliac rape. Significantly, the American maiden in distress rebels against her victimization when she turns upon her tormentor and stabs Ormond to death. Her act symbolizes a declaration of independence from the guiles of Europe, since Ormond's perverted theories of power are countered by an American heroine who represents the superiority of American democratic energy over European tyranny.

1-12. Edgar Huntly; or, The Memoirs of a Sleep-Walker. Philadelphia: H. Maxwell, 1799. Recommended edition: ed. by David Stineback. College & Univ. Press, 1973. A haunted castle becomes a haunted forest complete with hideous pit and spectral Indians in this early example of naturalized American Gothic. This novel is cast in the form of letters from Edgar Huntly to Mary Waldegrave describing his loss of rational control over his life, as he becomes a sleepwalker and possibly a murderer. The climax of Huntly's night journey into the depths of the forest occurs in the episode of the dreamer in the pit. Huntly awakens to find himself in a vast underground compartment whose exact shape he cannot determine and where delirium, hunger, the eyes of a panther and the silhouettes of marauding savages torment him. With his realization that there is an unprobed nightside to every human intelligence, or a pit which awaits us all, Brown fixes the American Gothic theme of the unexplored darkness of the self.

***

1-13. The Castle De Warrenne, A Romance. In: *Lady's Monthly Museum, or Polite Repository of Amusement and Instruction* (July–December 1800; 6 parts). Recommended edition: in *The Candle and the Tower*, ed. by R. D. Spector. Warner, 1974.
About: FG

A serialized Gothic novella typical of the installment Gothics which glutted the ladies' magazines from the mid-1790s through the 1820s. The reader follows the misadventures of four endangered maidens, Matilda, Lady Barome, Constantia and Olivia, with each heroine's plight associated with a sojourn at a different castle or abbey. Each heroine explores her place of confinement and rhapsodizes upon its Gothic sublimity as she is propelled toward discovery of her family identity and returned to the safe world of marriage and domestic safety outside the castle walls. Gothic novellas like *Castle De Warrenne* combined the dreadful pleasures of Gothic terror with the soothing myth of domestic security.

***

1-14. The Cavern of Horrors; or, The Miseries of Miranda, A Neapolitan Tale. London: T. Hurst, 1802.

About: FG

Eleven swoons over seventy-two pages by the miserable Miranda suggest the tear-stained pace of this Gothic chapbook. The Goth made certain that something horrid occurred on each page so that the heroine's "ability to totter into a state of utter oblivion" was the chief attraction. The main misery is the treatment she receives at the hands of her father, who abducts Miranda, then deposits her in the cavern of horrors. Miseries accumulate until Miranda is delivered by finding love in the arms of the reformed rake Napoli di Logano. The task of the chapbooker was to convey the heroine from anguish to the altar within the number of pages allotted by the rapacious publisher.

Crookenden, Isaac (U.K.), dates unknown.

About: FG

1-15. The Skeleton; or The Mysterious Discovery, A Gothic Romance. London: A. Neill, 1805.

Specializing in forged Gothics, Crookenden haunted the literary scene for more than two decades, turning out thirty-eight- and seventy-two-page chapbooks. The Crookenden plot offered splashes of bright red blood and spectral commotion against a backdrop of dismal shadows and toppled turrets. The horrific scenes in *The Skeleton* are taken from earlier Gothics in which the device of the animated skeleton appears. Mobile bones almost always belong to the murdered master of the castle and such is the case with Crookenden's dead Baron in this little Gothic. The castle tyrant is Maurice, or "the dark one," a composite of the villains of Walpole and Lewis, who is brought to justice at last by the ambulatory skeleton. The shilling shocker's haste and crudity are glaringly evident at the finale: Rotaldo's gore-clotted murder by Maurice having already been described, the young hero would not have been available to wed Almira on page 38 of the chapbook.

Curties, T. J. Horsley (U.K.), dates unknown.

About: FG

1-16. Ancient Records; or, The Abbey of St. Oswythe. London: Minerva Press for William Lane, 1801.

A Gothified history set in the reign of Henry VI, the novel duplicates plot elements taken from Mrs. Radcliffe's romances. Curties's heroine, Rosaline, is a reproduction of the Radcliffean hysteric as she anticipates with pleasure the worst of fates for herself when she is taken by force to the Abbey of St. Oswythe. The omnipresent villain, Gondemar, is also a standard figure of Radcliffean nightmare. While investigating the abbey, Rosaline enters a cell and discovers a closed casket, lifts the lid, then faints. In the tradition of Mrs. Radcliffe's technique of suspenseful delay, the reader is never told what Rosaline saw. Such horrid shocks and unexplained horrors carry the heroine from chamber to chamber and terror to terror until her release from the abbey and matrimony.

1-17. The Monk of Udolpho. London: D. N. Shury for J. F. Hughes, 1807. Recommended edition: ed. by Sister Mary M. Tarr. Arno, 1977.
Curties's malicious monk is Father Udolpho, "bold in guilt, triumphant in the success of his dark projects, cruel, bloodthirsty, insidious, remorseless and deceitful, formed to delude, and self-trained from boyhood to manhood in every vice." The victim of this monastic fiend and his agent, Sanguedoni, is Hersilia de Placenza. The peak of her peril comes when she is assailed by Sanguedoni during a drugged sleep. The phantom of Eloise enters to thwart the rape and to expose Sanguedoni as Father Udolpho. These events are handled with a crude vigor that unites the different Gothic methods of Mrs. Radcliffe and Monk Lewis. In the career of the Monk of Udolpho, Curties demonstrates that he who is capable of great good is also capable of great evil, a theme linking the Gothic hero to his nobler antecedent, the tragic hero.

Dacre, Charlotte (as by **Rosa Matilda**) (U.K.), 1782–1842.
About: GSF, FG

1-18. The Confessions of the Nun of St. Omer. London: D. N. Shury for J. F. Hughes, 1805. Recommended edition: ed. by Devendra P. Varma. Arno, 1972.
Dacre is perhaps the most accomplished female terror writer after Mrs. Radcliffe. Although her work would shift quickly to mainstream Gothic, her first book exhibits definite tendencies toward the novel of radical ideas as written by the Jacobin novelists of the 1790s. The narrative consists of the posthumous memoirs of Cazire de Arieni, a nun whose dissolute life is held up as a warning to her son, Dorvil Lindorf. She has been involved with two opposite men, the Byronic free-lover, Fribourg, and the conservative Count Lindorf. Because of her promiscuity, she undergoes a series of sexual falls which end in death for others and madness for herself. Dacre's characters represent some of the more extreme social theories of the era working in fatal conjunction with powerful sexual passions.

***1-19. Zofloya; or, The Moor, A Romance of the Fifteenth Century**. London: Longman, Hurst, Rees, Orme, 1806. Recommended edition: ed. by G. Wilson Knight. Arno, 1974.
The villainous role belongs to the devil-driven Victoria de Lorendani, who makes a diabolic pact with the Moor, Zofloya. In her character are concentrated all the bad energies which make for an exciting Gothic personage. "The wildest passions pre-dominated in her bosom; to gratify them, she possessed an unshrinking, relentless soul that would not startle at the darkest crime." Victoria travels to Venice to marry Berenza but schemes to seduce his brother, Henriquez. The thought of homicide is especially appealing to her, and to satisfy her lusts she enlists the aid of Zofloya. To evade the fires of the Inquisition, Victoria bargains away her soul to Zofloya who becomes an increasingly diabolic figure as the novel

progresses. Dacre attempted to surpass Lewis in shock in the annihilation of her wicked woman. Having saved her from the stake, Zofloya changes into Satan before her eyes, then "grasped firmly the neck of the wretched Victoria—and with one push he whirled her headlong down the fearful abyss."

1-20. The Libertine. London: T. Cadell & W. Davies, 1807. Recommended edition: ed. by John Garrett. Arno, 1974.
Dacre's Gothic probes the unconscious desires and discloses the sadistic aspects of human nature. The example of Richardson's rake, Lovelace, in *Clarissa* (1748) stands behind Dacre's conception of the libertine, the Count Angelo d'Albani. His victim is the child of nature, Gabrielle Montmorency, who is seduced, abandoned and subjected to all the Count's passions. That the Gothic novel is an extreme form of its literary predecessor, the sentimental novel, is evident in Dacre's character arrangement. All the debaucheries of the libertine are done with great psychological realism and the Count's one decent deed, the taking of his own life in a spasm of conscience, brings the book's Gothic action within range of two tragic themes, the wastage of intelligence and the destruction of innocence.

1-21. The Passions. London: T. Cadell & W. Davies, 1811. Recommended edition: ed. by Sandra Knight-Roth. Arno, 1974.
The correspondents in this epistolary Gothic represent polarities of destructive feeling. The passions become the new specters in Dacre's last Gothic as they assume an almost supernatural control over the characters, thus replacing supernatural horror with the force of the unknown self. The tale centers on two married couples, Count Wiemar and Julia, and Count Darlowitz and Amelia. Two independent characters, the deistic Baron Rotzendorf and the sensualist Apollonia Zulmer, infiltrate the lives of the couples. Apollonia arouses the sexual passions of the characters to the dismay of Baron Rotzendorf, who must watch helplessly as the marital paradises are ruined. The falls of the characters indicate how weak reason and self-control are when confronted by forces hidden just below the surface. Dacre's Gothic depicted the mind haunted by itself, a significant internalization of the basic Gothic conflict between villain and maiden.

Dana, Richard Henry, Sr., 1787-1879.

1-22. Paul Felton. In: **The Idle Man**, 2, no. 1 (1822). Recommended edition: in *The Idle Man*. Gordon Press, 1984.
Dana explored the darkness within the Gothic castle of the mind where the act of imagination might create not a vision of beauty but its opposite. His cerebral Gothic has affinities with the earlier psychological Gothicism of Brown's *Wieland* [1-9]. Paul Felton, the sensitive main character, is a prisoner of the castle of self and is tortured by an imagination which transforms all love into expressions of hatred. Like the insane Theodore Wieland, Felton is finally driven by a supernatural voice to kill his wife, Esther. He has had a terrible experience within a wilderness den called the "Devil's haunt" which has transformed him from misanthrope into mad murderer. Dana's interest in the vulnerability of the human mind and the proximity of that mind to madness link him with one of the central themes of the American Gothic: horror of self-encounter.

De Quincey, Thomas (U.K.), 1785-1859.
ABOUT: FG

1-23. Klosterheim, or The Masque. London: T. Cadell, 1832. Recommended edition: ed. by John Weeks. Woodbridge Press, 1982.
Klosterheim is a Gothified history of the Thirty Years War (1618-48) and of an imaginary Catholic city on the Rhine crushed by Protestant occupation. Blood flows; persecution abounds; fear stalks the streets as the deadly religious war rages outside the city walls. The "Masque" of the title refers to a mysterious being, half renegade and half champion of the people. He moves by night through the streets, sometimes performing deeds of justice. The novel also reuses the Gothic novel's female prisoner in Paulina whose sufferings at the hands of the Landgrave's mercenaries would be familiar to every Gothic reader. By preternatural if not supernatural means, the Masque eventually brings the Landgrave's wickedness to account, then unmasks himself to Paulina to reveal her dead lover, Maximilian. The mysterious events and revelation scenes are written in a kind of high Gothic rhetoric which blends the styles of Lewis and Radcliffe and gives the novel its unsurpassed moments of cold horror.

Diderot, Denis (France), 1713-1784.
ABOUT: SFE

1-24. La Rêligieuse [*The Nun*]. Paris: Buisson, 1796. Recommended edition: tr. by Leonard Tancock. Penguin, 1977.
Elements of the monastic shocker—including sexual fear—are present in *La Rêligieuse*. Except for its assault on the tyranny of parents and religious authority, the book could be classified as high Gothic fiction. The narrative is a first-person account by the involuntary novice, Suzanne Simonin, who has been condemned by her parents to a life of servitude in several nunneries. In a moment of Gothic horror, Suzanne is compelled to put on a shroud and occupy a coffin in a mock funeral so real that it causes her to fear that it will be followed by live burial. The young nun is the constant object of sexual lust by the authority figures of her closed world. The peril of Suzanne at the hands of a lesbian mother superior, the lugubrious chapels and the terrible cells of penance (called "In Pace Requiescat") add a strong Gothic décor to her psychological sufferings. Finally, *La Rêligieuse* uses the restrictive environment of the religious community as a metaphor for the repressive social structure and the warping of natural passion by unnatural institutions.

Drake, Nathan (U.K.), 1766-1836.
ABOUT: FG

1-25. "The Abbey of Clunedale" in *Literary Hours; or, Sketches Critical, Narrative, and Poetical*. London: J. Mitchell, 1798; T. Cadell & W. Davies, 1804. Recommended edition: in *Great Tales of Terror*, ed. by Peter Haining. Taplinger, 1972.
Drake's *Literary Hours* appeared in several editions from 1798 to 1804. He was the

first theorist of the Gothic to identify a Gothic pleasure principle whereby objects of terror could be "appalling, yet delighting to the reader." The sixty "hours" in the 1804 edition include essays on the operation of the Gothic aesthetic and response to various supernatural experiences as well as short tales of terror illustrating his discussions of Gothic narrative theory. "On Gothic Superstition" (Hour number 6), and "On Objects of Terror" (Hour number 15), are landmarks in Gothic criticism. The outstanding piece in the collection is the Radcliffean set piece "The Abbey of Clunedale." Terror in the tale arises entirely out of the eerie atmosphere which slowly builds to a sense of pleasing horror. Edward de Courtenay makes a round of nocturnal visits to the Abbey of Clunedale where he prostrates himself before the tomb of his father. As de Courtenay repeats his penance, the sister of his deceased wife mistakes him for a phantom. Drake is especially accomplished at making the natural world overlap with the supernatural in this encounter scene and others.

Ducray-Duminil, François Guillaume (France), 1761-1819.

1-26. Alexis; ou, La Maisonette dans les bois [*Alexis; or, The Cottage in the Forest*]. Paris: Maradan, 1789.
Alexis is a source for Mrs. Radcliffe's *Romance of the Forest* [1-82]. Another novel, *Victor; ou, L'Enfant de la forêt* (*Victor; or, The Child of the Forest*; 1796) was widely read in England and features a mixture of horrid and pastoral incident. Deep within the bandit-ridden forest of Chamboran stands the maisonette of Clairette and her father, Candor. This former criminal has abjured society and sought refuge in nature to escape the guilt of murdering his wife. Directly beneath the cottage is a maze of passageways leading to a hidden sepulcher containing her bones. Clairette descends to explore the secret underground, whose existence has been kept from her by her father. She encounters the stranger, Alexis, who guides her to the dark truth about her father and herself. The curious heroine, the homicidal father and Gothic melancholy in a subterranean setting were all attractive to the English Gothic imagination.

Dunlap, William, 1766-1839.

1-27. Fountainville Abbey. New York: David Longworth and the Dramatic Repository, Shakespeare Gallery, 1807. Recommended edition: in *Four Plays*. Scholar's Facsimiles, 1976.
America's "first native Gothic play" is a spectacularized version of Mrs. Radcliffe's third novel, *The Romance of the Forest* [1-82]. Character names and the sites of terror are preserved from the Radcliffean model. The villain, the Marquis of Montalt, the tearful Adeline and their ballet of death in the underground cells of the abbey give this stage adaptation a dramatic momentum not to be found in the slow-moving pages of Mrs. Radcliffe. When the trembling Adeline exclaims, "I must be cautious lest the sudden blast extinguish my faint guide. What's that I tread on? A dagger all corrupted by the rust," we can be certain that we have entered the Gothic world.

F., E. (U.K.), dates unknown.
ABOUT: FG

1-28. The Cave of St. Sidwell; A Romance. In: *Lady's Monthly Museum, or Polite Repository of Amusement and Instruction,* 2-3 (January–August 1807; 6 parts). Recommended edition: in *The Candle and the Tower,* ed. by R. D. Spector. 1974.
A serialized Gothic complexly plotted and ultra-sentimental in style. E. F. adheres to the maiden-centered formulas of Radcliffean Gothic. The heroine, "the hapless Rosa," must traverse abbey, cave, cottage and convent en route to her identity and a reunion with her parents. At the highpoint of horror, she is just barely prevented from marrying her father by the melodramatic intervention of a fearsome hag who later reveals herself to be Rosa's guilty mother, Julia. Periodical Gothics of this sort often prove to be well-made fables of danger and success and many commence their action within a cave or natural enclosure which symbolizes some genealogical secret. The cave or cavern also functions as an image for mental recesses where a concealed past is buried.

Fenwick, Eliza (U.K.), dates unknown.
ABOUT: FG

1-29. Secresy; or, The Ruin on the Rock. London: William Lane, Knight, 1795. Recommended edition: Garland, 1973.
Ideological fictions were sometimes marketed under Gothic titles to lure the reader. Such is the case with Fenwick's epistolary novel of radical ideas exposing the plight of women. Letters flow between two victims of despotic fathers and husbands, Sibella Valmont and Caroline Ashburn. To subdue her spirit, Lord Valmont had confined Sibella to a lonesome fortress, the ruin on the rock. Instead of being terrified into obedience, the young woman maintains her spirited correspondence with her friend and continues to protest her servitude. Both women are harassed by the repulsive Murden, thus strengthening their bond as objects of male privilege. Although Sibella's solitary situation duplicates that of the typical Gothic heroine, she responds intellectually rather than emotionally to these terrors with statements of protest instead of hysterical fainting fits and passive swoons.

Fitzball, Edward (U.K.), 1792–1873.

1-30. The Devil's Elixir; or, The Shadowless Man. London: J. Cumberland, n.d. Recommended edition: in *The Hour of One: Six Gothic Melodramas,* ed. by Stephen Wischhusen. Gordon Fraser, 1975.
Fitzball became famous in London theater for his dramatizations of popular Gothic novels. *The Devil's Elixir* is a Gothic melodrama stressing the morbid themes of its sources, Hoffmann's horror novel *Die Elixiere des Teufels* [1-39], and German legends concerning the folklore figure Peter Schlemihl, the man who lost his shadow to the devil. The tragicomic account of Peter Schlemihl's shadowless life was available to Fitzball from Chamisso's *Peter Schlemihls wundersame Geschichte* (*The Wonderful History of Peter Schlemihl*; 1814 [F2-27]).

Freneau, Philip, 1752-1832.

1-31. The House of Night. Philadelphia: Francis Bailey, 1788. Recommended edition: in *Poems of Freneau*, ed. by Harry Hayden Clark. Hafner, 1960.
Freneau's Gothic poem was first published in *The United States Magazine* for August 1779. The 136 quatrains echo the charnel imagery and scenery of the English Graveyard School, Blair's "The Grave" (1743) and Young's "Night Thoughts" (1742). Freneau's wanderer, an undertaker, enters the House of Night where he beholds Death himself as he lies dying in his own dark abode. Death ponders an epitaph for himself while the wanderer undertakes to assist him in this last task. The picture of Death upon his deathbed is rendered as a Gothic encounter with an animated skeleton. "Sad was his countenance, where only bones were seen,/And eyes sunk in their sockets, dark and low,/And teeth, that only show'd themselves to grin."

Godwin, William (U.K.), 1756-1836.

About: GSF, FG, H

***1-32. Things as They Are; or, The Adventures of Caleb Williams**. London: B. Crosby, 1794. Recommended edition: ed. by David McCracken. W. W. Norton, 1977.
Godwin used the Gothic to arouse the passions of the audience and move his readers to revolutionary action. His haunted castle is society itself, a social horror haunted by phantoms of injustice. The victim is no longer a maiden scurrying from a villain, but a young man of high principles harassed by the terrors of the law. Caleb Williams is the private secretary to the once decent Squire Falkland. Falkland has murdered a landowner named Tyrrel, but only Caleb Williams knows of his master's deed. Shielded by the law, Falkland permits another man to be tried and hanged for his offense. Debased by his crime and its concealment, Falkland pursues and persecutes Caleb Williams with the law behind him. The Gothic context was thus modernized, furnishing Godwin with a vehicle for expressing his moral horror over the entrapment of the liberal self within reactionary ideologies and a corrupt social structure.

1-33. St. Leon; A Tale of the Sixteenth Century. London: G. G. & J. Robinson, 1799. Recommended edition: ed. by Juliet Beckett. Arno, 1972.
Godwin placed the tale in the sixteenth century and revived the motif of the quest for the elixir of eternal life. When the knight, Reginald St. Leon, is visited by a Jew, Zampieri, he is granted the secret gift of immortality in the philosopher's stone. St. Leon immerses himself in alchemy, withdraws from human fellowship and causes the death of his wife, Marguerita. His activities draw the attention of the Inquisition and he is arrested for sorcery and made to watch the ceremony of the *auto-da-fé*, the public burning of heretics. This spectacle gives Godwin an opportunity to indict the institutionalized cruelties of church and state. St. Leon travels to Hungary where he begins a friendship with the giant Bethlem Gabor, the novel's most traditional Gothic character. The novel ends in a melodramatic fashion with the release of St. Leon from Gabor's dungeon, but physical freedom brings no accompanying spiritual freedom, and he becomes a type of Wandering

Jew figure himself. Godwin's theme of the corrupt consequences of knowledge and power impressed the Shelleys and left its imprint on his daughter's *Frankenstein* [1-97]. Also annotated as [F1-30].

Green, William Child (U.K.), dates unknown.
About: GSF, FG

1-34. The Abbot of Montserrat; or, The Pool of Blood. London: A. K. Newman, 1826. Recommended edition: ed. by Frederick Shroyer. Arno, 1977.
This novel holds its place in the final years of the Gothic movement as a brilliant flash of lightning even as the Gothic storm was passing from the literary landscape. Green's abbot is Obando, a creature of one virtue and a thousand crimes whose goals are religious power and sexual pleasure. He signs the contract of blood offered to him by the demon, Zatanai, then embarks upon a campaign of atrocities. Father Obando becomes the Abbot of Montserrat, murdering the previous abbot and converting this holy fortress into a vast torture chamber. The pool of blood in the abbey vaults might have succeeded as the ultimate horror of horrors, but Green undermined its effect by explaining it away as a chemical illusion. Green further violated the principle of victorious evil at the climax. Zatanai bears the criminal monk skyward through the roof of the burning abbey, then releases him to destruction. Looking down upon the conflagration beneath him, Father Obando repents in midair. Although his body now drops to its destruction, the reader must assume that his restored soul ascends to heaven.

Grosse, Carl (U.K.), 1768-1847.
About: GSF, FG

1-35. Horrid Mysteries. London: Minerva Press for William Lane, 1796. Recommended edition: ed. by Devendra P. Varma. Folio Press, 1968.
Few Gothics rival *Horrid Mysteries* for its horror and perplexity of plots, which resist synopsis. The pattern of flight and pursuit through midnight settings is globally enlarged; instead of moving through the catacombs of a haunted castle, the several victims' flights are from country to country. The international maze is presided over by a secret society which wields total power over its members. One of the heroes swears the blood oath to the society and finds himself enmeshed in a web of assassination and crime. He becomes a lethal automaton and may be responsible for several murders. The adventures are punctuated by the appearances of a phantasmic figure called Genius Amanuel who infiltrates the lives of various young men. One of Grosse's best Gothic scenes is the moment of cadaverous resurrection. Characters are casually killed off, then just as suddenly brought back to life, not once but many times. Elmira suffers at least three deaths and awakens after one of these while she is being transported in a coffin to a graveyard. No novel to survive from the Gothic period is more difficult to decipher or more surreal than *Horrid Mysteries*.

Harley, Mrs. (U.K.), dates unknown.
About: FG

1-36. The Priory of St. Bernard; An Old English Tale. London: William Lane, 1789. Recommended edition: ed. by William E. Coleman. Arno, 1977.
The Priory straddles an underground recess where Elgiva and her daughters, Maud and Laura, are held captive by an avuncular villain, Manston. Also known as the Knight Coucy, he schemes to have Lord Raby's estates along with his sisters, Laura and Maud. The novel abounds in Walpolesque contraptions. Lord Raby encounters the walking statue of his father as he roams the corridors of the Priory when the colossus points the way to rescue and revenge. But before the release of the sisters and the punishment of Manston/Coucy, Mrs. Harley permits the genealogical confusions to multiply to the point of absolute bewilderment. Yet Mrs. Harley was capable of writing thrilling scenes and her work does form a natural link between the Gothified histories of Clara Reeve and Sophia Lee and the masterworks of Mrs. Radcliffe.

Helme, Elizabeth (U.K.), 1758-1813.
About: FG

1-37. The Farmer of Inglewood Forest. 4 vols. London: Minerva Press for William Lane, 1796.
The domestic Gothic novel retained its popularity throughout the nineteenth century. These four volumes are crowded with catastrophic incident set off by the Romantic solitude of the forest. The story concerns the struggle of Farmer Godwin to preserve his children from the corruptions of city life. Edwin, William and Emma are lured away by a libertine pair, Mr. Whitmore and Mrs. Delmar. Each child succumbs to the vices of the city, then returns to Inglewood to engage in some cruel or disgraceful deed. Farmer Godwin can only moralize sadly over the decline of his family and the loss of their natural purity. The Gothic spirit dominates such scenes as Edwin's rape of his illegitimate daughter, Anna, and horror supersedes morality in another hideous scene in which Edwin stares down into Agnes Bernard's casket, there to behold a cadaverous infant with skeletal smile.

1-38. St. Margaret's Cave; or, The Nun's Story, An Ancient Legend. London: Earle & Hemet, 1801. Recommended edition: ed. by Devendra P. Varma. Arno, 1977.
A romance of the ruin in which the plot turns upon the device of the recovered manuscript which proves to be the biography of Sister Margaret. Much complicated action is dedicated to the genealogical tribulations of the heroine whose immurement in Castle Fitzwater in Northumberland brings her by a narrow passageway to St. Margaret's Cave, a place of mystery and destiny. The cave is the haunt of a hermit, the mad monk Austin, who befriends the nun and assists her against the machinations of Lord De Launcy. This is an orthodox Gothic plot in which every elaborate twist of fate brings the heroine one step closer to the reattainment of her good name. Both a cavern or grotto Gothic and its architectural opposite, tower or turret Gothic, this novel endows place with a supernatural

personality transforming the setting itself into the Gothic novel's most important character.

Hoffmann, E. T. A. (Germany), 1776-1822.

ABOUT: WW, GSF, SFW, NE, H, SMFL, SFE, RG, PE, ESF

***1-39. Die Elixiere des Teufels; Nachgelassene Papiere des Bruders Medardus** [*The Devil's Elixirs; Posthumous Papers of Brother Medardus*]. Berlin: Duncker & Humblot, 1815. Recommended edition: tr. by Ronald Taylor. J. Calder, 1963.
Hoffmann's horror novel was inspired by *The Monk* [1-58] and surpasses its English Gothic prototype in its portrayal of destructive psychological states. In presenting the crisis of multiple identity, the tale is "the analysis of a man who did not know where he began or ended." The story follows the criminal career of Father Medardus, a Capuchin monk whose outward holiness is a facade for his inward evil ways. Driven by fantasies of power, he drinks from a flask of liquor said to contain the elixir which Satan used to tempt Saint Anthony. He finds himself bedeviled by a twin or *doppelgänger* who threatens Medardus's identity. Medardus thinks that he witnessed the Count Viktorin's suicide when he seemed to plunge over a cliff, but Viktorin's presence in the life of the monk indicates the twin's supernatural survival. Fleeing from his demonic double, Medardus takes refuge in the monastery, where he discovers an ancient document forecasting his destiny and marking him for more monstrous deeds. Like Lewis's Ambrosio, Hoffmann's monk meets a spectacular death. Thematically, this Gothic version of the *doppelgänger* myth concerns the fatal collision of psychic forces ending in the violent disintegration of the self.

1-40. Nachtstücke [*Night Pieces*]. Berlin: Realschulbuchhandlung, 1817. Recommended edition: in *The Best Tales of E. T. A. Hoffmann,* ed. by E. F. Bleiler. Dover, 1967.
Hoffmann was steeped in the supernaturalism of the German *Schauerroman* or "shudder novel." To the physical horrors of Germanic Gothicism, Hoffmann appended a psychological dimension causing his tales to operate on the supernatural and psychological levels simultaneously. Such subjectified Gothic is the central quality of his *Night Pieces* and *Fantasiestücke* (*Fantasy Pieces,* 1814), "Der Sandmann" ("The Sandman"), *Das Majorat* (*The Entail* or *Inherited Estate*), "Der unheimliche Gast" ("The Weird Guest"), "Die Bergwerke zu Falun" ("The Mines of Falun") and "Automata" ("Robots"). In "The Sandman," the artist, Nathanael, is pursued by Coppelius, a phantom from his childhood whose object is to deprive Nathanael of his eyes. "The Entail" is a novella of inner deaths and architectural collapses that served Poe as a source for "The Fall of the House of Usher" [2-77]. "The Weird Guest" illustrates the theme of a supernatural world within that will not be denied. "The Mines of Falun" seizes upon the situation of subterranean mystery when a perfectly preserved body is discovered in a Swedish mine. "Automata" has as its subject robotics in its display of the mechanical talking doll, Olimpia.

Hogg, James (U.K.), 1770–1835.

ABOUT: WW, GSF, SFW, FG, H, SMFL, PE, ESF

***1-41. The Private Memoirs and Confessions of a Justified Sinner**. London: Longman, Hurst, Rees, Orme, Brown, & Green, 1824. Recommended edition: ed. by John Carey. Oxford Univ. Press, 1979.
Walpole's Gothic features a disintegrating castle; Hogg's Gothic features a disintegrating self. The narrative is a twice-told tale recited first as a case study of the schizophrenic sinner, Robert Wringham, and his murder of his half brother, George Colwan. The tale is then retold as a subjective narrative or confession from Wringham's point of view. The confession comes to light when Wringham's grave is exhumed and the manuscript taken from his casket. The structure of the novel creates a dual perspective on Wringham's disastrous double existence. Wringham tries to reunify himself by expelling the evil presence of his twin, Gil-Martin, who represents his darker half. Is the diabolic twin real or some hallucinated monster representing Wringham's unconscious self? Finding no exit from the dilemma, he expresses the new Gothic fate: "I was a being incomprehensible to myself. Either I had a second self who transacted business in my likeness, or else my body was at times possessed by a spirit over which it had no control." Hogg's Gothic novel opens a new vein of horror by denying the possibility or even the existence of any psychological unity.

[For other works by this author, see the companion guide to fantasy.]

Holcroft, Thomas (U.K.), 1745–1809.

1-42. A Tale of Mystery. London: Richard Phillips, 1802. Recommended edition: in *The Hour of One: Six Gothic Melodramas*, ed. by Stephen Wischhusen. Gordon Fraser, 1975.
A frequently performed Gothic drama by the radical novelist Thomas Holcroft, the play was first acted at Covent Garden on November 13, 1802. Holcroft based his plot on a contemporary source, René Pixérécourt's Gothic melodrama *Coelina; ou, L'Enfant du mystère* (*Coelina; or, The Child of Mystery*; 1801) which was itself taken from Mrs. Radcliffe's *Romance of the Forest* [1-82]. Holcroft's melodrama preserved the terror of the Radcliffean story line while expounding revolutionary ideas.

***

ABOUT: FG

1-43. The Horrors of the Secluded Castle; or, Virtue Triumphant. London: T. & R. Hughes, 1807.
A chapbook imitation of Reeve's *Old English Baron* [1-88] with an admixture of Radcliffean material. The time is the sixteenth-century period of devastation of the monasteries. The place is the secluded border castle of Glendenen, under siege by Lord Antley and his brother, Count Mortimer. Mortimer's daughter and Antley's niece, Anna, is installed in the secluded castle by her power-mad uncle. Successive events must have strained the credulity of even the most devoted Gothic reader. While Anna pines away in the deserted wing of the stronghold, her

lover, Lewis, sails for Madrid only to have his ship taken by pirates off the Barbary Coast. When Lewis is introduced to the consort of the Algerian pirate chieftain, he is shocked to see Anna. One must not ask how she managed to relocate from a secluded castle to a Moslem harem, but readers of the Gothic were not critical of such transportations among the shilling shockers.

Ireland, William Henry (U.K.), 1777–1835.
About: GSF, FG

1-44. The Abbess; A Romance. London: Earle & Hemet, 1799. Recommended edition: ed. by Benjamin F. Fisher. Arno, 1974.
Ireland's Gothic was no mere imitation of *The Monk*, but an original monastic shocker which reveled in sexual cruelty. His wicked abbess, Madre Vittoria Bracciano, never struggles with sexual temptation, as does Lewis's Ambrosio, but pursues her licentious goals without hesitation. The Count Marcello Porta lusts for Maddalena Rosa, a beautiful novice who is imprisoned in the abbess's Florentine Convent of Santa Maria del Nova. Aided by Father Ubaldo, the Count penetrates the cloister and violates a veiled beauty he takes to be Maddalena, only to learn later that his partner had been the Abbess Vittoria. As in *The Monk*, no erotic experience ever fulfills the character's cravings. The rape of Maddalena by Father Ubaldo is described graphically: "Already they began to tear the garments from her tender limbs; already the barbarians had rent the veil that had concealed her alabastrine bosom." The narrative is crowded with cold-blooded horror as Ireland's Gothic approaches an ideal of the hideous reached by the novel of horror only in its extremest state.

1-45. Gondez the Monk; A Romance of the Thirteenth Century. London: W. Earle & J. W. Hucklebridge, 1805.
E. F. Bleiler calls *Gondez* "an undisciplined and aggressive Gothic novel, so complex in plot as to be nearly unintelligible," a severe but accurate evaluation. The story chronicles the misfortunes of the warrior Huberto Avinco, who serves in the army of King Robert the Bruce. The narrative follows the trials of Huberto as he seeks to discover his identity, a quest which brings him into contact with Father Gondez, as loathsome a monk as ever stalked the pages of Gothic fiction. His Abbey of St. Columba is a warehouse of Gothic surprises. Along with the usual paraphernalia of supernatural shock, it contains a crucifix which bleeds and a specter in the person of the "Little Red Woman" who lurks about the plot and helps the Inquisition to bring Gondez to the justice of "a slow fire." Wild, outrageous, terrifying and fun to read, *Gondez* left its mark on the development of the Gothic novel's most exciting character, the satanic hero.

Irving, Washington, 1783–1859.
About: WW, GSF, SFW, SMFL, SFE, PE

1-46. "The Spectre Bridegroom" in *The Sketch-Book of Geoffrey Crayon, Gent.* New York: C. S. Van Winkle, 1819–20. Recommended edition: in *Romantic Gothic Tales, 1790–1840*, ed. by G. R. Thompson. Harper, 1979.
Gothic terror is mocked point by point in this Germanic hair-raiser. The narra-

tor's tone in the opening paragraph prepares the reader for his "sportive Gothicism": "It is well known that the forests of Germany have always been as much infested with robbers as its castles by spectres." One of these phantoms was the corpse bridegroom, a stock Gothic character. The names of the tale's rivals, the Baron of Katzenellenbogen (or cat's elbow) and Herman von Starkenfaust, show Irving's comic purposes and clear the path for the ghastly horseman who abducts the baron's daughter. The rider is no deceased hero after all, of course, but young Herman playing the same midnight charade as Brom Bones in "The Legend of Sleepy Hollow" (1820). Irving's wit was well attuned to one of the most stereotypical of Gothic ghosts, the demon horseman.

***1-47. "Adventure of the German Student"** in *Tales of a Traveller*. Philadelphia: Carey & Lea, 1824. Recommended edition: in *Washington Irving's Tales of the Supernatural*, ed. by E. F. Bleiler. Stemmer House, 1982.
Irving burlesqued the Gothic romance, but he was capable of telling a tale of terror free of comic ironies. The German student is Gottfried Wolfgang, a Frankensteinian recluse who takes chambers in Paris just as the Reign of Terror is reaching its full fury. His dreams are haunted by the image of a dark-haired woman who disturbs his pursuits. Seeking relief, he wanders near the scaffold of the guillotine where he discovers the figure of his dreams weeping on the steps of the "horrible engine." They return to the German student's apartments where she gives herself to him in a night of love. When he finds her corpse in his bed, the police are summoned, her black neck band is unfastened, and her severed head rolls off. Realizing that his evening of passion had been a necrophiliac encounter, he is carried screaming to the madhouse. No comic relief counters this *schauerromantik* climax nor is any explanation given for the student's cadaverous liaison.

[For other works of this author, see the companion guide to fantasy.]

Kahlert, Karl Friedrich (as by **Lawrence Flammenberg**) (Germany), dates unknown.

ABOUT: GSF, FG

1-48. The Necromancer; or, The Tale of the Black Forest. London: Minerva Press for William Lane, 1794. Recommended edition: ed. by Devendra P. Varma. Folio Press, 1968.
This Gothic has plenty of supernatural action but is encumbered by a plot which defies comprehension. The site is the Black Forest of Germany, primal Gothic territory. The story of the necromancer, Volkert, is buried so deep within the intertwined narratives that penetrating to the central story is a test for the experienced Gothic reader. The legend of Volkert is located within the frame stories of Hermann and Helfried, whose flight through the Black Forest has brought them to the funeral vault of Godfrey Hausinger, the repository of Volkert's memoirs dictated to Hausinger by the necromancer as he awaited execution. The papers describe his criminal career and terrible punishment when on the final night of his life "a flash of lightning hissed suddenly through the dreary vault" to cheat the executioner. When Jane Austen included *The Necromancer* in her list of Gothic titles, she had in mind a prime example of the German Gothic novel at its most outrageous.

Kelly, Isabella (U.K.), dates unknown.
ABOUT: FG

1-49. The Abbey of St. Asaph. London: Minerva Press for William Lane, 1795. Recommended edition: ed. by Devendra P. Varma. Arno, 1977.
There are reminders of Lewis's repulsive supernaturalism in this Gothic and the five other novels that Kelly produced for the Minerva Press. The story concerns the abbey confinement of the orphan Jennet Aprieu. She is victimized by Lord Belmont, a monster who derives from Ambrosio in *The Monk* [1-58]. When her pursuer overtakes her in an underground apartment, "He clasps her to his tumultuous bosom, while his hand, with indecent freedom, wanders over her lovely bosom." Jennet then undergoes what might be termed the abominable embrace as she gropes her way along a tunnel. The climax occurs in the burial vaults when she is approached by an airborne skull later revealed to be animated by a rat. Kelly's explanation of every supernatural crisis suggests the major weakness of many of Monk Lewis's followers in the 1790s; the novel of supernatural horror could easily be ruined by any attempt to combine it with the milder novel of suspense and terror.

1-50. The Baron's Daughter; A Gothic Romance. London: J. Bell, 1802.
Encouraged by Monk Lewis, Isabella Kelly enthralled the Gothic audience with this counterfeit of *The Monk* [1-58]. *The Monk* had allowed no redemption for its sufferers and sinners and no way back to a safe world for its crazed characters. This effect of permanent entrapment, or *Burgverliess* Gothic, is what Mrs. Kelly wanted to duplicate in *The Baron's Daughter*. Hence, the subtitle, "A Gothic Romance," implies something more gruesome than a tale of barbaric times. *Burgverliess* Gothic meant a Gothic "from which there was not the remotest possibility of escape." The novel's nauseous climaxes, picturesque gore and the terrible fates of all the characters, whether good or bad, render *The Baron's Daughter* a Gothic romance in the truest sense of the term.

Lamb, Caroline (U.K.), 1785-1828.
ABOUT: FG, PE

1-51. Glenarvon. London: Henry Colburn, 1816. Recommended editions: ed. by James L. Ruff. Scholars' Facsimiles & Reprints, 1972; ed. by Anne Fremantle. Curtis Books, 1973.
Lamb's Irish Gothic fictionalizes her love affair with the man who ruined her, Lord Byron. Her version of the Gothic was written as a warning against Byronic individualism. The storyline conforms to Radcliffean conventions. The heiress, Calantha Deleval, becomes the prey of Glenarvon, yielding to him because he fulfills her romantic image of the kind of male she desires. To save her from her impulsiveness, her father matches her with the Earl of Avondale and establishes the couple in an Irish castle. Glenarvon arrives during an evening of storms, and proceeds to the business of drawing the purest of women to the darkest of damnations. Lamb's Gothic novel is as much a critique of her own emotional profligacy as of Byron's exploitation of her life. The deflowered Calantha follows Glenarvon to London, falls ill and dies in his embrace. Glenarvon goes insane, loses his wealth and fatal handsomeness and perishes when he is afflicted with a nightmare of a death ship summoning him into a black ocean.

Lathom, Francis (U.K.), 1777-1832.
About: WW, FG, PE

1-52. The Midnight Bell; A German Story Founded on Incidents in Real Life. London: H. D. Symonds, 1798. Recommended edition: ed. by Devendra P. Varma. Folio Press, 1968.
From 1795 to 1830, Lathom manufactured one or several Gothic romances every year while pursuing his main career in the theater. *The Midnight Bell* is a sham translation from a nonexistent German source typifying that kind of horror novel which reveled in Germanism. A successful Gothic could sometimes be built around a sinister acoustic such as the bell which tolls without human hands, but the Midnight Bell of the title is scarcely audible until very late in the romance when the hero, Adolphus, learns the truth that his mother is his father's murderer. Since he has sworn to avenge the murder of his father, he must now grapple with the problem of matricide. A miraculous denouement releases him from this terrible duty and restores the Castle of Cohenburg to him. A special feature of the novel was Lathom's inclusion of descriptions of Paris during the Reign of Terror.

1-53. The Fatal Vow; or, St. Michaels Monastery. London: B. Crosby, 1807.
This historical Gothic is a fake chronicle which synthesizes history and horror. Events are set in the thirty-fourth year of the reign of Henry II when troubles with his son, Richard, were disturbing the realm. Action focuses on the unfortunate Christabelle whose name and identity are being withheld from her by her father, Glencowell. He exacts from Christabelle a pledge not to reveal her identity to a strange woman. Her word becomes a fatal vow since the woman is her mother and the object of a plot by her father. The ending shows Lathom's method of combining history with horror. Now calling herself Matilda de Clifford, Christabelle liberates Richard only to die in his arms from weariness and family guilt. In this complicated Gothic romance, Lathom shows great command over the multiple and overlapping plots, splicing real history with imaginary horror at every turn.

1-54. Mystic Events; or, The Vision of the Tapestry, A Romantic Legend of the Days of Anne Boleyn. London: Minerva Press for A. K. Newman, 1830.
Lathom's final novel is a webwork of Gothic enigmas and fabricated history. The account of Henry VIII's divorce and the fate of Anne Boleyn, a pawn in a deadly game, is rendered with historical exactitude. The Gothic segment of the novel is rearranged history involving the rivalry of the wandering knight, Sir Leolin, against his sovereign for the attentions of Anne when the two meet secretly at Hever Castle. The castle holds a tapestried chamber where Sir Leolin is approached by a ghostly monk who emerges from the tapestry with a prophecy on his lips: "The hour of your fate has arrived; embrace it with gratitude." Mystic events accumulate, and lead to Sir Leolin's discovery of his heritage by way of "the knight of the saffron plume." Sir Leolin is matched with Amabel, a fictitious sister of Anne Boleyn, to bring the Gothic to a satisfactory nuptial conclusion. Lathom thought of himself as an entertainer, not a moralist, and he never deviated from his purpose to write "books of this kind for an hour's relaxation from severe study."

Lawler, Dennis (U.K.), dates unknown.

1-55. The Earls of Hammersmith; or, The Cellar Spectre, A Comical, Tragical, Burlesque Drama in One Act. London: J. Duncombe's British Theatre Number 85, 1814. **Midnight Spells! or, The Spirit of St. Osmund**. London: A. Neil, 1815.
Lawler's satire of Gothic drama may be found in the Larpent Collection of Eighteenth Century Plays (Huntington Library). The complications of the Gothic plot are transmogrified into hilarious farce. The tyrant of the castle is Lord Bluster; the inept hero is Sir Walter Wisehead. He volunteers to spend a night alone in the castle's cellar cell to prove his valor to the most undesirable of Gothic virgins, Lady Margaret Marrowbones. Here, he receives a visitation in the shape of a phantom footman who bears a message from the dead Dowager Countess of Hammersmith: "Wed not Lady Margaret Marrowbones! She is your grandmother! Your father is imprisoned in the castle; yon secret door leads to his dungeon." Enter Lady Simple with torch and keys to assist Wisehead in the subterranean search for the father whose first request upon being released from his dungeon is for a shave. Lawler's ridicule was not the death blow for Gothic melodrama since Gothic plays continued to hold the boards for at least another decade. An anonymous chapbooker turned the Lawler play into the shilling shocker *Midnight Spells!*

Lee, Sophia (U.K.), 1750–1824.
ABOUT: FG

***1-56. The Recess; A Tale of Other Times**. London: T. Cadell, 1783–85. Recommended edition: ed. by Devendra P. Varma. Arno, 1972.
The features of Gothified history are complexity of plot, intensity of victimization, subterranean adventure, occasional supernatural happenings, the juxtaposition of chivalry and cruelty, and the interaction of royal or noble figures with fictitious heroines and villains. Lee's work was widely imitated by later Gothic writers. The "recess" refers to a network of underground apartments beneath the Abbey of St. Vincent, where the twin daughters of Queen Elizabeth's royal rival, Mary Queen of Scots, are concealed. Like their mother, Matilda and Ellinor are threats to Elizabeth's throne and are hunted by the Queen's agents. Flight, persecution, denial of freedom and disaster at "the savage hand of Elizabeth" are conditions which give the novel its Gothic momentum, which reaches a high point in Lee's use of a standard scene of the tale of terror, the specter at the bedside. The mad Ellinor makes a phantasmic visit to Elizabeth's bedchamber where she is taken by the guilty Queen for the ghost of one of her victims. The architectural device of the "recess" offers interesting symbolic possibilities suggesting the recessive condition of the feminine consciousness.

Leland, Thomas (U.K.), 1722–1785.
ABOUT: FG

***1-57. Longsword, Earl of Salisbury, An Historical Romance**. London: W. Johnston, 1762. Recommended edition: ed. by. R. D. Hume. Arno, 1972.
Longsword contains scenes and characters soon to become essential to the Gothic

novel. Lacking only supernaturalism, the work has fiendish barons, monastic villains, gloomy architecture, elaborate victimization, questions of paternity and identity and a displaced hero. The hero is the illegitimate son of King Henry III, William de Longspée, recognized in his disguise as a pilgrim by the long sword protruding from his cloak. This retired crusader hopes for a serene old age but finds that his castle at Canterbury has been usurped by Raymond and Count Mal-Leon. Their agent, Father Reginhald, is the prototype for the evil monk. Poetic justice is achieved when the good and bad characters are assembled at Longsword's castle. As Longsword is about to drink from a poisoned cup, his toast is stopped when the portals fly open to reveal the agent of justice, Les Roches, who presides over the hanging of Reginhald and the restoration of the castle to Longsword. With its high number of standard Gothic elements, it is impossible to deny to Leland's *Longsword* its status as a first Gothic novel.

Lewis, Matthew Gregory (U.K.), 1775–1818.
ABOUT: WW, GSF, SFW, F, FG, H, SMFL, PE, ESF

***1-58. Ambrosio; or, The Monk**. London: J. Bell, 1796. Recommended edition: ed. by Howard Anderson. Oxford Univ. Press, 1973.
The Monk is the locus classicus of the novel of horror. It brought its author instant notoriety and altered the course of Gothicism from the artificial terrors of Mrs. Radcliffe to the real horrors of a new Gothic spirit. Lewis combined the machinery of Walpole with Beckford's vision of the demonic irrational and unleashed an array of gruesome effects not before seen in Gothic fiction. Bleeding nuns, decomposing infants, Wandering Jews, matricide, soul-selling, subterranean fornication, incestuous rape, live burial, demonic interviews and erotic sadism are some of the elements leading to the destruction of the Monk at the hands of the Devil himself. Lewis spliced two plots and developed each story around the motifs of monastic fiendishness and depravity. The Monk's story traces the career of Abbot Ambrosio, leader of the Capuchins in Madrid, and a paragon of sanctity. But beneath this saintly surface, Ambrosio's soul is aflame with pride and lechery. Satan's agent, Matilda de Villanegas, penetrates his cloister in monastic disguise, then tempts Ambrosio to a sexual fall. Once aroused, his desire knows no limits and he feeds his lust by murdering his mother, Elvira, and violating his sister, Antonia, in the slimy vaults of the monastery. Condemned by the Inquisition, Ambrosio signs away his soul to Satan. The aeronautic death of the Monk is a climax that many Gothic writers imitated. Lucifer sinks his claws into the skull of the Monk, soars high above the Sierra Morena and releases him to impalement and death on the sharp rocks. The subplot tells the story of the separation of the lovers, Don Raymond and the pregnant nun, Agnes, who has been condemned to the convent. Agnes gives birth to her child in the depths of the Monastery of St. Clare, her "fingers ringed with the long worms which bred in the corrupted flesh of my infant." The impact of *The Monk* on the development of the Gothic novel needs no stressing. This arch-Gothic novel touched the psychopathic extremes of the Romantic consciousness and created a horror model without peer among the early Gothics. Also annotated as [F1-46].

1-59. The Castle Spectre. London: J. Bell, 1798. Recommended edition: in *The Hour of One: Six Gothic Melodramas,* ed. by Stephen Wischhusen. Gordon Fraser, 1975.
The Castle Spectre is hardly great drama, but it remained a sensational piece of Gothic theater. The scene is laid in Conway Castle where Earl Osmond plots against his brother, Earl Reginald, over possession of the family estate. Kenric, the seneschal, has remained loyal to Reginald and seen to his concealment from his brother's purposes in Conway Castle's underground cells. Also hidden away from Osmond's grasp is Reginald's daughter, Angela. Because she is a Gothic maiden in a Gothic drama, Angela must endure a confinement in the Cedar Room of Conway Castle. With the castle specter guiding her hand, Angela restores the castle to its rightful owner with one stroke of the family dagger. Conventional in plot, it was not the story but the contraptions of stagecraft (including a collapsing wall) that made *The Castle Spectre* so appealing.

1-60. Mistrust; or, Blanche and Osbright, A Feudal Romance in *Romantic Tales.* London: D. N. Shury for Longman, Hurst, Rees, & Orme, 1808. Recommended edition: in *Seven Masterpieces of Gothic Horror,* ed. by R. D. Spector. Bantam, 1966.
This Gothic novella is a horror tale based on a drama by Kleist, *The Family of Schroffenstein.* From the opening scene, in which we see Count Rudiger standing in the grave of his murdered son, Jocelyn, the novella is all crisis and climax. The scene is the Palatinate of Henry the Lion; the time is the late 1100s; the situation is the lethal conflict between the two great houses of Frankenheim and Orrenberg. Although raised in the code of mistrust, Blanche of Orrenberg and Osbright of Frankenheim have fallen in love despite the feud between their houses. Osbright's father, Count Rudiger, plans to end his son's love for the despised daughter of the Orrenbergs, but his men assassinate his son by mistake because the lovers have exchanged clothing. Thus, the bodies accumulate in Lewis's overloading of his bloody stage. Indeed, horrid shock in unbearable amounts seems the sole motivation for each episode in this Gothification of *Romeo and Juliet.*

Mackenzie, Henry (U.K.), 1745–1831.

ABOUT: FG

1-61. Julia de Roubigné. London: W. Strahan, 1777. Recommended edition: Garland, 1978.
No survey of Gothic fiction can omit the novel of sensibility at its tearful extreme. Mackenzie's *Julia de Roubigné* is a Gothic novel whose protagonist, Montauban, substitutes terror for tears in his maltreatment of Julia. Structurally, the novel is an epistolary quadrangle. One set of letters from Julia to Maria relates events from the victim's point of view while the other set of letters, from Montauban to Segarva, gives his sadistic account of his enclosure of Julia in the family mansion. Within its walls, Julia suffers all the anxious moments of the Radcliffean maiden before the fact. The motives for Montauban's sadism remain enigmatic, as is often the case with the high Gothic villain. Julia survives both persecution and an attempted poisoning by Montauban to communicate her new-found knowledge

of the evil of the world to her friend, Maria. Full of extreme emotions and decidedly Gothic in the situation of the heroine, the novel presents Mackenzie's moral picture of an unfeeling society in which the people of feeling are exploited and destroyed.

Maturin, Charles Robert (U.K.), 1780–1824.

ABOUT: WW, GSF, SFW, F, FG, H, SMFL, SFE, PE, ESF

1-62. The Fatal Revenge; or, The Family of Montorio. London: Longman, Hurst, Rees, & Orme, 1807 (as by Dennis Jasper Murphy), 3 vols. Recommended edition: ed. by Maurice Lévy. Arno, 1974.
Maturin's subject is guilt, not simply the alienation of one human being from others, but guilt in the character's separation from his better self. Maturin used a pair of brothers to show that the hero is lost in his own self-darkness. Gazing down upon the corpse of their father, Hippolito and Annibal are united in guilt when "the body extended one hand to Hippolito and the other to Annibal, seized on both, and drawing them under the pall, lapt them in total darkness." The novel is set in the Neapolitan Castle of Muralto, home of the Montorios. Count Montorio has cheated his brother, Orazio, out of the estate and now hides his deed from his two opposite sons, Hippolito and Annibal. The banished Orazio, having been driven to murder and madness, has returned secretly in monastic disguise as Father Schemoli, the fatal revenger. Orazio/Schemoli is the shadow-side of the self whose potential goodness has become complete evil. Unchecked by conscience, Schemoli destroys the family by corrupting the sons of Montorio, finally inciting them to parricide and later discovering that he is their father. Although the narrative is clumsy and complicated, the subterranean scenery is impressive and Maturin's major themes of guilt, self-destruction and the release of evil from the darker side of the self are already in place.

1-63. Bertram; or, The Castle of St. Aldobrand. London: John Murray, 1816. Recommended edition: Corti, 1956.
The drama fuses the characteristics of the Gothic villain and the Byronic hero into a single protagonist. Bertram is at once sophisticated and coarse, tender and cruel, virtuous and ruthless. His love for Imogine, although genuine, is struck through with powerful egotism. Bertram's antagonist is Imogine's father, who has had Bertram exiled. Secretly returning, he becomes a bandit chief and is shipwrecked on the coast just below the Castle of St. Aldobrand. Imogine has been married off to one of her father's cohorts, but Bertram vows to regain her, occupies the castle and stands off her besieging father who returns to the castle with a royal warrant for Bertram's death. Bertram slays St. Aldobrand, but is made mad by Imogine's grief over the death of her father at the hands of her lover. As she wanders off to die, Bertram follows her into death by committing suicide. Maturin's Gothic melodrama appealed to the romantic conflict between the passionate individual and the artificial codes of society.

***1-64. Melmoth the Wanderer, A Tale**. London: Hurst & Robinson, 1820. Recommended editions: ed. by William F. Axton. Univ. of Nebraska Press, 1961; ed. by Alethea Hayter. Penguin, 1977.
Maturin's epic Gothic impressed Goethe, Scott, Byron, Poe, Pushkin, Haw-

thorne, and later in the century influenced Balzac, Baudelaire and Wilde. It is several Gothics in one. The novel explores such crises as loss of self and soul, the riddle of suffering and the damnation of the never-ending life. The central situation of the romance is starkly simple. In the seventeenth century Melmoth had mortgaged his soul to Satan. He now roams the corridors of time seeking any sufferer whose agony is so unbearable that he will trade his fate for Melmoth's doom of eternal life. The novel is an odyssey of pain which sees this Wandering Jew figure fail in each attempt to regain his soul by tempting some fellow creature to damnation. Inside Melmoth's story are five tales, each a lesser Gothic novel in its own right and each positioned as a tale within a tale. As Melmoth wanders, he encounters the prisoner, Stanton, condemned to the madhouse; he meets the Spanish nobleman, Monçada, a victim of the Inquisition; in the third tale, Melmoth visits the innocent, Immalee, in her deserted tropical paradise and Godless Eden; the last two stories, "The Tale of Guzman's Family" and "The Lover's Tale" of Elinor Mortimer, are filled with starvation, cruelty, pathos and horror. Each sufferer resists Melmoth's temptation, thus compelling him to wander on through time. Previous Gothic villains had been condemned to the dark labyrinth beneath the castle, but Maturin's hero-villain wanders through a labyrinth that ultimately leads into the dark places of the human soul.

1-65. The Albigenses; A Romance. London: Hurst & Robinson, 1824. Recommended edition: ed. by Dale Kramer. Arno, 1974.
Maturin's final Gothic concerns one of history's blackest nightmares, the extermination of the Albigensians in 1209. The crusade symbolizes the depravity of the self abetted by a warped religious idealism. Two brothers, Sir Paladour and Sir Almirald, represent the good and evil instincts in their opposite treatment of the Albigensian heretics. Neither brother is aware of the fraternal relationship until the double wedding at the end. While hunting heretics, Sir Paladour comes upon the Castle of Courtenaye where he is welcomed by Isabelle. He learns that a strain of werewolfery infecting the Courtenayes has the power to change those who come into contact with the family into wolves. The novel ends on a note of hope and with religious bigotry dispelled by the double wedding of Sir Paladour and Isabelle and Sir Almirald and the Albigensian maid Genevieve. Maturin demonstrated that the historical novel and the Gothic tale could complement each other thematically. The Gothic devices indicated the darkness at the core of the human soul, thus pointing to the theme of guilt in a fallen universe.

Meeke, Mary (pseud. **Gabrielli**) (U.K.), died 1816.

ABOUT: FG

1-66. Count St. Blanchard; or, The Prejudiced Judge. London: Minerva Press for William Lane, 1795. Recommended edition: ed. by Devendra P. Varma. Arno, 1977.
Blood, mystery and terror flowed steadily from Mrs. Meeke's pen from her first novel, *The Abbey of Clugny* (1795), to her last Gothic, *The Veiled Protectress; or, The Mysterious Mother* (1819). She knew how to manipulate her reader's curiosity and how to concoct a diverting fable of success. The energies of Dubois, the hero of *Count St. Blanchard*, are devoted to countering the schemes of Adelaide's

father as he struggles to win both his name and the young woman. The prejudiced judge is De Ransal, who had lost his son in a kidnapping years before. His prejudices are exploited by Adelaide's father to keep Dubois from Adelaide and to implicate him in various crimes. The reunion of father and son is effected by means of the birthmark, and the elevation of Dubois to noble status is so gratifying to Adelaide's father that he offers to provide a dowry for the couple. The reader quickly forgets that this same father had had his daughter tied to a tree and threatened by one of his footmen, then confined to the worst convent in Paris. Mrs. Meeke's slick plots are as regular as clockwork, and her sense of the needs of her Gothic clientele nearly flawless.

1-67. Midnight Weddings. London: Minerva Press for William Lane, 1802.
Characters are moved around on her genealogical chessboard with authority in this slick Minerva Press best-seller. The title refers to two nuptials, the first between the ambitious Leonora M'Dougall and Octavius and the second between the title-seeking Leonora and an ugly substitute for Octavius. The first wedding is aborted when Leonora spurns the groom in mid-ceremony when Sir Edmund Browning announces that his son is not his heir. Gothic travails follow as Octavius attempts to legitimize his claim to the baronetcy of Vilmore. Not only is his lineage noble, it is royal, as a chain of circumstances reveals him to be the son of Louis XV. When he becomes the Duke de Valentinois and is given a handsome fortune, Leonora's interest in Octavius is rekindled. During a masked ball, she entices the new duke into elopement and a midnight wedding. But in her haste to become a duchess, Leonora fails to peer beneath her new husband's mask. Justice is dispensed by Octavius's royal father when he chooses a beautiful wife for his new-found son and invites the entire court to their midnight wedding. All of Mrs. Meeke's narrative tricks are invoked: unsubtle good and evil unsubtly punished; offspring locked away in foreign dungeons by parents; elopement, pursuit and mild violence; the miraculous elevation of a penniless young hero.

***

1-68. The Midnight Assassin; or, The Confessions of the Monk Rinaldi, Containing a Complete History of His Diabolical Machinations and Unparalleled Ferocity, Together with a Circumstantial Account of That Scourge of Mankind, the Inquisition, with the Manner of Bringing to Trial Those Unfortunate Beings Who Are at Its Disposal. In: *The Marvellous Magazine and Compendium of Prodigies,* 1 (May 1802).

About: FG

This periodical Gothic pilfers the final scenes of Mrs. Radcliffe's *The Italian* [1-84] and reduces her romance to 30,000 words. Father Schedoni becomes the Goth's Rinaldi who is depicted in the cover illustration bending with dagger raised over the sleeping Ellena di Rosalba. The Gothic novel in abbreviated form held its place beside sentimental fiction in the popular magazines. A common practice was to expropriate a terror episode such as the heroine's exposure to the black veil, then enlarge it into a short Gothic tale.

***

1-69. The Midnight Groan; or, The Spectre of the Chapel, Involving an Exposure of the Horrible Secrets of the Nocturnal Assembly. A Gothic Romance. London: T. & R. Hughes, 1808.

ABOUT: FG

The anonymous Goth was pressured by the publisher to bring the hero and heroine to the altar or to the grave within the thirty-six-page quota of this shilling shocker. Thus, the chapbook consists of abrupt horror scenes. Horatio and Miranda have been driven apart by her father who suggests that they are brother and sister. Horatio takes refuge in a castle where he is received by a specter who ushers him into a chamber which holds the corpse of a young woman who looks like the forsaken Miranda. A midnight groan rouses Horatio's curiosity and he descends to investigate. Beneath the chapel he beholds the "nocturnal assembly" engaged in a blood rite. The leader of this devil's band is Miranda's father. Having built the tale to this situation, the chapbooker was reluctant to permit a victory for evil. Miranda's father renounces the satanic fraternity and dispels all Gothic gloom by bringing forth the nubile Miranda. The details of the chapbook should not be dismissed as mere flummery. Hawthorne uses the pattern of a journey by night to a satanic meeting and the hero's fearful encounter with evil in the Puritan Gothic tale "Young Goodman Brown" [2-39].

Mitchell, Isaac, 1759–1812.

1-70. The Asylum; or, Alonzo and Melissa. Poughkeepsie, NY: J. Nelson, 1811. Haunted castles in colonial Connecticut? The Gothic novel could sink its roots anywhere, as this specimen of American Gothic shows. The fortresses of Mrs. Radcliffe's romances have been transported across the Atlantic, then reconstructed in the colonies. Mitchell knew how to turn the screws of terror when he placed Melissa Bloomfield in her father's Connecticut castle. Melissa has been encastled by her father for refusing his choice of husband and preferring the patriot, Alonzo. Separated from Melissa, he translates love into ardor and joins the naval war against the British. Captured at sea, he is aided by Benjamin Franklin, who makes his first and only appearance in a Gothic novel. The climax occurs in Charleston, and is worthy of any of Mrs. Radcliffe's finales. Alonzo casts himself upon Melissa's grave, believing that he has won his revolution but lost his beloved. She is not dead, of course, but has managed to slip away from Gothified Connecticut for a reunion with Alonzo. Mitchell's colonialized Gothic won the approval of American readers. It further reflected American Gothicism in its transitional phase from the high-minded horrors of Brown to the spooky excitement of Cooper's romances of the forest.

***

1-71. The Monk of Horror; or, The Conclave of Corpses. Tales of the Crypt. London: Dean & Munday, 1798. Recommended edition: in *Gothic Tales of Terror*, ed. by Peter Haining. Taplinger, 1972.

This tale's brevity contributes to its moods of horror. A brother of the monastery of Kreutzberg, anxious to discover what lies beyond the grave, descends into the charnel house where "the dead but imperishable bodies of the long-buried brothers of the convent sat erect in their lidless coffins." The leader of this conclave of corpses beckons him to look upon his name in the *Liber Obedientiae* which lies open atop a casket. The old monk exposes his breast where his heart burns hellishly. A vault opens and an army of skeletons emerges from the "den of death." Here, the narrative aborts with no description of the Monk's return to the upper world.

Moore, George (U.K.), dates unknown.

ABOUT: FG

1-72. Grasville Abbey; A Romance. In *Lady's Magazine, or Entertaining Companion for the Fair Sex*, 24–28 (March 1793–August 1797; 47 installments). London: G. G. & J. Robinson, 1797. Recommended edition: ed. by Robert D. Mayo. Arno, 1974.

This serialized Gothic romance "contains the sufferings of the Maserini family; by which the horrors of superstition are fully exposed, as was explained by Father Peter, the hermit who was found concealed in a cell." The abbey is filled with the hardware of horror. Percival Maserini helps Clementina to escape from a convent, then brings her to the abbey as his wife where she attracts the attention of his cousin, Count D'Ollifant. Percival disappears during an investigation of the ancestral home and Clementina dies, leaving Alfred and Matilda, the heirs to Grasville Abbey, with the mystery of their vanished father. Alfred resumes where his father left off by probing the forbidden chamber of the abbey, a search which turns up the long-missing father. A vile cousin has been responsible for all the "supernatural" occurrences. Lady readers who sought minimal violence and maximum suspense climaxed by the happiest of endings were never disappointed by this prolonged periodical Gothic.

Moore, John (U.K.), 1729–1802.

ABOUT: FG

1-73. Zeluco; Various Views of Human Nature, Taken from Life and Manners, Foreign and Domestic. London: A. Strahan & T. Cadell, 1789.

The protagonist of this novel of cruelty is an early version of the Gothic villain. The novel studies the growth of viciousness in a character who experiences aliveness only when inflicting pain. Zeluco begins his career at age ten by crushing a pet sparrow. The pleasure of this deed awakens a sadistic appetite which drives him to a series of detestable acts that he knows to be evil but cannot control. He marries the innocent Laura, then conspires with Nerina whose wickedness is on a par with that of any Gothic abbess. He orders his West Indian slave to be flogged to death and strangles Laura's infant because the child resembles the soldier Carlostein. The stiletto of a rival rake finally ends Zeluco's perverted career. The Gothic novelists knew and admired Moore's strange hero, an early example of innate brutality. No modern edition of this classic of sadism exists, certainly an omission in Gothic studies.

Parsons, Eliza (U.K.), 1748–1811.
ABOUT: GSF, FG

1-74. The Castle of Wolfenbach; A German Story. London: Minerva Press for William Lane, 1793. Recommended edition: ed. by Devendra P. Varma. Folio Press, 1968.
A fake German translation whose plot cannot be deciphered. The heroine, Matilda Weimar, flees from Rhine castles to Paris streets to London alleys with her homicidal uncle always in pursuit. Each hysterical moment is the same as any previous one. In London, Matilda hears the account of how the Count of Wolfenbach tortured Victoria's lover to death before her eyes, then sealed her up in a windowless chamber with his decapitated body. Of the seven "Northanger" novels, *The Castle of Wolfenbach* exhibits the least skill with the standard Gothic materials. Perhaps its inferiority was exactly the point which Jane Austen was making by including it among her horrid titles.

1-75. The Mysterious Warning; A German Tale. London: Minerva Press for William Lane, 1796. Recommended edition: ed. by Devendra P. Varma. Folio Press, 1968.
The device of ventriloquism as a terror motif is noteworthy, since this book preceded Brown's *Wieland* [1-9] by two years. Parsons also uses counterfeit Germanism to maintain her atmosphere of horror. Conflict develops around two brothers, Count Rhodophil and Count Ferdinand. Ferdinand is warned by a voice to beware of his brother and to shun his new wife, Claudina. Several volumes later, revelations of incest are made and Ferdinand learns that the supernatural voice was really that of the old steward, Ernest, protecting his master from his brother's schemes. Claudina's melodramatic demise clears the way for Ferdinand's marriage to Louisa. From this belabored management of a Gothic acoustic, Brown produced the potent ventriloquism of *Wieland.*

Peacock, Thomas Love (U.K.), 1785–1866.
ABOUT: FG

1-76. Headlong Hall. London: T. Hookham, 1816. Recommended edition: ed. by P. M. Yarker. Everyman's, 1961.
Peacock's novels are pastiches of crazy talk, much of it directed against romantic attitudes toward architecture, imagination and self. They are set in an eccentric host's country house where a group of literary lunatics have gathered. Among the talkers of *Headlong Hall* are the metaphysician, Mr. Panscope (Coleridge), whose opponent, Mr. Cranium, the ossuarian, hears him out while "seated in a pensive attitude, at a large table, decorated with a copious variety of skulls." The turkey stuffer, Mr. Gaster, Mr. Nightshade and Miss Philomela Poppyseed mock the cast of the Gothic novel while Mr. Milestone's commentaries on ruins ridicule Gothic building fads.

***1-77. Nightmare Abbey**. London: T. Hookham, Jr., Baldwin, Cradock, & Joy, 1818. Recommended edition: ed. by Charles B. Dodson. Holt, Rinehart & Winston, 1971.
This novel mocks the shrieking Gothic titles that glutted the circulating libraries.

The satire offers bits of conversation by monomaniacs representing the Romantic intellectuals of Peacock's era. Shelley is burlesqued in the son of the host, Mr. Scythrop Glowry. Byron is lampooned in the morbid Mr. Cypress. The incomprehensible Mr. Flosky is Coleridge at his worst. The most direct mockery of the Gothic imagination comes in the reading habits of Scythrop Glowry. He retreats to "the southwestern tower with a copy of Grosse's *Horrid Mysteries* [1-35] to dream of venerable eleutherarchs and ghastly confederates holding midnight conventions in subterranean caves."

Peake, Richard Brinsley (U.K.), 1792-1847.

1-78. Presumption; or, The Fate of Frankenstein. London: W. G. B. Whittaker, 1823. Recommended edition: in *Paradox*, 8 (September 1967): 3-31.
A *Frankenstein* opera featuring the talents of the actor Thomas Potter Cooke. Peake modified Mary Shelley's story and character relationships. Victor Frankenstein loves Agnes De Lacey and is served by an assistant named Fritz. Viewing his creation for the first time, Frankenstein threatens the monster with a sword and pursues it across a lake instead of into the arctic wastes. The noise of Frankenstein's musket causes an avalanche which buries monster and creator. Peake's melodrama omitted all of the psychologizing of the novel, but set the tone for cinematic treatments of the monster theme, particularly the garish horror of film Frankensteins.

Polidori, John William (U.K.), 1795-1821.
ABOUT: WW, GSF, SFW, FG, SMFL, PE

***1-79. The Vampyre**. London: Sherwood, Neely, & Jones, 1819. Recommended edition: in *Three Gothic Novels*, ed. by E. F. Bleiler. Dover, 1966.
The Vampyre began a trend culminating in the Victorian vampire pulps such as Prest's *Varney the Vampyre; or, The Feast of Blood* [2-87]. Beginning with Polidori's Lord Ruthven, the vampire assaults the spirits of its victims. Such psychological vampirism opened up themes of social and sexual fear. The main character, Aubrey, begins a friendship with Lord Ruthven, unaware that his companion with his "dead grey eye" is a vampire. The bond grows until a quarrel divides them. In Greece, Aubrey falls in love with Ianthe and is about to marry her when her whitened body is discovered, "and upon her throat were the marks of teeth." Lord Ruthven reenters the young man's life and they resume their travels until the Vampyre is shot by bandits. Expiring, he forces Aubrey to swear to keep the secret of his identity for one year and a day. When the body vanishes after being resuscitated by moonlight, Aubrey hurries back to London on the intuition that his sister is in peril. Hearing of her impending marriage, he finds Lord Ruthven escaped from the grave and preparing to feast on her soul. The rash oath causes Aubrey to burst a blood vessel and hemorrhage to death as Polidori intelligently chose not to dispose of the vampire or to rescue the good characters from his grasp.

Radcliffe, Ann (U.K.), 1764–1823.
ABOUT: WW, GSF, SFW, FG, SMFL, PE, ESF

1-80. The Castles of Athlin and Dunbayne; A Highland Story. London: T. Hookham, 1789. Recommended edition: ed. by Frederick Shroyer. Arno, 1972.
A Macbethian Gothic placed in medieval Scotland where the castles provide the locales of fear for the blood feud between the houses of Athlin and Dunbayne. The plot is standard for the early Gothic romance. A young man secures his birthright after nearly losing his life in a series of contests with his rival, Malcolm. Earl Osbert of Dunbayne vows to avenge his murdered father and is assisted by a peasant, Alleyn, who is too chivalrous to be lowborn. An assault on Dunbayne Castle is repulsed by Malcolm, who captures the two men and then demands Osbert's sister, Mary, in return for sparing them. Mrs. Radcliffe's revenge plot is secondary as she shifts most of her narrative attention to Gothic descriptions of the castle interior. The novel closes with a double marriage, but the major emphasis is on the terrors of the castles and their gloomy environs. Mrs. Radcliffe had found her subject, which was not the portrayal of character but the evocation of the mood of a dreamer entranced by a mighty Gothic building.

1-81. A Sicilian Romance. London: T. Hookham, 1790. Recommended edition: ed. by Devendra P. Varma. Arno, 1972.
Radcliffe's main method of suggestive terror is evident throughout her second Gothic. The year is 1580, the location, the palazzo of the Mazzini family on Sicily's northern coast. The daughters and son of the house must abide the schemes of their father and his lovely but deadly second wife, while ghostly noises and lights rise from the castle depths. Ferdinand, Julia and Emilia investigate the sounds while trying to locate a passageway to freedom. They escape from Mazzini Castle only to run directly into even worse perils in the Gothic countryside. Each returns to the castle, called back by the duty to bring their father to justice, but also lured back by the mysterious sounds and strange lights. When Ferdinand descends a staircase into total darkness, his curiosity is rewarded by a glimpse of a cell which holds the missing mother. Her sighs explain the ghostly sounds and her situation explains the cruel behavior of the father who had collaborated with their stepmother to deprive them of their heritage. Power now passes to Ferdinand as the pattern of terror slowly gives way to the light of reason. The device of the secret wife would find a wide following among Gothic writers and in Victorian sensation romances.

1-82. The Romance of the Forest, Interspersed with Some Pieces of Poetry. London: T. Hookham & J. Carpenter, 1791. Recommended edition: ed. by Devendra P. Varma. Arno, 1974.
The romance opens with the fugitive, de la Motte, threatened by a figure who pushes a girl into his arms: "If you wish to save your life, swear that you will convey this girl where I may never see her more." The girl is Adeline and the place of conveyance an abbey which holds the secret of Adeline's heredity. Proprietor of the abbey is Mrs. Radcliffe's first great villain, the Marquis de Montalt, "a votary of vice." While Adeline suffers, de la Motte looks on in horror, his will paralyzed by the Marquis's powers. Montalt is Adeline's uncle and the murderer of her father, but he is unaware of the blood tie as he pursues her. Now fearful of

incest, he has altered his strategy to homicide, but the villainy is exposed by the vigilant Theodore. As Montalt administers poison to himself and de la Motte resumes his exile, the wedding procession of Adeline and Theodore wends its way toward the repurified abbey. Because of its artful suspense, some critics have held that *The Romance of the Forest* should be placed ahead of *The Mysteries of Udolpho* as Mrs. Radcliffe's masterpiece, "a work in which we are aware of the first dawn of Radcliffe's mature powers."

***1-83. The Mysteries of Udolpho, Interspersed with Some Pieces of Poetry**. London: G. G. & J. Robinson, 1794. Recommended edition: ed. by Bonamy Dobrée. Oxford Univ. Press. 1966.
The Mysteries of Udolpho shaped Gothic taste in its own time and still casts its literary shadow over many modern Gothics. In her heroine, Emily St. Aubert, Mrs. Radcliffe created the character of the nervous observer whose terrifying experiences are also tantalizing. She converts natural danger into supernatural peril, thus adding a psychological dimension to the heroine's ordeal. Emily St. Aubert is cautioned by her dying father against fancy which clouds judgment and places one at the mercy of the passions. She is taken to Castle di Udolpho in the Apennines by her vile aunt, Madame Cheron, and her cohort, Montoni. Montoni is one of the model villains of Gothic literature. Lurking in the penumbra of the plot, he seldom speaks except to sneer: "You speak like a heroine. We will see if you can suffer like one." The chief terror of Castle di Udolpho is the portrait gallery where Emily faints after drawing aside a black veil which shrouds a picture. In a modern edition of the romance, the black veil is removed on page 248, but what she saw is not reported until page 662. Emily finally realizes that evil is neither a supernatural phenomenon nor a proper source of aesthetic pleasure, but a result of the unreliability of the passions. She is now ready to reenter the rational world as a woman and a bride with her rescuer, Valancourt, at her side. Mrs. Radcliffe differs fundamentally from the horror writers of the period because her values are conservative, depicting the power of the irrational while at the same time condemning it as monstrous and erroneous. *Udolpho's* far-reaching influence may be seen in the novels of the Brontës and in Shirley Jackson's *The Haunting of Hill House* [4-155]. Also annotated as [F1-68].

***1-84. The Italian; or, The Confessional of the Black Penitents**. London: T. Cadell, Jr. & W. Davies, 1797. Recommended edition: ed. by Frederick Garber. Oxford Univ. Press, 1968.
The focus of fear is not the heroine, but vulture-eyed Father Schedoni who presides over the persecution and near murder of Ellena di Rosalba. He begins his campaign against goodness by insinuating himself into the confidence of the Marquesa di Vivaldi and her son, Vincentio. Ellena becomes the object of something worse than rape as Schedoni installs her in the Convent of San Stefano and has Vincentio arrested and thrown into a dungeon. These events are subordinate to the dark images of Schedoni hovering over the petty humans caught in his net. He brings Ellena to a mansion on the shores of the Adriatic. In a scene copied by the chapbookers, Schedoni penetrates Ellena's chamber and raises his dagger above the sleeping maiden until her locket stops his hand. Ellena is his niece. He is the Count di Marinella, the slayer of Ellena's father and wanted by the Inquisition, that ever-present agent of Gothic justice. Readers who were accus-

tomed to the polite shudders of Mrs. Radcliffe's work must have been gratified by her new villain, a character on a par with Satan himself.

1-85. Gaston de Blondeville; or, The Court of Henry III Keeping Festival in Ardennes. London: Henry Colburn, 1826. Recommended edition: ed. by Devendra P. Varma. Folio, 1987.
A historical Gothic based on the reign of Henry III, deriving its atmosphere from the ruins of Kenilworth Castle. Radcliffe altered her practice by presenting a genuine ghost to dispense justice. The story originates with the manuscript account of the royal festival which brings the King's favorite, Gaston de Blondeville, to a reckoning. The wedding of de Blondeville to Lady Barbara is interrupted by the merchant, Hugh Woodreeve, who charges the knight with murder. Gaston de Blondeville has killed Sir Reginald de Folville to obtain his sword. Woodreeve's accusation is dismissed and he is imprisoned, an injustice which activates the supernatural intercessor. When the court gathers to witness the execution of Woodreeve, the visored specter of the murdered man intervenes and summons de Blondeville to confess his crime. Saluting the gallant ghost, King Henry supports Woodreeve's cause and keeps his festival by releasing the common man. In early Radcliffe, evil is overcome when the characters reject the supernatural as illusory and return to common sense; in late Radcliffe, evil is conquered through the acceptance of the supernatural.

Radcliffe, Mary Ann (U.K.), dates unknown.
About: FG

1-86. Manfroné; or, The One-Handed Monk. London: J. F. Hughes, 1809. Recommended edition: ed. by Coral Ann Howells. Arno, 1972.
The "other" Mrs. Radcliffe was often confused with her more famous namesake, and to her commercial advantage. Her sense of Gothic inclines toward the horror of Lewis. The novel commences when Rosalina di Rodolpho is seized by a sable-masked figure whose amputated hand will shortly be found on the castle pavement. Meanwhile, her father plays host at Castello di Coleredo to Prince di Manfroné whose "brows protended over his scowling eyes, whose lips were of livid hue and closely pressed together." Also on hand is Father Grimaldi, who lurks about the castle and never exposes his hands. When Rosalina finds a sable mask hidden in Father Grimaldi's cell, she realizes that the monk and Prince di Manfroné are one and the same man, but before she can make use of this evidence, she is seized by a figure who "had but one hand!" Before Manfroné can complete the rape he began in Rosalina's bedchamber, the sword of Montalto runs him through. "Here the pen pauses," sighs the second Mrs. Radcliffe, almost regretting that she had to extricate her heroine in this Gothic's Gothic.

***

1-87. The Recluse of the Woods; or, The Generous Warrior, A Gothic Romance. London: T. Maiden for J. Roe & Ann Lemoine, 1809.
About: FG

This "little" Gothic measures 4 × 6 inches and proves to be a plagiarized reduction of Reeve's *Old English Baron* [1-88]. The story concerns the ex-crusader Stephen de Raymond and his daughter, Eliza. The Earl's brother, Henry, perished under mysterious circumstances, and now a fratricidal suspicion hangs over the master of Montville Castle. Near the castle stands the cottage of Ambrose, a recluse of the woods. The genealogical gears turn rapidly to produce the denouement that the reader craves. The recluse of the woods is really Sir Everhard Lucie, friend of the murdered brother. He witnessed the slaying of Henry, but his conscience kept him silent for many years because he is Eliza's natural father. The Earl's son, Edgar, is rechristened Eugene, matched with Eliza and established as the new lord of Montville Castle. Before one dismisses this plot as trite, the insatiable demand for such formulaic Gothicism should be given its due. In fact, there could scarcely be a more typical fourpence chapbook of the period than this little Gothic.

Reeve, Clara (U.K.), 1729–1807.
About: WW, GSF, SFW, FG, SFE

***1-88. The Old English Baron; A Gothic Story**. London: Edward & Charles Dilley, 1777. Recommended edition: ed. by James Trainer. Oxford Univ. Press, 1967.
By toning down Walpole's Gothic, Mrs. Reeve included "a sufficient degree of the marvellous to excite attention." The interior of Lovel Castle is furnished with a haunted chamber where Edmund Twyford is granted an interview with an apparition in armor. Reeve's plot is probably the commonest of all Gothic story patterns, involving paternal murder, usurpation, disinheritance, supernatural disclosure and reinstatement of the young heir. During the minority of Henry VI, Sir Philip Harclay discovers that his friend, Lord Lovel, has been murdered and his castle claimed by Baron Fitz-Owen. Living near the castle and feeling that he has some bond with the murdered Lord is the peasant, Edmund Twyford. To test his worthiness, he performs a vigil within the haunted apartment, an event repeated so often in Gothic novels that its first usage by Mrs. Reeve needs to be stressed. A visored phantom rewards Edmund's courage by informing him that he is the natural son of Lord Lovel, whose bones lie in the compartment below. Edmund regains both the castle and his identity as his marriage to the highborn Emma ends the proceedings. The genealogical plot of *The Old English Baron* would be widely imitated, but it was the ordeal of the haunted chamber which attracted later Gothicists.

Roche, Regina Maria (U.K.), 1773–1845.
About: FG

1-89. The Children of the Abbey. London: Minerva Press for William Lane, 1796. Recommended edition: ed. by Devendra P. Varma. Folio Press, 1968.
A convent, a lonely mansion in Wales, an Irish castle and Dunreath Abbey are way stations for the heroine in her journey toward inheritance and bliss. Accompanied by her brother Oscar, Amanda endures the usual adversities to earn her name as the heir of the abbey's master, the Earl of Dunreath. The action of the novel takes the children from crisis to crisis as an assortment of villains block their path. The final obstacle to happiness calls for a sojourn within the abbey

and a series of supernatural tests. Intrigue, suffering and sexual peril beset the children until their chance return to Dunreath Abbey where a portrait-come-to-life advances toward Amanda with needed genealogical information. Although predictable at every point, this sentimental Gothic is a good replication of the Radcliffean model.

1-90. Clermont, A Tale. London: Minerva Press for William Lane, 1798. Recommended edition: ed. by Devendra P. Varma. Folio Press, 1968.
A high Gothic novel, its pure terror is confirmed by its placement in the "Northanger" septet. The ruin-loving Madeline Clermont has been called the "Gothistic super-heroine." Her cottage is adjacent to a ruin which tempts her nightly with "its horrid noises and still more horrid sights." Lurking about the ruin is the stranger, Sevignie, but before Madeline can form a love attachment to him, she is carried off to a chateau by D'Alembert, head of a gang of rakes who use the chateau as a meeting place. The exaggerated horrors of Madeline's confinement indicate the influence of the chapbooks on Mrs. Roche's nightmare scenes. Most exits from the haunted castle connect with a grotto which hides a hermit or a sanctuary, but the way out of the chateau brings Madeline amid D'Alembert and his men. Also waiting beyond the castle is Sevignie, absent from the plot for a lengthy period until the maiden has exhausted all of her avenues of escape. *Clermont*'s terrors attracted readers from all sections of the public as shown by the bookplate of the dramatist Richard Brinsley Sheridan in the Sadleir-Black Gothic Collection's copy of the novel.

S., R. (U.K.), dates unknown.

ABOUT: FG

1-91. The New Monk. London: Minerva Press for William Lane, 1798.
The goal of this parody is to undermine a single Gothic novel, *The Monk* [1-58]. Lewis's monk is converted into the bombastic Reverend Joshua Pentateuch, "the Boanerges of the pulpit." For the servant of Satan, Matilda, we have the sex-crazed Betsey. The horror scenes are lampooned in a paragraph-by-paragraph attack. The Convent of St. Clare where Lewis's Agnes gave birth to her child amid the corpses is modernized into Mrs. Rod's boarding school where Alice Clottleberry (Lewis's Agnes) is dragged from classroom to flogging chamber. Ambrosio's raid on Antonia's maidenhead is replaced by Pentateuch's invasion of Anna Maria Augusta's bedroom in quest of loose banknotes. Excoriating in style, *The New Monk* excels as one of the closest anti-readings of another work in the history of satire. R. S.'s satire merits a modern edition in order to show students of the Gothic that there was a light side to the dark side during the Gothic years.

Sade, Donatien-Alphonse-François Marquis de (France), 1740–1814.

ABOUT: WW

***1-92. Justine; ou, Les Infortunes de la vertu** [*Justine; or, The Misfortunes of Virtue*]. Paris: Girouard, 1791. Recommended edition: ed. and tr. by Richard Seaver and Austryn Wainhouse. Grove, 1965.
The sexual Gothicism of *Justine* cynically questions the moral life and mocks the

motto of "Virtue Rewarded." The novel thrusts the heroine into a spiked labyrinth of lust, perversion and depravity. Justine is the Gothic victim done in brutal caricature. Her life is a cycle of flagellations, rackings and rapes. She falls into the clutches of the freethinker Count Bressac, who whips her body as he lashes her mind with his arguments for the necessity of vice. She is placed in the academy of the child-flogger, Dr. Rodin, where she is punished with hot irons. Throughout these ordeals she clings to her virtuous opinions and hopeful view of human nature. For her pains, she is set upon by a pack of dogs, phlebotomized by monks, sealed into a coffin and made to endure a mock funeral, lowered slowly into a corpse-lined pit, and forced to witness the crucifixion of a nude girl. The death of Justine when she is incinerated by a bolt of lightning is a final cynical touch. The close relationship between English Gothic fiction and Sade's sexual Gothicism has never been sufficiently investigated.

***

1-93. Schabraco, A Romance. In *Lady's Monthly Museum, or Polite Repository of Amusement and Instruction*, 1 (August-November, 1798; 4 parts). Recommended edition: in *The Candle and the Tower*, ed. by R. D. Spector. Warner, 1974.

About: FG

A 12,500-word serialized Gothic which covered the entire range of taste from polite shudders to emetic horrors. Rinaldo and Sabrina are victimized by a villain operating under a triple identity from his mansion on the Calabrian coast. Schabraco is a figure of mystery "whose smile was the smile of spleen." Seen again, he becomes Father Stephano, "of blazing eye, pallid cheek, and trembling lip." At death, he is the nobleman Hernando Piozzi. Episode three of the romance concentrates on Sabrina's torments and contains a fantasy of subterranean rape. On the final page of the fourth installment, "the mansion with all its intricate subterranean apartments was totally destroyed," and Rinaldo is reunited with Sabrina.

Schiller, Johann Christoph Friedrich von (Germany), 1759-1805.

About: WW, GSF, SFW

1-94. Der Geisterseher: Eine Geschichte aus den Memoires des Graffen von O. [*The Ghostseer; A History from the Memoirs of the Count of O.*]. Berlin: G. J. Göschen, 1789. Tr. by Daniel Boileau, London: Vernor & Hood, 1795. Recommended edition: in *Gothic Tales of Terror*, ed. by Peter Haining. Taplinger, 1972. Schiller's theme of necromancy attracted both German and English Gothicists. The tale is a fragmentary memoir by the Count of O. concerning the odd adventures of a German prince. In Venice, this exile becomes involved with an Armenian Ghostseer who prevents the Prince's assassination and helps him to avoid the corruptions of a Sicilian alchemist. Cabalistic ceremonies, corpse raising, international conspiracy by a secret society and other occult practices complicate the life of the young Prince, but the reader is never sure whether the Ghostseer's role in the Prince's life is sinister or beneficial. These ambivalences foreshadow the attitudes of Schiller's successor in ambiguous Gothic, E. T. A. Hoffmann.

Scott, Sir Walter (U.K.), 1771-1832.
ABOUT: WW, SFW, FG, SMFL, PE

1-95. The Black Dwarf. London: Blackwood, 1816. Included in any modern set of Scott's works.
Scott's novel experimented with the Gothic theme of dwarfism. The plot elements, such as the sinister scenery around the dwarf's lair of boulders; the abduction of the heroine, Grace Armstrong; the persecution of Isabella Vere; and the disclosure of the Black Dwarf's noble lineage, are standard Gothic elements. The Black Dwarf is the freak, Elshender the Recluse, or Elshie of Mucklestanes. Living in a den of boulders, he emerges to perform anonymous deeds of charity for the local inhabitants who fear and loath him. The outlines of the pathetic monster story are present. Since Scott's novel precedes *Frankenstein* [1-97] by two years, we might surmise the book's influence on it. Scott touched on but did not develop, as Mary Shelley would later do, the monstrous attitudes of society toward its unfortunate freaks.

1-96. The Bride of Lammermoor. London: A. Constable, 1819. Recommended edition: ed. by W. M. Parker. Everyman's, 1963.
The Bride of Lammermoor takes a fatal view of human nature which shows the mark of Scott's friend among the Gothics, C. R. Maturin. The hero, Ravenswood, derives from the Gothic cast, and his physical and psychological attachment to the decaying Wolf's Crag Tower shows Scott's use of the motif of entrapment. Grim coincidence too plays a role. By a chance meeting, Ravenswood saves the life of his family's adversary, Sir William Ashton, and he falls in love with his rival's daughter, Lucy. Their fated love forms the core of the tale. Lucy shares many traits with the victimized maidens of Gothic fiction. She is persecuted by her aunt, Lady Ashton, and forced to marry against her wishes. Driven mad, she murders her would-be husband on the eve of her wedding day, and dies in agony. Lucy's death occasions Scott's best Gothic climax when Ravenswood is sucked down into the quicksand of the Kelpie Flow as he gallops toward his revenge. Scott lowers a black pall of horror over doomed love, thus endowing this novel with the note of tragedy also felt in the best work of Maturin.

Shelley, Mary Wollstonecraft (U.K.), 1797-1851.
ABOUT: WW, GSF, SFW, F, CA, FG, NE, H, SMFL, SFE, PE, ESF

***1-97. Frankenstein; or, The Modern Prometheus**. London: Lackington, Hughes, Harding, Mavor & Jones, 1818. Recommended editions: ed. by Harold Bloom. New American Library, 1965; ed. by James Rieger. Bobbs-Merrill, 1974. *The Annotated Frankenstein* includes the 1818 text, extensive notes by Leonard Wolf and many illustrations (Clarkson Potter, 1977).
Frankenstein is a special type of Gothic novel in its presentation of the destructive quest, and its version of the Gothic villain as a scientist. Victor Frankenstein seeks power over nature, a motive which recalls Beckford's *Vathek* [1-6]. The conflict between the scientist and his monster invites philosophical interpretations. The monster is only one in a book of many monsters. After the creation, Victor Frankenstein rejects his creature and attempts to resume a life of friendship,

courtship and marriage. The brute learns to hate his maker and the human community as he tries futilely to be accepted. The outcast avenges himself by strangling Frankenstein's fiancée, Elizabeth Lavenza, and killing his brother, William, and his friend, Henry Clerval. Asked by the creature to construct a mate, Frankenstein begins the task, then aborts it when he realizes that he may be manufacturing a monster race. The novel ends at the ends of the earth when the monster flees northward into the polar regions. Frankenstein's pursuit of the thing is an inversion of the usual Gothic pursuit. Dying aboard the ice-bound ship of Captain Walton, an explorer who is seeking the Northwest Passage, Victor warns Walton: "You seek for knowledge and wisdom as I once did. I ardently hope that the gratification of your wishes may not be a serpent to sting you as mine has been." The closing image shows the monster borne off on an ice floe into "the darkness and the distance"—only to reappear in Hollywood a century later. Without abandoning the Gothic, *Frankenstein* goes beyond the trappings of the popular horror tale to probe the darkest cave of them all, the human mind.

Shelley, Percy Bysshe (U.K.), 1792-1822.

ABOUT: GSF, SFW, FG, PE

1-98. Zastrozzi; A Romance. London: G. Wilkie & J. Robinson, 1810. Recommended edition: ed. by Frederick S. Frank. Arno, 1977.
The residue of Shelley's two Gothics infuses the poetry and contributes to his conception of the imagination. Both Gothics are allegories of the mind's dark places and self-destructive extremes. *Zastrozzi* contains demonic love, nocturnal pursuit, incestuous nightmare, sexual murder and charnel excitement. The villain is a colossus full of "pale ire, envy and despair." He plots against his half-brother, Verezzi, whom he blames for his wretched condition, and forms an alliance with Matilda to ruin Verezzi and Julia. A rondo of stabbings ends the intrigue. Exulting over the carnage he has caused, Zastrozzi laughs even as he is hoisted upon the rack. Shelley's shocker was actually a first portrait of the Promethean rebel whose defiant aim was to abolish divine authority and replace it with the human spirit.

1-99. St. Irvyne; or, The Rosicrucian, A Romance. London: J. J. Stockdale, 1811. Recommended edition: ed. by Frederick S. Frank. Arno, 1977.
The Gothic hero Ginotti (alias Nempere) is a composite of the villains admired by Shelley. Ginotti possesses the elixir of eternal life, but wants to dispose of this accursed gift which now blights his soul. The characters are allegorical embodiments of Shelley's ideas about God, nature and the human intellect. Wolfstein, the man chosen by Ginotti to receive the elixir, represents the torments of the imagination. The tale's three women symbolize love in its several forms. The Italian beauty, Megalena de Metastasio, is carnal love. The virtuous Olympia stands for the love that transcends the senses. Wolfstein's sister, Eloise St. Irvyne, combines both qualities to reconcile the opposite forces of heaven and earth. The temptation of Wolfstein by Ginotti is an allegorization of the fall of man. When Wolfstein refuses the secret of immortality, lightning flashes through the vaults of St. Irvyne, incinerating Ginotti but leaving him alive in death as the "frame

mouldered to a gigantic skeleton, yet two pale and ghastly flames glared in its eyeless sockets." Here, Shelley gives the animated skeleton new energy as an image of the soul's terrors.

Sleath, Eleanor (U.K.), dates unknown.

About: FG

1-100. The Orphan of the Rhine. London: Minerva Press for William Lane, 1798. Recommended edition: ed. by Devendra P. Varma. Folio Press, 1968.
The plot is intricate but accessible to the unhurried reader who savors a Gothic journey down the Rhine. Integrated into the story of the orphan, Laurette, are the chronicles of three other victims of Montferrat treachery. First we have Julia's memoir of her trials at the hands of the Marquesa of Montferrat and her henchman, Vescolini. The middle inset, a monastic shocker, is the account of the abused nun, Sister Cecilia, who may be Laurette's missing mother. The third inset is the biography of La Roque, the prisoner of the Marquis of Montferrat and later the agent of justice. This is a Gothic novel of insets in which the substories relate thematically to the genealogical progress of the heroine. The main narrative conveys Laurette down the Rhine until she enters the Castle of Elfinbach. Here, several of the characters who appeared in the inset stories assemble to effect her marriage to Enrico to the confusion of the Montferrats. The artificial medievalism and pleasing terrors resulted in a Gothic which earned Sadleir's praise as "a strangely attractive absurdity which excites a sort of sugary fascination over the reader."

1-101. The Nocturnal Minstrel; or, The Spirit of the Wood. London: Minerva Press for A. K. Newman, 1810. Recommended edition: ed. by Devendra P. Varma. Arno, 1972.
The heroine, Baroness Fitzwalter, is a Gothic Penelope who fends off suitors during the absence of her husband, who has joined the cause of the royal pretender, Perkin Warbeck, and is believed dead. The suitors are kept at bay by the Baron's musical ghost who patrols the halls of Castle Fitzwalter as he makes nocturnal minstrelsy. As the vicious Sir Reginald Harcland presses his case, the Baroness hears weird singing from the woods, and there are sightings of a spirit strolling in the picture gallery. Just as Harcland is about to force his suit, a stranger arrives and produces the castle specter by revealing the ghostly music to be his work since he had hidden himself in the forest to protect his wife. Nothing in the melodramatic patterning of the romance is unique or unexpected, but the desupernaturalized ending along with the pleasing terrors of the castle accommodated every need of the devotees of Radcliffean Gothicism.

Smith, Catherine (U.K.), dates unknown.

About: FG

1-102. Barozzi; or, The Venetian Sorceress, A Romance of the Sixteenth Century. London: Minerva Press for A. K. Newman, 1815. Recommended edition: ed. by Devendra P. Varma. Arno, 1977.
A "horror of the ruin" featuring midnight seizures, infanticide and satanic

rituals. The novel opens in the middle of a rape and finishes its first scene with the skewering of Rosalina's father, Ferrand St. Elmo. Her rescue from ruffians by Rosalva Barozzi only arouses the ire of his father, Augustino Barozzi. Getting a Venetian sorceress into the plot is accomplished by moving the young couple to a haunted castle in the Apennines. The castle offers the reader shape-shifting rooms and, in the deserted wing, a living female corpse bedecked in white robes. In another hidden apartment, Rosalina interrupts Augustino partaking of some obscene ritual conducted by the Venetian sorceress. Tearing aside her disguise, the Venetian sorceress declares her maternal tie with Rosalina and points the finger of justice at the astounded Augustino. With Augustino on the rack and Rosalina and Rosalva at the altar, Mrs. Smith's gore-stained curtain descends.

Smith, Charlotte (U.K.), 1749–1806.

ABOUT: FG

1-103. Emmeline, the Orphan of the Castle. London: T. Cadell, 1788. Recommended edition: ed. by Anne H. Ehrenpreis. Oxford Univ. Press, 1971.

Emmeline is the first heroine whose beauty is seen glowing against a grim background, or who is hunted along passages at night. The particulars of the plot, especially the heroine's efforts to establish her heritage against the operations of evil relatives, anticipate Mrs. Radcliffe's plots. Emmeline's father was the victim of a bad brother, Montreville, who now blocks her heritage. Her cousin, Delamere, opposes Montreville but lacks the power to be effectual. Pretending to yield Mowbray Castle, her uncle makes her a prisoner and proceeds with his schemes. For Mrs. Smith, the Gothic castle is not quite a supernatural site, although it is an arena of suffering. Emmeline's escape from the castle is an assertion of selfhood as the Gothic gloom clears in favor of her recovery of the title and her marriage to Mr. Godolphin. Mrs. Smith's first three novels are clear examples of muted Radcliffean romance as the older forms of the novel become Gothic under her direction.

1-104. The Old Manor House. London: J. Bell, 1793. Recommended edition: ed. by Anne H. Ehrenpreis. Oxford Univ. Press, 1969.

The story centers on decaying Rayland Manor, stronghold of the dowager Mrs. Rayland. Her protector is Orlando, who loves Monimia, an orphan taken in by the old woman and who later proves to be a blood relative. Instead of lecherous barons, the novel's villains are lawyers and fortune hunters who hover around the Old Manor House awaiting Mrs. Rayland's death. Lawyer Roker's harassment of old Mrs. Rayland is equalled by the sexual advances of the rake, Mr. Belgrave, against Monimia. Major Gothic scenes depict the young lovers fleeing through the mansion's vast network of rooms. The plot is given complexity when Orlando goes to the Americas to fight in the Indian wars, then returns to the Old Manor House to find Monimia missing and old Mrs. Rayland dead. Orlando had been named her beneficiary, but lawyer Roker has subverted the will. As in a true Gothic, a lost will comes to light and the Old Manor House is restored to the new generation. Lacking only an ancestral crime and a curse, Mrs. Smith's house novel impressed Gothic readers well into Victorian times.

Smollett, Tobias (U.K.), 1721-1771.
ABOUT: FG

***1-105. The Adventures of Ferdinand Count Fathom.** London: W. Johnson, 1753. Recommended edition: ed. by Damian Grant. Oxford Univ. Press, 1971.
Several episodes in Smollett's novel anticipate the Gothic. The Count's experiences while passing through the forest in Chapter 20 and the scenes in the graveyard in which the spirit of Monimia confronts Rinaldo have the Gothic tone. Count Fathom himself, however, cannot be considered a Gothic character. The bastard son of an unknown soldier and a camp follower, he has deserted from two armies. The pre-Gothic characters are his victims, Monimia and Rinaldo. Assaulted by the Count, Monimia's shame causes her to feign her own death and burial, a masquerade which brings Rinaldo to her tomb. When the amorous phantom of his dead beloved accosts Rinaldo, Smollett crosses from the picaresque to the Gothic world. Forty years before the apprehensive gropings of the Radcliffean heroine, Smollett's version of the Gothic seems firmly in place.

***

1-106. Spectre Mother; or, The Haunted Tower. London: Dean & Munday, 1800. Recommended edition: in *The Shilling Shockers: Stories of Terror from the Gothic Bluebooks,* ed. by Peter Haining. St. Martin's, 1979.
ABOUT: FG

In this chapbook condensation of *The Mysteries of Udolpho* [1-83], Montoni becomes Moresco. His habitat is Rovado Castle where Moresco has murdered Julia and is about to repeat the deed on her child when the Specter Mother interposes. Another wife, Angela Modeni, has been locked away in another castle and fears the worst when she is brought to Rovado Castle. But the Specter Mother is on hand to show the heroine the way downward "into an immeasurable chasm" which leads through a vault, which leads to a secret postern, which terminates in safety and sunlight. Awaiting Angela as she emerges from the tunnel of horrors is Montmorenci who announces that Moresco has fallen off a battlement. And the Specter Mother? The reader must assume that she retires to the interior of Rovado Castle to await the arrival of the next screaming maiden in need of a supernatural guide.

***

1-107. The Tomb of Aurora; or, The Mysterious Summons. London: Ann Lemoine & J. Roe, 1807.
ABOUT: FG

The shocker draws its power to thrill from the motif of the vocal tomb. At the Palazzo della Massina, the Marquis de Verezzi lives with his evil wife, Olivia, "the mistress of infamy." On his wedding day, a monk gives him a summons to the Convent of San Salvador, the burial place of his previous beloved, Aurora. Strange sounds have been coming from Aurora's tomb and the epitaph, "Aurora—The Victim of Perfidy," glows with an eerie light. A few swift strokes by the chapbooker bring the company to the tomb for the ensnaring of Olivia. To expose her infamy, the monk encourages Olivia's sexual advances as Verezzi watches. As Olivia gives herself to the monk, the portals of the tomb fly open to deliver the living Aurora to Verezzi. Literally every page of the chapbook exhibits some confiscation of name, event or device from the longer Gothics.

Walpole, Horace (as by **Onuphrio Muralto**) (U.K.), 1717–1797

ABOUT: WW, GSF, SFW, F, FG, SMFL, PE, ESF

***1-108. The Castle of Otranto; A Gothic Story**. London: Thomas Lownds, 1765. Recommended edition: in *Three Gothic Novels*, ed. by Mario Praz. Penguin, 1968.
The master plan for the Gothic was drafted by Horace Walpole in *The Castle of Otranto*. It generated terror in two ways: the installation throughout the castle of the machinery of supernatural shock; the placement of characters in "extraordinary positions." Gothic meant the suspension of reason and the triumph of disorder. The story line used by Walpole would become standard for the Gothic romance. A crisis induced by an ancestral curse, parental villainy and a conflict between natural and supernatural wills for possession of the castle became integral parts of Walpole's infernal machine. On the opening page, a huge helmet falls from the sky to crush the heir of Otranto, Conrad, on the eve of his wedding to Isabella. Crushed also are Manfred's plans for maintaining his control of the castle. Manfred is the patriarch of Gothic villains, figures of illegitimate power and tormented even as they torment others. With Conrad mangled by the helmet, Isabella becomes Manfred's prey in a subterranean chase that extends through "vaults totally dark." Doors grate on hinges and trapdoors open by themselves as the maiden seeks a way out of the darkness and into the arms of young Theodore. To oppose Manfred's villainy, supernatural forces, set in motion by the arrival of the enormous helmet, gather within the walls of the castle. The turrets vibrate with aliveness as if some giant figure were stirring inside the stones. The nose of Alfonso's statue exudes blood; a portrait of Manfred's guilty ancestor, Ricardo, leaves its frame; giant body parts are seen protruding through castle walls and pavement; an armored hand grasping after a mighty sword is seen over a staircase. The murder of Manfred's daughter, Matilda, at the crypt of Alfonso brings these forces into a spectacular convergence. Accompanied by Olympian thunder, the huge figure of Alfonso the Good, enlarged "to an immense magnitude," obliterates the walls of Otranto and stands amid the ruin. From the fall of the house of Otranto to the fall of the House of Usher, the Gothic universe would remain a place of instability and terror where universal darkness buries all. Also annotated as [F1-92].

1-109. The Mysterious Mother. Printed Privately by Walpole at Strawberry Hill, 1768; London: Dodsley, 1781. Recommended edition: ed. by Montague Summers. Constable, 1924.
Genealogical revelation furnishes the horror of *The Mysterious Mother*. The play set a standard for Gothic drama and influenced theatrical treatments of incest. Its sexual mysteries may be compared with Sophocles's *Oedipus Tyrannus* in the way Walpole constructs his dark fable of identity. The mysterious mother is the Countess of Narbonne. She has substituted herself for her son's mistress and secretly borne him a daughter, Adeliza. The stain of incest marks Edmund for

disaster since he cannot curb his sexual passion for Adeliza when she becomes a woman. When her crimes are disclosed, the mother takes her life, precipitating the death of her son. The sexual transgression that is hidden even from those who commit the deed is the drama's important contribution to the central mystery of the Gothic novel. The characters are their own worst enemies and are destroyed by psychotic drives that arise out of their hidden natures.

Warner, Richard (U.K.), 1763–1857.
ABOUT: FG

1-110. Netley Abbey; A Gothic Story. Southampton: T. Skelton, 1795. Recommended edition: ed. by Devendra P. Varma. Arno, 1974.
The story is prefaced by an overture on the wanderings of the crusader Sir Edward Villars. He was saved from death from a viper when the poison was sucked from the wound by Bertram, who is really his admirer, Isabel. Action passes to the next generation and to the children of Sir Edward and Isabel who suffer the machinations of Lord Hildebrand. Hildebrand's control of Netley is challenged by Edward Villars who is given the task of ending Hildebrand's domination. Guided by various phantoms, Edward is able to bring the crimes of Lord Hildebrand to light. One of his supernatural guides is Sir Raymond Warren, murdered uncle of Lord Hildebrand. The wronged natural and supernatural characters cooperate to bring about long-delayed justice when Edward and Sir Raymond foment a duel between Lord Hildebrand and the abbot which ends in their mutual deaths. Stability of family and the vindication of wrong were parts of the Gothic's reaffirming myth of dark passions brought under control.

Wilkinson, Sarah (U.K.), dates unknown.
ABOUT: FG

1-111. The Subterranean Passage; or, Gothic Cell. London: Ann Lemoine, 1803. Wilkinson's first work concentrates the apparatus of anguish that is usually distributed throughout the haunted castle into the two locales mentioned in the title. The maiden prisoner, Antoinette, and her tormentor, Father Anselmo, are impersonations of Mrs. Radcliffe's characters from *The Italian* [1-84]. Successfully abridging the best Gothic novels of her superiors, she managed to color her plots with her own distinctive shades of gore. Modern psychoanalytic criticism of the Gothic might relate her subterranean compartments to the male and female body. Corridors and passages are masculine; chambers and cells are female and vaginal. The villain who roams the corridors is a configuration of the terror of sex while the maiden trembling in dread within her Gothic cell is an emblem of sexual fear and desire. Examined from such a psychoanalytic perspective, the crudest bluebook made a powerful appeal to the repressed forces of the psyche.

1-112. The Mysterious Novice; or, The Convent of the Grey Penitents, Including the Memoirs of Augustus and Wilhelmina. London: Arliss, 1809. Recommended edition: in *The Shilling Shockers: Stories of Terror from the Gothic Bluebooks*, ed. by Peter Haining. St. Martin's 1979.
Wilkinson's Rosalthe is a refabrication of Mrs. Radcliffe's Ellena di Rosalba in

this imitation of *The Italian* [1-84]. The appended story of Augustus and Wilhelmina is taken from the Agnes-Lorenzo story of *The Monk* [1-58]. Wilkinson had used this combination of sources often in her more than twenty Gothic works, in which the tantalizing delays of Mrs. Radcliffe are combined with the horrid shocks of Lewis. The ability to produce the Gothic novel to the demands of popular taste kept this typical Gothic novelist in the public eye for almost two decades. In at least one instance, she was able to publish the same Gothic chapbook under two different titles without in any way disappointing her clientele. Her Gothic canon is typical of that of hundreds of Gothic writers who, in the words of the collector Robert K. Black, "in their own day held enthralled a nationwide reading public."

2

The Later Gothic Tradition, 1825–96

Brian Stableford

If there is one dominant theme in the post-Gothic weird fiction of the nineteenth century, it is the theme of the dead returning to pester the living. Different authors offered various theories about what business the dead might have with the living; they came most often to reveal the truth of hidden crime and to harry the guilty ones, but their visits were sometimes more kindly in intention despite the fright they caused, and in some stories they were reduced in status to mere purposeless echoes of the past. For whatever reason, though, they did come in great quantity and the idea of their returning received so much literary attention—despite this having been a relatively skeptical and rationalistic age—that the unwary might easily leap to the conclusion that nineteenth-century horror stories were symptoms of some kind of collective neurosis.

A preoccupation with the souls of the departed was not, of course, confined to the fiction of the day. Philippe Ariès, in his classic study of attitudes to death, *The Hour of Our Death* (1977; tr. 1981), calls the nineteenth century "The Age of the Beautiful Death," borrowing the phrase from Coraly de Gaïx, who wrote in her journal in 1825: "We live in an age of beautiful deaths; the death of Mme. de Villeneuve was sublime."

This quotation brings together, interestingly, the two ideas which Edmund Burke, in his *Philosophical Enquiry into the Origin of Our Ideas of the Sublime and Beautiful* (1756), had tried so carefully to separate. With the idea of the sublime Burke had associated awe, darkness, solitude, vastness and terror; with the idea of the beautiful he had associated light, delicacy, symmetry, smoothness and softness. Burke's meditations or the idea of the sublime—inspired in part by such literary productions as Edward Young's *Night Thoughts on Life, Death and Immortality* (1742-44) and James Hervey's *Meditations among the Tombs* (1745-47)—had been a key influence on the critical reception of Gothic fiction, which seemed to its apologists to embrace the sublime worldview wholeheartedly. But Coraly de Gaïx was quite correct; by 1825 the dialectical opposition of sublimity and beauty had begun to dissolve, and though it would be overstating the case to claim that a new synthesis was ultimately to emerge, there was a considerable effort of the imagination in that direction. It was as if nineteenth-century society (dragging nineteenth-century supramundane fiction in its wake) set out to tame—or at least to placate—the sublime, with beautification as its instrument.

Ariès calls our attention to the dramatic changes which overcame cemeteries in the nineteenth century. In Père-Lachaise Cemetery in Paris, he observes, the number of tombstones laid per year increased from 14 in 1805 to 76 in 1810 to 635 in 1815, and thereafter to something on the order of 2,000, as the practice spread even to the lower orders of society. The Victorian cemeteries of London abound in cracked and moss-covered angels and other such weighty memorials; the Victorian funeral processions, with their hired mutes and hired mourners, hearse and horses no less extravagantly decked in black than the people, represent an amazing fascination with death as well as a luxuriant indulgence of grief. In this era the dead were laid most carefully to rest, but clamored for attention nevertheless.

Ariès offers interesting comments on the variety of media in which the changing attitudes can be tracked. He refers, for instance, to the collection of funerary jewelry held in London's Victoria and Albert Museum, which spans the gap of time between England's two great queens, Elizabeth and Victoria; he notes that the items begin as *memento mori*, emblematic of the fear of death, and end as *memento illius*, reminding the living to remember the dead fondly and to include them in their prayers.

Victorian fiction accepted this fascination with death, and turned it to many purposes. The particular obsession which certain Victorian writers had with the glorious deaths of saintly children provides a key example of the struggle to combine solemnification with beautification. Realistic fiction, following the extravagant example set by Samuel Richardson in *Clarissa Harlowe* (1748), had taken the deathbed scene very much to its heart by the time the great nineteenth-century novelists appeared on the literary stage, and stories of Victorian domestic life are replete with melodramatic scenes of deathbed repentance and deathbed forgiveness.

Horror fiction, of course, bears eloquent testimony to the fact that the effort to beautify death and make it safe was a desperate one, which could not truly succeed. The extravagances of Victorian mourning, no matter how much genuine feeling was thus expressed, could not help being seen and felt by many as gross hypocrisies. Nothing is more guaranteed to stir up guilty feelings than the death of a relative, and attempts to exorcise guilty feelings by ostentatious displays of sorrow must frequently have had the contrary effect of magnifying those feelings. Thus, efforts made to soothe consciences by making more fuss about the dead often inflamed anxiety, and the angry psychological sores which resulted can be seen in the supernatural fiction of the period.

Britain was perhaps the nation most affected by the new attitude to death, but Ariès finds it in other European countries, and in America too. America was slow to fall prey to the same fashions in funerary practice which claimed nineteenth-century Europe (though studies of the modern American way of death suggest that the United States took over where Europe eventually left off) but was nevertheless touched by the same kinds of anxiety, as *Death in America* (1975), edited by David E. Stannard, reveals. It is entirely appropriate that it should have been America, with its strong cultural emphasis on practicality, which produced the joint-cracking Fox sisters, who began in 1848 to open up new channels of communication between the forgiving dead and the reassurance-seeking living, and were promptly put on public display by P. T. Barnum. As the nineteenth century progressed it became increasingly difficult for people in Europe and America to let the dead rest in peace, given that they seemed everywhere to be clamoring for attention with insistent rappings, levitating tables and clouds of ectoplasm, while they awaited impatiently their turn to use the overstrained vocal cords of countless entranced mediums.

The mediums were responding as best they could to audience demand, and what the members of the audience demanded above all else was to have their guilty anxieties soothed away. They wanted to know that their "loved ones" (emphatically so described, one cynically assumes, because they had not been loved enough) were safe in heaven, having a lovely time, and that they—the living—had been forgiven for all their petty trespasses and sins of neglect.

The success of the spiritualist cults is *prima facie* proof that guilty consciences ran riot in the late nineteenth century in a way they never had before. Never had the living mounted such an imaginative rebellion against the empire of fear ruled by the tyrant Mortality, and never had they been so anxious to retain the goodwill of those whom Mortality had claimed. Given all this, the rise of the Victorian ghost story, even in an age when sensible men had ceased to believe in ghosts, is an easily understandable phenomenon.

Whatever success people had in soothing their own fears of death by attempted beautification—and we must suspect that it was a self-confidence trick which hardly ever succeeded—had to be offset against the rise of further anxieties to supplement those they already had. The increased emotional investment in funerals and tombs had as one of its stranger corollaries a remarkable increase in taphephobia: the fear of premature burial. R. C. Finucane, in his book *Appearances of the Dead* (1982), notes that Tebb and Vollum's now-forgotten classic *Premature Burial and How It May Be Prevented* (2nd ed., 1905) had a bibliography which cited 120 books, 41 university theses and a series of 17 pamphlets published by the London Association for the Prevention of Premature Burial. We can find this anxiety manifest in a number of fine horror stories, the most notable by Edgar Allan Poe [2-77].

The growth of anxieties regarding premature burial was, however, a minor matter. A much more considerable growth of nineteenth-century anxiety can be seen in connection with the fear of madness. This growth complements attempts to defuse the menace of the supernatural, and may be regarded as its corollary. Hard-headed skeptics, who wanted to unburden modern society of the superstitions of the past, fought to demonstrate that horrific apparitions were *not* the malevolent spirits of the dead returned to torment and destroy the living; they insisted that apparitions were in fact *hallucinations*, products of the fevered imagination.

Of course they were right—but if empiricists hoped by this means to defeat and drive out fear, they had mistaken their enemy; the fear remained, and those sufferers who were convinced that the cause was internal rather than external simply accepted that they were haunted by demons within rather than demons without. Agnostics, who conserved doubt, could easily be persuaded that it surely did not really matter whether the source of the fear was external or internal—and that the very ambiguity of interpretation might itself become a further source of anxiety, amplifying confusion rather than eroding it.

Fear of madness had always been around, and it had probably been growing for some time in the Western world, but Michel Foucault's account of *Madness and Civilization* (1961) discovers a remarkably rapid growth in the second half of the eighteenth century when "the fear of madness grew at the same time as the dread of unreason; and thereby the two forms of obsession, leaning upon each other, continued to reinforce one another." The proliferation of asylums also began in the eighteenth century, but it was in the period now under consideration that the phenomena of madness were brought decisively into the context of medical research and medical explanation. The idea of *mental illness* achieved its final victory, so that the fear of the diseased psyche could take on its modern aspect. In stories of derangement written after 1825, therefore, we cannot help finding an advancing clinicality, a fascination with fear as *symptom* and an emerging notion of the bad conscience as a poisoner of the mind. This certainly helps to transform the business of writing horror stories, but it sharpens rather than blunts the horrific aspect of tales which feature disturbing encounters with enigmatic apparitions.

Bad conscience remained a prominent feature of stories of the unrationalized supernatural; despite all the effort which the Victorians invested in the hope that the dead were at peace, they never could free themselves of the conviction that many must be bitter in resentment, and that some must hunger for revenge upon the living. This does not mean that it was only the guilty who were pursued, but where the innocent are victimized in the Victorian story of the supernatural it is usually by *human* evil, or by their own folly. Equally, it is frequently the case that the guilty must flee, even though no man or actual ghost pursues them, haunted by a mysterious other part of their divided selves. In this way, nineteenth-century horror stories, though they may sometimes flirt with the idea of a morally chaotic universe, characteristically endorse the conviction that there must be a moral order of sorts, even if it works in more mysterious ways than had previously been thought likely. However clinicalized madness becomes in nineteenth-century fictions, it remains a disease with moral implications, like syphilis.

Because of its preoccupations with extraordinary extrapolations of guilt and with medically defined madness, the history of the horror story from 1825 to 1896 is very largely an account of growing introversion. The moaning specters and deformed monsters of the Gothic are gradually relocated within the psyche. They lurk there as ill-kept prisoners, like the monstrous Mr. Hyde within the personality of the noble and respectable Dr. Jekyll, in one of the period's most celebrated works [2-93]. Where the ghosts and monsters retain their independent existence, their connection with the people they haunt grows gradually more intimate, tending toward the covertly sexual; Le Fanu's "Carmilla" [2-50] adds a remarkable sensuality to the character of the seductive vampire first glimpsed in Polidori [1-79] and brought to eventual perfection in *Dracula* [3-186]. Victorian standards of decency had only to relax a little before the werewolf could be given a similar erotic charge by Clemence Housman [2-42], and the ghost by Vernon Lee [2-48].

In spite of its veiling in order to meet standards of literary decency, the intimacy of the relationships established between the haunters and haunted is striking in the most important writers, even in the earlier part of the period—it is especially obvious in Poe [2-77]. It is revealing that the painstaking primness which certain Victorian lady novelists carefully maintained in their mundane fiction is considerably compromised by the themes of their supramundane work; Mrs. Praed [2-78–2-79] and Florence Marryat [2-60] are obvious examples. Magically adept characters who turn their mesmeric talents to virtual rape become commonplace in fiction of the latter part of the period, figuring in Mrs. Praed's *The Soul of Countess Adrian* [2-79], Joseph Hocking's *The Weapons of Mystery* [2-41] and Conan Doyle's *The Parasite* [2-21].

There is nothing in the least surprising in this growing intimacy, given on the one hand the social melodramatization of death and on the other the clinicalization of madness. However the horrid specters of nineteenth-century supernatural fiction manifest themselves, and whatever ontological status they are given within the internal world of the story, it is something in the mind of their victim which summons them; the eye of the beholder is already prepared to catch sight of them.

A horror story is defined by the anxiety which is suffered by its characters, and communicated by imaginative identification to the reader. It is the threat of death (which subsumes the threats of pain, injury and rape) or the threat of madness which evokes the definitive anxiety, and is therefore its proximal cause. The ever-presence of such threats in horror fiction ought not, however, to blind us to the possibility of looking deeper, for more remote motive forces implicit in the aesthetics of the genre.

Threat and anxiety, despite their importance in horror stories, are not what horror fiction is really about. Horror stories are really about *evil*. Our ideas of evil are, of course, intimately bound up with our experiences of pain and violation; we identify an evil thing by its wanting and intending to hurt us. But whenever we ask questions about the nature of evil, we are attempting to go behind and beyond the mere fact of threat to ask why it is that we are threatened. The true project of horror fiction is to discover evil, to bring it out of hiding and to make it show its face; the horror fiction of the nineteenth century shows us the progress of contemporary anxieties about the evil which others did, whose consequences could not be "interred with their bones," and about the evil which we do, whose legacy will haunt us even while we live.

Western thought has always had its representations of an external force of evil—Satan and his demonic legions replaced various pagan analogues—but it has also located vulnerability to temptation firmly within the human person. This idea has a particularly striking representation in the Christian notion of Original Sin. In the pre-1825 Gothic tradition, though the instruments used to arouse anxiety may be inhuman, sometimes inert, and often lacking in particular purpose, the source and focal point of evil was always a man. But the Gothic villain was a crucially ambivalent figure, seductive as well as cruel; the pride and lust which disfigured his personality were, of course, merely ordinary inclinations recklessly and fatally unfettered. The excesses of the Gothic villain were exceptions, while moderation and repression were held to be the rule.

After 1825 the "classical" Gothic villain underwent an interesting process of evolution, which took his literary descendants in two opposed directions. In one direction he was reduced, becoming more human and much more like *us*; in the other direction he was surrealized, becoming unhuman and demonic, but in spite of that he retained his symbolic status and force. There is certainly no reduction of unease in such a bifurcated pattern of evolution.

In the direction of humanization we find post-Gothic characters less well acquainted with the Devil, whose powers are diminished by confusion; it is often their eccentricities rather than their actual malevolence that empowers them to create anxiety; their victims' anxieties are as likely to take the form of worrying that the person by whom they are awed might be mad as they are to engender suspicion of a diabolical pact. This species of post-Gothic villain, in fact, tends to move out of explicitly supramundane fiction into the baroque thriller—he features, for instance, in Wilkie Collins's *The Woman in White* [2-15], Sheridan Le Fanu's *Uncle Silas* [2-51] and Nathaniel Hawthorne's *The Scarlet Letter* [2-40], and in more Byronic guise in Emily Brontë's *Wuthering Heights* [2-10]. This humanization makes the relevant post-Gothic villains more vulnerable and more idiosyncratic, but the very domestication of the anxiety which they arouse serves to maintain the sharpness of its menace.

In the direction of dehumanization we find characters whose place in human society is much more precarious, who have been partly or wholly removed from such mundane roles as they once had. It is here that we find the flourishing tradition of nineteenth-century vampire fiction, which takes in Dumas [2-22], Gilbert [2-32], Rymer [2-87] and Von Degen [2-96] as well as those already cited, and the werewolves featured by Dumas [2-23], Erckmann-Chatrian [2-25], Housman [2-42] and Reynolds [2-82]. Also to this line of development belong certain magicians whose evil influence remains active after their deaths, animating the malevolence of haunted houses like Lytton's [2-54], or leaving more loathsome legacies in the early works of Arthur Machen [2-58–2-59]. This trend seems on a superficial level to represent an externalization of evil, running in the opposite direction to the general trend by which anxiety is internalized, but the matter is not so simple, because the supernaturalization of these agents of evil usually goes hand in hand with a more minute examination of the reactions of their victims. The more demonic the villains become, the more they become symbolic of the *forces* of temptation rather than the *dangers* of yielding to temptation.

It might be argued that in addition to these two counterbalanced directions of evolution there is a third line of development which the Gothic villain follows in the nineteenth century, and that is toward a frankly heroic status. There is a gradual emergence in the weird fiction of the period of the stereotyped figure of the wise and powerful magician who is also good; we meet him, for instance, in Lytton's Rosicrucian romances *Zanoni* [2-56] and *A Strange Story* [2-55], and he was later to become a familiar figure in credulous occult romance of the kind written by Mrs. Praed [2-78], where he is the Theosophical initiate or the Eastern "adept." Such characters have supposedly learned to transcend the temptations of pride and lust—but wherever they appear, it is in order to be carefully contrasted with characters who are weaker than they, including some who have been utterly corrupted by their failure to withstand temptation.

Such characters as these lead the reader in the direction of different imaginative territories—they are, of course, rather more familiar as the benevolent wizards of the fantasy genre than they are as significant characters in horror stories. Nevertheless, they have an important role to play in a kind of horror fiction which became increasingly popular as the nineteenth century progressed: the story of the inquisitive man who sets forth on a hard Faustian road of enlightenment, where the purity of his motives and the strength of his will must ultimately be subjected to an acid test, when conflicting forces tug at him from either side and threaten to tear him apart. The externalization of the supramundane powers of good and evil here serves merely to reify the impulses which are at war inside the mind of the key character, and however paradoxical it may seem, this too is a path to a more elaborate kind of introspection.

Despite the widespread popularity of supernatural fiction in the nineteenth century, there was a near-universal supposition that it was but a poor relation of the realistic novel. Before 1825, of course, the novel itself had been considered an essentially inferior form in the world of letters, not really literature at all, and the Gothic novel had consequently been at small disadvantage—but as the realistic novel formulated and won its claim to elite status, the more romantic varieties of prose fiction were ostentatiously left behind.

The early history of the novel (defined merely as a long prose fiction) shows no particular leaning toward realism; indeed, the popularity of the Gothic novel illustrates that the inherent verisimilitude of novelistic techniques—which give the impression that a real character is moving through actual space at a clearly defined time—was more often used to lend credence to a highly improbable narrative than to bring a new artistry to the depiction and interrogation of the ordinary and the everyday. By the middle of the nineteenth century, however, the novel had been claimed as the instrument of a particular kind of moral examination of actual emotions, projects and ambitions, and the nonrealistic novel was separated out, so that "novel" and "romance" were increasingly used as contrasting and mutually exclusive terms.

The aesthetic theories which elevated realism to its position of preeminence were not unopposed—most articulately, perhaps, by Lord Lytton, who belatedly became the most popular of all Victorian writers when his works were reissued as yellowback "railway novels" in the 1850s and 1860s. Lytton, influenced by the aesthetic theories of the German idealists, published a series of essays in *Blackwood's Magazine* in 1862-63, insisting that a work of art must go beyond the mundane to "imply the supernatural"—by which he meant that a key function of art was to explore a metaphysical framework without which the ordinary would lack a proper context.

In practical terms the most dedicated opponent of narrow realism was Dickens, who felt that space must be made for the sense of wonder. He was the prime mover in attempting to institute a tradition of Christmas ghost stories—a notion which, by implication, conceded the moral superiority of realism while insisting that such acceptance was not incompatible with a sense of the value of romance. All realism and no romance, according to Dickens, was a recipe for a dull mind.

First by his example, and later by his exploits as an editor, Dickens helped to inspire many of the most important Victorian writers to dabble in tales of the supernatural. He was aided by the editors of such annual volumes as *The Keepsake,* whose works were aimed at the gift-book market and who considered that a judicious mixture of literary confections ought to include a few tales of unease, and of course by the editors of *Blackwood's,* who were consistently hospitable to the *outré.* Without such editorial support, the supernatural fiction published in Britain would undoubtedly have comprised a thinner and less interesting tradition. It is unfortunate that America, despite the marvelous examples provided by Edgar Allan Poe [2-76–2-77] and Nathaniel Hawthorne [2-38–2-40], had so few middlebrow writers of supernatural fiction until the last few years of the period that it is difficult to speak of a "tradition" at all. Julian Hawthorne [2-37], perhaps the most important American-born writer of supernatural fiction in the years which separate his father's work from the period when Henry James [2-45], Ambrose Bierce [2-7] and Robert W. Chambers [2-12] came to prominence, lived mostly in England and published mainly in British periodicals.

Between 1825 and 1896 we can see the emergence of most of the themes which were to become staple elements of twentieth-century supernatural fiction. There are few supernatural characters who had not been glimpsed in Gothic fiction, but in terms of the modern mythology of the vampire, the werewolf and the ghost, Gothic fiction is no more "advanced" than classical mythology. The beginning of the next period in the history of horror fiction is marked by Stoker's *Dracula* [3-186], which presents a particularly elaborate "theorization" of its central character, in terms of his antiquarian connections and his supposed powers and weaknesses, but Stoker was building upon a trend laid down much earlier in the century, particularly by J. Sheridan Le Fanu [2-49–2-52]. The importance of Le Fanu in prefiguring Stoker was not so much that he too wrote a classic vampire story, but rather that he laid down the pattern of enquiry and investigation by which the apparatus of the supernatural was exposed to the interrogations of reason *not* in order to expose it as a hollow sham, but to enhance its power as a worthy opponent of sanity and scientific method.

Le Fanu is the most significant ancestor not only of Stoker but also of M. R. James [3-108], for Le Fanu was the first writer of academic and antiquarian ghost stories—much of his short work was published in the *Dublin University Magazine,* whose proprietor and editor he was for a while. In Le Fanu's best fiction a historian's sense of the past and an ethnologist's fascination with human belief become resources deftly used to heighten the implication of threat which is attached to his literary instruments of anxiety.

There were other trends which, though arguably less sensible, added further fuel to the antiquarian aspects of weird fiction. At the beginning of the nineteenth century, real belief in the supernatural was so obviously on the wane that where it survived it had become markedly defensive in tone—taking refuge, for instance, in studied piety or in stubborn but largely unarticulated conviction. By the end of the period, though, the die-hard believers had come to accept that the best defense might be attack, and were finding it politic to take the offensive again. They became flamboyantly strident, especially when the matters of faith at issue were unorthodox, and though their antiquarianism was essentially fake—the product of scholarly fantasy rather than authentic historical sensibility—the distinction did not seem to matter so much in terms of its expression in admitted fictions.

Several notable Spiritualists and Theosophists, including Madame Blavatsky [2-8], wrote ghost stories of their own, but what is more important from the point of view of the literary historian is that they also had an effect on the way in which nonbelievers wrote about the supernatural. They helped to liberate a new "supernatural brutality" such as can be seen in the works of apparent believers like Joyce Muddock [2-70] and obvious unbelievers like Edith Nesbit [2-72], simply by making it possible for writers to be less self-conscious about the deployment of apparitions, but their principal influence tended in the opposite direction, leading many writers to distance themselves, overtly and covertly, from those creeds which pretended to "explain" supernatural phenomena, and thus to be more thoughtful about the use of horrific motifs as carefully studied literary devices. One can see the emergence of this new self-consciousness quite clearly in works like Lanoë Falconer's *Cecilia de Noël* [2-26] as well as in the conspicuously arty ghost stories of Henry James [2-45], Vernon Lee [2-48] and Oscar Wilde [2-97].

Newly assertive stories of nasty supernatural horrors were only one aspect of a belated "backlash" against the constraints of realism. Lytton's *Blackwood's* essays were not content simply to enthuse about the pretensions of idealism—they also attacked the supposed realism of the Victorian novel as a hollow sham. In Lytton's view, the fact that novelists had begun to pay obsessive attention to certain minutiae of everyday life was inadequate to sustain the view that they were being "realistic." He observed that there were certain aspects of real life that were conscientiously ignored by the English novel, which was subject to an extraordinarily rigorous censorship (even Trollope, a die-hard champion of virtue, was once obliged to defend his works from the opinion that it was not morally adequate merely to have his characters refuse the temptations of vice—they should not, according to the most censorious opinion, even be allowed to contemplate the possibility of sin).

One curious consequence of this peculiarly English argument was that nonrealistic fiction began, as it were, to soak up the concerns which artificial realism was forced to treat with exaggerated circumspection. Though it often does so in coy and uncomfortable ways, English supernatural literature very often deals with the erotic themes which the newly respectable novel let alone. One can see this not only in prose fictions like Le Fanu's "Carmilla" [2-50], but also in some of the most elevated poetry of the period—Keats's "Lamia" [F2-97] and Christina Rossetti's "Goblin Market" [F2-140] are the most striking examples. As Victorian morality began to lose its grip, in the last years of the period, the lush eroticism which had always been an essential element in the work of writers like Gautier [2-30; F2-64–2-65] was zestfully seized by English writers eager to be decadent—Vernon Lee [2-48] and Oscar Wilde [2-97] prominent among them.

In America the battle to establish realism as the aim—or at least the norm—of the literary novel was fought in a later period, and though there were moralists in America who were every bit as fierce and bigoted as the English pillars of Victorianism, they never quite obtained the same imperialistic power over cultural products. For this reason, there was never the same peculiar separation of interests that was temporarily seen in Britain. The erotic elements in American horror stories—prominent enough in Poe, Lippard [2-53] and even Mrs. Spofford [2-90]—do not have the same air of self-conscious naughtiness about them. By extrapolation, posing as a decadent in America even in the yellow nineties was more or less restricted to Europeans determined to retain their alien status. But the doctrine of the innate superiority of realism won in America as it had won in Britain, and without a Dickens to create a literary reservation for it—despite even the noble example of Henry James—supernatural fiction in America was beginning in the 1890s to be relegated almost in its entirety to the lower strata of the market. Notwithstanding the efforts of Ambrose Bierce and the brilliance of Chambers's *King in Yellow* [2-12], the American weird tale was already earmarked for the pulp ghetto.

It still needs to be said, even today, that the poor regard in which supernatural fiction came to be held—on both sides of the Atlantic—was a dreadful insult to the literary quality of the best work being done, and to its aspirations as a species of art. The years 1825–96 produced some very fine work indeed—far better in every way than all but a handful of the Gothic tales of terror. That the Gothic has acquired a certain academic respectability is due much more to its antiquity and esotericism than to its essential merits in laying bare the darker side of the human soul. The post-Gothic fiction described in this bibliography deserves far more academic attention than has so far been given to it.

The bibliography which follows attempts to show the breadth of work done, as well as to pay due attention to the most interesting examples of it. Far and away the best sources for further research are Bleiler's *Guide to Supernatural Fiction* [6-19] and the anthology of essays on *Supernatural Fiction Writers* [6-20] which he edited; the second-named contains some impressive original research on several hitherto-neglected writers of the period. *The Penguin Encyclopedia of Horror and the Supernatural* [6-31] is highly selective in its coverage, but does have some useful commentaries on the better-known writers. David Punter's *Literature of Terror* [7-10] and Julia Briggs's *Night Visitors* [7-3] offer some useful insights into the literary and social contexts of late nineteenth-century horror fiction, while H. P. Lovecraft's study of *Supernatural Horror in Literature* [7-7] offers a fascinating, if slightly eccentric, commentary on the work of the period.

Bibliography

Ainsworth, W(illiam) Harrison (U.K.), 1802–1882.
ABOUT: WW, GSF, SFW, CA, PE, ESF

2-1. Auriol: Fragment of a Romance. London: Chapman & Hall, 1850.
The protagonist has the elixir of life, but must bring a woman to be sacrificed by his Rosicrucian mentor every ten years; he eventually rebels against this imposition. The story is complete but somewhat rough-hewn; Ainsworth presumably intended to rewrite it but never got around to it. The basic theme is borrowed from Maturin's *Melmoth* [1-64], but the imitation is weak.

***2-2. The Lancashire Witches**. 3 vols. London: Colburn, 1849.
Historical romance (loosely) based on England's most famous witch-trial, including a lurid description of the Sabbat. Here Alizon Device is made into a beautiful and virtuous heroine while her little sister Jennet (whose fanciful evidence sent the actual "witches" to the gallows) is a nasty piece of work; this makes an odd contrast with *Mist over Pendle* (1951) by Robert Neill, which reverses the roles.

Anonymous.

2-3. Terrible Tales: French; German; Italian; Spanish. 4 vols. London: Gibbings, 1891.
Set of anthologies presumably produced in imitation of [2-4], more interesting because of their use of unfamiliar European sources. The French volume features several tales by Erckmann-Chatrian [2-25]; the Spanish one includes some interesting folkloristic stories which are unattributed. The Italian volume mostly consists of lurid nonsupernatural romances.

2-4. Weird Tales: American; English; German; Irish; Scottish. 5 vols. Edinburgh: Paterson, 1888.
Anthologies of stories gleaned from various sources, mixing items by Poe, Defoe, Hoffmann, Le Fanu and Scott with anonymous tales drawn from cheap periodicals. Collections of horror stories of this kind usually thrive in the marketplace, and this set was reprinted several times.

Balzac, Honoré de (France), 1799–1850.
ABOUT: GSF, SFW, SMFL, SFE, PE

***2-5. The Magic Skin**. New York: Roberts Bros., 1888. Tr. by Katharine Prescott Wormeley of *La Peau de chagrin*, 1831.
Classic moralistic fantasy whose hero makes a diabolical bargain for the piece of shagreen, which grants his wishes but shrinks as it does so; in the end he can only watch helplessly as his boundless desires use up the measure of his life while he agonizes over his impending doom. A relentless Faustian melodrama. A similar account of horrific frustration is to be found in the lurid short story "The Elixir of Life" (1830), of which a measure depleted by carelessness will revivify only the head of a dead man. Balzac's fascination for the Gothic is also exhibited by the cynical "Melmoth Reconciled" (1835), which suggests that the doomed wanderer would have no difficulty in finding a volunteer to take his place were he to visit Paris.

Baring-Gould, Sabine (U.K.), 1834–1924.
ABOUT: WW, GSF, ESF

2-6. A Book of Ghosts. Methuen, 1904.
Collection of ghost stories, some dating back to the 1850s. Most are slight tales of apparitions; the most interesting are "Pomps and Vanities," a tale of possession; and "The Merewigs," a farce in which persons who made no spiritual progress in their last incarnation must now haunt the British Museum. Of much greater

interest are Baring-Gould's journalistic accounts of medieval legends and miscellaneous folklore, collected in various volumes, including *The Book of Werewolves* (1865) and *Curious Myths of the Middle Ages* (two series, 1866 and 1868).

Bierce, Ambrose, 1842–1914?
ABOUT: WW, GSF, SFW, CA, NE, H, SMFL, SFE, PE, ESF

***2-7. Tales of Soldiers and Civilians**. San Francisco: Steele, 1891. U.K. title: *In the Midst of Life*.
The first of two classic collections including several weird tales. Most notable are the classic "An Occurrence at Owl Creek Bridge"; "A Tough Tussle," about the delusions of a necrophobic soldier; "An Inhabitant of Carcosa," which had an important influence on Chambers [2-12] and Lovecraft [3-132]; and the Poesque "The Middle Toe of the Right Foot." All these stories are in the revised edition of 1908, issued as *In the Midst of Life*; so are the classic invisible monster story, "The Damned Thing," and the novella "The Eyes of the Panther," whose theme echoes Holmes's *Elsie Venner* [F2-83]. The second collection, *Can Such Things Be?* (1893), is slightly less fine, its most notable inclusions being the phantasmagoric tale of "The Death of Halpin Frayser"; "A Psychological Shipwreck," a tale of psychic bonding; and "A Fruitless Assignment," offering an ironic account of a skeptic's night in a haunted house. The revised edition of 1909 adds numerous stories, including the classic story of a temperamental chess-playing automaton, "Moxon's Master," and the neat ghost story "The Moonlit Road." An excellent modern collection is *Ghost and Horror Stories of Ambrose Bierce* (Dover, 1964). Bierce inherited the mantle of Poe [2-76] in producing striking and convincing accounts of the psychology of haunted men in guilty flight from the supra-rational; he is one of the finest architects of literary nightmares.

Blavatsky, H(elena) P(etrovna) (Russia), 1831–1891.
ABOUT: WW, GSF, ESF

2-8. Nightmare Tales. London: Theosophical Publishing Society, 1892.
Posthumous collection of ghost stories by the celebrated charlatan. The most notable is "The Ensouled Violin," in which a music teacher commits suicide to provide his protégé with strings made from human intestinal cord. The stories have little or no connection with the bizarre occult works which were supposedly dictated to her by Himalayan "masters."

Braddon, M(ary) E(lizabeth) (U.K.), 1835–1915.
ABOUT: GSF, CA, PE

2-9. Ralph the Bailiff and Other Tales. London: Ward, Lock, 1867.
Collection of short stories including "The Cold Embrace" and "Eveline's Visitant," both stories of erotically inspired hauntings; two more of the same stripe are in *Weavers and Weft and Other Tales* (1877). *Gerard; or, The World, the Flesh and the Devil* (1891) is a novel which begins as an acknowledged copy of Balzac's *Magic Skin* [2-5], but the supernatural is discarded half-way through. Braddon was obviously uncomfortable with supernatural themes, but the cited short stories

are interesting examples of the ambivalent Victorian preoccupation with the idea of passion transcending death.

Brontë, Emily (U.K.), 1818–1848.
ABOUT: F, CA, PE

2-10. Wuthering Heights. London: Newby, 1847.
Psychological Gothic romance in which the tempestuous changeling Heathcliff is driven to extremes of feeling and behavior following the double loss of his beloved, first by her marriage and then by her death. A marvelous extravaganza of morbid eroticism, disguised and displaced according to the dictates of Victorian repression.

Broughton, Rhoda (U.K.), 1840–1920.
ABOUT: WW, GSF, CA, SMFL, PE, ESF

2-11. Tales for Christmas Eve. London: Bentley, 1873.
Five short stories, four involving apparitions. The most interesting in post-Freudian retrospect is "The Man with the Nose," which compares interestingly with MacNish's account of a similar hallucination [F2-119]. Reprinted as *Twilight Stories* (1947).

Chambers, Robert W(illiam), 1865–1933.
ABOUT: WW, GSF, SFW, H, SMFL, SFE, RG, PE, ESF, HF

***2-12. The King in Yellow**. Chicago: Neely, 1895.
Collection including five supernatural tales, four of which are linked by references to the text of a play, *The King in Yellow,* which exerts an evil influence upon those who read it; the imaginary world in which the play is set (derived from Bierce's "An Inhabitant of Carcosa" [2-7]) somehow possesses the minds of the guilty and extracts nightmarish retribution for past misdeeds (usually unspecified). "The Repairer of Reputations" is magnificently bizarre, and "The Yellow Sign" is widely acknowledged as one of the finest horror stories ever written. "The Mask" is more sentimental, closer in tone to the fifth story, the deeply felt classic timeslip romance "The Demoiselle d'Ys," which echoes Gautier [F2-64]. There are more weird tales in *The Mystery of Choice* (1897), including "The Messenger," an effective tale of supernatural vengeance reaching across the ages; "The White Shadow" and "Passeur" are in the more romantic vein. Chambers had been strongly infected by the spirit of French decadent Romanticism while he was an art student in Paris, but he unfortunately made a complete recovery; his later work is determinedly trivial and rather colorless.

[For other works of this author, see the companion guide to fantasy.]

Cobban, J(ames) Maclaren (U.K.), 1849–1903.

2-13. Master of His Fate. Edinburgh: Blackwood, 1890.
Mystery story about a man who must continually renew his health and vitality by

draining the vital energy of others. Often compared to *Dr. Jekyll and Mr. Hyde* [2-93], but it is more closely related to stories of psychic vampirism, and in allowing the psychic vampire to give his own side of the story it anticipates such modern exercises in vampire existentialism as Charnas's *The Vampire Tapestry* [4-78].

Collins, Wilkie (U.K.), 1824–1889.

ABOUT: WW, GSF, SFW, CA, SMFL, PE, ESF

2-14. After Dark. London: Smith, Elder, 1856.
Collection of thrillers including a tale of attempted murder by bizarre means, "A Terribly Strange Bed." The one marginally supernatural story is "The Yellow Mask," about guilt punished by a horrific apparition, but Collins always preferred to create unease without recourse to ghosts. *The Queen of Hearts* (1859) has other macabre tales, including the first (shorter) version of an often-reprinted story of a premonitory dream, "The Dream Woman." *Little Novels* (1887) has two genuine ghost stories, "Miss Jéromette and the Clergyman" and "Mrs. Zant and the Ghost." The short novel *The Haunted Hotel* (1878) also features apparitions, though it is primarily a murder mystery.

2-15. The Woman in White. London: Sampson Low, 1860.
A celebrated thriller elaborately decorated with naturalized Gothic elements: the scheming fake nobleman Sir Percival Glyde and his exotic ally Count Fosco, and—of course—the mad Anne Catherick. Similarly Gothic in inspiration, and more bizarre in design, is *Armadale* (1866), whose eponymous hero is harried and persecuted by his diabolical twin, aided by an enigmatic *femme fatale*.

Cram, Ralph Adams, 1863–1942.

ABOUT: WW, GSF, PE, ESF

2-16. Black Spirits and White. Chicago: Stone & Kimball, 1895.
Weird short stories set in various European locales. The scariest of the apparitions is featured in "No. 252 Rue M. le Prince," but well-developed settings are what make the stories more than usually convincing.

Crawford, F(rancis) Marion, 1854–1909.

ABOUT: WW, GSF, SFW, CA, SMFL, PE, ESF

2-17. Wandering Ghosts. Macmillan, 1911. U.K. title: *Uncanny Tales*.
Posthumous collection of tales from the 1890s, featuring all-too-material apparitions of an unsubtle character. "The Dead Smile" is on the face of a detached head; "The Screaming Skull" bites as well; "For the Blood Is the Life" is an orthodox vampire story; but the star of the collection is the often-reprinted tale of a haunted stateroom, "The Upper Berth."

[For other works of this author, see the companion guide to fantasy.]

Dalby, Richard, editor.

2-18. The Virago Book of Victorian Ghost Stories. Virago, 1988.
An excellent anthology of twenty-one stories by female writers, ranging from classics like Mrs. Gaskell's "The Old Nurse's Story" [2-29] and Mrs. Oliphant's "The Open Door" [2-74] to an item of juvenilia by Charlotte Brontë and various pieces by forgotten writers; the short novel *Cecilia de Noël* by Lanoë Falconer [2-26] is also included.

Dickens, Charles (U.K.), 1812–1870.
About: WW, GSF, SFW, F, CA, SMFL, PE, ESF, HF

2-19. The Complete Ghost Stories of Charles Dickens. Ed. by Peter Haining. Michael Joseph, 1982.
Omnibus collection, including comic ghost stories and moral fantasies as well as horror stories. The most famous items are the tale of a haunted jury, "The Trial for Murder" (1865), which is often mistakenly labeled a collaborative work; and the excellent tale of premonitory apparitions "The Signalman" (1866), one of the best Victorian ghost stories. Also of interest are two bloodcurdling tales from *The Uncommercial Traveller* (1860), which Dickens recalled from his youth, attributing them to his nurse "Mercy" Weller. Dickens's unfinished novel, *The Mystery of Edwin Drood* (1870), appears to some readers to have been shaping up into a full-fledged occult romance, but it seems more likely that it would have been a pseudo-Gothic grotesque in the manner of Wilkie Collins, with the dream apparitions and the hypnotic powers of John Jasper afforded natural status.

[For other works of this author, see the companion guide to fantasy.]

Doyle, Arthur Conan (U.K.), 1859–1930.
About: WW, GSF, F, CA, NE, SMFL, SFE, TCSF, PE, ESF

2-20. The Captain of the *Polestar* and Other Tales. London: Longmans Green, 1890.
Collection including several weird stories. "The Captain of the *Polestar*" (1883) features an Arctic lorelei; in "The Ring of Thoth" (1890) an immortal born in ancient Egypt seeks release from life; "John Barrington Cowles" is a *femme fatale* story. The third is inexplicably omitted from the omnibus *The Conan Doyle Stories* (1929), which recovers Doyle's other early horror stories, most notably "Lot No. 249" (1892), which features reanimated mummies; and "The Los Amigos Fiasco" (1892), in which an electric chair accidentally endows a murderer with sinister superhumanity. All are in the Dover *Best Supernatural Stories of Arthur Conan Doyle* (1979). The stories are craftsmanlike, but somewhat lacking in intensity.

2-21. The Parasite. London: Constable, 1894.
Novella in which a repulsive medium falls in love with a young man, and uses her powers in an attempt to destroy him when he rejects her. Written before Doyle's conversion to Spiritualism; less credulous and better shaped than Mrs. Praed's *The Soul of Countess Adrian* [2-79] or Hocking's *Weapons of Mystery*

[2-41]. Doyle had earlier written a lackluster thriller about the occult revenge exacted by a party of Eastern adepts, *The Mystery of Cloomber* (1889).

Dumas, Alexandre (France), 1802–1870.
ABOUT: WW, GSF, CA, SMFL, PE, ESF

2-22. Horror at Fontenay. Sphere, 1975. Tr. by Alan Hull Walton of part of *Les Mille et un fantômes*, 1849.
Part of a long portmanteau work; other hands than Dumas's were probably involved in the full version, but the translator claims that the stories included here were all his. The tale-tellers meet after a grisly murder to debate the question of whether guillotined heads continue to be self-aware, and digress into a more general consideration of matters supernatural. Includes the vampire story "The Pale Lady" (first translated in *Tales of the Supernatural*, 1910).

***2-23. The Wolf-Leader**. Methuen, 1904. Tr. by Alfred Allinson of *Le Meneur de loups*, 1857.
A vainglorious peasant enlists the Devil's aid to obtain revenge upon an aristocrat; he obtains the assistance of a wolf pack but his progress toward damnation is marked by the discoloration of the hairs on his head, which proceeds in geometric series. In a breathless climax he is hunted in wolf form by his old enemy. An excellent story based in the folklore which Dumas encountered as a child, with a consequent undercurrent of nostalgic Romanticism.

Edwards, Amelia B(lanford) (U.K.), 1831–1892.
ABOUT: WW, GSF, SFW, PE

2-24. Monsieur Maurice. 3 vols. London: Hurst & Blackett, 1873.
Collection including four ghost stories set in various continental locales. In the interesting title novella a ghostly servant saves his imprisoned master from attempts to harm him; the ghosts in "An Engineer's Story" and "The New Pass" are also protectively inclined. Edwards's earlier collection, *Miss Carew* (1865), included several weird tales, most notably a quasi-folkloristic piece about the coach which collects the souls of the dead, "The North Mail" (also known as "The Phantom Coach"). *A Night on the Borders of the Black Forest* (1874) again deploys conventional supernatural motifs in varied European locales.

Erckmann-Chatrian (pseud. of **Emile Erckmann**, 1822–1899, and **Alexandre Chatrian**, 1826–1890) (France).
ABOUT: WW, GSF, PE, ESF

2-25. The Best Tales of Terror of Erckmann-Chatrian. Ed. by Hugh Lamb. Millington, 1981.
Includes two novellas which had earlier featured as the title stories of two collections: *The Man-Wolf and Other Stories* (1876) and *The Wild Huntsman and Other Stories* (1877); both are historical romances based in Germanic folklore; the former is one of the most important nineteenth-century werewolf stories. The six shorter pieces, most of which originate from the collection *Contes fantastiques*

(1847), include a classic story of arachnid giantism, "The Crab Spider," and a tale of a witch hoist by her own magical petard, "The Invisible Eye." Effective melodramas.

Falconer, Lanoë (pseud. of **Mary Elizabeth Hawker**) (U.K.), 1848–1908.
ABOUT: GSF, PE

2-26. Cecilia de Noël. London: Macmillan, 1891.
The narrator, crippled in a riding accident, listens to and learns from various reactions to the sight of a ghost whose aspect is that of a person condemned to pain and despair. The saintly Cecilia is the only one who understands the ghost's predicament and, by implication, shows the protagonist how to cope with his own troubles. A neat and touching story, written with obvious sincerity and unusual delicacy.

Falkner, John Meade (U.K.), 1858–1932.
ABOUT: WW, GSF, PE

***2-27. The Lost Stradivarius**. Edinburgh: Blackwood, 1895.
The protagonist is supernaturally guided to a hidden violin; its sinister influence leads him along a path to damnation mapped out by the instrument's former owner. A fine novel, in which the author cleverly draws on his knowledge of neo-Platonic mysticism to provide an unusual and fascinating grounding for the plot. Compare the works of Vernon Lee [2-48].

Field, Julian Osgood (U.K.), 1849–1925.
ABOUT: GSF

2-28. Aut Diabolus aut Nihil and Other Tales. London: Methuen, 1894 (published as by X. L.).
Collection including two weird tales. The title story, in which a priest witnesses the invocation of a handsome evil spirit by Satanists, caused a minor sensation on its first publication in *Blackwood's* when it was mistaken by some readers for nonfiction. "The Kiss of Judas" is an item of synthetic folklore about the curse borne by descendants of Jesus' betrayer.

Gaskell, Elizabeth (U.K.), 1810–1865.
ABOUT: WW, CA, PE, ESF,

2-29. Mrs. Gaskell's Tales of Mystery and Horror. Ed. by Mike Ashley. Gollancz, 1978.
Collection including the often-reprinted "The Old Nurse's Story" (1852), in which an old act of unkindness leaves a ghostly echo which recurs through time. "The Doom of the Griffiths" (1858) has a similar theme—the notion of family curses seems to have fascinated the author.

Gautier, Théophile (France), 1811-1872.

ABOUT: WW, GSF, SFW, SMFL, PE, ESF

2-30. The Works of Théophile Gautier. 24 vols. Sproul, 1900-1903. Tr. by F. C. de Sumichrast.
As well as the fantasies described in [F2-65] this collection includes the short novel *Jettatura* (1856), describing the misfortunes of a young man unknowingly cursed with the evil eye, whose fiancée is slowly destroyed by his loving gaze, leading him eventually to put out his eyes. An unusually cruel product of Gautier's preoccupation with the paradoxical nature of erotic attraction.

Gilbert, William (U.K.), 1804-1890.

ABOUT: GSF, CA

2-31. Shirley Hall Asylum; or, The Memoirs of a Monomaniac. London: Freeman, 1863 (published anonymously).
The protagonist, an inventor convinced that he has discovered a secret potentially capable of destroying mankind, is confined in the eponymous establishment, where he collects the stories of his fellow patients. The best is "Mainwaring's Confession," about a curious imaginary haunting; others include a study of alcoholism and an account of religious mania. *Doctor Austin's Guests* (1866) continues the series of case studies, including "Mr. Gurdon's Plight" (a curious phobia), "A Singular Love Story" (a man who believes he is getting younger), "L'Amour Medecin" (hysterical blindness), "The Old Maid" (hypnotically induced amnesia), "Banquo's Ghost" (guilt-induced delusion) and "The Imprisoned Demon" (a man who believes that he is possessed). Also present are two variants of the narrator's obsession with scientific matters: "Patent Mania" and "A Scientific Evening." An early exercise in speculative psychoanalysis, more interesting as such than Holmes's "medicated novels" [F2-83]. An odd combination of the tragic, the comic and the grotesque, cleverly exploring ways of accounting for classic supernatural motifs as phenomena of mental derangement.

2-32. The Wizard of the Mountain. London: Strahan, 1867.
Collection of linked stories of horror and fantasy. Various characters seek the aid of an astrologer and magician known as the Innominato, who also tells his own story by way of conclusion. The greedy and despicable are given advice or objects which rebound to their disadvantage—most gruesomely in the vampire story "The Last Lords of Gardonal," most ironically in the neat story of "Don Bucefalo and the Curate." The innocent receive modest assistance, for reasons explained in "The Innominato's Confession," which proposes that magic is essentially diabolical, tempting men to rebel against divine providence—though it is not at all clear that the story sustains this moral. An interesting book, especially read in conjunction with [2-31].

[For other works of this author, see the companion guide to fantasy.]

Gilchrist, R(obert) Murray (U.K.), 1868–1917.
ABOUT: WW, GSF, PE, ESF

2-33. The Stone Dragon and Other Tragic Romances. London: Methuen, 1894.
Collection of weird tales, self-consciously decadent in style though the motifs are conventional. The most effective is "The Return," about a rendezvous with a revenant lover; "Witch In-Grain" is a rather sadistic tale of witchcraft.

Gilman, Charlotte Perkins (earlier **Charlotte P. Stetson**), 1860–1935.
ABOUT: GSF, F, CA, PE

2-34. The Yellow Wallpaper. Small Maynard, 1901.
Classic short story first published in 1892, based on the author's experiences when she suffered a nervous breakdown and was ordered to remain completely inactive—a prescription which, she felt, drove her close to madness. The story's protagonist, in a similar predicament, is driven insane by forced confrontation with the awful wallpaper in her room.

Gotthelf, Jeremias (Switzerland), 1797–1854.
ABOUT: H

2-35. The Black Spider. Calder, 1958. Tr. by H. M. Waidson of *Die schwarze Spinne*, 1842.
Guests at a christening are told the story of a woman who made a bargain with a green huntsman (the Devil) on behalf of a peasant community given an impossible task to do by their liege-lord. The Devil completes the task, but the peasants then refuse to deliver an unbaptised child as promised, and the woman is changed into a monstrous poisonous spider whose depredations (an allegorical representation of the plague) decimate the community until the spider is magically trapped in a block of wood. Gotthelf wrote several other tales in this folkloristic vein, but they have not yet been translated.

Haining, Peter, editor.

2-36. The Penny Dreadful; or, Strange, Horrid & Sensational Tales. Gollancz, 1975.
Anthology of excerpts and short pieces taken from the penny part-works and periodicals whose popularity mapped the spread of literacy to the London lower classes in the 1840s and 1850s. The collection is strong on *grand guignol,* and replete with the bloody crimes of real and imaginary villains from Dick Turpin to Sweeney Todd, but has relatively little supernatural material save for a chapter of *Varney the Vampyre* [2-87]. An interesting assembly of period pieces.

Hawthorne, Julian, 1846–1934.
ABOUT: WW, GSF, CA, PE, ESF

2-37. The Laughing Mill and Other Stories. London: Macmillan, 1879.
Collection including three weird tales. In the title novella (also known as "The

Pearl-Shell Necklace") the mystery surrounding an old tragedy is explained by a ghost; "Calbot's Rival" is an eccentric tale of a curse put upon two lovers; "The Christmas Guest" is an allegory in which the contrasting attitudes of two lovers are tested when Death comes to take one away. *Ellice Quentin and Other Stories* (1880) includes the novella "Kildhurm's Oak," about a family curse whose effects are transmitted by a sinister tree, and "The New Endymion," about a strange vision seen through a telescope. *David Poindexter's Appearance* (1888) has the often-reprinted and atmospheric vampire story "Ken's Mystery" (1883) while *Six Cent Sam's* (1893; also known as *Mr. Dunton's Invention and Other Stories*) has an assortment of tales in a lighter vein, mostly involving hypnotism. Another novella from *Lippincott's Magazine,* "The Golden Fleece" (1892), also exists as a bound excerpt; as in *The Laughing Mill* and *Kildhurm's Oak* there is a treasure to be found. Other Hawthorne weird tales, including "The Rose of Death" (1876), are uncollected. Also of some interest because of Gothic elements are *Bressant* (1873) and the bizarre *Idolatry* (1874).

[For other works of this author, see the companion guide to fantasy.]

Hawthorne, Nathaniel, 1804–1864.
About: WW, GSF, SFW, NE, H, SMFL, SFE, PE, ESF

2-38. The House of the Seven Gables. Boston: Ticknor, Reed & Fields, 1851.
Gothic tale of unease concerning the history of an ill-starred house whose ugliness and atmosphere of decay infect its inhabitants. Highly regarded by H. P. Lovecraft (see [3-132]), many of whose grim edifices echo Hawthorne's house.

***2-39. Mosses from an Old Manse**. New York: Wiley & Putnam, 1846.
The earlier *Twice-Told Tales* (1837) has some horrific stories, notably "Lady Eleanore's Mantle," in which the reputedly magical object carried the seeds of destruction, but this collection contains two masterpieces: "Young Goodman Brown" (1835), whose hero is disillusioned by his encounter with Salem witchcraft; and "Rappaccini's Daughter" (1844), in which a girl whose father's experiments have made her nature venomous proves to be beyond redemption by love or science. These two stories show the potential which the horror story has to carry deep and disturbing moral implications.

***2-40. The Scarlet Letter**. Boston: Ticknor, Reed & Fields, 1850.
Psychological melodrama about the cruel and unusual punishment of a sin born out of love; the heroine must wear the stigma of the e nbroidered A which labels her an adulteress, while the clergyman lover whose identity she will not disclose is harassed and mentally tortured by the demonic husband who has disowned her. The surrounding wilderness seems pregnant with supernatural omens, its wildness reflected in the secret witchery masked by the hypocritical puritanism of the colony. To be compared (and sharply contrasted) with *Wuthering Heights* [2-10] as an allegory of the war between passion and morality, and the lust for vengeance which it inspires.

[For other works of this author, see the companion guide to fantasy.]

Hocking, Joseph (U.K.), 1860-1937.

2-41. The Weapons of Mystery. London: Ward, Lock, 1890.
The hero's rival for the hand of his beloved is an evil mesmerist who temporarily takes control of him and attempts to make him commit a murder. A rough-hewn thriller.

Housman, Clemence (U.K.), 1861-1955.
About: WW, GSF, PE

***2-42. The Were-Wolf**. London: John Lane, 1896.
Novella in which two brothers disagree about the strange *femme fatale* White Fell; the one who thinks her evil is proved right, and pursues her to a climactic meeting where their fates are decided. Highly stylized—almost a long prose poem—with a deeper and possibly unwitting sexual symbolism underlying the consciously wrought allegory. An excellent story. The much longer *The Unknown Sea* (1898) also features a young man alienated from his fellows and eventually drawn toward destruction by an enigmatic *femme fatale*.

Huysmans, Joris-Karl (France), 1848-1907.
About: WW, CA, SMFL, PE

***2-43. Down There; Là-Bas**. Privately printed in Paris, 1928. Tr. by Keene Wallace of *Là-Bas*, 1891.
The proto-existentialist hero is writing a book about Gilles de Rais and his researches lead him to encounters with contemporary Satanists; he almost succumbs to their seductions but settles for a quieter form of disillusionment (in later novels he reinvested in faith and eventually took Holy Orders—a sad fate for the alter ego of a writer who had set out in *À rebours* (1884) to take decadence to its limits). Despite its mannered luridness *Là-Bas* was assumed to be factual by some readers; it remains a key work in promoting the sensational mythology of the Black Mass.

James, G(eorge) P(ayne) R(ainsford) (U.K.), 1799-1860.
About: WW, GSF

2-44. The Castle of Ehrenstein. 3 vols. London: Smith, Elder, 1847.
A late novel in the typical Gothic mode; the eponymous edifice is subject to a whole series of mysterious apparitions, all eventually reduced by standard maneuvers to the level of natural phenomena. A competent deployment of genre stereotypes.

[For other works of this author, see the companion guide to fantasy.]

James, Henry, 1843-1916.
About: WW, GSF, SFW, F, CA, H, SMFL, PE, ESF

2-45. The Ghostly Tales of Henry James. Rutgers Univ. Press, 1948.
Collection of stories mostly dating from the period covered in this chapter (but see

also [3-107]). In "The Romance of Certain Old Clothes" (1868), jealousy between sisters and a broken promise invite supernatural punishment; in "Owen Wingrave" (1892), a pacifist must face the wrath of his ghostly militaristic ancestor; in "The Way It Came" (1896), a possibly supernatural encounter becomes magnified into an act of infidelity which spoils an engagement. James characteristically uses apparitions (whose supernatural status is very often ambiguous) to put to the proof moral convictions and obligations; they usually fail the test. He goes beyond the conventional links between hauntings and guilty conscience to explore more subtle moral issues, especially those concerned with family and sexual relationships.

Kipling, Rudyard (U.K.), 1865–1936.
About: WW, GSF, SFW, CA, NE, SMFL, SFE, RG, TCSF, PE, ESF, HF

2-46. The Phantom 'Rickshaw and Other Tales. Allahabad: Wheeler, 1888.
In the title story a jilted woman vainly pursues her lover in a 'rickshaw, continuing to pester him even after her death. Some trivial tales featuring real or apparent hauntings can be found in *Plain Tales from the Hills* (1888), but more important is "The Mark of the Beast" from *Life's Handicap* (1891), in which a boorish Englishman is punished for sacrilege by an appropriate curse. For later work see [3-116].

[For other works of this author, see the companion guide to fantasy.]

Lamb, Hugh, editor.

2-47. Victorian Tales of Terror. W. H. Allen, 1974.
The first of a series of anthologies; later volumes include *Terror by Gaslight* (1975); *Victorian Nightmares* (1977); *Forgotten Tales of Terror* (1978); and *Tales from a Gaslit Graveyard* (1979). Lamb's collections are unusually eclectic, featuring many neglected writers whose works are not often featured in the familiar and overstereotyped ghost story anthologies: R. Murray Gilchrist [2-33]; "Dick Donovan" [2-70]; Richard Marsh [3-142]; Guy Boothby [3-30]; Lady Dilke [F2-45]; and Erckmann-Chatrian, whose collected supernatural tales [2-25] he edited. The anthologies provide an interesting cross section of Victorian work.

Lee, Vernon (pseud. of **Violet Paget**) (U.K.), 1856–1935.
About: WW, GSF, SFW, CA, SMFL, PE

***2-48. Hauntings**. London: Heinemann, 1890.
Classic collection of four stories. In "Amour Dure" a historian falls under the ghostly spell of an irresistible *femme fatale* from the past; in "Dionea" a young artist falls under the spell of another *femme fatale* mysteriously rescued from the sea; in the novella "Oke of Okehurst" (published separately as *A Phantom Lover*, 1886) a wife becomes obsessed with a crime of long ago, and drives her husband to an extreme reaction; in "A Wicked Voice" a man is pursued by the ghostly and magical voice of a long-dead singer whose memory he has insulted. The stories

are powerful and very striking, among the finest of their kind. Fevered *amour dure* can also be found in "The Virgin of the Seven Daggers" (1889; reprinted in *For Maurice: Five Unlikely Tales*, 1927, which also contains an earlier version of "A Wicked Voice," "Winthrop's Adventure") and in the *Yellow Book* story "Prince Alberic and the Snake Lady" (1896; reprinted in *Pope Jacynth and Other Fantastic Tales*, 1907), which features a version of the lamia story much more cynical than Keats's [F2-97] or Gautier's [F2-64]. These collections were later reedited into two volumes: *The Snake Lady and Other Stories* (1954; reprinted with slightly different contents as *Supernatural Tales* and as *The Virgin of the Seven Daggers*) and *Pope Jacynth and More Supernatural Tales* (1956). No Victorian writer handles erotic supernaturalism better or more avidly than Lee, who had more reason than most to sublimate her own feelings in this curious fashion.

Le Fanu, J(oseph) Sheridan (Ireland), 1814–1873.

ABOUT: WW, GSF, SFW, F, CA, H, SMFL, RG, PE, ESF

2-49. The House by the Churchyard. 3 vols. London: Tinsley, 1863.
Historical romance set in rural Ireland at the time of the French Revolution, whose complex and intricate plot includes the gradual emergence of evil forces focused on the eponymous dwelling. The supernatural plays a minor but crucial role. Compare Hawthorne's *House of the Seven Gables* [2-38].

***2-50. In a Glass Darkly.** 3 vols. London: Bentley, 1872.
Classic collection including four supernatural stories. In "Green Tea" (1869) a doctor is consulted by a man whose perceptions, sharpened by green tea, have shown him a monkeylike malignant spirit which intends to drive him to suicide; in "The Familiar" (earlier published as "The Watcher") a guilty man is pursued by a vengeful spirit; in "Mr. Justice Harbottle" a hanging judge receives an appropriate judgment in a supernatural court; "Carmilla" is one of the great vampire stories, much invigorated by strong lesbian elements in the intercourse of vampire and victim. Very powerful stories, the first being the most elaborately theorized of Victorian horror stories; the three baleful spirits, plus the one which features in the novella "The Haunted Baronet" (1870; reprinted in *Chronicles of Golden Friars*, 1871), are among the most finely drawn in the genre. Le Fanu's earlier supernatural stories, mostly from the *Dublin University Magazine*, were assembled in the posthumous collections *The Purcell Papers* (1880) and *Madam Crowl's Ghost and Other Stories* (1923; edited by M. R. James); the best are the necrophiliac fantasy "Schalken the Painter" (1839) and "Squire Toby's Will" (1868), another story of the guilty pursued. The best material is all in the Dover *Best Ghost Stories* (1964), while the residue is gathered into the same publisher's *Ghost Stories and Mysteries* (1975).

2-51. Uncle Silas. 3 vols. London: Bentley, 1864.
Psychological horror story in which a young girl enters the household of her sinister uncle, which includes an equally sinister housekeeper, and is gradually possessed by a paranoia which turns out to be anything but delusion. Very much in the tradition of Mrs. Radcliffe's *Mysteries of Udolpho* [1-83]; an ancestor of the

stereotyped modern "Gothic romances" in which the heroine's anxieties are much more straightforwardly linked to a sense of sexual threat.

2-52. Wylder's Hand. 3 vols. London: Bentley, 1864.
Somber thriller in which the implacable working of fate brings the guilty to account, after the fashion of Le Fanu's best short stories (though the supernatural aspects are carefully understated). Similar in some ways to Wilkie Collins's melodramas [2-15], but grimmer in outlook.

Lippard, George, 1822–1854.
ABOUT: GSF, PE

2-53. The Quaker City; or, The Monks of Monk Hall. Philadelphia: Lippard, 1845.
Complex Gothic thriller with many subplots and much sensationalism in the vein of Eugène Sue [F2-150] or G. W. M. Reynolds [2-80–2-82]; apparently first issued as a part-work in 1844–45. Monk Hall is the central arena of Philadelphia's underworld, policed by the deformed but powerful Devil-Bug, who is initially dominated by an evil occultist but eventually attains an ambiguous autonomy.

Lytton, Lord (Edward Bulwer) (U.K.), 1803–1873.
ABOUT: WW, GSF, SFW, CA, SMFL, SFE, ESF

***2-54. The Haunters and the Haunted; or The House and the Brain**. Gowan, 1905.
First separate publication of a *Blackwood's* novella (1859), frequently reprinted (sometimes under the latter title) in abridged form. The two protagonists encounter extravagant supernatural phenomena whose source is a device abandoned in a hidden room by a magician, who materializes in the longer version to take control of the narrator. Although frequently nominated as an archetype of the haunted house story, it is actually very idiosyncratic (its nearest modern analogue is Matheson's *Hell House* [4-216]); it reflects Lytton's fascination with the reportage of spiritism.

***2-55. A Strange Story**. 2 vols. Leipzig: Tauchnitz, 1861.
A materialist is seduced by an enigmatic occultist who wishes to use his fiancée as a medium to assist in the quest for the elixir of life. Once caught up in the train of events he cannot escape it until the climactic conjuration, when the occultist fails to cope with the powers which he unleashes. A fevered half-credulous romance, which Lytton tried belatedly to redeem from silliness with an apologetic allegorical interpretation (as in [F2-113]). A key source of inspiration for writers of occult romance and life-style fantasists.

2-56. Zanoni. 3 vols. London: Saunders & Otley, 1842 (early editions published anonymously).
Rosicrucian romance which recovers material from an unfinished magazine serial, *Zicci* (1841; in book form 1876). The hero and the eponymous occultist are rivals in love; the former is forced to give way but is compensated by initiation

into occult mysteries. He fails in this too, attracting the evil attentions of the Dweller on the Threshold; Zanoni's love depletes his own powers, and he is similarly imperiled. An important example of Victorian fascination with the idea of occult enlightenment—Lytton's first flirtation with ideas which commanded his earnest fascination but never (quite) his faith. Many who came after him were less resolute in their skepticism.

[For other works of this author, see the companion guide to fantasy.]

MacDonald, George (U.K.), 1824-1905.

About: WW, GSF, SFW, CA, SMFL, SFE, RG, ESF, FL, HF

2-57. The Portent. London: Smith, Elder, 1864.
Subtitled "A Story of the Inner Vision of the Highlanders, commonly called the Second Sight." The case study features a young man who is victim of a family curse which subjects him at times of stress to a fearsome apparition. He falls in love with a disturbed girl given to sleepwalking in a haunted room, but their affair is frustrated and many years pass before he can use his gifts constructively to restore her sanity and her fortune. An underrated novel whose intricate linking of sexual stress and mental disorder may reveal more than the author intended and certainly provides an interesting comment on the psychology of Victorian morality.

[For other works of this author, see the companion guide to fantasy.]

Machen, Arthur (U.K.), 1863-1947.

About: WW, GSF, SFW, CA, H, SMFL, SFE, RG, PE, ESF, HF

***2-58. The Great God Pan and The Inmost Light**. London: John Lane, 1894.
Two novelettes. The first story (1890) is a celebrated example of decadent Romanticism, featuring a *femme fatale* whose mother had undergone a brain operation to free her sight from the effects of some kind of internal censor; after a long, destructive career she meets a gruesome end. The second story also involves experiments which touch the substance of the soul with awful consequences. Both are a little rough-hewn but very effective; their almost gleeful insistence that the truths of existence are too horrible to be made known was later to be taken over with equal fervor by Lovecraft [3-132].

***2-59. The Three Impostors**. London: John Lane, 1895.
Fix-up heavily influenced by Robert Louis Stevenson [2-92] in composition, featuring four stories contained by a clever frame. They include the often-reprinted "Novel of the Black Seal" and "Novel of the White Powder," the first of which describes the consequences of an ethnologist's attempts to discover the secrets of the fairy folk through experiments with a halfling boy, while the second is a story of metamorphoses induced by a medicine which has accidentally acquired satanic properties. Both are exceptionally effective tales presenting a subtler version of the worldview of [2-58]; the other stories are rather slight.

Marryat, Florence (U.K.), 1838–1899.
About: GSF, ESF

2-60. The Strange Transfiguration of Hannah Stubbs. London: Hutchinson, 1896.
Credulous occult romance in which a disgraced Italian nobleman discovers that the unsuspecting Hannah is a powerful medium. Through her he is able to enjoy again the company of the faithless wife whom he murdered; he marries her to secure the privilege, but the dead woman's personality is stronger than the girl's, and death has not cured her fickleness. Florence Marryat shares the fervor of her fellow believer Mrs. Praed [2-78–2-79], but has a less clotted narrative style. Her weird short stories, four of which are featured in *The Ghost of Charlotte Cray* (1883), are unremarkable.

Marryat, Frederick (U.K.), 1792–1838.
About: WW, GSF, CA, SMFL, ESF

2-61. The Phantom Ship. 3 vols. London: Henry Colburn, 1839.
The son of the Flying Dutchman has the means to release his father but is continually frustrated by the enigmatic villain until he finds a way to purify himself. Interpolated in the narrative is an often-reprinted werewolf story, which is structurally similar to Fouqué's *Undine* [F2-59] but much grimmer; it partakes of the same dubious moral propriety as the whole.

Maupassant, Guy de (France), 1850–1893.
About: WW, GSF, SFW, CA, SMFL, PE, ESF

2-62. The Complete Short Stories of Guy de Maupassant. Hanover House, 1955.
Authoritative collection of stories by the French master of the short story, whose work is a bibliographical minefield. By far the most notable among the horror stories is the classic "The Horla" (1887), whose narrator is persecuted by an invisible psychic vampire, which may be a forerunner of the race which will displace mankind. This tale, like Stoker's *Dracula* [3-186], has been interpreted by Freudian critics as a symbol of venereal disease. The psychopathology of fear, dread and guilt is featured in several other stories, most effectively in "On the River" and "Little Louise Roque."

Meinhold, Wilhelm (Germany), 1797–1851.
About: WW, GSF, SFW

2-63. The Amber Witch. London: H. G. Clark, 1844. Tr. by E. A. Friedlander of *Maria Schweidler, die Bersteinhexe*, 1843.
Historical novel which led early commentators into the trap of regarding it as an actual document of the period. An innocent girl is tried as a witch and condemned, but is saved in the nick of time. The authentic period flavor allows it to pass as an archetypal, if overcredulous, case study of the iniquities of the European witch-craze. Lady Duff Gordon's translation is now the standard one. An ancestor of François Mallet-Joris's fine collection *The Witches* (1969).

2-64. Sidonia the Sorceress. 2 vols. Belfast: Simms & McIntyre, 1849. Tr. by Lady Jane Wilde of *Sidonia von Bork*, 1848.
Historical novel in semi-documentary style describing the career of a celebrated witch, whose career is eventually terminated with the aid of white magic. More elaborate and less convincing than [2-63].

Meredith, Owen (pseud. of **Edward Robert Bulwer, Earl of Lytton**) (U.K.), 1831–1891.

About: GSF, CA

2-65. The Ring of Amasis. 3 vols. London: Chapman & Hall, 1863.
The eponymous object, found in an Egyptian tomb, carries a curse which falls upon its finder, whose life is blighted when he is tempted to let his brother drown. A rather awkward melodrama; a revised redaction, much preferable in terms of narrative pace, was later issued under the author's real name.

Mérimée, Prosper (France), 1803–1870.

About: GSF, SFW, PE

2-66. Tales from Mérimée. Nash & Grayson, 1929.
Collection including two classic weird tales. "The Venus of Ille" (1837) describes the baleful influence of an unearthed statue, which reaches a climax when a young man unwisely places a ring on its finger, and which cannot be laid to rest even though the statue is melted down. "Lokis" (1866) is the story of a nobleman whose mad mother was attacked during her pregnancy by a bear; he subsequently forsakes his human heritage for the royal one to which he is entitled by a more unusual line of descent.

Moffett, Cleveland, 1863–1926.

About: GSF, SFE

2-67. The Mysterious Card. Small Maynard, 1912.
Two short stories. The intriguing title story, first published in *Black Cat* in 1896, is the story of a man who is given a card containing some French words, which he cannot understand. When he asks others for a translation they are horrified and disgusted, and by degrees his life is utterly blighted. The story's refusal to give an explanation caused some controversy and led Moffett to write "The Mysterious Card Unveiled," offering an unlikely and anticlimactic "solution."

Molesworth, Mrs. (**Mary Louisa Stewart**) (U.K.), 1839–1921.

About: WW, GSF, PE, ESF, HF

2-68. Four Ghost Stories. London: Macmillan, 1888.
Collection featuring fairly conventional apparitions, which are here represented as mere echoes of personality, neither hostile nor significant. *Uncanny Tales* (1896) includes four more in the same anemic vein, though in the novelette "The

Shadow in the Moonlight" the supernatural phenomena do lead in the end to a modest revelation.

[For other works of this author, see the companion guide to fantasy.]

Morrow, William C(hambers), 1852-1923.

ABOUT: WW, GSF, PE, ESF

2-69. The Ape, the Idiot, and Other People. Philadelphia: Lippincott, 1897.
Collection of literary curios, with a certain calculated decadence. Most are *contes cruels,* including the deft "Over an Absinthe Bottle"; the most horrific is the Frankensteinian tale of "The Monster-Maker," a polished prototype of the medical-experiment-with-awful-results plot that became a Hollywood standard.

Muddock, Joyce E. Preston (U.K.), 1842-1934.

2-70. Stories Weird and Wonderful. London: Chatto & Windus, 1889.
Collection of twenty-two weird tales, some based on "true" cases (one offers an extravagant account of the career of the alleged satanist Major Weir), some of the remainder also being told in semi-documentary style. The best are the shocker "The Blue Star" and the quasi-documentary "Some Experiments with a Head." Muddock's later collection in the same vein, *Tales of Terror* (1899), was issued under the Dick Donovan pseudonym which he used for his crime stories.

Mudford, William (U.K.).

2-71. The Five Nights of St. Albans. Edinburgh: Blackwood, 1829.
Gothic grotesquerie featuring a series of supernatural phenomena which afflict an ancient abbey; not to be taken seriously, though parodies of a genre so intrinsically absurd are inevitably difficult to distinguish from the real thing. Mudford also satirized pseudo-Gothic tales of crime and lowlife in *Stephen Dugard* (1840), and wrote the archetypal shrinking room story, *The Iron Shroud* (*Blackwood's*, 1830; separate publication as a chapbook, 1839).

Nesbit, E(dith) (U.K.), 1858-1924.

ABOUT: WW, GSF, CA, SMFL, RG, PE, ESF, HF

2-72. Grim Tales. London: A. D. Innes, 1893.
Collection of seven stories, the most notable being "John Charrington's Wedding," in which the groom is forced by circumstance to attend the ceremony posthumously; and "Man-Size in Marble," in which the stone figures on a tomb come to life once a year to terrorize the neighborhood. Five of the seven (including these two) are reprinted in *Fear* (1910) along with six others, including the *conte cruel* "The Head" and the horror/SF story "The Three Drugs." The stories are frankly intended to shock; a noteworthy modern collection of Nesbit's weird fiction is *In the Dark* (Equation, 1988), edited by Hugh Lamb.

Ohnet, Georges (France), 1848–1918.

2-73. A Weird Gift. London: Chatto & Windus, 1890. Tr. by Albert D. Vandam of *L'âme de Pierre,* 1890.
A man facing ruin bequeaths his soul to an ailing friend and then vanishes; the friend recovers his health, but then finds himself falling prey to the same passions which ruined the other. All is not as it seems, however. Compare Robert Hichens's stories of partial personality exchange [3-86].

Oliphant, Mrs. (Margaret Oliphant Wilson) (U.K.), 1828–1897.

About: WW, GSF, SFW, CA, SMFL, SFE, PE, ESF

***2-74. A Beleaguered City**. London: Macmillan, 1880.
The inhabitants of a French town are expelled by the ghosts of their dead relatives, who are disappointed by their worldliness. They send ambassadors to the haunted streets, who promise that the citizens will mend their ways, but once matters are restored a perverted mythologization of the visitation begins. A brilliant moral fantasy, cynical and sentimental in equal proportions, with effective accounts of the supernatural phenomena as seen from various viewpoints. Some editions are abridged, including the first edition, published in the U.S. by Munro in 1879. The author revised and expanded her ghostly novella *The Lady's Walk* (Munro, 1883) into a full-length novel (1897) which similarly shows the passionate dead hopelessly attempting to direct the living to the path of redemption.

***2-75. Stories of the Seen and Unseen**. Blackwood, 1902.
Collection of four ghost stories. Mrs. Oliphant's work in this vein is closely related to her posthumous fantasies [F2-135] thematically and in terms of their moral sensibility, often featuring spirits who failed in life and who, craving forgiveness, try desperately to attract the attention of the living. "The Open Door" (1882) features a prodigal son; *Old Lady Mary* (separate publication in the U.S., 1884; editions differ) is guilty of a peculiar egoism. These two were coupled in an earlier Blackwood publication, *Two Stories of the Seen and the Unseen* (1885). In "The Portrait" (1885), which replaces *Old Lady Mary* in the U.S. edition of *Two Stories of the Seen and the Unseen* (1885), a son despairs of the miserliness of his father but is aided by the spirit of his mother to work for the old man's redemption. In "The Library Window" (1896) an alienated girl is not quite tempted from her voluntary isolation by a ghostly father figure. Much stronger than the Little Pilgrim stories, these melancholy tales of unease offer a subtle sense of desolation which stands at one extreme of the Victorian ghost story spectrum, the other being occupied by shocking accounts of supernatural vengeance.

[For other works of this author, see the companion guide to fantasy.]

Poe, Edgar Allan, 1809–1849.

About: WW, GSF, SFW, F, CA, H, SMFL, SFE, PE, ESF

***2-76. The Narrative of Arthur Gordon Pym of Nantucket**. New York: Harper, 1838 (published anonymously).
A stowaway is caught up in a disastrous mutiny and ventures into Antarctic

waters, where he discovers the strange people of Tsalal before continuing towards the pole and a highly enigmatic encounter with a gigantic "shrouded human figure." Commentators finding this ending unsatisfactory have tried to explain it in various ways (J. O. Bailey refers it to Symmes's theory of a hollow Earth with polar openings) and at least three sequels have been written: Jules Verne's rather feeble *An Antarctic Mystery* (1897; tr. 1898); Charles Dake's even feebler *A Strange Discovery* (1899); and H. P. Lovecraft's much more satisfying *At the Mountains of Madness* (1936; [3-132]).

***2-77. Tales of the Grotesque and Arabesque**. 2 vols. Philadelphia: Lea & Blanchard, 1840.
A landmark in the history of weird fiction, including three classic *femme fatale* stories, "Morella" (1835), "Berenice" (1835) and "Ligeia" (1838); the archetypal *doppelgänger* story "William Wilson" (1840); the prose poems "Shadow—a Parable" (1835) and "Silence—a Fable" (1838); and the magnificent "The Fall of the House of Usher" (1839), which epitomizes Poe's unparalleled ability to integrate abnormal states of consciousness into the literary texture of a story, obliterating the boundary between observation, hallucination and apparition. The book also contains two sarcastic fantasies featuring the Devil: "Bon-Bon" (1832) and "The Duc d'Omelette" (1832). There are many editions of Poe's complete works, the first omnibus having been issued in four volumes between 1850 and 1856. Other key horror stories in the Poe canon include the classic paranoid fantasies "The Black Cat" (1845) and "The Tell-Tale Heart"; the archetypal tale of taphephobia, "The Premature Burial"; the pseudoscientific account of death held at bay by mesmerism, "The Facts in the Case of M. Valdemar" (1845); and the magnificent extended prose poem "The Masque of the Red Death" (1842).

Praed, Mrs. Campbell (Rosa Murray Prior) (Australia), 1851–1935.
ABOUT: WW, GSF

2-78. The Brother of the Shadow. London: Routledge, 1886.
Credulous occult romance in which a doctor using "electricity" to cure the frail nerves of a friend's wife is tempted by his lust to forsake the path of virtue, encouraged by dreams in which he is visited by a black magician. A brief compendium of currently fashionable occult theories.

2-79. The Soul of Countess Adrian. London: Trischeler, 1891.
Credulous occult romance in which an aging female occultist becomes infatuated with a young man; following her death her soul possesses the body of the girl he loves. May have inspired Doyle's *The Parasite* [2-21].

Reynolds, G(eorge) W(illiam) M(acarthur) (U.K.), 1814–1879.
ABOUT: WW, GSF, SFW, CA, SMFL, PE

2-80. Faust. London: Vickers, 1847.
Rambling historical melodrama loosely based on the Faust legend; the main narrative follows the consequences of the diabolical bargain, but the subplots are more conventional. Heavily influenced by Eugène Sue [F2-150].

2-81. The Necromancer. London: John Dicks, 1857.
Very complicated historical melodrama serialized in *Reynolds' Miscellany* in 1851–52. The main narrative, modeled on Maturin's *Melmoth* [1-64], features a more elaborate version of the diabolical bargain than that featured in [2-80], including a rather improbable escape clause. Various other stories are haphazardly assimilated, in Reynolds's customary fashion.

2-82. Wagner, the Wehr-Wolf. London: John Dicks, 1848.
Repetitive penny dreadful serial from *Reynolds' Magazine* (1846–47); the diabolical bargain here secures eternal youth for Wagner in exchange for his accepting the burden of lycanthropy (though the Devil, apparently regretting his uncharacteristic generosity, periodically returns to bargain for his soul). Christian Rosenkreutz eventually gets involved, promising redemption. Reynolds's Suesque animosity toward the aristocracy is very much in the fore. Despite being overburdened by the shoddy padding and stereotyped melodrama which bring Victorian hackwork to the brink of unreadability, the story has a certain vigor; a modern edition was issued by Dover in 1976.

Riddell, Mrs. J(oseph) H. (Charlotte Cowan) (U.K.), 1832–1906.

ABOUT: WW, GSF, SFW, PE, ESF

***2-83. The Uninhabited House**. London: Routledge, 1875.
Short novel issued as a Christmas Annual. A haunted house proves difficult to rent, forcing an investigation by a solicitor's clerk. The ghost is that of a murdered man whose death has been recorded as a suicide, seeking to set matters right. Very highly rated by Bleiler, who reprinted it in his *Five Victorian Ghost Novels* (1971); its most interesting aspect is the investigative one, which prefigures much "psychic detective" fiction. *The Haunted River* (1877) is thematically very similar; *Fairy Water* (1872) is also an account of bad experiences in a haunted house.

2-84. Weird Stories. London: James Hogg, 1882.
Six stories, five featuring ghosts. They include the often-reprinted "The Open Door," which follows Mrs. Riddell's usual pattern of investigation of supernatural phenomena leading to the exposure of a past crime. The odd story out is "Sandy the Tinker," in which a clergyman trapped by the devil is terrorized into naming another to take his place. All are reprinted in *The Collected Ghost Stories of Mrs. Riddell* (Dover, 1977), along with six others, including a fine story of a guilty man pursued by a child's phantom footprints, "A Terrible Vengeance."

Ross, Ronald (U.K.), 1857–1932.

2-85. The Deformed Transformed. Bangalore: Spectator Press, 1890.
Verse drama revising and completing a fragment by Byron. The weakling Zozimo is tempted to exchange bodies with the Devil, who appears to him in the guise of the handsome and wealthy Count Azriman; the Devil seeks the exchange in order to achieve redemption through the love of a virtuous woman. Ross produced a prose version of the same story, *The Revels of Orsera* (1920), perhaps the most interesting example of late Gothic. Also of interest are the novel *The Child of Ocean* (1889), in which a boy castaway grows to manhood as a "Monster" and

then learns humanity from a female marooned on his island; and a gruesome tale of life artificially prolonged, "The Vivisector Vivisected'" (written 1881; published in Gawsworth's *Strange Assembly* [3-72]), which makes good use of the author's medical expertise (he was knighted for his pioneering work on the transmission of malaria).

Russell, W(illiam) Clark (U.K.), 1844–1911.

ABOUT: WW, GSF, SMFL, SFE, PE, ESF

2-86. The Death Ship. 3 vols. London: Hurst & Blackett, 1888.
A young Englishman is rescued from the sea by the Flying Dutchman's crew; he finds Captain Vanderdecken unaware that his unfortunate voyage has now lasted 150 years, and falls in love with a female fellow-captive. A strange and elaborate paranoid fantasy.

[For other works of this author, see the companion guide to fantasy.]

Rymer, James Malcolm (U.K.), 1814–1881.

ABOUT: WW, GSF, SMFL

2-87. Varney the Vampyre; or, The Feast of Blood. London: Edward Lloyd, 1847 (published anonymously).
The most famous penny dreadful Gothic, also attributed to Thomas Peckett Prest (though Bleiler's grounds for attributing it to Rymer, explained in the Dover edition of 1973, seem sound). The repetitive story, spun out far beyond its natural length because of its popularity as a serial, describes the depredations of the aristocratic vampire among the lower orders—the political allegory receives less stress than it might have in the hands of Reynolds [2-80–2-82], and the sexual allegory is handled with less intensity than in its model, Polidori's *Vampyre* [1-79].

Shelley, Mary Wollstonecraft (U.K.), 1797–1851.

ABOUT: WW, GSF, SFW, F, CA, FG, NE, H, SMFL, SFE, PE, ESF

2-88. Tales and Stories. London: W. Paterson, 1891.
Collection edited by Richard Garnett; most of the stories originally appeared in *The Keepsake,* the most famous of the early Victorian annuals. They include the personality-exchange story "Transformation" (1831), possibly inspired by Byron's "The Deformed Transformed" (see [2-85]); and "The Mortal Immortal" (1834) in which an apprentice of Cornelius Agrippa's takes a short measure of the elixir of youth, and finds his longevity a burden. The *Collected Tales and Stories* issued by Johns Hopkins Univ. Press in 1976 offers less corrupt texts of these items and adds some other supernatural trivia.

Shiel, M(atthew) P(hipps) (U.K.), 1865–1947.

ABOUT: WW, GSF, SFW, CA, NE, SMFL, SFE, TCSF, PE, ESF

2-89. Shapes in the Fire. London: John Lane, 1896.
Collection of highly ornamented and self-consciously decadent pieces, including

"Xelucha," which features a spectral *femme fatale*; "Vaila," a Poesque tale of a doomed house, later to be revised as "The House of Sounds"; and "Tulsah," the story of a man who must carry a murderous curse through many incarnations. The highly embroidered style and flirtatiously macabre eroticism of the first and third tales (also exhibited in the fantasy "Phorfor") make this a uniquely fascinating item, though it is not to everyone's taste.

Spofford, Mrs. Harriet Elizabeth, 1835–1921.
About: GSF

2-90. Sir Rohan's Ghost. Boston: J. E. Tilton, 1860 (published anonymously). The protagonist has been haunted for many years by the ghost of a woman he once loved and betrayed, but the haunting becomes much more assertive when he falls in love again; it proves that there is more than mere jealousy involved. An extravagant account of externalized guilty conscience.

Stenbock, Eric (Estonia), 1859–1895.
About: WW, PE

2-91. Studies of Death. London: Nutt, 1894.
Collection of seven stories, earnestly decadent and morbidly melancholy. "The True Story of a Vampire" has a sexual subtext which is both homoerotic and paedophilic; "Viol d'Amor" recalls Mme. Blavatsky's "The Ensouled Violin" [2-8], but is much more stylish; "The Other Side" is a werewolf story.

Stevenson, Robert Louis (U.K.), 1850–1894.
About: WW, GSF, SFW, F, CA, NE, H, SMFL, SFE, PE, ESF

2-92. The Merry Men and Other Tales and Fables. London: Chatto & Windus, 1887.
Collection including the curious moral fable "Markheim," in which a murderer will have no truck with a seductive tempter because he believes that he may yet be redeemed, and "Thrawn Janet," the story of an evil witch told in dialect. The omnibus *Stories of Robert Louis Stevenson* (1928) includes both of these plus "The Bottle Imp" (1893), which recasts a traditional story (also known in a literary version by Fouqué) for the Polynesian islanders among whom Stevenson lived his later years; "The Body Snatcher" (1884), a nasty tale inspired by the exploits of Burke and Hare; and [2-93].

***2-93. The Strange Case of Dr. Jekyll and Mr. Hyde**. New York: Munro, 1886. Classic story in which the monstrous Mr. Hyde is eventually revealed to be the alter ego of the upright Dr. Jekyll, whose incautious investigations into the nature of evil have liberated the urges and impulses whose repression has been the means by which he has achieved his moral probity. A pre-Freudian account of the workings of id and superego, mirroring the hypocritically concealed duality of Victorian London society, where a relentlessly repressive public morality had as its underside a clandestine underworld where perversity and prostitution were rife. Its origin in a nightmare is entirely appropriate and so (however regrettable it might be) is the fact that the author's morally upright wife forced him to burn the first draft because he had not exploited the potential which the tale had as moral fable. The film versions starring Fredric March (1931) and Spencer Tracy (1941) are outstanding among Hollywood fantasies, and are highly unusual in embellishing the plot in a coherent and constructive fashion, adding the fallen woman who becomes Hyde's mistress and victim while looking hopelessly to Jekyll for redemption.

Turgenev, Ivan (Russia), 1818-1883.

ABOUT: WW, PE

2-94. Dream Tales and Prose Poems. London: Heinemann, 1897. Tr. by Constance Garnett.

The "dream tales" comprise four phantasmagoric novellas. In the fine "Phantoms" (1863) a young man is taken night-riding by a lovely ghost who is mysteriously punished for her audacity; "The Song of Triumphant Love" (1881) is a lurid tale of supernatural seduction; "Clara Militch" (1882) tells of a young man's obsession with a dead girl who seems unaccountably to have committed suicide for love of him; in "The Dream" (1876) a young man suffers bizarre visions relating to his absent father. Some of the poems in prose (1878-82) are similarly nightmarish, especially "The Old Woman," "The Skulls" and "The Insect." Few other writers have so convincingly captured the disturbing quality of feverish nightmares.

Villiers de L'Isle-Adam, Comte de (France), 1840-1889.

ABOUT: WW, GSF, SFE, PE, ESF

2-95. Cruel Tales. Oxford Univ. Press, 1963. Tr. by Robert Baldick of *Contes cruels*, 1883.

Classic collection which gave its title to a subgenre of tales whose horrific effect stems not from the supernatural, but rather from a morbid contemplation of the manner in which people can be crushed and defeated by ironic circumstance, the bitter enmity of their fellow men or the perfidy of women (many stories in this vein are frankly misogynistic). An earlier translation was called *Sardonic Tales*, observing that many stories in this vein are cruel jokes (especially the ones of dubious authorship which circulate as "true" stories in urban folklore). The supernatural plays only a muted role here, though there are occasional echoes of Poe (in "The Sign"), of graveyard poetry (in "Occult Memories") and of Gothic antiheroes (in "The Messenger" and "The Duke of Portland"); instead, the human condition itself is made to seem macabre. It is a pity that the collection was not expanded to take in the similar tales which Villiers wrote after publication of the 1883 collection, including the often-reprinted "The Torture of Hope." To some extent the work carries forward a tradition established in Barbey d'Aurevilly's polished tales in *Les Diaboliques* (1874) (with which it has more in common than it does with its *grand guignol* descendants in the work of Level [3-129] and Leroux [3-127]), but it is a genuine landmark in the development of psychological horror fiction.

Von Degen (pseud. of **Baroness von Rabe**) (U.K.), born 1846.
About: GSF, PE

2-96. A Mystery of the Campagna and A Shadow on a Wave. London: Fisher Unwin, 1891.
Two novelettes set in Italy; the first is a vampire story in which the threat to a young composer is revealed by the delirious dreams of his friend, an artist—too late, alas, to save his life. Contrast Gautier's lushly romantic "Clarimonde" [F2-64].

Wilde, Oscar (Ireland), 1854–1900.
About: WW, GSF, SFW, F, CA, SMFL, RG, PE, ESF, HF

***2-97. The Picture of Dorian Gray**. London: Ward, Lock, 1891.
A highly moralistic fantasy (in spite of its prefatory claim that books can be neither moral nor immoral) in which the young protagonist wishes that the portrait painted by a man who loves him will bear the evident burden of his self-indulgence, sparing his own fair flesh from corruption. A masterpiece rejoicing in its own paradoxical nature; the brilliant light badinage of the early chapters does not intend to hide the fact that the book is very deeply felt—its presentation mirrors the calculated hypocrisy of the compromises which the homosexual Wilde tragically failed to sustain in the face of vicious persecution.

[For other works of this author, see the companion guide to fantasy.]

Wood, Mrs. Henry (**Ellen Price**) (U.K.), 1814–1887.
About: GSF, SFW

2-98. The Shadow of Ashlydyat. 3 vols. London: Bentley, 1863.
The story of a family curse, whose supernatural manifestations are ultimately traced to a buried skeleton which is the relic of an ancient crime. In the same theoretical vein as Mrs. Riddell's stories [2-84], but more ponderous. While she was editor of *The Argosy*, Mrs. Wood wrote a long series of anecdotal stories ostensibly told by the young Johnny Ludlow, which were issued in book form in six series between 1874 and 1899. They include numerous supernatural items, most notably "A Curious Experience" (Fourth series, 1890).

Wright, Thomas (U.K.).

2-99. The Blue Firedrake. London: Simpkin Marshall, 1892.
Historical novel based on the story of Elinor Shaw, the last witch executed in England (the novel's allegation that she was burned is supported by some contemporary sources, though the legal penalty in England was death by hanging). Offered as a first-person account by one Nathan Souldrop, whose glimpses of the ominous firedrake are ultimately written off as hallucinations. An eccentric novel, parallel in some ways to Meinhold's imitation historical documents [2-63–2-64]; superior to Ainsworth's *Lancashire Witches* [2-2].

3

Early Modern Horror Fiction, 1897–1949

Brian Stableford

The first words which Count Dracula speaks to Jonathan Harker are these: "Welcome to my house! Enter freely and of your own will!" The connoisseur of horror fiction will recognize in this speech an obscure point of the vampire mythology which Stoker elaborated in his book (partly borrowed from folkloristic tradition and partly invented): the predations of Dracula and his authentic kin are limited by the fact that they cannot trespass where they are not formally invited to enter; their victims must make them welcome, or go to meet them willingly. This is, of course, an ironic condition; Jonathan Harker has no idea of the danger in which he is placing himself by crossing Dracula's threshold, and the female victims who so often evade the precautions of their would-be protectors in order to invite male vampires to complete their own destruction have been so corrupted that their will is no longer their own. Nevertheless, the condition is made—horror does not simply descend upon the innocent; it responds to invitation.

We can see a similar perversity in another novel which, like *Dracula* [3-186], was published in the first year of this period in the history of horror fiction: Robert Hichens's *Flames* [3-86]. One of the two central characters of *Flames*, Valentine Cresswell, is one of nature's saints: a man who instinctively does right, and who never feels temptation. He is, however, discontented with this condition, and envies his friend Julian Addison, who feels the magnetism of sin in no uncertain terms, and might easily go bad were it not for Valentine's shining example. It is Valentine, not Julian, who suggests that they contrive a partial personality exchange, so that he may inherit a modicum of moral weakness, giving in return a charge of moral strength. The reader can hardly be surprised when this experiment turns out to be an invitation to disaster.

Each of these novels takes a moral stance which is fundamentally Victorian; the authors are stalwart champions of chastity. Yet each of the books is, in parts, vividly erotic. When Jonathan Harker discovers that he is a virtual prisoner in Dracula's castle, he becomes alarmed, as well he might. But his situation is still ironically misperceived; his imprisonment is intended to preserve him from harm, at least for the time being. Dracula, requiring his services as an estate agent, seems to have no immediate intention of making a victim of him, but wishes to secure him from the attentions of his three pale "brides"; it is they who come to threaten Harker's life, and though he issues no verbal invitation his feeling as he awaits the first sinister kiss is one of "languorous ecstasy." More than one critic has observed that the details of this passage are suspiciously reminiscent of a visit to a brothel, and have connected this with the theory that Stoker had contracted syphilis shortly before he wrote the novel.

Flames, though somewhat coy and inexplicit, leaves the reader in no doubt as to the general nature of the temptations which Julian Addison suffers; they are reflected in his fascination with the prostitutes of Piccadilly, for whose nightly parade the text co-opts a coincidentally remarkable metaphor, describing it as "the flight of the bats." Hichens's long and lyrical commentary on this phenomenon provides a fascinating example of the psychology of a particular kind of anxiety which arises from a competition within oneself of erotic attraction and moral panic.

> It is a great though secret army, the army of the bats. It scours through cities. No weather will keep it quite restful in camp. No darkness will blind it into immobility. The mainspring of sin beats in it as drums beat in a Soudanese fantasia, as blood beats in a heart. The air of night is black with the movement of the bats. They fly so thickly round some lives that those lives can never see the sky, never catch a glimpse of the stars, never hear the wings of the angels, but always and ever the wings of the bats. Nor can such lives hear the whisper of Nature and of the sirens who walk purely with Nature. The murmur of the bats drowns all other sounds, and makes a hoarse monotonous music. And the eyes of the bats are hungry, and the breath of the bats is poisonous, and the flight of the bats is a charade of the tragedy of the flight of the devils in hell. [*Flames,* p. 187]

Robert Hichens—who never married—went on to publish, in his aptly named collection *Tongues of Conscience* [3-87], one of the finest of all ghost stories, "How Love Came to Professor Guildea." It tells the story of a scientist whose prideful boast that he has no use for affection and has exorcised all passion from his being becomes an ironic invitation to disaster. He is subsequently driven to destruction by a doting, imbecilic spirit which poses no apparent threat to him, save only that it is drawn to him by exactly that helpless infatuation which he claims to have cut out of his own soul and thrown away: it is, in a way, his *doppelgänger,* his other half.

There is a sense in which Dracula, too, stands for something in his victims which they cannot entirely exorcise from themselves—something from the night-side of life which may be temporarily laid to rest by the daylight of reason, but which will always rise again when tired reason relaxes and the evening shadows of anxiety extend themselves. The bat is an apt symbol of this sinister fluttering entity, this animal spirit within the human soul—all the more so if the bat can metamorphose into a sexually seductive figure whose embrace leads to annihilation.

Dracula is one of only a handful of fictional characters to have become a modern legend. His name is instantly recognizable to everyone, like the names of Sherlock Holmes and Tarzan. He is one of the key figures in modern mythology: a monster, but a charismatic monster by whom we are attracted as well as repelled. Like the love which came to Professor Guildea, whose ruthless rationality was not sufficient to keep it at bay, or the night-flying "bats" of *Flames* (the one who figures prominently in the plot is called Cuckoo), Dracula is not a problem which can be conclusively solved. History was to prove that he could not be laid finally to rest; he returned again and again from the dead no matter what formulas were followed to ensure his destruction, and whenever he arose he never lacked for long that crucial invitation which allowed him to stir the feelings of his victim-lovers, and thus warm their blood to just that pitch of fever which makes it ripe for spilling.

It is, of course, easily arguable that *Dracula* contains nothing essentially new, and that the key features of his character were already incarnate in Polidori's Lord Ruthven [1-79]. This is true; the fundamental nature of horror is unchanged by literary fashions, and horror fiction has always been primarily interested in figures of menace which evoke a more complex response in us than unalloyed terror. Inspection of the ways in which characters wittingly and unwittingly invite the attention of monsters has always been a vital thread in the weft of horror fiction. Nevertheless, *Dracula* and *Flames* signify an advance, and the year which produced them both deserves recognition as a kind of benchmark. The thread had always been there, but in this new period its dance upon the loom began to draw more intricate and more hypnotically effective patterns than it ever had before.

The period in the history of horror fiction which began with the publication of *Dracula* and *Flames* has been discussed by several commentators—the pioneer was Peter Penzoldt, a Freudian who produced a reasonably wide-ranging study of *The Supernatural in Fiction* [7-9]—as an era most notable for its "psychological ghost stories." The introduction to the last chapter commented on the trend to introspection which was already well set in the nineteenth century, and it is only to be expected that the present period should have brought the trend to a new pitch of intensity; this was, after all, a period when psychological science made great strides and all manner of phenomena were brought under the clinical eye of the psychologist—not merely madness, but dreams and religious experiences too. Henry James, who was one of the most important ghost story writers at the turn of the century (see [2-45] and [3-107]), was the brother of one of the pioneers of the new science, William James, whose influence can also be seen in the clinicalized ghost stories of William Dean Howells [3-96]. The fascination which Freud had for the fiction of "the uncanny," which he developed elaborately in a famous essay on E. T. A. Hoffmann's "The Sandman" [1-40], was in part a mere peeping over the shoulders of writers who were every bit as intently interested in the mysteries of the human mind as he was, although their standpoint was very different.

This was a period when writers continued to explore, ever more elaborately, the ways in which the terror evoked by apparitions can and does reflect anxieties about those of our impulses and fascinations which pose a threat to moral order. That ghosts are often externalized representations of guilt had always been realized, but it was not until the eve of the twentieth century that writers of horror fiction developed (or were given) the right ideological tools to carry forward a particularly minute, careful and intense examination of the possible patterns which guilt might produce. Horror writers benefited not only from the gathering insights of psychological science (and psychological pseudoscience) but also from the literary evolution of cleverer methods of characterization, and the slackening of formal restrictions on the way that characters in stories were supposed to talk and otherwise conduct themselves. Despite its Romantic affiliations, horror fiction always gains from advances in the techniques and conventions of literary realism.

Under these various influences, the spirits unwittingly invited by their victims were able to enjoy a phenomenal adaptive radiation as they colonized a vast variety of psychological niches, moving all the time in the direction of a more disturbing intimacy with their reluctant hosts. Mere scarecrows dressed in the fleshy apparel of the dead were pushed out to the cruder margins of the genre.

The observation that horror fiction was influenced by advances in psychological science should not be taken to imply that what writers of this period did may be reckoned a straightforward exercise in dilettante psychoanalysis. Nor, for that matter, is horror fiction's increasingly sophisticated use of symbolism and concentration on moral stress points a matter of straightforward allegorizing. Even the most superficial consideration of the fiction of the period assures us that its leading writers were much less inclined to relate specific apparitions to specific violations of moral codes than their predecessors had been. The great majority were, in fact, less given to crudely analytical "explanations" in bringing their stories to a climax, and were much more frequently content to leave a good deal unexplained. Indeed, the inexplicability of the hypothetical events which they describe frequently comes to be a significant aspect of their power to create anxiety.

Some of the best writers of the period seem to be perfectly content not to be entirely certain what their own stories mean, as though they were working by some method of free association. Certainly they are much freer than nineteenth-century writers were in their employment of metaphor and symbolism, as if they were following—consciously or otherwise—Mallarmé's dictum that one should describe, not the thing itself (in this case, the guilty secrets of the soul), but the effect which it produces (the nightmare relationships of apparition and emotion).

The aesthetics of modern horror fiction are mainly based in this fascinated elaboration of symptom, often coupled with a marked reluctance to reduce and demystify supramundane phenomena by too specific an account of causality (whether in metaphysical or moral terms). Instead of attempting to expose the mechanics of the presumed link of association between apparition and anxiety, the ideal type of the twentieth-century psychological horror story attempts to draw out an increasingly elaborate image of the patterns that may be taken by the apparitions and the emotions which they induce. We can see different forms of this quest in the work of the most prestigious writers of the period: Henry James [3-107], M. R. James [3-108], Walter De la Mare [3-58–3-59], L. P. Hartley [3-80] and—in the less metaphysical mood of his shorter stories—Algernon Blackwood [3-26]. Numerous significant minor writers (examples include A. M. Burrage [3-43], Violet Hunt [3-99] and John Metcalfe [3-147]) can easily be assimilated to the argument.

This kind of literary strategy may help to produce a more detailed map of the deep anxieties underlying the images which have the power to frighten us, but what the writer is doing is adding detail to the map, not exploring the territory. Although horror fiction is intensely interesting to the psychoanalyst, that interest does not arise because the writer of such fiction is conducting a kind of psychoanalysis himself, but rather because the most effective writers *refuse* to move in that kind of analytic direction, concentrating instead on producing much more elaborate accounts of that which can be analyzed.

There is no contradiction between these observations and the fact that two of the significant subgenres of the period do indeed seem (on a superficial level, at least) to be preoccupied with methodical analysis. The kinds of analysis to which these subgenres—the psychic detective story and the academic/antiquarian ghost story—are devoted are not really reductions or explanations. Unlike the kinds of ratiocination which are celebrated by the true detective story or science fiction, they do not serve to precipitate a precious residue of certainty from a cloudy solution of doubt, but rather move in the opposite direction, dissolving the apparent safe solidity of the world we inhabit in a kind of metaphysical acid bath, which opens it up to the incursions of doubt, uncertainty and the horrific reflections of our inner fears.

Although there are precursors in Le Fanu [2-50], the popular fad for psychic detective stories began with magazine series featuring debunkers of spirits, like the hero of L. T. Meade and Robert Eustace's *Master of Mysteries* (1898), who ruthlessly exposed the mundane mechanics of supposed hauntings, after the fashion of Harry Houdini's ready penetration of the tricks of fake mediums. The credulous quickly hit back, however, with series of accounts of supposedly "authentic" hauntings, as can be found in E. and H. Heron's *Ghosts* [3-85]. The balance of power was decisively altered by the success of Algernon Blackwood's *John Silence* [3-27], whose mission to explain was not a reductionist one that would banish superstition, but rather a synthesist one that would reinterpret the metaphysics of supernatural phenomena to accommodate their literalness within a modern worldview. Silence does indeed go digging for the psychological roots of the various hauntings and transformations with which he comes into contact, but he is primarily concerned with matters of metaphysics, and with the description of a rather animistic universe.

To what extent Blackwood actually believed in what he was doing it is difficult to judge, but he certainly seemed more inclined to explore than to explain, and these explorations in hypothetical metaphysics are as much an exercise in map-making as they are elaborate extrapolations of the anatomy of fear. The same is true whenever stories of this species go beyond the production of pot-boiling puzzle stories, as Dion Fortune's stories of Dr. Taverner [3-69] and Margery Lawrence's stories of Miles Pennoyer [3-123] occasionally try to do, and Hodgson's Carnacki stories belatedly did in "The Hog" [3-89]. In these stories it is not so much supernatural characters—like Dracula or the ghost which haunted Professor Guildea—who become complex reflections of our inner conflicts and desperate anxieties, but the universe itself, which is remade in the image of the troubled psyche as an anxious entity of embodied disturbances. The Cartesian "animal spirits" which continually urge us into conflict with the externally defined moral order are here converted into elementary conditions of existence which can and do break through an environmental order which is merely a veneer.

The academic/antiquarian ghost story is similarly less paradoxical than it may appear. M. R. James, who was largely responsible for making it securely respectable for dons to dabble in weird fiction, initially associated his efforts in this vein with the Dickensian tradition of Christmas ghost stories. The point of this association was that Christmas was a holiday, when ordinary standards might be deliberately relaxed and indulgence not merely forgiven but encouraged. More specifically, the willing suspension of disbelief which supernatural fiction requires in a maturely credulous world might be granted at Christmastime (by definition the celebration of a miracle) with the same enthusiastic generosity with which presents are given.

The whole point of James's ghost stories [3-108] is that they celebrate the *limits* of academic expertise and scientific analysis; they focus upon the terror of moments when the rational worldview fails and collapses. The central characters of the stories are usually as careful and methodical in what they do as the author; their antiquarian interests characteristically lead them to pry into the past with an inquisitive attitude which contrives to be both prim and scrupulous, whose stark contrast with the brutal horror of what eventually turns up provides the stories with much of their power to shock.

The essence of an academic/antiquarian ghost story is that careful analysis is brought into contact with the unanalyzable, and that this in itself is (for an academic) a kind of tragedy. No matter how far the analysis can be carried—and in examples like Baker's *College Mystery* [3-10] it is very detailed indeed—the end result is no more (and, significantly, *no less*) than a more intricate account of an intractable mystery. We can see this not only in other British academic writers—A. C. Benson [3-13–3-14]; Arthur Gray [3-74]; Thomas G. Jackson [3-103]; E. G. Swain [3-193]—but in the American writers closest in spirit to the British tradition, especially William Dean Howells [3-96]. Ironically, we can see something of the same phenomenon in academic writing which sets out to analyze and explain what goes on in certain ambiguous ghost stories, as the mass of theories relating to Henry James's eternally evasive "Turn of the Screw" [3-107] readily shows.

That there is more to be gained by elaborating mysteries than by exposing their psychological roots was, as might be expected, very well appreciated by those who wanted to live fantasies as well as write them. When Violet Firth remade herself as Dion Fortune she understood well enough what she was doing, and when Aleister Crowley redefined himself as the Great Beast he understood it even better. Crowley was the first of the life-style fantasists to realize the attractions of monstrousness—to absorb, as it were, the lesson of *Dracula's* success—

and thus to luxuriate in representation of himself as "the most evil man in the world." He was happy to acknowledge, when drawing up the curriculum for study by initiates in his *Argentinum Astrum,* both those literary works from which he had borrowed—notably Edgar Jepson's *Number 19* [3-109]—and those which had repaid the compliment by borrowing from *him*—most notably W. Somerset Maugham's *The Magician* [3-144].

Crowley was no great shakes as a writer of fiction (see [3-56])—he shared with such overenthusiastic occult investigators as Lewis Spence [3-184] and Elliot O'Donnell [3-153] a crippling lack of detachment—but he certainly understood as well as anyone the evolving aesthetics of evil and it was a clever piece of opportunism which led Dennis Wheatley to invite him to dinner as a means of researching *The Devil Rides Out* [3-209]. Much the same spirit of opportunism has been involved in shaping the long career of Count Dracula as a star of stage and screen, whose ability to make comebacks is unrivaled even by Frank Sinatra.

Dracula's status as a modern archetype of evil was greatly assisted, if not actually secured, by the cinema, and in like manner the cinema of the period conferred archetypicality on a whole series of images of similar type. Second in notoriety only to Dracula was the monster made by Mary Shelley's *Frankenstein* [1-97], as portrayed by Boris Karloff; another character borrowed from an earlier period was the dual personality of *Dr. Jekyll and Mr. Hyde* [2-93]. Both of these images were used recurrently, the cinema in each case creating a somewhat remodeled legend according to its own formula.

The same sort of thing happened in a number of other cases. Several films were based on Gaston Leroux's novel *The Phantom of the Opera* [3-128]; another series developed the cinema's idiosyncratic version of the werewolf—seen to best advantage in *The Wolf Man* (1941; directed by James Whale and scripted by Curt Siodmak)—whose relative originality was forced not by any lack of literary models for adaptation but by the limitations of special effects and make-up, which were then inadequate to the task of allowing the central character to turn into an actual wolf. These two cases offer particularly clear examples of a Hollywood trend, also seen in the Karloff *Frankenstein* films, and to a greater extent still in *King Kong* (1933; see [F3-226]), by which concentration on the existential plight of the monster is used to generate sympathy.

Werewolves are very common in the fiction of this period—rather commoner than vampires. Often they are used as straightforward figures of menace, as by Alfred Bill [3-21], Gerald Biss [3-25], Greye La Spina [3-122] or Jack Mann [3-137], but there are a significant number of stories in which considerable sympathy for the werewolf is expressed, including H. Warner Munn's *Werewolf of Ponkert* and its sequels [3-151], Franklin Gregory's *White Wolf* [3-75], Aino Kallas's *The Wolf's Bride* [3-112] and—most significantly—Guy Endore's *Werewolf of Paris* [3-67]. The last-named was probably the work which most heavily influenced the scriptwriter of *The Werewolf of London* (1935), which provided the model that Siodmak, Whale and Lon Chaney, Jr. followed in *The Wolf Man.* These stories, like the films, depict unwitting or unwilling lycanthropes struggling after the fashion of Dr. Jekyll against the bestial alter egos which lurk within them; they represent the most interesting instances of a trend—

which was to become much more pronounced in later years—toward a reconciliation of the warring elements of the turbulent psyche.

By far the greater part of the fiction of the period is desperately pessimistic about the possibility of exorcising the evil within, but it is in stories where its inwardness has to be accepted (rather than denied, as it usually is in stories which externalize it in apparitions and vampires) that we begin to see explorations of the possibility of accommodating it. Endore's werewolf comes close to finding a way to live with his affliction, and though his failure is a tragedy, it is no worse than the failure of less evidently afflicted men to control their own wolfishness; in Jack Williamson's *Darker Than You Think* [3-214] we discover a more ambitious reconciliation which foreshadowed developments of a later period.

Werewolf stories stand at the figurative end of a continuum of representations of monsters-within-men, within which the key characters took many other forms. Lycanthropy figures more metaphorically as a derangement of the mind in stories like Jessie Kerruish's *Undying Monster* [3-114], Richard Bagot's *Roman Mystery* [3-9] and (with the metaphor slightly modified) in Leonard Cline's *Dark Chamber* [3-50]. There are many other representations which more directly and more idiosyncratically confront the issue of the evil within. Georges Bernanos's *Star of Satan* [3-20], Joseph Conrad's *Heart of Darkness* [3-51], Walter De la Mare's *The Return* [3-58] and Selma Lagerlöf's *Thy Soul Shall Bear Witness* [3-120] are the most prestigious examples, but there are less philosophically inclined works which explore the same ideative territory: Guy Boothby's *Curse of the Snake* [3-30], L. Ron Hubbard's "Fear" [3-97], the Syntons' *Possessed* [3-194] and Hugh Walpole's *Killer and the Slain* [3-202] all confront the reader directly with monstrous persons who are victims as well as instruments of the evil which moves within them.

Few of these works feature any actual challenge to conventional ideas of morality; even determinedly decadent works like those of Hanns Heinz Ewers [3-68] are content to flirt with a quasi-Sadeian denial or a vulgarized Nietzschean reconstruction of moral norms, without actually daring to embrace either. Nevertheless, they do seek to show us moral problems in a new light, questioning the internal authority of free will.

This skeptical account of our power over ourselves stands in close relationship with a deeper skepticism about the power of the human will to impose itself on external circumstance. The trend which was elaborately developed in the "psychological ghost story" runs parallel to the other major trend which is sometimes noted by historians of the period—the development of what H. P. Lovecraft in *Supernatural Horror in Literature* [7-7] called "cosmic horror." The premise of this kind of story, simply stated, is that the universe is not only lacking in a proper moral order but is actively hostile, and that penetration of its secrets can only lead to a terror far more absolute than mere existentialist *angst*.

The first great exponent of cosmic horror was William Hope Hodgson, who discovered this view of existence during his miserable years at sea, building it into his maritime horror stories [3-88; 3-90; 3-91] before extending it into the remarkable cosmic vision of *The House on the Borderland* [3-92]. Lovecraft himself became the second, developing in his Cthulhu Mythos [3-132] an elaborate account of mankind as the insignificant instrument of awesomely monstrous godlike creatures. A third writer who warrants close attention in this regard was

Lovecraft's correspondent and contemporary Clark Ashton Smith, whose flights of the imagination [3-182] took him to the very limits of time and space in search of menacing exotica. Donald Wandrei [3-204–3-205] was another who attempted to roll back the frontiers in similar fashion, but without the advantage of similar powers of imaginative vision. All of this work is, by necessity, close to the margin where horror fiction overlaps the science fiction genre.

The description of a grandiose metaphysical context in essentially horrific terms is a further exaggeration of the way in which the most impressive psychic detective stories work. One might also see this trend, in dialectical balance with the psychological ghost story, as a further extrapolation of the division whose effect on the character of the Gothic villain was noted in the introduction to the last chapter. The description of an entirely monstrous universe would then be seen as a logical destination of the lines of thought which had to be employed in making a thorough and convincing job of characterizing and rendering powerful such unhuman villains as Dracula.

In a sense, the premise that the universe is essentially hostile and hurtful, and that nothing can come of increasing wisdom but dreadful disillusionment, might be seen as the ultimate in horror. But consideration of the aesthetics of horror fiction is riddled with paradoxes and there is, in fact, an odd kind of comfort to be drawn from this kind of story. If the universe is hostile and essentially frustrating, and no success or achievement is really possible, then we do not have to take so much responsibility for our own failures; our inadequacies become simple reflections of the necessary features of our existential predicament. Thus, the awfulness of it all can become reassuring—and there is no real puzzle in the observation that in spite of the intensity of feeling which they put into their work, Hodgson, Lovecraft and Smith all appear to have been amiable and gentle men, by no means incapable of enthusiasm for life and contentment with circumstance.

By the time the trend which produced the most important works of cosmic horror was well set, horror fiction in America was in the process of being relegated to the status of a pulp genre. The psychological horror story had been reasonably well established in the upper strata of the marketplace, thanks to Henry James [3-107], Mary E. Wilkins Freeman [3-71] and Edith Wharton [3-208], but that tradition was allowed to ebb. When the pulps began to diversify and to specialize in the 1920s, the magazine *Weird Tales* [11-20] became the principal depository of American genre writing, and remained so for three decades.

Weird Tales became rather more than a useful market for American writers of horror stories—it became the focal point of a subculture. Although that subculture was never as large as the one which grew up around the science fiction pulps, it was certainly not without significance. The magazine gave writers of offbeat fiction a target for their submissions, but it also gave them a sense of common cause and community—a community whose lines of communication were anchored by the voluminous correspondence conducted by its father figure: H. P. Lovecraft.

That *Weird Tales* acquired this status is all the more remarkable given that the man who was actually in charge of the magazine during the crucial phase of its history, Farnsworth Wright (editor from November 1924 to March 1940), seems to have done little enough to encourage the cultivation of its distinct and unique identity. It seems to have been almost in spite of him that *Weird Tales* became the vehicle for development of the Cthulhu Mythos, and for extravagant explorations of the potential of "cosmic horror" by Smith and Wandrei; nevertheless, it did become the principal public arena for the literary exploits of the "Lovecraft circle," which (at least for a time) included—in addition to writers already cited—Robert Bloch [3-29], August Derleth [3-61–3-62], Frank Belknap Long [3-131] and E. Hoffman Price [3-159]. Other *Weird Tales* regulars, like Hugh B. Cave [3-48], Carl Jacobi [3-104], Seabury Quinn [3-163], Manly Wade Wellman [3-207] and Henry S. Whitehead [3-213], all brought their own independent resources to the magazine, but none remained untouched by Lovecraft's influence. That influence lasted long after Lovecraft's death in 1937 and spread beyond the pages of the magazine to Derleth and Wandrei's specialist publishing enterprise, Arkham House, which gave more permanent form to the best works of all the notable *Weird Tales* writers.

In Britain, meanwhile, the respectability conferred on weird fiction by M. R. James and the antiquarian school preserved the genre at a comfortably middle-brow level. This not only made it readily available to writers whose main intention was to shock or thrill in a clever manner, like E. F. Benson [3-15–3-17], Marjorie Bowen [3-32–3-33], A. M. Burrage [3-43] Frederick Cowles [3-53], William F. Harvey [3-81], John Metcalfe [3-147] and H. Russell Wakefield [3-200], it also offered useful scope to writers of greater ambition and greater finesse. Algernon Blackwood [3-26] and H. F. Heard [3-83] were able to use the genre for exercises in eccentric metaphysics, while the tradition of psychological horror stories which had been virtually abandoned in America was taken up and taken further by writers like Walter De la Mare [3-59], Violet Hunt [3-99], L. P. Hartley [3-80], Oliver Onions [3-155] and May Sinclair [3-178]. Many other writers found nothing amiss in occasionally dipping into the genre to produce distinctive and highly idiosyncratic works like Gerald Bullett's "Street of the Eye" [3-40], Robert Graves's "The Shout" [3-73] and Saki's "Gabriel-Ernest" [3-172].

There *was* crude "pulp fiction" of a kind in Britain, featured in series potboilers written by pseudonymous writers like M. Y. Halidom [3-77] and Mark Hansom [3-78]—a tradition which extended into the pioneering days of cheap paperbacks (unnaturally stretched in Britain because of World War II paper shortages) thanks to the writings of Eugene Ascher [3-4] and Ronald S. L. Harding [3-79]. This literary undergrowth absorbed some *Weird Tales* material, most notably that which was reprinted in Christine Campbell Thomson's *Not at Night* anthologies [3-195] and various works by Arlton Eadie [3-65]. It coexisted quite happily, however, with more sophisticated work, and the fondness which the British public had for anthologies of weird fiction readily accommodated the relatively upmarket series edited by Cynthia Asquith [3-6] and John Gawsworth [3-72] as well as the *Not at Night* series and the somewhat uneven *Creeps* series [3-23].

In America, by contrast, the one significant subgenre of horror fiction to survive (and, for a brief period, thrive) in parallel with *Weird Tales* was in the very lowest stratum of the marketplace. This was a curious subgenre of what has recently been dubbed "weird menace" fiction, which was propagated in flamboyantly lurid pulps with names like *Horror Stories, Dime Mystery* and *Terror Tales,* and which consisted mainly of "rationalized" shockers in which apparently supernatural events turn out to be elaborate pretenses hiding nasty criminal activities. There was no Arkham House to confer a measure of respectability on this kind of fiction, but it has recently attracted some interest as a subcultural phenomenon, as evidenced by the works annotated in [3-106].

Mention must, however, also be made here of the significant, if all-too-brief, encouragement lent to the development of American weird fiction by the fantasy pulp *Unknown* [11-18], which published several significant stories which might have been considered too offbeat by Farnsworth Wright's successor Dorothy McIlwraith, including key early works by Fritz Leiber [3-125–3-126] and Theodore Sturgeon [3-192], as well as interesting material by A. E. van Vogt [3-198], plus Hubbard's "Fear" [3-97] and Williamson's *Darker Than You Think* [3-214].

The effects of the pulp "ghettoization" of American horror fiction were various, but they are easily comparable to the effects which a similar ghettoization had on science fiction. In terms of orthodox literary merit the American horror fiction of the early twentieth century is, on average, distinctly inferior to British horror fiction of the same period. This general inferiority is, however, compensated in two ways.

First, relegation to the pulps liberated a number of American writers from the expectations of conventional fiction to an extraordinary extent, so that they did manage—albeit without much editorial encouragement—to explore new styles. There are still critics, even today, who will say of such eccentric stylists as Lovecraft and Clark Ashton Smith that they were simply bad writers, but that kind of offhand dismissal cannot possibly do justice to the experiments which they conducted. Both men wrote in an unusual fashion because they were attempting to affect their readers in a highly unusual way, and they succeeded with at least a significant minority of those whom they tried to reach.

Second, the relaxation of conventional literary standards allowed the pulp writers to be less inhibited in dealing with horrific imagery—not in terms of extremes of violence and repulsiveness, which were contained by relatively rigid standards of decency (the weird menace pulps could only *pretend* to be pornographic), but in terms of sheer bizarrerie. Just as the pulp science fiction writers quickly turned the universe into a gigantic stage for exotic costume dramas, so the pulp horror writers began to draw upon a vocabulary of ideas which accommodated the vastness of space and the more distant reaches of past time. The cosmic horror story thus overlapped both the SF genre and the subgenres of American fantasy which grew alongside it in *Weird Tales* and *Unknown*. Modern horror fiction and modern horror films owe a considerable debt to the work done by the pulp writers in consequence of this ideative boldness.

The bibliography which follows attempts to show the breadth of work done in the period, as well as to provide more detailed comments on the most significant writers. The above discussion explains why questions of definition become more vexing in relation to the work of this period than the work of the last, and there are significant elements of horror in some of the work covered in the companion volume on fantasy literature—the sword-and-sorcery stories written by Robert E. Howard [F3-181–3-182], C. L. Moore [F3-252] and Fritz Leiber

[F3-211] have a good deal of horrific imagery in them, and only a matter of degree separates them from the works of Clark Ashton Smith covered here [3-182].

As in the last chapter I have included here some ghost stories which are by no means wholeheartedly horrific, because of their obvious and close kinship with ones that are, though purely comic ghost stories have been allocated to the fantasy genre. Some stories which speculate clinically about the psychology and metaphysics of apparitions have been included because of their relevance to the discussions of the anatomy of horror which have been carried out in these introductory essays. Although the principal aim of the bibliography is to display the varieties of supernatural horror fiction, I have included representative examples of *contes cruels, grand guignol* fiction and rationalized exercises in grotesquerie, but I have not strayed very far into the borderlands where the more suspenseful kinds of crime fiction (usually featuring psychotic killers) overlap the horror genre.

Readers wishing to do further research will find the most useful tool by far to be Bleiler's *Guide to Supernatural Fiction* [6-19], which is especially useful in giving detailed accounts of the contents of hundreds of collections and anthologies from the period. There are good essays on many of the leading writers in the two-volume collection of essays on *Supernatural Fiction Writers* [6-20] which Bleiler edited. *The Penguin Encyclopedia of Horror and the Supernatural* [6-31] is at its best in covering this period, but remains a little patchy. More academically inclined histories like Penzoldt's [7-9], Punter's [7-10] and Briggs's [7-3] tend to be highly selective in their coverage, but offer worthwhile commentaries on the more respectable writers. Lin Carter's *Lovecraft: A Look behind the "Cthulhu Mythos"* (see [8-71]) has a good deal of interesting material about the *Weird Tales* school.

Bibliography

Alan, A. J. (pseud. of **Leslie H. Lambert**) (U.K.), 1883–1940.
About: GSF

3-1. Good Evening, Everyone! Hutchinson, 1928.
Collection of stories and anecdotes broadcast in the early days of the BBC, including several weird tales. The transfer to print is uncomfortable, the trick endings being designed to suit the art of the raconteur. *A. J. Alan's Second Book* (1933) offers more of the same. This tradition in British broadcasting was carried forward by others; Cynthia Asquith's anthology *My Grimmest Nightmare* [3-6] features tales by various hands, and SF writer John Gloag was another to write weird stories for broadcasting, some of which can be found in *First One and Twenty* (1946).

Andreyev, Leonid (Russia), 1871–1919.
About: WW, CA

3-2. Lazarus by Leonid Andreyev; The Gentleman from San Francisco by Ivan Bunin. Stratford, 1918. Tr. by Abraham Yarmolinsky.
Andreyev's story (1906) is a uniquely harrowing postscript to the gospels, in

which the reanimated corpse of Lazarus is sent to Rome, presenting such a dreadful appearance that all who meet him are blighted by the experience.

Arlen, Michael (formerly **Dikran Kouyoumidjian**) (Armenia), 1895–1956.

ABOUT: WW, GSF, CA, SMFL, SFE, PE, ESF

3-3. Ghost Stories. Collins, 1927.
Collection of seven stories mostly abstracted from the earlier collections *These Charming People* (1923) and *May Fair* (1925). The anecdotal stories are ironic recapitulations of familiar themes. Arlen's muddled satirical romance *Hell! Said the Duchess* (1934), a futuristic detective story about the hunt for "Jane the Ripper," parodies some horror story themes along with other aspects of popular fiction.

Ascher, Eugene (pseud. of **Harold Kelly**) (U.K.), 1900–1969.

ABOUT: ESF

3-4. There Were No Asper Ladies. Mitre Press, 1944.
Sensational thriller featuring occult detective Lucian Carolus, who also appears in the novella *The Grim Caretaker* (ca. 1946) and the collection *Uncanny Adventures* (ca. 1946). The series runs the gamut of traditional motifs: vampirism in the novel; demonic possession in the novella; a werewolf and a Black Mass in the collection. Among the better examples of cheap commercial fiction from the days when acute paper shortages led to a minor paperback boom in the U.K.

Asquith, Lady Cynthia (U.K.), 1887–1960.

ABOUT: WW, GSF, CA, PE, ESF

3-5. This Mortal Coil. Arkham House, 1947. U.K. title: *What Dreams May Come*.
Collection of stories, most of which first appeared in the author's fine series of ghost stories anthologies. Most notable are "God Grante That She Lye Stille" (1931), in which a woman is possessed by the spirit of a long-dead witch, and "The Playfellow," about a ghostly, invisible playmate.

As editor:

3-6. The Ghost Book. Hutchinson, 1926.
First of a notable series of anthologies, followed by *The Black Cap* (1927), *Shudders* (1929) and *When Churchyards Yawn* (1931). She later edited three more: *My Grimmest Nightmare* (1935; see [3-1]), *The Second Ghost Book* (1952) and *The Third Ghost Book* (1955). The stories featured are mostly original, by highly reputable British writers. Several of L. P. Hartley's weird tales [3-80] were written for these collections; Hugh Walpole [3-201] and Algernon Blackwood [3-26] were also regulars.

Atherton, Gertrude, 1857–1948.
ABOUT: WW, GSF, SFW, CA, SFE, PE, ESF

3-7. The Bell in the Fog and Other Stories. Harper, 1905.
Collection including four weird tales. In "The Striding Place" (1896) and "The Dead and the Countess" the living receive ambiguous signals from the dead; the title story, like the timeslip story "The Eternal Now" in *The Foghorn* (1934), supernaturalizes fascination with the past.

Atkins, John (U.K.), 1916– .
ABOUT: CA, SFE, TCSF, ESF

3-8. The Diary of William Carpenter. Resurgam, 1943.
Novelette about a man apparently driven to kill his wife by his experiences in a haunted house—but it becomes unclear which of them was actually driven to murder, and why. The introduction claims that the story takes its inspiration from Pirandello.

Bagot, Richard (U.K.).

3-9. A Roman Mystery. London: Digby Long, 1899.
Gothic novel in the manner of Mrs. Radcliffe [1-83], one of whose mysteries involves a case of lycanthrophy (here represented as a mental illness). The suspense is dulled by elaborate consideration of esoteric issues in ecclesiastical politics.

Baker, A(rthur) P(onsford) (U.K.).

3-10. A College Mystery. Heffer, 1918.
Novella in the form of a series of documents purporting to tell the story behind an apparition seen in Christ Church, Cambridge. A sideline from the tradition of such writers as M. R. James [3-108], A. C. Benson [3-14] and Arthur Gray [3-74]—a moral fantasy which makes its point very neatly.

Beale, Charles Willing, 1845–1932.
ABOUT: GSF, SFE

3-11. The Ghost of Guir House. Cincinnati: Editor Publishing Co., 1897.
The hero is mysteriously summoned to the eponymous dwelling, inhabited by a beautiful woman and her grandfather; after falling in love with her he discovers that she is a phantom, and they must decide whether he is to become part of her world, as she cannot be part of his. An unusually subdued and eccentrically embellished *femme fatale* story.

Bennett, Arnold (U.K.), 1867–1931.
ABOUT: GSF, CA, PE

3-12. The Ghost. Chatto & Windus, 1907.
A doctor falls in love with an opera star whose admirers are dogged by ill-fortune,

visited upon them by a jealous ghost. Sensational hackwork of which the author was not at all proud.

[For other works of this author, see the companion guide to fantasy.]

Benson, A(rthur) C(hristopher), 1862–1925.
ABOUT: WW, GSF, SFE, PE, ESF

3-13. Basil Netherby. Hutchinson, 1926.
Two novellas featuring haunted houses. The title story describes, obliquely, the composer Netherby's possession by an evil influence which perverts his art and life; "The Uttermost Farthing" is an account of attempts made by the ghost of an unlikable man to destroy the records of the occult experiments to which he was driven by bitterness. The style and tone are somewhat reminiscent of Robert Hichens [3-87].

3-14. The Hill of Trouble and Other Stories. Isbister, 1903.
Collection of academic ghost stories and classical fantasies; the most notable are "The Grey Cat," in which a demonic cat attaches itself to a boy and is driven away with difficulty; and "The Closed Window," about a window which looks out into a sinister parallel world; all are reprinted, with others, in *Paul the Minstrel and Other Stories* (1911).

Benson, E(dward), F(rederic) (U.K.), 1867–1940.
ABOUT: WW, GSF, SWF, CA, SMFL, SFE, PE, ESF

3-15. The Image in the Sand. Heinemann, 1905.
An occultist discovers an amulet which restrains an evil spirit; he releases it, but his attempts to control it go awry and it possesses his daughter, who then becomes an instrument in the researches of another occultist. An overelaborate exercise very much in the manner of Mrs. Praed [2-78–2-79; 3-158].

3-16. Raven's Brood. Barker, 1934.
Historical novel set in the 1870s, in which the travails of a farming family are complicated by supernatural intrusions. An interesting experiment, unlike the author's other works; the folkloristic supernatural elements are taken for granted and incidental, while the horrific and suspenseful elements of the story stem from human sources. It represents the culmination of a fascination with the idea of evil and misfortune whose development can be tracked in the novels *The Luck of the Vails* (1901), *Colin* (2 vols., 1923 and 1925) and *The Inheritor* (1930).

***3-17. The Room in the Tower and Other Stories**. Mills & Boon, 1912.
Collection of weird stories. In the title story the protagonist visits a house in his nightmares, and ultimately meets a nasty fate when he goes there in the flesh; "Caterpillars" describes a horrific vision and its symbolic meaning; "The Man Who Went Too Far" (a short version of *The Angel of Pain*, 1905) is an occult romance about a man seeking the ultimate experience. These shockers contrast strongly with the moralistic stories written by his brothers ([3-13–3-14] and [3-18]). The later collections *Visible and Invisible* (1923), *Spook Stories* (1928) and *More Spook Stories* (1934) are in the same tradition; the first includes another

invertebrate monster story, "Negotiam Perambulans . . . ," and the vampire story "Mrs. Amworth"; the second has the enigmatic "Bagnell Terrace" and yet another invertebrate monster in "And No Bird Sings"; the third has "James Lamp," in which a dead wife returns to bring her murderer to book, and "The Sanctuary," which features a haunted chapel. *The Flint Knife* (Equation, 1988), edited by Jack Adrian, recovers twelve previously unreprinted stories from periodicals and three from the collection *The Countess of Lowndes Square* (1920).

Benson, Robert Hugh (U.K.), 1871–1914.
ABOUT: WW, GSF, SFE, PE, ESF

3-18. A Mirror of Shalott. Pitman, 1907.
Collection of weird tales ostensibly related to one another by a group of Roman Catholic priests; improves considerably on the earlier collection *The Light Invisible* (1903) which similarly uses genre materials in the service of religious apologetics.

3-19. The Necromancers. Hutchinson, 1909.
The hero, grieving for his dead beloved, is seduced by Spiritualism, becoming a medium; by so doing he makes himself vulnerable to evil. A novel calculated to expose the supposed dangers of dabbling with heretical demonolatry, which only just fails to muster the same hysterial fervor as the author's apocalyptic romance *Lord of the World* (1907).

Bernanos, Georges (France), 1888–1948.
ABOUT: CA, ESF

3-20. The Star of Satan. John Lane, 1927. Tr. by H. L. Binsse of *Sous le soleil de Satan*, 1926.
Philosophical novel in which a priest throws himself all too enthusiastically into a battle with the Evil One, his preoccupation placing his own soul in jeopardy. Intended to demonstrate how easily and how unconsciously men surrender to the temptations of Satan. Also known as *Under the Sun of Satan*. Contrast the anxieties of the English Catholics R. H. Benson [3-19] and G. K. Chesterton [F3-79].

Bill, Alfred H(oyt), 1879–1964.
ABOUT: GSF, CA

3-21. The Wolf in the Garden. Longmans Green, 1931.
Historical novel in which the self-styled Comte de Saint Loup, having fled revolutionary France, settles in a small American town, which is soon being terrorized by a werewolf. Who can it possibly be?

Birkin, Charles (U.K.), 1907–1986.
ABOUT: WW, GSF, CA, SFFL, PE, ESF

3-22. Devil's Spawn. Philip Allan, 1936.
Collection of sixteen stories deploying familiar motifs, mostly reprinted from the

Creeps series anthologies [3-23], where they appeared under the pseudonym Charles Lloyd.

As editor:

3-23. Creeps. Philip Allan, 1932.
The first of a series of anonymously issued anthologies, which continued with *Shivers* (1932), *Shudders* (1932), *Horrors* (1933), *Nightmares* (1933), *Quakes* (1933), *Terrors* (1933), *Monsters* (1934), *Panics* (1934), *Powers of Darkness* (1934), *Thrills* (1935), *Tales of Fear* (1935), *Tales of Dread* (1936) and *Tales of Death* (1936); the first three were reissued as *The Creeps Omnibus* (1935). Single-author collections also affiliated to the series were *The Strange Papers of Dr. Blayre* [3-28], L. A. Lewis's *Tales of the Grotesque* [3-130], Vivian Meik's *Veils of Fear* (1934) and Achmed Abdullah's *Mysteries of Asia* (1935). The earlier volumes are all reprint and feature several fine stories by H. Russell Wakefield [3-200] and Tod Robbins [3-166]; the later ones are mostly original stories by minor writers, with the emphasis on shock value; Birkin's own contributions are credited to "Charles Lloyd" (see [3-22]).

Bishop, Zealia Brown.

ABOUT: GSF, ESF

3-24. The Curse of Yig. Arkham House, 1953.
Three stories from *Weird Tales,* all revised by H. P. Lovecraft from Bishop's first drafts. The title story (1929) features an Amerindian snake god; "Medusa's Coil" (1939) is a more conventional tale of a witch's remarkable hair; *The Mound* (1940) is a fine novella in which investigators of a haunting discover a manuscript describing a strange underworld. All three are reprinted in Lovecraft's *The Horror in the Museum and Other Revisions* (1970).

Biss, Gerald (U.K.).

ABOUT: WW, GSF, PE

3-25. The Door of the Unreal. Eveleigh Nash, 1919.
Mystery story in which disappearances following automobile accidents are traced to the activities of the sinister Dr. Wolff, who turns out, unsurprisingly, to be a werewolf. Better than [3-21] but not as good as [3-122] or [3-137].

Blackwood, Algernon (U.K.), 1869–1951.

ABOUT: WW, GSF, SFW, CA, H, SMFL, RG, PE, ESF, FL, HF

***3-26. The Empty House and Other Ghost Stories**. Eveleigh Nash, 1906.
The first collection by one of the great English writers of supernatural fiction. These early works are relatively conventional, and include "Keeping His Promise," in which the sound of breathing remains when a ghost periodically fades from sight, and "Smith: An Episode in a Lodging House," about the aftereffects of experiments in necromancy. It was quickly followed by the much stronger collection *The Listener and Other Stories* (1907), whose title story features a particularly scary phantom. There is also "The Willows," in which the narrator is marooned on a small island in the Danube where hostile entities impinge upon

the processes of nature; this was to set a pattern for many subsequent stories, several of them novellas, in which characters who have affinities with nature encounter natural substances imbued with or disturbed by strange elementals—examples include "The Man Whom the Trees Loved," "Sand" and "The Temptation of the Clay" in *Pan's Garden: A Volume of Nature Stories* (1912); and "The Regeneration of Lord Ernie" and "A Descent into Egypt" in *Incredible Adventures* (1914). These stories often combine a sense of threat and a sense of nostalgia in a fashion which was unique to Blackwood, where anxiety and consolation are often paradoxically interwoven. Another example of this curious alchemy can be seen in the title novella of *The Lost Valley and Other Stories* (1910), which also contains some fine pure horror stories, most notably the classic monster story "The Wendigo," and the curious paranoid fantasy "The Terror of the Twins." *Day and Night Stories* (1917) is the best of Blackwood's other collections. *Ten Minute Stories* (1914), *The Wolves of God and Other Fey Tales* (1921; with Wilfrid Wilson), *Tongues of Fire and Other Sketches* (1924) and *Shocks* (1935) are less successful. The best stories are recombined in a number of omnibus volumes, including *Strange Stories* (1929), *Tales of Algernon Blackwood* (1939), and the complementary pair *Tales of the Uncanny and Supernatural* (1949) and *Tales of the Mysterious and Macabre* (1967). *The Magic Mirror: Lost Tales and Mysteries by Algernon Blackwood*, edited by Michael Ashley (Equation, 1989), recovers some previously uncollected material.

***3-27. John Silence**. Eveleigh Nash, 1908.
Archetypal collection of five case studies featuring the eponymous occult detective. "A Psychical Invasion" is about the persecution of an author by a malign ghost; "Ancient Sorceries" is about an exotic witch-cult surviving in rural France; "The Nemesis of Fire" is an elemental associated with a mummy; "Secret Worship" involves Satanism in the Black Forest; "The Camp of the Dog" is a fine werewolf story. Silence also features in the metaphysical fantasy "A Victim of Higher Space" in *Day and Night Stories* (1917).

[For other works of this author, see the companion guide to fantasy.]

Blayre, Christopher (pseud. of **Edward Heron-Allen**) (U.K.), 1861–1943.
About: WW, GSF, CA, SMFL, SFE, TCSF, PE, ESF

3-28. The Purple Sapphire and Other Posthumous Papers. Philip Allan, 1921.
Collection of stories supposedly "selected from the unofficial records of the University of Cosmopoli" by its "sometime registrar"—the mock introduction is dated 1952. Nine stories are listed on the contents page but only eight appear, "The Cheetah-Girl" having been suppressed for alleged obscenity (a few copies were printed by the author for private circulation). The stories (not all supernatural) are satirical, mocking the gentility and earnestness of the academic school of supernatural writing developed by M. R. James [3-108]. Four new stories are added to the reprint issued in the *Creeps* series as *The Strange Papers of Dr. Blayre* (1932); four more were privately printed as *Some Women of the University* (1934), including two of the best ones: the vampire story "Zum Wildbad" and a sardonic tale of botanical discovery, "Passiflora vindicta *Wrammsbothame*." The ironic wit is not to everyone's taste, but these are among the best satirical weird tales.

Bloch, Robert, 1917– .
ABOUT: WW, GSF, SFW, CA, NE, H, SMFL, SFE, SFFL, RG, TCSF, PE, ESF, FF

3-29. The Opener of the Way. Arkham House, 1945.
Collection featuring the best of Bloch's weird fiction of the 1930s and early 1940s. It includes several Cthulhu Mythos stories (see [3-132]), including "The Shambler from the Stars" (1935), in which Lovecraft appears as a character, and several works in a similar vein drawing upon Egyptian mythology; the directions later to be taken by Bloch's work are foreshadowed in the classic "Yours Truly, Jack the Ripper" (1943) and the ironic tale of "The Cloak" (1939). Two of the stories had previously appeared, along with two others, in an odd booklet published in Britain, *Sea-Kissed* (1945). Eleven more early Bloch stories can be found, along with works from the early 1950s, in *Final Reckonings*, the first volume of the three-decker *Selected Stories of Robert Bloch* (1988) [4-47].

[For other works of this author, see the companion guide to fantasy.]

Boothby, Guy (Australia), 1867–1905.
ABOUT: WW, GSF, PE, ESF

3-30. The Curse of the Snake. F. V. White, 1902.
Weird mystery. The protagonist's love affair is blighted by the inconsistent malevolence of his friend, who has an enigmatic relationship with a sinister snake; the protagonist eventually inherits the snake and the relationship. The tired ending leaves much unexplained (as was Boothby's habit) and fails dismally to live up to the promise of the creepy opening, but this remains the most effective of his thrillers.

Bowen, Elizabeth (Ireland), 1899–1973
ABOUT: WW, GSF, SFW, CA, H, SMFL, PE, ESF

3-31. The Collected Short Stories of Elizabeth Bowen. Cape, 1980.
Omnibus which includes among many other stories a few idiosyncratic ghost stories and psychological tales of unease; most come from the collections *The Cat Jumps and Other Stories* (1934) and *The Demon Lover and Other Stories* (1945; U.S. title: *Ivy Gripped the Stairs*). Those stories which (like the title stories of the two collections) are tales of unease are highly ambiguous; in other stories, such as "The Storm" and "The Back Drawing Room," the ghosts are incidental, peripheral to the real point of the story. The timeslip story "The Happy Autumn Fields" is notable, but the author usually deploys fantastic intrusions merely as a device to heighten the mood of her delicate but slightly anemic stories.

Bowen, Marjorie (pseud. of **Gabrielle Long**) (U.K.), 1886–1952.
ABOUT: WW, GSF, F, CA, H, PE, ESF

***3-32. Black Magic**. Alston Rivers, 1909.
Historical melodrama subtitled "A Tale of the Rise and Fall of Antichrist," which perverts the legend of Pope Joan to tell the story of a female sorceress who

masquerades as a man and becomes pope, narrowly failing to bring down the Holy Roman Empire. It is very rare to find a female character aspiring to the role of magus rather than witch, and it is significant that the pronoun "he" is used throughout although the reader discovers early on that the protagonist is female, helping to make the novel a unique and fascinating commentary on sexist aspects of religious mythology and Christian superstition.

***3-33. The Last Bouquet: Some Twilight Tales.** John Lane, 1933.
Collection of weird tales including the very nasty "Kecksies," in which the Devil reanimates a corpse in order to commit rape, and the curious historical fantasy "Florence Flannery"; the title story and "The Crown Derby Plate" involve repressed spinsters with enigmatic hauntings. Follows two earlier collections, *Curious Happenings* (1917) and *Dark Ann and Other Stories* (1927); the title story of the latter is a sentimental ghost story; "The Accident," a neat posthumous fantasy, is also notable. Eclectic selections from Bowen's later work can be found in two overlapping reprint collections: *The Bishop of Hell and Other Stories* (John Lane, 1949) and *Kecksies and Other Twilight Tales* (Arkham House, 1976). Mrs. Long's perennial fascination with the psychology of haunting is expressed in the work published under this name by uncompromising physical manifestations; the results seem a little crude by comparison with the "Joseph Shearing" story *The Fetch* [3-176], but in the best stories the combination is very effective. She also compiled two fine anthologies as Bowen, reflecting her wide-ranging researches in the genre and including some of her own translations from French and German: *Great Tales of Horror* and *More Great Tales of Horror* (both 1935).

[For other works of this author, see the companion guide to fantasy.]

Bradbury, Ray, 1920–.

ABOUT: WW, GSF, SFW, F, CA, TCA, NE, H, SMFL, SFE, MF, SFFL, RG, TCSF, PE, ESF, HF

***3-34. Dark Carnival.** Arkham House, 1947.
Collection of twenty-seven stories (the U.K. edition has only twenty), mostly supernatural but with a few *contes cruels,* including the consummately repulsive taphephobic fantasy "Interim." Children feature sentimentally in many of the stories, including "Homecoming" and "The Traveller," which feature an Addamsesque family, but coziness always threatens to metamorphose into abomination, as in "The Emissary" or "The Man Upstairs." The necrophiliac aspects of "The Handler" and "The Dead Man" give them a polished sharpness. The collection stands at the head of a tradition in modern American horror fiction which combined stylistic deftness with a determination to deal forthrightly with the previously unthinkable—a tradition boldly carried forward by writers like Charles Beaumont [4-27] and Fritz Leiber [4-200]. Eleven of the stories were reprinted in *The October Country* (1955), and new material was added.

Briussof, Valeri (Russia), 1873–1924.
ABOUT: WW, GSF, CA, TCSF, PE, ESF

***3-35. The Fiery Angel**. Toulmin, 1930. Tr. by Ivor Montagu and Sergei Nalbandov of *Ognenny Angel,* 1907.
Historical fantasy whose hero is seduced by a witch, attends a Sabbat and becomes a student of black magic in spite of the nagging of his conscience. He meets Cornelius Agrippa and Doctor Faustus in the course of his adventures. A classic of its kind, elaborately developing the mythology of Satanism after the fashion of Huysmans's *Là-Bas* (1891); compare also Bowen's *Black Magic* [3-32] and Meinhold's *Sidonia the Sorceress* [2-64]. Anyone attempting to follow up the above-cited references should note that other transliterations of the author's name render it as Brussof or Bryusov.

Brodie-Innes, J(ohn) W(illiam) (U.K.), 1848–1923.
ABOUT: GSF, PE

3-36. The Devil's Mistress. Rider, 1915.
Novel based on the extraordinary confessions offered by the Scottish "witch" Isabel Gowdie (or Goudie)—one of the few educated women caught up by the witch-panic, whose fantasies of induction into the satanic cult (inspired by literary as well as folkloristic sources) became the main inspiration of Margaret Murray's scholarly fantasy representing witches as followers of a secretly preserved pagan religion. The original material offers far more to the novelist than the case of the Lancashire witches (see [2-2]) or that of Elinor Shaw (see [2-99]), and the credulous occultist Brodie-Innes, who had earlier written a similar historical romance, *For the Love of a Witch* (1910), takes up the task with evident relish and (despite his credulity) a good deal of sympathy for poor Isabel.

[For other works of this author, see the companion guide to fantasy.]

Broster, D(orothy) K(athleen) (U.K.), 1877–1950.
ABOUT: WW, GSF, SFE, PE, ESF

3-37. Couching at the Door. Heinemann, 1942.
Collection of five stories, including the often-reprinted title story, whose excellence is not given proper credit by summations which declare off-handedly that it is about a man haunted by a feather boa. "The Pestering" is a similar account of persecution by an enigmatic haunter; and "Juggernaut" features a guilty party hounded by a supernaturally enhanced chair. Effective and unusual tales.

Buchan, John (later **Baron Tweedsmuir**) (U.K.), 1875–1940.
ABOUT: WW, GSF, F, CA, SMFL, PE, ESF, FL

3-38. The Watcher by the Threshold and Other Tales. Blackwood, 1902.
Collection of weird tales. The title story is a curious account of neuralgia caused by demonic possession; "The Outgoing of the Tide" and "The Rime of True Thomas" are tales based in Scottish folklore. There are more fantasies in *The*

Moon Endureth (1912), including the metaphysical fantasy "Space" and a slightly sentimental story of antiquarian haunting, "The Grove of Ashtoroth." Many of the tales told by members of *The Runagates Club* (1928) are also weird, including Richard Hannay's account of "The Green Wildebeest." Buchan's work in this vein is marked by his anthropological interests in a way which prevents its being wholeheartedly horrific, but which lends it a persuasive authority.

3-39. Witch Wood. Hodder & Stoughton, 1927.
Historical novel about a witch coven in Scotland, with no actual supernatural intrusions. Interesting because of the author's attempt to explain the supposed activity of would-be witches as a response to certain religious doctrines. *The Dancing Floor* (1926) pursues similar metaphysical and anthropological issues in a Greek setting, but has not the same narrative strength.

[For other works of this author, see the companion guide to fantasy.]

Bullett, Gerald (U.K.), 1893–1958.
About: WW, GSF, PE, ESF

3-40. The Street of the Eye and Nine Other Tales. John Lane, 1923.
Collection including two horror stories. In the title story a young man becomes convinced that an immanent God is trying to compel him to do evil; in "Dearth's Farm" the hero's spirit takes possession of a horse in order to attempt murder. *The Baker's Cart and Other Tales* (1925) includes the macabre "Last Days of Binnacle," in which the ghost of a man cut in two by a sliding door unwittingly goes on his way with his severed legs; "Queer's Rival," a similar posthumous fantasy; and "The Dark House," a remarkable surreal grotesque. *Helen's Lovers* (1932) includes a curiously disturbing tale of an overexplained poltergeist, "Three Men at Thark" and a ghostly *conte cruel*, "The Elder." *Twenty Four Tales* (1938) has one new ghost story, "Dr. Jannock's Chair." Bullett's weird fiction is original and effective and would certainly warrant collection.

[For other works of this author, see the companion guide to fantasy.]

Burke, Thomas (U.K.), 1886–1945.
About: WW, GSF, CA, ESF

3-41. Night Pieces. Constable, 1935.
Collection of weird tales including "Miracle in Surburbia," which gruesomely explains what happens when a protective spell wears off; the excellent zombie story "The Hollow Man"; and "The Black Courtyard," about a criminal's odd obsession with the scene of his crime. The psychology of murder seems to have fascinated Burke, who invented an odd metaphysical explanation for it in his most famous (and best) story, *The Bloomsbury Wonder* (pamphlet 1929; reprinted in *Dark Nights*, 1944).

Burks, Arthur J., 1898–1974.
About: WW, GSF, SFE, ESF

3-42. Black Medicine. Arkham House, 1966.
Collection of Burks's work culled from the pulp magazines of the 1920s and 1930s (to which he was a prolific contributor in several genres). His supernatural stories are routine shockers, sometimes slightly enlivened (as in "Black Medicine" and "Guatemozin the Visitant") by a modicum of historical research.

Burrage, A(lfred) M(cClelland) (U.K.), 1889–1956.
About: WW, GSF, PE, ESF

3-43. Some Ghost Stories. Cecil Palmer, 1927.
Collection of twelve stories set solidly in the British tradition, sometimes more sentimental than horrific. The most notable are "The Green Scarf" and the timeslip story "Between the Minute and the Hour"; his second collection, *Someone in the Room* (1931), was issued under the pseudonym "Ex-Private X"; it includes "Smee," an eerie tale about a children's game, and the nasty visionary fantasy "One Who Saw." All four stories named, plus other reprints and five new stories, are in *Between the Minute and the Hour* (1967). Seventeen more previously unreprinted stories are in *Warning Whispers* (Equation, 1988), edited by Jack Adrian. Burrage's underrated short stories are deft and subtle, and include a number of poignant posthumous fantasies. His longer stories, *Seeker to the Dead* (1942) and the rationalized *Don't Break the Seal* (1946), are experiments in melodrama which do not make good use of his abilities.

Busson, Paul (Germany), 1873–1924.
About: GSF

***3-44. The Man Who Was Born Again**. Heinemann, 1927, Tr. by Prince Mirski and Thomas Moult of *Die Wiedergeburt des Melchior Dronte,* 1921.
The main narrative, ostensibly consisting of memories recovered from a previous incarnation, describes the career of an eighteenth-century Austrian nobleman who often falls victim to the forces of evil despite the guardianship of an enigmatic dervish. A very striking phantasmagoric tale with a good deal of memorable imagery; a key work of German expressionist fantasy. The 1927 translation is bowdlerized; the missing passages are restored by E. F. Bleiler in the Dover edition of 1976, which also includes Meyrink's *Golem* [3-148]. *The Fire Spirits* (1923; tr. 1929) is a similar allegorical fantasy of history, more modest in its fantastic embellishments.

Capes, Bernard (U.K.), 1870?–1918.
About: GSF, PE, ESF

3-45. At a Winter's Fire. London: Pearson, 1899.
Collection including several weird tales. "Dark Dignum" is a story of supernatural revenge; "The Black Reaper" is a curious allegory of death. Capes's later

collections *Plots* (1902), *Loaves and Fishes* (1906), *Bag and Baggage* (1913) and *The Fabulists* (1915) each contain a handful of supernatural tales. They include some unusual motifs, including a macabre ghostly rugby match in "The Ghost-Leech" (in *Loaves and Fishes*). An excellent sampler is *The Black Reaper* (Equation, 1989), edited by Hugh Lamb.

Carr, John Dickson (U.K.), 1905–1977.

ABOUT: GSF, F, CA, SMFL, SFE, ESF

3-46. The Burning Court. Hamish Hamilton, 1937.
Murder mystery in which much ingenuity is required to produce an explanation of apparently supernatural events echoing incidents in the days of the great witch-hunt. The dubious propriety of the double switch ending makes it an intriguing literary curiosity.

Casserly, Gordon (U.K.).

3-47. Tiger Girl. Philip Allan, 1934.
Thriller set in India in which devil-worshipping gypsies employ a powerful magician and a vampiric weretiger to further their nefarious ends. Less fantastic works in the same vein, drawing upon Casserly's experiences soldiering in India, are *The Elephant God* (1920) and *The Monkey God* (1933).

Cave, Hugh B., 1910– .

ABOUT: WW, GSF, CA, H

3-48. Murgunstrumm and Others. Carcosa, 1977.
Large collection of stories from various pulp magazines, including the "weird menace" pulps (see [3-106]) as well as *Weird Tales*. Cave's most famous story is the vampire tale "Stragella" (1932); vampires also feature in the extravagant title novella and in "The Brotherhood of Blood" (1932). A couple of the stories are tenuously linked to the Cthulhu Mythos. Occasionally striking imagery is all too frequently let down by mechanical plotting.

Christie, Agatha (U.K.), 1890–1976.

ABOUT: WW, GSF, CA, PE, ESF

3-49. The Hound of Death and Other Stories. Odhams, 1933.
Collection including several weird tales. The title story features a destructive spirit controlled by a psychic nun; several of the other stories exhibit a theoretical (but not entirely credulous) interest in spiritualism. None of the supernatural stories can compare with the classic crime story "Witness for the Prosecution."

Cline, Leonard, 1893–1927.

ABOUT: PE

3-50. The Dark Chamber. Viking, 1927.
The protagonist's experiments in memory stimulation ultimately open up the

store of ancestral memory, resulting in a gradual regression and devolution to proto-human consciousness. An intriguing story, prefiguring Paddy Chayevsky's *Altered States* (1978); highly praised by H. P. Lovecraft.

Conrad, Joseph (**Jozef Korzeniowski**) (Poland/U.K.), 1857-1924.
About: CA, H, SFE, PE

***3-51. Heart of Darkness**. Blackwood, 1902.
The protagonist travels up the Congo River in search of the mysterious Kurtz, who has absorbed (and been absorbed by) the dark heart of Africa, penetrating the veil of illusion which is civilization to confront the true desolation of the existential predicament. The allegory can be decoded in purely political terms, but really goes much deeper. Several of Conrad's shorter stories involve metaphorical hauntings, the most effective being gathered together in the aptly titled *Tales of Unrest* (1898), which includes the fine novella "Karain," and the grim "The Idiots."

Counselman, Mary Elizabeth, 1911- .
About: WW, GSF, CA, PE, ESF

3-52. Half in Shadow. Consul, 1964. The U.S. ed. (Arkham House, 1978) has somewhat different contents.
Collection of stories by a *Weird Tales* regular. Both versions include the notable story of misdirected fate, "The Three Marked Pennies" (1934), and the pseudo-folkloristic items of regional Americana, "The Tree's Wife" (1950) and "The Unwanted" (1951). Her stories are subtle, and usually sentimental in tone, though "Parasite Mansion" (1942; U.S. ed. only) is more frankly horrific.

Cowles, Frederick I(gnatius) (U.K.), 1900-1948.
About: WW, PE, ESF

3-53. The Horror of Abbot's Grange. Muller, 1936.
The first of two collections of weird tales in the M. R. Jamesian antiquarian vein, though somewhat crude by comparison with the originals [3-108]. The title story features a vampire; other motifs include possession and the inevitable haunted houses. *The Night Wind Howls* (1938) is a more accomplished collection in the same vein. A third collection, *Fear Walks the Night*, was assembled by the author but remained unpublished; an Equation edition has been announced for 1989.

Crompton, Richmal (pseud. of **Richmal C. Lamburn**) (U.K.), 1890-1969.
About: WW, GSF, CA, ESF

3-54. The House. Hodder & Stoughton, 1926. U.S. title: *Dread Dwelling*.
Minds and relationships begin to disintegrate when a family moves into a Tudor mansion; residues of evil within its walls eventually take the blame. A routine example of supernatural scapegoatism.

Cross, John Keir (U.K.), 1914–1967.
ABOUT: WW, GSF, CA, SMFL, SFE, TCSF, ESF

3-55. The Other Passenger. Westhouse, 1944.
Collection of eighteen stories (the Ballantine reprint has only nine). Most of the stories are nonsupernatural *contes cruels*; the surreal color plates in the U.K. edition add interest to the quirky tales.

Crowley, Aleister (U.K.), 1875–1947.
ABOUT: WW, GSF, CA, SMFL, PE, ESF

3-56. The Stratagem and Other Stories. Mandrake Press, 1929.
Three short stories by the extravert occultist. "The Testament of Magdalen Blair," in which a psychic records the decay of her husband's mind under the influence of a degenerative disease, and then tracks its experiences in a cruel afterlife, is spectacularly nasty-minded; the other two are distinctly weak-kneed by comparison.

[For other works of this author, see the companion guide to fantasy.]

Dane, Clemence (pseud. of **Winifred Ashton**) (U.K.), 1888–1965.
ABOUT: GSF, CA, ESF

3-57. The Babyons. Heinemann, 1927.
Four-part family history; the supernatural plays little or no part in the second and third novellas, but the first is the fine *Third Person Singular,* in which a man is haunted by the spirit of the cousin he jilted; the curse is finally worked out in *Lady Babyon,* though the supernatural is here reduced to a token presence.

De la Mare, Walter (U.K.), 1873–1956.
ABOUT: WW, GSF, SFW, CA, SMFL, PE, ESF, FL, HF

***3-58. The Return.** Edward Arnold, 1910; rev., 1922.
The protagonist goes to sleep in a graveyard and takes on the appearance of an eighteenth-century suicide; rejected by his family and friends, he is forced to reconstruct his identity, uncertain whether he must become a psychological as well as a physical replica of the dead man. An unusual exercise in speculative existentialism.

***3-59. The Riddle and Other Stories.** Selwyn & Blount, 1923.
The first of De la Mare's collections of weird tales, including the enigmatic title story about disappearing children; the often-reprinted "Seaton's Aunt," about a malevolent old lady; and the fine "Out of the Deep," about a man haunted by harrowing forces echoing the suffering of a child. *On the Edge* (1930) has three excellent ghost stories: "A Recluse," "Crewe" and "The Green Room"; *The Wind Blows Over* (1936) has six more, including a curious invocation of Edgar Allan Poe in "A Revenant." De la Mare's supernatural stories are atmospheric explorations in psychoanalytical metaphysics which treat death and the possibility of afterlife as fascinating mysteries. They are unparalleled in their subtlety, yet

succeed nevertheless in being very creepy. There are several collections selecting from his work; the most notable are *The Best Stories of Walter De la Mare* (1942) and *Ghost Stories* (Folio Society, 1956). Some early and more formularistic supernatural stories were collected posthumously in *Eight Tales* (Arkham House, 1971). The supernatural plays a significant part in De la Mare's poetry, most memorably in the famous poem "The Listeners."

[For other works of this author, see the companion guide to fantasy.]

Dennis, Geoffrey (U.K.), 1892–1963.
About: GSF, ESF

3-60. Harvest in Poland. Heinemann, 1925.
Apparently credulous occult novel in which a young man, forewarned by ominous prophecies, embarks upon a journey across Europe on the eve of World War I, and encounters supernatural evil in Poland. Despite allegorical pretensions the manner of narration is unusually realistic; though the story is dense and overburdened with detail, its descriptions of supernatural menace and temptation are curiously effective.

Derleth, August (William), 1909–1971.
About: WW, GSF, SFW, CA, NE, H, SMFL, SFE, SFFL, RG, TCSF, PE, ESF

3-61. The Lurker at the Threshold. Arkham House, 1945 (based on a fragment by H. P. Lovecraft, bylined as a collaboration).
Cthulhu Mythos story in which an estate near Arkham is blighted by the attentions of Yog-Sothoth, channeled through a mysterious tower which must be destroyed in order to banish the forces of evil. A lackluster exercise in pastiche. Derleth's solo Cthulhu Mythos stories are assembled in the collection *The Mask of Cthulhu* (1958), in which repeated gestures of homage to their models obstruct the stories; and in the fix-up novel *The Trial of Cthulhu* (1962), which combines five longer stories, including Derleth's best two Mythos stories, "The Keeper of the Key" (1951) and "The Black Island" (1952).

3-62. Someone in the Dark. Arkham House, 1941.
Collection, mostly drawn from the pages of *Weird Tales*. Some stories are Lovecraftian, others draw on the same sources as Derleth's many exercises in regional Americana; the best story describes the haunting of "The Sheraton Mirror" (1932). The stories use conventional motifs, and seem to consist mainly of exercises in pastiche. The later collections *Something Near* (1945) and *Not Long for This World* (1948) are similarly routine.

Dinesen, Isak (pseud. of **Baroness Karen Blixen**) (Denmark), 1885–1962.
About: GSF, CA, SMFL, SFFL, PE, ESF

3-63. Seven Gothic Tales. Putnam, 1934.
Long stories in a distinctive and highly decorated antiquarian mode. "The Monkey" is the only one which really qualifies as a horror story, but the rest are

fine examples of mannered grotesquerie. More stories in the same vein can be found in *Winter's Tales* (1942).

Doyle, Arthur Conan (U.K.), 1859–1930.

ABOUT: WW, GSF, F, CA, NE, SMFL, SFE, TCSF, PE, ESF

3-64. The Maracot Deep. John Murray, 1929.
The title short novel is an odd hybrid; it begins as Verneian scientific romance but is diverted by a strong injection of credulous mysticism to a climax involving a confrontation with an evil godling in Atlantis. The author's narrative gusto fails to save it from being profoundly silly. Also included are two SF shockers featuring Professor Challenger. The omnibus *Conan Doyle Stories* (1929) includes better examples of Doyle's later experiments in horror, including the classic horror/SF story "The Horror of the Heights" (1913) and a stylish account of a ghostly pugilist, "The Bully of Brocas Court" (1921). *The Supernatural Tales of Sir Arthur Conan Doyle* (Foulshan, 1988), ed. by Peter Haining, collects 18 tales.

Eadie, Arlton (U.K.), died 1935.

ABOUT: WW

3-65. The Trail of the Cloven Hoof. Skeffington, 1935.
Novel set in Devon about the horrible depredations of a half-human monster, previously serialized in *Weird Tales* (1934–35). Eadie contributed numerous other stories to *Weird Tales*, the most notable being "The Wolf-Girl of Josselin" (1938), and contributed a few rationalized horror stories to the "Piccadilly Novels" series of U.K. paperbacks; *The Veiled Vampire* (ca. 1935) is partly based on a *Weird Tales* story.

Endore, Guy, 1900–1970.

ABOUT: WW, GSF, F, CA, H, SMFL, SFE, PE, ESF

3-66. Methinks the Lady. Duell Sloan Pierce, 1945. Also known as *The Furies in Her Body* and *Nightmare*.
Murder mystery and courtroom melodrama in which a lawyer refuses to offer an insanity plea on behalf of his wife, who seems to be a victim of split personality. A remarkable study of the logic of psychosis, involving a rigorous application of Freudian analysis which makes it superior to most exercises in its subgenre, which ranges from Ben Hecht's *The Florentine Dagger* (1923) to Robert Bloch's *Psycho* [4-46].

***3-67. The Werewolf of Paris**. Farrar & Rinehart, 1933.
Classic novel which takes its inspiration from a reported case of necrophilia and cannibalism at the time of the Paris Commune. Endore makes his unlucky lycanthrope a victim of vile ancestry and sad circumstance; he has a chance of redemption by virtue of the self-sacrifice of the lover who nourishes him with her own blood, but it is lost in the violent madness of the time, when he is but one (and far from the worst) of countless men who seem to have fallen prey to a savage and bloodthirsty spirit. A sarcastic and bitterly misanthropic allegory, by far the

most effective of all the novels in which the werewolf becomes a symbol of divided and conflict-ridden human nature.

Ewers, Hanns Heinz (Germany), 1871–1943.

ABOUT: WW, GSF, CA, SMFL, SFE, PE, ESF

***3-68. The Sorcerer's Apprentice.** John Day, 1927. Tr. by Ludwig Lewisohn of *Der Zauberlehrling,* 1907.
Frank Braun, a young German intellectual secluded in a remote Italian village, hypnotizes his local mistress into the belief that she is a saint; when she is accepted as such by her neighbors, the masquerade becomes all too real and her progress to martyrdom becomes inevitable. *Alraune* (1911; tr. 1929) describes how Braun in his student days had conducted a complementary experiment in collaboration with his uncle, producing a female incarnation of evil who is supernaturally seductive but utterly destructive. The mature Braun falls in love with this *femme fatale,* whose nature is symbolized by the mandrake legend, but manages to save himself from destruction. *Vampire* (1921; tr. 1934) reveals that he might not entirely have escaped corruption; it follows his exploits in the United States in the early years of World War I, trying to recruit American support for the German cause while slowly turning into a vampire—a fate observed by the lovers on whom his appetite is inflicted long before he becomes aware of it himself. The salaciously provocative and self-indulgent decadence of the earlier stories make them repulsive to some readers, and they lack the artistry of Hecht's *Fantazius Mallare* [F3-170], but they are undeniably powerful. Ewers wrote numerous *contes cruels,* including a gruesome account of "The Execution of Damiens"; three are collected in *Blood* (1929).

Fortune, Dion (pseud. of Violet M. Firth) (U.K.), 1890–1946.

ABOUT: WW, GSF, SFW, SMFL, PE, ESF

3-69. The Secrets of Dr. Taverner. Noel Douglas, 1926.
Collection of occult detective stories; although they draw on the author's researches and her experience as a life-style fantasist (in the Golden Dawn and imitative organizations founded by herself), they are more pointed and less ponderous than her novels, with a few effective horrific motifs to offset occasional silliness; the most notable are the vampire/possession story "Blood-Lust" and the tale of "The Soul Who Would Not Be Born."

[For other works of this author, see the companion guide to fantasy.]

Fraser, Mrs. Hugh (Mary Crawford), 1851–1924.

ABOUT: PE

3-70. The Satanist. Hutchinson, 1912 (written in collaboration with J. I. Stahlmann).
The daughter of an Italian aristocrat becomes the victim of a cult of Satanists; marriage cannot save her from being terrorized, but she eventually brings about the downfall of the devil worshippers. A political Gothic in the vein of Bagot's

Roman Mystery [3-9], with some recherché touches borrowed from Huysmans's *Là-Bas* [2-43].

Freeman, Mary E(leanor) Wilkins, 1852–1930.
ABOUT: WW, GSF, SFW, CA, PE, ESF

3-71. The Wind in the Rose-Bush and Other Stories of the Supernatural. Doubleday, 1903.
Supernatural Americana set in New England; the title story and "The Lost Ghost" are sentimental accounts of ghost-children, but more horrific revenants feature in the effective psychic vampire story "Luella Miller" and in "The Southwest Chamber." Neat stories, crisply told.

Gawsworth, John (pseud. of **T. I. Fytton Armstrong**), editor.

3-72. Strange Assembly. Unicorn, 1932.
The first of several notable anthologies in which Gawsworth mixed reprint material with original stories. This one features regulars M. P. Shiel [2-89; 3-177], Arthur Machen [2-58–2-59; 3-135] and Frederick Carter, plus Sir Ronald Ross's gruesome "The Vivisector Vivisected" [2-85]. Many of the stories were reprinted in *Thrills, Crimes and Mysteries* (1935), one of several huge crime/horror anthologies produced as giftbooks by newspaper publishers; others are *Thrills* (1936); *Crimes, Creeps and Thrills* (1936), which includes an original weird novel by E. H. Visiak [F3-352]; and *Masterpiece of Thrills* (1936). Also notable is *New Tales of Horror by Eminent Authors* (1934).

Graves, Robert (U.K.), 1895–1985.
ABOUT: GSF, CA, SMFL, MF, SFFL, ESF

3-73. The Shout. Mathews & Marot, 1929.
Classic short story first published in 1924, in which a mental patient explains to a cricket scorer how he acquired the ability to kill or drive men mad by shouting, and how the power served him ill. A complex web of contradictory delusions. Reprinted in Graves's *Collected Short Stories* (1965), which also includes an odd tale of voodoo in Majorca, "She Landed Yesterday," and a story-cum-essay about hauntings, "The Whitaker Negroes."

Gray, Arthur (U.K.), 1852–1940.
ABOUT: GSF, PE

3-74. Tedious Brief Tales of Granta and Gramarye. Heffer, 1919.
Collection of antiquarian weird tales set in various periods of history. Quirkier than M. R. James's works [3-108]; "The Everlasting Club" and "The Necromancer" are true horror stories, the latter featuring a spectral cat, but the rest—especially the eleventh-century boat race tale "The Palladium"—are more ironic, comparable to the satires of "Christopher Blayre" [3-28]. "The Burden of Dead Books" addresses the idea of metempsychosis from an original and intriguing angle.

Gregory, Franklin, born 1905.
ABOUT: GSF, ESF

3-75. The White Wolf. Random House, 1941.
A French-descended Pennsylvania perfumer realizes that in consequence of a family curse his daughter has sold her soul to the devil and become (unknowingly) a werewolf. A boy who loves her is entrapped into a similar metamorphosis, but might yet be saved if she can be destroyed. A mature approach to a traditional theme, which compares and contrasts interestingly with Williamson's exactly contemporary *Darker Than You Think* [3-214].

Gresham, William Lindsay, 1909–1962.

3-76. Nightmare Alley. Rinehart, 1946.
Grotesque thriller in which a carnival huckster tries to exploit the tricks of his trade in carving out a career as a high society occultist. Its deployment of carnival bizarrerie links it to *The Circus of Dr. Lao* [F3-317] and *Something Wicked This Way Comes* [4-51].

Halidom, M. Y. (unattributed pseud.) (U.K.).
ABOUT: WW, GSF, ESF

3-77. A Weird Transformation. Burleigh, 1904.
Novel apparently begun as a mundane story, presumably converted into a horror story to cash in on the success of earlier Halidom titles [F2-50]. The body of a young man is possessed by the spirit of a malevolent Boer, who fails to impersonate him convincingly enough to benefit from the situation. Followed by *The Woman in Black* (1906), a vampire novel; *Zoe's Revenge* (1908), in which a girl's ghost inhabits a doll which contains her skeleton; and *The Poet's Curse* (1911), in which misfortune follows the desecration of Shakespeare's grave.

Hansom, Mark (unattributed pseud.) (U.K.).
ABOUT: GSF

3-78. The Ghost of Gaston Revere. Wright & Brown, 1935.
One of a series of lurid supernatural thrillers issued by the publishers of the "Jack Mann" Gees series [3-137]. Revere's body becomes comatose after a failed operation, but his evil spirit is freed to persecute the surgeon and the hero's inamorata. Others in the same vein are: *The Shadow on the House* (1934), *The Wizard of Berner's Abbey* (1935), *Master of Souls* (1937), *The Beasts of Brahm* (1937) and *Sorcerer's Chessman* (1939).

Harding, Ronald S. L. (U.K.).

3-79. One Dreadful Night. Modern Publishing Co., 1935.
A lurid murder mystery whose solution hangs on the question of whether the hero's experiments in resurrecting the dead have succeeded. Harding's work is overmelodramatic, but has an appealing frenetic verve. He wrote at least nine

novels in this rough-hewn vein, the most spectacularly gruesome effects being displayed in *The Blue Light* (ca. 1947).

Hartley, L(eslie) P(oles) (U.K.), 1895-1972.
ABOUT: WW, GSF, SFW, CA, SFE, SFFL, TCSF, PE, ESF

3-80. Night Fears and Other Stories. Putnam, 1924.
First of several Hartley collections to feature weird tales, drawing upon the author's theory that fear is an important creative force on which a writer may draw. The title story features a faceless apparition, but many of the others leave the fear at a psychological level. Other work in the same vein can be found in *The Killing Bottle* (1932), whose title story is a neat *conte cruel*. Both title stories and other materials are in *The Travelling Grave and Other Stories* (Arkham House, 1948), whose contents are also reprinted in *The Collected Short Stories of L. P. Hartley* (1968) and *The Complete Short Stories of L. P. Hartley* (1986). His later ghost stories tend to be wittier, often slyly so—Bleiler calls him "the master of the *double entendre*"—and echo the incipiently sadistic interest in psychological misfortune exhibited by his discomfiting mundane fiction.

Harvey, William F(ryer) (U.K.), 1885-1937.
ABOUT: WW, GSF, SFW, SMFL, PE, ESF

3-81. Midnight Tales. Dent, 1946. U.S. title: *The Beast with Five Fingers*.
Omnibus volume recovering the best items from three earlier collections of weird tales: *Midnight House* (1910); *The Beast with Five Fingers* (1928) and *Moods and Tenses* (1933). The title story of the second collection, made famous by an effective film, features a disembodied hand which sets out on a mission of vengeance. The other stories, which include the poltergeist story "Miss Cornelius" and the psychic vampire story "Miss Avenel," feature less striking motifs, but are enlivened by skillful construction and stylish prose. Four more weird tales are included in the posthumous collection *The Arm of Mrs. Egan and Other Strange Stories* (1952), but they are rather feeble.

Hawthorne, Hildegarde, 1871-1952.

3-82. Faded Garden: The Collected Ghost Stories of Hildegarde Hawthorne. Strange Company, 1985.
Slim collection of five stories and three poems by Nathaniel's granddaughter and Julian's daughter, edited by Jessica Amanda Salmonson. It includes "A Legend of Sonora," "Perdita" (1897) and "Unawares" (1908), all of which are deft and sentimental stories featuring ghostly children.

Heard, H(enry) F(itzgerald) (U.K.), 1889-1971.
ABOUT: WW, GSF, CA, NE, SMFL, SFE, SFFL, TCSF, PE, ESF

3-83. The Great Fog and Other Weird Tales. Vanguard, 1944. The U.K. edition has somewhat different contents.
Collection of stories including scientific romances, *contes philosophiques* and

stories of the supernatural. The most important of the latter is the novella *Dromenon,* in which an antiquarian discovers the true nature of medieval Christian worship by means of a restored church organ. A second collection, *The Lost Cavern and Other Stories* (1948), includes two more novellas of a similar stripe; *The Cup* is a remarkably fine story about an art forger who finds the Holy Grail but is supernaturally thwarted in his attempt to steal it; *The Chapel of Ease* is a theoretically elaborate account of a haunting. Together with Heard's novel *The Black Fox* [4-139] these stories develop an eccentric theology linked to the author's theory of psychological types and historical phases.

Heinlein, Robert A(nson), 1907–1988.

ABOUT: GSF, CA, NE, SMFL, SFE, SFFL, RG, TCSF, ESF, HF

3-84. The Unpleasant Profession of Jonathan Hoag. Gnome Press, 1959.
Collection whose title novella first appeared in *Unknown* in 1942. Hoag hires two private eyes to find out what he does during the blackouts he experiences daily; the revelation is appropriately appalling. Also included is the classic fantasy of solipsistic paranoia "They" (1941).

[For other works of this author, see the companion guide to fantasy.]

Heron, E. and H. (pseuds. of **Hesketh Prichard**, 1876–1922, and **Kate Ryall Prichard**) (U.K.).

ABOUT: WW, GSF, PE, ESF

3-85. Ghosts: Being the Experiences of Flaxman Low. London: Pearson, 1899.
Occult detective tales from *Pearson's Magazine* (where they were offered as two series of "real" cases) by a son-and-mother team; Low investigates numerous haunted houses—sometimes finding a rational explanation—and then moves on to combat the menace of evil occultist Dr. Kalmarkane. Cheap reprints redivide the two series, as *Ghost Stories* and *More Ghost Stories* (both 1917). Brisker than Blackwood's John Silence stories [3-27], probably inspired by the debunking efforts of L. T. Meade and Robert Eustace's *Master of Mysteries,* collected in 1898.

Hichens, Robert S(mythe) (U.K.), 1864–1950.

ABOUT: WW, GSF, SFW, PE, ESF

3-86. Flames; A London Phantasy. London: Heinemann, 1897.
A young man who finds moral uprightness effortless attempts to achieve psychic rapport with his friend, so that he may understand temptation; instead his soul is displaced by that of an evil occultist, whose corrupt example sets the friend on the road to damnation. A curiously intense moral fantasy, probably inspired by *The Picture of Dorian Gray* [2-97]. Hichens remained obsessed with the ideas in it, reexamining them in two other eccentric stories of personality exchange: the novel *The Dweller on the Threshold* (1911) and the novella "The Sin of Envy" (in *The Gardenia and Other Stories,* 1934). The title novella of his last collection, *The Man in the Mirror* (1950), also echoes *Dorian Gray* in its account of an artist

trying to paint his own *doppelgänger*. All are prolix, but offer fascinating material for psychoanalytic interpretation.

***3-87. Tongues of Conscience**. Methuen, 1900.
An unusual collection of stories which all feature guilt-induced hauntings, including the remarkably painful "The Cry of the Child" and the tragic "Sea Change" as well as Hichens's finest work—and one of the finest of all English ghost stories—"How Love Came to Professor Guildea" (extensively revised from its magazine publication as "The Man Who Was Beloved"), in which a scientist who boasts that he has put away sympathy and sentimentality as useless encumbrances finds his resolve tested to destruction by the attentions of a doting moronic spirit. The earlier collection *Bye-Ways* (1897) has two notable weird novellas; in "The Charmer of Snakes" a honeymooning wife is supernaturally seduced away from her husband, while "A Tribute of Souls" (based on a plot by Frederic Harrison) features a Faustian pact. Other supernatural novellas are scattered through Hichens's various collections, and include the romances of reincarnation "The Return of the Soul" (in *The Folly of Eustace*, 1896) and *The Black Spaniel* (in the collection of the same name, 1905), and the haunted house story "The Villa by the Sea" (in *The Last Time*, 1923).

Hodgson, William Hope (U.K.), 1877-1918.

ABOUT: WW, GSF, SFW, F, NE, H, SMFL, SFE, RG, TCSF, PE, ESF, FL, HF

3-88. The Boats of the *Glen Carrig*. Chapman Hall, 1907.
The longest of Hodgson's many stories of castaways threatened by monstrous creatures; as with all his exercises in teratology, it draws upon the scientific imagination rather than traditional Gothic motifs, but is a horror story nevertheless.

3-89. Carnacki the Ghost-Finder. Eveleigh Nash, 1913.
Collection of occult detective stories in the tradition of [3-85]. The stories in this edition are dull potboilers but the expanded Mycroft & Moran edition (1947) includes the novelette "The Hog", which presents an elaborate account of the distinctive metaphysical theory which underlay Hodgson's exercises in this vein, exploiting the horrific aspects thereof.

3-90. Deep Waters. Arkham House, 1967.
An eclectic selection of Hodgson's best sea stories, gathered from various collections, including *Men of the Deep Waters* (1914) and *The Luck of the Strong* (1916). Most of the stories are exercises in teratology after the fashion of [3-88]; they include the classic "The Voice in the Night" (1907), in which castaways undergo an awful metamorphosis after being forced to feed on a strange fungus; and "The Derelict" (1912), about a ship which has undergone a similar metamorphosis and has come to life. More of Hodgson's short works are reprinted in *Out of the Storm* (1975), which includes the remarkable "Eloi, Eloi, Lama Sabachthani" (written 1912), in which a scientist recreates the crucifixion in order to make contact with God, but discovers instead the corrupted cosmos of Hodgson's theories. R. Alain Everts has recently issued a series of booklets containing other recently discovered Hodgson stories.

***3-91. The Ghost Pirates**. Stanley Paul, 1909.
A ship bearing a mysterious curse slips into a hinterland between parallel worlds, where it becomes vulnerable to assault by bestial creatures from the other universe. Credibility is assured by virtue of the author's long experience at sea, and the suspense is handled with great skill. Though far less striking in its imagery than [3-92], it is superior in terms of its internal coherency, and is one of the great weird novels.

***3-92. The House on the Borderland**. Chapman & Hall, 1908.
Classic novel of supernatural menace and visionary experience. A manuscript found in a desolate spot tells of the material and visionary adventures of a man following the breakdown of the barriers protecting his existence and consciousness from a higher reality in which bestiality and corruption are the irresistible ruling forces. An imaginative tour de force whose power transcends its patchwork construction; the cosmic vision sequence makes it equally interesting as a scientific romance but it definitely strikes what its admirer H. P. Lovecraft sought to define as "the true note of cosmic horror." It is reprinted with [3-89], [3-91] and [F3-178] in an Arkham House omnibus of 1946.

[For other works of this author, see the companion guide to fantasy.]

Horler, Sydney (U.K.), 1888–1954.
ABOUT: WW, GSF

3-93. The Vampire. Hutchinson, 1935.
Convoluted thriller featuring the Stokeresque vampire Count Ziska. The inspiration of *Dracula* [3-186] is further acknowledged in Horler's short story "The Vampire" in *The Screaming Skull and Other Stories* (1930), whose title novella falls into the subgenre of lurid but ultimately rationalized "weird menace" stories, as does Horler's other "vampire story," *The Curse of Doone* (1928).

Howard, Robert E(rvin), 1906–1936.
ABOUT: WW, GSF, SFW, F, CA, SMFL, SFE, RG, PE, ESF, HF

3-94. Red Shadows. Grant, 1968.
Collection of stories, mostly from *Weird Tales,* featuring Solomon Kane, sixteenth-century Puritan adventurer. "Skulls in the Stars" is set in England but most of the rest are set in darkest Africa—the best are the title story (1928) and "The Hills of the Dead" (1930). Typically fast-paced and gaudy adventure stories; they were subsequently issued in three volumes by the Centaur Press: *The Moon of Skulls* (1969), *The Hand of Kane* (1970) and *Solomon Kane* (1971); and then in a two-volume set by Bantam as *Solomon Kane* (1979).

3-95. Skull-Face and Others. Arkham House, 1946.
Large memorial collection of Howard's best works, including several which do not belong to his various series. The best are the Lovecraftian "The Black Stone" (1931), the graphic prehistoric romance "The Valley of the Worm" (1934) and two items of eccentric Americana: "The Horror from the Mound" (1932) and "Black Canaan" (1936) (many of these stories are reprinted in the collection *Wolfshead,*

1968). The title novella, which features a Rohmeresque charismatic villain, is uncharacteristically weak. Other nonseries stories are to be found in *The Dark Man and Others* (1963), which has some odd supernatural westerns and some exercises in pastiche, as well as the effective "Pigeons from Hell" (1938); the bulk of the collection was reprinted as *Pigeons from Hell* (1979). More weird tales, unpublished in Howard's lifetime, can be found in *The Gods of Bal-Sagoth* (1979).

[For other works of this author, see the companion guide to fantasy.]

Howells, William Dean, 1837–1920.
ABOUT: GSF, CA, SFE, TCSF, ESF

3-96. Questionable Shapes. Harper, 1903.
Collection of three novellas in which the author describes and attempts to explain, by the theories of psychologist Wanhope, various apparently supernatural incidents. *Between the Dark and the Daylight* (1907) offers more painstaking rationalizations in the same vein. Slow and deliberately unsensational, these stories are interesting as earnest attempts to dissolve the characteristic forms of psychic phenomena into a skeptical worldview, where apparitions become mysterious products of the mind of the beholder.

Hubbard, L(afayette) Ron, 1911–1986.
ABOUT: WW, GSF, F, CA, NE, SMFL, SFE, TCSF, ESF

***3-97. Typewriter in the Sky; Fear: Two Science Fantasy Novels.** Gnome Press, 1951.
"Fear" (*Unknown*, 1940) is a classic mystery story in which a skeptical anthropologist is tormented by "demons" as he obsessively tries to figure out what happened during four hours which have been obliterated from his memory. The revelation is unusually modest by comparison with works such as *The Unpleasant Profession of Jonathan Hoag* [3-84], but all the more effective by virtue of its restraint. A tour de force amply demonstrating the creative power which was extravagantly wasted in reams of pulp hackwork before discovering a more perverse vocation in the invention of Dianetics (some of whose conceptual roots can be seen in "Fear"). Reprinted in *Fear and The Ultimate Adventure* (1970).

[For other works of this author, see the companion guide to fantasy.]

Hume, Fergus (U.K.), 1859–1932.
ABOUT: WW, GSF, CA, ESF

3-98. A Son of Perdition. Rider, 1912.
Credulous occult romance in which a practicer of black magic plots to win the hand of an acolyte's virtuous daughter and to obtain a younger and more virile body; he is ultimately thwarted by a rival lover and a rival adept, who thus redeem a moral debt incurred in a previous incarnation in lost Atlantis. Theosophical cant is not allowed to weigh down the sensational plot unduly, but the treatment is routine.

Hunt, Violet, 1866–1942.

ABOUT: WW, GSF, PE, ESF

3-99. Tales of the Uneasy. Heinemann, 1911.
Collection of stories in which the supernatural intrusions serve to dramatize the problems which arise in the relationships of the characters. The most interesting is "The Prayer," in which a wife's desperate plea succeeds in reviving her dead husband, but not in making the subsequent years of companionship worthwhile. The delicate irony of the stories is taken to bizarre lengths in "The Witness," in which a guilt-stricken woman pleads with a man who has committed murder on her behalf to kill his dog lest it spread the story of the crime to others of its kind. *More Tales of the Uneasy* (1925) has three further novellas in the same offbeat vein.

Ingram, Eleanor, 1886–1921.

ABOUT: GSF, SMFL

3-100. The Thing from the Lake. Lippincott, 1921.
The hero's dreams are troubled by a mysterious monster, which seems to be connected with an equally mysterious unseen woman whose ravings trouble his waking hours; hallucinatory vapors rising from a noisome pool may be to blame. Suggested as a precursor of Lovecraft [3-132], but not mentioned in his study of *Supernatural Horror in Literature* [7-7].

Irwin, Margaret (U.K.), 1889–1967.

ABOUT: WW, GSF, CA, SMFL, PE, ESF

3-101. Madame Fears the Dark. Chatto & Windus, 1935.
Collection including the title play and six short stories. These include "The Book," about a grimoire which can answer questions and impel its readers into evil; "The Earlier Service," about a timeslipped Black Mass; and "Monsieur Seeks a Wife," in which a man shopping around for a suitable bride gets far more than he bargained for. It is a great pity that Irwin, potentially one of the finest supernatural writers of her generation, abandoned this line of work.

[For other works of this author, see the companion guide to fantasy.]

Jackson, Shirley, 1919–1965.

ABOUT: WW, GSF, SFW, F, CA, H, SMFL, SFE, MF, SFFL, PE, ESF

3-102. The Lottery. Farrar, Straus, 1949.
Collection whose title story (1948) is a classic piece of invented folklore about human sacrifice in small-town America.

Jackson, Thomas G(raham) (U.K.), 1835–1924.

ABOUT: GSF, ESF

3-103. Six Ghost Stories. John Murray, 1919.
Collection of routine ghost stories in the M. R. Jamesian vein by a distinguished

architect. The most original, thanks to its setting, is "A Romance of the Piccadilly Tube."

Jacobi, Carl, 1908– .

ABOUT: WW, GSF, CA, SFE, SFFL, PE, ESF

3-104. Revelations in Black. Arkham House, 1947.
Collection of stories, mostly from *Weird Tales*. The title story (1933) features a deranged manuscript which helps discover the awfulness of the narrator's situation; "Carnaby's Fish" is a delicately gruesome monster story. Jacobi was one of the more stylish pulp writers, and uses some original motifs, though he failed to escape completely the straitjacket of pulp expectations. *Portraits in Moonlight* (1964) has more items in the same vein.

Jacobs, W(illiam) W(ymark) (U.K.), 1863–1943.

ABOUT: WW, GSF, SFW, CA, PE, ESF

3-105. The Lady of the Barge. Harpers, 1902.
Collection whose star item is the classic tale of wishes gone wrong, "The Monkey's Paw," which puts across its bitter message with unparalleled ferocity. A handful of other supernatural stories are scattered through Jacobs's various collections, but all are trivial.

Jaffery, Sheldon, editor.

3-106. The Weirds. Starmont House, 1987.
Anthology of stories from the "weird menace" pulps *Horror Stories* and *Terror Tales*. These magazines and their imitators specialized in bizarre thrillers in which apparently supernatural threats almost always turn out to be pretenses erected to conceal criminal conspiracies; the blurbs pretend that the stories are quasi-pornographic, though the texts are coy. Wonderfully tacky titles were a notable feature; stars of this collection are "The Mole Men Want Your Eyes" by Frederick C. Davis and "Mistress of the Blood-Drinkers" by Ralston Shields. Other reprints can be found in Robert Weinberg's series of *Weird Menace Classics* (5 vols., 1977–79). An interesting exercise in American *grand guignol*.

James, Henry, 1843–1916.

ABOUT: WW, GSF, SFW, F, CA, H, SMFL, PE, ESF

***3-107. The Two Magics: The Turn of the Screw; Covering End**. London: Heinemann, 1898.
The first story is the classic tale of a governess who comes to believe that the two children in her charge have been corrupted by two former servants who now manifest themselves as ghosts; her struggle for their redemption eventually reaches a tragic conclusion. The governess's unreliability as narrator of the tale-within-the-tale makes the story enigmatic and ambiguous, and has given rise to

so many different interpretations that the story is the most ludicrously overanalyzed in the genre. There is probably less in it than sometimes meets the scholarly eye, but it remains a historical landmark. The most notable of James's other ghost stories from this period is "The Real Right Thing" (1899), in which a biographer is put off by his subject's ghost. "The Jolly Corner" (written 1905) is a *doppelgänger* story thematically connected to his unfinished timeslip novel *The Sense of the Past* (1917).

James, M(ontague) R(hodes) (U.K.), 1862–1936.

ABOUT: WW, GSF, SFW, CA, H, SMFL, PE, ESF

***3-108. Ghost Stories of an Antiquary**. Edward Arnold, 1904.
The first and best of James's classic collections of stories, which he wrote at the rate of approximately one a year for reading to his friends at Christmas. In "Lost Hearts" a boy goes to live with his eccentric uncle, who has previously sacrificed two other children to his occult experiments. Most of the other stories feature sinister supernatural visitors accidentally summoned by dabblers in the antique who come to wish fervently that they had let well enough alone: "Count Magnus," "Oh, Whistle, and I'll Come to You, My Lad" and "The Treasure of Abbot Thomas" are all classics of this kind, as are "The Stalls of Barchester Cathedral" in *More Ghost Stories of an Antiquary* (1911), "An Episode of Cathedral History" in *A Thin Ghost and Others* (1919) and the title story of *A Warning to the Curious and Other Ghost Stories* (1926). Four other stories are added to *The Collected Ghost Stories of M. R. James* (1931). James introduces his horrors very methodically, building from ambiguous hints to awful climaxes. His hauntings are usually subtle, though he was not averse to more graphic imagery, such as is introduced into "The Ash-Tree" or "The Diary of Mr. Poynter." He wrote in a painstakingly realistic fashion whose power of conviction many others tried to capture, though few succeeded. He was a consummate artist of the creepy tale, and his best works are literary gems.

[For other works of this author, see the companion guide to fantasy.]

Jepson, Edgar (U.K.), 1863–1938.

ABOUT: WW, GSF

3-109. Number 19. Mills and Boon, 1910. U.S. title: *The Garden at 19*.
After moving into his new suburban house, the protagonist is disturbed by mysterious noises and monstrous presences in the neighboring garden, where an occultist is trying to reenact the Eleusinian Mysteries. He carries on a clandestine romance with the occultist's daughter while the research progresses to an invocation of Pan. An effective thriller, drawing on research conducted for Jepson's earlier exercise in anthropological allegory, *The Horned Shepherd* (1904); Aleister Crowley was inspired by the example of the fictional occultist to make his own attempt to invoke Pan (and acknowledged his debt by including the novel in the curriculum for initiates of the Argentinum Astrum).

Kafka, Franz (Austria), 1883-1924.
About: WW, F, CA, H, SMFL, SFE, PE, ESF

***3-110. Metamorphosis**. Parton Press, 1937. Tr. by A. L. Lloyd of *Die Verwandlung*, 1915.
Novella whose protagonist wakes to find that he has been transformed into a giant cockroach; his horrified family fulfill their obligations to him, but his existence becomes so dreadfully embarrassing that his death is a long overdue liberation. Other relevant short stories by Kafka include the classic *conte cruel* "In the Penal Settlement" (1919) and the bleak, posthumously published *conte philosophique* "Investigations of a Dog."

3-111. The Trial. Gollancz, 1937. Tr. by William and Edwin Muir of *Der Prozess*, written *ca.* 1915; published 1925.
The protagonist is arrested for an unspecified crime and must work his way through an incomprehensible legal process which will not permit any rational intrusion, proceeding gradually and irresistibly to the climax of his condemnation. A relentless allegory of contemporary man's alienation from society, his powerlessness in the face of social process and the hopeless absurdity of his endeavors. Thematically similar to, but more extreme in its "revelations" than Conrad's *Heart of Darkness* [3-51].

Kallas, Aino (Finland), 1878-1956.
About: GSF

3-112. The Wolf's Bride. Cape, 1930. Tr. by Alex Matson and Brian Rhys of *Sudenmorsian*, 1928.
Pious *Kunstmärchen* set in Estonia, in which the wife of a forester who carries the devil's mark is tempted by the *Diabolus sylvarum* to join the company of wolves, bringing disaster upon her family. A sentimental tale offered as a tragedy; its confused morality and essential sympathy for the werewolf are a first step in the direction of Angela Carter's apologetic tales of wolfwomen [F4A-63].

Keller, David H(enry), 1880-1966.
About: WW, GSF, SMFL, SFE, TCSF, PE, ESF

3-113. Life Everlasting and Other Tales of Science Fiction and Horror. Avalon, 1947.
Collection including several horror stories, the most notable being the often-reprinted "The Thing in the Cellar" (1932), about a child's fear of an "imaginary" monster. Keller's keen interest in psychiatry led him to produce a number of effective psychological horror stories; others in this volume include the excellent *conte cruel* "A Piece of Linoleum" (1933) and the delusional fantasy "The Dead Woman" (1934). These three stories are reprinted in *Tales from Underwood* (1952), which also contains some curious allegorical weird tales including, "The Bridle" (1942) and "The God Wheel," and the monster story "The Worm" (1929); and again in *The Folsom Flint and Other Curious Tales* (1969). *The Solitary Hunters and The Abyss* (1948) has two novellas, the first a *Weird Tales* serial (1934) about monstrous insects, the second an interesting horror/SF story about

the pollution of New York's water supply by a drug which obliterates the inhibitions of civilization.

[For other works of this author, see the companion guide to fantasy.]

Kerruish, Jessie Douglas (U.K.), 1890?-1949.

ABOUT: WW, GSF, PE, ESF

3-114. The Undying Monster. Heath Cranton, 1922.
The story of a family curse which is explained and exorcised thanks to the efforts of a female psychic detective. Long-winded theorizing slows down the action, but suspense is maintained and the explanation is interesting.

Kersh, Gerald (U.K.), 1911-1968.

ABOUT: WW, GSF, CA, SFE, PE, ESF

3-115. The Horrible Dummy and Other Stories. Heinemann, 1944.
Collection including two brief psychological horror stories: the often-reprinted title story about a paranoid ventriloquist, and the similar story of "The Devil That Troubled the Chess Board." Fantastic motifs crop up fairly frequently in Kersh's work of this period—his characteristic mordant misanthropy leads him to construct many black comedies and dark satires. *Neither Man nor Dog* (1946) has several examples, including the posthumous fantasy "In a Room without Walls," the metempsychotic "Fantasy of a Hunted Man" and the ghost-animal story "Who Wants a Liver-Coloured Cat?" *Sad Road to the Sea* (1947) has others, including the ghost story "The Scene of the Crime" and the post-holocaust fairy story "Voices in the Dust of Annan." His suspense novel *The Weak and the Strong* (1945) has a remarkable fantastic episode involving a man offered as a human sacrifice to the insect-god of a savage tribe.

Kipling, Rudyard (U.K.), 1865-1936.

ABOUT: WW, GSF, SFW, CA, NE, SMFL, SFE, RG, TCSF, PE, ESF, HF

3-116. Traffics and Discoveries. Macmillan, 1904.
Collection including the notable ghost story "They" and two interesting stories in which news media (radio and the cinema) open channels for apparent communication between dead and living: "Wireless" and "Mrs. Bathurst." *Actions and Reactions* (1909) has a haunted house story, "The House Surgeon," but the cerebral and speculative tone of these stories was set aside after World War I (in which Kipling's son was killed), and his later fantasies are redolent with poignancy and anguish. *Debits and Credits* (1926) has several weird tales, including the subtly bitter "A Madonna of the Trenches"; a delicate story of self-sacrifice, "The Wish House"; and a posthumous fantasy, "On the Gate," whose curious theology was to be further elaborated in "Uncovenanted Mercies" in *Limits and Renewals* (1932). A convenient, current and comprehensive collection is *The Complete Supernatural Stories of Rudyard Kipling* (W. H. Allen, 1987), ed. by Peter Haining.

[For other works of this author, see the companion guide to fantasy.]

Kneale, Nigel (U.K.), 1922- .
ABOUT: WW, GSF, SFE, TCSF, ESF

3-117. Tomato Cain and Other Stories. Collins, 1949.
Collection which won the Somerset Maugham Award, including numerous fantasies and *contes cruels*. The most notable are the sadistic fantasy "The Pond" and the poltergeist story "Minuke."

Kubin, Alfred (Austria), 1877-1959.
ABOUT: CA, SMFL

3-118. The Other Side. Crown, 1967. Tr. by Denver Lindley of *Die andere Seite*, 1909.
An artist is pleased to be invited to remove himself to a utopian "Realm of Dreams," but becomes disenchanted with its ruler and his achievements; ultimately the dreams turn to nightmare as the Realm is corrupted and destroyed. A remarkable work of surreal symbolism, which has strong affinities with the work of Kubin's similarly exiled fellow-countryman Kafka [3-110-3-111].

Lagerlöf, Selma (Sweden), 1858-1940.
ABOUT: GSF, CA

3-119. The General's Ring. Werner Laurie, 1928. Tr. by Francesca Martin of *Lowenskölda Ringen*, 1925.
Historical fantasy in which the ghost of a general visits ill-fortune upon all those who come into possession of a ring stolen from his corpse, although the later sufferers are innocent of any evil intent.

3-120. Thy Soul Shall Bear Witness! Odhams, 1921. Tr. by William Frederick Harvey of *Körkarlen*, 1912.
The last man to die on New Year's Eve must drive Death's ghostly cart for a year; the spirit of a man apparently marked for that fate is shown by his predecessor the evil effects of his actions, then given a chance to return to his body and make atonement. Moralistic melodrama; the basis of a notable silent film.

Laing, Alexander, 1903-1976.
ABOUT: GSF, CA, H, SFE, ESF

3-121. The Cadaver of Gideon Wyck. Farrar, Rinehart, 1934.
Fascinating murder mystery whose solution turns on matters of teratology (in the narrow medical sense of deformity and mutation in human beings). The graphic details are sufficiently repulsive to have been bowdlerized in some editions.

La Spina, Greye (Fanny Greye Bragg), 1880-1969.
ABOUT: WW, GSF, CA, SFFL, ESF

3-122. Invaders from the Dark. Arkham House, 1960.
Revised version of a 1925 *Weird Tales* serial. The widowed heroine, educated in occult matters by her husband, enters into rivalry with a female werewolf for the

body and soul of a young man. Rather awkward but more interesting than most werewolf stories of the 1920s and 1930s. The paperback edition is retitled *Shadow of Evil.*

Lawrence, Margery (**Mrs. Arthur Edward Towle**) (U.K.), 1896–1969.
ABOUT: WW, GSF, PE, ESF

3-123. Number Seven Queer Street. Hale, 1945.
Collection featuring the investigations of occult detective Miles Pennoyer, which includes "The Case of the Moonchild," an encounter with Crowleyesque magicians; and the "The Case of the Leannabh Sidhe," in which the fairies make clear their objection to having fairways at the bottom of their garden following the construction of a new golf course. *Master of Shadows* (1959) features further adventures of Pennoyer. Lawrence's earlier collections of anecdotal weird tales tend to be less wordy (and less credulous). *Nights of the Round Table* (1926) uses secondhand motifs effectively, notably in "The Priest's Story: How Pan Came to Little Ingleton" and "The Egyptologist's Story: The Curse of the Stillborn." *The Terraces of Night* (1932) places more tales in the same anecdote-swapping frame. *The Floating Café and Other Stories* (1936) is mostly less derivative; the title story is an unusual account of a nasty mermaid.

Lee-Hamilton, Eugene (U.K.), 1845–1907.
ABOUT: GSF, CA

***3-124. The Lord of the Dark Red Star**. Walter Scott, 1903.
Subtitled "The Story of the Supernatural Influences in the Life of an Italian Despot of the Thirteenth Century." The sadistic Ezelin (Eccelino da Romano), warlord of the Emperor Frederick II, promises the devil (whose son he believes himself to be) to deliver his unbaptized firstborn as a sacrifice, in return for the furthering of his ambition, but the child's exotic mother has the baby secretly baptized; Death, who has been dicing with Sin for Ezelin's body and soul, is thus enabled to make the winning throw. A marvelously lurid and stylistically extravagant melodrama.

Leiber, Fritz, 1910– .
ABOUT: WW, GSF, SFW, F, CA, NE, H, TCA, SMFL, SFE, MF, SFFL, RG, TCSF, PE, ESF, FL, HF

***3-125. Conjure Wife**. Twayne, 1953.
Novel from *Unknown* (1943), first issued in book form in the Twayne omnibus *Witches Three* (1952). A fine story developing the daring premise that the skeptical and scientific worldview is entirely a male product, while women have retained, both philosophically and practically, the magical worldview. A college professor is horrified to discover that his wife practices magic, but after he forces her to desist, they both become vulnerable to the witchcraft of the other campus wives. The first half is particularly brilliant, leading up to a marvelously chilling subclimax.

***3-126. Night's Black Agents**. Arkham House, 1947.
Collection of weird tales and heroic fantasies. The former include the fine "Smoke Ghost" (1941), whose hero wonders what form a modern urban ghost would take—and then finds out. This philosophy of procedure recurs in many of Leiber's finest tales; others here are "The Hound" (1940) and "The Dreams of Albert Moreland," while the excellent "The Girl with the Hungry Eyes" was the title story of a 1949 anthology. Leiber was the most stylish of all the *Weird Tales* writers.

[For other works of this author, see the companion guide to fantasy.]

Leroux, Gaston (France), 1868–1927.
ABOUT: WW, GSF, CA, PE, ESF

3-127. The Man with the Black Feather. Hurst & Blackett, 1912. Tr. by Edgar Jepson of *La Double Vie de Théophraste Longuet,* 1904.
The luckless protagonist is periodically possessed by the spirit of the long-dead villain Cartouche, which embarks upon various dangerous enterprises, not realizing how much time has passed. Feverish melodrama. An earlier translation appeared as *The Double Life* (1909).

3-128. The Phantom of the Opera. Mills & Boon, 1911. Tr. by Alexander Texeira de Mattos of *Le Fantôme de l'Opéra,* 1910.
Much-filmed novel set in and under the Paris Opera House, where a young singer is groomed for stardom by a mysterious person who haunts the theater. When the new managers will not bow to his demands, he takes murderous revenge, but his victory is short-lived. Key moments, like the girl's removal of the phantom's mask and the masquerade scene in which the phantom adopts the costume of Poe's Red Death, make this an archetypal melodrama. The silent film starring Lon Chaney is a classic; the recent opera by Andrew Lloyd Webber is also very effective.

Level, Maurice (France), 1875–1926.
ABOUT: WW, PE, ESF

3-129. Crises. Macdonald, 1920. Tr. by Alys E. Macklin; also known as *Grand Guignol Stories* and *Tales of Mystery and Horror.*
Level inherited the mantle of Villiers de L'Isle Adam [2-95] as a master of the *conte cruel,* though he was a less subtle exponent of the art; several of his stories were adapted for the stage by the notorious Grand Guignol Theater in Paris, and his ghoulish twists are unparalleled, save perhaps by Robert Bloch [3-29; 4-44–4-48]. "The Last Kiss" and "Blue Eyes" are the best examples.

Lewis, L(eslie) A. (U.K.), 1899–1961.
ABOUT: WW, GSF, PE

3-130. Tales of the Grotesque. Philip Allan, 1934.
Collection assimilated to the *Creeps* series. It features some unusual motifs, including the malevolently animated airplane in "The Iron Swine" and the sacred edifice gone wrong in "The Tower of Moab," but is generally routine.

Long, Frank Belknap, 1903- .
ABOUT: WW, GSF, SFW, CA, NE, SMFL, SFE, SFFL, RG, TCSF, PE, ESF

3-131. The Hounds of Tindalos. Arkham House, 1946.
Collection of horror and SF stories. The title story (1929) has an original motif: angular demons which cannot manifest themselves in curved environments; "Grab Bags Are Dangerous" (1942) is grimly ironic. Long was an important member of the Lovecraft circle, but few of the items here are Lovecraftian in style—not even "The Space Eaters," whose protagonist is modeled on Lovecraft. The contents of this collection are distributed in two paperback collections: *The Hounds of Tindalos* and *The Dark Beasts* (both 1963), and all but one story are in *The Early Long* (1975). Long's principal Lovecraftian pastiche is the short novel *The Horror from the Hills* (*Weird Tales*, 1931; in book form 1963).

Lovecraft, Howard Phillips, 1890-1937.
ABOUT: WW, GSF, SFW, F, CA, NE, H, SMFL, SFE, RG, TCSF, PE, ESF, HF

***3-132. The Outsider and Others**. Arkham House, 1939.
A landmark in genre publishing, reprinting thirty-two magazine stories (most from *Weird Tales*). They range from early exercises in Dunsanian pastiche to the mature and highly distinctive tales of the Cthulhu Mythos, which construct a horrific cosmological and historical context for human history. Luckless protagonists who stumble upon various dire intrusions of Cthulhu and his kin, or who unwisely pursue dangerous inquiries in the appropriate revelatory tomes, are inevitably brought to repulsively sticky ends. Lovecraft became the consummate master of the confirmatory ending, in which what has been suspected all along finally becomes manifest. The title story (1926) foreshadows many others in presenting a tale of discovery whose final revelation not only displays a corrupted cosmos but brings the protagonist into confrontation with his own monstrousness. Some effective stories, including "The Rats in the Walls" (1924) and "Dreams in the Witch-House" (1933) deploy traditional motifs, but the finest stories are those which elaborate Lovecraft's own mythos—and in so doing become borderline science fiction. These are "The Colour out of Space" (1927); the fine novellas "The Whisperer in Darkness" (1931), "The Shadow over Innsmouth" (1936) and "The Shadow out of Time" (1936); and the short novel *At the Mountains of Madness* (1936). Although Lovecraft's dense and adjectival style alienates some readers, his works remain one of the most remarkable literary products of their day and an enormously influential contribution to the genre, their influence extending not only to Lovecraft's many correspondents but to such significant modern writers as Ramsey Campbell [4-63-4-73] and Brian Lumley [4-209].

A second early Arkham House collection, *Beyond the Wall of Sleep* (1943), includes the short novel *The Case of Charles Dexter Ward* (*Weird Tales*, 1941; separate publication 1951) and assorted minor items, plus a few of the revisions which Lovecraft did for other writers. The Lovecraft canon was later distributed in three Arkham House collections: *The Dunwich Horror and Others* (1963), *At the Mountains of Madness and Other Novels* (1964) and *Dagon and Other Macabre Tales* (1965); these remain the standard editions, especially the reprints with texts corrected by S. T. Joshi. His "collaborations" with other authors (mostly undertaken as revisions of works sent to him for rewriting) were collected in *The Horror in the Museum and Other Revisions* (1970). Very many other collections present eclectic selections from his works. Notable anthologies of Cthulhu Mythos stories by Lovecraft and others include *Tales of the Cthulhu Mythos* (1969), edited by August Derleth, and *Spawn of Cthulhu* (1971), edited by Lin Carter.

[For other works of this author, see the companion guide to fantasy.]

Macardle, Dorothy (Ireland), 1889-1958.
ABOUT: GSF, PE, ESF

3-133. Uneasy Freehold. Peter Davies, 1941. U.S. title: *The Uninvited.*
A writer and his sister buy a haunted house; the granddaughter of the former owner is drawn back to the house where one ghost seeks her damnation and another tries to protect her. Overlong, but very effectively filmed (under the U.S. title).

Machen, Arthur (U.K.), 1863-1947.
ABOUT: WW, GSF, SFW, CA, H, SMFL, SFE, RG, PE, ESF, HF

3-134. The Green Round. Benn, 1933.
Short novel in which the protagonist, supposedly recovering from a nervous breakdown, experiences visions and becomes the focal point of various supernatural phenomena from whose torments he eventually flees. Lacks the intensity of Machen's earlier works.

3-135. The House of Souls. Grant Richards, 1906.
Collection which reprints much of Machen's fiction from the earlier period (see [2-58-2-59]) and adds some subsequent material, most importantly the fine documentary novelette "The White People" (1899), in which the metaphysical theories underlying much of Machen's work are elaborately laid out. The same ideas are in the background of "The Red Hand," and of the *The Green Round* [3-134]. Later work can be found in two different collections called *The Shining Pyramid* (U.S. 1923; U.K. 1924); in *The Children of the Pool and Other Stories* (1936); and in *The Cosy Room and Other Stories* (1936); most of it is rendered ineffective by comparison with Machen's early work because of its obliquity and overearnest concern with esoteric theory, but it is not uninteresting.

3-136. The Terror. Duckworth, 1917.
Short novel about a revolt of nature sparked by World War I, here seen as man's betrayal of his God-given hegemony. The mystery element is unconvincing, but this remains the most interesting of Machen's later weird tales.

[For other works of this author, see the companion guide to fantasy.]

Mann, Jack (pseud. of **Evelyn Charles Vivian**) (U.K.), 1882-1947.
ABOUT: WW, GSF, SMFL, SFE, ESF

***3-137. Grey Shapes**. Wright & Brown, 1937.
Second novel in the Gees series, which began as detective story hackwork but was here and afterward transformed into something far more unusual. This fairly conventional werewolf story was followed by *Nightmare Farm* (1937), in which Vivian borrowed some monsters from his lost race fantasy *City of Wonder* [F3-353]; an oddly downbeat ending established a pattern whereby poor Gees would be forever unlucky in love. *Maker of Shadows* (1938) is the best of the series, featuring an effective black magician and elaborating a syncretic mythological background which was to be further elaborated in subsequent volumes. *The Ninth Life* (1939) is an effective *femme fatale* story, but the series then began to run out of steam; *The Glass Too Many* (1940) redeploys material from *Maker of Shadows* in an ordinary country house murder mystery, and another *femme fatale* story, *Her Ways Are Death*, finds Gees surprisingly reluctant to get involved—perhaps anticipating the bitter ending which his creator had in store for him. Vivian was an accomplished writer whose commercially inclined books rarely do justice to his abilities, but his fascination with offbeat subject matter infuses such books as these with an intensity of feeling which stands in contradiction to their easy narrative flow.

Mannin, Ethel (U.K.), 1900-1984.
ABOUT: CA

3-138. Lucifer and the Child. Jarrolds, 1945.
A young girl is inducted by degrees into the mysteries of witchcraft by a handsome stranger who is probably her father; her teacher cannot believe that he is the devil, and unleashes the jealousy of the young witch when she falls half in love with him. A poignant story, reflecting the loss of confidence in moral order which war can bring—compare Edith Pargeter's *By Firelight* [F3-283].

Margulies, Leo, editor.

3-139. The Unexpected. Pyramid, 1961.
The first in a series of four anthologies selected from *Weird Tales*; the others are *The Ghoul Keepers* (1961), *Weird Tales* (1964) and *Worlds of Weird* (1965). The first two concentrate on the 1940s, the second two on the 1930s. The material is more varied than that featured in the earlier *Not at Night* series [3-195], whose early volumes reprinted heavily from *Weird Tales*. Other representative selections include Peter Haining's *Weird Tales* (1976) and Mike Ashley's *Weird Legacies* (1977). One of several attempts to revive *Weird Tales* was a short-lived series of paperback books, begun with *Weird Tales #1*, edited by Lin Carter (Zebra, 1980).

Marsh, John (U.K.), born 1907.
ABOUT: CA, ESF

3-140. Body Made Alive. Stanley Smith, 1936.
Horror/SF story in which an embittered scientist's experiments in resurrection are not uniformly successful. A pulpish thriller by a prolific writer of such works.

Marsh, Richard (U.K.), 1857–1915.
ABOUT: WW, GSF, PE, ESF

3-141. The Beetle: A Mystery. London: Skeffington, 1897.
Best-selling thriller which rumor claims to have been written as a result of a wager between Marsh and Bram Stoker (who reportedly wrote *Dracula* [3-186] as his part). The eponymous villain is an enigmatic figure whose alleged metamorphic abilities are never conclusively proven; while certainly more peculiar than Dr. Nikola [F2-19] or Sax Rohmer's Fu Manchu, he, she or it remains distinctly less charismatic.

3-142. The Seen and the Unseen. Methuen, 1900.
Collection including several weird tales. Routine work involving familiar motifs. Slightly better work can be found in *Both Sides of the Veil* (1902), but Marsh is quite unable to take supernatural themes seriously and his work is fatally enfeebled as a consequence.

[For other works of this author, see the companion guide to fantasy.]

Martens, Paul (pseud. of **Stephen H. Critten**, later **Stephen Southwold**) (U.K.), 1887–1964.
ABOUT: WW, GSF, SFE, PE, ESF

3-143. Death Rocks the Cradle. Collins, 1933.
Curious phantasmagoric romance in which the protagonist is temporarily stranded in Utopian Salabria, whose ascetic inhabitants indulge their one vice (sadism) by watching surgical operations carried out on morally lax individuals after their appetites have led them to spoil their bodies. A patchwork of themes, borrowing eccentrically from Hudson's *Green Mansions* [F3-186] and other sources.

Maugham, W(illiam) Somerset (U.K.), 1874–1965.
ABOUT: GSF, CA, SFFL, ESF

3-144. The Magician. Heinemann, 1908.
Occultist Oliver Haddo (very obviously modeled on Aleister Crowley) is offended by the protagonist and sets out to take revenge by seducing and wrecking the life of his fiancée, murdering her in the course of his loathsome experiments before he gets his comeuppance. Crowley, electing to be perversely flattered by the grotesque characterization, described it as "an amusing hotch-pot of stolen goods."

Meade, L. T. (**Elizabeth T. Meade Smith**) (U.K.), 1854?-1914?.
ABOUT: CA

3-145. The Desire of Men: An Impossibility. London: Digby Long, 1899.
An old man and his granddaughter are seduced into the power of an occult scientist who employs her vitality to restore his youth; they struggle to escape when they find that he has more ambitious plans for them. A readable thriller.

Merritt, A(braham), 1884-1943.
ABOUT: WW, GSF, SFW, F, CA, NE, SMFL, SFE, RG, TCSF, ESF, FL, HF

3-146. Burn, Witch, Burn! Liveright, 1933.
Thriller in which a psychiatrist and a mobster must team up in opposition to Mme. Mandilip, who uses stolen souls to animate the dolls which do her evil bidding; their efforts are ineffectual and she is ultimately overcome by other means. Suspenseful narration redeems the improbable plot and makes this one of the better stories of its kind. The unlikely heroes return in *Creep, Shadow!* (1934), where their efforts are equally ineffectual against the servants of an ancient godling, who are similarly defeated by other means. Merritt's narrative verve and colorful imagination again save the plot from incipient silliness.

[For other works of this author, see the companion guide to fantasy.]

Metcalfe, John (U.K.), 1891-1965.
ABOUT: WW, GSF, SFW, CA, PE, ESF

3-147. The Smoking Leg. Jarrolds, 1925.
Collection including several weird tales. The macabre title story involves opposing magic objects implanted in a sailor's leg by a drunken surgeon, but the most important stories are two highly distinctive metaphysical fantasies, "The Double Admiral" and "The Bad Lands." *Judas and Other Stories* (1931) has several more weird tales, including an intriguing account of "Mr. Meldrum's Mania," whose protagonist is becoming an avatar of an Egyptian god.

Meyrink, Gustav (formerly **Gustav Meyer**) (Austria), 1868-1932.
ABOUT: GSF, CA, SMFL, ESF

***3-148. The Golem**. Gollancz, 1928. Tr. by Madge Pemberton of *Der Golem*, 1914.
Key work of German expressionism; the narrator picks up the wrong hat and becomes privy to the late nineteenth-century sufferings of Athanasius Pernath, a jeweller of the Prague ghetto who is framed for murder, his predicament reflecting that of all the people of the ghetto. Among Pernath's weird experiences are visions of the Golem, a man of clay animated by the legendary rabbi Judah Loew (or Liva or Leib) to reveal the truth of the "blood libel" (the malevolent allegation that certain Jewish ceremonies employed the blood of innocents, used by Christians to justify pogroms). The Dover edition of 1976 offers a better (and un-

abridged) translation. Meyrink apparently borrowed the central symbolic figure from a pamphlet by Yudl Rosenberg published in 1909 (tr. in Joachim Neugroschel's *Great Works of Jewish Fantasy*, 1976); Chaim Bloch's novel *The Golem* (1920; tr. 1925) and Isaac Bashevis Singer's story *The Golem* (1969; tr. 1982) offer other versions of the legend.

Moore, F. Frankfort (U.K.), died 1931.

3-149. The Other World. Nash, 1904.
Collection of six stories; the most interesting, though marred by crude racism, is the novella *Black as He Is Painted,* set in Africa. An educated black man is rejected by a white woman and takes his revenge by using the magic of his tribe to superimpose upon the personality of the man she eventually marries the world-view of a baboon—but the curse ultimately rebounds upon its sender.

Munby, A(lan) N(oel) L(atimer) (U.K.), 1913-1974.
ABOUT: WW, GSF, CA, PE, ESF

3-150. The Alabaster Hand and other Ghost Stories. Dobson, 1949.
Collection of stories in the M. R. Jamesian antiquarian tradition, written while the author was a prisoner of war. The title story features an animated memorial figure; "*Herodes Redivivus*" involves the apparent serial reincarnation of Herod/Gilles de Rais, most recently in the person of a bookdealer; "The Devil's Autograph" has an unusual relic of a diabolical bargain. Unusual and subtle stories, lacking the climactic punch of James's works [3-108] but effective in their own understated way.

Munn, H(arold) Warner, 1903-1982.
ABOUT: WW, GSF, CA, SMFL, SFE, RG, PE, ESF, HF

3-151. The Werewolf of Ponkert. Grandon, 1958.
Two novelettes from *Weird Tales*. The title story (1925) explains how the protagonist became a reluctant member of a werewolf pack, then failed tragically in his attempt to rebel against the master of the pack. "The Werewolf's Daughter" (1928) follows the unfortunate career of his daughter, given to the pack in consequence of the failed rebellion. The series was extended in other stories (*Weird Tales,* 1927-30; revised as "Ten Tales of the Werewolf Clan" in Robert Weinberg's *Lost Fantasies,* nos. 4-6, 1976-77). The first story's unusual combination of sympathy for the protagonist with a strikingly cruel ending makes it exceptional.

[For other works of this author, see the companion guide to fantasy.]

Nesbit, E(dith) (U.K.), 1858-1924.
ABOUT: WW, GSF, CA, SMFL, RG, PE, ESF, HF

3-152. Salome and the Head. Alston Rivers, 1909.
Curious melodrama in which a strange young girl with a genius for dancing is

tricked into marriage by a loathsome music teacher; to avoid his blackmail, she must have a secret address while she becomes a star of the London stage. Madness threatens when the head of her tormentor is mysteriously substituted for the wax effigy she uses as a dancing partner. Stylistic flippancy fails to disguise the bitter feelings vented in the plot; the scene where the girl discovers the reality of the head is very effective.

[For other works of this author, see the companion guide to fantasy.]

O'Donnell, Elliott (U.K.), 1872–1965.

ABOUT: WW, GSF, CA, PE, ESF

3-153. The Sorcery Club. Rider, 1912.
Occult romance whose protagonist discovers magical documents and forms a mini-brotherhood to exploit their power; this brotherhood is ultimately vanquished by the forces of good. Not quite as rough-hewn as the earlier fix-up novel *For Satan's Sake* (1904), in which a minor recruit to the devil's cause is continually frustrated (and ultimately saved) by an angel, but awkward nevertheless. O'Donnell went on to produce many "nonfiction" works about ghosts and other supernatural entities, though he sometimes mingled works of fiction with supposedly "true" stories, reflecting the weakness of his powers of discrimination.

Oliver, John Rathbone, 1872–1943.

ABOUT: GSF

3-154. Priest or Pagan. Knopf, 1933.
The protagonist, disadvantaged by birth and breeding, becomes ripe for conversion to the cause of evil and is helped on that road by the aptly named Hell Fire, with whose aid he eventually embarks on catastrophic occult experiments. An overelaborate but intriguing allegory.

Onions, Oliver (later **George Oliver**) (U.K.), 1873–1961.

ABOUT: WW, GSF, SFW, H, SMFL, PE, ESF

***3-155. Widdershins**. Secker, 1911.
Collection whose star item is "The Beckoning Fair One," one of the finest of all ghost stories, in which a young writer's move to cheaper lodgings proves tragic when he falls under the spell of a vampiric and viciously jealous female ghost. Similar links between artistic creativity and abnormal mental states are drawn in "Benlian" and "Io," and the theme is extended to take in scientific creativity in "Rooum." Further play with related ideas can be found in "The Real People" (in *Ghosts in Daylight,* 1924), a variant on the common theme of an author's characters coming to life. A different hypothetical metaphysics underlies two of the three novellas in *The Painted Face* (1929); the title story and "The Rosewood Door" are both tragic romances of reincarnation. All these stories are in *The Collected Ghost Stories of Oliver Onions* (1935; "Io" is retitled "The Lost Thyrsus"), which also has some items not previously published in book form. Onions's work is stylishly suspenseful, and his best works are very effective.

Pain, Barry (U.K.), 1865–1928.
ABOUT: WW, GSF, SFW, CA, SMFL, PE, ESF, FL

3-156. Stories in the Dark. Grant Richards, 1901.
Collection including several tales of encroaching madness, of which the best is "The Diary of a God." "The Undying Thing" is a more conventional horror story about a family curse; and the often-reprinted "The Moon-Slave" tells the curious tale of a princess whose wild dances in the heart of a maze attract an enigmatic partner. Other weird tales can be found (with other items) in *Here and Hereafter* (1911), *Stories in Grey* (1911) and *Short Stories of Today and Tomorrow* (1928); the second-named includes the intriguing "Rose Rose," about an artist's model whose death does not prevent her continuing to pose, and the neat delusional fantasy "Linda."

[For other works of this author, see the companion guide to fantasy.]

Peterson, Margaret (U.K.), 1883–1933.
ABOUT: ESF

3-157. Moonflowers. Hutchinson, 1926.
Novel set in Africa in which a seductive female vampire marries a series of men, destroying them in turn until her true nature is discovered; with the aid of a priest, the characters put an end to her depredations. A familiar formula enlivened by the exchange of sex roles.

Praed, Mrs. Campbell (**Rosa Murray Prior**) (Australia), 1851–1935.
ABOUT: WW, GSF

3-158. The Insane Root. Unwin, 1902.
Credulous occult romance in which the power of a mandrake root enables a doctor to implant his own personality in the body of his handsome cad of a cousin in order that the girl whom they both love can be assured of a more loving marriage—but the displaced and disembodied persona can still make its presence felt. Prolix, but the passages dealing with the mandrake are effective.

Price, E(dgar) Hoffmann, 1898–1989.
ABOUT: WW, GSF, CA, RG, SFFL, ESF

3-159. Strange Gateways. Arkham House, 1967.
Collection of stories spanning some forty years; they include "The Stranger from Kurdistan" (1925), in which devil worshippers do not quite get what they bargained for when they invoke Melek Taus, and the ironic Oriental fantasy "Well of the Angels" (1940). Although he was a member of the Lovecraft circle, Price tends not to develop the horrific aspects of his stories fully, preferring to cultivate their Orientalism and exoticism. The larger collection *Far Lands, Other Days* (1975) reprints other stories from *Weird Tales* and items from the weird menace pulps, as well as exotic adventure stories.

Pryce, Devereux (U.K.).

3-160. Out of the Ages. Parsons, 1923.
Romantic entanglements among a group of friends are further complicated by their acquisition of an ancient Egyptian artifact which brings bad luck to all who have it; the tragedy which it precipitates conveniently solves all moral dilemmas. A restrained handling of the curse-of-the-mummy's-tomb theme.

Quiller-Couch, Arthur T(homas) (U.K.), 1863-1940.

ABOUT: WW, GSF, SFW, CA, PE, ESF

3-161. Old Fires and Profitable Ghosts. Cassell, 1900.
Collection including five weird tales; the best is "The Lady of the Ship," set in sixteenth-century Cornwall and telling the story of a shipwrecked witch. Cornwall is also featured in the Wandering Jew story "The Mystery of Joseph Laquedem," and in several other weird stories scattered through the author's many collections (earlier ones appeared under the pseudonym Q). *The Laird's Luck* (1901) includes the ambitious "Phoebus on Halzaphron," based on the legend of Lyonesse; *The White Wolf and Other Fireside Tales* (1902) includes the notable nautical ghost story "The Haunted Yacht."

Quinn, Seabury, 1889-1969.

ABOUT: WW, GSF, F, CA, SMFL, SFE, RG, PE, ESF

3-162. Is the Devil a Gentleman? Mirage Press, 1970.
Collection of Quinn's nonseries stories, including two odd *femme fatale* stories—"Glamour" (1939) and the title story (1942)—plus the interesting Mardi Gras ghost story "Masked Ball" (1947) and the werewolf story "Uncanonized" (1939). Quinn's more famous werewolf story, "The Phantom Farmhouse," (1923), is not included.

3-163. The Phantom-Fighter. Mycroft & Moran, 1966.
Collection of stories involving the occult detective Jules de Grandin, who was featured in ninety-three adventures in *Weird Tales* between 1925 and 1951. The one novel in the series was *The Devil's Bride* (1932; in book form 1976); other paperback collections are: *The Adventures of Jules de Grandin* (1976), *The Casebook of Jules de Grandin* (1976), *The Skeleton Closet of Jules de Grandin* (1976), *The Hellfire Files of Jules de Grandin* (1976) and *The Horror Chambers of Jules de Grandin* (1977). Structurally the stories are weak pastiches of the Sherlock Holmes stories, whose supernatural apparatus is unenlivened by any interest in metaphysical theory; Quinn recklessly plundered motifs from many sources without any real attempt at consistency.

[For other works of this author, see the companion guide to fantasy.]

Renard, Maurice (France), 1875-1940.
ABOUT: SFE, TCSF, ESF

3-164. The Hands of Orlac. Dutton, 1929. Tr. by Florence Crewe-Jones of *Les Mains d'Orlac,* 1920.
Classic macabre murder mystery in which the hands of a murderer are transplanted to replace the mangled hands of a concert painist, then seem to take on a life of their own when a gruesome series of killings follows. Three films based on the story fail to do it justice, as does this somewhat free translation; a better one was made by Iain White for the Souvenir Press edition of 1981.

Robbins, Tod (Clarence Aaron Robbins), 1888-1949.
ABOUT: WW, GSF, ESF

3-165. Mysterious Martin. Ogilvie, 1912.
The story of a writer whose depiction of the psychology of a murderer is so accurate that people who read the book are inspired with the urge to murder—but how has the author coped with the problem of auto-suggestion? An intriguing story, possibly owing its inspiration to Chambers's *The King in Yellow* [2-12]. It was reprinted as *For Art's Sake* in the collection *Silent, White and Beautiful* (1921) and revised as *The Master of Murder* (1933).

***3-166. Who Wants a Green Bottle?** Philip Allan, 1926.
Collection of stories, mostly previously featured in the *Creeps* series [3-23]. Two—the title story and "Wild Wullie the Waster"—also feature in *Silent, White and Beautiful* (1921). Most are boisterously vivid tall stories set in the British Isles, but the stars of the collection are the metaphysical fantasy "Toys" and the excellent *conte cruel* "Spurs," on which the famous Tod Browning film *Freaks* (1932) was based—though standards of decency required that the spurs be left out of the film. Robbins also wrote the macabre crime story *The Unholy Three* (also known as *The Terrible Three* and *The Three Freaks*), which was twice filmed—once by Browning.

Rohmer, Sax (pseud.—later legal name—of Arthur Sarsfield Ward) (U.K.), 1883-1959.
ABOUT: WW, GSF, SFW, CA, NE, SMFL, PE, ESF

3-167. Brood of the Witch-Queen. Pearson, 1918.
Thriller in which the evil adopted son of an occultist uses various magical and murderous means to gain control of his adoptive father's fortune, but is ultimately thwarted when his true (but unlikely) identity is revealed. Pulp action-adventure exhibiting Rohmer's predilection for supposedly charismatic villains, which became habitual after the success of the early books in the long-running Fu Manchu series (1913-59).

3-168. The Green Eyes of Bast. Cassell, 1920.
Occult mystery thriller involving a villainess marked by prenatal influences with feline stigmata. Creepier and less chaotic (at least in its earlier stages) than most of Rohmer's work in this well-worn vein. *Grey Face* (1924) is more typical, featuring

a rejuvenated supervillain with various occult powers; *The Bat Flies Low* (1935) is rather more interesting by virtue of getting away from the straightforward supervillain formula in its use of a more engimatic occultist.

3-169. The Haunting of Low Fennel. Pearson, 1920.
Perhaps the best of Rohmer's several short story collections; the title story features a haunted house, while the other weird stories draw on the author's Oriental interests, as do the supernatural marginalia in the earlier *Tales of Secret Egypt* (1918) and the later *Tales of Chinatown* (1922) and *Tales of East and West* (Cassell, 1932; the U.S. collection of the same title is a selection from the three U.K. collections). Several of the stories in the later collections feature Paul Harley, who is also the hero of the macabre murder mysteries *Bat Wing* (1921) and *Fire-Tongue* (1921).

Rolt, L(ionel) T(homas) C(aswell) (U.K.), 1910–1974.
About: WW, GSF, CA, PE, ESF

3-170. Sleep No More. Constable, 1948.
Collection of weird tales featuring conventional motifs. The best is the murder-will-out story "Hawley Bank Foundry," but "Music Hath Charms," about the supernatural influence of an old music box, is also interesting.

Ross, Charles (U.K.), 1864–1930.
About: CA, ESF

3-171. When the Devil Was Sick. Murray, 1924
The caves associated with ancient Cornish mine workings are opened to the public, but are troubled by apparitions and a mysterious death. The owner and his friends investigate, and become caught up in a reenactment of ancient rites of human sacrifice first practiced when a temple of Astarte was taken over by worshippers of Moloch. An effective thriller.

Saki (pseud. of **Hector Hugh Munro**) (U.K.), 1870–1916.
About: WW, GSF, SFW, CA, SMFL, SFE, PE, ESF

3-172. The Complete Short Stories of Saki. John Lane, 1930.
Omnibus edition containing *Reginald* (1904), *Reginald in Russia* (1910), *The Chronicles of Clovis* (1911), *Beasts and Super-Beasts* (1914), *The Toys of Peace* (1923) and *The Square Egg* (1924). "Saki" is without peer as a writer of sardonic tales which take malicious delight in visiting cruel and ironic fates upon the blinkered members of the British upper classes. The tales include such classics as "Gabriel-Ernest," which features a juvenile werewolf; "Sredni Vashtar," in which a small boy deifies his ferret; "The Music on the Hill," in which country life might be idyllic were it not for the spirit of Pan; and "Laura," in which a shrewish woman resolves while dying to return from beyond in unconventional guises.

Sampson, Ashley (U.K.), born 1900.
About: GSF

3-173. The Ghost of Mr. Brown. Fortune Press, 1941
The story of a ghost who attempts to redeem himself from his anguished predicament by forming new relationships with the family whose house he haunts—but the corruption of his nature, which was responsible for his condemnation, inevitably reasserts itself. Grimly effective.

Savage, Richard (pseud. of **Ivan Roe**)(U.K.), 1917- .
About: SFE, ESF

3-174. The Horrible Hat. Jarrolds, 1948
Psychological horror story in which an artist becomes obsessed and mentally ill after seeing visions of the horribly transfigured face of a fellow artist long presumed dead; a psychoanalyst tries to sort out the actual from the illusory. Effective, but rather coy about filling in the details of its final explanation, avoiding use of the word "syphilis."

Sayers, Dorothy L(eigh), editor.

3-175. Great Short Stories of Detection, Mystery and Horror. Gollancz, 1929.
First of three similarly titled classic anthologies; a *Second Series* followed in 1931 and a *Third Series* in 1934. The U.S. editions, published as *The Omnibus of Crime, The Second Omnibus of Crime* and *The Third Omnibus of Crime,* have somewhat different contents. The "Mystery and Horror" sections of the first two anthologies are excellent eclectic selections from the British tradition of supernatural fiction; the third is somewhat weaker.

Shearing, Joseph (pseud. of **Gabrielle Long)** (U.K.), 1886-1952.
About: WW, GSF, F, CA, H, PE, ESF

3-176. The Fetch. Hutchinson, 1942. U.S. title: *The Spectral Bride.*
Psychological horror story. A sensitive young aristocrat obsessed by a girl supposedly murdered by his ancestor is taken in by the charade of a fantasizing girl who poses as her ghost; the consequence is ironically tragic. Richly detailed by courtesy of Mrs. Long's own intense fascination with case studies involving occult experiences and impostures.

Shiel, M(atthew) P(hipps) (U.K.), 1865-1947.
About: WW, GSF, SFW, CA, NE, SMFL, SFE, TCSF, PE, ESF

3-177. The Pale Ape and Other Pulses. Werner Laurie, 1911.
Collection including several weird tales. The most interesting are "Huguenin's Wife" and "The Bride," both of which feature remarkable revenants bent on vengeance. *Here Comes the Lady* (1928) has the curious *conte à clef* "The Primate

of the Rose" and the magnificent "Dark Lot of One Saul" in which a shipwrecked sailor finds himself in a dreadful underworld. *The Invisible Voices* (1935) embeds various stories in a frame narrative, including the excellent visionary fantasy "The Place of Pain." All of these except the last-named are in *The Best Short Stories of M. P. Shiel* (1948) and *Xelucha and Others* (1975).

[For other works of this author, see the companion guide to fantasy.]

Sinclair, May (U.K.), 1865–1946.

ABOUT: WW, GSF, SFW, CA, PE, ESF

***3-178. Uncanny Stories**. Hutchinson, 1923.
Collection of weird tales including two fine posthumous fantasies—"Where Their Fire Is Not Quenched" and "The Finding of the Absolute"—and the very striking "The Nature of the Evidence," in which the ghost of a man's first wife intrudes upon his second marriage. The supernatural is here used in the Henry Jamesian manner (see [2-45; 3-107]) to symbolize and extrapolate the stress points which arise within human relationships, emphasizing the importance of matters of moral choice. *The Intercessor and Other Stories* (1931) includes a further posthumous fantasy, "Heaven," and the excellent title story about a ghostly child. Sinclair's stories are among the most outstanding examples of the ghost story as moral fable.

Siodmak, Curt (Germany/U.S.) 1902- .

ABOUT: WW, CA, NE, SFE, SFFL, TCSF, ESF

3-179. Donovan's Brain. Knopf, 1943
Twice-filmed horror/SF story about the disembodied brain of a gangster which gradually acquires the power to compel others to do its evil bidding. An effective melodrama by a prolific scriptwriter of Hollywood shockers.

Sitwell, Osbert (U.K.), 1892–1969.

ABOUT: CA, SFE

3-180. A Place of One's Own. Macmillan, 1941.
Novella in which a childless couple move into their "dream house" but find the dream turning slowly to nightmare as they and their servant-girl are confronted by supernatural manifestations which gradually escalate from annoyance to tragedy. A darkly ironic study of skepticism defeated.

[For other works of this author, see the companion guide to fantasy.]

Sloane, William M(illigan) 1906–1974.

ABOUT: GSF, F, CA, SFE, TCSF, PE, ESF

3-181. The Edge of Running Water. Farrar & Rinehart, 1939.
The protagonist is summoned to the home of a longtime friend whose attempts to build a device to communicate with the dead have injured his health and given rise to nasty rumors; the experiments are brought to a seemingly successful

conclusion, but the achievement brings tragedy in its wake. An effective and suspenseful mystery story.

Smith, Clark Ashton 1893-1961.
About: WW, GSF, SFW, F, CA, NE, H, SMFL, SFE, RG, TCSF, PE, ESF, FL

3-182. Out of Space and Time. Arkham House, 1942.
The first of Smith's several collections of ornate and phantasmagoric fantasies, most of whose contents fall into the borderlands between fantasy, SF and horror. Closest to the orthodox horror tradition are the stories set in the imaginary French province of Averoigne in various phases of history; examples here are the lamia story "The End of the Story" (1930) and the vampire story "A Rendezvous in Averoigne" (1931). Also included are the taphephobic fantasy "The Second Interment" (1934); several nightmarish fantasies set in ultimately decadent far-future Zothique, most notably "The Dark Eidolon" (1934) and "The Death of Ilalotha" (1937); and three grotesque tales set in prehistoric Hyperborea, including the Lovecraftian "Ubbo-Sathla" (1933) and the black comedy "The Testament of Athammaus." Equally varied and colorful material can be found in *Lost Worlds* (1944), which includes the best of Smith's Hyperborean grotesques, "The Seven Geases" (1933), and two of the nastiest tales of Zothique: "The Empire of the Necromancers" (1932) and "Necromancy in Naat" (1936). Some early stories featuring more conventional motifs can be found in *Genus Loci and Other Tales* (1948), as well as Smith's reprise of Mérimée's "Venus of Ille," "The Disinterment of Venus" (1934) and the gruesome "The Charnel God" (1934). The rest of Smith's stories were collected in *The Abominations of Yondo* (1960), *Tales of Science and Sorcery* (1964) and *Other Dimensions* (1970). As Lovecraft remarked, Smith was "unexcelled by any other writer dead or living" in "sheer daemonic strangeness and fertility of conception"; he was an unparalleled artist of the phantasmagoric literary nightmare. A recent representative collection of his stories is *A Rendezvous in Averoigne: The Best Fantastic Tales of Clark Ashton Smith* (Arkham House, 1988).

Snow, Jack, 1907-1957.
About: WW, GSF, ESF

3-183. Dark Music and Other Spectral Tales. Herald, 1947.
Collection of stories partly drawn from *Weird Tales*; the bizarre title story features a hermit who has coopted musical bats into a sinister orchestra; "The Dimension of Terror" features a nasty parallel world; "Midnight" (1946) is about a diabolist who unwisely seeks union with the principle of evil. Standard pulp fare enlivened by a touch of grotesquerie.

Spence, Lewis (U.K.), 1874-1955.
About: GSF, CA, ESF

3-184. The Archer in the Arras and Other Tales of Mystery. Grant & Murray, 1932.
Collection of weird tales by a noted writer of "nonfiction" about Atlantis and the

supposed roots of British folklore. The most interesting are "The Sorceress in Stained Glass" and "The Horn of Vapula," both of which are examples of M. R. Jamesian pastiche (see [3-108]). Many of the stories are anchored in Scottish folklore. Like Elliott O'Donnell [3-153], Spence was not a sufficiently artful writer to produce convincing fiction.

Stevens, Francis (pseud. of **Gertrude Bennett**), 1884–1939?

ABOUT: GSF, F, SMFL, SFE, TCSF, ESF

3-185. Claimed. Avalon, 1966.
Novel first serialized in *Argosy* (1920). A mysterious box (which turns out to have been recovered from an island where an ancient city seems to have been destroyed by a volcano) is bought out of a curio shop by a plutocratic collector, but it soon becomes apparent that something monstrous and powerful is following its trail. An effective thriller by one of the better pulp writers.

Stoker, Bram (i.e., **Abraham**) (U.K.), 1847–1912.

ABOUT: WW, GSF, SFW, F, CA, NE, H, SMFL, SFE, RG, PE, ESF

***3-186. Dracula**. London: Constable, 1897. A useful edition is *The Annotated Dracula,* with extensive notes by Leonard Wolf (Clarkson Potter, 1975).
The most famous and most influential of modern horror stories, which marks the beginning of this period in the history of the genre. The novel is a patchwork of documents which tell the story of Jonathan Harker, who visits the mysterious Count Dracula in Transylvania and subsequently makes it possible for him to come to England, where resistance to his vampiric depredations depends upon the expert knowledge of Professor van Helsing. The eroticism of the story and the power of its melodramatic imagery easily override the technical faults of the narrative, producing a modern archetype of seductive evil. Some critics have suggested that Stoker had recently contracted syphilis, and unwittingly wrote a symbolic account of his malady, but one can equally well argue that Dracula, who threatens to turn chaste young women into voluptuous ravening predators, is simply a monstrous symbol of the fearful Victorian attitudes to sexuality which were then reaching their time of crisis.

3-187. Dracula's Guest and Other Weird Stories. Routledge, 1914.
Posthumous collection of Stoker's shorter works; the title story is a melodramatic fragment wisely dropped from the novel; "The Judge's House" is an exercise in Le Fanuesque pastiche; "The Secret of the Growing Gold" is the story of a murderer brought to account by the hair of his victim. "The Burial of the Rats" and "The Squaw" are effective *contes cruels.*

3-188. The Jewel of Seven Stars. Heinemann, 1903.
Occult romance involving an attempt to revivify the mummy of an ancient Egyptian queen. The vague and sketchy ending is "repaired" in subsequent editions, probably not by Stoker. The story has interesting elements and a few creepy moments but ultimately fails to achieve coherency.

3-189. The Lady of the Shroud. Heinemann, 1909.
Long and confused political Gothic with a few supernatural intrusions and a vaguely science fictional conclusion. Most subsequent editions are heavily abridged, but fail to find much of a story to extract from the literary morass.

3-190. The Lair of the White Worm. Rider, 1911.
Spectacularly ridiculous novel about a vermiform monster which can manifest itself as a sinisterly beautiful woman. Possibly based on an actual nightmare from which the author could make little sense; invites interpretation (in the eyes of those critics who read a similar meaning in [3-186]) as a symbolic transfiguration of venereal disease.

[For other works of this author, see the companion guide to fantasy.]

Stonier, G(eorge) W(alter) (U.K.), 1903- .
ABOUT: GSF, ESF

3-191. The Memoirs of a Ghost. Grey Walls Press, 1947.
Surreal novella very extensively revised from a short story of the same title; the narrator is a casualty of war who settles gradually into his post-existential situation but gradually loses touch with reality. A strange and bitter work whose allegorical implications are difficult to trace.

Sturgeon, Theodore (formerly **Edward Hamilton Waldo**), 1918-1985.
ABOUT: WW, GSF, SFW, CA, TCA, NE, SMFL, SFE, SFFL, RG, TCSF, PE, ESF

3-192. Without Sorcery. Prime Press, 1948.
The first of Sturgeon's many collections, including SF and fantasy as well as horror stories. Includes the excellent monster story "It" (1940) and a gruesomely ironic story of a man given the power to see ghosts, "Shottle Bop" (1941). *E Pluribus Unicorn* (1953) has a typically nasty-minded story of a demonic toy, "The Professor's Teddy-Bear" (1948); a brilliant story of perverse love, "Bianca's Hands" (1947); and a story of a prison inmate who has a weird invisible twin, "Cellmate" (1947); as well as stories from a later period. In these early works, and in his famous SF/horror story "Killdozer!" (1944), Sturgeon demonstrates considerable imaginative vision in discovering unusual horrific situations as well as consummate artistry in drawing them out.

Swain, E(dmund) G(ill) (U.K.), 1861-1938.
ABOUT: WW, GSF, PE, ESF

3-193. The Stoneground Ghost Tales. Heffer, 1912.
Ghost stories by the chaplain of one of the Cambridge colleges; dedicated to M. R. James but not really following his method (see [3-108]). The stories are subtle, the supernatural intrusions preserving reminders of past crimes but rarely hurting anyone. Reprinted as *Bone to His Bone: The Stoneground Ghost Tales* (Equation, 1989), with introduction by Michael Cox and six original stories in the same series by David Rowlands.

Synton, Rosalie and Edward (U.K.).

3-194. Possessed. Hutchinson, 1927.
The story of a mother's apparent attempts to destroy her daughter by a kind of psychic vampirism, told from three successive viewpoints: that of a doctor who intervenes to help the daughter; that of the daughter's husband, who murders the mother; and that of the woman herself. An interesting and very unusual study of evil, which ends on a striking note of cruel irony.

Thomson, Christine Campbell, editor.

3-195. Not at Night. Selwyn & Blount, 1925.
The first in an important series of anthologies which continued with *More Not at Night* (1926), *You'll Need a Night Light* (1927), *Gruesome Cargoes* (1928), *By Daylight Only* (1929), *Switch on the Light* (1931), *At Dead of Night* (1931) *Grim Death* (1932), *Keep on the Light* (1933), *Terror by Night* (1935) and *Nightmare by Daylight* (1936). There was also a *Not at Night Omnibus* (1937), and some stories are recombined in various paperback reprints. The series used some domestic material but reprinted many stories from *Weird Tales,* including first book publication of several stories by the great *Weird Tales* triumvirate H. P. Lovecraft [3-132], Robert E. Howard [3-95] and Clark Ashton Smith [3-182]. The editor included some of her own stories (usually bylined Flavia Richardson) and some of her first husband, Oscar Cook.

Thorndike, Russell (U.K.), 1885–1972.

About: GSF, CA, ESF

3-196. The Master of the Macabre. Rich & Cowan, 1947.
Fix-up novel in which the narrator stays with the eponymous collector of exotica, hears some of his stories and is bothered by phantoms and mysterious men in search of an ancient Islamic relic. Crude melodrama by the author of the Dr. Syn books.

Tweedale, Violet (U.K.), 1862–1936.

About: CA, ESF

3-197. The House of the Other World. John Long, 1913.
Credulous and portentous novel about a haunted farmhouse whose phenomena are ultimately explained and laid to rest by careful investigation. The plot is continually interrupted by theoretical dialogues about metaphysical matters, which are less inventive and less interesting than those in Blackwood's John Silence stories [3-27], on which the story is seemingly modeled. The author produced two volumes of supposedly true stories about her experiences as a psychical researcher, *Ghosts I Have Seen* (1919) and *Phantoms of the Dawn* (1924).

van Vogt, A(lfred) E(lton), 1912- , and **Hull, E(dna) Mayne,** 1905-1975.
ABOUT: GSF, F, CA, NE, SFE, SFFL, TCSF, ESF

3-198. Out of the Unknown. Fantasy Publishing Co., 1948.
Collection including five weird tales from *Unknown*. "The Wishes We Make" (1943) and "The Ultimate Wish" (1943) are wry tales of wishes gone wrong; "The Ghost" (1943) is a convoluted and very unusual ghost story. Despite the use of conventional themes, the stories are clever and innovative, ideally suited to the spirit of the magazine in which they appeared.

Viereck, George Sylvester, 1884-1962.
ABOUT: WW, GSF, CA, SMFL, SFE, PE, ESF

3-199. The House of the Vampire. Moffet, Yard, 1907.
A young musician becomes the protégé of an older man, whose artistic talents are abundant and varied; as their acquaintance extends, he finds his own powers weakening, and is forced to conclude that the other is drawing them from him in vampiric fashion. Like Wilde's *Picture of Dorian Gray* [2-97] it has an obvious homosexual subtext; it also has affinities with the work of Hanns Heinz Ewers [3-68].

[For other works of this author, see the companion guide to fantasy.]

Wakefield, H(erbert) Russell (U.K.), 1888-1965.
ABOUT: WW, GSF, SFW, CA, SFFL, PE, ESF

***3-200. They Return at Evening.** Philip Allan, 1928.
The first and best of the author's several collections. Includes "Professor Pownall's Oversight," about a chess player harassed by the spirit of a murdered rival; "The Third Coach," a study in madness involving a nasty confidence trickster; and "The Seventeenth Hole at Duncaster," about a haunted golf course. Some of the stories are derivative ("He Cometh and He Passeth By!" is a virtual pastiche of M. R. James [3-108]) but they are handled with consummate craftsmanship. *Old Man's Beard* (1929) is not quite up to the same standard, but features several fine studies of supernatural malevolence, two of the best being "The Cairn" and "Blind Man's Buff." *Imagine a Man in a Box* (1931) is a more varied collection whose best weird story is the haunted house story "The Frontier Guards." The stories in *The Clock Strikes Twelve* (1940; the Arkham House edition of 1946 adds four additional stories) tend to be more ambiguous in dealing with the supernatural, often accommodating the apparitions to various kinds of metaphysical theory. *Strayers from Sheol* (1961) [4-31] further extrapolates this trend to produce some complex and unusually sophisticated stories, including the excellent story of human bondage "Monstrous Regiment." Two collections which recombine stories from earlier books but add a few new items are *Ghost Stories* (1932) and *A Ghostly Company* (1935). Wakefield was a consistently competent writer who took up where M. R. James left off in extending the core of the British tradition through the period between the wars.

Walpole, Hugh (U.K.), 1884-1941.
ABOUT: WW, GSF, CA, H, PE, ESF

3-201. All Souls' Night. Macmillan, 1933.
Collection of strange stories, including the often-dramatized tale of psychological menace "The Silver Mask" and the ironically nasty "Tarnhelm; or, the Death of My Uncle Robert," in which the unflattering "true self" of the eponymous uncle is revealed. Some other uneasy tales of a similarly ambiguous stripe are in *The Silver Thorn* (1928). Walpole's interest in paranoid fantasy was compromised by his reluctance to use overtly supernatural themes, but he produced some artful stories closely akin to those of his fellow contributor to Cynthia Asquith's anthologies [3-6], L. P. Hartley [3-80].

3-202. The Killer and the Slain: A Strange Story. Macmillan, 1942.
The life of the ineffectual and repressed narrator is made miserable by the teasing bonhomie of an uninhibited sensualist; the fear that this false friend may seduce his wife drives him to murder, but he gradually takes on the psychological and physical characteristics of his victim, eventually embarking upon a merciless persecution of a man who strongly resembles his old self. Has an evil spirit transferred itself from victim to killer? Much more effective than Walpole's earlier exercise in "romantic macabre," *Portrait of a Man with Red Hair* (1925), which features a deranged sadist of a less subtle stripe.

Walton, Evangeline, 1907- .
ABOUT: WW, GSF, CA, SMFL, RG, PE, ESF, FL, HF

3-203. Witch House. Arkham House, 1945.
Baroque thriller in which a house owned by the descendants of a sorcerer is the focal point of much supernatural activity, including the harassment of a young girl; a psychiatrist and occult expert comes to her defense. The imagery is overcrowded but occasionally very effective, and the mystery element is well handled.

[For other works of this author, see the companion guide to fantasy.]

Wandrei, Donald, 1908-1987.
ABOUT: WW, GSF, SFE, PE, ESF

3-204. The Eye and the Finger. Arkham House, 1944.
Collection of short stories, mostly SF of an outrageously melodramatic stripe, including the horror/SF story "The Red Brain" (1927). The title story (1936) is a case study of an all-too-real vision; "It Will Grow on You" (1937) is a moral fable featuring macabre stigmata. *Strange Harvest* (1965) is a similar mixture, including a nasty fantasy about an unlucky grave robber, "The Chuckler" (1934).

3-205. The Web of Easter Island. Arkham House, 1948.
Cthulhu Mythos novel (see [3-132]) in which an archaeologist is unlucky enough to find the key which will open a dimensional gateway for the monstrous titans which set in train the evolution of mankind. As with most of Wandrei's work, the

novel deploys SF motifs as well as supernatural ones in the service of unrestrained melodrama; the result is saved from silliness only by its zest.

Warren, J. Russell (U.K.).

3-206. This Mortal Coil. Melrose, 1947.
A man anaesthetized in a dentist's chair awakens to find himself within the body and sharing the memories of a man wanted for a brutal murder. One of the more intense and detailed accounts of metempsychosis; compare Christopher Evans's similarly bleak *The Insider* (1981).

Wellman, Manly Wade, 1903–1986.

About: WW, GSF, SFW, CA, H, SMFL, SFE, SFFL, RG, TCSF, PE, ESF

3-207. Worse Things Waiting. Carcosa, 1973.
Huge collection of pulp stories, mostly from *Weird Tales*. The most interesting stories are those which deploy folkloristic themes in an American context, including four linked stories set in the Civil War period: "His Name on a Bullet" (1940), "The Valley Was Still" (1939), "Fearful Rock" (1939) and "Coven" (1942). Also included are a nice story featuring Edgar Allan Poe, "When It Was Moonlight" (1940); the Dracula story "The Devil Is Not Mocked" (1943); and a Cthulhu Mythos story, "The Terrible Parchment" (1937). *Lonely Vigils* (1981) is a collection of occult detective stories, mostly from two series featuring Judge Pursuivant (bylined Gans T. Field when they appeared in *Weird Tales*) and John Thunstone; several of the latter feature the sinister false humans called Shonokins. Though many of the stories are hackwork, Wellman's exercises in supernatural Americana have a certain fascination, and their plots are sometimes sharpened by awkward moral dilemmas.

Wharton, Edith, 1862–1937.

About: WW, GSF, SFW, CA, SMFL, SFE, PE, ESF

***3-208. Ghosts**. Appleton-Century, 1937.
Collection reprinting the ghost stories from the earlier collections *Tales of Men and Ghosts* (1910), *Xingu and Other Stories* (1916) and *Here and Beyond* (1926), and adding four others. Like her contemporary May Sinclair [3-178], Wharton uses ghosts to emphasize the moral stress points which shape human lives and relationships; the apparitions usually dramatize guilt but can also signify love and duty (as in "The Lady's Maid's Bell"). The most outstanding stories are "Afterward," "Kerfol" and "The Triumph of Night." *The Ghost Stories of Edith Wharton* (1975) adds one more story to the contents of *Ghosts.*

Wheatley, Dennis (U.K.), 1897–1977.

About: WW, GSF, SFW, CA, SMFL, SFE, SFFL, TCSF, PE, ESF

3-209. The Devil Rides Out. Hutchinson, 1935.
Lurid thriller in which the three heroes of the spy story *Forbidden Territory*

become involved with a Crowleyesque sorcerer who has one of them in his thrall; a second falls in love with one of the magician's female pawns. After much frenetic action, including a Black Mass, the situation is belatedly saved by a mind-bogglingly extravagant *deus ex machina.* The same characters figured in several other novels, not all supernatural; the same basic plot is replayed in *Strange Conflict* (1941), an exercise in wartime jingoism in which they must combat Nazi black magic.

3-210. Gunmen, Gallants and Ghosts. Hutchinson, 1943.
Collection including several weird tales; four feature occult detective Niels Orsen, while "The Snake" is an often-reprinted story of African magic. Wheatley's own efforts in this line are weak, but he is named as editor of the excellent eclectic anthology *A Century of Horror Stories* (1935).

3-211. The Haunting of Toby Jugg. Hutchinson, 1948.
The young hero, injured in the war, is beset by supernatural horrors unleashed by those bent on possessing the fortune to which he is heir. His situation seems hopeless, but the Wheatley brand of *deus ex machina* can reach depths never plumbed by more scrupulous plotters.

[For other works of this author, see the companion guide to fantasy.]

White, Edward Lucas, 1866-1934.

ABOUT: WW, GSF, PE, ESF

3-212. Lukundoo and Other Stories. Doran, 1927.
Collection of horror stories whose often-reprinted title story features a curse which makes tiny homunculi erupt periodically from the flesh of a man who has wronged an African tribeswoman. "Sorcery Island" also has an unusual motif. *The Song of the Sirens and Other Stories* (1919) also contains some (mostly nonsupernatural) macabre tales.

Whitehead, Henry S(t. Clair), 1882-1932.

ABOUT: WW, GSF, PE, ESF

3-213. Jumbee and Other Uncanny Tales. Arkham House, 1944.
Collection of stories mostly reprinted from *Weird Tales.* All but one are set in the West Indies and are redolent with local color. A distinctive brand of witchcraft is featured in the title story (1926), in the excellent "Sweet Grass" (1929) and in "The Tree-Man" (1931), while voodoo in the narrow sense crops up in "The Passing of a God" (1930). The novella "Seven Turns in a Hangman's Rope" (1932) is a nice account of a man condemned to a special hell when his soul is captured in a painting. This is a much stronger collection than *West India Lights* (1946), which reprinted the remainder of the author's work, but the latter does have the interesting phantasmagoric novella "The Great Circle" (1932). Whitehead was a cut above the general run of pulp writers and his stories feature some remarkable motifs, occasionally let down by inept plotting.

Williamson, Jack, 1908- .

ABOUT: GSF, F, CA, TCA, NE, SMFL, SFE, MF, SFFL, TCSF, ESF, HF

***3-214. Darker Than You Think**. Fantasy Press, 1948.
Classic novel from *Unknown* (1940). An investigative reporter enthralled by a female werewolf becomes the hapless instrument of a plot by which members of a second human species, *Homo lycanthropus*, seek to win ascendancy in the evolutionary struggle. A fine translocation of science fictional sympathy for the supermen-to-come into a more traditional framework; the narrative is gripping and the imagery very effective. Williamson wrote several highly melodramatic novellas for *Weird Tales* and similar pulps, including *Dreadful Sleep* (1938; reprinted as *Lost Fantasies #7*, 1977) and "Wolves of Darkness" (1931; reprinted in *Beware More Beasts*, edited by Vic Ghidalia and Roger Elwood, 1975).

Wren, P(ercival) C(hristopher) (U.K.), 1885-1941.

ABOUT: GSF, CA, ESF

3-215. Dew and Mildew. Murray, 1916.
A fakir places a curse on a bungalow whose erection involved the desecration of a tomb. The story follows the effects of the curse on later inhabitants of what comes to be known as Sudden-Death Lodge. Less emotionally intense than Wren's later works. Several weird tales based in the folklore of India and the Far East are in Wren's collections *Rough Shooting* (1938) and *Odd—But Even So* (1941); the best are "Elephantasy," in which a strange tree is worshiped by an elephant, and "Ordeal by Water," which features a werepanther.

3-216. The Disappearance of General Jason. Murray, 1940.
The inhabitants of the lost island of São Thomé wish to remain lost, giving short shrift to adventurers attracted by rumors of its radium deposits; the hero goes there in search of his vanished friend, only to discover that the general has met with a particularly horrible fate. Displays Wren's curious penchant for subjecting his characters to harrowing ordeals as a result of apparently trivial mistakes and misapprehensions.

Wylie, Philip, 1902-1971.

ABOUT: GSF, CA, NE, SFE, SFFL, TCSF, ESF

3-217. Night unto Night. Farrar & Rinehart, 1944.
Philosophical novel in which an epileptic scientist becomes involved with two women, one of whom is the focal point of supernatural phenomena which expand their scope to involve him; a ghost is seeking to reveal a secret regarding the second woman. A typically idiosyncratic novel of ideas, by no means up to the standard of Wylie's *tour de force* of *avant-garde* realism *Finnley Wren* (1934), but interesting nevertheless.

[For other works of this author, see the companion guide to fantasy.]

Young, Francis Brett (U.K.), 1884–1954.
About: GSF, CA

3-218. Cold Harbour. Collins, 1924.
A young couple become acquainted with the sinister Mr. Furnival, whose enervated wife is seemingly being driven mad by the forces which haunt their awful house and which have fatally corrupted her husband. Powerless to intervene, the outsiders can only watch the matter run its tragic course. An atmospheric story of malevolence extending across the centuries.

4

Contemporary Horror Fiction, 1950–88

Keith Neilson

Two Legacies: Wheatley and Lovecraft

In terms of contemporary dark fantasy, the two most important horror writers in the decades between the world wars were Dennis Wheatley in Great Britain and Howard Phillips Lovecraft in America.

Wheatley began his career relatively late in life, but achieved commercial success almost instantly, and continued to produce best-sellers for forty years. Lovecraft began early and wrote constantly throughout his short lifetime, but his output was small, some sixty-odd stories in twenty years, published only in low circulation pulps, primarily *Weird Tales* [11-20]. Thus, during their lifetimes, Wheatley achieved immediate and continuing fame and fortune throughout a long life and prolific writing career, while Lovecraft lived a short, modestly productive life in relative obscurity and poverty.

But although dead only a decade, Wheatley is generally ignored by contemporary horror writers and critics. The most recent and comprehensive survey of the field, *The Penguin Encyclopedia of Horror and the Supernatural* [6-31], grants him one short paragraph. Lovecraft, on the other hand, is universally regarded as the most important American writer of dark fantasy since Edgar Allan Poe.

It was only after the failure of the family wine business that Dennis Wheatley took up the writing of fiction, initially with a spy novel, *Forbidden Territories,* in 1933. His first and best horror novel, *The Devil Rides Out* (1935) [3-209], was a best-seller, and his commercial success continued unabated until his death in 1977. Mixing horror with spy novels, historical adventure novels and a few exercises in nonfiction, Wheatley produced over sixty volumes. His total sales exceeded twenty-three million books and he has been translated into twenty-seven languages. Thus, for over four decades, Wheatley was the most widely read horror writer in the world.

Much of this success was deserved. Wheatley was an excellent storyteller, especially adroit at creating vivid, exciting dramatic scenes. He was also a scrupulous researcher, whose novels are filled with significant, appropriate details, particularly in areas of arcane, occult information. The "black magic" books are a veritable catalogue of supernatural lore—Satanism, Black Masses, demonic possession, magical incantations, the conjuring of demons, necromancy, hypnotism, clairvoyance, numerology, palmistry, astrology, ghostly apparitions, enchanted pentacles, astral travel, curses, crystal ball gazing, sex orgies, child sacrifice and time manipulation, to mention a few. In his best works, Wheatley integrates these supernatural elements into a solid, realistic milieu at those moments in the story when they fit most easily into the narrative flow. By doing so he creates a world in which the laws of black and white magic operate naturally and inevitably, the unseen becoming a palpable presence.

The second ingredient in Wheatley's success was his ability to fuse popular genres into exciting hybrids that defy precise categorization, but utilize some of the most stimulating elements of each. For example, Wheatley's most successful post-World War II novel, *They Used Dark Forces* [4-323], is a sophisticated integration of the occult, espionage and historical adventure forms. This mixture of dark fantasy and spy novel also served Wheatley well in two subsequent novels, *To the Devil—a Daughter* [4-324] and *The Satanist* [4-322]. Both novels, despite serious flaws, again demonstrate Wheatley's ability to merge the excitement and topicality of the spy thriller with the power of the horror story.

All of which is not to say that Wheatley's current lack of recognition is inexplicable. Although a fine storyteller, he was a terrible preacher, and unfortunately, preaching replaces storytelling in too many of his books, particularly in the later works where his obsessive hatred of Communism and his abstract metaphysical speculation more often than not overwhelm his narrative. This tendency also brought out the worst in his prose, which could be quite efficient in telling a story but, when used rhetorically, turned into a kind of late-blooming pseudo-Victorian prose, heavy on abstraction, ornate in diction and syntax, glutted with sentimental clichés.

Even if understandable, however, the present dismissal of Wheatley is unfortunate—and ironic—because, although the fact is unacknowledged and probably unrecognized, the *form* of the most popular contemporary horror novels, the operatic wide-screen novels with large casts and elaborate plots that mix the elements of several genres—horror, social melodrama, mystery, spy, etc.—written by King, Farris, Straub, Koontz, Herbert, and others was pioneered and perfected by Dennis Wheatley.

If Wheatley provided contemporary horror with its most popular form, it was H. P. Lovecraft who gave it much of its substance. Although he died in 1937, his influence on the contemporary scene is pervasive and acknowledged—even if, as so often happens to artistic revolutionaries, he has become the "old" to be reacted against. But when critic Darrell Schweitzer says "the Lovecraftian tradition is about as vigorous as the poetry of the Byzantine Empire,"[1] he is at best only half right. Lovecraft contributed two things to dark fantasy: a mythology and a set of metaphors.

It may be that the Mythos has run its course. But even if it is no longer on the cutting edge of dark fantasy, it has still generated a number of excellent stories, although the emotions evoked are closer to nostalgia than fear. Particularly notable are Mythos stories by Ramsey Campbell (*Cold Print*, 1985), Robert Bloch [3-29; 4-47], Brian Lumley [4-209], Colin Wilson [4-330–4-331], Michael Shea [4-268] and Fred Chappell [4-77].

And behind the Mythos are the metaphors.

> The most merciful thing in the world, I think, is the inability of the human mind to correlate all its contents. We live on a placid island of ignorance in the midst of black seas of infinity, and it was not meant that we should voyage far. The sciences, each straining in its own direction, have hitherto harmed us little; but some day the piecing together of dissociated knowledge will open up such terrifying vistas of reality, and of our frightful position therein, that we shall either go mad from the revelation or flee from the deadly light into the peace and safety of a new dark age.[2]

That opening paragraph from "The Call of Cthulhu" is a succinct summary of Lovecraft's own thinking. It is this cosmic vision which gives primary stature to Lovecraft among modern horror writers. Lovecraft was a materialist who viewed all supernatural ideas, whether conventionally religious or occult, as make-believe. Thus, his Old Ones, with their indifferent cruelty and overwhelming powers, are metaphors for a cruelly indifferent universe that provides a fragile, temporary refuge for that most ephemeral of creatures—man.

In essence, Lovecraft's cosmic view resembles that of many modern writers, including artists as different as Thomas Hardy and Robinson Jeffers. The power of his work lies in the fact that despite the clumsiness, turgidity and triteness of much of the writing, it presents a powerful metaphorical construct of the modern world and man's extremely precarious place in it. Eliminate the labels and particulars of the Cthulhu Mythos, streamline the language and bring the monstrous forces to bear on the mundane world of today and the metaphors behind the Mythos can bring great scope, power and resonance to the horror story, as many of the best contemporary authors have discovered.

The Thing from the Sugarbowl, or: From Cthulhu to Paranoia

The most obvious continuity in contemporary horror fiction is that most of the genre writers who came into prominence after the end of World War II—Robert Bloch, Ray Bradbury, Fritz Leiber, Richard Matheson—saw early publication in *Weird Tales* and then reacted, in one way or another, against the *Weird Tales* "type" of story.

H. P. Lovecraft stated that "In every detail *except* the chosen marvel, the story should be accurately true to nature. The keynote should be that of scientific exposition . . . and should not change as the story gradually slides off from the possible to the impossible."[3]

Compare what Richard Matheson has said about his fiction: "In a way, as a fantasy writer, I'm a mainstream writer. Once I've established the twist, I proceed in a non-fantasy manner." Or, at another point in the same interview, "the typical Richard Matheson story is where a husband and wife are sitting down to have coffee and cake when something strange pops out of the sugar bowl. I just think people identify with fantasy more if you can get the story closer to their daily lives."[4]

It sounds as though Lovecraft and Matheson are saying almost the same thing—that the fantastic must proceed from the realistic, mundane, everyday experience of the characters—yet Stephen King cites Matheson as one of the writers most responsible for making "the break from the Lovecraftian fantasy that had held sway over serious American writers of horror for over two decades or more. . . . [He is] an almost entirely new breed of American fantasist. . . ."[5] How can this be?

The answer is that whatever his intention, Lovecraft does not give us a picture that is "accurately true to nature." Arkham may be based on Salem, Miskatonic University on Brown University, and so on, but like his spiritual father, Edgar Allan Poe, Lovecraft's special talent was to create a completely real but thoroughly alien world, hermetically sealed off from our own but offering a grotesque reflection of it. This distancing effect gives his best works much of their special power, but it also deprives them of the thing that Matheson and his like-minded colleagues wanted to bring—or perhaps restore—to horror fiction, a sense of everyday immediacy, "the thing from the sugar bowl." The final irony is that Matheson and his contemporaries reacted against the Lovecraftian mode of dark fantasy by succeeding at what Lovecraft himself said he was trying to do.

The point can be made even more vividly by another Lovecraft-Matheson comparison, this one contrasting the climactic moments from two stories, Lovecraft's "The Outsider" and Matheson's "Where There's a Will" (written with his son, Richard Christian Matheson; see *Dark Forces* [4-346]). Both stories are about fugitives from the "underground" who seek and make contact with the real world—and then look at themselves in a mirror.

> I cannot even hint what it was like, for it was a compound of all that is unclean, uncanny, unwelcome, abnormal, and detestable. It was the ghoulish shade of decay, antiquity, and desolation; the putrid, dripping eidolon of unwholesome revelation, the awful baring of that which the merciful earth should always hide. God knows it was not of this world—or no longer of this world—yet to my horror I saw in its eaten-away and bone-revealing outlines a leering, abhorrent travesty of the human shape; and in its moldy, disintegrating apparel an unspeakable quality that chilled me even more.[6]

> Staring back at him was a face that was missing sections of flesh. Its skin was grey, and withered yellow bone showed through.[7]

In the usual Matheson short story, the "thing from the sugar bowl" may threaten the entire world, as does the irrational urge to mass self-destruction in "Lemmings" [4-218], but more often the focus is on a single person—almost always a sensitive, intelligent male, usually moderately successful, family-oriented but sometimes estranged, comfortable in bourgeois surroundings and modest in desires, but acutely aware (or made aware) of the precariousness of life and the ambiguity of reality—who finds himself in a trap.

These traps range from straightforward physical ones—a chain on a wall, a closed car, an apartment, a casket; to very complicated, elaborate ones—a barricaded house in a world full of vampires, an unorthodox haunted house, a time loop; to personal afflictions—a shrinking sickness, a wild talent, a terminal illness, death itself. They are products of the bizarre worlds which they reflect, worlds that are overwhelmingly threatening, regardless of whether they exist in reality or only within the heads of the beleaguered protagonists. In short, the *paranoia theme* is central to Matheson's vision.

This paranoia can be simple and straightforward, as in "Legion of Plotters," but it is usually more complex. In "Mad House," not only do people plot against Neal, but even the objects in his house become animated and kill him. Even more extreme are those stories—among Matheson's best—which involve a collapsing mental process and/or a world that is going mad or disintegrating into nothing. Robert Graham, in "The Curious Child," progressively forgets everything about the life he is living; Don Marshall ("The Edge") goes out for lunch one day and inadvertently wanders into a parallel universe; the protagonist of "Disappearing Act" sees his world vanish around him—the story ends in mid-sentence.

But bleak as the implications of these stories may be, they are also often quite funny. In "Lemmings," for example, the spectacle of hordes of people dutifully driving up to the beach, parking their cars and then casually walking en masse into the ocean dressed in business suits, fur coats and police uniforms is horrific and hilarious. Like Finney, Leiber, Bloch and Bradbury, Matheson laces his stories with humor and irony. Wheatley and Lovecraft had only one thing in common: no sense of humor. With Matheson and his peers, humor, satire, irony, even playfulness and deliberate silliness—admittedly of a very dark and grotesque sort—became a major element in contemporary horror.

That this paranoia theme can easily wed a Lovecraftian worldview to a Norman Rockwell setting can be seen in Jack Finney's *The Body Snatchers* [4-116], the archetypal 1950s science fiction/horror novel. Alien invaders from beyond the stars drift to Earth in seed pods and systematically take over the bodies of the citizens in Mill Valley, a typical, idyllic rural small town. The invasion is half completed before the book's hero, Dr. Miles Bennell, and his girl friend, Becky Driscoll, understand the danger, attempt to expose it and finally flee it.

Here we have a Lovecraftian idea of a cosmic power beyond our knowledge or experience, from the remotest depths of space, moving in and displacing man for reasons never clear or even relevant. But the monsters are not incredible, disgusting arrangements of tentacles, scales and discolored pulsating flesh; they occupy our own bodies, and they do not eat or rip their victims apart, they simply drain those qualities from people that make them distinctively human: feelings, imagination, intuition, love. We have met the monsters and they are us. To cosmic horror is added cosmic paranoia.

Carr Makay, the hero of Fritz Leiber's *The Sinful Ones* [4-204], and his girl friend Jane face a similar dilemma, that of a sensitive couple facing pursuit in a world filled with automatons. In this novella, however, otherworldly or alien planetary invaders are not needed to accomplish the dehumanization process; it has already happened. The modern world has become so mechanized that any human who is able to act outside of his/her programmed pattern is simply not *seen* by anyone else. Thus, Carr and Jane are free to live and love as they please—except that other free souls, wanting to indulge their inclinations and perversities at will, are out to destroy them. *The Sinful Ones* delineates Leiber's paranoid landscape with a combination of deft irony, biting satire, realistic precision tinged with the grotesque, and just a touch of the romantic sentimentality characteristic of his best work in a variety of genres.

Although several of his earliest efforts are in the Lovecraft tradition ("To Arkham and the Stars"), Leiber articulated his own brand of literary paranoia as early as 1941 in his classic short story "Smoke Ghost," in which the protagonist, Catesby Wran, suggests that the modern ghost

> would grow out of the real world. It would reflect the tangled, sordid, vicious things. All the loose ends. And it would be very grimy. I don't think it would seem white or wispy, or favor graveyards. It wouldn't moan, but it would mutter unintelligibly, and twitch at your sleeve. Like a sick, surly ape.[8]

The "smoke ghosts" Wran speculates about become progressively real to him, until he is almost taken over by one—or by his own overwrought imagination. Thus, supernatural horror not only intrudes into the modern world, but may actually be a product of it. Or the horrors may originate in the psyche of contemporary man as he is overwhelmed by the world he lives in.

All of these elements—a realistic depiction of everyday contemporary life, the paranoid theme, the updating of traditional materials, and the inclusion of humor and irony side by side with horror—came together in the most important dark fantasy novel of the 1960s, Ira Levin's *Rosemary's Baby* (1967) [4-206]. Like most pivotal works, *Rosemary's Baby* can be read as a synthesis of what preceded it and a blueprint for what was to come.

On the one hand, *Rosemary's Baby* follows the pattern of the classical Gothic novel. A young, naive, basically innocent woman is put into a strange environment, which initially seems safe and comfortable, but which grows increasingly menacing, and she is introduced into a circle of people who seem at first to be friendly and trustworthy, but who become progressively hostile and devious—progressive paranoia à la *The Body Snatchers*. In the case of Rosemary Woodhouse, the traditional dangers are made more ominous because, since she is pregnant, she becomes more dependent, both physically and emotionally, on those people—including her own husband—that she is becoming more suspicious of and threatened by. As her insight increases, so does her vulnerability. By the time her suspicions are confirmed, the birth is imminent.

But Rosemary is not simply a passive victim. Again in the Gothic tradition, the threatened young woman develops spunk and, cast on her own resources, tries to fight back. In part, *Rosemary's Baby* is the story of Rosemary's growth and emancipation, as she attempts to take charge of her own life in the face of increasing adversity.

In typical Lovecraftian fashion, Rosemary's real enlightenment comes through a book, *All Those Witches,* sent to her by a dying friend (killed, of course, by witchcraft). The book confirms all of her suspicions and reveals the true identity of Ramon Castevet, the aged Satanist behind it all. Levin's sophisticated use of the details, lore and paraphernalia of witchcraft is probably the most effective use of such materials since the heyday of Dennis Wheatley.

But if the plot structure and occult trappings are traditional, the context and use of these materials is strikingly contemporary. The site of the action, the Bramford Apartments, although old and possessing an unsavory history, is no dark, creaking haunted house isolated in the middle of nowhere, but is a very fashionable, upscale building in the middle of New York City. The book is rife with details of everyday life and topical references are constant: the New York City power failure, the Pope's visit, echoes of John Kennedy's assassination. On a more metaphysical level, the "God-Is-Dead" controversy offers an ironic counterpoint to the "Satan-Is-Born" theme of the novel.

The novel's contemporaneity becomes most striking in the book's remarkable, controversial ending. When Rosemary awakens, she is told that the baby has died. Convinced that the baby was used in a sacrificial rite, she determines to seek revenge. Taking a long knife, she sneaks down to the Castevets' apartment to wreak her vengeance. When she arrives, she finds a party in progress and discovers that, rather than being a sacrificial object, her baby is the honored center of attention. The "child" was, she learns, fathered by Satan, not her husband, and its appearance confirms this: "His eyes were golden-yellow, all golden-yellow, with neither whites nor irises, all golden-yellow, with vertical black-slit pupils."[9]

When Roman Castevet tells Rosemary that the child-devil "has his father's eyes," it is, as Stephen King has suggested, "almost like the punch-line of a long, involved shaggy-dog story."[10] The collection of elderly, oddball Satanists in the Castevets' apartment, as well as the old couple themselves, are more comical than frightening, and their antics border on farce. The creature is not so much a monster as a cute little demon, again in King's words, "the comic-book version of Satan, the L'il Imp."[11] And Rosemary herself, in her rapid metamorphosis from horrified victim to fond mother, also becomes a comic figure. Thus, the book's last revelation and confrontation with evil is more humorous than horrific. This semicomic finale, in King's opinion, "is a splendid confirmation of the idea that humor and horror lie side by side and to deny one is to deny the other."[12]

Traditional horror in a modern context, a tone that balances the humorous and ironic with the grotesque and horrific, and an exploitation of the child as monster are three important elements in *Rosemary's Baby* that would become central in contemporary dark fantasy.

Pastoral Paranoia

Although the big city has flourished as the setting for paranoia in Matheson, Leiber, Levin and others, that more traditional demonic stamping ground, the rural small town, has become an even more popular landscape for contemporary dark fantasy.

Pastoral horror can be divided roughly into two types, those in which an outside menace invades the small town and, perhaps combining with evil already dormant in the environment, spreads its corruption until it is either thwarted or takes over completely; and those in which the evil is already present, waiting to destroy or absorb innocent outsiders, generally ex-urban dwellers seeking a rural refuge. Both types can be distinguished from those narratives, like many haunted house stories, that simply happen in the country, because the *town itself* is a dynamic element, either as a collective victim or as an active accomplice in the evil, often as both.

Two Stephen King novels, *'Salem's Lot* [4-172] and *The Tommyknockers* [4-177], serve as examples of the small town overwhelmed by external evil. In *'Salem's Lot,* King's updating of and homage to *Dracula* [3-186], the external evil is simple: Kurt Barlow, a classic European vampire, invades and infects 'Salem's Lot. As in Stoker's original, a small group of citizens battle the evil that slowly, systematically overwhelms the Lot. They succeed in killing Barlow, his familiar and a number of the local undead, but at the end of the novel the Lot is still overrun with mindless vampires wandering about aimlessly, a loose end presumably to be taken care of in King's promised, but as yet unwritten, sequel.

The emerging evil in *The Tommyknockers* is more interesting and ingenious. Bobbi Anderson releases forces emanating from a buried flying saucer which gradually transform all of the citizens, except a few who just happen to have metal in their heads or mouths, into physical and mental grotesques, toothless, hairless, gelatinous blobs with extraordinary intellectual and psychic powers, totally dominated by the enigmatic consciousness of the saucer. These gradual, pervasive, weird—yet humorous—transformations are among the most disturbing collective images in the genre.

The evil that pervades Harlowe, New Hampshire, in Joan Samson's *The Auctioneer* (1975) [4-260] is even more frightening, because the menace is both inexorable and human, drawing its strength from the weakness, confusion, self-doubts and latent evil of the townspeople themselves. *The Auctioneer* ia a powerful novel that works on a variety of levels—as a thriller, as a psychological study of men under severe stress and as a moral parable.

Often the evil force does not simply invade the community from the outside, but emerges/bursts forth from within, a latent malignancy brought suddenly to life. Occasionally it is a periodic visitor—as in Straub's *Floating Dragon* [4-285] or King's *It* [4-168]—appearing on a regular schedule; more often it is inadvertently released by accident or folly, as in Ramsey Campbell's *The Hungry Moon* [4-68], or even deliberately summoned as in Charles L. Grant's *The Nestling* [4-126].

In *The Nestling,* primal evil resurfaces in the form of a huge winged serpent or carnivorous eagle, summoned by a female shaman to "warn off" the whites, but the entire town, Shoshone Indians as well as Caucasians, are put under siege as the summoner loses control, the evil spreads and its motives change from serving a "cause" to general malevolence. *The Nestling* illustrates an important point: ancient evil may be summoned for a specific—even worthy—reason, but once released, it assumes an agenda of its own, perhaps even destroying those who would have used it.

Alan Ryan's first two novels, *The Kill* (1982) [4-257] and *Dead White* (1983) [4-256], involve encounters with small-town evil that illustrate additional aspects of the motif. In *Dead White,* demonic clowns seek revenge for evil done to them many years earlier, an evil which must be expiated. This notion of a collective past injustice that must be sought out, recognized and atoned for in order to placate the intruding malevolent force is common to many small-town horror stories.

In *The Kill,* New York couple Megan Todd and Jack Casey escape from the big city to Deacons Kill, where they are menaced by an invisible, bloodthirsty monster. This basic set-up—the young city dwellers, seeking a respite from urban chaos, come to the small town where they encounter some sort of malevolent force—is perhaps the most common situation in the pastoral nightmare. The major difference between *The Kill* and the majority of such narratives is that in this book the outsiders are welcomed and easily combine with their new neighbors to defeat the evil; in the majority of such novels the newcomers are at best outsiders who must pay a high price to become part of the community, and at worst, become victims of that community.

Occasionally the newcomer to the rural enclave is responsible, inadvertently or deliberately, for triggering an evil that had been dormant. In Ramsey Campbell's *The Hungry Moon,* an outsider, American evangelist Godwin Mann, enters the small town of Moonwell and quickly imposes his rigidly disciplined, fanatical brand of neo-puritanism on the citizenry. He challenges the "thing" at the bottom of the "pit"—which had been contained for eons by local rituals—and unleashes forces latent since the time of the druids. Thus, the outsider, acting out of self-righteous arrogance and self-deluded feelings of power, destroys the delicate barrier that had insulated the citizens of Moonwell from the primal evil that had long threatened them.

More often the outsider is the victim, as in the Robin Hardy–Anthony Shaffer novelization of *The Wicker Man* (1978) [4-134]. Police Sergeant Neil Howie finds himself gradually transformed from pursuer to pursued and finally to sacrificial victim. Originally an outstanding 1973 film, *The Wicker Man* presents the outsider-as-victim motif in its purest form: the occult powers, whether real or imaginary, demand a sacrifice and the outsider is the inevitable choice, whether he is lured into the community by design or simply blunders into it by unlucky happenstance, as does Ned Constantine in Thomas Tryon's *Harvest Home* (1973) [4-305].

Harvest Home is a much more elaborate and complex variation on *The Wicker Man* situation. Constantine, an artist, becomes gradually suspicious of the isolated New England village, Cornwall Coombe, into which he has ventured with his wife and daughter. His interference is finally punished in a harsh but appropriate manner, with, most cruelly, the complicity of his wife and daughter. *Harvest Home* is easily the best and most sophisticated of the "fertility cult" novels, beautifully written and structured, with fine characterizations and a savagely ironic worldview.

A more recent elaboration of a similar situation can be found in T. E. D. Klein's *The Ceremonies* [4-182]. The general atmosphere of Gilead, New Jersey, is reminiscent of Cornwall Coombe, but the evil comes from an outsider, the cherubic-seeming Mr. Rosebottom, who is actually in the service of an ancient evil, which he hopes to resurrect. Although overly long, *The Ceremonies* is one of the best examples in recent horror of a successful, imaginative revitalization of old dark fantasy images and myths, like Arthur Machen's "Little People" [3-135] and H. P. Lovecraft's "Cthulhu Mythos" [3-132], given a new twist in a thoroughly contemporary context.

Of course, the urban sprawl and the rural enclave are not the only two environments that harbor dark forces. The middle-size city and the suburbs also host their share of the demonic. Neither big city nor small town, Charles L. Grant's Oxrun Station, Connecticut, can serve as the prototype of the middle-size community with a predilection for evil. In Grant's own words:

> I didn't want to create another Arkham. I didn't want to use the stereotypical small town or small village that's falling apart and a little spooky. I wanted a Greenwich-type community where people—for practical reasons as well as for the contrast—are just different. Upper-middle-class and upper-class people are more mobile and have more free time. . . .[13]

Thus, Oxrun Station is large and modern enough to allow Grant the mobility and flexibility necessary to present a variety of characters, social levels and situations, but small enough to project a sense of the isolated small town with its mysterious past, obscure traditions and long-entrenched evils. To be sure, the entire town of Oxrun Station is never quite under siege like King's Haven, Samson's Harlowe or Campbell's Moonwell, nor is it saturated with evil like Cornwall Coombe, but as a general breeding ground for malevolence it has few equals. Its pervasive atmosphere of tension and dread—reinforced by continuing characters, locations and cross-references—is a primary reason why the best of the Oxrun novels and stories—*The Sound of Midnight, The Last Call of Mourning, The Bloodwind* [4-125], the "historical" novel *The Soft Whisper of the Dead* [4-128], and the novellas in *Nightmare Seasons*—rank with the best of the genre.

But perhaps the ultimate vision of those special horrors uniquely suited to suburbia—albeit in an exaggerated fashion—is Ira Levin's only post-*Rosemary's Baby* dark fantasy, *The Stepford Wives* [4-207]. As in *Rosemary's Baby,* we have a threatened female, Joanna Ingalls Eberhart, a thirty-five-year-old wife and mother of two, who moves into an apparently idyllic environment, which slowly but relentlessly becomes progressively ambiguous and threatening. But instead of the Devil, malevolence in *The Stepford Wives* comes in the form of an idealized middle-class ethos pushed to the nth degree. Stepford men will settle for nothing less than good old-fashioned girls, dedicated mothers, committed housekeepers and eager bed partners—with no independent thoughts or activities of their own. Joanna comes to believe, with mounting dread, that the husbands, including her own, will do whatever they must to achieve that ideal. *The Stepford Wives* may be a little too satirically broad to take completely seriously, but Levin's details of suburban living and his handling of Joanna's mounting terror are handled with great skill, economy and flashes of black humor.

Old Monsters, New Skins

Ghosts

As Ira Levin reworked the traditions and clichés of witchcraft and satanic worship in *Rosemary's Baby,* so other authors have updated those other traditional horror monsters—the ghost, the vampire and the werewolf—giving them new qualities and possibilities while retaining and manipulating the metaphorical power of the originals.

The shifting attitude toward the classical ghost has been articulated by Peter Straub. In his first supernatural novel, *Julia* [4-288], Straub deliberately evoked the classical approach:

> I was burdened by everything I thought I knew about supernatural literature—a kind of Henry James lesson: that to be good books of this kind had to be ambiguous, modest, and restrained. They had to have good manners. *Julia* was written more or less in that spirit. I was trying to write a scary book in which the horror could either be inside or outside, attached to the people or to some external force. . . . I was thinking, as I often do, of "The Turn of the Screw."[14]

But soon Straub began to question those assumptions, particularly after reading Stephen King.

> . . . after reading *Salem's Lot, The Shining*, and *The Stand*, I realized that my notions about a well-bred novel didn't apply to this kind of book. In fact, they were inhibiting. Better that this kind of book be bad-mannered, noisy, and operatic.[15]

The result was his extravagant, complicated masterpiece, *Ghost Story* [4-286], which, despite its simple, generic title, is not really about ghosts at all.

All of which is not to say that significant examples of traditional ghost stories have not been written in the decades since the war. The classical British ghost story has endured, if not thrived, in novels such as Arthur Calder-Marshall's *The Scarlet Boy* [4-62] and R. Chetwynd-Hayes's *The Grange* [4-79].

Even better examples of the traditional English ghost story can be found in short fiction, where it has always been more comfortable. Outstanding examples have been written by several contemporaries including L. P. Hartley [3-80] and Elizabeth Walter [4-312–4-313] among others. But the author most identified with the classical ghost story in a modern context is Robert Aickman.

Part of this identification is due to Aickman's long stint as editor of *The Fontana Book of Great Ghost Stories* (1964–72), but most important has been a series of subtle, atmospheric, stylistic stories that rely for their unnerving effect on suggestion, ambiguity and, to use M. R. James's famous slogan, "a nicely managed crescendo." The typical Aickman story develops slowly and indirectly—some might even say aimlessly—with a careful modulation of tone and a gradually thickening atmosphere that draws the reader uneasily into the tale. The emphasis is psychological, there is rarely physical violence or graphic detail, and more often than not the climax is muted and ambiguous, with the reader suspended between uncertainty and dread. His best stories balance delicately on that thin line between the real and the hallucinatory so that the reader cannot quite be sure whether he is dealing with the truly supernatural or with psychic projections of the narrator's own inner needs, drives and fears—or with both.

But if Aickman's approach and manner seem traditional, even old fashioned, contemporary attitudes, preoccupations and fears permeate the stories, giving them a distinctly original mix of the old and the new: M. R. James meets Franz Kafka. In even the most traditional ghost stories, the expected revelations usually have a nasty, contemporary edge. In "Ringing the Changes," for example, the really unnerving twist is not so much that the incessant church bells raise the dead to interrupt a couple's honeymoon, as it is the way the new bride moves so easily and nonchalantly into the festivities. A more complex story, "The View," also takes a common ghost story situation—a man meets a beautiful woman, has an idyllic affair and awakens to discover the woman and the affair to be nonexistent. He goes to sleep a young man with his lover beside him on an isolated estate on a deserted island, but awakens alone, an old man in the hustle and bustle of the modern world; bizarre as this transformation may be, he accepts it as a matter of course, as something he almost expected.

Despite Aickman's association with the ghost story, his most persistent theme is the strangeness and precariousness of life. His is a world in which ghosts fit naturally, but which sensitive humans rarely find comfortable. The most common situation in his stories, whether ghostly or otherwise, is for the protagonist to enter, usually accidentally and arbitrarily, a world that is just slightly skewed and becomes more so as the story progresses, until it consumes the protagonist or at least leaves him or her changed in some fundamental way—a destruction or change that is accepted as inevitable and natural.

It is this final acceptance of the bizarre as mundane that gives many of his tales their most chilling twist. For example, in "The Swords," a young man has his first sexual experience with a girl who is a carnival freak capable of taking sword stabs in her body and removing her limbs at will. The really awful thing, however, is the sheer dull normality of the girl in every other way. Molly Sawyer, heroine of "In the Woods," is drawn slowly into the nightmare world of permanent insomniacs. She moves from curiosity, to unease, to irritation, to fascination, and finally to acceptance as she, too, becomes one of them, an end she accepts with an odd combination of resignation and eagerness. In a slightly lighter vein, the salesman who spends the night at "The Hospice" encounters not only eerie premonitions of his own death, but also an absurd bureaucracy, a set of complicated, ludicrous regulations and a series of comic grotesques. Indeed, grotesque humor underscores much of Aickman's writing.

Although the traditional ghost story has never enjoyed a comparable popularity in America, its partisans—like Russell Kirk [4-181], Joyce Carol Oates [4-244] and Shirley Jackson—have produced a respectable quantity of good work. By common consent, the single best contemporary ghostly novel is Jackson's *The Haunting of Hill House* [4-155].

Although none of Jackson's other novels deals explicitly with ghosts and the supernatural, they all center on profound dislocations of everyday reality. The young protagonists of *Hangsaman* [4-154] and *The Bird's Nest* [4-152], Natalie Waite and Elizabeth Richmond respectively, each make their own personal ghosts, Natalie by creating a companion named Toni, Elizabeth by fragmenting her personality into four independent identities. The characters in *The Sundial* [4-156] and *We Have Always Lived in the Castle* [4-157] all live in their own peculiar brand of haunted house where they can deny the outside world and recreate reality in whatever manner they choose.

Although a number of her stories do boast specters, Hill House is Shirley

Jackson's only bona fide haunted house. Even in this more traditional novel, however, Jackson's real interest is not in the hauntings, but in the *effect* of those hauntings on the investigators, especially on her heroine, Eleanor Vance. Eleanor is, in fact, a slightly older version of Jackson's tormented teenagers. Thirty-two years old, she has spent most of her adult life nursing her ailing mother, who has only recently died in a manner that has triggered deep guilt feelings. Living in a state of resented dependence with her married sister, Eleanor goes to Hill House in her first really independent act. Once there, Eleanor attempts unsuccessfully to establish a personal relationship with two of the other investigators, the tantalizing Theodora, would-be artist and very sophisticated lady, and Luke Sanderson, playboy nephew of the house's owner, but it is the house itself that finally attracts and makes her its own.

Or does it? Or is Eleanor herself doing the haunting? As a teenager she had had a poltergeist interlude. Could that talent have been revived and intensified by the experience of coming to Hill House? This possibility occurs only to the reader, never to Eleanor. The book ends with this delicious ambiguity, an ambiguity that takes us back to the very best of the classical ghost story tradition.

More characteristic of the contemporary scene is Richard Matheson's *Hell House* [4-216], a novel which uses an almost identical set-up to a very different effect. Again we have investigators sealed in an ostensibly haunted house to discover the truth of the hauntings. But the investigators in this novel are professionals—a scientist with a machine that measures psychic energy, a clairvoyant whose seances have produced tangible results, a burned-out psychic who was the only survivor of a previous experiment—and the phenomena they encounter are neither gradual nor subtle. Almost from the beginning of the novel, the group is attacked by every conceivable form of psychological, visual, auditory, hallucinatory, sexual and sadistic horror. These assaults are reinforced by a pervasive atmosphere of decadence, sexual perversion, moral chaos, depravity and cruelty. The most powerful thing in *Hell House* is the mansion itself, which projects an aura of evil comparable to that in Lovecraft's classic "Rats in the Walls." The final explanation for the hauntings at Hell House, while supernatural, is thoroughly physical.

Another pair of important novels that demonstrate the shift from psychological to visceral ghost are Jack Cady's *The Well* [4-61] and Stephen King's *The Shining* [4-173]. In both books the protagonist is trapped, along with his loved one(s), in a haunted house, one that exploits his personal history and weaknesses in order to open him up to its machinations. In the former, John Tracker ultimately comes to terms with his own moral and psychological vulnerability to battle with and, although severely damaged, at least temporarily defeat the evil that has long fed on the Tracker family, while saving his fiancée from an awful fate. In the latter, internal weakness and overwhelming evil combine to destroy Jack Torrance and threaten his family.

But it is not the fate of the protagonists, but the contrasting approaches taken by Cady and King, that signals the differences between these two books. Although written three years later than the King book, *The Well* is firmly rooted in the classical tradition. When developer John Tracker and his fiancée-secretary, Amy, make a final visit to his family home prior to having it leveled for a highway, they are trapped inside the decaying mansion by physical barriers—a series of deadly booby traps set for the Devil by Tracker's great-grandfather—but more strongly by the evil presence that pervades the house and seeks to destroy not only their bodies, but also their souls. Although most often personified by the ghosts of Tracker's grandparents, the evil seems more general, pervasive and ambiguous. It seems to embody not only the compounded evil of the Tracker family, but also a larger, more general malevolence that somehow emanates from the ancient well that sits beneath the house's foundations.

But none of this is explained. We experience the house through John and Amy. Very little is seen; everything is felt. The psychological and emotional tension, as well as the sheer physical danger, increases deliberately throughout the novel. Even at the end, after John has finally learned enough of the truth about the family past and his father's place in it to escape the house relatively unscathed, we cannot—in the best classical tradition—be completely sure where the evil came from, or how much of it resulted from deliberate human malfeasance, how much from the would-be victims' imaginations and how much from otherworldly influences.

Prior to *The Shining*, King demonstrated his kind of ghosts in an early story, "Sometimes They Come Back" (in *Night Shift* [4-170]). The protagonist, Jim Norman, an insecure high school teacher, is continually plagued by nightmares in which he is forced to relive the time when, as a young boy, he witnessed the murder of his brother, barely escaping with his own life. One by one, three of the four young thugs who killed Wayne appear in his "Living with Lit" class, taking seats vacated by students mysteriously killed or missing. Norman quickly determines that they are, of course, ghosts, but not of the traditional variety: they are flesh and blood, have names, smell of sweat, beer and pizza, even possess elaborate high school transcripts (from a "school" that turns out to be a cemetery).

Thus, for King, ghosts are concrete physical beings and their haunting is a very real, palpable thing. In contrast to *The Well*, everything in *The Shining*, living people and ghosts, reality and hallucinations, is quite concrete. The Overlook Hotel, where Jack Torrance has accepted employment as the winter caretaker, is no dilapidated ancestral home; it is a very ritzy Colorado resort, old but modernized, and always, except for a few winter months, filled with America's best and most well-heeled vacationers. The evil that saturates the building makes up a collage of twentieth-century violence, including a bathtub suicide, a gangland triple killing and a mass murder committed by a crazed caretaker, as well as a multitude of lesser crimes and corruptions. Thus, when the ghosts appear, there is no doubt that they are real, hostile and capable of physical as well as psychic damage.

Although it is the psychic power—or "Shine"—generated by the young son, Danny, that fully energizes these evil presences in the Overlook, it is his father, Jack Torrance, who is the focus of the novel. *The Shining* is basically the story of how, under the malevolent pressures of the Overlook, he gradually changes from a loving, if troubled, husband and father and a talented aspiring playwright into a maddened, vengeful monster, the human agent and embodiment of the Overlook's evil history.

This approach broadens and dramatizes the action, but it makes all but impossible the kind of subjective identification necessary for the classical ghost story. While we are watching Jack Torrance's psychic disintegration, we are not imaginative participants in that disintegration; we sympathize with Jack, but we do not really identify with him. His strengths and weaknesses are laid out in front of us; the supernatural powers of the Overlook that work against him are presented in vivid, even gross, detail, with an inevitable result that is dramatic and powerful, but not mysterious or ambiguous. King's physicalization of the ghost is one of the most graphic examples of the shift from inward, psychological horror to external, visceral horror that characterizes contemporary dark fantasy.

This idea of the palpable ghost as a catalyst for the very human fears and instabilities of living characters is put to even more original use in Chet Williamson's *Ash Wednesday* [4-328]. Its ghosts function not as spectral threats, but as visceral stimuli, or even visual evidence, of suppressed guilt that forces the characters to come to terms with their own living problems.

But not all solid ghosts are demonic or accusatory. The specters in Alan Ryan's *Cast a Cold Eye* [4-255] are victims who come to the living for solace and help. More poignant—even tragic—than horrific, *Cast a Cold Eye* is one of the most original and moving ghost stories in modern literature.

At the other extreme, realistic ghosts are also perfectly suited to comic, even farcical horror stories. Although ghosts, even solid ghosts, are more benign than most of the creatures in Clive Barker's menagerie, they appear in a number of his clever, lighter stories. In "Confessions of a (Pornographer's) Shroud," for example, the ghost assumes the form not of the traditional bedsheet, but of the cloth burial shroud, with which he pursues his vengeance. The ghostly couple in "Revelations" return to the motel room where the woman murdered the husband many years previously only to replay their earlier scene vicariously through a pompous, hysterical evangelist, his pill-popping wife and their horny assistant. The cast of specters in "Sex, Death, and Starshine" is much larger, the entire cast of a production of Shakespeare's *Twelfth Night,* Barker's most extended and effective more-or-less light handling of the ghost story. The production in question is in serious jeopardy until the ghosts of former stars of the theater, alarmed at its pending demise, take over the production. In all three of these stories, Barker's wit and ironic sense of humor shine through, relatively unburdened by the dark, bitter edge that characterizes most of his humor.

The humor is even more blatant in two other contemporary exercises in dark fantasy as black comedy, Peter Beagle's *A Fine and Private Place* [4-25] and Thomas M. Disch's *The Businessman* [4-98].

In *A Fine and Private Place* the line between the living and the dead is almost nonexistent. The living protagonist, Rebeck, a disillusioned druggist, has chosen to live with the dead, having voluntarily spent the previous nineteen years of his life in a cemetery, while the ghosts, Michael Morgan, a pompous history professor, and Laura Durand, an unloved woman, stimulated by a love they cannot act upon, become more alive after death. Pursued by a Jewish widow, forced to help the lovers reunite in a new cemetery, generally hassled by the raven who feeds him and castigated by the ghost of the widow's husband, Rebeck is finally forced to choose life and leave his cemetery sanctuary.

But while *A Fine and Private Place* is a rather cozy, old-fashioned, bittersweet dark comedy, *The Businessman* is a thoroughly contemporary exercise in very black farce. Upper-echelon corporate executive Bob Glandier murders his wife, Giselle, setting in motion a complicated, hilarious, grotesque set of hauntings that include his wife, identified by the thick scent of chocolate; her mother, Joy-Ann, who has a pipeline to Paradise by way of Sears and later turns into a plaster statue of the Virgin Mary; a halfling child, who has returned after an abortion in an attempt to help his deteriorating father; and the poet John Berryman, still in search of recognition and good scotch, a failure with Ouija boards due to his dyslexia, who ends up as a black iron lawn jockey. *The Businessman* is a wonderfully funny dark satire of contemporary American society, a delicious send-up of horror fiction clichés and an exercise in slapstick surrealism that is entertaining, occasionally moving and always intellectually stimulating.

Of course, the line between the solid, realistic ghost and the reanimated corpse—the zombie—is a thin one. For example, how does one label the Larkin family in Michael McDowell's *Cold Moon over Babylon* [4-231]? Murdered by their aristocratic landlord, they return from the Styx River, occupying their original bodies, albeit in a somewhat squishy, decomposed condition, to seek vengeance. Ghosts, zombies, or both?

The traditional zombie figure, the body reanimated by the evil sorcerer/scientist to do his bidding, was probably destroyed as a viable metaphor by George Romero's *The Night of the Living Dead* in 1968. That film, its sequels and its clones displaced, for better or worse, the zombie as individual menace, replacing it with the mindless mobs of resurrected corpses that have glutted horror movies from the *Living Dead* series through Michael Jackson's *Thriller* video and beyond.

But, ironically, Romero's success in creating such a powerful film image has probably come close to eliminating the zombie from most good narrative horror fiction. As a visual image, hordes of stumbling, mindless, decomposing zombies can be overwhelming, but it is very difficult to make a strong narrative subject out of mindless cannibal hordes.

Thus, it is not surprising that the only really memorable zombie novel of the last decade is one that ignores zombies as mob members, restoring them to the bosom of the family: Stephen King's *Pet Sematary* [4-171]. When his youngest son is killed accidentally, Dr. Louis Creed buries him in an old Indian cemetery reputed to reanimate the dead. The boy returns with terrifying results.

But, of course, even at its best the fictional zombie has rarely been one of the most metaphorically potent figures. Even in pre-Romero times he was rather limited, dependent primarily on the malevolence of whoever/whatever was using him/her. The notion of the reanimated dead has been much more extensively and elaborately explored in that most provocative of all undead creatures, the vampire.

Vampires

Contemporary revisions of the classical vampire figure have been even more imaginative and complicated than those of the ghost. Much of the continued potency and popularity of the vampire figure is due not only to the essential power of the archetype, but also to the elaborate, complex mythology that has grown up around it. The best writers have not only reinterpreted the vampire to suit their own needs and aims, but have also freely redesigned the lore that goes with it. Thus, as well as traditionally evil vampires in the classical mold, we also have mindless zombie-like vampires, existential vampires, outer space vampires, misunderstood vampires, even heroic, do-gooder vampires. Count Dracula himself has gone from Stoker's evil aristocrat to heroic, misunderstood nobleman to super-hero on the side of truth and justice.

The novel that opened up new possibilities for the vampire metaphor was Richard Matheson's *I Am Legend* [4-217]. Published in 1954, it completely redefined the vampire for contemporary fiction. In *I Am Legend* nuclear war and a series of severe dust storms unleash a virulent disease, semilatent for centuries, that turns everyone into a vampire except the hero, Robert Neville, who lives barricaded in his home, venturing out only during the day to forage and kill as many of the creatures as he can. The book's central irony is that in a world of vampires, the normal man is the real "vampire." Like that of his nemeses, Neville's life is regulated by the sun; he must return to his "casket"—his fortress home—before the sun sets or be destroyed by hordes of rampaging vampires. It is he who ravages the countryside, indiscriminately killing sleeping victims. And, like the traditional vampire, he kills not only in the name of survival, but also—defining the term broadly—for pleasure. Neville finally gives up when he realizes that he is an anomaly in a world that has no place for him. The vampires are not only mindless animated corpses fit only for destruction, but are also a new breed of still-living human beings. His hatred is too intense and narrow to enable him to consider the nature and implications of the living vampires, so he is unprepared for their metamorphosis into the new society.

Matheson's new image—or rather *images*—of the vampire influenced contemporary horror fiction and film as profoundly as Stoker's aristocratic Count Dracula had fixed that image in the Victorian mind. "I got the idea," he told *Twilight Zone* magazine, "when I was seventeen years old in Brooklyn and saw *Dracula*. I figured that if one vampire was scary, then a whole world full of vampires should really be scary."[16] Thus, Matheson is the first novelist to follow through on the mathematical implications of traditional vampirism: a vampire makes a vampire, who makes a vampire, who makes . . . and so on: the world soon becomes completely vampirized.

The first image Matheson gives us of such a world offers crowds of zombie-like vampires, newly revived corpses whose brains have remained dead; only their appetites have survived the grave. It is *I Am Legend* that gave film director George Romero the idea for the cannibal-zombies that populate his "living dead" films. The second group of vampires Neville encounters, the brutal but living, intelligent creatures who finally inherit the Earth, suggest another contemporary vampire concept: the vampire as a separate race with its own life-style, needs and mores. And finally, by telling the story from Neville's point of view and by delineating Neville's isolated, problematical existence, Matheson sets the stage for the existential vampires of Anne Rice and Somtow Sucharitkul.

Which is not to say that the old, thoroughly evil Count Dracula-type of vampire has become obsolete, only that when he does appear, he does so with a much greater arsenal of weapons and, perhaps, a much more ambiguous role. For example, Stephen King's *'Salem's Lot* [4-172]—his first best-selling novel—was an attempt to reintroduce the Dracula-style vampire into the contemporary scene.

The structure of *'Salem's Lot* is also similar to that of *Dracula.* The stranger moves in and slowly, gradually, odd and terrible things begin to happen in town—a dog is mutilated, a child vanishes, a series of increasingly frequent and peculiar deaths occur—but the town as a whole remains oblivious to the danger. Slowly a small group of perceptive, imaginative people emerge to engage in what appears to be very unequal combat with the forces of evil. By the time evil makes itself known, the town has been decimated and the ranks of the good combatants considerably thinned. But finally, as in Stoker's novel, courage, tenacity, common sense, the vanity of the antagonist and a little luck (or divine intervention?) combine to give the surviving protagonists—novelist Ben Mears and twelve-year-old Mark Petrie—a final victory.

One difference between the two books, however, is the vampire's scale of operations—and this is where the Matheson influence is evident. Stoker's Count had quality standards, concentrating on a few well-chosen victims, while King's Kurt Barlow is completely indiscriminate. When the beleaguered heroes start turning out stakes on a home lathe and scour the town in daylight hours looking for hidden vampires, we are reminded of Neville's solitary crusade against a world filled with nothing but the undead. Thus, unless he is presented as a figure of nostalgia, as in Charles Grant's *The Soft Whisper of the Dead* [4-128], the Old World vampire must be perceived in a contemporary context if he is to retain his traditional impact.

But while *'Salem's Lot* and *Soft Whisper of the Dead* are deliberate exercises in nostalgia set in isolated rural areas, other current writers have brought the classical vampire to the big city in straightforward contemporary horror stories. Interesting examples of the traditional vampire's assault on the modern big city can be seen in Leslie Whitten's *Progeny of the Adder* [4-326], John Skipp and Craig Spector's *The Light at the End* [4-275] and Robert R. McCammon's *They Thirst* [4-225].

Whitten marries the traditional vampire tale to the contemporary police procedure novel, and what begins as a routine serial murder investigation gradually develops into a confrontation with a classical vampire. *The Light at the End* also involves a manhunt for a vampire in an urban setting. Although the vampire himself is disappointing—a street punk converted into a rampaging blood drinker by an ancient master vampire—Skipp and Spector's gritty, realistic evocation of contemporary New York City and especially of terror in the subway system powerfully mixes ancient evil with contemporary social chaos to produce a memorable work.

The marriage of Stoker and Matheson is even more harrowing and ambitious in the McCammon book, where a very traditional Old World monster, Count Vulcan, overwhelms contemporary Los Angeles with hordes of the undead. From his hideout in an old Hollywood horror castle, the Count recruits a band of followers and slowly, systematically begins to spread his evil over the city: vampires create new vampires by the dozens, with even the elements—darkness, snow, ultimately earthquake—forwarding his plot. The salvation of mankind rests with several very different, unlikely individuals scattered all over the Los Angeles basin. Thus, the vampire, the dimensions of his world extended and his possibilities expanded, is perfectly suited to the large, panoramic novel that has come to dominate the contemporary scene.

Like the Whitten novel, Barbara Hambly's *Those Who Hunt the Night* [4-133] weds the mystery story to the vampire tale, but with an ingenious twist—the vampire becomes the victim. In the London of Sherlock Holmes, the novel's protagonist, James Asher, professor and ex-spy, is coerced into service—his wife's life is in jeopardy—by London's oldest vampire, Simon Ysidro, to find a serial killer who preys exclusively on vampires. The man—or thing—hunt is adroitly handled, but the most ingenious aspect of the novel is Hambly's collection of vampires, a crew of believable, understandable, individualized almost-human beings, with their own distinctive society, history and morality. They are, in fact, like a separate parallel race of alien beings existing among and feeding off men. By turning to a human being for help, Ysidro—over the protests of his fellow vampires—brings the two races into contrast; these relationships—vampires with humans in general and Ysidro with Asher in particular—are the most provocative elements in the novel.

While this notion is ancillary to the mystery in *Those Who Hunt the Night*, it is the major concern in two of the most stimulating vampire novels of the early 1980s, Suzy McKee Charnas's *Vampire Tapestry* [4-78] and Whitley Strieber's *The Hunger* [4-290]. Charnas avoids most of the traditional trappings—her vampire drinks blood and lives a very long time, but has neither bizarre abilities nor peculiar vulnerabilities. Charnas has created her own vampire myth and developed a fascinating, subtle book around it. Whitley Strieber is even more successful in creating a believable alien vampire—although the book never uses that word—in Miriam Blaylock, primarily because we view the world from *her* perspective. She is wholly evil, from a human perspective, yet curiously sympathetic, even, perhaps, marginally tragic.

The alienated vampire who reluctantly kills to live is even more powerfully and subtly developed in the novel that restored the vampire to respectability for general readers, Anne Rice's best-selling *Interview with a Vampire* [4-250]. Louis, the vampire protagonist, not only tells his story in intimate, sensual detail, he also ruminates on it; his life becomes a vehicle for exploring profound and disturbing philosophical, even religious questions. Having given himself up to vampirism as an act of guilty self-destruction, Louis learns what it really meant to be human. Prompted by the tauntings of his master vampire, Lestat, Louis attempts to become wholly vampiric, but his human desires, needs and mores will not be completely suppressed.

This is intensified when Louis and Lestat acquire a vampire companion, Claudia, transformed when a five-year-old girl and thereby doomed to live eternally with a grown woman's intellect and desires trapped in a small child's body. Louis and Claudia embark on a search for other vampires, which leads them eventually to Paris and the *Théâtre des Vampires* where the last enclave of the undead, led by Armand, the oldest living vampire, live together in their own strange society. It is here, primarily from Armand, that Louis learns the meaning of not only vampiric, but also human, existence: in a world where the existence of God is at best problematic, the vampire may represent the highest form of life, perhaps even of morality. This is a powerful, disturbing line of reasoning which elevates the vampire myth to a higher level of seriousness. Unfortunately, Rice backs away from the disturbing implications of these ideas in her subsequent vampire novels, *The Vampire Lestat* (1985) and *The Queen of the Damned* (1988).

The evolution of Anne Rice's vampire myth demonstrates a cardinal rule of dark fantasy mythmaking—writers should not overwhelm their readers with a completely comprehensive personal mythology, however clever. The most effective vampire novelists—Charnas, Strieber, Sucharitkul, Kast, the Rice of *Interview*—do reinvent the vampire myth to suit their own purposes, but they resist the temptation to explain *everything*, and thus to reduce the myth to a set of ideas. Literary myth thrives on suggestion and is most convincing when the final, awful truth lies just out of reach and sight; myths, like boogeymen, live best in shadows.

There is no more ingenious proof of this than *Vampire Junction* [4-278] by Somtow Sucharitkul (writing as S. P. Somtow). Like Rice's Louis, Sucharitkul's vampire, in the guise of Timmy Valentine, a teenaged rock star, questions his own meaning and existence. Through Timmy, Sucharitkul poses the question "what is a vampire?"

Several centuries of killing for blood, coupled with participation in many of history's most horrible events, and a fear that he is developing some uncomfortable sympathies for his victims have taken their toll on Timmy's psyche, so he enters Jungian analysis. The idea sounds comical, a variation on the situation in Jeremy Leven's *Satan: His Psychotherapy and Cure by the Unfortunate Dr. Kassler, J.S.P.S.* [F4A-167], and it *is* funny—but also very serious. Indeed, *Vampire Junction* may be the most sophisticated—as well as the most gory—black comedy in the genre.

Vampire Junction is not an easy book to read. Even in a conventional straight-line narrative, the several plot lines and complex ideas would be hard to keep straight—and the plot line is anything but conventional. The stories are told in bits and pieces and juxtaposed against each other. The prose style is visual, energetic, nervous, highly ironic, often lyrical and very dense, relying on suggestion and fragments more than direct statements and clear descriptions. The overall pattern emerges slowly and it is the reader's responsibility to fit the pieces together as they come along. The underlying ideas, especially the smattering of Jungian theory, are not simple and some prior familiarity with them is assumed. Obviously, *Vampire Junction* is not your typical pop horror novel, but the reader willing to accept the book on its own terms will experience a novel that is original, gory, funny and extremely provocative, both intellectually and viscerally.

If, after Rice and Sucharitkul, a reader feels the need for a less taxing novel dealing with the moral ambiguity of vampirism, he or she might look to George R. R. Martin's *Fevre Dream* [4-213], where there is a clear division between good vampires and bad ones, and the ensuing clash is colorful and exciting, if not profound.

The combination of an exotic historical setting and a morally ambiguous or reclaimed vampire is used even more elaborately in the historical vampire novels of Les Daniels [4-92], Chelsea Quinn Yarbro [4-340], and Pierre Kast [4-159]. Daniels and Yarbro use basically the same formula. Their ambiguous vampire heroes/villains, Don Sebastian de Villanueva and Count de Saint Germain respectively, are thrust into exotic locales at moments of historical trauma to confront the really corrupt human monsters of that time and place.

Don Sebastian is the more traditional vampire of the two, a classical hero-villain in the Byronic mold—larger than life, aristocratic and savage, his evil mitigated only by moments of sympathy for his victims, occasional gestures of mercy and the fact that the human villains around him are even more monstrous.

As the Countess de Corville puts it in *Citizen Vampire*: "What good is a fiend with a conscience?"

If Don Sebastian is an ambiguous hero/villain, Yarbro's François Ragoczy Count de Saint Germain is pure hero in the five novels and one collection that chronicle his career. Yarbro has fashioned a blend of the historical romance and the horror story that is entertaining and provocative. As a vampire, Saint Germain is neither villainous nor invincible, but his humanity, cultivation and erotic appeal make him a contemporary hero in a comfortably old-fashioned series of books—indeed, Saint Germain is the moral standard in the books; the real horror, as Yarbro has indicated, is man.

If Chelsea Quinn Yarbro utilizes historical settings and a reinterpreted vampire myth to develop first-rate entertainments, Pierre Kast does so to produce one of the most provocative, intellectually stimulating novels of the genre. In Kast's *The Vampires of Alfama* [4-159], the figure of the morally regenerated vampire in a setting of historical crisis becomes a serious new metaphor with profound and disturbing implications. Simply as a historical intrigue-adventure novel, *The Vampires of Alfama* is a very strong book.

But it is a good deal more than that. Kast's concept of the vampire, while borrowing much from the tradition, is strikingly original. His vampires do not age and are generally robust, but beyond that they have no special powers, nor must they kill to live. Kast's undead eat, drink and, most importantly, make love in a thoroughly human fashion. Although they must avoid sunlight, even their preference for coffins seems more ritualistic, even symbolic, than necessary. Their only weapons are the wisdom and skills gained through very long lives.

The parallels between the vampire cult exemplified by Kotor and early Christianity are deliberate and obvious, as are the contrasts between them: Kotor preaches a doctrine of Earthly physical immortality, rather than an otherworldly, spiritual one. This new religion is dangerous. The social implications of universal immortality undermine all civil and traditional authority, which is based on temporal power over life and death, coupled with an otherworldly mythology that sanctifies those power relationships as part of a divine scheme. Thus, the war against the vampires is a war of repression against intellectual, political, social and sexual freedom. Kotor the vampire is the new Prometheus.

Unlike the writing of Yarbro, which creates exotic historical settings with lengthy, elaborate descriptions and copious, minutely detailed descriptions, Kast's writing is austere and compressed. Period atmosphere is evoked by simple, direct descriptions, suggestion and carefully selected, but extremely graphic details. The characters are not complicated or well rounded; they are obsessed, larger-than-life, even grotesque exemplars of the ideas they animate. The novel presents a heightened, intensified, almost surrealistic landscape, in Kast's words, "a Portugal of fantasy, let us say of a dream."[17] For dream, read nightmare. *The Vampires of Alfama* is at once the most detached and the most passionate of contemporary vampire novels.

Even the greatest vampire of them all, Count Dracula, has been refurbished and restored. Count Dracula has, of course, especially in his Bela Lugosi incarnation, long been an icon of popular culture to the point where it is difficult to take the character seriously. Can a figure that has appeared as a *Sesame Street* puppet, an animated duck and a breakfast cereal still evoke reactions of fear or sophisticated irony? The answer is yes, if the author returns to the source and builds on, or takes off from, the archetypal power of the original.

Thus, Count Dracula has been resurrected from the grave, unstaked and thrust into dozens of novels and stories ranging in quality and insight from the serious and powerful to the trivial and ridiculous. One of the more ridiculous examples of the ways in which the legend can be jazzed up for a set of current potboilers can be seen in the Dracula books of Robert Lory. Lory's gimmick is that his scientist hero, Dr. Damien Harmon, has implanted an electrical device in the Count's skull that more or less keeps him in line. Thus, directed by Harmon, the Count is forced to take the side of good in clashes with implacably evil foes. For example, in *The Witching of Dracula* (1974), the Count clashes with Sabor, a reanimated Egyptian princess, who "sucks the brains until their skulls are dry and empty." After Harmon engineers the destruction of Sabor's powers, he lets the Count savage her body. But the Dracula myth is revised in far more interesting directions by Peter Tremayne (Peter Berresford Ellis) and Fred Saberhagen.

Tremayne's trilogy [4-304]—*Dracula Unborn, The Revenge of Dracula* and *Dracula, My Love*—is carefully built on the original, although each novel takes progressively increasing liberties with it. Accepting Stoker's idea that Dracula was the historical Vlad the Impaler, Tremayne carefully fleshes out the historical Count and gives him an agenda for taking over the world. In *The Revenge of Dracula,* Tremayne takes two characters Stoker mentions in passing and weaves a novel around them as a kind of prequel to *Dracula.*

But in *Dracula, My Love,* Tremayne veers in an entirely new direction. In this novel the Count tells his side of the story and, without denying his need for blood or even his evil, presents himself as a noble, even tragic hero.

If Tremayne fleshes out the Dracula myth, Fred Saberhagen turns it on its head, particularly in *The Dracula Tape* [4-258], the novel that inaugurated his series. On a tape sent to Mina Harker's grandson, Dracula defends himself as a much maligned victim of misunderstanding and deliberate slander: he meant no harm; he turned Lucy Harker into a vampire to save her from Van Helsing's medical bungling; Mina's diary was a fictitious cover for their love affair; the Count actually saved Mina from her real enemy, the crazed Renfield; Van Helsing was a maniacal religious fanatic and the other men his dupes; and so on. It is a deliciously clever, ironic, humorous, touching pastiche. The second book, *The Holmes-Dracula File,* is less deliberately ironic, but is, in its own way, probably just as ingenious. In this novel, Saberhagen offers the hypothesis that the Count and Sherlock Holmes were not only acquainted, they were, in fact, related look-alikes (Holmes having been fathered by the Count's brother, Radu). Once they meet, Holmes and Dracula form an alliance to prevent a mad scientist from loosing the bubonic plague on London.

With *The Holmes-Dracula File* Saberhagen established the Dracula-as-Old-World-Superhero formula that would become increasingly simplified in the three subsequent series novels. While Yarbro's Saint Germain and Saberhagen's Dracula are both heroic vampires with extraordinary powers, the two authors approach their protagonists quite differently. Yarbro's Saint Germain is a figure out of historical romance; Saberhagen's Dracula is almost pure comic book.

Werewolves

Such an elaborate restoration/reformation of the werewolf figure has not been necessary, since he has always been at least partially sympathetic. By and large, vampires are volunteers, while werewolves are usually unlucky, arbitrarily chosen, cursed. Vampires kill because they need human blood to survive and they do so in a calm, calculated manner, often slowly, elaborately, even ritualistically. Werewolves kill because they must, and they do so in uncontrolled frenzy. Vampires are undead; they are in no sense human. Werewolves are ordinary human beings who change involuntarily—generally provoked by the full moon—into monsters and then, their rage satiated and the moon down, revert again to human state to face the aftermath of their carnage, usually with feelings of fear and remorse. Who can forget the plaintive pleas of Larry Talbot (Lon Chaney, Jr.) to the old Gypsy Woman (Maria Ouspenskaya) to relieve him of his curse in Universal's *The Wolf Man* (1941) and *Frankenstein Meets the Wolf Man* (1943) films?

Roughly speaking, there are two types of werewolf story, those in which the werewolf—or wolves—threaten the protagonist and his friends, and those in which the action is described from the werewolf's point of view. The former tend to be mysteries in which the werewolf's identity is not revealed until the end of the story and he is usually, although not always, evil; in the latter, since we share the werewolf's perceptions, we are more sympathetic to his plight, even if appalled by his behavior. Occasionally the two approaches merge, as in Whitley Strieber's *The Wolfen* [4-291].

Excellent examples of the werewolf novel as mystery story can be seen in Charles Grant's *The Dark Cry of the Moon* [4-128], Basil Copper's *The House of the Wolf* [4-86] and Leslie Whitten's *Moon of the Wolf* [4-325]. These novels gain additional resonance by being set in colorful locales and periods: Grant's in his favorite New England town, Oxrun Station, immediately after the Civil War; Copper's in an ancient castle in rural, turn-of-the-century Hungary; Whitten's in an isolated town in the Mississippi delta. Thus, the werewolf legend interacts with an exotic setting and cultural milieu to thicken the atmosphere and intensify the sense of danger.

The Dark Cry of the Moon is the second in Grant's "historical trilogy" of traditional horror novels set in Oxrun Station. Werewolf depredations have terrified the town. Detective Chief Lucas Stanton comes to suspect the arrogant, aristocratic Bartholomew Drummond, his rival for the novel's heroine, Johanna Pendleton. As Lucas investigates the Drummond clan (Bartholomew; his war-battered brother, Lawrence; and his crippled old father, Claude) the werewolf attacks increase, finally putting Johanna into jeopardy. *The Dark Cry of the Moon* is a simple, direct, economical novel that generates considerable suspense and ends with a surprising reversal.

The House of the Wolf is as elaborate and circuitous as *The Dark Cry of the Moon* is simple and direct. It is a very traditional book that uses all of the trappings of the old-fashioned Gothic: a huge, mysterious castle near a rural village in turn-of-the-century Hungary in the dead of winter; an aristocratic family, headed by a mysterious, vaguely sinister Count and featuring a beautiful daughter; a body of unsavory local legend; terrible ancestors; hidden torture chambers; gypsies; peasants; stoic priests; and, of course, werewolves. Copper moves slowly and indirectly, more interested in creating atmosphere and a pervasive sense of impending doom than in rushing his story along. If the final resolution in *The House of the Wolf* is somewhat disappointing, the moment-to-moment pleasures of an old-fashioned horror story rooted in setting, atmosphere and gradually intensifying menace are quite rewarding.

As did his *Progeny of the Adder* [4-326], Leslie Whitten's werewolf novel *Moon of the Wolf* blends the police procedure novel with the horror story, although in this novel his investigator is a part-time deputy sheriff in a small Mississippi town, rather than a big-city detective. For most of the novel Whitten concentrates, not on the werewolf, but on the investigation, the delineation of interesting, sympathetic characters and the creation of a believable milieu. He economically sketches in the social and racial hierarchies and distinctions of the Mississippi delta community with considerable precision and subtlety. Most impressive is Whitten's conception of the werewolf itself. Mixing a little science, a large dose of pseudo-science and a smattering of ambiguous occultism, he almost convinces us that his werewolf is a perfectly natural, if rare, phenomenon. The bloodletting in *Moon of the Wolf* is sufficient and graphic enough to serve the plot's needs, but the overall impression the novel gives is one of restraint and intelligence, rather than emotional and visceral overkill. As in *Progeny of the Adder,* Whitten demonstrates in *Moon of the Wolf* that less is frequently more in monster novels, that carefully managed details and hints of the supernatural which take advantage of common monster myths can be more convincing and chilling than rehashes of old stereotypes made current by being more blatant and bloody.

In Thomas Tessier's *The Nightwalker* [4-297], we meet Bobby Ives, an American Vietnam War veteran living in London, who gradually, painfully realizes that he is a werewolf. Like Whitten in *Moon of the Wolf,* Tessier balances on the line between the psychological and the supernatural in his exploration of Bobby's condition, although, unlike Whitten, he leans toward the supernatural. The writing is intense, sensual and intimate; we are forced to identify with Bobby's anguish even as we are horrified by his actions.

As he did with vampires in *The Hunger* [4-290], Whitley Strieber presents the werewolf as a separate race in *The Wolfen* [4-291]. Wolfen are not monsters, supernatural or otherwise, but a species that fits logically into the natural scheme of nature, preying only on weak, sick, superfluous members of society. The police procedural elements, along with the romance between the two detectives, dominate the first half of *The Wolfen,* but the focus shifts gradually to the wolfen themselves in the latter part of the novel. The reader discovers a very tight, loyal, devoted family unit. As carnivores, their pride and pleasure lies in killing, but they do so without cruelty and carefully choose only the weak and old as victims. It is a rigid code, and its violation—by the young and foolish—is responsible for their downfall. The leader of the pack, the old father, accepts full responsibility for his children's errors. His feelings for his pack-family, his acceptance of responsibility and his final sacrifice of self for them evoke the same admiration the reader would have for a human. He is perhaps the novel's most remarkable character, yet—and this is Strieber's most memorable accomplishment—he, and the other wolfen, are not just humans with a taste for human blood, but a believably separate species whose animal characteristics are as real as their human ones. We end the novel with divided sympathies—glad that the hero and heroine survive and triumph, but moved by the destruction of the wolfen, which ends the book on a pathetic, even tragic note.

The werewolf as an innocent child of nature also appears in several recent novels. The most touching element in the King-Straub collaboration *The Talisman* [4-178] is the relationship between the young hero, Jack Sawyer, and Wolf, the powerful, benevolent, child-like werewolf. Wolf manages to control his bestial appetites, and avoid hurting his friend, by locking Jack up during the time of the full moon. A more sophisticated and interesting exploration of this character type can be found in Robert Stallman's The Book of the Beast series [4-279]. The werewolf protagonist of the series takes the shape of boys of various ages, so we see the action through their eyes, rather than those of the "beast" behind them. For example, in *The Orphan*, the first book in the trilogy, as the boy, Charles, grows into adolescence, the tension between his human identity and his bestial nature becomes increasingly powerful and dangerous.

At the other extreme, the werewolf as superhero appears in *The Wolf's Hour* [4-227], Robert McCammon's intriguing mix of spy thriller and horror story. Here Michael Gallatin combines his werewolf skills and his human resourcefulness—more often the latter—to extricate himself from seemingly impossible predicaments in this exciting adventure/horror hybrid that deftly combines the appeals of both genres.

The Psychopath as Werewolf

At first glance, Stephen King's notion that Stevenson's *Dr. Jekyll and Mr. Hyde* [2-93] is the archetypal werewolf story—"Gaze, if you dare, on the face of the *real* Werewolf. His name, gentle reader, is Edward Hyde."[18]—seems dubious. There are numerous differences between Hyde and the traditional werewolf, even in the modified forms described. Without fangs or claws, Hyde is completely human in form, if vaguely deformed. Nor is he particularly strong or agile. Most important, Hyde does not represent uncontrolled bestiality; he is a thoroughly civilized monster—he drinks, parties, dresses in evening clothes and is thoroughly articulate. If he is driven and unable or unwilling to control his appetites, he nevertheless gratifies them in his own calculating ways. In short, Hyde is not so much a werewolf as he is a psychopath.

Or is that King's point? Is the psychopath, along with his psychiatric flipside the psychotic, particularly in such extreme manifestations as the serial murderer, a valid variation on the werewolf? Is he perhaps the primary variation on the werewolf in contemporary horror fiction?

Two novellas by David Case, *The Cell* and *The Hunter* [4-75], illustrate this notion of the psychopath/psychotic as werewolf. The protagonist of *The Cell* claims to have inherited the "werewolf disease" from his mysterious family. Despite having been locked into a basement cell by his wife every time the full moon appears, the smug, arrogant, snobbish narrator claims responsibility for the deaths of three people who, he casually suggests, deserved to die. Since the story is told from his viewpoint, without any outside corroboration, we have no way of knowing whether he is truly monstrous or simply insane.

From believing oneself to be a werewolf, to behaving consciously and deliberately like a werewolf, is a small step. In *The Hunter*, the nature and rationale of the killer is never in doubt. A series of savage, bizarre killings—the bodies brutally shredded but the heads neatly decapitated and taken—have terrified a rural British country community and induced retired big-game hunter Jake Wethersby to join in the search for the killer. The trail leads Wethersby to his best friend, another hunter (ironically named Byron), who is civilized, self-controlled and completely rational. The killings, Byron states, are justified as stimulants, since only in the face of death can man, individually or collectively, really live. He then invites Wethersby to join the hunt with himself, Byron, as the game.

Thus, the man in *The Cell* kills—or thinks he kills—because he must; the man in *The Hunter* kills because he wants to—for pleasure, or excitement, or entertainment, or perverse whim. Both monsters are central to the modern consciousness and to contemporary dark fantasy. *The Hunter* has an additional element that is integral to the best of such stories, the *relationship* between the killer and his victim and/or his pursuer. When Byron confesses to his serial killings, he challenges Wethersby with his philosophy and dares him to recognize in himself those same murderous impulses—which Wethersby, and perhaps the reader, does. In *The Hunter*—as in *Dr. Jekyll and Mr. Hyde*—the werewolf motif merges with another major dark fantasy archetype, that of the psychic double or *doppelgänger*, allowing us to categorize such books as true horror stories rather than as police procedure novels on the one hand or psychiatric case histories on the other.

The novel, along with the classic film made from it, that set the pattern for the contemporary suspense-horror story was Robert Bloch's *Psycho* [4-46]. In King's words:

> But Norman is the Werewolf. Only instead of growing hair, his change is effected by donning his dead mother's panties, slip, and dress—and hacking up the guests instead of biting them. . . .
>
> *Psycho* is effective because it brings the Werewolf myth home. It is not outside evil, predestination; the fault lies not in our stars but in ourselves. We know that Norman is only outwardly the Werewolf when he's wearing Mom's duds and speaking in Mom's voice; but we have the uneasy suspicion that he's the Werewolf *all* the time.[19]

After his Lovecraftian apprenticeship, Bloch turned increasingly to psychological aberration for his subject matter. The psychopath shows up in several short stories and especially in the novels *The Scarf* (1947) and *The Kidnapper* (1954). Bloch tried out the split personality motif in two interesting pre-*Psycho* short stories, briefly in "Lucy Comes to Stay" (1952) and at greater length in one of his best efforts, "The Real Bad Friend" (1957), both of which withhold the truth about the main characters until the stories' climaxes.

In *Psycho,* Norman's split personality is likewise concealed through most of the book. The importance of this, beyond the mystery story ruse, is that by seeing things through Norman's eyes, we identify with his skewed view of the world for much of the novel. We understand and sympathize with him, sharing his confusions, anxieties, insecurities and attempts to repress his hostility and violence.

Even after he has been revealed as the killer, we continue to feel sorry for him. The scary thing about *Psycho* is not that Norman is an otherworldly monster, but that he is one of us.

John R. Maxim takes the split personality a step further in *Abel/Baker/Charley* [4-221]. As the result of a traumatic experience, Jared Baker's personality fragments into three classically Freudian parts, ego, superego and id. The id—"Abel"—then goes on a vengeful rampage, which stimulates a manhunt by police, underworld and scientists.

More conventional and disturbing is Ramsey Campbell's venture into the psychotic mind in *The Face That Must Die* [4-66]. His protagonist, a self-righteous, moralistic, homophobic paranoic, who reeks of sexual confusion and repression, is absolutely revolting and thoroughly believable.

The killers in Dean R. Koontz's *Whispers* [4-194] and (as Leigh Nichols) *Shadowfires* [4-189] go beyond psychosis; their evil is enhanced by extraordinary powers, genetically induced "immortality." *Whispers* is the story of Hillary Thomas, a successful young woman stalked by the murderer, Bruno Frye, she has already killed in self-defense. In *Shadowfires*, Eric Leben, a wealthy Californian who heads a genetics firm performing secret government work, is killed in an accident shortly after threatening his estranged wife, Rachel.

An earlier Koontz novel, *The Vision* [4-192], also features an apparently resuscitated serial killer stalking a beautiful woman, but Koontz adds an extra wrinkle, a telepathic connection between the killer and the would-be victim. Having survived a near-fatal assault and named her attacker, who subsequently kills himself, Mary Bergen develops telepathic abilities, which she uses to predict and prevent homicides. Her gift backfires, however, when she has a vision of herself being murdered, but can do nothing to prevent it except look into her own troubled mind for the clues to the truth about her would-be killer's resurrection.

Stephen King also uses the connection between psychic and serial killer in *The Dead Zone* [4-165]. After his hero, John Smith, awakens from an accident-induced four-and-a-half-year coma, he discovers that he possesses clairvoyant powers. As these dubious gifts increasingly isolate him from a normal life, he tries to suppress them, but society demands that he use them for the common good—even though that will eventually destroy him. The crucial sequence in this process is Smith's telepathic tracking of the "Castle Rock Strangler," a demented serial murderer who hides behind a police badge.

The psychological identification between psychic and killer takes a heavy toll on Mary Bergen and John Smith. The psychological dangers of such an identification—the psychic/killer *doppelgänger* theme—are explored even further in James Herbert's *Moon* [4-143], Owen Brookes's *Deadly Communion* [4-56] and Thomas Harris's *Red Dragon* [4-135].

Before *Moon* begins, the life of Jon Childes has been disoriented by a psychic connection to a serial killer. He resists the psychic intrusions, but they become increasingly severe and begin to be directed at Childes and his loved ones. Herbert's delineation of Childes's mental landscape is thorough and intense, with the progressive absorption of the killer's madness into Childes's mind handled in a convincing manner. As a depiction of a mind in conflict with its own powers and dark possibilities, *Moon* is impressive.

In *Deadly Communion*, Owen Brookes pushes the notion of psychic identification even further. Steven Coles experiences the secondhand thoughts of a serial murderer of young boys, first in hints and random flashes, but gradually as a palpable presence that threatens to take over his mind.

But in the most powerful variation on the killer-pursuer as *doppelgänger* theme, Thomas Harris's *Red Dragon* [4-135], there are no extrasensory or clairvoyant talents, just an intense psychological identification between the killer and his pursuer. Ex-FBI agent Will Graham's pursuit of the "Tooth Fairy" killer is similar to Marlow's quest for Kurtz in Conrad's classic *Heart of Darkness* [3-51], and the message of *Red Dragon* echoes Kurtz's final lament—"The horror! The horror!"

Another Turn of the Screw—The Child as Victim and Villain

The title of Henry James's most famous ghost story comes from the notion that putting a child in jeopardy gives a ghost or horror story an additional "turn of the screw." That formula remains powerful today as contemporary authors have exploited the threatened child from embryo through adolescence in every conceivable way, but yet another "turn" has been added: the child as villain as well as victim—and sometimes both.

The child can simply be a victim—of supernatural powers as in Thomas Tessier's *Phantom* [4-298] and Stephen King's "Gramma" and *The Shining* [4-173]; of a psychotic murderer as in Davis Grubb's *The Night of the Hunter* [4-130]; and even of its own mother as in V. C. Andrews's *Flowers in the Attic* [4-12].

The child, especially in horror fiction, is vulnerable not only because of age, size, physical weakness and dependency on adults, but also because he or she is simply not taken seriously by that adult world—especially when claiming belief in the unbelievable. The child is also more vulnerable to internal terrors, subject not only to external forces, but to his or her own imagination as well. As Mark Petrie, teenaged co-hero of Stephen King's *'Salem's Lot* [4-172], drifts off to sleep:

> he found himself reflecting . . . on the peculiarity of adults. They took laxatives, liquor, or sleeping pills to drive away their terrors . . . and their terrors were so tame and domestic: the job, the money . . . does my wife still love me, who are my friends. They were pallid compared to the fears every child lies cheek and jowl with in his dark bed . . . the thing under the bed or in the cellar every night, the thing which leers and capers and threatens just beyond the point where vision will reach. The same lonely battle must be fought night after night and the only cure is the eventual ossification of the imaginary faculties, and this is called adulthood.[20]

George, unfortunate boy hero of Stephen King's "Gramma," is a pure example of the child victim. Left to care for his ancient, sick, perhaps dying grandmother, George is terrified of the woman—with good reason; she is a witch who wants to take over George's body before she dies. George has the perception and imagination to know the truth about the woman, but neither the strength nor the credibility with the adult world to do anything about it.

Ten-year-old Ned Covington is in a similar situation in Thomas Tessier's *Phantom,* in which the "phantom"—perhaps the ghost of a bereaved mother, perhaps the spirit of a violated scarecrow, perhaps Death itself—stalks Ned both as a tangible force and as a psychological dread.

Ned is not completely passive, but he has no real defense against the vague but terrifying menace that seems to be toying with him. A solitary, sensitive boy, Ned is ripe for picking. His father, well meaning but distant, and his mother, physically ailing and nervous almost to the point of hysteria, are of little help. Two old fishermen offer him companionship, but their storytelling only feeds his vulnerable, receptive imagination. Although he knows better, Ned seeks confrontation with his phantom in the ruins of a long-abandoned health spa, where his worst nightmares are confirmed. The serious illness that threatens his life may seem contrived, but it is actually a necessary, even inevitable plot development, given Ned's essential passivity. Because we can never be completely sure to what extent Ned's phantoms are real and to what degree they are projections of his inner fears, *Phantom* balances on that ambiguous line between outer evil and internal dread that is the essence of refined terror.

But if imagination and youth make the child especially vulnerable, they also provide him or her with the weapons needed to confront these menaces. Danny Torrance in King's *The Shining* is in many ways similar to Ned Covington—both are sensitive, imaginative, emotionally precarious and seriously disturbed by family tensions (Danny's father's potential violence, Ned's mother's serious illness). But Danny has one additional vulnerability, the dubious gift of extrasensory perception (called his "shine" by King, inspired by the line "We all shine on" in John Lennon's song "Instant Karma"), which intensifies his sensitivities, overwhelms him with upsetting information and energizes the diabolical powers in the Overlook Hotel, where he and his parents are snowbound for the winter.

Thus, Danny's shine is at best a mixed blessing, even before the Overlook experience. Danny is forced to know too much, both from the thoughts he reads in the minds of others and in the erratic glimpses he has of the future. He is aware of his father's weaknesses and the precariousness of his parents' marriage. All this has driven him into himself. The tensions have been increased in the months preceding the trip to Colorado by a series of frightening but unintelligible images that he has been receiving with increasing power and clarity. These are, of course, premonitions of his encounter with the dark forces of the Overlook, and as they close in on the Torrance family, Danny sees exactly what is happening, although he does not always understand what he is seeing. But in the end it is not Danny's shine, but his physical courage and faith that even as the monster he has become, his father retains enough of his real self to be redeemed, or at least restrained, which saves Danny and his mother from death.

The ill-fated George and Danny Torrance are just two of many threatened youngsters King has featured from his first novel, *Carrie,* through *It,* one of his most recent. King has often left it to the child—ranging in age from five-year-old Danny and eight-year-old Charlie McGee (*Firestarter*), through thirteen-year-old Jack Sawyer (*The Talisman*), fourteen-year-old Marty Coslaw (*Cycle of the Were-*

wolf) and Gordon Lechance ("The Body"), the teenaged outcasts in *It* and high school seniors Carrie White and Arnie Cunningham and Dennis Guilder (*Christine*)—to confront the dark forces, both without and within, sometimes being destroyed by them, sometimes triumphing over them, sometimes "helped" by "wild talents" of one kind or another, sometimes armed with no more than courage, intelligence and luck.

Thus, in several of his best works King mixes the horror story with the rite-of-passage narrative. Mark Petrie's intelligence and imagination make him the natural ally for Ben Mears as they confront Kurt Barlow and his vampiric hordes in *'Salem's Lot.* In the final confrontation between man and beast in *Cycle of the Werewolf* (1983), it is wheelchair-bound Marty Coslaw and not his grown uncle who has the strength and nerve to kill the werewolf. It is left to Dennis Guilder to challenge Arnie Cunningham's demonic car in *Christine* [4-163] to a final duel. To save his mother's life, Jack Sawyer must undertake a quest for a magical talisman by traveling not only in this world, but also in the dangerous, primitive alternate world of the "Territories." And the seven teenaged loners who band together in *It* [4-168] to track the evil things in the Derry, Maine, storm drains all undergo a rite of passage in coming to terms not only with the external evil confronting them, but also with their own personal and social demons.

But in King's most poignant coming-of-age story, and the one that seems closest to King himself, the boy faces no supernatural horror, only the knowledge of his own mortality. Although very grim at the center, "The Body," (in *Different Seasons* [4-166]) is laced with a nostalgia for the freedom, camaraderie and, with qualifications, innocence of boyhood in a manner somewhat reminiscent of one of King's favorite predecessors, Ray Bradbury. Indeed, "The Body" could be called King's *Dandelion Wine* [F4A-44]. The two works are celebrations of childhood and sad introductions to the pains and limitations of adulthood, with the central motif of each being the boy-protagonist's first real confrontation with death.

But the two works also emphasize the difference between these two masters of dark fantasy. The boyhood landscape of *Dandelion Wine* is seen through a soft, sentimental filter, however sad the book's thematic center, and even the fact of death hovers only at the novel's edge, never becoming much more than a poetic abstraction. But "The Body" is about just that, a corpse: a solid mass of dead, rotting, slug-infested flesh that had been a living boy, of the same age as the protagonist. This concrete physical reality permeates the story, qualifying and darkening King's homage to youthful hope and exuberance.

"The Body" recounts the pilgrimage of twelve-year-old Gordon Lachance and three friends to recover the body of a teenaged boy hit by a train and left in an undeveloped Maine woods near the fictional town of Castle Rock. The story is told from the viewpoint of the adult Lachance—now a successful writer of horror fiction—looking back on the primary formative experience of his boyhood.

As the boys struggle through their difficult, sometimes comic trek into the woods, beset by natural and human barriers including a harrowing brush with death on the train trestle, they also struggle with themselves—their fears, insecurities, confusions—and with each other. Secondary to the mortality theme of the story is the notion of boyhood camaraderie, a kind of pure, elemental companionship, made more intense by its necessarily transitory quality. Two of the boys,

Lachance and Chris Chambers, who is the product of a deprived, quasi-criminal background, come to understand this. The others, Teddy Duchamp and Vern Tassio, remain blissfully ignorant, despite their terrifying shared experiences. In the end, after their arduous, dangerous trek, they are confronted by a gang of older boys, led by Chris's older brother, who beat them up. Thus, human injustice and brutality, as well as natural mortality, are a legacy of their quest. And perhaps the saddest insight of all comes when Gordon realizes that he must desert his boyhood friends in order to avoid the traps laid for them and achieve his own potential, a potential that he does in fact achieve, but at no small price.

Two other examples of the effective blend of dark fantasy with coming-of-age story are Ray Bradbury's *Something Wicked This Way Comes* (1962) [4-51] and Peter Straub's *Shadowland* (1980) [4-289].

The title of Bradbury's novel comes from the witches' chant in *Macbeth*—"By the pricking of my thumbs/Something wicked this way comes"—and that something wicked is "Cooger and Dark's Pandemonium Shadow Show," which comes to disrupt Green Town, Illinois, Bradbury's idyllic midwestern small town. The novel centers on two thirteen-year-old boys, best friends Will Halloway and Jim Nightshade, and Will's father, Charles, a middle-aged library custodian. Born one minute before midnight on Halloween eve, Will has a positive, sunny disposition; born one minute after, James is his "darker twin." Both boys—and finally Charles, too—are tempted by the carnival's black magic: a carousel that runs time backwards or forwards, a mirror maze that reflects images of what one wants to be or most fears, a sinister fortune teller; in short, magical devices that pervert the normal order.

Because *Something Wicked* is about change, Dark offers tempting but ultimately malevolent change. The boys' teacher, Mrs. Foley, sees herself as young in the Mirror Maze and succumbs to Dark's temptation, becoming a little girl in his freak show. The boys are also tempted and must learn to know, accept and even celebrate time and the right kinds of change in themselves, in others and in the world in which they live. Charles should know this already, but he falters. *Something Wicked* is a coming-of-age novel for him as well. At age fifty-four, with a precarious heart condition, he feels his vitality slipping, his mortality looming.

The counterpoint to the dark carnival is the library where Charles works. The characters retreat there to find the wisdom to deal with Dark & Co. as Bradbury once again celebrates books and accumulated wisdom, and there they learn at least the nature of their enemy. Dark, Cooger and the other freaks represent the "Autumn People," beings who have wandered the world for eons, feeding on the guilt, fear, misery and greed of mankind. But in the end it is not knowledge but affirmation that defeats the Autumn People. Facing sure destruction by the Dust Witch, Charles laughs at her and she is vanquished. Laughter also brings Jim back from the edge of the grave. And, finally, Charles hugs Dark—who has regressed into a young boy—destroying him with affection.

In *Shadowland* [4-289] young friends Tom Flannigan and Del Nightengale also encounter darkly magical forces, in the person of Del's uncle, Coleman Collins, a magician, who tempts them—especially Tom—with real magic. The first section of the book, which takes place at Carson, an expensive, mediocre prep school, introduces the theme of magic, both its possibilities and its dangers, culminating in the boys' magic show, which ends in a general conflagration that consumes the school. All of that, however, is only a preparation for the boys' summer at Shadowland, where Del's uncle attempts to seduce them with magical extravaganzas and dramatized fairy tales.

Life at Shadowland becomes increasingly weird and sinister: the shows become darker and more cruel, as well as more fantastic; thug-like men threaten the boys; and a beautiful young girl, Rose Armstrong, becomes an object of both desire and fear. Collins's true motive is slowly revealed: he wants to recruit Tom, the more talented youth, to be his successor. Thus, Tom is faced with a terrible dilemma: if he develops his gifts, he risks succumbing to Collins's temptation and the evil power that goes with it, but if he denies his gifts, he and Del will be defenseless against the dark forces that permeate Shadowland. Despite strong literary echoes—of Bradbury's *Something Wicked This Way Comes* [4-51], John Fowles's *The Magus* [4-117; F4A-108] and John Knowles's mainstream novel *A Separate Peace* (1960)—*Shadowland* is one of the most exciting and inventive blends of horror and coming-of-age novel in the genre.

But, while the notion of children as victims is an old one, the demonic child is relatively recent. In 1948, Ray Bradbury shocked his readers with "The Small Assassin" and its idea that a baby could be a killer. A much wider audience found William March's *The Bad Seed* [4-211] disturbing in its initial form as a novel and also in its incarnations as a successful play (dramatized by Maxwell Anderson) and popular film. Although March's simplistic notion of inherited evil may seem quaint today, it is probably no more absurd than demonic or alien possession. Despite its naturalistic facade, *The Bad Seed* established the formula of the evil child novel. Whether *that* "seed" is a bad one has been the subject of much critical dispute (see Büssing's *Aliens in the Home* [7-69] for a detailed discussion of the child in horror fiction).

Given a few years, March's Rhoda Penmark would probably come to resemble Rynn Jacobs, heroine of Laird Koenig's *The Little Girl Who Lives Down the Lane* [4-184]. Rynn wants nothing more than to be left alone with her unseen poet father (fled? dead? murdered? comatose?), but strangers keep trying to force themselves on her. She welcomes a shy boy magician, but resists the others, especially the realtor who rented the house to her father, and the realtor's conniving son, and she deals with them in a way that would have won Rhoda's warm approval.

All of the psychopathic youngsters in contemporary horror are not, of course, females. Although King has not generally subscribed to the demonic child theory, he has created one classical young male psychopath in "Apt Pupil," one of the four novellas in *Different Seasons*. The main character is Todd Bowden, "the total all-American kid," a typical California teenager. Bowden confronts Alfred Denker, an aged German recluse, with the fact that he, Todd, has discovered Denker's true identity, that of Kurt Dussander, a Nazi war criminal in hiding, once the *Untercommandant* of the Patin death camp. Bowden threatens Dussander with exposure and demands, not money, but a detailed, firsthand account of the German atrocities (all the "gooshy" stuff) and Dussander's part in them.

The first half of "Apt Pupil" is an engrossing study in progressive corruption, as the relationship between the boy, fascinated by evil-as-fun, and the old survivor, long numb to his own decadence, evolves and changes both of them. In the end the old man dominates the boy, but neither can control the corruption the boy's curiosity and perverse make-believe have set in motion. As a study of moral corruption "Apt Pupil" is very provocative, but as a story it fails because King cannot resolve the conflict on the psychological level. Prodded by their mental deterioration, both Todd and Dussander almost gratuitously become mass murderers. Thus, physical gore finally replaces psychological violence and plot contrivance substitutes for characterization.

Todd Bowden may be a monster, but he is a human one, possible and explainable, if frightening and disgusting. But, at least from *Rosemary's Baby* [4-206] on, the evil child has been often aligned with supernatural malevolence in works that range from the superficially sensational, like David Selzer's *The Omen* (book and film) and the novels of John Saul, to more serious and sophisticated treatments by such authors as Lawrence Block, Bernard Taylor, Thomas Tryon, James Herbert, William Peter Blatty and Stephen King.

The sinister little girls in Lawrence Block's *Ariel* [4-49] and Bernard Taylor's *The Godsend* [4-295] can probably also be categorized as psychopathic except that the explanation seems inadequate. Both girls are, if not overtly supernatural, at least too strange and ambiguous to fit neatly into clinical case histories. Ariel's guilt is never proven and the book's ensuing violence is the product of clashing personalities, misunderstandings and irrational behavior—with an aura of supernatural malevolence hovering in the background.

There is no doubt about the guilt of Bonnie, the title character in *The Godsend.* She is clearly more than a precocious psychopath. The realistic possibility that a six-year-old girl could murder several children and then fight off an adult man is remote, but one of the brilliant touches in the novel is that Taylor creates no elaborate history or mythology to explain Bonnie's malevolent powers, only the simple metaphor of the cuckoo bird who deposits her eggs to hatch in a foreign nest and displace the natural offspring (a metaphor also central to another fine evil child novel, John Wyndham's *The Midwich Cuckoos* [4-338]).

The line between the insane and the supernatural is even more brilliantly blurred in Thomas Tryon's *The Other* [4-306]. The summer games of twin thirteen-year-old boys Holland and Niles Perry turn dark as mysterious "accidents" begin to happen, apparently engineered by the evil twin, Holland—except that we learn that Holland has been dead for months. Has the good brother, Niles, influenced by his mystical grandmother, established psychic contact with his dead twin? Has Holland taken full possession of Niles, using him as a vengeful agent? Or is Niles simply psychotic, having been pushed over the edge by Holland's death? Tryon deftly manipulates these ambiguities through shifting viewpoints, jumps in time, fragments of action and conversation and, above all, Niles's fervent, almost hysterical, yet colorful and ironic voice talking incessantly to his dead brother. Of all the evil child narratives, *The Other* takes us most deeply and intimately into the distorted, anguished, obsessed mind of the child villain-victim.

The possession motif has the advantage of giving us the child as both villain and victim. Because the child does the evil deeds, he/she is a villain, but being under the dominance of another being, the child is actually innocent. This mix, the child as both villain and victim, has produced the most subtle and sophisticated of the evil child/teenager stories, whether the rationale be psychiatric, religious, paranormal or simply demonic.

The possession idea is most often presented in a traditional religious context. Two excellent examples are James Herbert's *Shrine* [4-146] and William Peter Blatty's *The Exorcist* [4-42]. The possession in *The Shrine* focuses on eleven-year-old Alice Pagett, whose vision of the Immaculate Conception turns the parish of St. Joseph's and the surrounding town of Benfield into a shrine overnight. In the novel's finale, a huge outdoor ceremony that turns into a riot, Herbert's talents for depicting mass hysteria and pervasive evil, while still maintaining his focus on the main characters, is particularly impressive.

But it was the best-selling novel *The Exorcist* (1971), followed two years later by William Friedkin's film adaptation, that firmly fixed the evil child/demonic possession story in the public mind. As eleven-year-old Regan MacNeil begins to exhibit increasingly weird traits, she puzzles and alarms those around her—her mother, Chris; her psychiatrist-priest, Damien Karras; and others who attempt, in various ways, to deal with her bizarre, obscene behavior.

The major conflict, however, is not between demon and exorcist, but between the war of faith within the book's real protagonist, Damien Karras. As a psychiatrist, Karras is committed to a rational view of life and a conviction that, where religious belief cannot be reconciled with reason, belief must give way; as a priest, Karras fervently believes—or wants to believe—in his traditional religious heritage. Panzuzu's possession of Regan brings this conflict within Karras to a test, one that costs him his life but, the reader is left to assume, saves his soul.

The Exorcist is a thoughtful, provocative book—Blatty's philosophical and theological musings are not intrusive, but are nicely integrated into the action, and the novel is briskly written with deft, if not overly deep characterizations, and a number of vivid, memorable scenes. It was certainly one of the better books of its period.

But that alone does not explain the enormous popularity of the book and film. Like *Rosemary's Baby* and the novels of Stephen King, *The Exorcist* touched a nerve in the American public that caused it to appeal to a far wider audience than did the most skillfully written, critically lauded horror novels. This point is underscored by the fact that Blatty's next dark fantasy, *The Ninth Configuration* [4-43], received relatively little general attention either as a book or a film, even though it is artistically and intellectually a far superior work. And perhaps the popularity of *The Exorcist* can in part illuminate the surprising popularity of the whole evil child subgenre.

The most common observation is that Regan was, in a sense, a symbol of her generation. Commenting on the film version, Stephen King has observed:

> The movie (and the novel) is nominally about the attempts of two priests to cast a demon out of young Regan MacNeil. . . . Substantively, however, it is a film about explosive social change, a finely honed focusing point for that entire youth explosion that took place in the late sixties and early seventies. It was a movie for all those parents who felt, in a kind of agony and terror, that they were losing their children and could not understand why or how it was happening. . . . Religious trappings aside, every adult in America understood what the film's powerful sub-

> text was saying; they understood that the demon in Regan MacNeil would have responded enthusiastically to the Fish Cheer at Woodstock.[21]

True enough, but it may be a mistake to push the "religious trappings aside." One need not be a Catholic or even religious to appreciate the moral structure that religion gives to the novel. Blatty handles the Catholicism quite adroitly. It is not so intrusive as to bog the book down or annoy non-Catholics, but it naturally provides an institutional framework for marshalling the forces of good and a set of procedures for focusing those powers. His skillful use of ritualistic detail is reminiscent of Dennis Wheatley at his best.

Thus, *The Exorcist* is very contemporary in its scenes of graphic horror and obscenity, but it is very conservative, even old-fashioned, in the worldview that provides the context for these actions. Evil is awesomely powerful, man is weak, and divinity seems ambiguous, but in the end, evil is vulnerable, man finds the courage and determination needed, and divine help is strongly implied, if not overtly demonstrated. Blatty's resurrection of Divine Order coupled with his keen sense of the contemporary scene and his precise use of graphic detail make *The Exorcist* a popular classic deserving of its readership.

The traditional view that horror fiction dealing with the Devil suggests—even proves—the existence and supremacy of God has been muted or ignored in contemporary dark fantasy. This new attitude may be acceptable or even favored by many hardcore devotees, but writers who move beyond the perimeters of the genre to achieve a widespread following, like King, Dean Koontz, John Farris and James Herbert, almost invariably combine an essentially traditional worldview with a contemporary sensibility that makes use of explicit language and graphic depiction in treating violence, sex and current issues.

Although there is no overtly divine design in the works of Stephen King, there is a sense of moral order in his writings, including those featuring troubled teenagers. Carrie White (*Carrie* [4-162]) and Arnie Cunningham (*Christine* [4-163]) are not evil, nor are they possessed, at least not in the usual sense, but they are ultimately destructive, overwhelmed by forces they can neither anticipate nor understand, but which take their frustrations and deprivations and turn them into forces that lash out, destroying the guilty and innocent alike.

Both Carrie and Arnie are persecuted high school outsiders who long for acceptance. Both suffer under oppressive mothers, although Arnie's is merely overbearing and severely neurotic, while Carrie's mother is an actively psychotic religious fanatic. Both receive an unexpected opportunity to become normal, at least for a short time. Carrie is invited to the junior-senior prom by the handsomest boy in school; Arnie begins an affair with the prettiest girl in class. And, most importantly, both have or acquire a spectacular power. Carrie's awesome telekinetic abilities are unleashed by her first, belated menstrual period and her persecution by her female schoolmates; Arnie buys "Christine," a demonic 1958 Plymouth Fury that comes to life to minister to his needs. These gifts initially invigorate their recipients, but they are dangerously volatile, needing only a spark to ignite a terrible conflagration.

The spark for Carrie is a cruel, dangerous joke played on her at the prom by the most vindictive of the girls; the spark for Arnie is his blossoming love affair, which excites Christine's jealousy. The result for Arnie is that Christine attempts to kill all enemies or rivals, real or imagined, including finally Arnie's girlfriend and his lifelong chum. Carrie's response is more spectacular: she kills all the promgoers, destroys the gym, ravages a good deal of the town, kills the girl whose vicious prank sent her over the edge and then kills her own mother, after she herself has been mortally wounded by Mrs. White.

But both Arnie and Carrie are ultimately redeemed. Despite all the carnage, they are both more victim than villain. Their outsider status—the fault of their narrow-minded, vindictive classmates—has made them vulnerable to seduction: Carrie by her own powers, Arnie by Christine. In the early stages of both books, we identify with each of them and share the pleasures of their apparent good fortune—although we sense the trap being set. And when, in their own ways, they go over the edge, we pity them. In *Christine* the shift of focus from Arnie to his friend, Dennis Guilder, somewhat distracts us from Arnie's fate. Since we hear about his death secondhand, we don't share the poignancy of the moment. But we do learn that in the end, Arnie did not succumb to the lure of Christine or of her depraved owner, Ronald LeBey. In the final fight with LeBey's ghost for life and soul, Arnie loses his life but, we are meant to believe, saves his soul.

Carrie's explosion was inevitable and completely beyond her control. To be given a glimpse of wholeness and acceptance only to have it viciously snatched away and replaced by public scorn and laughter was a shattering vindication of her mother's hellish vision. Thus, given the powers of a god, she strikes back with the wrath of a god. Yet she knows her powers are demonic, a final proof of her personal damnation, a damnation she cannot resist. As she destroys her enemies, she punishes herself.

But there is a final reconciliation between Carrie and Sue Snell, a girl whose ill-advised plan to loan her boyfriend to Carrie for the prom unwittingly provoked the catastrophe. As Sue attempts to confront the moribund Carrie in her last moments, they experience a moment of lucid understanding and Sue receives, if not forgiveness, at least an insight into her own responsibility and mortality. Thus, the violence and destruction in *Carrie* and *Christine* are resolved in a final calm that is, if not tragic, at least satisfying.

Stephen King and the Return to Otranto

Occasional best-sellers like *Rosemary's Baby* [4-206] and *The Exorcist* [4-42] notwithstanding, horror novels and collections have rarely competed with social melodramas, spy novels or historical romances on the best-seller lists—until the emergence of Stephen King in the mid-1970s. The "Stephen King phenomenon"—it has become almost one word—must be a dominant consideration in any analysis of contemporary dark fantasy.

The most common defense of popular writers is that they are "good storytellers," and King certainly is that. The essence of successful storytelling is solid plotting, and the structural principles of King's plots, while hardly unique, are remarkably effective. His characters are believable, sympathetic and thoroughly contemporary; his settings are realistic, his dialogue colloquial, his writing clear and vivid. To readers whose taste for the visceral have been sharpened by movies, especially post-George Romero horror films, King offers gory details galore, as he himself has admitted: "First I try to terrify my readers. If I can't achieve terror, then I try for horror. And if I can't manage horror—I'm not proud—I try at least to gross 'em out."[22]

But none of this fully accounts for King's extraordinary popularity. Horror fiction has had other good storytellers whose work is distinguished by solid plotting, sharp characterizations, vivid sets, scenes, dialogue and ample gore. King is obviously doing more than "just" telling his stories well—and what he is doing has radically changed the shape of contemporary horror fiction. As already noted in discussions of *Rosemary's Baby* and *The Exorcist,* in order for a horror novel to achieve best-seller status, it must touch subjects, themes and attitudes of more general public concern than is usual in hardcore genre products, while also exploiting the characteristic appeal of the genre. Stephen King has done this more efficiently and consistently than any other horror writer, past or present.

To those who suggested, upon the 1982 publication of *Different Seasons* [4-166], that he was moving away from horror, King responded:

> there are a lot of people who are convinced that, just as soon as I have made enough dough, I will just leave all this silly bullshit behind and go on and write *Brideshead Revisited* and spy novels and things like that. You know, this [horror fiction] is all I've ever wanted to write. . . .[23]

But it is not only the critics' disdain of the horror category that has inclined them to believe King will follow such predecessors as Ira Levin and Thomas Tryon into other genres or into that large literary puddle called the mainstream, but also King's own apparent ambivalence toward the genre he so admires. In a sense, he *has* been writing "*Brideshead Revisited* and spy novels and things like that." Rarely is a King novel a "pure" horror story; most of his books also contain bits and pieces of science fiction, mystery fiction, spy fiction, epic quests and westerns.

Thus, one ingredient in the King best-seller recipe is his utilization not only of the formulas and devices of horror fiction, but also of those of other popular genres. While he has systematically offered his own versions of all the classical horror figures—the vampire (*'Salem's Lot*), the ghost ("Sometimes They Come Back," *The Shining*), the zombie (*Pet Sematary*), the werewolf (*Cycle of the Werewolf*), the gypsy curse (*Thinner*), other-dimensional monsters (*The Mist*), ancient evil periodically unleashed (*It*), to mention only a few—he has also picked plot ideas, characters and situations from other genres.

King's first published novel, *Carrie,* features a "wild talent," telekinesis, usually thought of as the province of science fiction, to horrific effect. Wild talents also occupy the center of *The Dead Zone* [4-165] (clairvoyance), and *Firestarter* [4-167] (pyrokinesis), two books that double as political intrigue stories and science fiction horror novels. *The Stand* [4-175] and *The Tommyknockers* [4-177] utilize standard science fictional situations, the post-end-of-the-world catastrophe novel and the flying saucer story respectively. *The Talisman* [4-178], King's collaboration with Peter Straub, is an alternate world epic fantasy. And *The Gunslinger*, the first volume in his *Dark Tower* series [4-164], is a veritable catalogue of popular genres: the gunslinger protagonist comes from the western; his name, Roland, and background are out of pseudo-medieval romance; on his travels he encounters mutant creatures out of science fiction or horror; and the basic story is an alternate world quest fantasy.

King also manipulates different genre devices within the individual works. In the climax of *The Shining,* Danny Torrance confronts his demented father; *Christine* concludes with Dennis Guilder fighting it out with Christine in a tanker truck named "Petunia"; at the end of *Firestarter,* Andy McGee stands up to the villainous John Rainbird in a horse-filled barn—three modern versions of the western "walkdown."

But King has done more than simply borrow elements of other popular categories: his primary contribution to the development of contemporary dark fantasy is to marry the subjects and paraphernalia of the traditional horror novel to the shape and conventions of the most important best-seller formula, the "social melodrama," a term coined by critic John Cawelti:

> within the diversity of best-sellers there is a certain type of novel that has almost invariably been represented on best-seller lists . . . [it] so often achieves best-seller status that it has become, in effect, a best-selling formulaic type. I will call it the social melodrama, since it synthesizes the archetype of melodrama with a carefully and elaborately developed social setting in such a way as to combine the emotional satisfactions of melodrama with the interest inherent in a detailed, intimate, and realistic analysis of major social or historical phenomena. . . .
>
> . . . social melodrama is a type defined by the combination of melodramatic structure and character with something that passes for a "realistic" social or historical setting. The appeal of this synthesis combines the escapist satisfactions of melodrama—in particular its fantasy of a moral universe following conventional social values—with the pleasurable feeling that we are learning something important about reality.[24]

At first glance it would seem difficult to reconcile the "realistic" aspect of the social melodrama with the fantastic elements of horror fiction. But, as noted above, the mix of realistic surface and supernatural or horrific intrusion—the "thing from the sugar bowl"—is one of the major characteristics of contemporary dark fantasy. King goes further in this than such predecessors as Matheson and Leiber in that, like the mainstream social melodramatist, he not only describes a realistic surface, he also examines the social and political contexts, the life-styles and institutions, the professional and domestic realities of his characters, often counterpoising them with a growing supernatural menace.

Carrie, for example, is as much about the politics of high school life as it is about the horrors of unleashed telekinesis. The novel has three major plot lines: Carrie's awakening, first to womanhood and then to insane destructiveness; Sue Snell's misguided, well-intentioned but self-righteous plan to "help" Carrie; and Christine Hargensen's vindictive conspiracy to humiliate, even destroy her. Sue's do-gooder activities actually set Carrie up for Christine's malevolence. The precarious emotional state that makes Carrie vulnerable to Christine's machinations has little to do with her telekinetic powers. Like all of King's best work, *Carrie* would be a gripping novel even *without* the horrific elements; they intensify and dramatize conflicts that already exist.

But while *Carrie* contains the seeds of the King method, it was in his second novel—and first best-seller—*'Salem's Lot* that he fully developed the potential of the social melodrama plot as adapted to the contemporary horror novel.

'Salem's Lot is divided into three long parts, "The Marsten House," "The Emperor of Ice Cream" (the title is taken from a Wallace Stevens poem) and "The Deserted Village," which embody the major movements of the novel. Within each section, the chapters bear a character's name ("Ben I," "Matt," "Danny Glick and Others") or the general heading "The Lot." Thus we have, presumably, a constantly shifting focus from character to character, but this is only partly true. There are, in fact, only three major characters in *'Salem's Lot* and each represents a separate plot line, the three lines gradually converging as the novel progresses.

These three characters are Ben Mears, the hero; Kurt Barlow, the villain; and the Lot, the setting. Ben is our point of identification for most of the novel. We enter Jerusalem's Lot with him and perceive the growing menace mostly through his eyes. The other characters around him—the "good guys" of the novel—have their own stories, but they still function primarily in relation to him. The Ben Mears line of action begins with his entry into town; explores, via his memories, his reasons for being there; accompanies him during his courtship of Susan Norton; shares his observations of the Lot as well as his growing awareness of the pervasive evil that surrounds them all; and finally identifies with his attempt to direct his group in a counterattack against Barlow and company. We also share his growing anguish as, one by one, his lover, friends and allies are picked off by the growing evil, until only he and teenaged Mark Petrie are left to share the burden of confronting Barlow in his lair and saving what is left of 'Salem's Lot.

Kurt Barlow is never much of a character, but that is not his function: he is the *menace.* Emulating Stoker's strategy in the original *Dracula,* King keeps his villain mostly offstage, letting the horror grow, in a sense, from the ground up, as the vampiric infection spreads throughout 'Salem's Lot.

Which brings us to the third character, "The Lot" itself. Perhaps the most impressive thing about this novel is the way in which King has reinforced his main lines of action with a network of subplots that give an impressive density to the story. King is a master of the narrative snapshot, the brief, concise sketch of an intense situation dramatized with great color, immediacy and believability. He takes several small groups of ordinary 'Salem's Lot folk and tells us of their individual plights, in stories that have considerable impact in their own right, but gain even more potency from the reader's knowledge that these mundane crises will soon be swallowed up by the larger, more terrible evil that waits in the background.

These vignettes run the gamut from the coyly amusing to the vicious and violent, but always the characters are very real and generally sympathetic. We see the nostalgic romance between Ben's landlady Eva Miller, an aging but still attractive widow, and her ex-lover Weasel Craig, a down-and-out but amiable drunk mired in terminal despair. We understand the frustrations of the well-meaning, dull-witted Sandy McDougall, trapped into premature motherhood and poverty, who gradually and necessarily drifts into serious child abuse. We see violence emerge when Bonnie Sawyer's promiscuity attracts Corey Bryant, a telephone lineman, who must face the shotgun of Bonnie's bitter, enraged husband. We watch Dud Rogers shooting rats and cavorting in the town dump—

until Barlow arrives one night. In sort, we have a pattern of minidramas juxtaposed against each other and against King's larger pattern. The effect is that of a large but finely detailed canvas, impressive both for its general scope and for its attention to minute, revealing detail. Even without Barlow in the background, it would be an impressive panorama of small-town rural life in America; with him, it is an extremely powerful, realistic vision of cosmic evil overwhelming a mundane, vulnerable world.

As the characters work out their individual destinies, we are caught up in their immediate problems, dramatized in a sequence of brief, intense scenes, while the larger menace hovers in the background and gradually closes in, finally culminating in a grand, gory finale. Thus, in *Salem's Lot* the supernatural menace offers King that "overarching structure sufficiently commodious to accommodate a vast variety of exciting incidents and a plethora of characters as well as a detailed discussion of the workings of major social institutions"[25] necessary to the social melodrama.

This plot structure is most noticeable in King's other *big* novels, *The Stand* [4-175], *It* [4-168], *The Tommyknockers* [4-177], *The Talisman* (with Peter Straub) [4-178] and his open-ended epic *The Dark Tower* [4-164]. All of these novels have overarching structures, taken from traditional horror or science fictional motifs, that give the books coherence and direction, as well as frameworks upon which King can hang his numerous subplots and digressions, many, perhaps most, of which could be deleted from their respective novels without in any way disturbing the main plot line, but which are, to the traditional best-seller reader, the real "meat" of the book. As Cawelti notes, "Because the overall shape of melodrama tends to be complicated and diffuse, there is a special premium on the writer's ability to make individual episodes engrossing."[26] No contemporary writer in any genre—or in the mainstream—is more adroit at quickly creating self-contained minidramas with sharply defined characters, conflicts and sudden intense climaxes and then juxtaposing those little stories against his major plot lines. This explains why long, complicated novels like *The Stand* and *It*, which fizzle badly at the end, are still enjoyable reading experiences.

King is not, of course, the first horror writer to successfully combine the social melodrama and the horror story, along with ingredients from other popular forms. Dennis Wheatley has already been mentioned, although Wheatley's combinations are largely confined to the spy novel, historical romance and, occasionally, science fiction, and his novels are not big or elaborate in the King manner. For a really apt comparison one must go back almost to the beginnings of modern dark fantasy to a time when the horror novel enjoyed a general popularity it has not been able to claim since. What King has actually done is to reinvent the classic Gothic novel of the sort written by Horace Walpole [1-108], Mrs. Radcliffe [1-83], "Monk" Lewis [1-58], Charles Maturin [1-64] and Mary Shelley [1-97]. Hence, "Stephen King and the Return to Otranto."

These classical Gothics were long (except for that of Walpole), complicated, elaborate, gory, grotesque and sensational. The plotting, while formulaic, was diffuse, with numerous and frequent digressions, subplots and very large casts of characters. The action, usually spread over large areas and covering considerable spans of time, was largely external. While the narratives might contain considerable surface ambiguity, the outcomes clearly distinguished between good and evil and conformed to Cawelti's requirement that they reinforce the "fantasy of a moral universe following conventional social values."[27] Thus, the novels closely reflected contemporary events, concerns, attitudes, mores and assumptions, which contributed greatly to both their contemporary popularity and their subsequent neglect.

Like the Gothic novelists, King uses a very broad canvas, stresses topicality in subjects and attitudes—his "brand name" obsession is practically a trademark—and combines classical horror subjects with vivid, careful delineations of current manners, institutions and problems. For example, the public's deeply rooted suspicion of government, provoked by the Vietnam War and the Watergate scandal, is reflected in such King works as *The Stand, The Dead Zone,* "The Mist" and *Firestarter.* Alcoholic English professor Jim Gardner, the hero of *The Tommyknockers,* fulminates against the dangers of nuclear plants in the early chapters of the novel, then later encounters a mysterious energy source that promises miraculous technological wonders, but ultimately destroys all those it touches; the metaphorical equation is blatant and effective.

But it would be a mistake to ascribe King's popularity solely to topicality. Behind the social and political issues is a view of the world and modern man's place in it that touches what King calls his readers' "phobic pressure points."[28] This overview can be clearly seen in the novella "The Mist," one of King's finest stories.

In "The Mist," a group of people are trapped in a small market that has been surrounded by a mysterious thick white mist, which, the group learns the hard way, contains hordes of monsters of every size, shape and description. These creatures are not evil, only hungry; they are pure, primitive appetites that respond to the smell of anything organic (they consume bags of dogfood as eagerly as they eat people). It is the thick white mist that makes them especially dangerous. We subsequently learn that the mist and its creatures have leaked into our world from another dimension through a hole opened by a combination of a severe storm and a miscalculated, clandestine government experiment. Thus we have human, technological culpability, from a government whose ineptitude is more disturbing than its malevolence (dangerous toys in the hands of moral and intellectual idiots), and natural disaster accidentally combining to produce chaos. Yet this is a model for King's world. That other dimension of concealed, horrible creatures is *always* there, waiting for *something* to poke a hole in the very thin wall that separates the two worlds.

In a metaphorical way, this touches the fears of many middle-class Americans. Take the great general fear of annihilation by nuclear war. Few expect the U.S.S.R. to launch a deliberate attack upon us, nor are we likely to do so to them, but we all fear that by bureaucratic misadventure, protracted political ineptitude, technological glitch, bad timing, paranoia, local terrorism or plain accident, the bombs *will fall.* Most people agree that the arms race is folly, that it must lead to mutual destruction, but few can see any way out of it.

Or, on the personal level, we all know we will eventually die, and hope that it will be at the end of a long, useful and satisfying life, but we harbor the fear that our end will be the foolish product of a trivial cigarette, of driving ten miles over the speed limit, of eating, or drinking, or smelling, or being in the wrong place at the wrong time. In short, it is not evil, but the arbitrariness of life that we most fear. It is this sense of chaos and danger beneath the safe and placid surface of contemporary life that King has capitalized on in his fiction.

At the same time, there is in King's writings, as in those of the classical Gothic authors, a consoling sense of order, almost a hint of divine providence. This appears most obviously in the long, apocalyptic novels like *The Stand, The Talisman* and *It,* but it is present in one form or another in most of his stories. And, at the very least, his characters are tough, strong-willed and sympathetic and the best of them usually survive, however battered, to pick up the pieces or even to do battle again, if need be.

The author most often associated with Stephen King is Peter Straub. When *Ghost Story* [4-286] soared to the top of best-seller lists in 1979, not long after King's dominance had been established, the two dark fantasists were naturally paired in the public mind. Their friendship and King's admitted influence on Straub's development, which culminated in a collaborative effort, *The Talisman* [4-178], in 1983, cemented this identification.

For the most part, the identification is valid. Straub's major novels, *Ghost Story* and *Floating Dragon* [4-285], are certainly big enough, echoing King's blend of traditional, if elaborated, horror motifs with the social melodrama formula.

At the same time, there are obvious differences in approach, style, technique and theme. Straub is the most literary of contemporary horror writers. While King novels are replete with references to 1950s and 1960s writers like Bloch, Matheson, Bradbury, Shirley Jackson, and others, or E.C. comics or B-movies, Straub is more likely consciously to echo Poe or Hawthorne or Machen or his favorite, Henry James. King laces his books with references to rock performers such as the Rolling Stones, Bruce Springsteen or the Who, while Straub's taste runs to classical jazz; the name of the hero of *If You Could See Me Now,* Miles Teagarden, is an amalgam of the names of jazz greats Miles Davis and Jack Teagarden.

More important, King is an almost entirely external writer. That is, all of King's landscapes, internal as well as external, are solid, factual, *real.* In Straub, the interiority and Jamesian ambiguity of his first two novels are incorporated into his big books to create, at times, a tension between the real and the unreal, between the interior and the exterior, that is largely absent from King's work. And it is these tensions, coupled with the large canvas and operatic structure that makes *Ghost Story* one of the most important contemporary works in the genre.

Despite its simple, generic title, *Ghost Story* is neither simple nor typical. Traditional ghosts are, in fact, almost the only common horror creature/situation not in the novel. In bald summary it sounds very much like, in King's words, "an extravagant mishmash of every horror and gothic convention ever yarned in all those B-pictures."[29]

The basic story is simple enough. Milburn, an isolated town in upstate New York, is gradually invaded and taken over by a mysterious malevolent force. The plot is almost identical to that of *'Salem's Lot* and, of course, that novel's progenitor, *Dracula.*

The most obvious thing setting *Ghost Story* apart from the conventional horror novel is Straub's manner of telling the story. The primary story, which takes place in the late 1970s, is continually broken up by other bits and pieces of narrative: stories within stories, time shifts, scenes, images, events real and imagined, glimpses of the future, seemingly irrelevant incidents and details, bizarre yet realistic hallucinations, terrifying nightmares. But the sudden shifts between the external and the internal, the real and the hallucinatory, the past and the present, are not ultimately confusing, because they are presented as part of a consistently changing whole. The reader comes to expect radical shifts because that is the nature of Straub's reality.

At the center of each man's story is a woman and a guilty secret associated with her. The key to the mystery—and the ways to fight against it—lies in the men's personal histories. They must come to terms with their own pasts, first by reliving them in order to understand their meanings, and then by finding the strength to break free of them. Those who can, survive; those who cannot, die. The turning point in the novel occurs when the group plays a tape left by the "woman"—actually a demonic shapeshifter inspired by Arthur Machen's *The Great God Pan* [2-58]—whose accidental "murder" by the original Chowder Society men began the long sequence of events culminating in their present danger. In that tape the female describes her/its nature and taunts them with their inevitable fate. "We chose to live in your dreams and imaginations because only there you are interesting. . . . You are at the mercy of your human imaginations, and when you look for us you should always look in the places of your imagination. In the places of your dreams."[30] But if it is the men's imaginations that make them vulnerable, these same imaginations are also the sources for their defense and ultimate victory.

Straub has said that "the novel refers back to the classic American novels and stories of the genre by Henry James and Nathaniel Hawthorne. . . . I was moved by a desire to look into, examine, and play with the genre—to take those 'classic' elements as far as they could go."[31] It is probably this classic dimension, given a striking contemporary twist, that sets *Ghost Story* apart.

Following *Ghost Story* Straub wrote his "fairy tale," *Shadowland* [4-289] and then returned to the *big* novel with *Floating Dragon* [4-285]—which is even bigger, more elaborate and more ambitious than *Ghost Story.* In *Floating Dragon,* Straub juxtaposes a contemporary evil with an ancient one. Critics have disagreed over the novel's merit. To some it is his best: a profound and complex message realized in a masterful form. Others admire the book's ambitions, but find it uneven, out of balance, excessive and illogical.

Despite the King-Straub connection, three other authors are much closer to King in style, technique and subject matter: John Farris, Dean R. Koontz and Robert McCammon. All three write big, ambitious, operatic novels that blend genres and boast large casts of characters and elaborate narratives that juxtapose several plot lines with themes, situations and concerns that reach beyond the usual genre perimeters. And all three have enjoyed impressive commercial popularity.

Farris actually predated King as a successful writer. The high school melodrama *Harrison High* (1959), published when Farris was in his early twenties, was an important influence on King's early writing. Farris edged into dark fantasy with *When Michael Calls* (1967), a mystery-horror story about a series of killings that follow mysterious phone calls supposedly made by a long-dead ten-year-old boy, and *Sharp Practice* (1974), a psychotic killer narrative in the *Psycho* [4-46] tradition, but it was with *The Fury* [4-112] that Farris first balanced the elements of dark fantasy with the conventions of other popular forms. *The Fury* is a mix of psychic horror story and intrigue thriller.

Farris touches on many contemporary preoccupations and fears in *The Fury*—psychic experimentation, government secrecy and mendacity, fear of, as well as exploitation of, young people, loss of control over self, suspicions of neighbors, casual violence as a way of life. Thus, while the book may sound complex in summary, it is in fact a simple morality play. Childermass and MORG are unmitigated evil, Peter Sanza is an avenging angel who destroys the evil at the expense of his own life. Gillian and Robin are victims both of nature and of man. Gillian survives because she comes to terms with her own psychic talents; Robin tries to do too much too fast and is destroyed by his. The novel thus combines the psychic horror of *Carrie* with the adventure-thriller excitement of a Robert Ludlum novel. Farris's variety and virtuosity have been further confirmed in such impressive efforts as *All Heads Turn When the Hunt Goes By* [4-110], *Catacombs* [4-111], *The Uninvited* [4-114], *Son of the Endless Night* [4-113] and *Wildwood* [4-115]. With the exception of *The Uninvited*—the weakest of the five—these are all large-canvas works with complicated plots, a large and varied cast and a thematic complexity that pushes beyond the horror genre, yet they are all very different. *All Heads Turn When the Hunt Goes By* is a steamy Southern Gothic with the traditional old decaying plantation house, the family curse, racial conflict, sexual tensions and voodoo. *Catacombs* is a spy novel with a dose of quasi-Lovecraftian supernaturalism—James Bond meets Cthulhu. *Son of the Endless Night* is an eschatological horror novel in which Good and Evil fight it out in a courtroom. *Wildwood* features a haunted mountain, paranormal visions, flying people, a black magician, dislocations in time and space and a one-hundred-room chateau that vanishes along with the five hundred people in it. Even the relatively modest *The Uninvited* features a thoroughly original ghost/demon and several provocative characters.

As he demonstrates in these works, Farris may be the most consistently imaginative and daring of contemporary dark fantasists. Especially in such novels as *The Fury, Son of the Endless Night* and *Wildwood* he takes big risks—these novels tread perilously close to absurdity in their scope, complexity and extremity. In the hands of a lesser talent they could be ludicrous, but Farris does not lose control. The convolutions of his plots finally fit together; his extreme characters may strain credibility, but they never lose it; beneath the gore and the pyrotechnics he deals with questions and problems of concern to a very wide readership. John Farris rates the commercial success he has achieved and deserves greater recognition and appreciation from horror fiction *cognoscenti*.

Dean Koontz's mastery of the mixed genre novel is not surprising given his long, varied, prolific career. From the late sixties to the present Koontz has published more than sixty books under his own name and several pseudonyms (Leigh Nichols, Brian Coffey, Owen West, Deanna Dwyer, among others), not to mention over three dozen stories in several genres.

> I've not only written SF and horror but psychological suspense like *Shattered*, and *Whispers*. And caper novels like *Blood Risk, Surrounded*, and *The Wall of Masks* as by "Brian Coffey." And international intrigue

> as in *The Key to Midnight* by "Leigh Nichols." The large novel I just sold to Putnam's [*Strangers*] . . . contains elements of the fantastic and many techniques of the horror novel—and is in some ways *weirder* than any other book I've done—but it is solidly in the mainstream and not easy to slot in *any* genre.[32]

Few popular writers have studied their genres as diligently and deliberately as Koontz. Hard work, coupled with meticulous analysis of his own work and that of others, have given him a thorough, precise knowledge of the mechanics and appeals of each as evidenced in his *Writing Popular Fiction* (1972) and *How to Write Best Selling Fiction* (1981), which remain two of the best books on the subject.

Thus, it is not surprising that Koontz's evolution has taken him increasingly into dark fantasy as his primary genre, but in a very impure way. The impulses and moods are horrific ("there's one constant in my books . . . I love to scare the readers, grip them by the throat, make them sweat, make them beg for mercy"[33]), but the menaces usually have a pseudo-scientific rationale and the size, shape and form increasingly resemble the best-selling social melodrama. His recent novel *Strangers* [4-190] illustrates this very well.

Koontz has described his intentions for *Strangers*:

> Yes, *Strangers* was an attempt to take the strengths of genre fiction—story, pace, vitality of imagination—and combine them with the strengths of mainstream fiction—layered characterization, tight thematic structure and purpose, a sense of the melodies and rhythms of language, emotional depth, and a multifaceted realistic portrayal of the world in which we actually live, as opposed to a fantasy world.[34]

In *Strangers* Koontz deftly juxtaposes the separate stories of several characters against one another as he moves his central mystery forward to a climax that underscores Koontz's deep suspicions of the government as well as his fundamental optimism about man in general—an unbeatable thematic mix for a contemporary novel. Not surprisingly, *Strangers* enjoyed great commercial success, as did its successor, *Watchers* [4-193]. Koontz's most recent novel, *Midnight* [4-187], soared to the top of the *New York Times* best-seller list soon after publication.

After serving his apprenticeship with three fairly conventional horror novels, *Baal* (1978), *Bethany's Sin* (1979) and *The Night Boat* (1980), Robert R. McCammon hit his stride with his massive vampire novel *They Thirst* [4-225]. Since then, his books have been big, complex horror stories which utilize structural elements of the social melodrama, while remaining firmly within the perimeters of dark fantasy. He is quite happy with horror: "I don't believe there's any other kind of literature that has as much to say, or is as strong. Or as important."[35]

Like King in his big books—*Swan Song* [4-224] is in fact a mirror image of *The Stand* [4-175]—McCammon likes to set up several narrative lines, crosscut between them, then bring things together in a rousing finale. But despite their size and complexity, the novels originate in simple, dramatic ideas that can be articulated in a single sentence: "an old world vampire sets out to enslave the world from a Hollywood castle," "a Choctaw boy who talks with the dead and an evangelist's son with the power to heal engage in a deadly competition, egged on by a diabolical supernatural being," "the descendants of Poe's Usher family gather at the deathbed of the clan patriarch to confront the awesome, dangerous Usher legacy." It is this combination of a simple, ingenious premise and complicated, elaborate plotting that makes McCammon one of the most impressive writers of his generation.

They Thirst has the biggest canvas and *Mystery Walk* [4-223] the most sensitive characterizations, but it is *Usher's Passing* [4-226] that offers the best example of McCammon's virtuosity. Taking Poe's Usher clan as a starting point is an inspired idea, particularly in the way McCammon fits Roderick and his ailments neatly into his Usher history. Not only does this create literary resonances, but it also gives McCammon a framework—the family chronicle—to develop his story around.

And it is a story that has almost everything: a rich, decadent, aristocratic family with a tainted, mysterious history and a terrifying, disgusting inherited illness, financial and domestic intrigue, an awesome secret weapon, a haunted mansion, a pair of colorful, malevolent, seemingly supernatural monsters, a wise old man with psychic abilities, a young boy with even stronger powers a burned-out city once inhabited by witches, a magical cane, sex, violence, murder, even cannibalism. The book teeters on the edge of absurdity, but in the end everything fits together logically and—considering the highly charged, grotesque atmosphere of the book—naturally.

The Usher family history gives the novel narrative density. As McCammon jumps back and forth between generations to uncover gradually the dark secrets that have given the Ushers both their powers and their vulnerabilities, we are completely absorbed. But, while the mood and atmosphere of *Usher's Passing* evoke Lovecraftian feelings of archaic, long-buried evils, the immediate clash of personalities is more reminiscent of Tennessee Williams. Indeed, this duel of siblings at the deathbed of the dying patriarch seems almost a grotesque reflection of Williams's *Cat on a Hot Tin Roof* (1955). One could—admitting exaggeration—describe *Usher's Passing* as combining the atmosphere of Poe, the generational sweep of Faulkner and the dramatic vitriol of Williams in a cosmos out of Lovecraft.

This marriage between the family chronicle and the dark fantasy has also yielded impressive results in novels by Michael McDowell. By the time he wrote his epic dark fantasy/family chronicle, the *Blackwater* series [4-230], McDowell had established himself as the southern regionalist among recent dark fantasists, thus feeding off not only the contemporary horror scene, but also that rich Southern Gothic tradition that includes William Faulkner, Flannery O'Connor, Carson McCullers, Reynolds Price and, most important for McDowell, Eudora Welty. "A lot of the extravagance of speech that I allow my characters," McDowell has said, "comes from Welty, from seeing how she did it."[36] So it is not surprising that he renders the atmosphere and details of the southern small-town milieu with such fidelity in *The Amulet* [4-229], *Cold Moon over Babylon* [4-231], *The Elementals* [4-232] and especially the *Blackwater* books.

The *Blackwater* series is a six-volume family chronicle horror novel that traces the fate of the Caskey family of Perdido, Alabama, from Easter 1919, when Elinor Dammert, later to become the clan matriarch, is rescued from the flooding Perdido River, to her death in the spring of 1970, during a second great flood.

Early in the series we learn that she is really an elemental water creature from the depths of the Perdido, who has chosen to live a mortal existence as a wife, mother and matriarch. Monster though she may be, Elinor is one of the most sympathetic, even tragic characters in contemporary dark fantasy. The internal tension between her supernatural origin and her human characteristics is the center of her story and is passed on to her female offspring.

But despite the novel's supernatural premise, the real conflicts in the *Blackwater* series are human ones as Elinor guides the family fortunes. The fantastic elements in *Blackwater* are integral to the book's structure, characterizations and themes, but only as part of a larger whole; this artistic decision may blunt the series' popularity among some hardcore fans, but it gives the book strong appeal beyond the confines of the genre readership—and underscores the point that the most successful examples of horror are those featuring real people encountering monstrous things, and not monsters for their own sakes.

John Blackburn emerged in the 1960s as the logical successor to Dennis Wheatley as Britain's most effective cross-genre dark fantasist. Like Wheatley, Blackburn is a prolific writer in several genres—mystery, spy thriller, science fiction—who brings the conventions of these other popular genres into his horror stories. But unlike Wheatley—fortunately—Blackburn has no distracting ideological axe to grind. His novels feature adroit plotting, sharply drawn characters and clever, original underlying concepts.

In his five major horror novels—*Children of the Night* [4-38], *Bury Him Darkly* [4-37], *For Fear of Little Men* [4-40], *Devil Daddy* [4-39] and *Our Lady of Pain* [4-41]—Blackburn has, with varying degrees of precision, utilized a simple, ingenious formula that blends the horror story and the science fiction thriller: a series of apparently random events leads a small group of perceptive outsiders first to identify the menace and then to fight a desperate battle against the horror unleashed by it. The mysterious menance is supernatural in origin, although often glossed with science fiction elements, and the mystery usually turns on some sort of arcane discovery—but once loosed, the menace is very real in nature and cosmic in scope—a rampaging monster (*Bury Him Deadly*), a world-threatening plague (*Devil Daddy*), an ancient malevolent god (*For Fear of Little Men*).

Blackburn's formula works most effectively in his best horror novel, *For Fear of Little Men*. The catalogue of things that Blackburn convincingly integrates into the novel is impressive: a magnate who tries too hard to please the locals; his mysterious, promiscuous wife and her brutish, feeble-minded lover, an ex-Nazi scientist; the unnaturally hostile townspeople; a murdered judge; a hippie commune; an archeological dig; international industrial intrigue; germ warfare; and above all, Allt y Cricht, a dangerous, sinister mountain, which supposedly houses the body of Daran, demonic demigod of a once-powerful pre-Celtic race, who awaits resurrection. This mass of material threatens to split the novel open, but the seams never give; they don't even show. This is the sort of ambitious synthesis that Peter Straub attempted—at at least twice the length—in *Floating Dragon* [4-285] with very mixed results. Although Blackburn's other novels are less ambitious and more transparent, they are all clever, interesting, skillfully plotted blends of popular genres.

Since the mid-1970s, James Herbert has established himself as England's most popular writer, although his critical reception has generally been less than enthusiastic. To a large degree, both his popularity and the adverse critical reactions can be explained by Herbert's most obvious device—graphic, visceral, imaginative, sustained gore. The title of his first novel, *The Rats* [4-144], tells it all: huge mutant rats attack the citizens of London in increasing numbers, leaving death and plague in their wake. Herbert tells his story by a simple, old-fashioned formula: while the depredations continue, increasing in size, scope and bloodiness, a small group of men, led by Harris, an ordinary high school art teacher, search for the key to defeat the seemingly implacable enemy, with the hero, at great personal risk, finally finding and destroying the source of the enemy's power.

Herbert uses and elaborates the same formula in the two sequels to *The Rats*, *Lair* (1979) and *Domain* (1984), as well as in *The Fog* (1975) [4-141] and *The Dark* (1980) [4-140]. In *Lair*, the rats simply return to challenge man again, but in *Domain* nuclear holocaust forms a backdrop to the human-rat conflict. In *The Fog*, an insanity-inducing yellow fog, a government experiment gone wrong, is accidentally released to turn the London environs into a raging madhouse. In *The Dark*, the agent that spreads madness and violence is Evil itself, in the palpable form of a spreading blanket of darkness that infects the minds of all with whom it comes in contact, exploiting their repressed anger and violence, turning them into raging, zombie-like creatures.

The elements of this formula account for much of Herbert's initial commercial success: an implacable enemy that, while fantastic, is also clearly related to commonly held fears—rats, a secret weapon gone awry, Evil itself—and that strikes quickly, pervasively, arbitrarily; a desperate conflict that threatens total destruction; individual scenes of great visceral power—like Stephen King, Herbert is a masterful miniaturist—juxtaposed against larger movements of mass chaos (Herbert's mob scenes are unexcelled); and a "common man" hero thrust into crisis who survives and triumphs through ordinary intelligence, tenacity and courage.

But the popularity and visceral impact of these early mass-disaster novels have obscured the real variety in Herbert's works, which include a ghost story (*Survivor*, 1976), a "Catholic" horror novel (*Shrine*, 1983 [4-146]), a pair of occult thrillers (*The Spear*, 1978 [4-147] and *Sepulchre*, 1987 [4-145]), a haunted house tale (*The Magic Cottage*, 1986 [4-142]), horror-mysteries involving psychic identification (*Moon*, 1985 [4-143]) and a mysterious jinx (*The Jonah*, 1981) and even a reincarnation fantasy about a murdered man who returns as a dog (*Fluke*, 1977).

Clearly, Herbert has been exploring all the popular genres, reaching toward the kind of horror/social melodrama mix favored by his most popular contemporaries. His early, gory successes fixed him in the public and critical minds and this perception was reinforced by imitators like Shaun Hutson in *Slugs* (1982) and *Breeding Ground* (1985) and Guy N. Smith in his "Crabs" tetralogy, whom the critics have lumped together as "nasties."

But Herbert has certainly developed well beyond such a simple label into an eclectic, intense, provocative writer of the first rank, whose popularity is well merited and understandable: direct, vivid, sometimes gruesome writing; sharp characterizations; a sympathetic, believable "ordinary" hero; and behind it all, a moral universe in which, despite all the violence and carnage, Good does finally triumph, however tentatively, over Evil—a crucial ingredient in the successful social melodrama. As Herbert observes:

> I think I preach goodness, strangely enough. I hate to sound pretentious about it, but I think overall I do preach goodness. In all these battles of good against evil, good always comes out on top. Although there's usually a twist at the end, to say you haven't completely won. And again, that is life.[37]

An even more original and provocative writer who mixes his genres is J. G. Ballard. Definitional purists have always had problems with Ballard. As a leading figure of the 1960s British science fiction avant-garde, he is strongly identified with the genre he so radically influenced. Yet even in his early short stories and his global disaster novel quartet, which use the paraphernalia of science fiction, the primary focus is on inner space, or the psychological adjustments of his isolated, traumatized characters to their changing, usually disintegrating situations. In the tetralogy, each of the four elements—air in *A Wind from Nowhere* (1962), water in *The Drowned World* (1962), fire in *The Drought* (1964), earth in *The Crystal World* [4-17]—provokes worldwide disaster. But unlike the actors in the usual science fiction catastrophe scenario, the characters in these novels do little to alter or even understand their situation. Ballard cares only that they attempt to understand *themselves* and their own reactions to what is happening. The most successful characters in these books are actually those, like Dr. Kearns in *The Drowned World* and Dr. Sanders in *The Crystal World,* who not only adjust to, but actually embrace, the new, bizarre, inhuman world that has come into being.

Thus, it would seem an easy step for Ballard to move, as many science fiction writers have, into dark fantasy, where themes of psychological deterioration, madness and paranoia, and the ambiguities of reality are more characteristic. But he has not done that either. While Ballard jettisoned the science fiction apparatus from most of his stories and novels in the 1970s, he has taken on few of the usual dark fantasy trappings. There are no supernatural powers or otherworldly monsters in *Crash* [4-16], *Concrete Island* [4-15] or *High-Rise* [4-18], only contemporary man and the world he has built for himself, and that is quite enough. These novels, his "Urban Disaster Trilogy," come as close to being the definitive big city horror story as anything in the literature.

Ballard's modern man is physically and psychologically alienated, uncomfortable but obsessed with the technological world he lives in, isolated from other people yet the product of social conditioning, suppressed and preoccupied with sex, horrified and attracted by death, especially violent death.

Crash takes our current obsessions—technology (more precisely machines), speed, sex, violence—and mixes them together in a surrealistic parable of contemporary life. Ballard creates further tension by treating his highly charged material in a cool, graphic, meticulously detailed, almost clinical prose style. *Crash* is an obsessive, upsetting, unforgettable book.

Concrete Island lacks the surrealistic intensity of *Crash,* but is just as unnerving in its own way. A tire blowout sends Robert Maitland into a littered, undeveloped traffic island beneath three converging highways, where he finds himself trapped with two other castaways, a disturbed young woman and a brain-damaged ex-acrobat. Eventually Maitland comes to enjoy his isolation as a kind of primitive chief to a small tribe.

In *High-Rise* Ballard broadens his canvas to encompass the denizens of a luxury high-rise apartment building. Segregated by floor according to financial and social status (the higher the floor, the richer the individual), the occupants move from latent hostility to overt gesture to outright savagery as the building gradually turns into a war zone. It is not the bizarre behavior and violent activity that Ballard offers in his heightened, grotesque vision of the world that is so upsetting, it is the matter-of-fact, even eager way in which his characters—and his readers—accept this vision as perfectly natural, predictable, even inevitable.

Ramsey Campbell is probably the last major writer to make the transition from Cthulhu Mythos acolyte to a personal mythology that utilizes Lovecraftian metaphors in the contemporary landscape in a genuinely unique and powerful body of work. As Lovecraft encouraged the young Robert Bloch to write, so his "successor" as keeper of the Mythos, August Derleth, gave personal advice, counsel and stimulation to Campbell. The result was Campbell's first book, *The Inhabitant of the Lake* (1964), a number of pastiches in the Lovecraft mode but set in a realistic Liverpool environment.

Like several of his predecessors, Campbell moved away from the restrictions of the Lovecraft mythology to develop a personal vision, an evolution that can be traced in his three subsequent collections, *Demons by Daylight* (1973) [4-64], *The Height of the Scream* (1976) [4-67] and *Dark Companions* (1982) [4-63]. *Demons by Daylight* demonstrates Campbell's transition from the Lovecraft pastiches to his own style. Labelled "elliptical" by Campbell, these stories are characterized by vivid dramatic vignettes, extreme compression, suppressed or nonexistent transitions, and a blurring of the lines between the rational and the insane, the real and the nightmarish. But these stories are, by Campbell's own admission,

> all very enigmatic. . . . Instead of explaining everything, I wasn't explaining anything at all. You've got stuff like "The End of Summer's Day" which is *totally* enigmatic. I mean *I* can't explain it to you any more than anyone else can explain it to me. . . . I had to get beyond that, too, and write stories that were more coherent.[38]

The stories in *The Height of the Scream* retain much of the compressed ambiguity of the earlier stories, but also show more willingness to expand and develop the characters and ideas, relying less on suggestion. By *Dark Companions*, Campbell's short fiction techniques have become fixed.

Campbell's first attempt at the novel came in *The Doll Who Ate His Mother* (1976) [4-65], an essentially realistic suspense story with some supernatural trappings. His second novel, *The Face That Must Die* (1979) [4-66], a tautly written thriller about a homophobic paranoic who stalks a gentle homosexual he believes to be a serial murderer, is a much tighter, more finely structured book with a truly chilling central character, but it was with his third novel, *To Wake the Dead* (1980) [4-73] that Campbell fully realized his talents as a novelist.

To Wake the Dead (retitled *The Parasite* in the U.S.) is perhaps Campbell's scariest novel, the one that most closely fits the label of "humanist tale of terror," which can be defined, in Campbell's words, as a

> tale of the supernatural which is very closely related to the psychology of the protagonist, whoever it might be. . . . I tend to write more stories

> where the supernatural element does relate very directly to something in the victim's psychology. More often than not, it's a childhood fear or a childhood trauma that was apparently dealt with, but was really repressed and pops up in a much worse form. But the important thing, I think, is that in those stories you can't just explain it away. You can't use the psychology to explain the supernatural and say "*That* is what it's all about." Equally, the supernatural in these stories has got to have a distinct power of its own. It can't just be a symbol of whatever is within the victim.[39]

The Nameless (1981) [4-71] is a bit of a letdown after *To Wake the Dead.* As the figure of Hitler hovers in the background of *To Wake the Dead,* so the Manson Family occupies a similar place in *The Nameless*—and that is a clue to the more modest scale and implications of the latter book.

Like *To Wake the Dead, Incarnate* (1983) [4-69] and *Obsession* (1985) [4-72] are both novels about evil seeds planted in characters that remain latent for years, only to burst forth finally in terrible forms to threaten and attack the sanity and lives of the victims. But in these two novels, Campbell broadens his focus to tell the stories of several characters, juxtaposing their experiences and fates against one another, finally bringing them together in finales that fuse plot, theme and character.

Campbell's most recent novels, *The Hungry Moon* (1986) [4-68] and *The Influence* (1988) [4-70], may or may not signal a shift in Campbell's emphasis. *The Hungry Moon* is Campbell's oddest book—for him. It is a large-canvas big book, with a complicated plot and a very large cast—much closer to the type of operatic horror/social melodrama novel practiced by King and his followers or perhaps more precisely to the horror thrillers of John Blackburn than to Campbell's previous works. It contains almost none of the powerful ironies and ambiguities that characterized his earlier works.

The Influence represents at least a partial return to the smaller-scale novel of "humanistic terror." In it Campbell returns to the possession theme of several short stories and *To Wake the Dead. The Influence* is a strong book, closer in style and approach to the earlier books than to *The Hungry Moon,* but still one in which good and evil, reality and illusion, and so on, are relatively solid.

All of this is not to say that Campbell's last two novels are not good—they are both excellent—only that perhaps what has been most unique and distinctive in his work is being muted in favor of a more solid, matter-of-fact good vs. evil horror story.

With the publication of the first three volumes of his *Books of Blood* [4-20] in 1984, Clive Barker's impact on contemporary horror fiction was immediate, visceral and controversial. As Ramsey Campbell notes in his introduction to the set, "Clive Barker is the most original writer of horror fiction to have appeared for years, and in the best sense, the most deeply shocking writer now working in the field."[40]

"Originality" and "shock" are the two words that best describe Barker's work. He is a writer of many and mixed talents, the most impressive of which is his unfettered imagination, both in the large concepts that form his stories and novels and in the relentlessly visceral details of individual characters, scenes and settings. The shock comes from Barker's willingness to follow his ideas, however outlandish, quirky or excessive, wherever they may lead. Add to this Barker's highly visual prose style, his knack for dialogue (he has written plays), his strong sense of cinematic movement and pacing, and a sharp, ironic sense of humor and the reasons for his success are evident—although Barker's offbeat, extravagant imagination also leads to his predictable failures—excess in concept.

Barker's world is violent, sensual, chaotic and often quite funny. It is a world in which supernatural menaces and casual bloodshed move easily in and out of the mundane world, the living mix with the dead and it is often difficult to tell them apart, everyone and everything are obsessed with sex in all possible variations and permutations, with vivid, spectacular, protracted violence at the center of it all. Perhaps most upsetting, it is world in which the characters accept all of this as routine, with responses that range from indifferent fatalism to positive glee.

Often the most interesting things in Barker's stories are his monsters. Some are more admirable than the citizens they confront, but most of them are not so benign. From the monster who appears human to the human who becomes monstrous is a very slight shift, one that occurs in several of Barker's better stories. The most obvious transformation human beings undergo is from living body to corpse, but in Barker this transition is rarely simple. In his hands the ghost can become an entirely new kind of creature, as, for example, in "In the Flesh," Barker's most complicated and disturbing ghost story.

This story also brings together two of Barker's preoccupations, the interrelationship between the living and the dead and the concept of the alternate world. The empty, silent city with the bare desert behind it and the gradual revelation of what it means is the most chilling element in the story. In a number of his other stories, Barker creates a nightmare secondary world that his characters are gradually drawn into, at first fearing it, then resisting it, finally embracing it. This world is not always fantastic. The "Spector Street" slum that draws a middle-class academic into her final confrontation with the Candyman in "Forgiven" is thoroughly realistic, but to Helen and the reader it is quite foreign and threatening.

"Midnight Meat Train" is one of the stories that will test Barker's readers. His originality, imagination, ability to write powerfully visual scenes and images, and his dark humor are in ample evidence in this story, as is his exuberant taste for extreme and graphic gore. The person who can read, enjoy and appreciate "Midnight Meat Train" is ready for just about anything that the genre has to offer.

The same can be said with some qualification about Barker's first full-length novel, *The Damnation Game* [4-22]. In general outline *The Damnation Game* resembles a John Farris novel, with its mixture of international intrigue and graphic supernaturalism, but the adventure element central to Farris is largely absent from this book. While the initial situation echoes the intrigue novel—a reclusive millionaire with a secret, tainted past hides terrified in a fortress sanctuary, while his empire crumbles about him—Barker has little interest in thriller paraphernalia. The focus is on the dramatic confrontation between Whitehead, the industrialist, and Mamoulian, a sinister European with supernatural powers, and his helper, Breer, a huge, sadomasochistic child murderer, as filtered through the viewpoint of Whitehead's ex-con bodyguard, Marty Strauss. *The Damnation Game* demonstrates growth over the *Books of Blood* stories because of the control Barker exerts over his materials.

Many of the virtues and vices of *The Damnation Game* can be seen in Barker's most ambitious work to date, *Weaveworld* [4-23; F4A-18], an epic fantasy with horrific overtones. The central concept in *Weaveworld* is one of the most imaginative and brilliant in modern fantasy and horror fiction. The novel is imaginative, exciting and vivid, with Barker's usual attention to graphic visceral detail and imagery. He carries out the broad outline of his audacious concept with great skill, manipulating his plot lines with considerable dexterity. Many of the individual scenes are highly impressive. The writing is quite good; the principals, especially the villains, are vivid and interesting, if not overly consistent; the pacing is energetic; and the novel offers many imaginative surprises.

But it also highlights some typical Barker shortcomings. Several of his short stories, even otherwise effective efforts, are badly overwritten. A playwright as well as fiction writer, Barker's dialogue is generally good—sharp, incisive, revealing—but it sometimes reads more like stage dialogue than narrative speech, and goes on too long, providing information that could be more economically presented in narrative. At times the graphic details or grotesque images seem gratuitous, meant for momentary shock rather than as integral parts of the whole. Barker's weakest stories are like those bad horror movies in which plot, character and logic are lost in a storm of special effects, a failing that *Weaveworld* occasionally shares.

A surprising weakness in *Weaveworld*, however, is the lack of solidity in Barker's alternate world. It may sound odd to say that a 584-page book is too short, but so much happens to so many characters in the novel, it is so conceptually big and thematically complicated, that it requires even more exploration. Once again, Barker excites us with his concept, fascinates us with his grotesques, but fails to touch us with his characters as living human beings.

In terms of the triumvirate of "terror," "horror" and "gross-out," Barker offers much horror, even more gross-out, but relatively little terror. Terror demands a sympathetic identification with the principal characters so that readers will not only be appalled by their fates, but will also, on an imaginative level, share them. Because it is almost impossible to identify closely enough with Barker's characters, the reader tends to stare with detached horror, fascination and often disgust, but from the outside, as spectators of the traffic accident, not as passengers in the wrecked vehicles.

Contemporary horror writers, particularly in the wake of Stephen King and his followers, have not so much changed the substance and direction of horror literature as they have consolidated the traditional character types, myths and appeals of horror literature, while infusing them with new color, vitality and sweep. The canvas is larger, the language freer, the imagery more extreme and the plotting more grandiose, spilling over into other popular genres. If dark fantasy has lost some of the psychological subtlety and finely tuned terror of the classical ghost story, it has gained a scope, drive and energy well suited to the agitated decades it reflects. In terms of originality, creativity, popularity and literary merit the period from 1950 through 1988 has been one of the most interesting, stimulating and productive in the history of dark fantasy.

Notes

1. Darrell Schweitzer, *Discovering Modern Horror Fiction: I* [7-13] (Starmont House, 1985), p. 2.
2. H. P. Lovecraft, "The Call of Cthulhu," *The Dunwich Horror and Others* (Arkham House, 1963), p. 130.
3. Quoted in Lin Carter, *Lovecraft: A Look behind the "Cthulhu Mythos"* [8-71] (Ballantine, 1972), p. xv.
4. James E. Burns, "TZ Interview: Richard Matheson," *Twilight Zone*, September 1981, p. 47; October 1981, p. 15.
5. Stephen King, *Danse Macabre* [7-6] (Everest House, 1981), pp. 293–294.
6. Lovecraft, "The Outsider," *The Dunwich Horror and Others*, pp. 57–58.
7. Richard Matheson and Richard Christian Matheson, "Where There's a Will," *Dark Forces* [4-346], ed. by Kirby McCauley (Viking, 1980), p. 110.
8. Fritz Leiber, "Smoke Ghost," *Night's Black Agents* [3-126] (Gregg Press, 1980), p. 110.
9. Ira Levin, *Rosemary's Baby* [4-206] (Random House, 1967), p. 235.
10. King, *Danse Macabre*, p. 283.
11. Ibid.
12. Ibid.
13. Interview with Douglas Winter, *Fantasy Newsletter*, February 1982, p. 31.
14. Jay Gregory, "TZ Interview: Peter Straub," *Twilight Zone*, May 1981, p. 14.
15. Ibid., p. 15.
16. "TZ Interview: Richard Matheson," *Twilight Zone*, September 1981, p. 46.
17. Pierre Kast, "Author's Note," *The Vampires of Alfama* [4-159] (W. H. Allen, 1976), p. 24.
18. King, *Danse Macabre*, p. 78.
19. Ibid., pp. 84–85.
20. Stephen King, *'Salem's Lot* (Doubleday, 1975), p. 253.
21. King, *Danse Macabre*, p. 168.
22. Quoted in Don Herron, "Horror Springs in the Fiction of Stephen King," *Fear Itself: The Terror Fiction of Stephen King* [8-43], ed. by Tim Underwood and Chuck Miller (Underwood-Miller, 1982), p. 59.
23. Quoted in Douglas E. Winter, *Stephen King: The Art of Darkness* [8-42] (NAL, 1984), p. 110.
24. John Cawelti, *Adventure, Mystery, and Romance* [F7-11] (Univ. of Chicago Press, 1976), p. 261.
25. Ibid., p. 266.
26. Ibid., p. 263.
27. Ibid., p. 261.
28. King, *Danse Macabre*, p. 18.
29. Ibid., p. 247.
30. Peter S. Straub, *Ghost Story* (Coward, McCann, 1979), p. 401.

31. Quoted on *Ghost Story* book jacket.
32. Interview with Bill Munster, *Sudden Fear: The Horror and Dark Suspense Fiction of Dean Koontz* [8-48], ed. by Bill Munster (Starmont House, 1988), p. 5.
33. Ibid., p. 30.
34. Interview by "Leigh Nicholls," *Horror Show*, Summer 1987, p. 23.
35. Interview with Stanley Wiater, *Fantasy Review*, May 1987, p. 23.
36. Quoted in Douglas E. Winter, *Faces of Fear* [8-112] (Berkley, 1985), p. 186.
37. Interview with Lisa Tuttle, *Twilight Zone*, December 1984, p. 42.
38. Interview with Darrell Schweitzer, *Fantasy Newsletter*, April 1980, p. 15.
39. Ibid., p. 16.
40. Ramsey Campbell, Introduction to Clive Barker, *Books of Blood: Volume One* (Berkley, 1986), p. xi.

Bibliography

Annotations written by Mike Ashley, Bentley Little and Brian Stableford are identified by their initials in parentheses following the annotation. My thanks to them, especially Bentley Little, for sharing their knowledge and talents. Of the 340 annotations, 76 are of single-author collections. Mike Ashley annotated an additional 23 anthologies, most of whose contents were published since 1950. See also the anthologies annotated in chapter 3 and those recommended but not annotated in the core-collection list in chapter 13. The argument for the importance of short horror fiction is made by David Hartwell in the introduction to his *The Dark Descent* [4-345].

Ackroyd, Peter (U.K.), 1949- .
ABOUT: F, H, MF

4-1. Hawksmoor. Hamish Hamilton, 1985.
Hawksmoor is a very British, very literary horror novel in which the narrative style alternates between contemporary prose and a well-crafted eighteenth-century writing style. In the 1700s, an orphan whose parents died of plague is reared and educated by Satanists and grows up to design cathedrals. The legacy of the evil Satanists' still reverberates in twentieth-century London, where a series of murders is taking place. Despite its intelligence and obvious stylistic attributes, *Hawksmoor* is not an entirely successful novel. At times Ackroyd elicits the frightening sort of surreal half-connections that du Maurier achieves in "Don't Look Now" [4-101], but his stubbornly cold prose and inability or unwillingness to pursue the horrific elements of his story result in a rather static and inconclusive narrative. Too often, *Hawksmoor* reads like a horror novel by Nabokov, filled with intellectual mind games and literary allusions but ultimately devoid of substance. Nevertheless, despite its problems, *Hawksmoor* is an interesting effort and is obviously the work of an ambitious and original writer. (B.L.)

[For other works of this author, see the companion guide to fantasy.]

Adams, Richard (U.K.), 1920- .
About: CA, SMFL, SFFL, RG, PE

4-2. The Girl in a Swing. Knopf, 1980.
The love affair between Alan Desland, a conservative country gentleman, and Käthe Wasserman, a mysterious, exotic beauty, gradually moves from passionate fulfillment to ambiguous dread and finally to death and grief. The question of Käthe's true nature and history—lover? child murderer? ghost? demon?—reverberates throughout the novel and beyond. Adams is best known for such epic animal fantasies as *Watership Down* (1972) [F4B-1] and *Shardik* (1974) [F4A-2]; his sole venture into dark fantasy is a powerful, lyrical, thoughtful book, as well as an intensely satisfying love story, which blends the spirit of the classical ghost story with a thoroughly contemporary sensibility. Adams's mixture of dark fantasy, eroticism, and philosophical-religious speculation is reminiscent of Amis's *The Green Man* [4-11] and, to a lesser degree, Calder-Marshall's *The Scarlet Boy* [4-62].

Aickman, Robert (U.K.), 1914–1981.
About: WW, GSF, SFW, CA, H, SMFL, SFFL, PE, ESF

4-3. Cold Hand in Mine. Gollancz, 1975.
Eight stories by the acknowledged contemporary master of the classical Victorian ghost/horror story—subtle, ambiguous, stylistically elegant, quietly creepy stories with a touch of unnerving humor. The "nicely managed crescendo" of M. R. James in a landscape out of Kafka. Especially noteworthy are "The Hospice," in which a traveling salesman is forced to take overnight accommodations in a "hospice," a weirdly bureaucratic cross between a hotel and a hospital, where he has a series of strange encounters that may or may not predict his own demise; "Meeting Mr. Miller," in which a reclusive editor of pornography and would-be novelist becomes increasingly fearful of the strange, sinister and vaguely comic activities of his downstairs neighbor; "The Clock Watcher," in which a happily married man becomes progressively disturbed by his wife's obsession with grotesque clocks and her ambiguous relationship with the mysterious man who sells and services them; and "Pages from a Young Girl's Journal," a quietly chilling chronicle of a girl's transformation from bored teenager to fresh and eager neophyte vampire, told in her own chatty style, and which won the World Fantasy Award in 1975. Compare the traditional stories of Daphne du Maurier [4-101], on the one hand, and the more experimental efforts of Ramsey Campbell [4-63, 4-64, 4-67], on the other.

4-4. Intrusions. Gollancz, 1980.
Six stories reflecting the more elegiac mood characteristic of Aickman's later stories. Most remarkable is "The Fetch," one of his best. The narrator tells his long, complicated but essentially barren life story, which is dominated by memories of his overbearing father, the early deaths of his adored mother and his first wife, his failed second marriage and career and the family "fetch," a witch-like figure who, from beneath her hood, shows the intended victim his or her own face at the moment of death. A truly chilling tale.

4-5. Night Voices. Gollancz, 1985.
One of the last collections of Aickman's fiction. The best story of the five in the volume, and one of the finest of Aickman's career, is "The Stains." Stephen, a recently widowed man recuperating in the country, meets and falls in love with Nell, a hearty, nymph-like young girl with a powerful, mysterious, unseen father and an odd stain on her back. Their love grows, but so does the stain, which spreads to Stephen and to the outside world. Finally, love and death are reconciled in what is perhaps Aickman's most poignant and satisfying conclusion. Other impressive stories are "Laura," another variation on the theme of an ordinary man's encounter with a mysterious, seductive, dangerous female. Much lighter in tone than "The Stains," "Laura" ends with comic relief rather than tragic reconciliation. In "Mark Ingestre: The Customer's Tale," the figure of the dangerous female—two of them, in fact—appears again in an odd, darkly erotic retelling of the Sweeney Todd story from the viewpoint of a resourceful customer.

4-6. Painted Devils: Strange Stories. Scribner's, 1979.
Nine stories reprinted from earlier volumes. "The View" is one of his best. A mysterious, aristocratic female takes Carfax, an ex-Foreign Office official recovering from a depression, to her mansion on a semi-deserted island. Their affair becomes increasingly idyllic and mysterious until neither Carfax nor the reader can be sure how much of it really happened. "The Waiting Room," a more traditional story, concerns a salesman who spends the night in a supposedly deserted railway waiting room. In "Ringing the Changes," an older man and his young bride spend a honeymoon night in a small town where the church bells raise the dead to dance with the living. In "Ravissante," a self-taught Surrealistic artist visits an aged female painter who lures him into a bizarre ritual with her "adopted daughter's" clothing. In "House of the Russians," a mysterious holy medal apparently saves the narrator from an awful, if undefined, fate. And in "Marriage," Lanning's complicated, problematical relationship with the sexually energetic Ellen and her more proper, mundane sister, Helen, demonstrates the fundamental unreality of relations between the sexes.

4-7. Powers of Darkness. Collins, 1966.
Six stories. Most impressive is "The Visiting Star," about Anabella Rokeby, a mysterious, possibly ghostly stage star, whose effort for a provincial theater is both demonic and exhilarating. Compare to Langley's "The Fall of the Fothergays" [4-197] and Leiber's "Four Ghosts in *Hamlet*" [4-201]. Also quite interesting are "Your Tiny Hand Is Frozen," about a mysterious telephone caller who haunts a typically lonely Aickman protagonist during the Christmas season, and "The Wine-Dark Sea," about a man who encounters three ancient Greek sorceresses on an Aegean island.

***4-8. Sub Rosa: Strange Tales.** Gollancz, 1968.
Eight threatening, mysterious, subtle stories, two later reprinted in *Painted Devils*. Three stories are outstanding: "The Inner Room," in which Leni, as a girl, receives and loses a large Gothic dollhouse with a mysterious inner room; as an adult she encounters it again, full-sized and waiting for her. In "The Unsettled Dust," a government bureaucrat, spending several days in a once grand English

estate now gone to seed, encounters hostility and tension between the last of the clan, the aging Brakespear sisters, a ghost and mysterious, continually swirling dust that coats everything. In "Into the Wood," Molly Sawyer, inadvertently enters the strange, threatening world of the permanent insomniac.

4-9. Tales of Love and Death. Gollancz, 1977.
Seven stories. Outstanding is "Compulsory Games," in which the protagonist, Colin, finds his trivial, mundane existence abruptly turned into a nightmare and his self-image shattered by his wife's sudden departure. These themes of estrangement and psychic disintegration are also picked up in "Wood" and "*Le Mirror*." Also worthy of note are "Growing Boys," about twins who grow to monstrous sizes, and "Residents Only," a chronicle of the inhabitants of a cemetery.

Aldiss, Brian W(ilson) (U.K.), 1925- .
ABOUT: CA, NE, SFE, MF, SFFL, TCSF, ESF

4-10. Frankenstein Unbound. Cape, 1973.
In the year 2020 nuclear war has ruptured the infrastructure of time, sending politician Joseph Bodenland through a time slip to Lake Geneva in May 1816, where he encounters Mary Shelley in the midst of writing *Frankenstein* [1-97], has an affair with her, then meets the real Dr. Victor Frankenstein and, eventually, his Creature. More science fiction than dark fantasy, but important for anyone interested in *Frankenstein*, the "Frankenstein Myth" or Mary Shelley. A highly entertaining, intellectually stimulating, thoroughly ingenious novel. Compare Saberhagen's *The Frankenstein Papers* [4-259].

Amis, Kingsley (U.K.), 1922- .
ABOUT: F, CA, NE, H, SMFL, SFE, MF, SFFL, TCSF, ESF, HF

4-11. The Green Man. Cape, 1969.
The proprietor of the Green Man Inn, Maurice Allington, troubled by fears of declining virility and intimations of mortality, becomes fascinated by the history of Dr. Thomas Underhill, a lecherous seventeenth-century black magician, whose ghost was said to haunt the inn. Encountering both Underhill's specter and a mysterious young man, who may be God, Allington is finally forced to choose between good and evil, with his sanity and soul, along with the life of his daughter, Amy, at stake. A sophisticated, provocative, unorthodox ghost story, with serious philosophical and religious themes. Compare Adams's *The Girl in a Swing* [4-2] and Calder-Marshall's more conventional but thematically similar *The Scarlet Boy* [4-62].

Andrews, V(irginia) C(leo), died 1986.
ABOUT: CA, PE, FF

4-12. Flowers in the Attic. Pocket Books, 1979.
The beautiful Dollanganger children are locked away in an attic by their greedy mother as part of a scheme to claim an inheritance. In their attic prison the

children attempt to create a world of their own until they are finally forced to come to terms with their mother's treachery. Andrews continued the Dollanganger saga in *Petals in the Wind* (1980), *If There Be Thorns* (1981), *Seeds of Yesterday* (1984) and *Garden of Shadows* (1987; completed by Andrew Neiderman). Critic Douglas Winter has praised the way Andrews presents sensational stories in "romantic, fairy tale tones, producing the most highly individualistic tales of terror of this generation." Other, less generous critics have found her work excessively melodramatic, sentimental and exploitative of such subjects as incest and child abuse. But whatever the critical dispute, Andrews was the best-selling female author of horror-related material in the 1980s.

Baker, Frank (U.K.), 1908–1982.
ABOUT: WW, GSF, SFW, CA

4-13. Stories of the Strange and Sinister. Kimber, 1983.
A posthumous collection of ten stories. Early pieces like "Art Thou Languid?" (1947) and "Quintin Claribel" are whimsical, and include the marvelous "My Lady Sweet, Arise" in which a virtuous old lady hears from a medium that there is no music in Heaven and becomes adamant that she won't go; later ones, mostly stories set in Cornwall from Denys Val Baker's original anthologies, are deft and subtle weird tales, the most delicately horrific of which is "The Chocolate Box" (1973). (B.S.)

4-14. Talk of the Devil. Angus & Robertson, 1956.
Novelist Philip Hayes becomes intrigued by the mysterious deaths several years earlier of two women amid rumors about a black magic cult headed by an Aleister Crowley-like figure. His investigation reanimates old hostilities, raises new questions and stimulates new threats of violence. A complicated, interesting mystery/horror story, with the emphasis on the mystery. The supernaturalism is muted and most important for the psychological and intellectual effects it has on the characters. Baker's delineation of the Cornish environment is superior and his characters are complex, believable and generally sympathetic. However, the intrusion of an unforeshadowed political element upsets the book's mood and strains the credibility of the ending.

Ballard, J(ames) G(raham) (U.K.), 1930– .
ABOUT: F, CA, NE, H, SMFL, MF, SFFL, TCSF, ESF

4-15. Concrete Island. Cape, 1974.
A traffic accident leaves Robert Maitland stranded and injured on a littered, undeveloped traffic island beneath three converging highways. He survives on radiator water and food litter and by manipulating the two other castaways he meets on his island, a disturbed young woman and a brain-damaged ex-acrobat. Another of Ballard's original, provocative parables of physical and psychological isolation in the modern world. Although *Concrete Island* can be identified with the tradition of castaway novels from *Robinson Crusoe* to Golding's *Pincher Martin*, it is thoroughly original in concept and execution.

4-16. Crash. Cape, 1973.
After the narrator, named "Ballard," survives a serious automobile accident, he becomes fascinated and excited by car crashes, especially after he meets Vaughan, a fanatical "hoodlum scientist," whose ultimate ambition is to die with Elizabeth Taylor in a fiery car accident. Perhaps Ballard's darkest, most unsettling book. The identification between sex, automobiles and violent death is made complete and explicit. But while the details of sex and violence are graphic, Ballard's tone is detached, almost clinical. A fascinating book, neither easily read nor easily forgotten.

4-17. The Crystal World. Cape, 1966.
Traveling into the West African interior to see an ex-lover, Dr. Edward Sanders discovers that the jungle is crystalizing, with all flora, fauna and animal life gradually hardening into a glittering mineral formation, a process that threatens to spread all over the world and perhaps even the universe. Ballard's focus is not on the disaster, but on the characters' psychological reactions to it, as they must alter themselves to adjust to their new, inhuman environment. A powerful, puzzling, disturbing book that blends a traditional science fiction motif with a psychological concern with man's dark side in a lush, grotesque landscape more typical of dark fantasy. Critics have noted similarities between the novel and Conrad's classic *Heart of Darkness* [3-51]. *The Crystal World* was the fourth in Ballard's quartet of global disaster novels, which includes *A Wind from Nowhere* (1962), *The Drowned World* (1962) and *The Drought* (1964).

***4-18. High-Rise**. Cape, 1975.
The occupants of a forty-story luxury condominium building, roughly organized according to financial and social status (the higher the floor, the richer the individual), gradually move from hostility to anger to violence as the building erupts in a civil war between the floors and finally deteriorates into pure savagery. Ballard's delineation of the gradual transformation of this luxury building, through the shifting viewpoints of three characters, one from each faction, from an upper-middle-class playground into a guerrilla battlefield is done with such care and precision that each phase of the conflict seems reasonable and believable, even inevitable. The book has been called an adult version of Golding's *Lord of the Flies* [4-123].

[For other works of this author, see the companion guide to fantasy.]

Banks, Iain (U.K.), 1954- .
ABOUT: CA, H, MF, PE

4-19. The Wasp Factory. Macmillan, 1984.
Sixteen-year-old Francis Cauldhame contemplates ritual animal and insect sacrifice, casual murder and family secrets as he waits for the cataclysmic return of his older brother, an escaped lunatic. A brilliant if eccentric first novel that manages to be thought-provoking, funny, revolting and poignant, at the same time.

[For other works of this author, see the companion guide to fantasy.]

Barker, Clive (U.K.), 1952– .
About: CA, H, PE, FF

***4-20. Books of Blood**. 6 vols. Sphere, 1984–85. Vols. 1–3 reprinted with corrections and some rewriting as a boxed set by Scream/Press, 1985. Retitled U.S. reprints include *In The Flesh* (vol. 4) and *The Inhuman Condition* (vol. 5), both Poseidon, 1986, and *Cabal* (Poseidon, 1988) [4-21], which reprints vol. 6 with a short novel, *Cabal*, published separately in the U.K.

In the frame story, a grisly updating of Ray Bradbury's *The Illustrated Man* (1951) by way of Kafka's "In the Penal Settlement" [3-110], the "books of blood" are etched on the skin of Simon McNeal, a fake psychic, by the annoyed dead. The stories are violent, sensual, chaotic and often quite funny, with strikingly original concepts and explicit details of sex, violence and cruelty, indicating a bleak worldview relieved only by Barker's often bitter, but always lively sense of humor. Even his more or less conventional stories, such as "Rawhead Rex," about a giant cannibalistic monster who decimates the countryside, contain visceral descriptions that set them above their B-movie formulas. More original monster stories like "Skins of the Fathers" combine Barker's offbeat imagination with his impressive talent for visual detail and grotesque imagery. These qualities are also evident in "The Inhuman Condition." When Kelley steals a knotted string from an apparently harmless old derelict, he does not realize, until he unties the first of them, that each of the knots binds a demon. The "Candyman" in "Forgiven" is equally monstrous, but much closer to human. It is not until the heroine of the story meets him face to face and looks upon his disintegrating face and the hive of bees that replaces his chest that she realizes that he is not an ordinary serial murderer, but an inhuman monster who represents the collective violence and cruelty of the slum neighborhood she has unwisely intruded into. The ghost of a hanged murderer lures his grandson into a terrible pact in "In the Flesh"; the pact also leads the boy's cellmate protector to murder and its terrible, otherworldly aftermath.

In between the realistic slum of "Forgiven" and the total otherworld of "In the Flesh" are the underground subway caverns of "The Midnight Meat Train." A series of ghastly murders on the New York subway has panicked everyone except the blasé Leon Kaufman. Attacked by the Butcher, Leon kills him; when the subway car reaches its final destination, a cavern below the city, he learns that he must take over the job of supplying fresh meat for the City Fathers, the army of ghoulish city founders who have lived for eons on the flesh brought to them by Leon's predecessors. And since the central figure in this story is an ordinary, mediocre human being who turns into a monster, it illustrates another important point: the real monster is man himself. This point is made most vividly in what is probably the best story in the *Books of Blood*, "Dread." Stephen Grace, a student, meets Quaid, a "philosopher" with the theory that the basic motivating force in human behavior is "fear" of one kind or another. Quaid sets out to prove his theory by experimenting first on a female student and subsequently on Grace, subjecting him to tailor-made tortures that succeed in breaking him, but in the process turn him into a mindless axe murderer whose first victim is Quaid. "Dread" is an unnerving exploration of the dark side of the psyche in which the physical tortures that Grace endures are reflections of inner torments that are much more severe. In "Dread" Barker mutes his pyrotechnics and extravagant imagery to focus on characterization, and it pays off. As long as Barker exerts control over his imagination, extravagant imagery and taste for explicitly detailed sex and violence, he offers some of the most exciting and original stories in the genre. It is only when these elements spin out of control, in stories like "Jacqueline Ess" and "Pig Blood Blues," or when he tries to build stories out of very thin ideas, as in "The Body Politic" or "Babel's Children," that he falters. Compare the stories of Ramsey Campbell [4-63, 4-64, 4-67].

4-21. Cabal. Poseidon, 1988.
The title novella and four longish short stories (the last comprising vol. 6 of the *Books of Blood*). In "Cabal," Boone, a psychotic who fears he is a brutal serial murderer, flees to Midian, a town rumored to welcome monsters, where he encounters the violent undead creatures of the Nightbreed. After being pursued by the real killer and the police, cornered and killed, he becomes one of them. His girlfriend, Lori, comes after him in Midian, precipitating a gory, protracted confrontation between the living and the dead. An interesting contemporary zombie novel, filmed as *Nightbreed,* that makes up in imagination and stylistic gore what it lacks in plot credibility. The best of the short narratives is "Twilight at the Towers," which combines the spy story with a highly original, exciting werewolf tale. Also effective is "The Life of Death," in which the heroine falls in love with death, giving her life a new meaning (compare Disch's "Death and the Single Girl" [4-99]).

4-22. The Damnation Game. Weidenfeld & Nicolson, 1985.
Barker's first full-length novel. Marty Strauss is released early from prison to take a job as bodyguard for Joseph Whitehead, an aging, reclusive, mysterious millionaire, who is being stalked by Mamoulian, a sinister European with supernatural powers, and his helper, Breer, a huge sadomasochistic child murderer. As Mamoulian closes in, Strauss learns the dark secrets of Whitehead's past and falls in love with Carys, his psychic, heroin-addicted daughter. The past and the present, the living and the dead, the real and the unreal all come together in a broken-down hotel in the novel's harrowing conclusion. Despite the triteness of the initial situation—the reclusive millionaire with a secret, tainted past, hiding, terrified, in a fortress sanctuary—*The Damnation Game* is a highly original novel, a complex reworking of the Faust theme in a contemporary context. It is a beautifully structured novel, all of whose elements fuse perfectly at the end. Although the book has several scenes of graphic violence and messy, perhaps perverse gore, the scenes are carefully prepared for and are integral to the book's structure and themes. The novel's only real flaw is that we must see everything through the eyes of the novel's least interesting character, Marty Strauss, who is neither bright nor sympathetic. The terrified yet defiant Whitehead, the demonic, totally evil, yet oddly vulnerable Mamoulian, the wonderfully disgusting Breer, even the enigmatic Carys are powerful dark creations that deserve more space than Barker allots them. Compare Herbert's *Sepulchre* [4-145].

4-23. Weaveworld. Poseidon, 1987.
The magical world of the Seerkind is woven into a rug to escape the ravages of the Scourge. After the death of its last human keeper, the rug falls into evil hands. It is

unwoven and attacked, initially by the Immacolata, a disgruntled Seerkind, and her human lover, Shadwell the salesman, and finally by the reactivated Scourge. The novel moves back and forth between this world and the world of the Seerkind, as a small group of humans and Seerkind, led by Susanna, granddaughter of the rug's last protector, and Cal Mooney, insurance clerk, bird keeper and would-be poet, fight to save the Seerkind's world from extinction. An exotic, imaginative, ambitious mix of horror and fantasy that only occasionally realizes the potential of its brilliant concept. The writing is quite good, the principals, especially the villains, are vivid and interesting, if not overly consistent, and the pacing is energetic, but the world of the Seerkind lacks solidity and the plotting is somewhat strained, the resolution contrived. Also annotated as [F4A-18].

Barker, Nugent (U.K.), born 1888.

4-24. Written with My Left Hand. Percival Marshall, 1951.
A regular contributor to the literary reviews of the 1920s and 1930s, Barker developed a talent for writing short, offbeat stories. Twenty-one of them, not all supernatural, but all, as the title implies, sinister, are collected here. The best is "The Curious Adventure of Mr. Bond," a tense story of a traveler ensnared by three related inns. "One, Two, Buckle My Shoe" gives a bleak interpretation of the old nursery rhyme. Barker's style is tight and controlled, with a knack for delivering a strong final line. (M.A.)

Beagle, Peter S(oyer), 1939- .

ABOUT: WW, GSF, SFW, CA, SMFL, MF, SFFL, ESF, FL, HF

4-25. A Fine and Private Place. Viking, 1960.
Beagle's first novel, perhaps most readily available in *The Fantasy Worlds of Peter Beagle* (1978). From his home in a cemetery mausoleum, disillusioned druggist Jonathan Rebeck converses with his only living friend, a cynical, tough-talking raven; acts as a matchmaker for a recently deceased couple; and resists, for a time, the romantic advances of a Jewish widow. A charming, funny, bittersweet fantasy that uses death as a device to affirm the value of life. Compare Disch's much darker comedy, *The Businessman* [4-98]. Also annotated as [F4A-22].

Beaumont, Charles (pseud. of **Charles Nutt**), 1929–1967.

ABOUT: WW, GSF, CA, SMFL, SFE, SFFL, RG, TCSF, PE, ESF

4-26. Best of Beaumont. Bantam, 1982.
Twenty-two stories which focus, in Beaumont's own words, on "the most terrifying monster of them all . . . The Mind." Few writers have so effectively fused humor and horror, although in his weaker stories, the humor becomes somewhat arch and the plotting forced in the manner of an overlong shaggy dog story. The most memorable stories in this collection are "Blood Brother," in which a newly transformed vampire complains to a psychiatrist about the complications and irritations of being undead; "The New People," a truly frightening story about

the dark side of a typical suburban neighborhood; "The Crooked Man," about a man's futile attempt to have an old-fashioned heterosexual love affair in a society where homosexuality is compulsory; and "The Jungle," in which a new modern city, carved out of a jungle, is reclaimed by the dark forces it was meant to displace.

***4-27. Charles Beaumont: Selected Stories**. Ed. by Roger Anker. Dark Harvest, 1988.
Twenty-nine stories and one novel excerpt (from *The Intruder*) that span Beaumont's short but relatively productive career. Six repeats from the *Best of . . .* volume, four original with this collection. Several of the individual stories are introduced by such former Beaumont associates as Ray Bradbury, Richard Matheson and Roger Corman. The gentler side of Beaumont shows in such Bradburyish stories as "Fair Lady," in which a lonely spinster finds imaginative romance with a bus driver, and "Magic Man," in which a traveling magician regretfully learns that his audience does not want to know how his tricks are done. More characteristic are such disturbing stories as "The Howling Man," "Perchance to Dream," "Miss Gentlebelle" and "The Hunger." Overlapping the line between horror and science fiction, Beaumont's best stories are clever, funny and unique, usually ending with a sharp, ironic twist that not only serves as a "punchline," but also underscores the seriousness beneath the humor. Compare the stories of Bloch [4-45, 4-47], Bradbury [4-52], Matheson [4-218] and William F. Nolan [4-242].

Bell, Neil (pseud. of **Stephen Southwold**) (U.K.), 1887–1964.

ABOUT: WW, GSF, SFE, PE, ESF

4-28. Who Walk in Fear. Alvin Redman, 1953.
Collection of three novellas, with a prefatory essay on horror fiction. In "Culver Island," a group of castaways is terrorized by monstrous crabs; in "Thirty-Six Hours," a young woman is seduced by a modern Jack the Ripper; in "The Mate of the *S. S. Vega*," a castaway forced to eat human meat in order to survive becomes addicted to it. The themes were brutally shocking in their day, but they are addressed in an uneasily clinical manner. (B.S.)

Benchley, Peter, 1940– .

ABOUT: CA

4-29. Jaws. Doubleday, 1974.
A great white shark invades the waters of the resort town of Amity, Long Island. Police Chief Martin Brody is joined by Quint, a professional shark hunter, and Matt Hooper, an oceanographer, in an attempt to find and kill the hungry shark. A cleanly written, energetic book, with sharp, if shallow, characterizations. Vivid descriptions and lively action scenes help to account for its popularity as well as its adaptability to the screen. Steven Spielberg's streamlined 1975 film version, with a more heroic ending, became the highest grossing horror movie ever made. Compare du Maurier's "The Birds" [4-101].

Bernanos, Michel (France), 1924–1964.
About: SMFL

4-30. The Other Side of the Mountain. Houghton, 1968. Tr. by Elaine P. Halperin of *La montagne morte de la vie,* 1967.
The Narrator and Toine, the ship's cook, are the only survivors of a mutiny, shipwreck and whirlpool. They find themselves on a mysterious island with no animal life, but fantastic, carnivorous vegetation and, at the center, a huge mountain. As they attempt to climb the mountain, their skins are gradually encrusted by a stony substance until they become totally immobilized and fused into the mountain itself. A surrealistic nightmare, with some echoes of Poe's *Narrative of Arthur Gordon Pym* [2-76], that can be read as pure horror fantasy or can be probed for a variety of allegorical or symbolic possibilities. Also annotated as [F4A-31].

Birkin, Charles (U.K.), 1907–1986.
About: WW, GSF, CA, SFFL, PE, ESF

4-31. The Kiss of Death. Tandem, 1964.
Introduction by Dennis Wheatley. Fifteen stories in which Birkin's precise, detached style moves from a placid, often elegant setting with ordinary characters involved in mundane activities to intense, visceral finales. Although supernatural or science fiction elements sometimes enter the stories, the major thrust of Birkin's fiction is psychological, with an emphasis on the bizarre, obsessional, insane and often purely evil. In the title story, twice-married and very rich beauty Sylvia Nicolson encounters her old lover bearing a hideous gift. In "Les Belles Dames Sans Merci," Virginia McLean's idyllic marriage to Conrad gradually deteriorates until she finally learns what happened to her three predecessors. "'The New Ones'" is a kind of mini-*Body Snatchers* [4-116] in which the Earth is invaded by alien spores that *gradually* take over the body, whether living or dead. Most of the entries are quite short, which is perfect for Birkin's compression, savagely ironic humor and clever final twists. Compare the psychological horror stories of Robert Bloch [4-45, 4-47].

***4-32. My Name Is Death**. Tandem, 1966.
Eight stories that move from the mundane and detached to the cruel and gruesome. Sometimes the shift is abrupt, as in "Hard to Get," in which an elegant seduction turns at the midpoint into a ghoulish alien invasion tale. In the best stories, however, the menace is gradually, unobtrusively developed from several apparently casual details until the final twist brings the story together in a painful, violent, often grotesque and bloody climax. The best examples include "My Name Is Death," in which two female campers encounter a sinister force on an island (compare Blackwood's "The Willows" [3-26]); "King of the Castle," in which a dull-witted son strikes back at his vicious father; "The Finger of Fear," about a ghoulish remedy for toothache; and best of all, "Hosanna," in which an intellectual hitchhiker encounters an artist who is overly dedicated to the purity of his work.

4-33. The Smell of Evil. Tandem, 1965.
Thirteen *contes cruels*. Particularly unnerving are the title story, in which a crippled young beauty is the victim of a bizarre conspiracy involving flesh-eating crabs; "Ballet Negre," in which reporter Simon Cust learns, too late, that zombies make excellent ballet dancers, but very bad interviewees; "The Lesson," in which Uncle Oscar, as a party joke, is tied up and gagged, with a plastic bag over his head, and left in the care of seven-year-old Milo; "'Is There Anybody There?'" about Millie Ackland who, obsessed with a murder committed in her cottage many years earlier, becomes convinced that the spirits of the principals have returned; and "The Cornered Beast," about an encounter between Vera, a prostitute, and Leonard, a sideshow freak.

4-34. The Spawn of Satan. Award, 1970.
Ten stories. Most are longer than Birkin's usual fare, and depend more on characterization and development than on shock value and final twists—although they have the usual quota of cruelty and violence. Excellent examples are "Spawn of Satan," a contemporary tale about the eruption of racial tensions and violence that occurs when school teacher Venetia Palmer moves into the Arbour Hotel with her black husband; "The Beautiful People," an ironic treatment of the contemporary rich and amoral; and "Wedding Presents," a long, cruel story about infanticide (one of Birkin's favorite subjects) and blackmail.

Bishop, Michael, 1945- .
ABOUT: CA, NE, H, SFE, MF, TCSF

4-35. Who Made Stevie Crye? Arkham House, 1984.
Forced to support her two children as a freelance writer following the untimely death of her husband, Mary Stevenson Crye is upset when her typewriter begins to write on its own. Are the messages from her dead husband? From the mysterious repairman who services the machine? Or his pet monkey? Or from her own subconscious? A provocative, entertaining novel that is both charming and chilling—although never quite horrific. In its author protagonist and diabolical machinery, it is reminiscent of such lighter Stephen King efforts as "Word Processor of the Gods" [4-174]. Not quite a pure horror novel and not quite a parody of the genre, *Who Made Stevie Crye?* is *sui generis*.

Black, Campbell (U.K.), 1944- .
ABOUT: CA

4-36. Letters from the Dead. Villard, 1985.
A subtle, quiet horror novel about the effect of the past on the present and the endless reverberations of evil. Two women, one divorced, one separated, rent a beach house for the summer in a small Virginia town and bring with them their adolescent son and daughter, respectively. The boy and girl begin receiving messages on an old Ouija board found in a closet, and as the summer progresses all four of them begin to notice strange events occurring at and around the house. *Letters from the Dead* is Straubian in its theme, with many conscious parallels

with *The Turn of the Screw* [3-107]. Black effectively creates an atmosphere of mounting tension and unseen menace, investing even seemingly innocent occurrences with chilling overtones. The climax seems too quick and easy and does not really live up to the promise of the preceding pages, but even here Black carefully avoids the pitfalls of a clichéd ending. An excellent work. (B.L.)

Blackburn, John F(enwick) (U.K.), 1923- .

ABOUT: WW, CA, SFE, SFFL, PE

4-37. Bury Him Darkly. Cape, 1969.
A small circle of devotees fights the Church of England to gain access to the tomb of Sir Martin Railstone, an eighteenth-century artist, scientist, sensualist and murderer, even though opening the crypt may unleash terrible forces that threaten all mankind. A superior mystery suspense novel with a disappointingly facile monster-on-the-rampage resolution.

4-38. Children of the Night. Cape, 1966.
The Yorkshire village of Dunstonholme's long history of bizarre crimes and unnatural disasters reaches a peak in the mid-1960s. The search for the causes of these events leads to a fanatical religious cult, supposedly destroyed in the Middle Ages, and their prophecy that the world will end on June 24, 1966. Another fast-paced, adroitly plotted horror-thriller that conforms to Blackburn's characteristic mix of mystery thriller and horror story.

4-39. Devil Daddy. Cape, 1972.
Suspected of raping an English schoolgirl—who suddenly and mysteriously dies of old age—bacteriologist-hero Marcus Levin sets off, with his wife, Tania, on the trail of John Batterday, a sinister art dealer. Batterday, who is Levin's double, seems impervious to injury and may be the target of a satanic cult. The Levins discover a terrible connection between Batterday, a terrifying virus that could loose a deadly plague on the world and the fulfillment of an ancient Christian prophecy. An exciting read, although not up to Blackburn's very best. The menace is ingenious and the plot twists are adroit, but Blackburn's characters are less sympathetic than usual and his reliance on coincidence to bring things together is too transparent.

***4-40. For Fear of Little Men**. Cape, 1972.
Investigating a case of unexplained mass food poisoning in the Welsh village of Treflys, bacteriologist Marcus Levin and his wife, Tania, are plunged into a complicated, dangerous mystery that ultimately threatens the human race. Blackburn mixes an assortment of strange characters and apparently unrelated incidents and convincingly integrates them into a tightly structured, compressed, suspenseful narrative that merges modern techno-horror with prehistoric black magic. Compare Straub's *Floating Dragon* [4-285], which attempts a similar combination with considerably less success at about three times the length, and Campbell's *The Hungry Moon* [4-68].

4-41. Our Lady of Pain. Cape, 1974.
The mysterious, self-destructive insanity of three petty thieves stimulates an investigation that leads a newspaper reporter and a female psychiatrist to a hidden treasure, a sadistic plastic surgeon, an egomaniacal, vindictive actress and,

ultimately, to the demonic spirit of Krisia, equally evil sister of the "Blood Countess" Elizabeth Bathori. At some sacrifice of character and setting, *Our Lady of Pain* is probably Blackburn's most tightly structured, exciting book.

Blatty, William Peter, 1928- .
ABOUT: CA, H, SMFL, SFFL, PE, FF

***4-42. The Exorcist**. Harper, 1971; **Legion**. Simon and Schuster, 1983.
Eleven-year-old Regan MacNeil begins to exhibit increasingly weird traits, which puzzle and alarm those around her—her mother, Chris; her psychiatrist-priest, Damien Karras; and others who attempt, in various ways, to deal with her bizarre, obscene behavior. Convinced that Regan is possessed by a demon, Father Karras recruits an exorcist, Father Lankester Merrian, to purge the girl of her demon. One of the most generally popular books of the 1970s, *The Exorcist* is a well-written, skillfully paced novel, with several graphically potent scenes, that touched on then-current generation gap concerns while at the time presenting a traditional good vs. evil conflict in a contemporary context. William Friedkin's 1973 film adaptation, scripted by Blatty, was even more commercially successful than the book. Compare Herbert's *Shrine* [4-146]. The long-awaited sequel to *The Exorcist, Legion,* did not appear until a dozen years later. The primary connection between the two books is police lieutenant Kinderman, who moves from the periphery of *The Exorcist* to center stage in *Legion.* A series of particularly brutal murders convince Kinderman that he is up against some form of supernatural horror. As he tracks the killer, he ponders the ancient questions of guilt and innocence, human depravity and divine indifference. The mystery/horror elements in the novel are generally good and the final twist is clever, but Blatty's expertise in plotting takes a back seat to his metaphysical speculations, which, whatever their merits as theology, are deadly dull in a horror thriller.

4-43. The Ninth Configuration. Harper, 1978.
An earlier version, *Twinkle, Twinkle, Killer Kane!*, was published in 1966. Marine psychiatrist Colonel Hudson Kane takes over treatment of the inmates at Center 18, an isolated facility housing twenty-seven ex-military officers who have developed inexplicable mental aberrations. By his eccentric methods and enigmatic personality, Kane manages to break through the men's bizarre defenses while, at the same time, his own mysterious background and instabilities become increasingly evident, until his true identity and past provoke a violent finale. An original grotesque comedy of reality and illusion, good and evil, guilt and responsibility that is, despite its savage humor, Blatty's most serious, provocative novel. Scripted and directed by Blatty, *The Ninth Configuration* was effectively brought to the screen in 1981 with Stacy Keach as Kane.

Bloch, Robert, 1917- .
ABOUT: WW, GSF, SFW, CA, NE, H, SMFL, SFE, SFFL, RG, TCSF, PE, ESF, FF

4-44. American Gothic. Simon and Schuster, 1974.
During the 1893 World's Fair in Chicago, spunky reporter Crystal Wilson jeop-

ardizes her life when she investigates G. Gordon Gregg, a suave, kindly pharmacist, whom she suspects of being a serial murderer of young women. Loosely based on the career of turn-of-the-century mass murderer H. H. Holmes, *American Gothic* is a fast-paced, suspenseful period mystery with strong overtones of the Gothic romance mitigated by typical Bloch ironies, especially his villain's gruesome taste in keepsakes. Compare Copper's *Necropolis* [4-87] and Oates's *Mysteries of Winterthurn* [4-244].

4-45. Pleasant Dreams. Arkham House, 1960.
Fifteen stories published between 1938 and 1958, including several important items not available in the *Selected Stories* [4-47]. The usual adroit mix of humor, horror and biting irony is present. Humorous standouts are "The Dream-Makers" (1953), a Hollywood story that suggests that life is, indeed, the acting out of a script in which any improvisation risks the wrath of the "cutter," and "The Proper Spirit" (1957), in which aging bon vivant Roland Cavendish, lover and confidant of many great female spirits, utilizes his otherworldly contacts to give his greedy relatives their comeuppance. For straight horror, "The Lighthouse" (1953), Bloch's completed version of Poe's last tale, is more interesting as a historical oddity than as a story, but "The Hungry House" (1951), in which a young couple discover ghostly presences in the mirrors of their newly rented home, and "Sleeping Beauty" (1958), in which a nostalgic tourist's amorous fling turns into an encounter with a larcenous skeleton, are two of his most chilling stories.

***4-46. Psycho**. Simon and Schuster, 1959; **Psycho II**. Whispers Press, 1982.
Psycho is Bloch's most famous and impressive novel of psychological aberration. Mary Crane steals $40,000 and heads toward her boyfriend. En route she stops off—permanently—at the Bates Motel. She is pursued by a private detective, who also encounters Norman Bates's "Mother," and subsequently by her boyfriend, Sam Loomis, and her sister, Lila. A masterful, suspenseful study of paranoia, split personality and homicide. Norman Bates is one of the great characters in the genre. We can identify and sympathize with his agitated confusion and feeble attempts at repressing his hostility, while we are appalled by his actions. Adulation for Alfred Hitchcock's classic film adaptation has obscured the fact that the original concept, characterizations and narrative structure are all present in Bloch's original. *Psycho* is a genre masterpiece which set the pattern for the psychological suspense-horror novel (compare Campbell's *The Face That Must Die* [4-66]). In *Psycho II* Norman escapes from the hospital and heads toward California, where a film about his exploits is being made. Deaths begin to occur on the studio backlot and Norman is—perhaps—seen haunting the area. *Psycho II*—which bears *no* connection or resemblance to the film of the same title—is no masterpiece, but it is a clever, suspenseful mystery thriller with horrific overtones and a nasty, ironic final twist.

***4-47. The Selected Stories of Robert Bloch: I, Final Reckonings; II, Bitter Ends; III, Last Rites**. Underwood-Miller, 1987.
The three volumes span Bloch's entire career, demonstrating his versatility, facility, bleak vision and savage sense of humor. *Final Reckonings* contains thirty-one stories first published between 1939 and 1956. Bloch's sense of horrific

tradition can be seen in "The Skull of the Marquis de Sade" and "The Man Who Collected Poe," two stories in which his protagonist literally comes into contact with the remains of his literary forebears. The latter story is an especially effective Poe pastiche with echoes of "The Fall of the House of Usher" and "The Facts in the Case of M. Valdemar" [2-77]. Bloch's fascination with psychological obsession is illustrated in "The Head Man," in which the official executioner for the Third Reich dooms himself by becoming enamoured of the heads of his victims. "Lucy Comes to Stay" is one of his most interesting pre-*Psycho* explorations of split personality. The ambiguities of persecution and madness are described in "Terror in the Night" as a female patient in frenzied flight from a mental hospital claims she is being kept prisoner. Bloch's more humorously ironic mode is evident in "The Pin," in which an artist meets Death, who turns out to be a middle-aged man who chooses his victims by sticking a pin arbitrarily in a big book of names (compare Bradbury's "The Scythe" [4-52] and Disch's "Death and the Single Girl" [4-99]).

Bitter Ends covers the years 1956 to 1960 with thirty-one stories. The split personality theme is presented even more powerfully in "The Real Best Friend." Psychological aberration is also central to "The Gloating Place," in which an ugly girl becomes a celebrity by claiming she was assaulted by a mysterious man, a fantasy that leads to violence. Other effective murder stories include "Water's Edge," in which a scheming drifter receives ironic justice, "Man with a Hobby," which happens to be mass murder, and "Crime in Rhyme," about a murder mystery writer's penchant for authentic research. One of Bloch's best Hollywood stories is "Terror over Hollywood," in which the narrator finally reveals the terrible secret behind the longevity of great movie stars. Other good Hollywood stories include "Sock Finish" and "Betsy Blake Will Live Forever."

Last Rites includes thirty-nine stories published between 1960 and 1979. Murder, psychological aberration and revenge continue to be Bloch's dominant subjects. In "Method for Murder," a wife plans to kill her husband with the help of a lover—who turns out to be a madman. The ventriloquist protagonist of "The Final Performance" gets revenge on his wife and her lover by killing her and using her body as a dummy to coax a confession out of the lover. "Nina" is a *femme fatale* who resents her lover's wife and baby to the point that her snake-like inheritance intervenes. In "A Toy for Juliette," the historical figure her grandfather brings Juliette as a plaything turns out to be more than she expected. Three of Bloch's best "movie" stories are "The Plot Is the Thing," "Talent" and "The Movie People." In the best of these stories Bloch demonstrates a cleverness, facility with dialogue and adroitness in plotting, especially in his final "punchlines," that has rarely been equalled. The bleakness of his vision is redeemed by the richness of his irony and humor. Occasionally the plotting is forced and the wit strained, but among contemporary horror writers, Bloch has best demonstrated and exploited the proximity of horror and humor. Compare the short fiction of Charles Beaumont [4-26, 4-27], Charles Birkin [4-31–4-34] and Richard Matheson [4-218].

4-48. Strange Eons. Whispers Press, 1978.
An updated Cthulhu pastiche and homage to H. P. Lovecraft. After Albert Keith buys the original "Pickman's Model," he, then his ex-wife, Kate, and finally a

young reporter, Mark Dixon, are swept up in a giant conspiracy that pits the disciples of the Great Old Ones, led by Nyarlathotep himself, against the U.S. government in a struggle to keep Cthulhu and his eldritch horrors from reestablishing their dominance over man. Taking the idea that Lovecraft's stories were disguised fact rather than fiction, Bloch punctuates the narrative with references to particular stories that parallel the action of the novel. The results of this ingenious premise are mixed. The associations stimulated by the references give resonance and solidity to the novel, as well as a nostalgic treat for hard-core Lovecraft fans, but they also contribute to the top-heavy exposition that slows down and blunts the action. Of all the Lovecraft pastiches, *Strange Eons* most emphatically takes the bleak implications of his mythos to their logical conclusion. Compare the mythos stories by Fred Chappell [4-77], Brian Lumley [4-209] and Michael Shea [4-268].

[For other works of this author, see the companion guide to fantasy.]

Block, Lawrence, 1938- .
About: CA, PE

4-49. Ariel. Arbor House, 1980.
A female specter visits Roberta Jardell three times prior to the sudden, unexpected death of her baby son. She is distraught and suspicious, especially of her adopted daughter Ariel, whose behavior becomes increasingly peculiar and sinister. A rekindled romance with an old flame adds the third dangerous ingredient to the volatile mixture that threatens to destroy the Jardell family. The novel moves back and forth between Roberta and the wonderfully strange and ambiguous Ariel, with occasional side-trips with Jeff Channing, the lover, to develop an intriguing, disturbing mystery horror story. *Ariel* is a highly literate, carefully written novel with sensitive, ambiguous characters. One of the best and most subtle of the evil children novels. Compare the novels of John Saul [4-264] and Taylor's *The Godsend* [4-295].

Boileau, Pierre (France), 1906- , and **Thomas Narcejac** (France), 1908- .
About: ESF

4-50. Choice Cuts. Dutton, 1966. Tr. by Brian Rawson of *Et mon tou est un homme*.
An interesting novel by the scriptwriters of *Vertigo* and *Diabolique*. A scientist develops a technique enabling him to transplant any part of the human body from one person to another. He grafts the limbs, organs and head of an executed murderer onto seven victims of life-threatening accidents, and the body parts soon begin developing wills of their own. The idea is not original—it was previously explored in *The Hands of Orlac* [3-164] and its several film versions among other works—but here it is handled uniquely, on a larger scale than before, with as much humor as horror, and the result is a compellingly absurdist novel. The ludicrous science, explained from the objective viewpoint of a trained observer and ostensibly supposed to lend the work verisimilitude, is particularly hilarious. A very sophisticated, blackly funny novel. (B.L.)

Bradbury, Ray, 1920– .
ABOUT: WW, GSF, SFW, F, CA, TCA, NE, H, SMFL, SFE, MF, SFFL, RG, TCSF, PE, ESF, HF

***4-51. Something Wicked This Way Comes.** Simon and Schuster, 1962.
Something wicked is "Cooger and Dark's Pandemonium Shadow Show," which comes to Green Town, Illinois, to lure its citizens to their doom. Initially attracted to the carnival, thirteen-year-old Will Halloway and his best friend, James Nightshade, gradually learn the frightening truth about the carnival and its sinister owners, G. M. Dark and J. C. Cooger: it destroys people by granting them their darkest wishes. *Something Wicked* is a virtual compendium of Bradbury's strengths and weaknesses. It echoes several earlier works, notably its lighter companion piece, *Dandelion Wine* (1957) [F4A-44], and the short story "The Black Ferris" (1948), which, considerably revised and expanded, provides the substance of chapters 18 through 23. Although it may lack the irony and suggestiveness of the book's major literary inspiration, Charles Finney's *The Circus of Dr. Lao* (1935) [F3-137], *Something Wicked* is a provocative, stimulating coming-of-age dark fantasy. An exuberant, inventive, colorful book, written in a somewhat ornate, highly charged prose style that some critics have found overblown, but which others consider beautifully lyrical. Filmed in 1983 from a script by Bradbury with Jason Robards as Charlie. Also annotated as F4A-45.

***4-52. The Stories of Ray Bradbury.** Knopf, 1980.
One hundred short stories spanning Bradbury's career from its beginnings through the 1970s. The usual mix of science fiction, horror stories, fantasies, magic realism, wit, whimsy, nostalgia and lyricism. Approximately one-third of the items can be properly categorized as dark fantasies, including stories from *Dark Carnival* [3-34] and *The October Country* (1955), his best collections in the genre. The horror stories range from the playfully grotesque to the overtly horrific. At his most fanciful Bradbury plays with traditional horror creatures—vampires, succubi, ghouls and the like—in the weird family that animates "Homecoming," "Uncle Einar" and "The April Witch." Many of the horror stories look at the dark side of things that he celebrates in other writings. For example, small-town America, eulogized in *Dandelion Wine* [F4A-44], becomes a horrible trap for Mars colonizers in "Mars Is Heaven." The evil side of childhood is exposed in "The Veldt, "The Small Assassin" and "The Playground." Humor often gives an extra grotesque twist to Bradbury's images, as in "The Jar," where a rustic, irritated at his wife's infidelity and mockery, replaces the "thing" in a jar purchased from a freak show with her head, or in "The Skeleton," where a man obsessed with the notion that his skeleton symbolizes his mortality succeeds in getting rid of it. Most horrific are those stories that lack humor, lyricism or sentimentality to mute the bleak vision. In "October Game," one of Bradbury's most disturbing and visceral stories, a husband uses his daughter to get a terrible vengeance on his wife. In "The Crowd," a man, obsessed by the idea that a crowd of the dead gather to observe traffic accidents and recruit specters, learns the truth of his delusion. "The Next in Line" is a less fantastic, more chilling development of a similar situation. A woman visits the mummies in a small Mexican town and, despite her husband's assurances, becomes increasingly convinced that she is "next in line." Told in clean, sparse language without Bradbury's usual lyricism,

"The Next in Line" has the anguished foreboding of a Robert Aickman tale. While Bradbury's dark fantasies make up only a fraction of his oeuvre, they number some of his most powerful, disturbing and beautiful stories. Compare the short fiction of Charles Beaumont [4-26, 4-27] and Richard Matheson [4-218].

[For other works of this author, see the companion guide to fantasy.]

Brennan, Joseph Payne, 1918- .

ABOUT: WW, CA, H, SFFL, PE, ESF

4-53. The Casebook of Lucius Leffing. Macabre House, 1973; **The Chronicles of Lucius Leffing**. Donald M. Grant, 1977.

Two collections of short stories featuring psychic sleuth Leffing and his confidant "Brennan," which originally appeared in such publications as *Macabre, Mike Shayne's Mystery Magazine* and *Alfred Hitchcock's Mystery Magazine*. The stories follow the formula of the classical detective story: the problem (a crime, a haunting) is presented to the detective, who apprehends the guilty party and/or solves the problem, and then explains his solution to the awestruck Brennan. Leffing specializes in haunted houses, although he does encounter a variety of malevolent forces, both supernatural and routinely criminal. Leffing, passionately Victorian by habit and inclination, laments constantly to Brennan about the contemporary world as he solves cases that have a distinctly old-fashioned flavor. The result is a kind of cozy, deliberately archaic tale reminiscent of Seabury Quinn's Jules de Grandin stories [3-163] or even those of Hodgson's Carnacki [3-89] and Blackwood's John Silence [3-27]. Diverting and entertaining, if not particularly horrific.

4-54. Nine Horrors and a Dream. Arkham House, 1958.

Brennan's first published collection. The stories are simple, direct and clean, usually with deft, ironic twists, such as the ending of "Levitation," in which a hypnotist dies of a heart attack in the middle of a performance. Other notable short entries include "The Hunt," a powerful exercise in mounting paranoia, and "The Mail for Juniper Hill," featuring a letter carrier who takes the slogan "the mail must go through" a little too far. The most important in the volume, however, are his two most famous stories, "Slime" and "Canavan's Back Yard." "Slime" features a primordial black mass that is loosed on mankind by an underwater explosion. It emerges to eat everything in its path in the best tradition of 1950s monster movies. "Canavan's Back Yard," which turns ordinary people into wild beasts, may be an entryway to Hell.

4-55. The Shapes of Midnight. Berkley, 1980.

Twelve stories first published between 1953 and 1973, plus a laudatory introduction by Stephen King. In addition to the classics "Slime" and "Canavan's Back Yard," the collection features "Diary of a Werewolf"—a self-explanatory title—(compare to Case's *The Cell* [4-75]); "The Corpse of Charlie Rull," which, reanimated by electronic waste from a government project, ravages the countryside; "The Willow Platform," a Lovecraftian story about the sad fate of a village deadbeat who summons forces he can neither understand nor control; "Disappearance," about a brotherly feud that ends in a gruesome discovery; and, most original and chilling, "The Horror at Chilton Castle," in which the narrator learns the terrible truth behind the legend of the castle's "hidden room." Simple, direct and vivid, Brennan's short stories evoke the flavor and energy of the pulp adventure-horror tale without its frequent crudities.

Brookes, Owen (pseud. of **Dulan Friar Whilburton Barber**) (U.K.), 1940- .
About: CA, H, PE

4-56. Deadly Communion. Holt, Rinehart, 1984.
Made especially vulnerable by the collapse of his marriage and the general chaos of his personal life, Steven Cole is subjected to a psychic intrusion by a serial murderer of young boys. Aided by a compassionate psychic researcher/lover, Cole attempts to control and utilize his psychic capacities to track the killer before he, Cole, disintegrates into violence himself. A superior psychic thriller, especially good in delineating the complex, painful relationships between Cole, his estranged wife, teenaged son and psychic lover. Compare Harris's *Red Dragon* [4-135], Herbert's *Moon* [4-143], King's *The Dead Zone* [4-165], Koontz's *The Vision* [4-192] and Matheson's *A Stir of Echoes* [4-220].

4-57. Inheritance. Holt, Rinehart, 1980.
Regina acts as a foster mother to a group of teenagers possessing extraordinary psychic talents. Peter, a boy with no apparent extrasensory skills, is slowly drawn into the group and becomes the focal point for a mysterious conspiracy that threatens him and his mother, as well as the other members of the remarkable group. To save himself and the others, Peter must unravel the mystery of his past and discover the talent—if any—that he possesses. A suspenseful, ingenious mix of SF, mystery and horror. Although *Inheritance* definitely belongs under the dark fantasy umbrella, the psi-talented youngsters are reminiscent of the group in Theodore Sturgeon's science fiction classic *More Than Human* (1953).

Burke, John (U.K.), 1922- .
About: WW, SFFL

4-58. The Devil's Footsteps. Coward, McCann, 1976; **The Black Charade**. Coward, McCann, 1977; **Ladygrove**. Coward, McCann, 1978.
Three novels featuring psychic detective Dr. Alexander Caspian. Ostensibly a stage magician (Count Caspar), Caspian possesses real psychic powers as well as formidable analytical abilities, which enable him, in partnership with his wife, Brownwen, a professional photographer, to deal with a variety of malevolent threats. In *The Devil's Footsteps*, he journeys to the rural village of Hexney, where he meets Brownwen for the first time and encounters a community caught up in the fervor of a primitive religion. Caspian must put his psychic powers into direct combat with an ancient demonic force. Compare Tryon's *Harvest Home* [4-305]. In *The Black Charade*, Caspian and Brownwen, now married, investigate the peculiar behavior of a young girl and are drawn into conflict with Ilona, a mysterious, sinister female whose psychic abilities and knowledge of the secret arts may exceed Caspian's. In *Ladygrove*, Caspian and Brownwen battle an

ancient curse at Ladygrove Manor that threatens a close friend and her unborn child. The Caspian novels are lively and entertaining, even if they fall rather easily into the usual young-girl-in-jeopardy formula. Caspian is a convincing, colorful psychic detective and the Caspian-Brownwen partnership works well. Compare to Mann's "Gees" series [3-137].

Buzzati, Dino (Italy), 1906–1972.

ABOUT: CA, PE, ESF

4-59. Catastrophe: The Strange Stories of Dino Buzzati. Calder and Boyars, 1965. Tr. by Judith Landry and Cynthia Jolly.

Fifteen stories published between 1949 and 1958. All except the disappointing final story, "The Scala Scare," are quite short, a perfect length for expressing Buzzati's bizarre, ironic, pessimistic vision. In his best sketches Buzzati pictures ordinary people in a very mundane world that suddenly collapses into chaos in a way that seems both shocking and inevitable. Sometimes this destruction is the result of accident, as in "The Collapse of the Baliverna," where the narrator inadvertently pulls a small metal spike out of a wall, initiating the collapse of a huge, people-filled building. Sometimes the horror comes from other people, as in "Just the Very Thing They Wanted," where a young girl's need for a quick dip in an outdoor fountain sets off a violent mob. And sometimes the horror just drops on the victims from the unknown, as in "Catastrophe," where the riders of a modern high-speed train notice that the people outside are fleeing in terror from their train's destination. These short, highly charged, understated tales take on the power of terrifying parables in a manner reminiscent of Kafka. Compare also Topor's *Joko's Anniversary* [4-302].

Cady, Jack, 1932– .

ABOUT: CA, PE

4-60. The Jonah Watch. Arbor House, 1981.

A spectral sea novel based, Cady states in his "Author's note," on personal experience: "Each incident in this story actually occurred in one form or another." The crew of the Coast Guard cutter *Adrian* is plagued by the ghost of the ship's "Jonah," or bearer of bad luck, the former engineer who was lost at sea. Tensions among the crew members increase as the hazards of duty, coupled with real or imagined encounters with the supernatural, turn the crew in on themselves as they hunt the "Jonah" in their midst. Meticulously written, with sensitive characterizations and a pervasive atmosphere of dread, *The Jonah Watch* is perhaps the best nautical horror story since the heyday of William Hope Hodgson [3-88–3-92].

***4-61. The Well**. Arbor House, 1980.

Prior to having it leveled for a highway, developer John Tracker returns with his fiancée to the mansion that has housed three generations of the Tracker family. To save both of them from the diabolical powers of the house, he must avoid a series of deadly booby traps planted by his great-grandfather, come to terms with the Tracker family's dark past, deal with the ghosts of his grandparents and learn the truth about his father's life and death. A superior scary ghost story in the classical tradition featuring a most original haunted house. Compare Jackson's *The Haunting of Hill House* [4-155], King's *The Shining* [4-173] and Matheson's *Hell House* [4-216].

Calder-Marshall, Arthur (U.K.), 1908- .

ABOUT: CA, SFFL

4-62. The Scarlet Boy. Rupert Hart-Davis, 1961.

When George Grantley agrees to negotiate the purchase of a nearby estate for an old school friend, he inadvertently evokes the ghost of a childhood playmate who committed suicide. Grantley is forced to reexamine the meaning of his own past, his relationship to the dead boy and his family, and his present relationships, beliefs and religious faith in order to rescue his friend's daughter from a similar self-destructive act. A classic ghost story in a strict Christian context. Calder-Marshall's careful, leisurely, apparently diffuse narrative gradually narrows to a powerful climax that is emotionally gripping and thematically stimulating, even though the forces of evil are vanquished with disappointing ease. A more classical treatment of themes also developed in Adams's *The Girl in a Swing* [4-2] and Amis's *The Green Man* [4-11].

Campbell, Ramsey (U.K.), 1946- .

ABOUT: WW, SFW, CA, H, SMFL, MF, SFFL, RG, PE, FF

***4-63. Dark Companions**. Macmillan, 1982.

Twenty-one stories, all written between 1973 and 1982, with the exception of "Napier Court" (1967). Campbell's third collection amplifies and develops themes and techniques of his earlier short stories without the agitated surface and extreme compression that mar some of his earlier efforts. In the typical Campbell short story, an innocuous individual finds him or herself gradually cornered or smothered by an increasingly bizarre, threatening, but essentially mundane environment and/or by his or her own obsessive, irrational, intensifying fears until a final, sudden confrontation demoralizes and/or destroys the character completely. The best of the stories include "Macintosh Willy," about the ghost of an old drunk who takes revenge for a young boy's cruelty; "Baby," one of Campbell's most viscerally ghoulish stories, about a derelict who brutally murders a bag lady and is then pursued by her most unusual familiar; "The Chimney," in which a young boy encounters, not Santa Claus, but a burned "thing" from the fireplace—which may or may not be his own father; and two tales that would have fit neatly into the pages of an EC comic book: "Call First," in which a librarian's curiosity leads him into a most unpleasant confrontation; and "Heading Home," in which the severed head of a "mad scientist" struggles valiantly to rejoin its body. Campbell occupies a middle ground among contemporary British horror short story writers, more radical than Robert Aickman [4-3–4-9], but less extreme than Clive Barker [4-20, 4-21].

4-64. Demons by Daylight. Arkham House, 1973.

Fifteen stories divided into three sections: *Nightmares, Errol Undercliffe: A Trib-*

ute and *Relationships*. Except for the Undercliffe stories, the volume demonstrates Campbell's progress from the early Lovecraft pastiches to his own unique, disturbing style. Noteworthy stories include "Potential," in which a conventional but curious young man, enticed into a mid-1960s counterculture ritual, unleashes his own dark potential; "The Sentinels," in which two couples make a nighttime visit to "the sentinels," a group of oddly shaped and peculiarly arranged rock formations atop a hill—which may or may not come to life and surround them; and "The Telephones," a sexually charged *doppelgänger* story about a man pursued for an assignation from phone booth to phone booth by a voice that may be his own.

4-65. The Doll Who Ate His Mother. Bobbs-Merrill, 1976.
Four individuals—an elementary schoolteacher, a writer of sensationalized crime stories, a middle-aged theater owner and a street actor—form an unlikely team to track down a psychotic killer with cannibalistic tendencies. An essentially realistic suspense story with some supernatural trappings, Campbell's first novel is well paced and has vivid, believable characters and sharp details, but is marred by some awkwardness in handling the supernaturalism, an ambivalence toward the book's villain and a rushed ending.

4-66. The Face That Must Die. Wyndham/Star, 1979.
Hardcover edition with previously deleted text restored and an autobiographical essay, "At the Back of My Mind: A Guided Tour," published by Scream/Press, 1982.
John Horridge, a homophobic paranoic, is convinced by a police "Identi-kit" picture that Roy Craig, a gentle, innocent homosexual, is a serial murderer of young boys. As Horridge begins stalking his prey, a young couple, Cathy and her drug-taking husband, Peter, are gradually drawn into the madman's gruesome plot. A thoroughly chilling book with one of the most disturbing and convincing characters in the genre. The paranoid landscape of the 1970s urban Great Britain has rarely been presented with such frightening precision and intensity. Compare Bloch's *Psycho* [4-46].

4-67. The Height of the Scream. Arkham House, 1976.
Eighteen stories (two repeats from *Demons by Daylight*) that explore Campbell's grotesque, obsessional, paranoic landscape with great subtlety, precision and intensity. Especially notable are "The Scar," a contemporary *doppelgänger* story; "The Dark Show," about a hypnotic and apparently demonic rock group; "Missing," in which a progressively unstable narrator becomes involved with a female who may have killed her husband in a voodoo ritual and who may even be a ghost; "The Cellars," one of Campbell's earliest stories, in which a fungus gradually transforms a young explorer of London's catacombs into a blob of white stuff while his female companion watches in horror; "The Height of the Scream," in which the protagonist develops the bad habit of foreseeing his friends' deaths; and "Litter" and "Ash," similar stories in which the protagonists are progressively trapped by the debris mentioned in the titles.

4-68. The Hungry Moon. Macmillan, 1986.
An American evangelist, Godwin Mann, enters the small town of Moonwell and quickly imposes his rigidly disciplined, fanatical brand of neo-puritanism on the

citizenry. He challenges the "thing" at the bottom of the pit and unleashes forces latent since the time of the druids. As the religiosity of the citizens of the isolated, darkened town becomes increasingly hysterical, a small group of skeptical citizens, led by Diana Kramer, an elementary schoolteacher with visionary insights, searches for a defense against the evil that threatens to engulf everything. A well-structured, carefully paced novel that gradually intensifies to an exciting conclusion, *The Hungry Moon* is much more conventional than the typical Campbell novel. The menace is entirely external, good and evil are clearly defined, and heroism wins a clear and unambiguous victory. The novel is most impressive in Campbell's delineation of the progression from religious dogmatism to fanaticism to violence-tinged hysteria. Compare Blackburn's *For Fear of Little Men* [4-40].

4-69. Incarnate. Macmillan, 1983.
Five very different individuals take part in an experiment in prophetic dreaming, an experiment that is abruptly terminated for ambiguous, sinister reasons. Eleven years later, each of them experiences a frightening resumption of their nightmare worlds. Campbell alternates chapters between characters as their frightening visions become increasingly vivid and threatening, and their conviction grows that there is some conscious, malevolent power guiding these nightmares to a terrible end. *Incarnate* is the novel in which Campbell takes the reality/illusion theme to its fullest, most powerful and enigmatic conclusion. A brilliant book.

4-70. The Influence. Macmillan, 1988.
An old woman, Queenie, dies and leaves her huge Victorian mansion to her nièce Alisoun. Soon after Alisoun, her husband, Derrick, and their seven-year-old daughter, Rowan, move in, they begin to have premonitions of danger, especially to Rowan. Then follow the mysterious deaths of two other relatives, and the appearance of a little girl named Vicky—which happens to be Queenie's real name. Alisoun, a woman with a history of emotional problems, must learn how to deal with the malevolent spirit of her aunt if she is to save her daughter from a terrifying fate. A more conventional horror story than usual for Campbell, *The Influence* is a carefully constructed, suspenseful narrative with a scary climax. This is an elaborate, sophisticated variation on the possession notion also found in Stephen King's "Gramma" [4-174].

4-71. The Nameless. Macmillan, 1981.
Barbara Waugh, a literary agent, receives a pleading phone call from her daughter Angela—whom Barbara believed had been murdered seven years earlier. Helped by a boyfriend, an underground reporter and psychic, she sets out to track down and rescue her daughter. The search brings her into contact with a vicious satanic cult reminiscent of the Manson Family. Essentially a thriller with strong supernatural overtones, *The Nameless* evokes an atmosphere of corruption and decadence that is most unnerving, although the novel lacks the psychological intensity and, except in its strange finale, the imaginative flights that make *To Wake the Dead* [4-73] so impressive.

4-72. Obsession. Macmillan, 1986.
Four teenagers—Peter, Steve, Jimmy and Robin—answer an advertisement that promises "WHATEVER YOU MOST NEED I DO." They each submit a request, which is

fulfilled, but in a disturbing way. Twenty-five years later, as adults, they must pay for their answered prayers. Campbell's variation on the "Monkey's Paw" theme is essentially a psychological study, especially of Peter, the most disturbed and extreme of the four, with a supernaturalism that is at best ambiguous. An intriguing, stimulating novel, but lacking Campbell's usual horrific bite.

***4-73. To Wake the Dead**. Millington, 1980. U.S. edition, with an alternate epilogue, retitled *The Parasite*. Macmillan, 1980.
As a small girl, Rose Tierney suffers a traumatic "cosmic rape." Grown to adulthood, she has apparently suppressed the incident and developed into a successful film critic and wife. Her stable life-style is disoriented, however, when, after a mugging, she finds herself developing psychic abilities, especially a capacity for astral projection. After her initial euphoria over discovering her new powers subsides, Rose finds herself pursued by bizarre external and internal forces: a mysterious bald man, hallucinatory visions, a sinister psychiatrist, an occult society, increasingly frightening out-of-body travel and, most terrifying of all, an internal "parasite" which may be the spirit of Peter Grace, a black magician. The novel gains additional resonance by a running thematic association between Grace and Adolf Hitler. Opinions differ as to which "Epilogue" is preferable, but both give the book a bitterly ironic final twist. A truly scary book that brilliantly balances supernatural horror with psychological disintegration. Rose Tierney is a powerfully sympathetic heroine-victim caught up in a frighteningly believable dilemma. The tensions between reality and illusion and between the mundane and the horrific are manipulated with surgical precision. One of the classics of contemporary dark fantasy. Compare Levin's *Rosemary's Baby* [4-206].

Cantrell, Lisa W.

4-74. The Manse. Tor, 1987.
The Manse won the 1988 Bram Stoker Award for Best First Novel, and it is indeed an admirable first effort. In the North Carolina town of Merrillville, the Jaycees put together an annual haunted house at a local mansion. The mansion is really haunted, however, and the power of the house increases each year, gradually affecting the entire town. Cantrell's characters are believable and well-motivated, and the hints of real horror intercut with the intentional scares of the Jaycees are quite effective. There are signs of strain—the explanation of the house's evil is awkwardly handled through the monologue of an old woman, and Cantrell unfortunately opts for a pyrotechnic "Poltergeist" ending—but the novel is an assured debut. (B.L.)

Case, David, 1937- .

About: WW, CA, SFFL

***4-75. The Cell, and Other Tales of Horror**. Macdonald, 1969.
Three novellas. The protagonist of *The Cell* admits to being a werewolf who, under the spell of his disease, may have been responsible for at least three deaths. The question whether he is a supernatural monster or a homicidal psychotic is never answered. In *The Hunter*, a retired big game hunter is forced to test his

rusty skills as well as his ethical standards and assumptions in tracking a gruesome, possibly supernatural killer on the moors of Dartmoor. The Dead End explores the relationship between a renegade scientist and a dangerous "missing link" in the isolated mountains of Terra del Fuego. Three chilling, evocative, thought-provoking novellas told with great precision, economy and intensity. Compare *The Cell* to Tessier's *The Nightwalker* [4-297] and *The Hunter* to Harris's *Red Dragon* [4-135].

4-76. Fengriffen: A Chilling Tale. Macdonald, 1971.
Dr. Pope, a turn-of-the-century psychologist, is summoned by Charles Fengriffen to the family estate to treat his pregnant wife's erratic, hostile, mysterious behavior. There he discovers a family curse provoked by a demented ancestor; a grotesque, sinister woodsman; and, perhaps, an otherworldly demon. A vintage Gothic story told with the streamlined plotting and dramatic immediacy of a contemporary work. One of the first and best of recent horror stories dealing with the incubi/succubi theme. Filmed as *And Now the Screaming Starts* (1973).

Chappell, Fred, 1936- .
About: CA, PE

4-77. Dagon. St. Martin's, 1968.
Minister/scholar Peter Leland, accompanied by his wife, Sheila, spends the summer at the southern farm inherited from his grandparents in order to write a monograph on "Remnant Pagan Forces in American Puritanism." His researches lead him to discover that his grandparents were not the simple, hardworking Puritans he had thought, that the squatters on his property are not ordinary backwoods rustics and, most important, that the ancient, obscure gods of his studies are actually alive, well and hungry—for him. Perhaps the most artistically successful of the contemporary Lovecraft pastiches because it focuses, not on any grand, monstrous conspiracy, but on one individual as he is slowly, painfully drawn into the world of the dark gods. Compare the pastiches by Robert Bloch [4-48], Brian Lumley [4-209] and Michael Shea [4-268].

Charnas, Suzy McKee, 1939- .
About: CA, NE, SFE, MF, TCSF, PE

4-78. The Vampire Tapestry. Simon and Schuster, 1980.
Five linked stories about Dr. Edward L. Weyland, Ph.D., noted anthropologist and the last living vampire. Told from a variety of perspectives, the novel is more interested in human reactions to the undead than in vampirism itself. Weyland is a fascinating creature, inhuman yet cultivated, even noble, as he attempts to satisfy his needs, evade exposure and, most dangerous of all, avoid developing a sympathetic relationship with the "herd" he must feed on. The most intense moments in the book occur when the hunter becomes the hunted—psychologically, by a female psychotherapist who, after discovering his true nature, falls in love with him; and physically, by a self-styled Satanist, who makes him a captive. Like Rice in *Interview with a Vampire* [4-250], Charnas uses the vampire as a measure of what it is to be human. A generally restrained novel with only one

deserved scene of graphic violence. Eschewing the usual paraphernalia—aside from his blood diet and longevity, Weyland has none of the traditional vampiric traits, capacities or weaknesses—Charnas has produced an original, subtle, highly provocative reinvention of the vampire myth. Compare also Somtow's *Vampire Junction* [4-278] and Strieber's *The Hunger* [4-290].

[For other works of this author, see the companion guide to fantasy.]

Chetwynd-Hayes, R(onald) (U.K.), 1919- .

ABOUT: WW, CA, SFFL, PE

4-79. The King's Ghost. Kimber, 1985. U.S. title: *The Grange*.
The King's Ghost is an unlikely horror novel. A page-turning romance in the tradition of Sir Walter Scott, it concerns the adventures of a noble bastard in the late sixteenth century who is hired to oversee the day-to-day operation of Clavering Grange, a haunted English estate. Chetwynd-Hayes has written the novel in a unique first-person style which retains the flavor of the period while jettisoning some of the more cumbersome verbiage and awkward sentence structure of the era. The novel is at once easy to read and superbly evocative, filled with sly digs at the mores and manners of the English nobility. Not as literary or original as Süskind's *Perfume* [4-293], *The King's Ghost* is nonetheless an admirable historical horror novel. (B.L.)

4-80. A Quiver of Ghosts. Kimber, 1984.
A prolific writer, R. Chetwynd-Hayes has received limited critical attention despite publishing over twenty collections of supernatural stories and a half dozen novels. A possible reason for this neglect is his tendency not to take his stories seriously; there is frequently a misplaced strand of humor that lessens their effect. But among his works are a number of serious stories with genuinely original ideas and treatments. *A Quiver of Ghosts* offers a good, representative selection of fourteen shorter works, including "The Ghost Who Limped," which is possibly his best. (M.A.)

4-81. Tales of Darkness. Kimber, 1981.
Chetwynd-Hayes is often at his best in longer stories where he can build tension into his narrative. *Tales of Darkness* contains five long stories, including "Tomorrow's Ghost," one of the first of his many stories about the multi-haunted Clavering Grange. (M.A.)

Christopher, John (pseud. of **Samuel Christopher Youd**) (U.K.), 1922- .

ABOUT: CA, NE, SFE, SFFL, TCSF, ESF

4-82. The Possessors. Simon and Schuster, 1964.
A small group of skiers in an isolated Swiss chalet are taken over one by one by alien life forms, who then use their bodies to trick the remaining survivors. Similar in concept to Finney's *The Body Snatchers* [4-116] but lacking its scope, *The Possessors* gains intensity from the claustrophobic situation of being snowbound and isolated with monsters. See also King's *The Shining* [4-173].

Cook, Robin, 1940- .

ABOUT: CA, PE

4-83. Coma. Little, Brown, 1977.
When medical student Susan Wheeler discovers that comatose patients are being used to supply a black market organ bank, she attempts to expose the medical conspiracy before she, too, is made a victim of it. Although Michael Crichton (writing as John Lange) had published the medical thrillers *Drug of Choice* and *A Case of Need* in 1968, it was Cook's *Coma* that established the formula for the medical horror story that led to the flood of such books, including Cook's own *Brain* (1981), *Fever* (1982) and *Godplayer* (1983), as well as similar books by Michael Palmer (*The Sisterhood*, 1982), Michael Stewart (*Monkey Shines*, 1983) and David Shobin (*The Unborn*, 1981). For a savagely dark-humored approach to the subgenre, see Boileau and Narcejac's *Choice Cuts* [4-50]. Crichton scripted and directed the successful film version of *Coma* in 1978.

Copper, Basil (U.K.), 1924- .

ABOUT: WW, GSF, SMFL, SFFL, RG, PE, ESF

4-84. From Evil's Pillow. Arkham House, 1973.
Five stories. The title is taken from Baudelaire's *Les Fleurs du mal* (1857): "From evil's pillow/Thrice great Satan smiles." The first of Copper's works to appear in the United States, this collection demonstrates the verbal precision, meticulous attention to detail, mastery of tone and implication, and adroit narrative structuring that have established him as one of Great Britain's masters of the genre. The most impressive of the stories are "The Gossips," in which a supernaturally indestructible statue of three women, with an evil, cursed past, spreads disaster wherever it is taken; "The Grey House," a haunted house tale which both exploits and rejuvenates the traditional paraphernalia of the story type; and the strikingly original "Amber Tint," about a haunted print of the movie *The Cabinet of Dr. Caligari*, which integrates disturbing new scenes into the film and then gradually exerts a malevolent power over the two unfortunate film buffs who have acquired the print.

4-85. The Great White Space. Robert Hale, 1974.
Professor Clark Ashton Scarsdale leads the Great Northern Expedition into the bowels of the earth in search of the "Great White Space" and the door to another universe, where they encounter a powerful alien race of Slug-Creatures. A deliberate echo of Poe's *The Narrative of Arthur Gordon Pym* [2-76], Doyle's Dr. Challenger books [3-64] and Lovecraft's *At the Mountains of Madness* [3-132], *The Great White Space* has the old-fashioned, exaggerated excitement of a pulp magazine adventure story.

4-86. The House of the Wolf. Arkham House, 1983.
A fine period horror story, rich in atmospheric detail, slow and calculated in its plotting, with carefully modulated suspense and believable characters. The mystery, as well as the horror, is developed adroitly, but the final revelations, coming from a secret report by a minor character, seem contrived. Compare Grant's *Dark Cry of the Moon* [4-128].

4-87. Necropolis. Arkham House, 1980.
Detective Clyde Beatty's investigation into the death of the father of beautiful Angela Meredith puts him on the trail of the sinister Dr. Horace Couchman, who leads him to mystery and intrigue in London and finally to the catacombs beneath Brookwood Cemetery. Copper demonstrates his skill at rendering period atmosphere and intricate plotting in this well-developed, if occasionally slow, mystery-melodrama. Compare Bloch's *American Gothic* [4-44], Hambly's *Those Who Hunt the Night* [4-133] and Oates's *Mysteries of Winterthurn* [4-244].

Cowper, Richard (pseud. of **John Middleton Murry, Jr.**) (U.K.), 1926- .

ABOUT: SFE

4-88. Shades of Darkness. Kerosina, 1986.
Although considered more a science fiction writer, Cowper has written several fantasies as well as this full-length ghost story. A journalist returns to a remote seaside bungalow in East Anglia to write a novel about his African experiences. The house had once been owned by a woman tried for murder in the 1950s in Kenya during the days of the Mau-Mau. Her spirit remains attached to the house through an old dress. Cowper is a skillful and tender writer and the supernatural elements are suppressed, with only a few moments of heightened tension. The result rather suggests a modern-day M. R. James (whose "Oh, Whistle, and I'll Come to You, My Lad" [3-108] has similar bleak seashore scenes) writing "The Beckoning Fair One" [3-155]. (M.A.)

Coyne, John, 1937- .

ABOUT: CA, PE, FF

4-89. Hobgoblin. Putnam, 1981.
Scott Gardiner, a teenaged boy addicted to "Hobgoblin," a fantasy role-playing game, is further destabilized by a series of traumatic events: the sudden death of his father, the move with his mother into Ballycastle, an ancient Irish mansion rebuilt on the Hudson River, and his transfer to Flat Rock High School, where he is scorned and humiliated. At the same time, his mother's investigation into the history of the mansion uncovers dark secrets about its late owner and activates long-suppressed evil forces. Everything comes together in a terrifying showdown when the senior class holds a "Hobgoblin" dance at Ballycastle. An adroitly plotted, cleanly written, rapidly paced book, with sharp, sympathetic characters. The ending is vivid and intense, but a bit excessive and contrived.

4-90. The Shroud. Berkley, 1983.
Like John Farris, John Coyne does not get the attention he deserves. His novels consistently sell well (though not as spectacularly as those of King or Koontz), his work is always literate and intelligent, yet he does not receive the critical respect and recognition accorded to many less well selling, less talented writers. *The Shroud* is a fine example of Coyne at his best. The novel concerns the disappearance of homeless New York street people, and the plight of a young priest who has reason to believe that their disappearances are the result of supernatural

events to which he is connected. A very human horror story, peopled with believable, likable characters, *The Shroud* is at once an interesting horror/mystery, a convincing plea for greater political activism and a criticism of the social agenda of organized religion. (B.L.)

Cunningham, Jere

4-91. The Abyss. Wyndham, 1981.
A flawed but interesting novel whose parts are greater than their sum. An old coal mine is reopened in a dying Appalachian town and initially brings prosperity to the community. As the miners dig deeper, however, the town starts to change: water turns to blood, streets are overgrown with strange thorny plants, and the people degenerate into violence and decadence. There is a definite problem with the time transitions within the novel, and a subplot involving an astrophysics student from Massachusetts seems oddly out of place, but the disintegration of the town, the occurrences at the mine and the atmosphere of creeping surrealism are all expertly handled. Unfortunately, the disparate elements of the plot are never tied together effectively and the denouement is far too protracted. Although less ambitious than *Floating Dragon* [4-285], *The Abyss* is similar in many ways to Straub's novel and suffers from many of the same weaknesses. (B.L.)

Daniels, Les, 1943- .
ABOUT: CA, PE

4-92. The Black Castle. Scribner's, 1978; **The Silver Skull**. Scribner's, 1979; **Citizen Vampire**. Scribner's, 1981; **Yellow Fog**. Donald M. Grant, 1986.
Four novels featuring the aristocratic, morally ambiguous vampire Don Sebastian de Villanueva. *The Black Castle* takes place during the Spanish Inquisition (1496) when Don Sebastian clashes with his ambitious, depraved brother, Diego, the Grand Inquisitor, over the fate of Margarita de Mendoza, a beautiful witch. In *The Silver Skull*, Don Sebastian is brought back to life by an Aztec priestess. They form an alliance against Cortez's destruction of the Aztecs, finally merging in death while attempting to summon the god Smoking Mirror to their cause. In *Citizen Vampire*, Don Sebastian comes to Paris at the height of the French Revolution. Against a backdrop of carnage, he engages in a vampiric conspiracy as two aristocratic females, one a witch, the other a vampire, pursue an aristocratic young man. In *Yellow Fog*, Don Sebastian, posing as Sebastian Newcastle, a medium, becomes involved with a young girl fascinated with the afterlife, even to the point of courting death, and her hedonistic fiancé. Don Sebastian is a traditional larger-than-life Byronic hero-villain, a "fiend with a conscience," as one character puts it. Aristocratic and savage, Don Sebastian is nevertheless horrified by the monstrous behavior of the humans he encounters. The stories are vivid, fast-paced and—except for *Yellow Fog*—very gory. The characters are sharply drawn, if stereotypical. Daniels's ability to create convincing historical epochs with a minimum of period detail and paraphernalia is his most impressive talent. Compare Kast's *The Vampires of Alfama* [4-159] and Yarbro's Saint Germain series [4-340].

Davies, Hugh Sykes (U.K.), 1909–1984?
About: CA, SFE, ESF

4-93. The Papers of Andrew Melmoth. Methuen, 1960.
Reclusive, enigmatic scientist Andrew Melmoth gradually detaches himself from friends and lover as he pursues his researches into the effects of nuclear radiation on rats. Written in a low-key, detached, almost deliberately archaic style, *The Papers of Andrew Melmoth* is more thoughtfully disturbing than overtly horrific. Its initial chapters seem slow and indirect and the characters subdued and distant, but the patient reader is rewarded with a provocative, original variation on a common SF/horror theme of the 1950s. For a more typical horror story treatment of a similar idea, see Herbert's *The Rats* [4-144].

DeFelitta, Frank, 1921– .
About: CA

4-94. Audrey Rose. Putnam, 1975.
Like Konvitz's *The Sentinel* [4-185], *Audrey Rose* was an enormously popular horror novel of the 1970s, which was made into a fairly successful movie. Also like *The Sentinel,* DeFelitta's novel has received very little respect from the horror community. Part of this is deserved: *Audrey Rose* is far too long, and the horror in the work is relegated to almost secondary status. But DeFelitta is a competent writer, and his story of a woman who discovers that her daughter is the reincarnation of the daughter of another man is undeniably powerful. *Audrey Rose* is a horror novel for people who don't like horror, but it is well done, and DeFelitta deserves credit for helping to bring horror to a broader, more mainstream audience. A sequel, *For Love of Audrey Rose,* appeared in 1982. Compare Ehrlich's *The Reincarnation of Peter Proud* [4-103], Hallahan's *The Search for Joseph Tully* [4-132] and Stewart's *The Possession of Joel Delaney* [4-284]. (B.L.)

4-95. Golgotha Falls: An Assault on the Fourth Dimension. Simon and Schuster, 1984.
Golgotha Falls combines the preoccupation with religious mysticism evident in the Audrey Rose books with that of parapsychology (*The Entity,* 1978) in DeFelitta's most ambitious novel. The first and most interesting half of *Golgotha Falls* focuses on the personal conflict between two humanistic parapsychologists from Harvard, who want to study a seemingly possessed church, and a mystical Jesuit priest, as they encounter, record and apparently defeat the evil forces that permeate not only the church, but also the entire town of Golgotha Falls. But midway through the book, *Golgotha Falls* becomes an eschatological horror story focusing on the Pope, Francis Xavier, an odd combination of millennialist mystic and solid peasant. The fate of the universe comes down to a conflict between the Pope and the forces of evil that have retaken the church. This ambitious book has much to recommend it, especially to readers sympathetic to its themes, but DeFelitta's intentions exceed his ability, and the novel finally seems more pretentious than profound. Compare Farris's more successful *Son of the Endless Night* [4-113].

Dick, Philip K(indred), 1928–1982.

ABOUT: CA, TCA, NE, H, SFE, SFFL, TCSF, ESF

4-96. The Three Stigmata of Palmer Eldritch. Doubleday, 1965.
In the year 2016, which is made bearable by Can-D, a powerful mind-altering drug, Leo Bulero, the man behind Can-D, finds himself challenged by the mysterious Palmer Eldritch, who has returned from Proxima Centuria with Chew-Z, an even more potent hallucinogen. When Eldritch forces Chew-Z on his rival, Bulero is thrust into a totally hallucinatory world dominated by Eldritch, where everything—reality, time, space, even his own being—is in flux, the only constant being the dominance of Eldritch, whoever or whatever he may be (an alien? a monster? God? Bulero himself?). Dick is one of the twentieth century's premier science fiction writers, and his explorations of inner space, his exploitation of the continually blurring lines between sanity and madness, between reality and illusion, between the sentient and the mechanical, between life and death, between past, present and future, and his pervasively paranoic landscape, all strongly resemble the development of similar themes in dark fantasy writers like Matheson, Leiber and Ellison, as well as younger authors like King, Farris, Campbell and Barker. Indeed, no writer in any genre has so thoroughly dissected the fundamental unreality of the contemporary world as has Philip K. Dick.

4-97. Ubik. Doubleday, 1969.
Joe Chip, "psi tester" for Runciter Associates, is almost killed, along with several other employees, while on a mission. Almost immediately, time begins to regress around him, and his companions disintegrate one by one. In order to survive Joe must discover the reason for this dissolution of reality as well as the nature of "Ubik," the mysterious cure-all that promises salvation. Another venture into Dick's hallucinatory, paranoid, darkly comic landscape, and one of his best. The implications of *Ubik* are among the most disturbing yet hopeful in all of Dick's works.

Disch, Thomas M(ichael), 1940– .

ABOUT: F, CA, TCA, NE, SFE, MF, SFFL, TCSF, PE, ESF

4-98. The Businessman. Harper, 1984.
A surrealistic slapstick dark fantasy about an upper-echelon corporate executive, Bob Glandier, who is reluctantly haunted by Giselle, the wife he murdered. This bizarre, grotesque, hilarious novel also features the shades of a mother who goes to Paradise via Sears; a vindictive aborted child; poet John Berryman, still seeking recognition and good Scotch; glimpses of Paradise (*not* Heaven); HBO, where incidents from one's own life and those of relatives can be viewed in any order; and, most important, Tom Disch's Boschian vision of contemporary America. Also annotated as [F4A-88].

4-99. Getting into Death. Knopf, 1976.
Contents differ from the 1973 British edition. Sixteen highly original, ironic, biting, funny, and often moving stories representing the best of Disch's early short fiction. Disch's vision of modern society is pessimistic, his image of man negative, his conclusions usually bleak. But there is a streak of romanticism in the

stories, often a basic sympathy with his central characters, coupled with comedic sense and stylistic virtuosity that leaves the reader both disturbed and elated. The biting wit can be seen in "Death and the Single Girl." Having decided to commit suicide, the heroine phones death. When he arrives, he turns out to be dull, middle-aged and impotent. The most memorable story in the volume is "The Asian Shore," in which an American visitor to Istanbul finds himself followed by a Turkish woman and a small boy. Although he tries to evade them, he gradually loses his own identity, until he is finally absorbed completely and metamorphosed into the ordinary Turk the woman had mistaken him for.

[For other works of this author, see the companion guide to fantasy.]

Drake, David, 1945- .

ABOUT: CA, NE

4-100. From the Heart of Darkness. Tor, 1983.
Fourteen stories previously published between 1974 and 1982 plus two originals. The book demonstrates Drake's full range of versatility and power. As Karl Edward Wagner notes in his introduction, "*From the Heart of Darkness* is an excellent introduction to Drake's work, offering examples of his Vettius and Dama stories, historical pieces, Viet Nam horrors, contemporary nightmares, and bleak visions of the future." Written in a spare, hard prose, Drake's most impressive stories are those in which he juxtaposes a tangible human horror against an otherworldly menace. For example, "Than Curse the Darkness" mixes the supernatural horror from Lovecraft with the vicious inhumanity and dangerous atmosphere of Conrad's *Heart of Darkness* [3-51] in a prose reminiscent of Dashiell Hammett. But most impressive are his Viet Nam stories—such as "Firefight," "Best of Luck," "The Dancer in the Flames"—in which ambiguous, awful jungle warfare is made even more nightmarish by the intrusion of supernatural menaces.

du Maurier, Daphne (U.K.), 1907–1989.

ABOUT: WW, GSF, SFW, CA, SMFL, SFFL, PE, ESF

***4-101. Echoes from the Macabre**. Doubleday, 1976.
Nine stories that represent the best of du Maurier's short fiction. An appropriate title: "macabre" because they deal with the irrational, dark forces lying beneath the placid surface of everyday life; "echoes" because the approach is indirect, suggestive and ironic. While the dominant mood of the stories is bleak, they are laced with subtle humor. Most famous and important are "The Birds" and "Don't Look Now," which were made into outstanding films by Alfred Hitchcock and Nicolas Roeg respectively. By focusing on a single family in "The Birds" and by only hinting at what is happening in the rest of the world, du Maurier creates one of the bleakest end-of-the-world scenarios in the genre. John, the hero of "Don't Look Now," denies his psychic talents and the reality of the "message" being sent to him by his deceased daughter and suffers the consequences. Classical in style and method, but contemporary in sensibility, du Maurier's stories are comparable to the best of Robert Aickman [4-3–4-9].

4-102. The House on the Strand. Doubleday, 1969.
A hallucinogenic drug propels Richard Young backward in time from the 1960s to fourteenth-century Cornwall, where he can monitor, but not participate in, the lives of the Manor House. The conflict between his identification with the people he observes and his mundane life in the twentieth century becomes progressively more disturbing as his hold on reality becomes increasingly tenuous until, finally, the past and the present flood together. A superior time travel Gothic with modest science fiction trappings. Compare Laski's *The Victorian Chaise Longue* [4-198] and Millhiser's *The Mirror* [4-237]. Also annotated as [F4A-92].

Ehrlich, Max, 1909- .

ABOUT: CA, SFE, SFFL, TCSF, PE, ESF

4-103. The Reincarnation of Peter Proud. Bobbs-Merrill, 1974.
Peter Proud begins to have increasingly convincing intimations, including terrifying dreams, that in a "previous life" he was murdered—and that the killer is still at large. He feverishly explores his past to avoid undergoing the same fate again. An ingenious if predictable supernatural suspense-mystery novel. Compare DeFelitta's *Audrey Rose* [4-94], Hallahan's *The Search for Joseph Tully* [4-132] and Stewart's *The Possession of Joel Delaney* [4-284].

Ellison, Harlan, 1934- .

ABOUT: GSF, SFW, CA, TCA, NE, H, SMFL, SFE, SFFL, TCSF, PE, ESF

***4-104. The Essential Ellison: A 35-Year Retrospective**. Ed. and Intro. by Terry Dowling. Nemo Press, 1987.
Sixty-seven items, mostly short stories, but with a healthy selection of essays and one unproduced teleplay. As noted in the introduction, it is not a "Best of" book, but a "sound representation . . . warts and all" of Ellison's work, arranged by subject matter in fifteen titled sections, each prefaced by the editor. The collection demonstrates the full range and diversity of Ellison's talent from juvenilia to stories and essays published in the early 1980s. Although he was initially categorized as a science fiction writer, the stories prove Ellison's claim that his work is *sui generis*. Such classics as "A Boy and His Dog," "I Have No Mouth and I Must Scream" and "The Prowler in the City at the Edge of the World" utilize the paraphernalia of science fiction, but they are horrific in mood and implication. Other particularly noteworthy stories with a horrific emphasis include "The Whimper of Whipped Dogs," a savage "homage" to the "god" of the Big City; "Adrift Just Off the Islets of Langerhans: Latitude 38° 54′ N, Longitude 77° 00′ 13″ W," in which the contemporary Wolfman searches within himself for death and finds life; "Shattered Like a Glass Goblin," about a search for love that ends in drug-induced self-destruction; "Pretty Maggie Moneyeyes," another love story, this one about a dead hooker, an unlucky gambler and a slot machine; and "The Deathbird," Ellison's rewrite of the Book of Genesis from the Serpent's point of view. Ellison combines a bitter vision of man, society and an unfeeling cosmos with an intense and essentially romantic and moral commitment to the individual, an extravagant imagination pushed to its limit, a prose style that combines

fervent lyricism with savagely ironic humor and, on occasion, old-fashioned sentimentality (as in "Jeffty Is Five"). *The Essential Ellison* is an excellent introduction to his work, and his work is absolutely essential to any serious evaluation of contemporary dark fantasy. Other good, less comprehensive collections include *Alone against Tomorrow* (1971) and *Deathbird Stories* (1975). Also annotated as [F4A-96].

Ely, David, 1927- .

ABOUT: CA, PE, ESF

4-105. Seconds. Random, 1963.
Wilson, a bored, middle-aged banker, is "reborn" by the "company" into a new identity. Adjusting to his new life, he is even less happy than he was before and gradually understands that the price paid for a second chance is too high. A Kafka-like exploration of the depersonalization of modern life. The benign indifference, bureaucratic efficiency and courteous reasonableness of the company are more disturbing than overt malevolence. John Frankenheimer's 1966 film version, with Rock Hudson as the protagonist, was one of the scariest films of that decade. For a more benign and fantastic view of the second chance motif, see Ken Grimwood's *Replay* (1986) [F4A-125].

Etchison, Dennis, 1943- .

ABOUT: WW, CA, PE, FF

4-106. The Dark Country. Scream/Press, 1982.
Sixteen stories originally published between 1972 and 1981. The introduction by Ramsey Campbell concludes: "Dennis Etchison is the finest writer of short stories now working in this field, and the rest of us ought to learn from him." Etchison's horrors are rarely supernatural and never traditional, and his locations, such as highway rest stops, laundromats and convenience stores late at night, department stores and butcher shops, etc., are ordinary, everyday places—made horrific. Outstanding stories in this volume include "It Only Comes Out at Night," about a highway rest stop filled with apparently abandoned automobiles; "The Late Shift," in which the reader learns why clerks at convenience stores look and act like zombies; "Sitting in the Corner, Whimpering Quietly," in which the narrator listens unwillingly to a late-night murder confession while doing his laundry; and "Dark Country," about a violent encounter between American tourists and Mexican scavengers, a starkly realistic story that—ironically—won the British Fantasy Award and World Fantasy Award.

4-107. Darkside. Charter, 1986.
Soon after moving to Beverly Hills, Doug Carlson and his family are pursued by the "Darkside," a cult that experiments with near death experience, and which lures one teenaged daughter, Erin, into suicide and a second, Lori, almost into emulating her. To save the lives of Lori and his unstable wife, Casey, Doug must finally plunge himself into the darkside. Etchison's first novel (except for film novelizations) displays the qualities that have made him a premier short story writer. *Darkside* is told in a series of intense dramatic scenes with energetic, at

times almost manic dialogue, colorful, precise details, in economical, highly charged language. Although the density of the narration occasionally slows the story, Etchison's original, adroit plotting, colorful if grotesque characterizations and semi-surrealistic rendering of the Southern California landscape combine to present a stimulating, memorable novel.

4-108. Red Dreams. Scream/Press, 1984.
Dennis Etchison is widely regarded as one of the premier short story writers of the genre, and *Red Dreams* provides ample evidence why. The stories are uniformly well written, and a common thread of urban alienation runs through each. Particularly noteworthy is the final story, "Not from Around Here." Etchison's writing is quiet, harkening back to subtle classic ghost stories while remaining undeniably contemporary. The stories are mercifully free of the literary trendiness and self-conscious artsiness found in the work of many similarly praised "serious" horror writers, and also avoid the obtuseness which occasionally mars the short fiction of Ramsey Campbell [4-63, 4-64, 4-67], Etchison's only real rival for the throne. An excellent collection. (B.L.)

Eulo, Ken, 1939- .

About: CA, PE

4-109. The Brownstone. Pocket Books, 1980.
The first and best book in a trilogy, *The Brownstone* is a work whose strong points are also its shortcomings. The novel concerns a New York couple who rent one floor of a building from the owners, two old women who live upstairs. The apartment is haunted, and the sisters turn out to be worshippers of Ahriman, the Zoroastrian god of evil. The husband and wife's mental health and relationship deteriorate as strange incidents increasingly occur and lead to an inevitable climax. *The Brownstone* is written from a selectively omnipotent point of view; this partial illumination of characters' thoughts, feelings and motives lends the work a surrealistic, at times almost hallucinogenic, quality. Unfortunately, this also tends to distance the reader from the characters, none of whom ever become as sympathetic as they should. *The Brownstone* owes an obvious debt to *Rosemary's Baby* [4-206] and was followed by the sequels *The Bloodstone* (1981) and *The Deathstone* (1982). (B.L.)

Farris, John.

About: CA, H, SMFL, PE

4-110. All Heads Turn When the Hunt Goes By. Playboy Press, 1977.
At his wedding, Cliff Bradwin goes insane, killing his bride, father and self with his saber. Years later his brother, Cliff, returns to Dasharoons, the family estate, where he encounters not only the tragic legacy of his brother's madness, but also the tainted family history and the voodoo magic that permeates the area. A powerful, complex dark fantasy that mixes racial and sexual themes with the tradition of the cursed southern family. Although it may not have quite the imaginative sweep of Farris's other major novels, *All Heads Turn When the Hunt Goes By* is probably his most finely crafted, fully realized horror story. Compare

such southern horror stories as McCammon's *Usher's Passing* [4-226] and McDowell's *Blackwater* series [4-230].

4-111. Catacombs. Delacorte, 1981.
Adventurer Matthew Jade leads an expedition to find the "bloodstones," mysterious red diamonds, hidden in catacombs deep in Mt. Kilimanjaro, that contain the secrets of an ancient lost race and a weapon that could radically change the world balance of power. To secure the stones Jade must combat both a ruthless Russian adversary and, even more dangerous, the ancient dark powers unleashed by the stones. Although more Rider Haggard and Ian Fleming than H. P. Lovecraft, *Catacombs* is an exciting, fast-paced adventure/horror story which blends fantastic action, a large, vivid, if not overly subtle cast of characters and a realistically rendered African landscape.

***4-112. The Fury**. Playboy Press, 1976.
"Psychic twins" Robin Sanza and Gillian Bellaver are pursued by MORG, a clandestine government agency, which wants to harness and develop their potentially extraordinary powers. Robin's father, Peter, an ex-government assassin, attempts to rescue the youngsters from MORG. An exciting, tightly structured narrative—despite its considerable complexity—with strong characterizations. An ingenious mix of science fiction, horror and political intrigue, *The Fury* covers much of the same ground as King's *Firestarter* [4-167] with considerably more success.

4-113. Son of the Endless Night. St. Martin's, 1985.
Richard Devon kills Karyn Vale and is brought to trial for murder. He is defended on the grounds that he was possessed by the demon Zarach's Bal-Tagh in a trial that becomes a contest between ultimate good vs. evil. A complex, powerful novel that ends in one of the most harrowing courtroom scenes in the literature. Although common Christian concepts of good and evil offer the novel its general thematic structure, Farris gives the book a complete and consistent mythology of its own so that, unlike such books as *Golgatha Falls* [4-95] or even more modest efforts like *The Sentinel* [4-185], *Son of the Endless Night* is satisfying on its own terms and not dependent on sympathy with or knowledge of any separate belief system. An audacious, imaginative, beautifully structured eschatological novel.

4-114. The Uninvited. Delacorte, 1982.
Barry Brennan accidentally runs over a mysterious naked man, who bears an uncanny, if idealized, resemblance to Barry's dead ex-fiancé. The man recovers, moves into the Brennan household over everyone's objections—except Barry's—and grows increasingly powerful and sinister, seemingly draining the psychic and artistic energies from those about him. The characters—especially Barry, her artist father and Alexandra Chatellaine, an elderly neighbor with occult powers—are sharply drawn and sympathetic; the premise is ingenious and adroitly handled; and the menace grows with subtle, steady, inexorable force. Only at the end does the book falter somewhat; it all comes together just a little too completely and neatly.

4-115. Wildwood. Tor, 1987.
Ex-Army Colonel Whit Bower and his teenaged son Terry journey to a mountain-

ous area in North Carolina to visit an old Army buddy, Arn Rutledge, and his psychic Cherokee wife, Feran, and, more important, to explore Tormentil mountain for Whit's developer employer. Undeterred by legends of dangerous magic, unnatural phenomena, beast-humans and Wildwood, a hundred-room chateau owned by a mad millionaire-scientist-sorcerer that vanished on Midsummer Eve 1916, Whit and Arn set out to explore the area, followed shortly by Terry and Feran, who has had a psychic premonition of danger. Farris crosscuts the narrative between the explorations of the mountain (in 1958) and historical flashbacks to 1916 to show the events leading up to the vanishing. The two time lines eventually come together in a finale that is extravagant even for Farris. The characters are a little flatter than usual, but Farris's imagination goes over the top—without a loss of control—in this very ambitious book.

Finney, Jack (Walter Braden Finney), 1911- .

ABOUT: GSF, CA, TCA, NE, MF, RG, TCSF, ESF, HF

***4-116. The Body Snatchers**. Dell, 1955; "Revised and updated" as **The Invasion of the Body Snatchers**. Dell, 1978.

Originally published as a short novel in *Colliers* in 1954. In the idyllic rural community of Mill Valley, Dr. Miles Bennell gradually learns that his friends and neighbors have been taken over by aliens as a prelude to a total invasion of Earth. He and girlfriend Becky Driscoll attempt to warn others of the plot while avoiding a similar fate for themselves. A chilling classic, somewhat marred by an overly optimistic *deus ex machina* resolution. Don Siegel's 1956 film adaptation remains one of the classic films of the period; Philip Kaufman's gorier 1978 remake is also quite scary, although it lacks the straight-line intensity and thematic suggestiveness of its predecessor. Compare Christopher's *The Possessors* [4-82], Leiber's *The Sinful Ones* [4-204] and the short fiction of Richard Matheson [4-218].

[For other works of this author, see the companion guide to fantasy.]

Fowles, John (U.K.), 1926- .

ABOUT: CA, MF, ESF

4-117. The Magus. Little, Brown, 1965. Rev. ed. with Foreword. Cape, 1977.

Nicholas Urfe, a teacher in retreat on the Greek Islands, encounters Maurice Conchis, an old man who may or may not be a wizard. As Urfe participates in the increasingly bizarre and fantastic rituals of Conchis's "godgame," he is forced to question the very nature of reality and the meaning of his own existence. A fascinating, intricate, ambiguous work by one of the outstanding modern British fiction writers. *The Magus* was, by Peter Straub's admission, a strong influence on his *Shadowland* [4-289]. Despite the interesting casting of Michael Caine as Urfe and Anthony Quinn as Conchis, the 1968 film version was feeble. Also annotated as [F4A-108].

Furey, Michael (pseud. of **Arthur Sarsfield Ward**, later **Sax Rohmer**) (U.K.), 1883–1959.
About: WW, GSF, CA, NE, SMFL, SFE, PE, ESF

4-118. Wulfheim. Jarrolds, 1950.
Historical melodrama deliberately recapitulating classic Gothic themes; evil is unleashed when the heart of a long-dead black magician is exhumed, compounding the confusions of his descendant, who is torn between a dubious religious vocation and an incestuous passion for his sister. Ward/Rohmer may have been trying—only partially successfully, if so—to transcend the cheap thriller vein of his earlier works. On the other hand, he may have been trying to move into the best-selling territory of the somewhat *recherché* occult romances of Dennis Wheatley [4-319–4-324]. Either way, he draws upon the early occult researches which he conducted during his days with the Golden Dawn and for his study of *The Romance of Sorcery* (1914). (B.S.)

Gallagher, Stephen (U.K.), 1954- .

4-119. Valley of Lights. New English Library, 1987.
A group of brain-dead bodies being kept alive on minimal sustenance is found in a sleazy motel in Phoenix, Arizona. A cynical police sergeant soon discovers that the bodies are hosts for an ancient being which uses these human forms to commit grotesque murders, and the creature and the cop face off for a game of chess with human lives at stake. Although the central premise of *Valley of Lights* is similar to that of *Ghost Story* [4-286], Gallagher takes his work in a different direction, writing a hard-boiled police procedural rather than an inbred novel of literary preciousness. His Phoenix is a film noir city, a low-rent metropolis under scorching skies. Although British, Gallagher writes with such an authentic American voice, with such a perfect eye and ear for cultural details, that *Valley of Lights* reads as though it had been written by a native Arizonan. A very interesting book. Compare also Strieber's *The Wolfen* [4-291] and Whitten's *Progeny of the Adder* [4-326]. (B.L.)

Gardner, John, 1933–1982.
About: CA, H, MF, FL, HF

4-120. Mickelsson's Ghosts. Knopf, 1982.
Peter J. Mickelsson, a disillusioned, financially and emotionally overwhelmed academic, retreats to an old farmhouse in rural Susquehanna, Pennsylvania, where he encounters sexual misadventures, religious fanaticism and a house full of articulate ghosts. An interesting, stimulating, if somewhat chaotic mix of a realistic character study of an intellectual in crisis with a Gothic thriller. Although not one of Gardner's best novels, *Mickelsson's Ghosts* is an excellent example of a mainstream novelist's use of dark fantasy materials to facilitate complex character analysis and thematic development.

[For other works of this author, see the companion guide to fantasy.]

Gaskell, Jane (U.K.), 1941- .

ABOUT: WW, GSF, F, CA, SFE, SFFL, RG, ESF, HF

4-121. The Shiny Narrow Grin. Hodder and Stoughton, 1964.
Cruising the London party scene, "promiscuous but pure" teenager Terry Slade is captivated by a delicate blond vampire who offers an alternative to her frenzied, complicated life-style. More amusing than horrific, *The Shiny Narrow Grin* offers a gleefully amoral heroine and a bright, lively picture of "Mod" London in the early 1960s.

[For other works of this author, see the companion guide to fantasy.]

Geary, Patricia.

4-122. Strange Toys. Bantam, 1987.
Strange Toys traces the bizarre life of Pet in three stages, as a nine year old, as a girl of sixteen and as a woman of thirty as she attempts to come to terms with the strange, dangerous legacy of her older sister, a voodoo practitioner. An interesting, eccentric book, not exactly horror, not exactly fantasy, not exactly science fiction, but an odd blend of all three. Pet's manic, slightly mad voice has echoes of Merricat Blackwood, the even wackier heroine of Shirley Jackson's *We Have Always Lived in the Castle* [4-157].

Golding, William (U.K.), 1911- .

ABOUT: WW, NE, H, SFE, MF, SFFL, TCSF, ESF

4-123. Lord of the Flies. Faber, 1954.
The airplane carrying a group of British schoolboys is forced down on an isolated tropical island. At first, led by Ralph and the intellectual Piggy, they attempt to reconstruct a civilized society, but under the primitive survival conditions this soon dissipates into savagery, even cannibalism. The novel can be read as an exciting jungle adventure story with horrific overtones and/or as a parable of man's basic savagery. Enormously popular, especially with younger readers, *Lord of the Flies* is an acknowledged masterpiece of modern fiction. A powerful variation on the same concept, but from an adult point of view, can be seen in Ballard's *High-Rise* [4-18]. Peter Brooks's stark 1963 film of *Lord of the Flies* captures the spirit and energy of the book.

Goldman, William, 1931- .

ABOUT: CA

4-124. Magic. Delacorte, 1978.
Corky, a ventriloquist, is psychologically overwhelmed by his dummy, Fats. When Corky attempts to break away, Fats takes revenge. Novelist-screenwriter Goldman excels in crisp, biting dialogue and vivid, fast-moving dramatic scenes. *Magic* is an original, provocative novel of psychological disintegration. The Corky-Fats relationship, as told from Fats's point of view, is reminiscent of the relationship of the twins in Tryon's *The Other* [4-306]. The low-keyed 1978 film,

scripted by Goldman, starred Anthony Hopkins in a strong performance as Corky.

[For other works of this author, see the companion guide to fantasy.]

Grant, Charles L., 1942– .

ABOUT: CA, H, SMFL, SFE, PE, FF

4-125. The Hour of the Oxrun Dead. Doubleday, 1977; **The Sound of Midnight**. Doubleday, 1978; **The Last Call of Mourning**. Doubleday, 1979; **The Grave**. Popular Library, 1981; **The Bloodwind**. Popular Library, 1982.

Five novels set in Oxrun Station, Connecticut, which Grant describes as "a Greenwich-type community," large and modern enough to allow Grant the mobility and flexibility necessary to present a variety of characters, social strata, and situations, but small enough to project a sense of the isolated small town with its mysterious past, obscure traditions and long-entrenched evils. Four of the five novels have as their protagonists young women who are outsiders in Oxrun Station. As each attempts to adjust to the nature and mores of the enigmatic town, she finds herself mysteriously threatened by increasingly dangerous assaults, both external (direct attacks on her person, possessions, friends) and internal (nightmares and/or hallucinations). In the end she must come to terms with both supernatural menace and diabolical human machinations. In *The Hour of the Oxrun Dead,* a young widow, Natalie Windsor, faces her suspicions about the mysterious death of her husband as well as the hostility of his colleagues and friends. Ultimately the trail leads to a mysterious millionaire and a quasi-satanic cult. The supernatural elements in *The Sound of Midnight* are more convincing. Dale Bartlett, owner of a toy store, is drawn by the murder of a young customer into a diabolical plot involving a strange set of chessmen and an ancient Welsh religious cult. The mystery in *The Sound of Midnight* is intricate and well developed, with the nature of the evil adroitly concealed until the book's final moments. The external danger facing Cyd Yarrow, heroine of *The Last Call of Mourning,* is a mysterious automobile that tries to run her down, but even more threatening is the evil that seems to emanate from her own family. This novel is the most emotionally intense of the five, but it, too, suffers from dubious plot rationalizations and a thin climax. *The Bloodwind* pits Pat Shavers, professor of art at Hawkested College, against the "bloodwind," a destructive elemental wind that takes the shape of a huge beast. In *The Grave,* Grant departs from the practice of using a female protagonist to focus on Josh Miller, freelance hunter for antiques and curios, who is drawn into a mystery surrounding the sudden disappearance of several people on their birthdays. The use of a male hero gives the book a more visceral quality, and the sex and language is freer, but Josh is the least effective of Grant's protagonists. Despite weakness in plotting and climaxes, Grant's delineations of the inner landscapes of horror, fear and loneliness in these novels are among the most sensitive and intense in recent dark fantasy, and Oxrun Station is one of the primary locations on any contemporary map of outstanding dark fantasy.

4-126. The Nestling. Pocket Books, 1982.
Against a background of general unease and white vs. Native American tensions in Windriver, Wyoming, a flying monster—alternately described as a "winged serpent" and a huge carnivorous eagle—savagely attacks, kills and devours its victims. Reporter Jason Clarke investigates the killings and discovers a connection between the Shoshone Indians' complex attempt to reclaim the valley for their own and the summoning of the creature by a dying female shaman. *The Nestling* features a larger canvas and considerably more bloodletting than usual for Grant. Especially effective is his delineation of the causes, complexities and contradictions in the Caucasian-Indian conflict. The novel's only serious flaw is a rather thin and imprecise rationale for the supernatural elements.

4-127. The Pet. Tor, 1986.
Troubled teen Don Boyd is picked on by the jocks at school, blamed by his teachers for things he did not do and ignored by his self-centered parents. He must also compete with his best friend for the affections of a girl in whom they are both interested. Don's darkest desires manifest themselves as a demonic black horse which roams the town acting as the boy's emotional guardian, killing those who cause him distress. *The Pet* is atypical Grant. Much of the poetic imagery and carefully established atmosphere ordinarily found in his work is gone, but so is the overwriting which occasionally mars his prose. The result is a compelling study of adolescence and its inherent emotional horrors. Compare King's *Carrie* [4-162] and *Christine* [4-163]. (B.L.)

4-128. The Soft Whisper of the Dead. Donald M. Grant, 1982; **The Dark Cry of the Moon**. Donald M. Grant, 1986; **The Long Night of the Grave**. Donald M. Grant, 1986.
All three novels were issued in signed, numbered, limited editions as well as trade editions. A historical trilogy of traditional horror stories set in the fictional small town of Oxrun Station, Connecticut, during the latter part of the nineteenth century. *The Soft Whisper of the Dead* chronicles the machinations of the evil Count Braslov as his vampiric influence gradually decimates Oxrun Station. In *The Dark Cry of the Moon*, a werewolf stalks the Station, and suspicion focuses on the aristocratic but eccentric Drummond clan. *The Long Night of the Grave* focuses on a plan to gain immortality through the use of magical ancient Egyptian artifacts that unleashes a reanimated mummy who kills all those who threaten the conspiracy. In this trilogy Grant succeeds admirably in his stated goal of recreating the simple thrills of the classic movies from the Universal, RKO and Hammer studios. The writing is simple, clean and direct. The characters are vivid, if uncomplicated, and the pace is energetic. Deliberately one-dimensional, the novels make up in color, action and nostalgia what they lack in sophistication.

4-129. Tales from the Nightside. Arkham House, 1981.
Laudatory introduction by Stephen King. Fifteen stories, five set in Oxrun Station, four on Hawthorne Street and six without specific locales. Grant's careful control of tone and atmosphere, deft, subtle characterization and precise, suggestive use of language are evident in all of these finely crafted stories, which emphasize the terror of the unseen rather than overt violence and carnage. Especially noteworthy are "Coin of the Realm," in which strange coins with Egyptian

symbols begin appearing in the Oxrun Station toll booths; "If Damon Comes," in which a son's obsessive devotion to—or hatred of—his father extends beyond the grave; "The Gentle Passing of a Hand," a contemporary reworking of the "Monkey's Paw" theme; "When All the Children Call My Name," in which young children discover how to use their playground magic to get revenge on the older boys; "Come Dance with Me on My Pony's Grave," in which a young Vietnamese boy uses his father's magic to avenge his pony's death; and "White Wolf Calling," about the strange friendship between an old man and an odd boy who believes in the white wolf that signals imminent death.

Grubb, Davis, 1919-1980.

About: WW, GSF, SFFL, PE, ESF

4-130. The Night of the Hunter. Harper, 1953.
Children John and Mary are relentlessly pursued by the Preacher, who believes—correctly—that they have access to stolen money given them by their executed father. A classic suspense thriller with Gothic overtones. Brilliantly filmed by Charles Laughton in his only directorial assignment, with Robert Mitchum as the Preacher.

4-131. Twelve Tales of Suspense and the Supernatural. Scribner's, 1964. U.K. title: *One Foot in the Grave.*
Stories largely set in rural West Virginia that combine the gruesome, the wistful and the darkly humorous, evoking a folktale mood, somewhat similar to that of the work of Manly Wade Wellman [4-316, 4-317]. Perhaps Grubb's best-known story is "One Foot in the Grave," in which a severed foot takes on a life of its own, which includes seduction and murder. Other notable stories include "Busby's Rat," in which the death of rat-keeper Busby is avenged by his surviving rodents; "Radio," in which Will's wife assumes the incessant voice of the radio he had smashed in anger; "The Horsehair Trunk," in which a vindictive husband attempts to use astral projection to kill his wife; and "Where the Woodbine Twineth," about a little girl who vanishes when her imaginary playmates are driven away.

[For other works of this author, see the companion guide to fantasy.]

Hallahan, William H(enry).

About: CA, PE

4-132. The Search for Joseph Tully. Bobbs-Merrill, 1974.
Well-written, peopled with interesting characters, and containing some powerful scenes of horror. Unfortunately, it is an occult mystery novel with no mystery. A good book, but it could, and should, have been better. Compare Ehrlich's *The Reincarnation of Peter Proud* [4-103] and Hjorstberg's *Falling Angel* [4-149]. (B.L.)

Hambly, Barbara.

4-133. Those Who Hunt the Night. Ballantine, 1988. U.K. title: *Immortal Blood.*
Oxford professor and ex-British spy James Asher is hired by a vampire to discover

who—or what—is killing vampires in Victorian-era London. Refusal, betrayal or failure will result not only in his own death, but also in that of his beloved, resourceful wife. But if he succeeds—can he trust a vampire? Asher is a bland hero and the Victorian age never comes to life, but Hambly's ingenious plot is handled with great skill, the mystery is clever, and the suspense is adroitly sustained and intensified throughout the book. Most impressive, however, is Hambly's vampiric subculture and her manipulation and enhancement of the vampire myth. Although *Those Who Hunt the Night* lacks the intellectual fervor and sensual intensity of *Interview with a Vampire* [4-250], it compares favorably with the Rice novel in its depiction of vampires as distinct, credible, not-quite-human beings, whose life-style, motivations and even ethical system are understandable, if evil. Locus award for best horror novel. Compare also Strieber's *The Hunger* [4-290] and Whitten's *Progeny of the Adder* [4-326].

[For other works of this author, see the companion guide to fantasy.]

Hardy, Robin (U.K.), and **Anthony Shaffer** (U.K.), 1926- .

About: CA, PE

4-134. The Wicker Man. Crown, 1978.

That rarest of all literary hybrids, the film novelization that is also a fine book in its own right. Venturing to a coastal island, ruled by the aristocratic Lord Summerisle, to search for a missing girl, Scottish police Sergeant Neil Howie finds himself gradually transformed from the pursuer to the pursued. Although the supernaturalism is marginal, *The Wicker Man* is a suspenseful, intriguing occult mystery thriller with serious thematic overtones. The novel also boasts two remarkable characters, the solid, stoic, courageous Howie and the elegant, mysterious, sinister Lord Summerisle, as well as a devastating, if inevitable, finale. The classic 1973 film on which the novel was based starred Edward Woodward as Howie and Christopher Lee as Lord Summerisle. Compare Burke's *The Devil's Footsteps* [4-58] and Tryon's *Harvest Home* [4-305].

Harris, Thomas, 1940?- .

About: CA, H, PE

***4-135. Red Dragon**. Putnam, 1981.

Ex-FBI agent Will Graham is pressured into joining the manhunt for a serial killer who specializes in happy families. Graham's technique of tracking the killer by psychologically identifying with him transforms *Red Dragon* into an extremely powerful and sophisticated *doppelgänger* story. *Red Dragon* was sensitively filmed as *Manhunter* in 1986. Compare Brookes's *Deadly Communion* [4-56], Herbert's *Moon* [4-143] and Koontz's *The Vision* [4-192].

Harrison, M(ichael) John (U.K.), 1945- .

About: F, CA, SFE, MF, SFFL, ESF

4-136. The Ice-Monkey and Other Stories. Gollancz, 1983.

Seven stories first published between 1975 and 1983. Although some stories, like

"The New Rays," contain strong physical details, most, like the title story, are realistic psychological studies of characters caught up in ambiguous personal crises. Most characteristic and effective is "Egnaro," in which a grubby book-dealer is obsessed by "Egnaro," a mysterious idyllic world that is constantly hinted at but never revealed; the obsession gradually overwhelms the story's narrator.

Hartley, L(eslie) P(oles) (U.K.), 1895–1972.

ABOUT: WW, GSF, SFW, CA, SFE, SFFL, TCSF, PE, ESF

4-137. The Complete Short Stories of L. P. Hartley. 2 vols. Hamish Hamilton, 1973; Beaufort, 1986.
Contains one novella and the four collections of stories first published between 1924 and 1971 (*The Travelling Grave and Other Stories* [1948], *The White Wand and Other Stories* [1954], *Two for the River* [1961] and *Mrs. Carteret Received and Other Stories* [1971]), which mix genteel horror stories with social comedies. Firmly fixed in the Henry James/M. R. James tradition, Hartley's stories are carefully crafted, restrained, grimly ironic and often laced with biting humor. Although several of his best-known tales, such as "The Travelling Grave," "The Killing Bottle" and "A Visitor from Down Under," were published early in Hartley's career, some of his best stories were written in the period between his late fifties and his death, notably "W. S.," in which an artist must come to terms with an evil character of his own creation; "The Waits," about a greedy business-man who gets his comeuppance at the hands of the ghosts of two starving Christmas Eve carolers; "Someone in the Lift," a gruesome, upsetting vignette about a young boy's involvement in the death of his father; "Fall in at the Double," in which a barracks of soldiers reenact the murder of their C.O.; "Paradise Paddock," about a jinxed scarab that returns to its corrupt owner; and the macabre comedy of "Please Do Not Touch," in which a London bachelor uses cyanide-laced sherry to discourage burglars.

4-138. The Go-Between. Hamish Hamilton, 1953.
Leo Colston recalls his boyhood experience as the innocent go-between for the aristocratic Marian Maudsley and her tenant-farmer lover, Ted Burgess. This premature exposure to adult complexity and sexuality becomes the crucial event in shaping Leo's adult life. Realistic in incident and character, *The Go-Between*'s status as dark fantasy depends on Hartley's rich, suggestive use of tone, Leo's imaginative flights of fancy and the elaborate, symbolic subtext that infuses the novel. Joseph Losey's 1971 film adaptation, scripted by Harold Pinter and starring Julie Christie and Alan Bates, beautifully captured the realistic dimensions of the text, but largely ignored its fantastic implications.

Heard, H(enry) F(itzgerald) (U.K.), 1889–1971.

ABOUT: WW, GSF, CA, NE, SMFL, SFE, SFFL, TCSF, PE, ESF

4-139. The Black Fox. Cassell, 1950.
When Canon Charles Throcton, an Anglican clergyman, uses a magical Arabic ritual to kill a rival, he unleashes ancient dark forces, focused in the form of

Anubis, a leprous jackal, that haunt him. His sister, aided by a Sufi master, learns of his predicament and offers to sacrifice herself to save him. An interesting old-fashioned occult story in a well-rendered Victorian setting. Excellent use of period and ecclesiastical detail, but somewhat slow and pretentious.

Herbert, James (U.K.), 1943- .

ABOUT: WW, GSF, SFW, CA, SFE, PE, FF

4-140. The Dark. New English Library, 1980.
Evil, as a solid blanket of darkness, spreads across England, inducing madness and violence in its wake. Psychic investigator Chris Bishop joins blind paranormal expert Jacob Kulek and his daughter, Jessica, to trace its origins to Boris Pryslak, a deceased monomaniac. As Bishop and his friends search for a way to stop the spreading Dark, their efforts are challenged by the remaining members of Pryslak's cult. Although it strains credulity at times—particularly in its confusing ending—*The Dark* is an exciting narrative which poses some interesting questions about the nature of good and evil.

***4-141. The Fog**. New English Library, 1975.
An earthquake in a small rural town releases a yellow fog—a long-buried biological warfare experiment—that induces madness in all who breathe its fumes. Led by John Holman, the only person to experience the madness and survive, a small group of scientists and government officials attempt to track down and neutralize the deadly gas before it devastates the entire country. Herbert adroitly balances sharp, grotesque, occasionally comic acts of individual violence against larger movements of mass chaos. The potentially deadening effect of such repeated and intense violence is avoided by Herbert's focus on the personal struggles of his strong, believable protagonist. Predictably plotted, but skillfully paced and strongly written. Compare Ballard's *The Crystal World* [4-17] and McCammon's *They Thirst* [4-225].

4-142. The Magic Cottage. Hodder & Stoughton, 1986.
Midge, an artist, and Mike, a musician, move into an idyllic isolated house in the New Forest, where initially their creative energies flourish. Contact with the Synergists, a bizarre religious cult, triggers a series of strange, slowly intensifying menaces that challenge the resources of the beleaguered couple, forcing them to discover and use their hidden talents. A strong pastoral horror novel that emphasizes gradually mounting terror rather than Herbert's usual physical gore.

4-143. Moon. New English Library, 1985.
Three years after a traumatic psychic experience, Jon Childes has gotten his life together—a new job teaching computer science at an exclusive girls school, a serious romance with a fellow-teacher—when the terrible psychic visions return to signal a mad serial murderer, who leaves a moonstone inside each victim's body. As the psychic identification grows stronger, Childes himself becomes the object of the killer's hostility and he must embrace his talent, as well as the dark secrets of his past, to save himself and his loved ones. An intense, suspenseful novel. Childes's gradual melding with the mind of the demented killer is compelling. The rationale of the moon killings is handled weakly, however, and the

novel falls down when Herbert's predilection for gore dissipates the finale. Compare Brookes's *Deadly Communion* [4-56] and Koontz's *The Vision* [4-192].

4-144. The Rats. New English Library, 1974; **Lair**. New English Library, 1979; **Domain**. New English Library, 1984.
Huge mutant rats attack the citizens of London in increasing numbers, leaving death and plague in their wake. The authorities attempt to destroy the rodents with an antirat virus, while two men, Harris, an art teacher, and Foskins, a Minister of Health agent, go after the telepathic intelligence that is directing the rats in their depredations. In *Lair,* a mutant rat that has survived the initial killing breeds even larger, nastier, tougher rats to attack humankind again. This time it is Lucas Pender, an entomologist, who leads the search to discover and destroy the mutant rat-king in its lair. In *Domain,* nuclear war has devastated the world, and the battered human survivors must hide from masses of newer, bigger, smarter and even more vicious rodents. Forced out of their bunker, the humans, led by helicopter pilot Steven Culver and Alex Dealey, a minor government functionary, fight the creatures in the ruins of London. The most ambitious novel of the trilogy, *Domain* is, despite vivid moments, too diffuse in plotting and shallow in characterization to sustain the power of its predecessors. *The Rats* was Herbert's first novel and established him as England's best-selling horror writer. Poorly filmed under the title *Deadly Eyes* (1982). Compare du Maurier's "The Birds" [4-101].

4-145. Sepulchre. Hodder & Stoughton, 1987.
Bodyguard extraordinaire Liam Halloran is hired to protect Felix Kline, whose amazing psychic abilities—especially his talent for locating buried mineral deposits—have made him invaluable to Magna Corporation, a huge multinational company. During his tour of duty Halloran encounters a kinky love affair, a terrorist assault, terrifying psychic phenomena and a Sumerian devil-god. An exciting, suspenseful, sometimes very gory occult thriller, with a harrowing, if slightly farfetched, finish. Good, if not overly deep, characterizations: Halloran is a surprisingly sympathetic and believable superhero in the James Bond tradition; Kline is a marvelously devious, mysterious villain; and the weird bodyguards are vivid grotesques in the best comic-strip tradition. Compare Barker's *The Damnation Game* [4-22] and Blackburn's *For Fear of Little Men* [4-40].

4-146. Shrine. New English Library, 1983.
Eleven-year-old Alice Pagett, spontaneously cured of deafness and dumbness, has a vision of the Immaculate Conception, demonstrates the power of healing and is even seen to levitate. The parish of St. Joseph's and the surrounding town of Benfield become a shrine overnight, but a series of bizarre and violent incidents convince Gerry Fenn, a newspaper reporter, that Alice's powers are demonic rather than angelic. Assisted by the parish priest, Fenn searches for the dark secret behind Alice's extraordinary career in hopes of thwarting whatever malevolent design is behind it. A superior novel that utilizes Herbert's talent for depicting mass hysteria and pervasive evil, as in *The Rats, The Fog* and *The Dark,* in the service of a much more sophisticated and complex treatment of the good-vs.-evil theme. Deft characterization in a subtle, intricate plot marred only by a gratuitous twist that compromises the ending.

4-147. The Spear. New English Library, 1978.
Former agent Harry Steadman is recruited by the Mossad to locate one of their missing agents. The trail leads to an ancient castle where a neo-Nazi cult, using the occult powers of the spear that pierced Christ's side, is attempting to resurrect Heinrich Himmler. Herbert's first foray into the occult thriller is exciting, fast-paced and ingenious, with an ample ration of Herbert's characteristic gore. An impressive move in the direction of the cross-genre best-seller. Compare McCammon's *The Wolf's Hour* [4-227], Wheatley's *They Used Dark Forces* [4-323] and Yarbro's *Tempting Fate* [4-340].

Hill, Susan (U.K.), 1942– .
ABOUT: CA

4-148. The Woman in Black. Hamish Hamilton, 1983.
When solicitor Arthur Krips travels to the English countryside to manage the affairs of the late Mrs. Drablow, an aged, unpopular recluse, he encounters an apparently haunted house, a deadly marsh and a sinister, spectral "woman in black with a wasted face." The woman's story and the terrible curse that resulted from it give *The Woman in Black* a nasty final twist that keeps it from being a run-of-the-mill exercise in updated M. R. James. Compare Calder-Marshall's more sophisticated *The Scarlet Boy* [4-62].

Hjorstberg, William, 1941– .
ABOUT: CA, H, SFE, SFFL

***4-149. Falling Angel**. Harcourt, Brace, 1978.
Private detective Harry Angel is hired by Louis Cyphre to find a missing pop singer, Johnny Favorite. Pursuing his quarry in the black magic underground of New York City, Angel sees his witnesses, including the voodoo priestess who becomes his lover, gruesomely murdered one by one, with himself as the chief suspect. A brilliant synthesis of the hard-boiled detective story and the horror novel, with thematic echoes of *Heart of Darkness* and *Faust*. Alan Parker's film version (1987), with Mickey Rourke and Robert De Niro, was faithful to the novel in all but setting, which became New Orleans, and title, which became *Angel Heart*.

Household, Geoffrey (U.K.), 1900–1988.
ABOUT: F, CA

4-150. The Sending. Michael Joseph, 1980.
After the mysterious death of a friend, Algif Hollaston, landowner, ex-Indian Army colonel and painter, is plagued by irrational, pervasive, almost debilitating feelings of fear. To come to terms with these emotions, Hollaston must search within himself, accept the psychic gifts he has tried to ignore, and confront the supernatural evil that threatens not only his own sanity, but also that of his dearest friend. A rare excursion into dark fantasy by the author of the classic thriller *Rogue Male* (1969), *The Sending* exhibits the elements that make House-

hold's thrillers so popular—clean, direct writing, a thoughtful, sensitive, believable hero, finely controlled pacing and deft use of significant detail.

Hutson, Shaun (U.K.), 1958- .

ABOUT: PE

4-151. Shadows. W. H. Allen, 1985.
When psychic experimenters unleash the astral bodies of their patients, they learn two disturbing facts: that the astral body is capable of physical acts—like murder—and that it is the province of the "shadow," the evil, destructive side of the personality. When someone begins to use this knowledge for personal gain, carnage and violent death follow. One of Britain's most popular horror writers, Hutson has been labeled one of the "nasties," a group of authors generally criticized for extreme, protracted gore. *Shadows* is a solid cut above such other Hutson novels as *Slugs* (1982) and *Breeding Ground* (1985). Hutson's excesses are muted in *Shadows,* which offers an original horror concept, fast pacing and a cleverly developed mystery. The writing is mundane but efficient, and the gore, although frequent and vivid, is integral to the plot. Compare Campbell's much more sophisticated *Incarnate* [4-69] and Wheatley's *The Ka of Gifford Hillary* [4-321].

Jackson, Shirley, 1919-1965.

ABOUT: WW, GSF, SFW, F, CA, H, SMFL, SFE, MF, SFFL, PE, ESF

4-152. The Bird's Nest. Farrar, Straus, 1955.
The book's title, from an old riddle, tells the whole story: "Elizabeth, Lizzy, Betsy and Bess/All went together to see a bird's nest;/They found a nest with five eggs in it;/They each took one and left four in it." Elizabeth Richmond has four personalities—Elizabeth, Beth, Betsy and Bess—which fight for dominance. Jackson dramatizes this struggle by using multiple viewpoints both from within Elizabeth's fragmented personality and from outsiders, her doctor and her aunt. A powerful, compassionate, fascinating profile of psychological disintegration laced with Jackson's typical irony and humor.

4-153. Come Along with Me. Viking, 1968.
Edited by Stanley Edgar Hyman, the volume contains "Come Along with Me," the existing fragment of Jackson's last novel, sixteen previously uncollected stories spanning her entire career and three lectures on the writing of fiction. "Come Along with Me" chronicles the initial adventures of one of Jackson's most interesting characters, Mrs. Motorman, a rotund, middle-aged woman recently set free by the death of her husband, but the fragment unfortunately ends before the plot really gets into motion. "The Lottery" [3-102], Jackson's most famous story, is reprinted along with an essay on its origin and development. Among the previously uncollected stories, the most memorable are "The Beautiful Stranger," "The Island," "The Bus," "The Summer People" and "A Visit." In "The Beautiful Stranger," a young wife is so estranged from her husband that she perceives him to be a "beautiful stranger" when he returns from a business trip. In "The

Island," an old woman dreams of freedom and quietly challenges the insensitive nurse-companion who controls her life. In "The Bus," an old woman falls asleep on a bus and subsequently finds herself stranded in an ambiguously hostile world which may or may not be a bad dream. The menace is more concrete in "The Summer People," when a vacationing couple decide to remain in their cabin after the end of the tourist season. While visiting a classmate in "A Visit," the most ambiguous and disturbing of the stories, Margaret, the young heroine, meets her younger brother and her elderly aunt, also named Margaret, both of whom may be real, hallucinatory or ghosts from the past—or future. An outstanding collection.

4-154. Hangsaman. Farrar, Straus, 1951.
Natalie Waite, a shy, introspective, imaginative college freshman, tests her precarious sense of reality through a series of subtle, ambiguous relationships: with her hyper-intellectual, domineering father, with her college English professor and his coed wife, and finally with Tony, a mysterious girlfriend, whose contact with reality seems even more tenuous than Natalie's. More of an exercise in psychological suspense than horror, *Hangsaman* demonstrates Jackson's ability to develop rich, complex, subtle characters in language that is precise, economical and graceful, with a gentle irony that edges into the sinister.

***4-155. The Haunting of Hill House**. Viking, 1959.
Four individuals—a college professor, a sheltered spinster, a free-spirited female and the playboy nephew of the house's owner—move into Hill House, a mansion with an unsavory history, to study psychic phenomena. As apparently otherworldly intrusions become increasingly evident, the researchers' relationships with each other, with themselves and with the house become increasingly complicated and intense. The arrival of two additional investigators, the professor's wife and a prep school headmaster, provides the final impulse that drives the novel to its powerful, unexpected conclusion. An excellent novel in every way. Two characters are especially noteworthy: Eleanor Vance, the spinster, who finds in the frightening atmosphere of Hill House her first real home, and the house itself, which is, in Jackson's own words, "not sane." Effectively filmed as *The Haunting* (1963). Compare Matheson's *Hell House* [4-216] and Williamson's *Soulstorm* [4-329].

4-156. The Sundial. Farrar, Straus, 1958.
Following the death of the owner, a small group of eccentrics gather in the Halloran mansion to fight for household dominance as they wait for the end of the world. A highly imaginative, provocative and funny book.

***4-157. We Have Always Lived in the Castle**. Viking, 1962.
In a quietly mad voice, a teenaged would-be witch, Mary Katharine ("Merricat") Blackwood, tells the story of her comically grotesque, playfully menacing family: her older sister Constance, accused of murdering her parents, brother and aunt; Uncle Julian, obsessed with the past and out of contact with the present; and Charles, the normal cousin, whose intrusion into the Blackwood sanctuary leads to hostility, confusion, fire, death and mob violence. A delightful, disturbing book. In critic Louis Untermeyer's words: "It achieves the incredible: an unbelievable combination of terror and tenderness, of horror and pity." Named one of

the ten best books of 1962 by *Time* magazine and winner of the National Book Award.

Jeter, K(evin) W., 1950- .
ABOUT: NE, MF, TCSF

4-158. Soul Eater. Tor, 1983.
The "soul eater" is a young woman in a drug-induced coma, and the soul she eats is that of her daughter, Dee. Dee's attempt to knife her father, David Braemer, alerts him to his daughter's plight and leads him to investigate the parapsychological experiments that turned his wife into a psychic vampire. A tightly developed, suspenseful novel, with well-drawn, sympathetic characters and an expert rendering of the contemporary Southern California landscape. *Soul Eater* touches on several contemporary thematic concerns, notably psychic experimentation, psychic possession and the evil child.

Kast, Pierre (France).
ABOUT: SMFL

***4-159. The Vampires of Alfama.** W. H. Allen, 1976. Tr. by Peter de Polnay of *Les Vampires de l'Alfama*, 1975.
Historical fantasy set in the eighteenth century. A liberal politician and rebel churchman who is trying to bring the Enlightenment to Portugal is opposed by the combined forces of dogma and repression. The conflict is brought to a violent climax by the arrival in the criminal *quartier* of Lisbon of a vampire scientist who seeks to discover the means to a less inconvenient immortality in which all men may share. A brilliant novel by a noted film critic, spectacular in its grotesquerie and eroticism; it boldly offers the vampire a role more aptly heroic than those subsequently popularized by such writers as Saberhagen [4-258] and Yarbro [4-340]. (B.S.)

Kersh, Gerald (U.K.), 1911-1968.
ABOUT: WW, GSF, CA, SFE, PE, ESF

***4-160. Men Without Bones.** Heinemann, 1962.
Thirteen stories that mix horror, science fiction, fantasy and mystery. The title story is an especially unnerving SF/horror blend. Professor Goodbody is horrified by his discoveries in a South American jungle of the remnants of a crashed space ship; a race of short, fat men without bones; and the secret of the origins of human life. Other interesting stories include "Oxoxoco Bottle," in which a collector discovers Ambrose Bierce's last manuscript, which tells of a lost race in Mexico with unpleasant culinary practices; "Epistle of Simple Simon," about an early Christian in Roman Palestine who tries to convert an old hermit who saved his life, not realizing the man is Jesus Christ; and "The Ape and the Mystery," a kind of literary joke in which we meet Leonardo da Vinci and learn the secret of Mona Lisa's smile. Clever, imaginative, energetic stories, generally told in a clean, direct prose style, although Kersh is capable of considerable stylistic virtuosity when required. A very strong collection.

4-161. Nightshades and Damnations. Fawcett Gold Medal, 1968.
Eleven stories (two repeats from [4-160]), plus "Introduction: Kersh, the Demon Prince" by Harlan Ellison. The centerpiece of the volume (along with the repeated "Men without Bones") is the SF/horror classic "The Brighton Monster." A Japanese man is blown back by the H-bomb to eighteenth-century England, where he is believed to be a monster from the deep. Other provocative stories include "'Busto Is a Ghost, Too Mean to Give Us a Fight!,'" "Voices in Dust of Annan" and "Whatever Happened to Corporal Cookoo?"

King, Stephen, 1947- .

ABOUT: WW, GSF, SFW, CA, NE, H, SMFL, SFE, MF, SFFL, RG, PE, ESF, FF

4-162. Carrie. Doubleday, 1974.
Stephen King's first published novel. In defiance of her religious fanatic mother, Carrie White, a much-abused teenaged girl with awesome telekinetic powers, accepts an invitation to the Senior Prom, where she momentarily tastes acceptance and popularity before they are cruelly torn away. The result is a cataclysm of violence and gore. Ironically, King's first novel is his least conventional. Although it lacks the control of the later works, *Carrie* remains one of his more interesting novels. King's rapid ascendancy to popularity must in part by credited to Brian De Palma's powerful 1976 film adaptation. Compare Wood's *The Killing Gift* [4-335].

4-163. Christine. Viking, 1983.
Arnie Cunningham, teenaged loner, buys a battered 1958 Plymouth Fury named "Christine" from Ronald LeBey, a degenerate ex-soldier. As he becomes increasingly obsessed with restoring the car, Arnie seems to become more normal and his confidence grows to the point that he starts a romance with Leigh, the prettiest new girl in school. But Christine grows possessive and jealous. She/it begins to kill Arnie's enemies, and even threatens his girl friend and his best friend, Dennis Guilder. The story is told primarily by Dennis, who desperately searches for a way to defend himself, Leigh and finally Arnie from the demonic, seemingly invulnerable Christine. A strong mixture of supernatural horror and 1960s high school nostalgia. The last word on the automobile as *femme fatale*. Arnie and Dennis are strong, sympathetic characters. The novel suffers from awkwardness in the handling of point of view as King abandons Dennis's first-person narration in the middle of the book but returns to it in the final third. Compare Grant's *The Pet* [4-127].

4-164. The Dark Tower: The Gunslinger. Donald M. Grant, 1982; **The Dark Tower II: The Drawing of the Three**. Donald M. Grant, 1987.
The first two volumes in a projected epic fantasy of "six or seven books" inspired by Robert Browning's poem "Childe Roland to the Dark Tower Came." *The Gunslinger* stories were originally published in *The Magazine of Fantasy and Science Fiction*. More readily available trade editions of *The Gunslinger* and *The Drawing of the Three* were published by New American Library in 1988 and 1989. *The Gunslinger* begins the quest by Roland, the gunslinger, to track and confront the "man in black," who knows, perhaps, the secret of the "Dark Tower."

As he travels across the barren landscape of King's alternate world, sometimes alone, sometimes with a boy named Jake, Roland recalls fragments of his own past. He finally confronts the man in black, who reads his future with a Tarot deck. In *The Drawing of the Three,* the doorway between King's alternate world and our own opens to admit allies from our world to help Roland in his quest. *The Gunslinger* is a wonderfully ambiguous, exciting mix of horror, science fiction, western and epic fantasy. Although longer and more detailed, *The Drawing of the Three* seems more mundane and predictable, with protracted physical horror predominating. King describes future volumes as follows: "The third, *The Waste Lands,* details half of the quest of Roland, Eddie, and Susannah to reach the Tower; the fourth, *Wizard and Glass,* tells of an enchantment and a seduction but mostly of those things which befell Roland before his readers first met him. . . ." Compare the King/Straub *The Talisman* [4-178]. Also annotated as [F4A-150].

4-165. The Dead Zone. Viking, 1979.
When John Smith awakens from a four-and-a-half-year coma, he discovers he possesses clairvoyant powers. As his insights increasingly isolate him from society and normality, he resists them, but is inexorably forced to use them to protect society against "monsters," particularly a vicious serial killer and, ultimately, a political demagogue who will, unless stopped, launch World War III. One of King's most moving cross-genre novels, a fusion of horror story, science fiction and political intrigue thriller. John Smith is a poignant, perhaps tragic, hero. Compare Brooke's *Deadly Communion* [4-56] Koontz's *The Vision* [4-192], Matheson's *A Stir of Echoes* [4-220] and Silverberg's *Dying Inside* [4-271].

4-166. Different Seasons. Viking, 1982.
Four novellas, each "written after completing a novel"—"The Body" (*'Salem's Lot*), "Apt Pupil" (*The Shining*), "Rita Hayworth and the Shawshack Redemption" (*The Dead Zone*) and "The Breathing Method" (*Firestarter*)—and an afterword by King discussing the composition of each piece along with some general comments on the nature and state of the novella. The best horror story in the volume is *The Breathing Method,* a somewhat Henry Jamesian story-within-a-story about a feisty unmarried pregnant girl who refuses to let even mortality prevent her from giving birth. The story is told by a member of a mysterious gentlemen's club where elite males gather to eat gourmet food, drink fine whiskey, read books available in no other library and tell tales of the supernatural. Both outer frame and inner story are excellent, literate, provocative narratives. Much less successful is "Apt Pupil", about a teenaged California boy who browbeats an elderly neighbor, who happens to be an ex-Nazi death camp commander, into telling him all the "gooshy stuff" about the Holocaust. The stories eventually trigger dramatic reactions in both the boy and the old man. "Apt Pupil" is an inspired idea which works very well as a study of psychological disintegration, but King's rather facile, gory ending dissipates most of the story's effectiveness. In "The Body," four fourteen-year-old boys go in search of a body in the woods and confront death—literally and psychologically—while also exploring the possibilities of friendship and commitment. "The Body" was memorably filmed by Rob Reiner as *Stand by Me* (1987). "Rita Hayworth and the Shawshack Redemption" is a realistic nonhorror story about a weak but shrewd convict's

attempts to deal with the brutal prison world into which he has been thrust. Along with "The Mist" [4-174], these four works demonstrate King's thorough mastery of the novella form.

4-167. Firestarter. Viking, 1980.
The McGee family is persecuted and pursued by "The Shop," a clandestine government agency, whose chemical experiments of the 1960s have produced extraordinary psi powers in the McGees, especially in the pyrokinetically inclined young daughter, "Charlie." The most memorable character in the book, however, is John Rainbird, the gigantic, malevolent, philosophical villain. *Firestarter* is an interesting mix that is part horror novel, part science fiction story and part political intrigue adventure, with a climax that evokes the classical western formula. The contrived, improbable plotting, however, makes *Firestarter* one of King's weaker novels. Sometimes dismissed by critics as "Carrie II," the novel actually seems more indebted to John Farris's *The Fury* [4-112].

4-168. It. Viking, 1986. (First edition published in German as *Es*, Edition Phantasia, 1986.)
One of King's longest books, with his shortest title. In the summer of 1958, seven oddly assorted children—losers all—band together as a defense against the hostility of their more rugged, "normal" peers, but are gradually drawn into a confrontation with a powerful, primal malevolent force that feeds off the young. In 1985, the same group, now more or less successful adults, are reunited once again to confront It, this time, they hope, to end the menace for good. The novel's loose structure gives King the space to tell *everybody's* story in intimate detail. Some of the stories are interesting and well worth the digression; others are dull. In general, the narrative of the children is moving and exciting; the parallel story of the adults is uneven. Unfortunately, the book dissipates badly in the latter chapters, and the final confrontation is very disappointing—long, painful, improbable and anticlimactic. By far the weakest thing in *It* is It. But if the whole is much less than the sum of the parts, there are nevertheless enough strong parts to more than justify a reading. Winner of the 1987 August Derleth Award.

4-169. Misery. Viking, 1987.
"Misery" is the heroine of Paul Sheldon's historical romances and misery is his fate when he becomes the captive of his most devoted and demented fan, Annie Wilkes. Angered by Sheldon's desire to kill off his heroine, Annie destroys his serious novel and forces him, under threat of torture and mutilation, to create a new Misery novel for her alone. A tense, suspenseful two-character duel. Paul Sheldon is King's most thorough delineation of the artist figure and Annie Wilkes is a monster of heroic proportions. "Misery's Return," the novel within the novel, is an especially entertaining pastiche of the historical romance. *Misery* is seriously marred, however, by unnecessary and protracted physical torture and mutilation. Minor but memorable King. Co-winner of the 1988 Bram Stoker Award.

***4-170. Night Shift**. Doubleday, 1978.
Twenty stories that are a veritable catalogue of modern horror fiction subjects: the obligatory tribute to H. P. Lovecraft ("Jerusalem's Lot"); horror/science fiction ("Night Surf," "I Am the Doorway"); vengeful ghosts ("Sometimes They Come

Back"); vampires ("One for the Road"); grotesque transformations ("Gray Matter"); monsters ("The Boogeyman"); pagan gods ("The Lawnmower Man," "Children of the Corn"); psychotic killers ("Strawberry Spring," "The Man Who Loved Flowers"); demonic children ("Children of the Corn"); black magic ("I Know What You Need"); and vindictive machines ("The Mangler," "Trucks," "Battlefield"). These stories, originally published between 1970 and 1978, clearly demonstrate the growth and development of King's powers as he perfected the blend of qualities that would make him the most successful of modern horror writers.

***4-171. Pet Sematary**. Doubleday, 1983.
Louis Creed learns of an old Indian burial ground with the power to reanimate animal—including human—flesh. Against his better judgment he gives way to the temptation to make use of the cemetery. King's variation on the "Monkey's Paw" theme, which he has called his most "painful" and "unpleasant" book. The primary reason for this is that the one thing in most King stories that offers hope—the power of *love*—becomes, in *Pet Sematary*, the destructive force.

***4-172. 'Salem's Lot**. Doubleday, 1975.
His first best-seller, *'Salem's Lot* is Stephen King's updating of, and homage to *Dracula* [3-186]: the classic vampire, in the character of Kurt Barlow, invades and infects 'Salem's Lot, a small town in southern Maine. Novelist Ben Mears, despondent over the recent death of his wife, returns to 'Salem's Lot and organizes a small group of citizens, including his girlfriend, an English teacher, an alcoholic priest, a doctor and a teenaged boy, to battle the evil that is slowly, methodically overwhelming the Lot. In this novel King introduced the technique of building a panoramic novel by setting up several separate plot lines and juxtaposing them while systematically moving the main story forward until everything coalesces by book's end. Compare Peter Straub's *Ghost Story* [4-286]. In 1979 *'Salem's Lot* was adapted for television in a generally mediocre four-hour miniseries directed by Tobe Hooper.

***4-173. The Shining**. Doubleday, 1977.
As the caretaker of the Overlook Hotel in the Rocky Mountains, Jack Torrance is snowbound with his wife, Wendy, and son, Danny, for three months. Energized by Danny's psychic powers—called his shine by King—the malevolent ghosts from the Overlook's violent past manifest themselves to claim the Torrance family as their latest victims. Despite Danny's shine, the focus of the book is on Jack, the most vulnerable of the trio, as he battles with his own demons as well as those present in the Overlook. A powerful character study and chronicle of domestic tension, as well as a first-rate, very visceral ghost story, *The Shining* is one of King's best books and one of the major horror novels of the 1970s. Jack Nicholson's portrayal of Jack Torrance as a one-dimensional madman rather than as a basically decent man who disintegrates gradually under internal and external pressures made Stanley Kubrick's 1980 film adaptation a disappointing if interesting and intermittently gripping film.

***4-174. Skeleton Crew**. Putnam, 1985.
Nineteen short stories, one novella and two prose poems that span King's career from his first publication ("The Reaper's Image," 1969) through 1985 and show

the full range of his ability. The novella, "The Mist," is particularly impressive. The combination of a secret government experiment and a severe storm breaks open a hole between dimensions through which pours a thick white mist filled with voracious monsters of every size, shape and description. A small group of shoppers trapped in a grocery story fight among themselves as they try to formulate a plan for dealing with the horror that surrounds them. In *The Mist,* King adroitly combines a menagerie of the most extravagant and bizarre comic book/horror movie monsters with an intensely realistic setting and a collection of believable characters in conflict to produce one of his best and most viscerally scary stories. Compare Heard's "The Great Fog" [3-83] and Hodgson's *The Night Land* [F3-178]. Equally impressive is the gentle ghost story "The Reach," in which an old woman meets and rejoins the specters of her past. Other outstanding examples of King's short fiction are "Mrs. Todd's Ride," about a gutsy female whose passion for shortcuts takes her into some very bizarre territory; "The Word Processor of the Gods," in which a homemade computer allows its owner to reprogram his own life; "Nona," about a female who is either a vicious *femme fatale* or a creature of the narrator's imagination; and "Gramma," about the terrors that gradually overwhelm a young boy when he is left alone with his sinister, dying grandmother. These stories demonstrate, in a compressed form, the qualities that have made King the genre's most popular author: adroit plotting, sharply and quickly drawn characters, and a vivid sense of detail and visual imagery.

***4-175. The Stand**. 1978.

The accidental release of a germ-warfare superflu virus wipes out most of the human race. The scattered survivors gradually wend their way to one of two rendezvous points: Boulder, Colorado, where Mother Abagail, an ancient black woman, draws the Good, and Las Vegas, where Randall Flagg, the dark man, recruits followers for Evil. Thus, a post-holocaust SF novel evolves into an epic morality play of good vs. evil. The sweep of the novel is impressive, with several plot lines juxtaposed, more than a dozen major characters in a variety of believable relationships and a meticulously detailed landscape that covers most of the United States. Tension builds gradually but inexorably to the apocalyptic confrontation between Good and Evil in Las Vegas. Only at the end does King falter with a *deus ex machina* finale. The early chapters are reminiscent of George Stewart's SF classic *Earth Abides* (1949). Compare McCammon's *Swan Song* [4-224].

4-176. Thinner. New American Library, 1984 (as by Richard Bachman).

King did not initially admit to the Bachman pseudonym, which appeared earlier on four Signet original paperbacks. The story is unmistakably King, as a number of reviewers commented before King's admission of authorship in February 1985. An elderly gypsy puts curses on an attorney who killed the gypsy's daughter in an automobile accident, and on the police chief and judge who exonerated him of guilt. The overweight lawyer begins losing weight inexorably, and other misfortunes are visited upon the other two men. King's use of brand-name realism to create belief in gypsy curses is effective. The lawyer's attempt to shift the curse has unexpected and horrific results. Expertly plotted, but—unusual for King—completely devoid of sympathetic characters. Compare Matheson's *The Shrinking Man* [4-219].

4-177. The Tommyknockers. Putnam, 1987.
When Bobbi Anderson trips over the protruding tip of a flying saucer, she releases long dormant forces that threaten not only herself, but also her friends, neighbors, the citizens of Haven, Maine, and ultimately the world. Only her best friend, self-destructive alcoholic ex-English professor and poet Jim "Gard" Gardener, offers any continuing opposition to the gradual, grotesque transformations that will culminate in the "Becoming," when the mission of the saucer will be completed. A "big" King book with a large canvas, many characters of all types and a host of minidramas juxtaposed against one another and against the larger plot. At times these secondary actions and characters threaten to obscure the main thrust of the book, but in the end the book holds together and—unlike some of his other "big" novels—the finale is logical and satisfying. Compare to Finney's *The Body Snatchers* [4-116] and Koontz's *Strangers* [4-190].

—— and **Peter Straub,** 1943- .

4-178. The Talisman. Viking, 1984.
An ambitious collaboration between two preeminent dark fantasy authors. To save his mother's life—as well as that of Laura DeLoessian, Queen of "The Territories," a dangerous, bizarre alternate world—thirteen-year-old Jack Sawyer must journey to a hotel on the California coast to find and secure a mysterious, magical "talisman." As Jack pursues his quest, he "flips" back and forth between our world and the Territories, encountering increasingly grotesque and dangerous obstacles, doggedly chased by his late father's evil partner, Morgan Sloat. The lengthy, episodic, open-ended plot gives King and Straub ample space and freedom to indulge their imaginations. The result is, not surprisingly, a quite uneven, but generally strong mix of quest fantasy and horror story. Jack is a sympathetic, well-drawn (if overly precocious) character, particularly in his touching relationship with Wolf, a powerful, benevolent child-like werewolf. Several individual sequences are powerful, particularly in the early chapters, and the book's overall design is audacious, but about three-fourths of the way through the novel, weariness sets in and violence replaces careful plotting. Compare to King's *Dark Tower* series [4-164]. Also annotated as [F4A-152].

[For other works of this author, see the companion guide to fantasy.]

Kirk, Russell, 1918- .

ABOUT: WW, GSF, CA, SMFL, PE, ESF

4-179. Old House of Fear. Fleet, 1961.
Attempting to purchase the "Old House of Fear," agent Hugh Logan is thrust into a complex political intrigue involving the sinister Dr. Jackman, romance with the lovely Mary MacAskival and possible otherworldly intrusions. A contemporary adventure-Gothic mix that does not resolve the question of supernaturalism until the final few pages. The conservative social, political and religious attitudes of Kirk are freely expressed throughout the novel.

4-180. The Princess of All Lands. Arkham House, 1979.
Five new stories and four reprints from *The Surly Sullen Bell*. The centerpiece is

"There's a Long, Long Trail A-Winding," a chilling haunted house tale about an old derelict who, seeking refuge in a deserted mansion, encounters the ghosts of the people killed there years earlier. By helping the spectral victims, he is able to right an old personal wrong. World Fantasy Award, 1977. Also outstanding are the title story, about a psychically talented woman haunted by a ghostly teenaged hitchhiker, and "The Last God's Dream," about the spectral return of an ancient Roman emperor.

4-181. The Surly Sullen Bell. Fleet, 1962.
Ten stories plus "A Cautionary Note on the Ghost Tale," Kirk's defense of the classical ghost story as a moral allegory in the Christian tradition. In the title story, a man visits an old flame who is dying—by the hand of her husband, who has further plans for all three of them. In "Uncle Isiah," David Kinnaird's mysterious, perhaps deceased uncle returns to defend Kinnaird from extortion by local gangsters. When local planners in "Ex Tenbris" attempt to displace old Mrs. Oliver, she calls upon her deceased vicar for support. In "What Shadows We Pursue," Mr. Stonburner, a bookseller, must deal with the ghost of the former owner of a recently purchased collection. Kirk's stories are carefully, cleanly written, with the classical qualities of his major influences—M. R. James, Henry James, Arthur Machen, Algernon Blackwood and Sheridan Le Fanu—clearly evident. Excellent rendering of a variety of milieus, from the English countryside to the American big city to the American backwoods. Kirk's conservative political, social and religious biases are clearly evident in these stories, although the rhetoric is somewhat more muted than in the novels.

Klein, T(heodore) E(ibon) D(onald), 1947- .
ABOUT: CA, H, PE, FF

4-182. The Ceremonies. Viking, 1984.
An expansion and elaboration of the novella "The Events at Poroth Farm" (1974), which originally appeared in *The Year's Best Horror Stories: Series II* [4-363]. Graduate student Jeremy Freirs rents a summer cottage in rural Gilead, New Jersey, from farmers Sarr and Deborah Poroth, devotees of the Brethren of the Redeemer religious sect. As he settles in to his academic research, Freirs acquires a girlfriend, becomes friendly with the Poroths and explores the cultural idiosyncrasies of the community—unaware that he and the others are being manipulated by the cherubic, evil Mr. Rosebottom into a series of increasingly demonic ceremonies that will ultimately unleash a terrible primal evil on the world. *The Ceremonies* has echoes of Arthur Machen and H. P. Lovecraft, but in a thoroughly contemporary context. The novel's length allows time for a thorough development of plot, characters and setting—the delineation of the religious culture is especially good—but it also bogs down at times. Winner of the August Derleth Award in 1986. Compare Burke's *The Devil's Footsteps* [4-58] and Tryon's *Harvest Home* [4-305].

4-183. The Dark Gods. Viking, 1985.
Four novellas. "Children of the Kingdom," which appeared originally in *Dark Forces* [4-346], features an ancient race of malevolent, but fortunately blind, creatures noticed only by the perceptive—or paranoid—narrator, until they erupt

to assault New York City during the 1977 blackout. Compare Barker's less subtle "The Midnight Meat-Train" [4-20]. In "Petey," the Kurtzes and their guests celebrate their new bargain house, gradually becoming aware of the horrors that lie within and the horror—the unfed "Petey"—that lies without. In "The Black Man with a Horn," a story in the Lovecraft mode, the narrator, investigating the death of a recently returned missionary, becomes slowly aware of the "black man"—actually the monstrous "Sho Goran," or "sucker fish" man—hovering nearby. "Nadleman's God" is evoked when his old poem is used as lyrics for a rock song which, in turn, attracts a sinister fan, who forces Nadleman to see the horror at the "center of things." The story touches on ideas developed at greater length in Martin's "The Armageddon Rag" [4-212] and Skipp and Spector's *The Scream* [4-276]. Carefully written and developed, the horrors in *The Dark Gods* are more chilling because they are largely unseen. Because of their greater compression, these novellas avoid the wordiness that marred Klein's otherwise successful novel, *The Ceremonies.*

Koenig, Laird.

About: PE

4-184. The Little Girl Who Lives Down the Lane. Coward, McCann, 1974.
Living alone with her poet father—who is never seen—thirteen-year-old Rynn Jacobs resents intruders, particularly the nosy realtor who rented them the house and her suspicious, conniving son. Recruiting a shy young magician, she defends the sanctity of her little world against all threats by whatever means necessary. A slick, lively, darkly humorous—if fairly superficial—novel with several clever plot twists. Compare March's *The Bad Seed* [4-211].

Konvitz, Jeffrey, 1944- .

About: CA, SFFL

4-185. The Sentinel. Simon and Schuster, 1974.
The Sentinel is a book entirely without pretensions. A straightforward popular page-turner, it is also one of the seminal works of horror from the mid-1970s. An up-and-coming model, Allison Parker, moves into a New York apartment building peopled with eccentric characters, including an old man who holds birthday parties for his pets, a pair of lesbian lovers and a blind priest who never leaves his apartment and stares unseeingly out the window. The neighbors are at first interestingly comic, but Allison soon learns that she has no neighbors save the priest, that the other tenants do not exist and that the building is situated over the gates of Hell. Although *The Sentinel* deals with God, Satan and the Catholic Church, it is refreshingly free from the pseudo-serious trappings of *The Exorcist* [4-42] and its clones. The novel was followed by a sequel, *The Guardian* (1979), which, while equally hard to put down, nonetheless relies on too many tricky twists and cheating revelations to be truly effective. *The Sentinel* was relatively faithfully filmed in 1976. Compare *Rosemary's Baby* [4-206]. (B.L.)

Koontz, Dean R(ay), 1945– .
About: CA, NE SFE, SFFL, TCSF, PE, ESF

4-186. Darkfall. Berkley, 1984.
Originally written under the pseudonym Owen West and later reissued under Koontz's own name, *Darkfall* is the story of a widowed police officer, his young daughter and a female partner who are terrorized by demons summoned from hell by a voodoo priest. *Darkfall* is atypical Koontz in both its setting and subject matter: the novel takes place in New York, and the horror is straight and hardcore, without even a trace of science fiction. Koontz's deft characterization and page-turning suspense are here in abundance, however, as are many of his familiar thematic elements. *Darkfall* is probably Koontz's best novel written under the West pseudonym. (B.L.)

4-187. Midnight. Putnam, 1989.
In the small northern California town of Moonlight Cove, local authorities have been covering up the true causes of a series of "accidental" deaths. An FBI agent is assigned to investigate, and he meets the sister of one of the victims, in town for similar reasons of her own. They team up with a local girl whose parents have turned into monsters, and a paraplegic veteran who has discovered that the same thing has been happening throughout the town. There are elements of *The Body Snatchers* [4-116] and *The Island of Dr. Moreau* (1896) in the plot of *Midnight,* but thematically the novel is pure Koontz, who here not only celebrates the redemptive power of love and the joy of life, but also examines what it means and what it costs to be human. *Midnight* is a horrific cautionary tale, and an assured, sophisticated, playfully self-aware work. (B.L.)

4-188. Phantoms. Putnam, 1983.
Phantoms was one of Koontz's first crossover successes, and it is still one of his best. In the small ski town of Snowfield, California, a third of the population has been gruesomely murdered. The rest have disappeared without a trace. Into this nightmare stumble an innocent young female doctor and her little sister, who try desperately to find out what has occurred before they become the next victims. *Phantoms* is extremely well written and set the tone for Koontz's later big best-sellers: horror/mystery/suspense stories peopled with likable, believable characters, containing a pseudo-scientific explanation for the horrific events. In this novel, the scientific ties also have vaguely Lovecraftian overtones, which makes for a particularly interesting amalgam. (B.L.)

4-189. Shadowfires. Avon, 1987 (as by Leigh Nichols).
The subject of genetic engineering, which Koontz explores under his own name in *Watchers,* he here addresses under a pseudonym. A wealthy California businessman, head of a genetic-engineering firm performing secret work for the government, is killed in an accident shortly after threatening his estranged wife and returns from the dead to terrorize her. Unlike Koontz's previous pseudonymous books, *Shadowfires* is a complex cross-genre novel which is virtually indistinguishable from the work published under his own name. There are obvious plot similarities with *Whispers,* but *Shadowfires* is a fine book in its own right. The novel was the last written under the Nichols pseudonym. (B.L.)

4-190. Strangers. Putnam, 1986.
A number of widely scattered individuals, all suffering from severe neurotic reactions and puzzling memory blanks, are mysteriously drawn to a rendezvous at the Tranquility Motel on the plains of northern Nevada. As the group coalesces and their thoughts clarify, they uncover a terrible/wonderful secret as well as a desperate conspiracy to keep that secret from ever being made public. Koontz's surprisingly euphoric resolution may annoy some hard-core horror fans, but his skill in the manipulation of the intricate plotting and diverse characterizations, while maintaining a high level of intensifying suspense, is impressive. Compare King's *The Tommyknockers* [4-177].

4-191. Twilight Eyes. Berkley, 1987.
A slightly different version of Part One was published in a hardcover collector's edition in 1985; Koontz has referred to Part Two as a "sequel" to Part One. Slim MacKenzie is both cursed and blessed with "twilight eyes," a psychic sensitivity that enables him to see "goblins"—an implacably hostile race of animal-like creatures that assume human shapes and plot continuing evil against man. In Part One, Slim, a fugitive because he murdered his goblin uncle, joins a carnival where he finds contentment, love—in the person of the beautiful but dangerously mysterious Rya Raines—and deadly competition with the goblins of Yontsdown, a small town dominated by the creatures. In Part Two, Slim and Rya return to Yontsdown to seek out and destroy the goblins in their underground retreat. Part One, with its moving characterizations, especially the Slim-Rya romance, and its realistic, colorful observation of the carnival milieu, is especially strong.

4-192. The Vision. Putnam, 1977.
Mary Bergen, a clairvoyant, sees her own murder at the hands of a vicious serial killer—even after he is dead. To understand her danger and save herself, Mary must concentrate her powers on her own tortured psyche. A tightly focused, increasingly suspenseful book. Compare King's *The Dead Zone* [4-165] and Matheson's *A Stir of Echoes* [4-220].

***4-193. Watchers**. Putnam, 1987.
Although the subject matter of his novels is dark, Koontz has always been an optimist, a firm believer in the ability of human beings to triumph over adversity and emerge stronger and healthier. Nowhere is this theme dealt with more effectively than in *Watchers*, the story of an emotionally abused woman and an emotionally barren man who find love and strength while helping a genetically engineered dog escape from a laboratory-spawned monster. There are obvious parallels with *Frankenstein* [1-97], and Koontz uses the novel to address moral and ethical concerns, but at its core *Watchers* is a love story and a testament to human survival. The cross-genre approach which brought Koontz mainstream success is much in evidence, and his blending of horror, suspense, science fiction, social melodrama and romance has never been achieved more skillfully. A tightly focused novel of psychological complexity. A wonderful book. (B.L.)

4-194. Whispers. Putnam, 1980.
A big, ambitious novel, *Whispers* is the story of a successful young woman stalked by a man she killed in self-defense. With the help of a policeman with whom she becomes romantically involved, she tracks down the man to learn the

secret of his apparent immortality and to stop him from terrorizing her. Many of Koontz's recurring motifs and themes can be found in this novel—the emotionally battered female protagonist, the redemptive power of love—and he uses the work to address several social, political and interpersonal concerns. Koontz has also laced the book with an uncharacteristically strong dose of libertarian philosophy which, though obvious, does not become propagandistic and does not detract from the novel's artistic merit. *Whispers* is not only an excellent horror novel, it is also a fascinating and large-scale work of contemporary fiction. (B.L.)

Kosinski, Jerzy (Poland), 1933– .

ABOUT: CA, H

4-195. The Painted Bird. Houghton Mifflin, 1965. Rev. ed., 1976.
In 1939, a six-year-old boy is forced to wander the European countryside for four years, surviving by luck and his wits. Among the peasants he encounters every imaginable type of prejudice, ignorance, misery, superstition, cruelty, deprivation and violence, while the Nazi war machine hovers in the background, before he is finally rescued by the Allies. Although there is nothing overtly fantastic in the book, the extremity of the events rendered in meticulous detail by the boy's flat, almost clinically detached voice gives the novel the feeling of a long, protracted surrealistic nightmare. Compare J. G. Ballard's more conventionally realistic *Empire of the Sun* (1985).

Kressing, Harry (pseud. of **Harry Adam Ruber**).

4-196. The Cook. Random, 1965.
The Cook is a tight, extremely well-written story of a mysterious cook and his influence over the wealthy family for whom he works. The cook, Conrad, slowly and subtly gains control of the household through the politics of food, and though he remains ostensibly a servant, the members of the family are soon coming to him for advice, and eventually end up obeying his orders. The novel works as both a simple horror story and as a Machiavellian study of influence and evil. A brilliantly conceived novel and a frightening allegory, *The Cook* is an obvious precursor of Joan Samson's similarly themed and structured *The Auctioneer* [4-260]. (B.L.)

Langley, Noel (U.K.), 1911–1980.

ABOUT: WW, GSF, CA, SFFL

4-197. Tales of Mystery and Revenge. Arthur Barker, 1950.
Seven stories. The best of them, "The Fall of the Fothergays," chronicles the decline and fall of the Fothergays, one of the foremost British theatrical clans, triggered by the family's black sheep, an admitted black magician (compare Aickman's "The Visiting Star" [4-7] and Leiber's "Four Ghosts in *Hamlet*" [4-201]). Other notable stories include two tales, "Serenade for Baboons" and "The Bead Necklace," involving African black magic, and "Little Miracle," in which a drowned sailor returns to salvage his fiancée's life. Langley's stories of

genteel horror are clever, compact, ironic and generally humorous. The best have a sharp bite, although others are damaged by a touch of mawkishness.

Laski, Marghanita (U.K.), 1915–1988.
About: CA, ESF

4-198. The Victorian Chaise Longue. Cresset, 1953.
Confined to an ornate Victorian chaise longue by a touch of tuberculosis and a difficult childbirth, Melanie Langdon awakens in the year 1844 occupying the body of Milly Baines, a terminally ill young woman. She desperately tries to understand the bizarre situation she has been thrust into, to convince someone that she is telling the truth about her transformation and, most important, to discover some way to return to her own time, place and body. Since the story is told entirely from Melanie/Milly's point of view, we can never be sure whether we are sharing a nightmare, an extended hallucination or an actual time migration caused by a magical couch. A very engrossing, suspenseful, skillfully developed short novel. Compare du Maurier's *The House on the Strand* [4-102] and Millhiser's *The Mirror* [4-237].

Laymon, Richard.
About: CA, H, PE

4-199. The Cellar. Warner, 1980.
Filled with graphically titillating scenes of child molestation, sexual abuse and violent torture, *The Cellar* is without a doubt one of the most viscerally disgusting novels ever written. It is also extraordinarily original. The plot is simple: a woman and her daughter, fleeing her escaped convict husband, end up in a small California town which is home to the Beast House, scene of a series of gruesome murders. The horror at the core of the novel, however, and the cause of the events at the Beast House, is unique and archetypally primal. *The Cellar* is a precursor of the more widely publicized, but considerably less graphic and interesting work of the so-called splatterpunks. The novel's unrelentingly nihilistic ending was diluted somewhat by a tamer sequel, *The Beast House* (1987). (B.L.)

Leiber, Fritz, 1910– .
About: WW, GSF, SFW, F, CA, NE, H, TCA, SMFL, SFE, MF, SFFL, RG, TCSF, PE, ESF, FL, HF

4-200. The Best of Fritz Leiber. Doubleday, 1974; Sphere (U.K.), 1974 (stories are the same in both, but the secondary material differs).
"Introduction" by Poul Anderson, "Afterword" by Leiber. Twenty-two stories that mix science fiction/fantasy with supernatural horror. Especially interesting are "Gonna Roll Them Bones" (Nebula and Hugo Awards, 1967), a grotesque, surrealistic Faustian bargain story in which Joe Slattermill tries to outplay, outwit and finally outfight the "Big Gambler," the Devil himself; "The Ship Sails at Midnight," a poignant, ironic account of a clash between alien innocence and human sexual jealousy; "A Deskful of Girls," in which a maniacal psychiatrist collects the "ghosts" of beautiful women to file in a locked desk; "Rump-

titty-titty-tum-tah-tee," which features an obsessive primal rhythm that threatens to enslave mankind; and "The Man Who Made Friends with Electricity," in which Mr. Leverett loves the sound of electricity, listens to its voice and finally comes to understand its plans for the human race. Vintage Leiber—inventive, witty, ironic, occasionally touching. The satirical barbs aimed at modern life in particular and human nature in general are especially well placed. Compare the short fiction of Matheson [4-218] and Beaumont [4-26, 4-27].

4-201. The Ghost Light. Berkley, 1984.
Nine stories first published between 1950 and 1984 plus an extended autobiographical essay. Along with such Leiber standards as "Coming Attraction," "A Deskful of Girls," and "Gonna Roll Them Bones," *The Ghost Light* features the title story, in which an oil portrait and a mysterious nightlight draw out old Cassius Kruger's repressed memories and guilty secrets as a severe storm batters his northern California home; "Four Ghosts in *Hamlet*," in which the shade of Hamlet's father turns out to be none other than the Bard himself; "Midnight by the Morphy Watch," about an old watch, once owned by a crazy chess champion, that carries its haunted history with it; and "Black Glass," in which an elderly writer, on a walking tour of New York City, inadvertently wanders into that city's dismal future. The links between the stories are provided by Leiber's chatty, rambling, intimate memoir, "Not Much Disorder and Not So Early Sex," which ties each story to the event in Leiber's life which inspired it.

4-202. Night Monsters. Gollancz, 1974.
Seven short stories, two of which are science fiction. The Ace "double edition" (bound with *The Green Millennium*, 1969) drops four stories but adds "The Casket Demon." Most impressive are "The Black Gondolier," which postulates that oil is not an inorganic mineral substance, but is actually a conscious, deliberate force that controls human development and punishes any who become aware of its true nature and purpose; "Midnight in the Mirror World," a strange, touching "romance" between a rich recluse and a ghostly presence in a mirror; and "The Girl with the Green Eyes," a vampiric *femme fatale* tale with a very contemporary slant.

***4-203. Our Lady of Darkness**. Putnam, 1977.
San Francisco novelist Franz Weston, recovering from the recent death of his wife and a bout of alcoholism, learns about "paramental entities," malevolent spirits produced by the modern big city. In the process of investigating the nature and meaning of these paramentals, Weston becomes increasingly vulnerable to them while, at the same time, coming to terms with his personal emotional crisis. A powerful, original, scary, deeply moving novel, with strong autobiographical elements, as well as a plethora of in-jokes and much name dropping for the *cognoscenti*. World Fantasy Award, 1978.

***4-204. The Sinful Ones**. Universal, 1953; rev. ed., Pocket Books, 1980.
Awful title, great book. Originally called *You're All Alone* when published in a much shorter version in *Fantastic Adventures* (1950) and as a 1972 Ace paperback, the first book publishers retitled it *The Sinful Ones*, and added snappy chapter headings and some gratuitous soft porn scenes, without the author's knowledge or permission. Upon retrieving the rights to the book for a 1980 edition, Leiber

revised or deleted the sex scenes but let the title and headings remain: "after all, they'd been there for twenty-seven years and they helped identify the book." *The Sinful Ones* follows the adventures of Carr Mackay after he suddenly realizes that most people are actually pre-programmed machines and that a "real person" can do almost anything he/she wants without being noticed. Mackay uses this freedom to pursue his dream girl, Jane, another real person. But he soon learns the catch: most real people use their freedom to indulge their perversities, lusts and greed—and they hate and fear others so endowed. Thus, Mackay and Jane must flee the homicidal wrath of a dangerous trio and their pet panther. Clever, witty, touching and provocative. Ranks with Finney's *The Body Snatchers* [4-116] and the works of Richard Matheson [4-216–4-220] as an early exploration of the "paranoid theme" in contemporary horror literature.

Leslie, Josephine (U.K.), 1898–1979.

About: GSF, CA

4-205. The Devil and Mrs. Devine. Millington, 1975.
Historical fantasy by the author of the pseudonymous comic ghost story *The Ghost and Mrs. Muir* [F3-112]. A grieving young widow makes a reckless diabolical bargain from which she can be redeemed only by the love of a good man; it takes a long time to find. An intriguing sexual inversion of the Faust theme, appropriately sentimental but somewhat contrived. (B.S.)

Levin, Ira, 1929- .

About: F, CA, NE, SMFL, SFE, MF, SFFL, TCSF, PE, ESF

***4-206. Rosemary's Baby**. Random, 1967.
Guy and Rosemary Woodhouse move into the elegant, fashionable but sinister Bramford Apartments and are quickly befriended by an elderly couple, the Castevets, who become quite helpful when Rosemary learns she is pregnant. Rosemary becomes increasingly worried and suspicious, however, as her difficult pregnancy progresses, and decides that a demonic conspiracy is being directed against her and her baby. Her flight, the birth of the child, the revelation of the baby's true father and Rosemary's reaction to that revelation comprise one of the greatest finales in contemporary dark fantasy. Incisive dialogue, vivid dramatic scenes, sharply defined characters and clean, controlled writing that balances wit and irony against the grotesque and horrific make *Rosemary's Baby* one of the most sophisticated and stimulating books in the genre. Roman Polanski's outstanding and very faithful 1968 film adaptation of the novel enhanced its already great popularity and consolidated its reputation as the most important horror novel of the 1960s and the book that launched the "horror boom" of the 1960s and 1970s. Compare Campbell's *To Wake the Dead* [4-73].

4-207. The Stepford Wives. Random, 1972.
After moving with her husband and two children to Stepford, Connecticut, an idyllic small town, Joanna Ingalls Eberhart, wife, mother and would-be professional photographer, quickly becomes disillusioned by the local women, who seem interested only in home, family and housekeeping. Gradually she discovers

that these women are not "real," that they have been turned into machines of domesticity and conformity, and that she is in danger of a like fate. A slick, scary, provocative novel that puts a feminist twist on the paranoia theme. Does Stepford represent the ultimate backlash against the feminist movement?

Lofts, Norah (U.K.), 1904–1983.

About: CA, SFFL, ESF

4-208. The Devil's Own. Doubleday, 1960 (as by Peter Curtis). Reprinted as *The Witches*, Pan, 1966.

Deborah Mayfield slowly becomes aware that a sinister witch-cult is flourishing in Walwyk, the small English village where she has accepted a position as head mistress, and that she is being gradually drawn into its machinations. Lofts skillfully blends creditable occult materials with the strong sense of place and detail characteristic of her historical romances to create a superior dark fantasy. Filmed as *The Witches* (1967). Compare Burke's *The Devil's Footsteps* [4-58].

Lumley, Brian (U.K.), 1937- .

About: WW, CA, PE

4-209. The Burrowers Beneath. DAW, 1974.

Lumley's first full-length H. P. Lovecraft pastiche. The title comes from the list of stories attributed to "Robert Blake," hero of Lovecraft's "The Haunter of the Dark" [3-132]. A group of anti-Cthulhu crusaders, led by Titus Crow, fight to destroy the offspring of the earth-burrowing Shudde-M'ell, along with other Cthulhu-type beings. Using a multiple-narrator, semi-documentary style reminiscent of Lovecraft's "The Call of Cthulhu" [3-132], Lumley succeeds in the first two-thirds of the book in evoking that sense of cosmic horror characteristic of Lovecraft's best, but the novel becomes fragmentary and loses focus toward the end. Crow reappears in *The Transition of Titus Crow* (1975), *The Clock of Dreams* (1978), *Spawn of the Winds* (1978), *In the Moons of Borea* (1979) and *The Compleat Crow* (1987). Compare Bloch's *Strange Eons* [4-48], Chappell's *Dagon* [4-77] and Shea's *The Color Out of Time* [4-268].

Marasco, Robert.

About: CA, H

4-210. Burnt Offerings. Delacorte, 1973.

Marian and Ben Rolfe, along with their son David and Aunt Elizabeth, rent a spectacular summer house at a ridiculously low rent in exchange for a promise to care for the owner's invalid mother who never leaves her upstairs room. It soon becomes clear to the Rolfes that the house is haunted, and the house begins to affect their relationships, their mental health and their lives. Like *Hell House* [4-216], *Burnt Offerings* is a direct descendant of *The Haunting of Hill House* [4-155]. But whereas Matheson essentially rewrote Jackson's story, substituting a more traditional ghost for Hill House's terrifying ambiguous haunting, Marasco has chosen to go a step beyond Jackson's concept of a sentient house, to produce not only a frighteningly original tale, but an extremely literary and influential one as well. Marasco knows the genre and its conventions, and he manipulates them brilliantly. Compare also King's *The Shining* [4-173]. (B.L.)

March, William (pseud. of **William Edward March Campbell**), 1893–1954.

ABOUT: CA

4-211. The Bad Seed. Holt, Rinehart, 1954.
Christine Penmark gradually comes to suspect that her eight-year-old daughter, Rhoda, inheritor of her grandmother's homicidal tendencies, is guilty of three murders. Blaming her "bad seed" for her daughter's evil, she vows to terminate the evil, even at the cost of her own life. A very popular novel, subsequently adapted to both stage (by Maxwell Anderson) and screen. Although Rhoda's evil is inherited, rather than supernatural, *The Bad Seed* established the pattern of the "evil child" novel that was to become one of the most popular subgenres in contemporary dark fantasy.

Martin, George R(aymond) R., 1948– .

ABOUT: CA, NE, SFE, TCSF, PE

4-212. The Armageddon Rag. Poseidon, 1983.
Sandy Blair, former underground journalist and successful novelist experiencing writer's block and relationship problems, accepts an assignment to investigate a brutal murder. The trail leads him back into 1960s politics, life-styles and music, as well as a bizarre, horrific plot to resurrect the "revolution" through rock music, focusing on Nazgûl, a sinister, legendary sixties rock group. The first half of *The Armageddon Rag* is unabashed nostalgia, but the second half becomes increasingly dark and menacing, with strong supernatural overtones. A strong, evocative novel. Compare Skipp and Spector's *The Scream* [4-276].

4-213. Fevre Dream. Poseidon, 1982.
Vampire Joshua York, assisted by Mississippi riverboat captain Abner Mann, sets out on a mission to reform his fellow vampires by giving them a new drink to relieve their need for blood. This ignites a civil war among the undead. Less sophisticated than revisionist vampire novels by Kast [4-159] and Rice [4-250], *Fevre Dream* is a fast-moving, exciting book, with a colorful period flavor.

4-214. Portraits of His Children. Dark Harvest, 1987.
Introduction by Roger Zelazny. Eleven stories ranging from science fiction to high fantasy to humorous sketch to dark fantasy that demonstrate Martin's virtuosity and versatility. The best story in the collection, however, is the title story, which is the most realistic. Provoked by a series of portraits, a famous novelist confronts his own characters as he struggles with the painful dilemma posed by the conflict between his life and his art. A poignant, even tragic, delineation of a man whose passion to create destroys his human relationships.

4-215. Songs the Dead Men Sing. Dark Harvest, 1983.
Seven stories anchored by two of his best known, "Sandkings" and "Nightflyers," which tread the line between science fiction and horror. In "Sandkings," Simon

Kress's quest of the ultimate pet is satisfied by the purchase of "sandkings," small creatures that build castles, make war and worship their owner as a god. Kress, unfortunately, makes a very poor god. "Nightflyers," on the other hand, is a disappointingly routine science fiction/horror story about a group of scientists trapped on a spaceship determined to kill them off one by one. Other noteworthy stories include: "The Monkey Treatment," a funny-grotesque story about a weight-loss program that features the nastiest monkey this side of Le Fanu's "Green Tea" [2-50]; "The Needle Men," in which the title characters kidnap unattached poor folk to supply cadavers for medical education and experiment; "Meathouse Man," which traces the career of Greg Trager, a corpse handler, from his boyhood experiences with dead whores in the "meathouse," to his search for love, to his final disillusionment—a moving character study told in a provocative fragmentary style; and "Remembering Melody," an eerie tale about Melody, the failed and dissipated member of the old bohemian college gang, who keeps returning to her old friends—even after she's dead. Compare the short stories of Harlan Ellison [4-104].

Matheson, Richard, 1927- .

About: WW, GSF, SFW, CA, TCA, NE, H, SMFL, SFE, MF, SFFL, RG, TCSF, PE, ESF, HF, FF

4-216. Hell House. Viking, 1971.

Three experts—a scientist, a spiritualist and a former child psychic—are hired by an eccentric millionaire to prove or disprove afterlife through an investigation of the mysterious phenomena that pervade the Emerick Belasco mansion. Attacked by every conceivable form of psychological and physical horror, two of the three investigators are destroyed before the diabolical force behind the hauntings is revealed. The basic concept is ingenious and the atmosphere of sexual perversion and moral chaos is very strong, but the characters are generally unsympathetic and the final revelation seems contrived. Matheson scripted the film adaptation, *The Legend of Hell House* (1973). Compare Jackson's *The Haunting of Hill House* [4-155] and Williamson's *Soulstorm* [4-329].

***4-217. I Am Legend**. Fawcett, 1954.

In a world filled with vampires, the "normal" man becomes the real vampire. Atomic war unleashes a long-dormant disease that turns everyone into a vampire except the hero, Robert Neville, who barricades himself in his home, emerging during the day to kill as many of the creatures as possible. Neville's determination and security are threatened when he meets Ruth, who is either another survivor or a new type of vampire. A classic reversal of the traditional vampire novel: provocative, moving, imaginative. One of the central novels in the shaping of contemporary horror fiction. Filmed twice (*The Last Man on Earth*, 1964; *The Omega Man*, 1971), both times badly; the novel's primary film influence was as the inspiration for George Romero's *The Night of the Living Dead* (1968).

***4-218. Shock!** Dell, 1961; **Shock II**. Dell, 1964; **Shock III**. Dell, 1966; **Shock Waves**. Dell, 1970.

Four volumes that gather the best of Matheson's short fiction, fifty-three stories written between 1950 and 1970. Scream/Press announced for 1989 Matheson's

Collected Stories, which collects eighty-six stories. Matheson's stories often present threats to couples or family units: nuclear holocaust ("The Last Day," "Descent" and, with an unusual twist, "Third from the Sun"), mass self-destruction ("Lemmings"), rampaging insects ("Crickets") or more domestic concerns like alien impregnation ("Mother by Protest"), voodoo curses ("From Shadowed Places"), kidnapping ("Being," "Dying Room Only"), a vanishing child ("Little Girl Lost"), an unruly child ("The Doll That Does Everything") and a grotesque, radiation-mutated child ("Born of Man and Woman"). Even more typical is the isolated male thrust into a trap of some kind. Sometimes there is no escape, as in "The Children of Noah," where the vacationing Mr. Ketchum is arrested for a traffic violation and, before he realizes what is happening, is put into a huge oven. A different, more complicated sexual trap confronts David Lindell in "Lover When You're Near Me." Left to manage the mining operations on Space Station Four, he is overwhelmed by the strong mind and grotesque lusts of his "Gnee" servant, a pink, hairless, one-nostriled female with telepathic powers. Even more frightening is the fate of John in "Wet Straw," who is pursued by the ghost of his murdered wife. As her presence grows and erotic memory vies with fear, John's mind deteriorates rapidly. Still more harrowing than mental collapse is being trapped in a world that is going mad or disintegrating altogether, as does that of Robert Graham in "The Curious Child," who progressively forgets everything about the life he is living, although he is rescued by a happy ending. Less fortunate is Don Marshall in "The Edge," who goes out for lunch and wanders into a parallel universe. Still more unlucky is the protagonist of "Disappearing Act," whose world simply disappears around him. The story ends in mid-sentence. Not all Matheson heroes accept their fates passively; some fight back despite the odds. Unbeknown to his fellow passengers, Arthur Jeffrey Wilson in "Nightmare at 20,000 Feet" saves them all from a destructive gremlin on the airplane wing, despite his almost hysterical fear of flying. In these and other equally ingenious, biting, funny stories, Matheson established himself as one of the premier charters of the paranoid landscape of the 1950s and after. Compare Beaumont [4-26, 4-27], Bloch [4-45, 4-47], Leiber [4-200–4-202] and Nolan [4-242].

4-219. The Shrinking Man. Fawcett, 1956.
Accidental exposure to radioactive mist plus the ingestion of a pesticide trigger a process that shrinks Scott Carey one inch every week. Vignettes dramatizing the stages of Carey's decline alternate with scenes of his battle with a spider in his own cellar—as the hero's loss of humanity is juxtaposed against his courageous defiance. An exciting, poignant, thought-provoking book, perhaps Matheson's best. Filmed from Matheson's screenplay—his first—*The Incredible Shrinking Man* (1957) was a superior film. Compare King/Bachman's *Thinner* [4-176].

4-220. A Stir of Echoes. Lippincott, 1958.
When Tom Wallace is hypnotized at a party, his psychic powers are set free. He begins to foresee events, to read the minds and feelings of those around him and to see a female ghost in his living room. As these powers expose his neighbors' dark secrets, he is drawn into their deceitful, lustful, even murderous intrigues. But the real focus is on Wallace's internal struggle, as his wild talent threatens his career, his marriage and even his sanity. An engaging, provocative story. Sympathetic characters in a sharply drawn southern California suburban milieu. Compare

King's *The Dead Zone* [4-165], Koontz's *The Vision* [4-192] and Silverberg's *Dying Inside* [4-271].

[For other works of this author, see the companion guide to fantasy.]

Maxim, John R., 1937- .

ABOUT: CA, PE

4-221. Abel/Baker/Charley. Houghton Mifflin, 1983.

After his wife is killed and his child injured by a reckless motorcycle rider, Jared Baker has an emotional breakdown in which his primal personalities—in Freudian terms his id, ego and superego—split into separate identities, "Abel," pure vengeful instinct and "Charley," total concentration. Abel/Baker/Charley then becomes both hunter—in his quest for revenge—and hunted—by police, gangsters and scientists. A fast-paced, suspenseful, perhaps overcomplicated but thoroughly original novel that combines elements of science fiction, horror story and thriller.

4-222. Platforms. Putnam, 1980.

Platforms is a novel with a central idea so original that even if the writing were stilted and the characters flat, it would still be an excellent and unforgettable work. The writing is consistently first rate, and Maxim's spare use of a modified and limited stream-of-consciousness style is highly effective. Characters throughout the book are complex and believably motivated. The plot concerns a New England suburb in which train commuters are behaving oddly, respected businessmen are suddenly becoming murderously violent and the ghosts of dead townspeople are appearing to the living. All these events center around a commuter train station and one of the most complex and intricate theories put forth in a contemporary horror novel. In addition to creating a rounded New England community, Maxim hypothesizes a believable afterlife, with specific details, and throws in some pointed social commentary as well. (B.L.)

McCammon, Robert R(ick), 1952- .

ABOUT: CA, H, PE

4-223. Mystery Walk. Holt, Rinehart, 1983.

A bizarre recurring dream of a smoke-eagle battling a fire-snake is shared by two boys with extraordinary psychic talents: Billy Creekmore, a Choctaw capable of communicating with the dead, and Wayne Falconer, an evangelistic faith healer. As the novel juxtaposes their lives and careers, the competition between them becomes increasingly dangerous, because another force, an evil Shape Changer, lurks in the background, maneuvering them toward mutual destruction. A suspenseful, provocative book, with surprising twists and turns in the plotting and several memorable characters, especially Billy and his extraordinary mystical mother, Ramona. Vintage McCammon.

***4-224. Swan Song**. Pocket Books, 1987.

McCammon's debt to Stephen King is nowhere more evident than in *Swan Song*, whose similarities to *The Stand* [4-175] are almost overwhelming. Plot and structural differences between the novels are so slight and superficial that it is impossible not to notice the parallels. In *Swan Song* the holocaust is a result of nuclear war rather than a strain of flu, the dark man's name is Friend instead of Flagg, and the old black woman has become a young white girl. That said, *Swan Song* is an eminently readable and enjoyable work, despite its length. Its depiction of the day-to-day lives of the survivors, both evil and good, is superbly handled, and personalities are so well drawn that it is easy to keep track of the book's numerous characters. The novel also improves in many ways upon King's work, particularly in the final confrontation between the forces of good and evil, which is mercifully free from the *deus ex machina* that mars *The Stand*'s climax. *Swan Song* is by no means an original work, but it is well written, consistently entertaining and an impressive, ambitious effort. Co-winner of the Bram Stoker Award in 1988. (B.L.)

4-225. They Thirst. Avon, 1981.
From his hideout in an old Hollywood horror castle, Count Vulkan begins his campaign to vampirize the world in Los Angeles. He recruits a band of followers and slowly, systematically begins to spread his evil over the city: vampires create new vampires by the dozens, with even the elements—darkness, snow, ultimately earthquake—forwarding his plot. The salvation of mankind rests with several very different, unlikely individuals scattered all over the Los Angeles basin. An extremely ambitious, extravagant vampire novel filled with interesting characters, adroit plot twists and vivid, if extremely gory, descriptions. Similar in scope and structure to King's *The Stand* [4-175] and *Swan Song* without the pretensions that mar those books.

***4-226. Usher's Passing**. Holt, Rinehart, 1984.
Still feeling grief and guilt over the death of his wife, Rix Usher returns to Usherland to join his brother, Boone, and sister, Katt, in a vigil at his father's deathbed. There he must come to terms with the Usher legacy, which includes Usher Armaments, a $10 billion weapons business; Usher's Malady, a lingering terminal illness in which the body decomposes before the onset of death; and the vast family estates, rumored to contain a legendary child-stealing monster, the Pumpkin Man, and his companion, the bloodthirsty panther, Greediguts. Beginning with his inspired use of Poe's masterpiece, McCammon has written a highly imaginative, extravagant novel filled with horrific elements, all of which come together in the novel's exciting conclusion. Despite the near comic-strip exaggeration in the plotting, the story is convincing, the characters believable, if grotesque, and the domestic conflict rings true—a kind of mix of Tennessee Williams and H. P. Lovecraft. Compare to Cady's *The Well* [4-61], McDowell's *Blackwater* series [4-230] and Oates's *Bellefleur* [4-243].

4-227. The Wolf's Hour. Pocket Books, 1989.
During the waning days of World War II, the Allies learn of a Nazi plan that could affect the outcome of the D-Day invasion. The only man able to get behind enemy lines, learn the details of the plan and successfully return is Michael Gallatin, a British spy and werewolf. Unlike F. Paul Wilson's *The Keep* [4-333], which is a horror novel set during World War II, *The Wolf's Hour* is essentially a World War II adventure novel with horror overtones. Michael Gallatin is Indiana

Jones as a werewolf, a fearless adventurer who uses fantastic escapes to get out of seemingly impossible predicaments. Surprisingly, Michael does not become a wolf nearly as often as the premise of the work would lead one to expect or the plot of the novel would seem to dictate. McCammon, in fact, purposely keeps the supernatural aspects to a minimum, and succeeds in his attempt to create an adventure/suspense/horror hybrid. One might wish for more background on Michael—too much time is spent on the specifics of the mission while intriguing aspects of his past are either dropped abruptly or not explored at all—but *The Wolf's Hour* is still a fine book and a rather bold step for McCammon into mainstream territory. Compare Wheatley's *They Used Dark Forces* [4-323] and Yarbro's *Tempting Fate* [4-340]. (B.L.)

McCloy, Helen, 1904- .

About: CA, ESF

4-228. Through a Glass, Darkly. Random, 1950.
Sensitive, fragile Faustina Crayle is dismissed from her teaching job because several people have been frightened by the sight of her "double." Psychiatrist Basil Willing attempts to learn the truth behind these apparitions before they drive Faustina to madness or worse—but he is unable to do so before Faustina's "double" commits murder. A suspenseful, nicely developed Gothic mystery with a disappointing final rationale.

McDowell, Michael, 1950- .

About: CA, PE, FF

4-229. The Amulet. Avon, 1979.
A fine first novel. In the small town of Pine Cone, Alabama, a beautiful gold amulet circulates from person to person, leaving death and destruction in its path. The action is predictable, but the gore is ingenious and the underlying rationale and purpose of the cursed pendant are clever. In *The Amulet,* McDowell establishes his most impressive talent, his ability to delineate the southern small-town milieu with an accuracy and vividness worthy of comparison to such regionalists as Reynolds Price, Carson McCullers, Flannery O'Connor and Eudora Welty.

***4-230. Blackwater: I, The Flood; II, The Levee; III, The House; IV, The War; V, The Fortune; VI, Rain**. Avon, 1983.
A six-volume family chronicle/horror novel that traces the fate of the Caskey family of Perdido, Alabama, from Easter 1919, when Elinor Dammert, later to become the clan matriarch, is rescued from the flooding Perdido River, to her death in the spring of 1970, during a second great flood. The novel follows the lives and fortunes of the Caskeys as they rise through periods of great social, political and personal turbulence to positions of power, wealth and influence. At the same time there is the mystery of Elinor and the dark forces she represents. But despite the novel's supernatural premise, the real conflicts in the *Blackwater* series are human ones as Elinor guides the family fortunes through the 1920s, the Depression, World War II and the postwar boom of the 1950s and early 1960s. An

ambitious, impressive social melodrama/dark fantasy with sensitive characterizations, strong plotting and a very effective rendering of the southern small-town milieu—although hard-core fans may be disappointed at the relatively modest use made of the horror elements. Compare McCammon's more extravagant *Usher's Passing* [4-226] and Oates's *Bellefleur* [4-243].

4-231. Cold Moon over Babylon. Avon, 1980.
Shortly after the Larkin family, struggling berry farmers in Babylon, Florida, are systematically murdered and their bodies cast into the Styx River, mysterious watery specters emerge and pursue the killer. Although the motivations of the murderer are not fully developed and the plot is fairly predictable, *Cold Moon over Babylon* is a superior novel, distinguished by its characterization of the Larkins, its careful presentation of the rural southern environment and its gradually intensifying, increasingly hallucinatory narrative thrust.

4-232. The Elementals. Avon, 1981.
The Elementals is probably McDowell's best novel. The *Blackwater* books may be more ambitious, but *The Elementals* is equally fine in its depiction of a southern matriarchy and is far superior in its handling of horror. Here, two families related by marriage spend the summer in twin Victorian houses by the beach, joined by the black sheep and his daughter, who now live in New York. A third beach house, adjoining the vacation homes, has been gradually filling with sand over the years, and creatures called "elementals" are said to live inside. McDowell's descriptions are richly Faulknerian, and his characters are worthy of Tennessee Williams at his most bitterly satiric. The novel works as social criticism, but the horror in *The Elementals* is real and deadly serious, frighteningly well done, and the final scene in the abandoned sand-covered house is one of the most unforgettable in all of contemporary horror fiction. A truly frightening work. (B.L.)

McEwan, Ian (U.K.), 1948- .
ABOUT: CA, PE

4-233. The Cement Garden. Simon and Schuster, 1978.
After their mother dies, four children—Julie, Sue, Tom and the narrator, Jack—bury her in the cellar in a cement-filled trunk and attempt to create a private world of their own in the family house. McEwan's first novel is a fascinating exercise in psychological suspense that covers territory similar to that of V. C. Andrews's *Flowers in the Attic* [4-12] in a much more sophisticated, subtle manner.

McGrath, Patrick (U.K.).

4-234. Blood and Water and Other Tales. Poseidon, 1988.
Thirteen provocative short horror stories. McGrath's combination of cultivated, restrained narrative and gruesome physical detail is reminiscent of Charles Birkin [4-31–4-34]. However, McGrath's stories have a bitterly ironic, darkly humorous tone, as well as an imaginative eccentricity that is uniquely his own. Strong examples of this can be seen in "The Black Hand of the Raj," a contemporary variation on Edward White's classic "Lukundoo" [3-212]; "The Angel," about

the perils of physical immortality; the title story, about an aristocratic family plagued by sexual ambivalence, madness, decapitation and bad plumbing; and the gentler, almost wistful "The Lost Explorer," about a young girl who finds a lost, dying explorer in her parents' garden. McGrath's stories may be too offbeat for some readers (the type who find stories narrated by "frogs" or "boots" too whimsical), but others will be delighted and chilled by McGrath's elegant, oddball tales.

McKenney, Kenneth, 1929- .
ABOUT: CA

4-235. The Moonchild. Simon and Schuster, 1978; **The Changeling**. Avon, 1985.
Edmund and Anna Blackstone, already shocked and saddened by the sudden, mysterious death of their young son, Simon, are horrified to learn that he is not really deceased, that he is an undead "moonchild," with an insatiable thirst to kill. Upon discovering that the only way Simon can be put to rest is by being buried where he was born, they begin a dangerous, increasingly violent trip home. A slick, ingenious novel that combines elements of the zombie, evil child and even werewolf motifs. In the sequel, *The Changeling*, Simon is freed from his grave and, now a handsome adult, moves easily in the world, loving and killing as he goes along.

Metcalfe, John (U.K.), 1891-1965.
ABOUT: WW, GSF, SFW, CA, PE, ESF

4-236. The Feasting Dead. Arkham House, 1954.
Walter Hapgood is increasingly baffled and disturbed by the bizarre friendship between his ailing son, Dennis, and Roul, a sinister French handyman with a mysterious past and apparently inhuman qualities. After his friend vanishes, Dennis flees to the estate where he first met Roul, pursued by his desperate father. Although Roul never reappears, the mystery becomes progressively ambiguous, sinister and dangerous. Initially refused publication in Great Britain as "too gory," *The Feasting Dead* is a provocative mix of overt horror and ambiguous menace which leaves many questions unanswered, particularly in its puzzling finale. An irritating but fascinating book.

Millhiser, Marlys, 1938- .
ABOUT: CA, SMFL, SFFL

4-237. The Mirror. Putnam, 1978.
Shay Garrett, a modern coed, and Brandy McCabe, her grandmother, exchange places when, on their respective wedding days, they simultaneously look into a magical mirror and exchange bodies. Each woman then lives out the life of the other. Although *The Mirror* is more interested in exploring women's roles in different historical epochs than in providing scares, the Gothic paraphernalia, especially the enigmatic magical mirror, give the book a sinister edge. Compare du Maurier's *The House on the Strand* [4-102] and Laski's *The Victorian Chaise Longue* [4-198]. Also annotated as [F4A-180].

Monteleone, Thomas F(rancis), 1946- .

ABOUT: CA, SFE, TCSF, PE

4-238. Night Train. Pocket Books, 1984.

The subways of New York City have proved to be a popular setting for horror stories, the claustrophobic darkness of the underground tunnels an obvious and effective location in which to make manifest subliminal and not-so-subliminal fears. *Night Train* is a fine example of the subway tale of terror. Television reporter Lya Marsden and policeman Michael Corvino, with the help of Lane Carter, a parapsychologist, discover the secret behind the disappearance of a turn-of-the-century subway train and find that there are more than just man-made tunnels running under the city of New York. Monteleone is a fine writer, and his depiction of quiet menace and subtle horror is excellent. The more overt, straightforward scenes do not work as well, however, and the novel is marred slightly by what seem like obtrusive elements of fantasy. Compare Clive Barker's "The Midnight Meat Train" [4-20] and Skipp and Spector's *The Light at the End* [4-275]. (B.L.)

Mordane, Thomas.

4-239. Bloodroot. Dell, 1982.

Bloodroot is a post-*Harvest Home* [4-305] novel of rural religious rites in contemporary New England. Laura and Mark Avery move to the town of Hubley's Gore, whose inhabitants belong to a Druidic cult which worships and offers sacrifices to a huge sentient oak. Not enough is done with the oak itself and the outcome of the novel is fairly predictable, but *Bloodroot* is consistently interesting and the background of the town's tree worshipping is unique. There is an excellent sense of place, and despite the obviousness of the ending, tension is sustained throughout the work. While not as good as *Harvest Home, Bloodroot* is free of the plodding plotting and meandering digressions of T. E. D. Klein's pretentious and less successful *The Ceremonies* [4-182]. (B.L.)

Morrell, David C., 1929- .

ABOUT: CA, H, PE, FF

4-240. The Totem. M. Evans, 1979.

Nathan Slaughter, police chief in a small Wyoming town, encounters a reanimated corpse, savage animals, insane children and widespread, irrational violence. The cause is a mysterious strain of rabies originating in a hippie commune, a type of plague, that Morrell suggests, provides the scientific and historical explanation for lycanthropy, vampirism and the like. Told in 107 brief, intense chapters, juxtaposed in a cinematic fashion, *The Totem* is a vivid, ferociously paced mix of horror and SF by the author best known for creating the popular character Rambo in his novel *First Blood* (1972). Compare Herbert's *The Fog* [4-141].

Murdoch, Iris (Ireland), 1919- .
About: CA

4-241. The Unicorn. Chatto and Windus, 1963.
Marian Taylor accepts a governess position at Castle Gaze and is immediately drawn into a sinister intrigue involving the beautiful, possibly deranged Hannah Crean-Smith, who has been "imprisoned" in the castle for seven years. The complex plot touches all the Gothic clichés, ancient and modern, including incest, suicide, several violent murders, homosexuality and lesbianism. But for all the dark fantasy trappings, *The Unicorn* is—like all Murdoch's works—a serious novel of ideas.

Nolan, William F(rancis), 1928- .
About: GSF, CA, TCA, NE, SFE, SFFL, TCSF, ESF

4-242. Things Beyond Midnight. Scream/Press, 1984.
Introduction by Richard Christian Matheson. Preface and comments on each story by the author. Nineteen stories and a short teleplay mixing horror, science fiction and psychological suspense. Most of the stories are brief—nothing over twenty pages—crisp, ironic, often humorous and usually with a grim final twist. At his best, in such stories as his well-known "The Underweller," which gives a brilliantly nasty, original turn to the clichéd last-man-on-earth scenario, Nolan puts a likable character into a terrible crisis and watches him squirm until a surprising, generally unpleasant conclusion is reached. The brevity of his stories intensifies their impact when they are good, but sometimes results in the wasting of a good idea ("Lonely Train A-Comin'") or the underdevelopment of an interesting character ("Kelly, Fredric Michael: 1928-1990"). Other notable narratives include "Dead Call," in which a deceased caller offers posthumous relief to an old friend, and "Something Nasty," in which a beleaguered young girl turns the tables on an unpleasant uncle. It is ironic and illuminating, however, that in a volume of short fiction Nolan's most entertaining and provocative effort should be a short teleplay, "The Party," in which a committed party-goer, heavy drinker and wife abuser learns that there can be too much of a bad thing. Compare the stories of Beaumont [4-26, 4-27] and Matheson [4-218].

Oates, Joyce Carol, 1935- .
About: CA, SMFL, PE

***4-243. Bellefleur**. Dutton, 1980.
A Gothic family saga that chronicles six generations of the Bellefleurs, a rich, notorious family living in a vast mansion on Lake Noir, a mythical lake in a region similar to the Adirondacks, where they breed a bizarre set of descendants that include a mass murderer, a mountain hermit in search of God, a vampire, a brilliant scientist, landowners, millionaires, gamblers, lechers, profligates, politicians and the book's more-or-less heroine, Germaine, a woman born with the lower half of a male twin protruding from her abdomen. Big, complicated,

colorful, grotesque, often funny, infused with supernaturalism, but never overtly fantastic, *Bellefleur* is a Gothic romance that more than transcends the genre, becoming a modern epic and a culmination of Oates's dark vision of the American psyche. Compare Cady's *The Well* [4-61], McCammon's *Usher's Passing* [4-226] and McDowell's *Blackwater* [4-230].

4-244. Mysteries of Winterthurn. Dutton, 1984.
The third of a trilogy of nineteenth-century genre novels (*Bellefleur*; *A Bloodsmoor Romance* [1984], a historical romance), *Mysteries of Winterthurn* presents three classical detective stories with Gothic overtones featuring detective-hero Xavier Kilgarvan. In the first, "A Virgin in the Rose-Bower," a sixteen-year-old Kilgarvan attempts to solve a series of bizarre murders in the ancestral mansion of the rich Kilgarvans and uncovers a shocking family secret. In the second, "Devil's Half-Acre," the twenty-eight-year-old detective investigates the murder of local factory girls, focusing his attention on one of Winterthurn's most respected citizens. In the third narrative, Kilgarvan's arduous struggles to solve the mystery of "The Bloodstained Bridal Gown" force him out of the detective profession at age forty. Although these investigations are separate, they dovetail at the end to make *Mysteries of Winterthurn* a single, coherent, impressive work of art. Elaborately written, frequently in imitation of the style and topography of the nineteenth-century popular novel, Oates's work convincingly recreates an era and a milieu as well as a literary form, although the sheer wealth of detail and density of the writing may discourage some readers. A powerful, complex, thought-provoking narrative that is well worth the effort required to read it. Compare Bloch's *American Gothic* [4-44] and Copper's *Necropolis* [4-87].

4-245. Night-Side. Vanguard, 1980.
Eighteen stories ranging from darkly realistic sketches to overtly supernatural fantasies with settings as diverse as upstate New York, southern Ontario, nineteenth-century Massachusetts and contemporary Eastern Europe. The horrors in these tales are primarily psychological, and most of the action is internal, the revelation of a disturbing insight or perception of a potential evil. In the title story, a skeptical spiritualist investigator is converted with disastrous and disturbing results. The "Two Widows" are the emotionally unbalanced Beatrice and the apparently self-contained Moira, who explore themselves, each other and their relationships to their deceased husbands. In "Lover," an M.D., obsessed with his work, identifies with his female patients to the point of losing contact with his own life. In "Famine Country," a disturbed young man identifies God with a dead turtle. Perhaps the best story in *Night-Side* is "The Snowstorm," an extended interior monologue of a young woman who, as she attempts to walk several miles to her home in a snowstorm, reflects on her life, her isolation, her unhappiness and her potential death. It is a brilliant *tour de force*. As a master of finely crafted, expertly written psychological horror stories, Oates must be ranked with Shirley Jackson (see [4-153]).

O'Donnell, Elliott (U.K.), 1872–1965.
ABOUT: WW, GSF, CA, PE, ESF

4-246. The Dead Riders. Rider, 1952.
An occult adventure novel that splits into two parts. While searching for the tomb of Genghis Khan, soldier-of-fortune Burke Blake is captured by the Lovonans, a group loyal to the spirit of an ancient black magician, Shadna Rana, and his ghostly troop of "black riders." After much peril, Blake escapes and returns to England. Years later he again encounters the lost members of the earlier expedition and does battle with a black magic cult. A straight-ahead, fast-paced pulpish adventure yarn with some chilling injections of supernaturalism by an author whose primary writings were a series of "nonfiction" studies of the occult.

Raucher, Herman, 1928– .
ABOUT: CA, SFFL

4-247. Maynard's House. Putnam, 1980.
Herman Raucher, author of *Summer of '42* (1971), here tells the story of Austin, a Vietnam veteran, who is willed a cabin in Maine by his platoon buddy, Maynard. The cabin is isolated, far away from the nearest town, built next to a supposedly haunted spot known as the Devil's Dancing Rock. After moving into the cabin, Austin meets two strange young children who may or may not be the unearthly creatures called Minnawickies, and a beautiful, mysterious woman with whom he falls in love. The cabin becomes creepier and more confining and his contacts with the children and woman more confusingly surreal. Austin is not sure whether he is suffering from cabin fever or some sort of delayed post-traumatic stress syndrome or whether the cabin and surrounding woods are really a residence of evil. *Maynard's House* is a thought-provoking and consistently well-written novel which addresses both postwar trauma and supernatural horror. It covers much the same territory as T. M. Wright's equally good *Strange Seed* [4-337]. (B.L.)

Raven, Simon (U.K.), 1927– .
ABOUT: CA, ESF

4-248. Doctors Wear Scarlet. Anthony Blond, 1960.
Richard Fountain's studies in ancient Greek rites and religions lead him to an involvement with Chriseis, an ancient female vampire. A cultivated, calculated horror story that builds slowly—too slowly—to its inevitable finale. The university atmosphere is expertly rendered. Long on interesting conversations, short on action and overt horror.

Rees, Simon (U.K.).

4-249. The Devil's Looking-Glass. Methuen, 1985.
Caught between the ambitions of parapsychologist Thomas and the arcane knowledge and influence of the vindictive Wiston, John Born disintegrates physi-

cally and mentally during a course of parapsychological experimentation. His obsession with the image of a black obsinian looking-glass, once owned by Elizabethan magician John Dee, pushes him to an encounter with the real mirror that ends in disaster. An interesting, restrained, unusual novel of style and subtlety that treads the realistic-supernatural line very carefully.

Rice, Anne, 1941- .
ABOUT: CA, H, PE

***4-250. Interview with a Vampire**. Knopf, 1976; **The Vampire Lestat**. Knopf, 1985; **The Queen of the Damned**. Knopf, 1988.
Three works originally projected as a trilogy, now an open-ended series. In *Interview with a Vampire,* Louis, the vampiric protagonist, dictates his life story into a tape recorder manned by a young man and would-be acolyte. Turned into a vampire in the 1790s by Lestat, a master vampire, Louis chronicles his early life as a Louisiana plantation owner, his early experiences with Lestat and their acquisition of Claudia, who, having been vampirized as a five year old, harbors in a child's body the intelligence and lusts of a grown woman coupled with the amorality of a vampire. The trio argue, fight and split up, with Louis and Claudia setting out in search of others of their kind, finally reaching Paris, where, at the *Théâtre des Vampires,* they encounter the only remaining group of vampires and their leader, Armand, the oldest vampire of all. *Interview with a Vampire* is easily the best of the three books. In "adjusting" to the vampire life, Louis probes serious questions of what it means to be truly human, of the meaning of life in a world where the existence of God seems at best problematical, of guilt and responsibility. In *The Vampire Lestat,* the title character defends himself against the picture Louis has painted of him. He then goes on to tell of his transition and adjustment to the vampiric life and of his search for the truth of the vampire myth. The first half of the novel, which chronicles this search, is fascinating, but, unfortunately, the myth that he uncovers is a huge disappointment and the second half of the book falls down badly. In *The Queen of the Damned,* Lestat continues his career as a rock singer, openly proclaiming himself a vampire, revealing the ancient secrets in his music. This act rouses Akasha, the Mother of all vampires, who, claiming to save mankind, unleashes terrible evil on the world. *The Queen of the Damned* is superior to its immediate predecessor, but is still not in a class with the initial novel. In *The Vampire Lestat* and *The Queen of the Damned,* Rice has elaborated and consolidated her vampire myth and, in the process, has made it increasingly contrived and mundane, no longer able to suggest the serious ambiguities and provocative suggestions of *Interview with a Vampire.* Compare the revised vampire mythologies found in Charnas's *The Vampire Tapestry* [4-78], Kast's *The Vampires of Alfama* [4-159], Somtow's *Vampire Junction* [4-278] and Strieber's *The Hunger* [4-290].

Russell, Ray(mond), 1924- .
ABOUT: WW, CA, SFFL, ESF

4-251. The Case Against Satan. Ivan Obolensky, 1962.
A precursor to *The Exorcist, The Case Against Satan* treads the same territory but

in a more naive, less gruesome and, ultimately, less frightening and effective manner. A girl appears to be possessed by Satan, and two clergymen, a conservative bishop and a priest who is also a student of psychology, must exorcise the demon. *The Case Against Satan* is less a horror novel than a discussion of contemporary philosophical/religious questions wrapped around a fictional situation. Most of the action takes place within a rectory as the bishop and the doubting priest discuss the existence of God and Satan, and argue whether faith and rationality, science and the church, can coexist. Along the way, shots are taken at both pious churchgoers and radical atheists. Simplistic, but highly readable, *The Case Against Satan* is supposedly based on a true incident. (B.L.)

***4-252. Haunted Castles: The Complete Gothic Tales of Ray Russell**. Maclay, 1985.
Haunted Castles brings together the seven "Gothic" short fictions (some expanded for this edition) that Russell completed between 1959 and 1969. The volume is anchored by his three best-known stories, "Sardonicus," "Sagittarius" and "Sanguinarius" (previously published as *Unholy Trinity*, 1964). His most famous story, "Sardonicus," an oddly disturbing story about a rich and ruthless man with a grotesque smile permanently fixed on his face, best illustrates the effectiveness of Russell's Gothic trappings. In "Sagittarius" Russell uses his self-conscious archaism to spin a deft, ironic nest-of-boxes puzzle that manages to mix Gilles de Rais, Dr. Jekyll and Mr. Hyde, Hyde's "son" and Jack the Ripper in a single ingenious narrative stew. "Sanguinarius," a fictional (but "historically accurate") exploration of the mind and motives of Elizabeth Bathory, is disappointing, not so much from weakness in execution as from Russell's failure to realize the potential inherent in the idea. The other four tales are less ambitious, but no less skillfully wrought. By and large Russell succeeds very well in his attempt to emulate the plotting, diction, structuring devices, characterization, atmosphere and sensibility of the mid-nineteenth-century Gothic novella. A unique contribution to contemporary dark fantasy.

4-253. Incubus. Morrow, 1976.
A small town is besieged by a rapist who virtually tears his victims to pieces. Gradually it becomes clear that he—or it—is no ordinary sexual criminal, but a voracious supernatural being with extraordinary powers. A strong, graphic, original novel, with a surprise ending that some readers will find ingenious, others annoying.

Ryan, Alan, 1943- .
About: CA, PE, FF

4-254. The Bones Wizard and Other Stories. Doubleday, 1988.
"The Bones Wizard" is about Sean who, in order to evoke the primeval sounds from his instrument, must have special bones, whatever the cost. "The Bones Wizard" won a World Fantasy Award in 1985. Other excellent stories include "Babies from Heaven,' about a woman who satisfies the desire for a child in a fantastic manner; "Sand," about a young mother who increasingly confuses blood with red sand; "Sheets," about a salesman who is overwhelmed by the designs on the sheets he sells; and "Hear the Whistle Blowing," about Wayne, a

young man who gradually becomes obsessed with the ease of killing with an automobile. The dozen stories range from almost slice-of-life realism to extravagant fantasy, but are uniformly well crafted and cleanly written, with vivid characters. Compare the short fiction of Etchison [4-106, 4-108] and Martin [4-214, 4-215].

***4-255. Cast a Cold Eye**. Tor, 1984.
The title comes from the conclusion of W. B. Yeats's poem "Under Ben Bulben": "Cast a cold eye/On life, on death/Horseman, pass by"—and the book is worthy of its title. When Jack Quinlan visits the village of Doolin on the remote western coast of Ireland to write a book about the Famine, he encounters more than he had anticipated: romance in the person of Grainne Clarkin; evasiveness, even hostility, from the townfolk; and, most disturbing, specters of the famine victims. As he investigates these strange experiences, Jack is drawn into the strange, dangerous practices and rituals of the Doolin inhabitants as they try to make peace with their terrible history. *Cast a Cold Eye* is an original, deeply moving, beautifully written book. The characters are vivid and memorable, the setting very real. More poignant—even tragic—than horrific, the novel fulfills the promise of Ryan's first two horror novels. One of the best dark fantasies of the 1980s.

4-256. Dead White. Tor, 1983.
"Stanton Stokely's Stupendous Circus" train arrives on a long-unused track during a blizzard that has isolated the small Catskills town of Deacons Kill. Featuring only clowns, the circus prepares a special performance for the citizens of the Kill. A small group of townspeople, led by bright, energetic Susan Lester, Rich Mead, the reluctant sheriff, and Doc Warren, an elderly G.P., search for the truth about the sinister circus and then race to prevent it from unleashing a catastrophe on the town. A strong follow-up to *The Kill,* with sharp, if not overly deep characters. Ryan's evocation of an oppressive snowbound atmosphere is reminiscent of Peter Straub's *Ghost Story* [4-286], and his use of the clown figure as an object of menace is more effective than Stephen King's in *It* [4-168].

4-257. The Kill. Tor, 1982.
Ryan's first horror novel. New York couple Megan Todd and Jack Casey escape from city life to the rural enclave of Deacons Kill in the nothern Catskills, where they are menaced by a mysterious, invisible, bloodthirsty evil. Joining forces with their neighbors—a sheriff, a doctor and the former owner of their new home—they investigate, pursue and finally confront the creature hiding in the woods. The set-up is not particularly original and the resident monster strains credulity, but the novel moves along briskly with sharply drawn, sympathetic characters in a vividly delineated milieu.

Saberhagen, Fred, 1930- .

About: CA, TCA, NE, SMFL, SFE, SFFL, RG, TCSF, PE, ESF

***4-258. The Dracula Tape**. Warner, 1975; **The Holmes-Dracula File**. Ace, 1978; **An Old Friend of the Family**. Ace, 1979; **Thorn**. Ace, 1980; **Dominion**. Ace, 1982.
The Dracula Tape tells the Count's side of the story through a tape sent to Mina Harker's grandson. Dracula defends himself as a much-maligned victim of mis-

understanding and deliberate slander: he meant no harm; he turned Lucy Harker into a vampire to save her from Van Helsing's medical bungling; Mina's diary was a fictitious cover for their love affair; the Count actually saved Mina from her real enemy, the crazed Renfield; Van Helsing was a maniacal religious fanatic and the other men his dupes; and so on. The book is a clever, ironic, humorous, touching pastiche. The sequel, *The Holmes-Dracula File*, offers the hypothesis that not only were the Count and Sherlock Holmes acquainted, they were, in fact, related look-alikes. Once they meet, Holmes and Dracula form an alliance to prevent a mad scientist from loosing the bubonic plague on London. More of an adventure than a satire, *The Holmes-Dracula File* is thoroughly enjoyable, although its Dracula is more of a modern superhero than an ironic counterpart to Stoker's original. This concept of Dracula as superhero, with its consequent loss of humor and irony, becomes central to the remaining series books. In *An Old Friend of the Family*, the Count comes to Chicago in the 1970s to protect Mina Harker's descendants and encounters a coven of evil vampires who seek his final destruction. In *Thorn*, the Count travels to the American Southwest, where he clashes with the rich, decadent Seabright family; the reader is also given scenes from his prevampire days in flashback. In *Dominion*, the Count, now renamed Talisman and living in Chicago, becomes involved in a conflict between two ancient magicians, a conflict in which he is little more than an observer. The series thus grinds to a somewhat confusing halt. On the whole, however, Saberhagen's Dracula books are thoroughly enjoyable, especially for devotees of the original. Compare Daniels's Don Sebastian series [4-92], Tremayne's Dracula trilogy [4-304] and Yarbro's Saint Germain series [4-340].

4-259. The Frankenstein Papers. Baen, 1986.
Saberhagen's version of the Frankenstein myth is told by the Creature himself, who, it turns out, is not an artificial human, but an extraterrestrial alien. Saberhagen deftly manipulates the events from the novel—while pointing out problems in the original—within appropriate historical settings, sprinkled with a few historical figures like Benjamin Franklin and Anton Mesmer. While not quite up to *The Dracula Tape, The Frankenstein Papers* is a highly entertaining, amusing and, especially for devotees of the original, provocative novel. Compare Aldiss's *Frankenstein Unbound* [4-10].

[For other works of this author, see the companion guide to fantasy.]

Samson, Joan, 1937–1976.
ABOUT: CA

***4-260. The Auctioneer**. Simon and Schuster, 1975.
Perly Dunsmore moves into Harlowe, New Hampshire, and initiates a series of auctions to benefit the local police force. He begins by taking discards, unused equipment, and so on, but, as his success and powers grow, makes increasingly severe demands on the farmers and landowners, until he has his own police force and virtual control of the area. A group of townspeople, led by farmer John Moore, belatedly start a guerrilla war to recapture their town and personal integrity. A truly frightening story because, without benefit of any supernatural intervention, Perly's ascent to power seems logical, believable and inevitable,

given the greed, weakness, confusion and self-doubts of the Harlowe residents. The writing is clean, direct and vivid; the characters are sharply drawn; and the movement of the book, from its ominous beginning to its violent, chaotic finale, is a masterful exercise in mounting tension and suspense. As a realistic thriller, as a moral parable and as, perhaps, an oblique critique of America's involvement in Vietnam, *The Auctioneer* remains a minor genre masterpiece.

Sarban (pseud. of **John William Wall**) (U.K.), 1910–1989.
ABOUT: WW, GSF, SFW, CA, H, SMFL, MF, TCSF, PE, ESF

4-261. The Doll Maker, and Other Tales of the Uncanny. Peter Davies, 1953.
In "The Doll Maker," Clare Lydgate, a bored eighteen-year-old student who is home for Christmas vacation, is attracted to her rich, handsome neighbor, Niall Sterne, who carves extraordinarily realistic dolls for an elaborate model world he keeps in his house. As her feelings for Niall grow, Clare also begins to perceive that the dolls are *too* lifelike, particularly the one being made in her image. Sarban takes the basic heroine-in-jeopardy situation and gives it a strikingly original twist. The writing is precise and sensual, the characterization subtle and suggestive and the sexual subtext most provocative. In "A House of Call," a man returns from India only to find himself thrust back in time to the Roman occupation. In "The Trespassers," two schoolboys break into a house and encounter an older girl who has trapped a unicorn.

4-262. Ringstones and Other Curious Tales. Peter Davies, 1951.
In the novella *Ringstones*, we read the unfinished diary of Daphne Hazel, recounting her experiences as governess to three strange children, especially the oldest boy, Nuaman, at Ringstones, a house near a ring of stones, remnants of some ancient civilization. Gradually she finds herself isolated and mesmerized by Nuaman, who increasingly takes on a peculiar, even inhuman aura, and she is drawn to the ringstones, which may have sinister ancient powers, until her very being is—perhaps—threatened. Sarban's suspenseful, sensual prose and careful delineation of his heroine's psychological awakening give this relatively simple story the evocative power of a dark fairy tale. The other stories include "Capra," in which lovers at a masquerade party foolishly go to the ruined Temple of Pan; "Calmahain," in which displaced children in World War II build a boat and disappear; and "The Khan," in which a dispute between a husband and wife over a pet bear is resolved when the woman, walking in the woods, meets a king bear and moves in with him.

4-263. The Sound of His Horn. Peter Davies, 1952.
Alan Querdilion tells how, after escaping from a World War II POW camp, he stumbled into an alternate world, one hundred years after the Nazis won the war. He finds himself on the estate of the massive, grotesque Count Hackelnberg, Master of the Hunt, in which humans are used instead of foxes. The hunt proceeds with, of course, Querdilion as the number one fox. Despite its science fiction premise, *The Sound of His Horn* is pure horror—frightening, grotesque, exotic and terrifying, both in its action and in its implications. *The Sound of His Horn* manages to convey both the horror of a modern technological society and

the horror of a primitive natural one. The relative shortness of the book makes its impact that much stronger.

Saul, John, 1942– .

About: CA, PE

4-264. Suffer the Children. Dell, 1977.
Stimulated by an (imagined?) Ouija board message from a dead rape/murder victim, Elizabeth kidnaps and kills two children, along with one cat, to create a "family" for herself. In *Suffer the Children* Saul developed the child-as-villain/victim formula that would make him one of the most widely read—if not critically appreciated—writers of the late 1970s and 1980s. For more sophisticated handlings of the same motif see Block's *Ariel* [4-49] and Taylor's *The Godsend* [4-295].

Saxon, Peter (pseud. of Wilfred McNeilly [U.K.],) 1921–1985.

About: WW, CA, ESF

4-265. The Killing Bone. Berkley, 1969; **Dark Ways to Death**. Howard Baker, 1968; **The Curse of Rathlaw**. Lancer, 1968; **Through the Dark Curtain**. Lancer, 1968.
Four novels featuring The Guardians—Gideon Cross, Steven Kane and Father John Dyball, assisted by their secretary, Anne Ashby, and Lionel Marks, a private detective—a team of occult investigators who seek out and do battle with the dark forces of the universe. In *The Killing Bone,* the Guardians do battle—a battle they admit is a morally ambiguous one—with a Stone Age witch doctor from the Australian outback who uses a "killing bone" to strike down victims from afar. In *Dark Ways to Death,* the enemy is Doctor Obadiah Duval, chief of the voodoo Satan worshippers. In *The Curse of Rathlaw,* the Guardians attempt to aid Sir Alistair Rathlaw, who has been cursed by Fergus Trayle, hermit of Black Loch, and must fight not only the ancient magic of Fergus, but the modern methods of his equally corrupt brother, Cosmo. In *Through the Dark Curtain,* the spontaneous, mysterious madness of a beautiful young woman draws the Guardians to the small town of Frenton where they encounter a druidic cult. The cult leader, inspired by his daughter, who may or may not be the reincarnation of a warrior queen, seeks to change history by unleashing the dark forces against the Roman legions in the crucial battle for control of Britain. An ingenious novel marred by an off page climax. The Guardian series reads like a streamlined Dennis Wheatley. The novels lack the density and occult detail of Wheatley's better books, but also have none of his reactionary politics, sentimental moralizing and fuzzy metaphysics. Compare Wheatley's *The Devil Rides Out* [3-209] and *Gateway to Hell* [4-319].

Seignolle, Claude (France), 1917– .

About: WW, CA, PE, ESF

4-266. The Accursed: Two Diabolical Tales. Allen and Unwin, 1967. Tr. by Bernard Wall of *Les Maledictions,* 1963.
Introduction by Lawrence Durrell. "Malvenue" juxtaposes the story of the title

character, a sixteen-year-old girl apparently possessed by evil impulses, against the story of her father's life and death. Both characters are doomed by the influence of a mysterious ancient stone head unearthed by the old man. In "Marie the Wolf," a "gift" of healing given to Marie, a farm girl, by a sinister wolf drover, provokes a series of events that lead to turmoil and violence in a small rural community. A noted ethnographer, Seignolle combines a highly charged but matter-of-fact prose style, complicated but compressed plotting and an authentic feel for the details of turn-of-the-century French rural farm life. Bizarre events and otherworldly intrusions are taken in stride by his earthy, vital, if grotesque, characters. The tension between this mundane surface and the fantastic content creates a kind of semi-surrealistic folk tale that is particularly unnerving.

4-267. Nightcharmer: and Other Tales. Texas A & M Univ. Press, 1983. Tr. by Eric Hollingsworth Deudon.
Eight stories plus a foreword by Lawrence Durrell as well as Deudon's introduction and selected bibliography. The stories can be divided into two types, rustic tales, which depict the folklore and popular traditions of the French countryside, and "modern" stories, which demonstrate primitive superstitions and the supernatural in modern situations. "The Healer," about a gardener who accepts a stranger's "ailment" for a fee, only to discover, too late, what he has accepted, is a good example of the former, while "A Dog Story," in which the narrator is forced to kill a mangy dog twice during World War II, is a particularly vivid example of the latter.

Shea, Michael.

About: SFE

4-268. The Color Out of Time. DAW, 1984.
This sequel to Lovecraft's "The Colour Out of Space" [3-132] begins some years later, when the haunted valley has become a lake popular with vacationers. Three characters unite to oppose the creature, which is more precisely described than Lovecraft's ambiguous horror, but—perhaps because this is a novel—lacks the terrifying immediacy of Lovecraft's creation. The language is Lovecraftian, the sensibility contemporary. Compare Bloch's *Strange Eons* [4-48], Chappell's *Dagon* [4-77] and Copper's *The Great White Space* [4-85].

4-269. Polyphemus. Arkham House, 1987.
Through his novels, Shea has become regarded as a fantasist of high order, and it is easy to forget his talent as a writer of horror fiction. All of his shorter fictions are imbued with a colorful surrealism that breathes an air of rich decadence into their often gross and intense frames. *Polyphemus*, with its laudatory introduction by Algis Budrys, brings together seven stories, ranging from his first, "The Angel of Death" (1979), to "The Extra" (1987). Although roughly half the stories could be classed as science fiction by setting or theme, they are all horrific by treatment, and none more so than "The Autopsy," in which a pathologist must physically destroy himself to avoid being taken over by an alien. "Uncle Tuggs" is perhaps the most successful story, with ghostly revenge being enacted through a sequence of murderous mechanical objects. Shea is one of the most visually powerful creators of horror images writing today. (M.A.)

Siddons, Anne Rivers, (U.K.), 1936- .
ABOUT: CA, SMFL

***4-270. The House Next Door.** Simon and Schuster, 1978.
Certainly the most original haunted house story of the 1970s, and one of the best. Insanity and bloodshed descend on each of the three families who move into a beautiful, newly built, thoroughly contemporary "dream house" in an affluent suburban neighborhood in Atlanta. Although there are evidences of supernatural intrusion, the malevolence of the house acts by turning its occupants into violent, monstrous extensions of their normal selves. Although not similar in plot or tone, *The House Next Door* can be compared to Updike's *The Witches of Eastwick* [4-308] in its mix of supernaturalism and social satire.

Silverberg, Robert, 1935- .
ABOUT: CA, TCA, NE, SFE, SFFL, RG, TCSF, ESF

4-271. Dying Inside. Scribner's, 1972.
David Selig's extraordinary psychic powers have made him an outcast. He is unable to come to terms with his talents, yet he is terrified of losing them—as he seems gradually to be doing. A powerful and moving psychological study, *Dying Inside* explores from a unique perspective the psychological, moral and social implications of psychic powers, a major concern in contemporary dark fantasy, especially in such works as King's *The Dead Zone* [4-165] and Matheson's *A Stir of Echoes* [4-220].

Simmons, Dan, 1948- .
ABOUT: CA, H

4-272. Song of Kali. Bluejay, 1985.
An accomplished and impressive debut novel, *Song of Kali* concerns an American man and his Indian wife whose baby has been kidnapped by cult worshippers of the god Kali. Simmons is an excellent writer, particularly adept at portraying the horrific poverty and claustrophobic overcrowding of Calcutta. The work makes considerable use of nineteenth-century framing devices, but the alternation between gritty reality and a hallucinogenic surrealism is strictly contemporary. The novel is marred only by an overly literal climax which undercuts the poetic mystery and ambiguity of the rest of the work. World Fantasy Award, 1986. (B.L.)

Singer, Isaac Bashevis (Poland), 1904- .
ABOUT: CA, SMFL, PE, ESF

4-273. Collected Stories. Farrar, 1982.
This volume gathers the most important of Singer's stories. Many are realistic, but even those are often infused with hints of the otherworldly. Singer accepts the supernatural as a fact of life—"two sides of the same coin"—and this is evident in his tales. In the overtly supernatural tales, the Devil, ghosts, demons and the like move freely among the living, and it is often difficult to tell them apart: the hero in "A Wedding in Brownsville" meets his deceased former sweetheart at a wed-

ding; the heroine of "The Cafeteria" sees Hitler eating with the rest of the customers. One of the great storytellers of the twentieth century, Singer offers the reader rare and memorable pleasure, through his control of voice and tone, and his warmth and imagination, edged with darkly ironic overtones.

4-274. Satan in Goray. Noonday, 1955. Tr. by Jacob Sloan from the Yiddish. Based loosely on a real historical event, the emergence in the mid-seventeenth century of a Messianic pretender named Sabbatai Zevi and the disastrous effect he had on the Jewish community. *Satan in Goray* chronicles the gradual usurpation of the town of Goray by a Messianic cult and finally by Satan and his dominions. A very sophisticated folk-horror story that draws us into Singer's exotic world where the distinctions between the natural and the supernatural, the real and the demonic, are dissolved. A deeply satisfying reading experience.

Skipp, John, 1957- , and **Craig Spector**, 1958- .

4-275. The Light at the End. Bantam, 1986.
An interesting mix of the classical vampire story in a gritty urban setting. After a powerful Old World vampire turns street punk Rudy Pasco into one of his kind, Rudy goes on a rampage in the New York subway system. He is discovered, tracked and finally destroyed by a mixed group of street people. The master vampire hovers in the background, but the book's focus is on Rudy, who is not quite up to the demands of the classical vampire. Although extremely gory, *The Light at the End* is a very fast-paced, exciting book. Skipp and Spector are especially good at delineating the sights, sounds and squalor of the modern urban environment. Compare McCammon's *They Thirst* [4-225] and Monteleone's *Night Train* [4-238].

4-276. The Scream. Bantam, 1988.
Heavy Metal band "The Scream" is exactly the type of rock group that fundamentalist organizations try to ban or censor—in this case, with good reason. The Scream does have a message in its music, and it is converting fans, using them for its evil purposes. Rock star and Vietnam veteran Jack Hamer leads the fight to stop the demonic doings and thwart The Scream's plans. *The Scream* is not a subtle novel. It is loud, obvious and defiantly contemporary, influenced (perhaps overinfluenced) by King both in style and structure. It also picks easy and overdone targets, treading familiar territory with a familiar point of view. The novel's shortcomings, however, are also part of its charm. *The Scream,* like good rock and roll, is rough, ragged, fast-paced and extremely entertaining. Compare Martin's *The Armageddon Rag* [4-212], Rice's *Queen of the Damned* [4-250] and Somtow's *Vampire Junction* [4-278]. (B.L.)

Smith, Guy N(ewman) (U.K.), 1939- .

ABOUT: WW, PE

4-277. The Sucking Pit. New English Library, 1975.
Stephen King has called the title of *The Sucking Pit* an "all-time pulp horror classic." The novel is somewhat less than that, but this lively mix of sex, violence,

possession, sinister gypsies and the swamp of the title—home of the devil—demonstrates the formula that Smith has used in a multitude of best-selling paperbacks: one-dimensional characters, neatly divided between good and evil, in a series of brief dramatic scenes, which more or less alternate sex and violence, culminating in the deaths of most of the characters, save a hero and heroine, told at a furious pace in very simple, functional prose. Smith's novels can by no stretch of the imagination be called literature, but as fast, lively, "no-brainer" entertainment they are hard to beat.

Somtow, S. P. (pseud. of **Somtow Sucharitkul**) (Thailand), 1952- .

ABOUT: CA, NE, TCSF

***4-278. Vampire Junction**. Donning/Starblaze, 1984.

Timmy Valentine, teenaged rock singer and vampire, attempts to come to terms with his nature and past by undergoing Jungian analysis. With Timmy we move back and forth in time between the present and the past, witnessing such events as the destruction of Pompeii, the sadistic acts of Gilles de Rais and the Nazi atrocities as we probe his long, colorful, gory life. At the same time, a small group of eccentric, grotesque old men, who call themselves "The Gods of Chaos," plot to kill Timmy. It all comes together at "Vampire Junction," Timmy's Gothic castle retreat. An extraordinarily original vampire novel. Told in fragments in a prose style that is visual, energetic, nervous and often lyrical, *Vampire Junction* requires the reader's active participation in putting together the pieces of this very complex puzzle. The characters are vivid and larger than life, closer to comic-strip grotesques than to human beings, yet they—especially Timmy—do command our attention and identification. *Vampire Junction* is sensational, gory, funny and extremely provocative, both intellectually and viscerally. It ranks with Kast's *The Vampires of Alfalma* [4-159], Matheson's *I Am Legend* [4-217] and Rice's *Interview with a Vampire* [4-250] as a major reworking of the vampire myth and one of the most original novels of the 1980s.

Stallman, Robert , 1930-1980.

ABOUT: RG, TCSF

4-279. The Orphan. Timescape, 1980.

First book in a trilogy entitled The Book of the Beast. The "Beast" is a werewolf-like creature able to assume human form at will. To protect himself, he initially changes into a young boy and joins a farm family; then, following a crisis, he assumes the shape of an older, larger boy and moves in with a widow. As the boy, Charles, grows into adolescence, the tension between his human identity and his bestial nature becomes increasingly powerful and dangerous. An original, ingenious book, with a lyrical charm, a mix of reality with fantasy, and a sensitivity in the descriptions of rural boyhood that are reminiscent of early Ray Bradbury. Stallman continued his contemporary fable in *The Captive* (1981) and *The Beast* (1982).

Stanwood, Brooks (pseud. of **Susan Stanwood Kaminsky**), 1937- .
ABOUT: CA

4-280. The Seventh Child. Linden Press/Simon and Schuster, 1982.
Shortly after the Richardsons—Hal, Judy and nine-year-old Annie—settle in Ripton Falls, odd accidents begin to happen to the new kids in town. Things become more sinister when an old legend surfaces that puts all the children, especially Annie, in real jeopardy. A fast-moving, dramatic, intricate novel that is one of the better examples of the child-in-jeopardy motif.

Stewart, Desmond (U.K.), 1924-1981.
ABOUT: CA

4-281. The Vampire of Mons. Hamish Hamilton, 1976.
A vampire may or may not be stalking Malthus College, an English boarding school, but the boys come to believe it and act accordingly. More of a character study of adolescents under pressure (World War II is going on in the background), *The Vampire of Mons* is a thoughtful, intelligent, well-developed book. Compare the first half of Straub's *Shadowland* [4-289].

Stewart, Fred Mustard, 1936- .
ABOUT: CA, SFFL

4-282. The Mephisto Waltz. Coward, McCann, 1969.
Shortly before his death, piano virtuoso Duncan Ely takes on writer Myles Clarkson as a protégé. Soon thereafter Myles blossoms—to the puzzlement of his wife, Paula, particularly when he starts emulating Ely in other ways, including an interest in the late pianist's wife. Paula begins to suspect black magic, but the only way she can learn the truth is to investigate the dark powers for herself. A lively, dramatic book, with good dialogue and clever twists, similar in style and approach, if not in complexity and sophistication, to *Rosemary's Baby* [4-206]. *The Mephisto Waltz* was unevenly filmed in 1971 with Alan Alda as Myles and Curt Jurgens as Ely.

Stewart, J. I. M. (pseud. of **Michael Innes**) (U.K.), 1906- .
ABOUT: CA

4-283. Cucumber Sandwiches and Other Stories. Gollancz, 1969.
Four carefully written, subtle stories that brush the supernatural lightly. In "Laon and Cythna," the longest story in the book, skeptical psychic investigator Holroyd cannot decide whether the spectral lovers seen by a young girl are real ghosts or projections of her own mind. "Cucumber Sandwiches," the shortest of the stories, is a Henry Jamesian story about a biographer who feels obligated to tell the principal heir of his subject a very dark family secret—only to learn the real truth of the situation.

Stewart, Ramona, 1922- .

ABOUT: SFFL

4-284. The Possession of Joel Delaney. Little, Brown, 1970.
Despite the promise of its title, *The Possession of Joel Delaney* is surprisingly devoid of supernatural occurrences, although the occult trappings of spiritualism, voodoo and Santeria are all explored in detail. Read today, the novel seems clearly to be a metaphoric examination of the counterculture phenomenon of the late 1960s/early 1970s. A young man, Joel Delaney, suddenly changes from a mild-mannered middle-class WASP into a crazed killer. At first, drugs are blamed for the radical change in Joel's personality, but as his sister explores further, she comes to believe that he has been possessed by the spirit of a psychotic Puerto Rican teenager. *The Possession of Joel Delaney* is open-ended—there may or may not be a supernatural explanation for Joel's sudden transformation—but the horror is very real. The novel provides an interesting look at the emotions generated by young people's rejection of middle-class values and life-styles during the so-called hippie era. Compare to Blatty's *The Exorcist* [4-42]. (B.L.)

Straub, Peter, 1943- .

ABOUT: CA, H, SMFL, RG, PE, FF

4-285. Floating Dragon. Putnam, 1982.
Two evils, one modern and one ancient, systematically decimate the city of Hampstead, Connecticut. The modern threat, an experimental drug (DRG-16) accidentally let loose, induces unconsciousness, sickness, insanity, death and severe "leaking" in a manner reminiscent of Herbert's *The Fog* [4-141]. The ancient evil, a malevolent spirit, has reappeared approximately every thirty years to wreak havoc. The last descendants of the four original families gather to battle the evil spirit in a reenactment of the first settlers' combat with cosmic evil. This is Straub's most ambitious novel, but critics have differed over its merit. To some it is his best: a profound and complex message realized in a masterful form. Others appreciate the book's ambitions, but find it uneven, out of balance, excessive and illogical. August Derleth Award, 1984. Compare Blackburn's *For Fear of Little Men* [4-40].

***4-286. Ghost Story**. Coward, McCann, 1979.
Ghost Story is a veritable catalogue of traditional and nontraditional horror characters and motifs including nightmares and hallucinations, animal slaughter, murders both simple and complex, rumors of U.F.O.'s, suspected vampirism, lycanthropy, ghoulishness, spiritualism, occult societies, a haunted house, a series of *femmes fatales,* illicit and dangerous sexuality, and demonic children, both male and female. For all that, the basic plot is simple: the town of Milburn, New York, is under siege from a malevolent being that usually takes the shape of a beautiful woman. Particularly vulnerable are the four elderly members of "The Chowder Society," a young novelist and a teenaged boy. At the center of each man's story is a woman and a guilty secret associated with her. The key to the mystery—and to the ways to fight against it—lies in the men's personal histories. They must come to terms with their own pasts, first by reliving them in order to

understand their meanings, and then by finding the strength to break free of them. Those who can, survive, those who cannot, die. Straub's narrative technique is unorthodox and sophisticated: the story is broken up by other bits and pieces of narrative: stories within stories, time shifts, events real and imagined, glimpses of the future, seemingly irrelevant incidents and details, bizarre yet realistic hallucinations, terrifying nightmares. But the sudden shifts between the external and the internal, the real and the hallucinatory, the past and the present, are not ultimately confusing, because they are presented as part of a consistently changing whole. *Ghost Story* is one of the seminal works of modern dark fantasy. Compare King's *'Salem's Lot* [4-172].

4-287. If You Could See Me Now. Coward, McCann, 1977.
Miles Teagarden returns to his hometown of Arden, Wisconsin, to keep a rendezvous with Alisoun Greener, a girl he may or may not have killed twenty years earlier. Upon his return, he finds himself not only resented for his boyhood reputation, but also suspected of being the murderer who stalks local girls. Hostilities intensify, new murders are committed, old crimes and mysteries resurface, and Alisoun's ghost becomes increasingly pervasive. Although the ghost's motivations and actions are never really clear or logical, *If You Could See Me Now* is a strong horror novel—subtle, complex, intense. Straub's rendering of the small-town milieu and his development of Miles—intelligent, pompous, erratic, perhaps demented—are especially impressive.

4-288. Julia. Coward, McCann, 1975.
Straub's first venture into supernatural fiction. A ghost story in the classical manner with deliberate echoes of "The Turn of the Screw" [3-107]. Obsessed by guilt over accidentally killing her daughter while attempting a tracheotomy, Julia Lofting retreats to a house in Kensington where she encounters the ghost of a child murderer—which may or may not be real. As Julia pursues the truth of the twenty-five-year-old crime, her own identification with the "ghost" intensifies and her grasp on reality becomes increasingly tenuous. A subtle, beautifully atmospheric novel of psychological disintegration and ambiguous supernaturalism. Compare du Maurier's "Don't Look Now" [4-101].

4-289. Shadowland. Coward, McCann, 1980.
The novel traces the friendship between Tom Flannigan and Del Nightengale from their early struggles at Carson, an expensive, mediocre prep school, through their summer with Del's uncle, Coleman Collins, a magician, at his summer estate, Shadowland. As Tom, the more talented of the pair, gradually begins to explore his psychic gifts, life at Shadowland grows increasingly bizarre and threatening. Weird shows and hallucinatory experiences disrupt the line between reality and illusion, sanity and madness, as Collins pursues his design of grooming Tom as his successor. Despite strong literary echoes—of Bradbury's *Something Wicked This Way Comes* [4-51], John Fowles's *The Magus* [4-117] and John Knowles's mainstream novel *A Separate Peace* (1960)—*Shadowland* is an inventive, beautifully written, intellectually provocative book.

Strieber, Whitley, 1945- .

ABOUT: WW, CA, H, SMFL, MF, PE, FF

4-290. The Hunger. Morrow, 1981.

Miriam Blaylock possesses the secret of physical immortality and has shared that secret—imperfectly—with a long line of lovers over the centuries. As her current mate, John, begins to age dramatically, she seeks a new lover in Sarah Robert, a sleep researcher who has herself, perhaps, stumbled onto the secret of unlimited longevity. Tensions between life, death, aging, fear, jealousy, desire and love finally come together to threaten Miriam's immortality. Although he never uses the term, Strieber has written one of the very best of the contemporary vampire novels. As in *The Wolfen*, he postulates a separate race that lives with and feeds upon humanity. From a human perspective, Miriam Blaylock is wholly evil, yet she is also curiously sympathetic, and even, perhaps, marginally tragic. A beautifully crafted, sensual, original book. Compare Charnas's *The Vampire Tapestry* [4-78], Rice's *Interview with a Vampire* [4-250] and Somtow's *Vampire Junction* [4-278]. Tony Scott's 1983 film adaptation was sensitive and relatively faithful, but confusing to viewers unfamiliar with the novel.

***4-291. The Wolfen**. Morrow, 1978.

Strieber's first novel, a radical reinterpretation of the werewolf story. Wolfen are not actually werewolves, but are a separate species of carnivorous humanoid wolves that prey on marginal inhabitants of modern urban society. An impulsive, sloppy killing by two young wolfen begins a homicide investigation by the unlikely police team of George Wilson, a cynical, chauvinistic middle-aged bachelor, and Becky Neff, a pretty, bright, assertive female. As they learn about the wolfen, they become frustrated by their inability to convince their superiors of the beasts' existence and are themselves threatened by the wolfen, who fear exposure. The book becomes a race between the Wilson-Neff team's attempt to prove the existence of the wolfen and the creatures' efforts to hunt and kill the pair. A superior, original blend of the horror story and the police procedure novel. The characters of Wilson and Neff are convincing and their improbable romance is surprisingly believable, but it is the characterization of the wolfen that gives the novel its stature. It was director Michael Wadleigh's failure to characterize the wolfen with any ingenuity that doomed the intelligent 1981 film adaptation of the novel to the category of well-intentioned, effectively rendered failure. Compare Whitten's *Moon of the Wolf* [4-325] and *Progeny of the Adder* [4-326].

Sturgeon, Theodore (formerly **Edward Hamilton Waldo**), 1918–1985.

ABOUT: WW, GSF, SFW, CA, TCA, NE, SMFL, SFE, SFFL, RG, TCSF, PE, ESF

4-292. Some of Your Blood. Ballantine, 1961.

Although he is an essentially sympathetic character, George Smith's taste for human blood labels him a monster in the eyes of society and, more importantly, in his own. Even though the novel is more case history than horror story and Smith's eccentricities lack the shock value they had in 1961, Sturgeon's careful, beautifully developed delineation of Smith's painful struggle for emotional wholeness still makes for a sensitive, poignant short novel.

[For other works of this author, see the companion guide to fantasy.]

Süskind, Patrick (Germany).

4-293. Perfume. Knopf, 1986. Tr. by John E. Wood of *Das Perfum,* 1985.
Perfume is a lyrical European horror novel which owes more to Günter Grass than Stephen King. The novel chronicles the picaresque life of an eighteenth-century perfumer, a completely amoral man with the most highly developed sense of smell in the world, who discovers how to manipulate those around him through the use of particular scents. Süskind is literary without being pretentious, and his refreshingly straightforward narrative style perfectly suits the inventive and unpredictable story. He also manages to capture and bring to life the squalid world of the eighteenth century much more effectively than does Peter Ackroyd in the interesting but labored *Hawksmoor* [4-1]. Winner of the World Fantasy Award in 1987, *Perfume* is a unique novel and an outstanding work of contemporary fiction. (B.L.) Also annotated as [F4A-242].

Talbot, Michael, 1953- .
ABOUT: CA

4-294. The Bog. Morrow, 1986.
David Macauley's euphoria at making the archeological discovery of the century, two preserved bodies from Roman times in the Hovern Bog, soon turns to horror when he and his family are taken prisoners in the small English town of Fenchurch St. Jude and find themselves at the mercy of a black magician and his carnivorous, shape-shifting demon. A cleanly written, well-paced novel with strong characterizations, particularly effective in the delineation of family relationships. The demon-monster is vivid and original and the sorcerer is a worthy exemplar of the aristocratic villain tradition. The book runs down toward the end, however, as Talbot's ingenious mythology becomes strained and his chaotic conclusion falls back on a *deus ex machina.* Compare Blackburn's *For Fear of Little Men* [4-40].

Taylor, Bernard (U.K.), 1936- .
ABOUT: CA, H, PE

4-295. The Godsend. St. Martin's, 1976.
Alan and Kate Marlowe befriend an oddly apathetic pregnant woman, who gives birth and immediately abandons her child. The Marlowes adopt the baby girl, naming her Bonnie. Shortly thereafter, terrible "accidents" threaten the lives of their own children—until Alan becomes convinced that Bonnie is deliberately destroying the family so that, like the cuckoo bird, she can have possession of the entire nest. Narrating in a brisk first-person style in short, spare, highly dramatic short scenes, Taylor commands strong reader identification with his protagonist, gradually intensifying suspense from the first page to the last. A truly terrifying

novel. Compare Block's *Ariel* [4-49], March's *The Bad Seed* [4-211] and Saul's *Suffer the Children* [4-264]. The "cuckoo" metaphor is also used quite effectively in another, very different evil child novel, Wyndham's *The Midwich Cuckoos* [4-338].

4-296. Sweetheart, Sweetheart. Souvenir Press, 1977.
David Warwick travels to the English countryside to discover the truth about the fate of Calvin, his twin brother, and Calvin's wife. Sharing a cottage, David and his fiancée, Shelagh, are gradually threatened by the malevolent forces that doomed his twin. A powerfully original manipulation of traditional ghost story materials, featuring the nastiest she-ghost since Onions's "The Beckoning Fair One" [3-155]. Compare Theroux's *The Black House* [4-299].

Tessier, Thomas, 1947- .
ABOUT: PE

***4-297. The Nightwalker**. Atheneum, 1979.
Bobby Ives, American Vietnam veteran living in London, finds himself gradually changing into a werewolf, killing several people, including assorted girl friends, in the process. But because the story is told from his viewpoint, we identify with Bobby and share his anguish, even as we are horrified by his behavior. Although not exactly likable, Bobby is one of the more compelling characters in contemporary dark fantasy. Tessier's writing is highly charged, sensual and intimate. One of the most important werewolf stories in the literature. Compare Seignolle's "Marie the Wolf" [4-266], Strieber's *The Wolfen* [4-291] and Whitten's *Moon of the Wolf* [4-325].

4-298. Phantom. Atheneum, 1982.
Ten-year-old Ned Covington fears that a "phantom" wants to kill and/or possess him and perhaps also his mother. These fears intensify as he explores the woods near his home and especially the ruins of a long-abandoned health spa where he encounters—perhaps—the ghost of a woman who lost her child at sea and wants him as a replacement. A touching, scary book. The child's point of view is handled quite believably and sensitively, and Ned's final hallucinatory confrontation with the "woman" is as harrowing and imaginative as anything in current horror fiction. The unanswered question of whether the phantom is real or a projection of Ned's emotional confusions adds additional ambiguity and tension to this fine novel. Compare King's *The Shining* [4-173].

Theroux, Paul, 1941- .
ABOUT: CA

4-299. The Black House. Houghton Mifflin, 1977.
Alfred Munday, an anthropologist, and his wife, Emma, return after a long stay in Africa to an English country house in Dorset, where they encounter the spectral presence of a lovely woman who makes increasingly strange, disturbing demands upon Alfred. A mainstream nonfiction (*The Great Railway Bazaar*, 1975) and novel writer, best known for his portrayals of eccentric characters in

exotic locales (*Saint Jack,* 1973; *The Mosquito Coast,* 1982), Theroux utilizes the formula of the classical ghost story to write an intriguing study of a haunted man. Compare Taylor's *Sweetheart, Sweetheart* [4-296].

Thompson, (Eu)Gene, 1924- .

About: CA

4-300. Lupe. Random, 1977.
The title character of *Lupe* is a demonic, sexually precocious eleven-year-old Hispanic boy who terrorizes a doctor's wife and kills the woman with whom her husband is having an affair. The first third of the novel, the portion dealing with Lupe's "haunting" of the wife, is by far the scariest and most successful segment of the work. Here Thompson explores to a greater extent the fear of children's sexuality and its association with evil, which is hinted at but never fully explored in Straub's *Julia* [4-288]. The second part of the novel concerns the wife's trial for murder; while parallels with the Salem witchcraft trials are obvious, they are not overdone, and real tension is generated as to the outcome of the proceedings. The third and weakest section of the book is a *Rosemary's Baby*-like posttrial denouement. *Lupe* is not a perfect novel, but it is well written, fast paced, scary and literary. (B.L.)

Tonkin, Peter (U.K.), 1950- .

About: CA

4-301. The Journal of Edwin Underhill. Hodder & Stoughton, 1981.
Subsidence in a graveyard leads a mild-mannered schoolmaster to impale his hand on the sharpened stake driven through a vampire's heart, whereupon he begins a slow metamorphosis into dreadful superhumanity, becoming perversely attractive to the woman who had previously repulsed his advances. One of the more nasty-minded ventures into vampire existentialism, which attempts to explore and expose the underlying psychology of the widespread contemporary fascination with the vampiric condition. (B.S.)

Topor, Roland (France), 1938- .

About: PE

4-302. Joko's Anniversary. Calder & Boyars, 1970, Tr. by J. A. Underwood of *Joko fête son anniversaire,* 1969.
En route to work, Joko encounters conventioneers in bathing suits who demand to be carried on his back. He initially refuses, but then agrees to become an all-purpose conveyance in order to regain acceptance and popularity. Eventually seven riders become permanently attached, whereupon they commence to insult, humiliate and torture him, driving the distraught Joko to madness, violence, self-destruction and beyond. In contrast to the activities described, the writing is simple and direct, almost childlike, with narrative segments alternating with play-like dialogue exchanges. The novel (if it can be called such) is a surrealistic nightmare of grotesque, hilarious carnage that satirizes man's capacity for social and self-enslavement. As an example of the black comic fantasy, it would be

difficult to find a work more black, more comedic or more fantastic than *Joko's Anniversary*. Compare the stories of Dino Buzzati [4-59].

4-303. The Tenant. Doubleday, 1966. Tr. by Francis K. Price of *La locataire chimérique*, 1964.
A unique, disturbing novel about the effects of peer pressure, *The Tenant* concerns a young man, Trelkovsky, who moves into a Paris apartment whose previous occupant has committed suicide. The other tenants in the building immediately begin requesting that he conform to their standards, and Trelkovsky is eager to win their approval. A quiet man, the neighbors insist that he makes too much noise, and he obligingly changes his personal habits—refusing to let his friends visit, wearing women's slippers when he is home—in order to placate them. The demands of the neighbors grow, and Trelkovsky first suspects that they are trying to turn him into a copy of the former tenant and then that they are trying to drive him to suicide. It is never clear whether the increasing and increasingly bizarre demands of the tenants are real or are merely the product of Trelkovsky's disturbed mind, and this Poe-like ambiguity lends to the work a literary credibility not often found in contemporary horror. *The Tenant* is Kafkaesque in its worldview, and there are echoes of both Camus and Dostoyevsky in the self-conscious alienation of the protagonist. This distinctly European novel was effectively filmed by Roman Polanski (1976). (B.L.)

Tremayne, Peter (pseud. of **Peter Berresford Ellis**) (U.K.), 1943- .
ABOUT: CA

4-304. Dracula Unborn. Bailey Bros. & Swinfen, 1977. [U.S. title *Bloodright: Memoirs of Mircea, Son to Dracula*]; **The Revenge of Dracula**. Bailey Bros., 1978; **Dracula, My Love**. Bailey Bros., 1980.
In an autobiographical fragment discovered by Abraham Van Helsing, Mircea, estranged son of Vlad the Impaler, tells the story of his awful heritage. Having returned to Wallachia for a reunion with his half-brothers, following the "death" of his father, Mircea slowly, reluctantly becomes aware of the pervasive evil in Castle Dracula and of the terrible role that he is expected to play in spreading that evil around the world. An effective historical horror story that firmly connects Stoker's Dracula with the historical Vlad the Impaler. Tremayne adroitly integrates historical detail, Dracula lore and deft characterization to create an exciting, believable amplification of the Dracula myth. In *The Revenge of Dracula*, Upton Welsford, a diplomatic functionary, buys a statue of the god Draco, which draws him, along with the beautiful Clara Clarke, to Transylvania for an encounter with Dracula. In *Dracula, My Love,* governess Morag MacLeod gradually comes under the Count's power, but this time he is presented not as a villain, but as the supreme romantic lover. Although separate novels, the three books extend the Dracula character in interesting directions, from the consummate evil of Stoker's Count to the romantic hero/villain who is more to be pitied than censored. The first novel is the best of the three, the third the most interesting. Compare Les Daniels's Don Sebastian series [4-92], Saberhagen's *The Dracula Tape* and its sequels [4-258], and Yarbro's Saint Germain series [4-340].

Tryon, Thomas, 1926– .
ABOUT: CA, H, SMFL, SFFL, PE

***4-305. Harvest Home**. Knopf, 1973.
Artist Ned Constantine, his wife and his daughter settle in Cornwall Coombe, a quaint, isolated New England village. Despite evasions and warnings from townspeople, Ned investigates the true nature of Cornwall Coombe and uncovers a matriarchal society rooted in a fertility religion that reconciles man to nature through a series of secret, dangerous rituals—which he and his family are finally drawn into. Beautifully written, deftly structured, suspenseful and ironic, *Harvest Home* is the best of the "fertility cult" novels by a wide margin. Compare Burke's *The Devil's Footsteps* [4-58], Hardy and Shaffer's *The Wicker Man* [4-134] and Klein's *The Ceremonies* [4-182]. Filmed from a script by Tryon as a 1978 television miniseries under the title *The Dark Secret of Harvest Home*.

***4-306. The Other**. Knopf, 1971.
A genuine horror classic, *The Other* is a unique, disturbing novel that has never been successfully imitated. The story of identical twins Niles and Holland, their invalid mother and their mystical grandmother, the work initially seems to be treading Bradbury territory with its tale of a magical pastoral summer. But Tryon's worldview is much darker than Bradbury's and *The Other* metamorphoses from sepia-tinted nostalgia to American Gothic, turning from a ghost story into something much more frightening. Continually inventive, the novel has at its core an unrevealed secret, and it keeps the reader guessing, revealing only parts of the puzzle in snatches of conversation, overheard verbal exchanges and imaginary games of childhood which take on a dark ritualism. Tryon's prose is worthy of Shirley Jackson, and is characterized by finely crafted understatement which invests even the most innocent events with hints of evil. In Tryon's universe, everything is slightly off, subtly altered, and this sense of indefinable wrongness is transferred to the reader, instilling a feeling of increasing paranoia. *The Other* is a powerful artistic statement, and a horror novel of authentic literary merit. A great book. Robert Mulligan directed the film version of *The Other* in 1972 from a strong script by Tryon. (B.L.)

Tuttle, Lisa, 1952– .
ABOUT: CA, NE, H

4-307. A Nest of Nightmares. Sphere, 1986.
Short stories published between 1980 and 1985, except "Stranger in the House" (1972). The horrors in *A Nest of Nightmares* grow out of the everyday experiences of Tuttle's female protagonists/victims (problems with men, with children, with careers), often complicated by supernatural intrusions (otherworldly visitors, Celtic witches, possessed horses). Tuttle combines the classical emphasis on tension, suggestion and unseen horror with a strong contemporary, feminist sensibility. Especially noteworthy are "The Nest," about a haunted attic; "The Other Mother," in which a Celtic goddess fulfills the needs of neglected children; and "Flying to Byzantium," in which an author becomes trapped in a world of her own creation. A superior collection.

Updike, John, 1932- .

ABOUT: CA, MF, SFFL, ESF

4-308. The Witches of Eastwick. Knopf, 1984.

The three "witches" of Eastwick, Rhode Island—Jane, Sukie and Alexandra—are captivated by a darkly mysterious, perhaps diabolical stranger, Darryl Van Horne. As they find their own talents, powers and inhibitions released, they also find themselves increasingly manipulated and dominated by Van Horne. Finally, pooling their psychic resources, the trio attempt to turn the tables on their errant lover-mentor. Updike's rare venture outside the realistic mainstream is excellent as humorous satire, thin as fantasy. His picture of contemporary small-town New England life is funny, perceptive and thought-provoking, particularly in his view of male-female relationships; his dark fantasy lacks imaginative drive, dissipating badly in the latter chapters as Van Horne, the novel's central figure, almost disappears from view. But while the novel fails due to Updike's unwillingness, or inability, to follow through on his fantasy premises, the 1987 film adaptation fails for an opposite reason, its finale that loses plot logic and characterization in an arbitrary excess of special effects. Compare Leiber's *Conjure Wife* [3-125]. Also annotated as [F4A-255].

[For other works of this author, see the companion guide to fantasy.]

Wagner, Karl Edward, 1945- .

ABOUT: WW, CA, H, SFE, SFFL, PE, ESF

4-309. In a Lonely Place. Warner, 1983.

Seven stories originally published between 1973 and 1982, plus an introduction by Peter Straub. Wagner combines an original contemporary sensibility with a thorough immersion in the dark fantasy tradition. "In the Pines," for example, is a ghost story that is both thoroughly original and reminiscent of "The Beckoning Fair One" [3-155] and *The Shining* [4-173]. A more practical kind of horror story is "The Fourth Seal," about a doctor who discovers that his cure for cancer is not as popular with his colleagues as he would have supposed. The two really outstanding stories in the volume, however, are "Where the Summer Ends" and "The River of Night's Dreaming." In the first, a small group of people gradually realize—too late—that something is alive beneath the masses of kudzu that grows thickly on their property. In the second, a crazed girl escapes and enters an old house, where she becomes trapped in a fantasy based on Robert W. Chambers's *The King in Yellow* [2-12]. When she finally escapes—to her death—we are left uncertain as to whether the madness was within or without.

4-310. Why Not You and I? Tor, 1987. The Dark Harvest hardcover edition, 1987, adds two stories to the nine in the Tor paperback.

Wagner is an interesting writer whose horror stories contain surprisingly little horror. He is more concerned with the vicissitudes of real life than with the workings of a supernatural world, and he chronicles in believable detail the human and societal problems which lead his characters into the realm of horror. This collection is a fine sampling. He paints portraits of emotionally abused porno actresses, fanatic science fiction conventioneers and a slew of sad people who for one reason or another cross into the twilight zone. The book suffers somewhat from sameness of approach—the retelling in dispassionate biographical fashion the events of a character's life—but the works are interesting enough to overcome this minor drawback. A worthwhile collection. Compare the short fiction of Dennis Etchison [4-106, 4-108] and George R. R. Martin [4-214, 4-215]. (B.L.)

Wakefield, H(erbert) Russell (U.K.), 1888–1965.
About: WW, GSF, SFW, CA, SFFL, PE, ESF

4-311. Strayers from Sheol. Arkham House, 1961.
Wakefield's last book of ghost stories, as he wryly states in his "Introduction: Farewell to All Those!" Fourteen stories in the classic mode with some contemporary touches. The most interesting stories include: "The Gorge of the Churels," an uncharacteristically humorous piece in which an Indian servant overcomes his justified distaste for his English employers and saves their young boy from the "churels," ghosts of women who have died in childbirth and seek the souls of living children for solace; "'Immortal Bird,'" about a mathematics professor, "accidentally" responsible for his predecessor's death, who is haunted by a "white blackbird" which had been the dead man's favorite; "Four Eyes," in which a dead husband gets revenge on his murderess-wife through his spectacles; "The Middle Drawer," in which a recent widower is questioned about his wife's death and denies everything, despite the presence of bad smells, peculiar noises and his wife's ghost; and "Monstrous Regiment," in which the narrator, writing from a madhouse, tells how his mother's ghost coaxed him into murdering his governess to be free of her sexual enticements. Effective examples of the genre by a generally underrated master. Compare the stories of Robert Aickman [4-3–4-9].

Walter, Elizabeth (U.K.).
About: PE, SFFL, ESF

4-312. In the Mist. Arkham House, 1979.
This volume of seven stories represents the author's own selection of her best work from her five earlier collections, which have been published only in Britain. Walter writes in the traditional style, making much use of local legends and tales either from her native Welsh border country, the setting of "The Sin-Eater," or wherever her travels take her. The author's introduction explains the origins of the stories and discusses her belief in the supernatural. The stories are of novelette length, which allows for optimum development of atmosphere, which is delivered in a polished and effective style. A solid volume of weird fiction. (M.A.)

4-313. Snowfall and Other Chilling Events. Harvill, 1965.
The first of the author's five collections of weird tales, featuring five stories. Each story builds painstakingly to a cruel climax, and though the motifs employed are relatively stereotyped, they are carefully adapted to the modern settings. The most interesting is "The Island of Regrets," which features a particularly seductive islet where "there is always a madman." Walter's later collections are *The Sin Eater* (1967), *Davy Jones' Tale* (1971), *Come and Get Me* (1973) and *Dead Woman* (1975). (B.S.)

Watson, Ian (U.K.), 1943– .
About: CA, NE, SFE, SFFL

4-314. Evil Water. Gollancz, 1988.
Better known for his science fiction, Watson has recently turned his imaginative talents to the horror field. *Evil Water* is a collection of ten stories somewhat more traditional and uniform than his longer fiction, although not lacking in original ideas. He has tried to give a 1980s face to the simple concepts of fantasy and horror, which do not always totally succeed but nevertheless have a refreshing sense of endeavor to bolster them. (M.A.)

4-315. The Power. Headline, 1987.
Watson has started a series of novels that could be called social protest narratives, fired by Watson's own views as a member of the Campaign for Nuclear Disarmament. *The Power* is an anti-nuclear novel which lets loose all manner of horrors on a small British village facing a nuclear disaster. Although Watson overdoes the horror and thereby suffocates the effect, *The Power* is a strong novel all the same. (M.A.)

Wellman, Manly Wade, 1903–1986.
About: WW, GSF, SFW, CA, H, SMFL, SFE, SFFL, RG, TCSF, PE, ESF

4-316. John the Balladeer. Baen, 1988.
This volume reprints the contents of *Who Fears the Devil?* (1963), and adds several previously uncollected stories. Silver John, balladeer and white magician, travels the mountains and backwoods of North Carolina, singing and encountering various kinds of supernatural evil, which, with the aid of courage, ingenuity, arcane knowledge and his magically stringed guitar, he vanquishes. John is at his best in the short stories, where the conflict is simple, direct and immediate. Excellent examples of Wellman's method can be seen in "O Ugly Bird," wherein John encounters a witch-man who uses a huge bird to terrorize the local citizens; "Vandy, Vandy," in which John's encounter with a survivor of the Salem witch trials almost costs him his life; and "Little Black Train," in which John uses his magic to bring the "little black train"—a coffin—to collect the wicked. Using the language, geography, manners and songs of the area that he knows so well, Wellman evokes such a strong sense of place that the stories take on the aura of folk tales (and, indeed, Wellman does mix folk legend with his original stories).

4-317. The Old Gods Waken. Doubleday, 1979; **After Dark**. Doubleday, 1980; **The Lost and the Lurking**. Doubleday, 1981; **The Hanging Stones**. Doubleday, 1982.
Four novels featuring Silver John the Balladeer. In *The Old Gods Waken*, Silver John and an Indian medicine man battle Old World druids, who have invaded Wolter Mountain with the aim of reawakening and harnessing the pre-Indian spirits that lie dormant at the top of the mountain. In *After Dark*, the ancient Shonokin race attempt to trick Silver John into using his magical talents to restore them to power. In *The Lost and the Lurking*, Silver John responds to a government request to investigate strange happenings in the town of Wolver, where he encounters a beautiful, malevolent witch who offers John the choice of

joining her devil-worshippers or being sacrificed by them. In *The Hanging Stones,* John happens on an industrialist whose attempts to construct a new Stonehenge have unleashed a succession of wood-haunting ghouls. The Silver John novels offer the same charms as the short stories: a strong central character; a colorful, believable setting; and an ingenious, offbeat supernaturalism based on folk magic. Occasionally the pacing is off and the plotting contrived, but the longer Silver John narratives offer a stimulating diversion for horror fiction readers.

4-318. The School of Darkness. Doubleday, 1985.
In this novel Wellman brings back John Thunstone, psychic investigator, hero of several stories in the 1930s. Thunstone confronts black magician Rowley Thorne at a symposium at Buford State University. This conflict triggers evils latent in the university, which reputedly had a centuries-old devil pact. An entertaining, well-plotted novel that demonstrates Wellman's storytelling capabilities, although it lacks the charm of the better Silver John tales.

[For other works of this author, see the companion guide to fantasy.]

Wheatley, Dennis (U.K.), 1897–1977.

ABOUT: WW, GSF, SFW, CA, SMFL, SFE, SFFL, TCSF, PE, ESF

4-319. Gateway to Hell. Hutchinson, 1970.
Wheatley's last black magic novel featuring his "four musketeers," Duc de Richleau, Rex Van Ryn, Simon Aaron and Richard Eaton, first introduced in *The Devil Rides Out* [3-209]. The Duc, Simon and Richard travel to Argentina to rescue Rex from a satanic cult. An efficient but somewhat tired rehash of Wheatley's basic black magic formula.

4-320. The Irish Witch. Hutchinson, 1973.
The only one of Wheatley's black magic novels to feature Roger Brook, aristocratic soldier-of-fortune hero of a dozen historical adventures. With the fall of Napoleon as a backdrop, Roger fights the Irish Witch, a *femme fatale* who has revived the notorious Hell Fire Club, for the soul of his daughter Susan. Another interesting, effective mix of popular literary genres that takes advantage of the approaches and formulas of both.

4-321. The Ka of Gifford Hillary. Hutchinson, 1956.
Having been killed by a death ray, Gifford Hillary's "Ka"—or astral body—travels freely and discovers a Russian plot against the British military. His problems: to communicate this information to the world of the living, to reanimate himself and, finally, to face the accusation that he killed his murderer. Another interesting mix of the horror novel and spy novel with a narrower focus, briefer time span and greater concern with character than usual for Wheatley. Compare Hutson's *Shadows* [4-151].

4-322. The Satanist. Hutchinson, 1960.
The first half of the book focuses on the protagonist's attempts to infiltrate the Satanic Order of the Great Ram and emphasizes occult paraphernalia. In the second half, the book shifts into the spy thriller mode, with the supernatural

giving way to secret formulas, stolen H-bombs and political terrorism on a grand scale. One of Wheatley's liveliest, if more chaotic, novels. The heroine, Mary Morden, is Wheatley's most interesting emancipated female character. Compare Blackburn's *For Fear of Little Men* [4-40].

***4-323. They Used Dark Forces**. Hutchinson, 1964.
The sixth and last novel in Wheatley's fictionalized history of World War II chronicles the exploits of Gregory Sallust, a dashing, amoral, but stridently patriotic hero. In the only novel of the series with supernatural elements, Sallust forms an alliance with black magician Ibrahim Malacou to fight the Nazis. With Malacou's help, Sallust eventually becomes occult adviser to Hitler and is perhaps instrumental in the Führer's suicide. A vivid, exciting adventure punctuated by real historical incidents. The supernaturalism is minimal, but *They Used Dark Forces* is probably Wheatley's best post-World War II novel. Compare McCammon's *The Wolf's Hour* [4-227] and Yarbro's *Tempting Fate* [4-340].

4-324. To the Devil—a Daughter. Hutchinson, 1953.
Another mix of politics and horror. Satanist Canon Copley-Syle attempts to create an army of homunculi to war against the free world. The first step in the plan is to animate his prototype creature with the soul of the heroine, Christina, who was pledged to Satan at birth by her father. A small group of friends, led by Intelligence chief "Conky Bill" Verney, fight to save Christina and disrupt the unholy satanic-communistic alliance. The politics are absurd, but the action is lively and the villain is one of Wheatley's best.

Whitten, Leslie H(unter), 1925- .

ABOUT: CA, SFFL

4-325. Moon of the Wolf. Doubleday, 1967.
The body of a bright, pretty black girl is found savaged in an open field and her militant brother is charged with the crime, but deputy Aaron Whitaker knows the killer is someone else, perhaps the man, probably white, who fathered her unborn child. After two additional murders, superstitious locals raise the cry of "werewolf," but the book's focus is on Whitaker's meticulous investigation which leads him to suspect the town's leading citizen—while he falls in love with his suspect's sister. An excellent novel in which the supernaturalism is muted and ambiguous. The characters are believable and, even including the murderer, sympathetic. Whitten's depiction of the Mississippi delta region is authentic and the question of black-white relations, which is crucial to the story, is handled with balance and subtlety. Compare Strieber's *The Wolfen* [4-291] as a mix of horror story and mystery and Tessier's *The Nightwalker* [4-297] in its characterization of the werewolf.

4-326. Progeny of the Adder. Doubleday, 1965.
Investigating the murders of three prostitutes, homicide detective Harry Picard gradually realizes that he is tracking, not a typical serial killer, but an awesomely powerful vampire. An adroit, exciting mix of the police procedure novel with the horror story. Whitten is especially adroit at integrating bits and pieces of traditional vampire lore smoothly and unobtrusively into his fast-paced narrative. The

book is somewhat marred by a too facile conclusion. Compare Hambly's *Those Who Hunt the Night* [4-133] and Strieber's *The Wolfen* [4-291].

Williams, Mary (U.K.).

4-327. The Dark God. Kimber, 1980.
One of the author's eleven collections of ghost stories, featuring the title short novel and five short stories. "The Dark God" novella is set, as is much of the author's work, in Cornwall and based in Celtic mythology; it describes the reemergence of ancient evil to haunt and hurt the inhabitants of a group of new cottages. Although marred by bad habits carried over from the author's many works of historical romantic fiction, it makes interesting use of its materials. Equally flawed but equally interesting is the title short novel of the later collection *Haunted Waters* (1987). Williams's stories are unfortunately close in spirit to modern "Gothic romances," but are redeemed by her interest in and obvious affection for the mythologies from which she draws her motifs. (B.S.)

Williamson, Chet, 1948- .

4-328. Ash Wednesday. Tor, 1987.
Real but blue-tinged, incorporeal ghosts suddenly appear in Merridale, Pennsylvania, frozen in position as they were at the moment of death, upsetting and frightening the local citizenry, while turning the town into a media circus. These vivid reminders of mortality force several individuals to come to terms with their own past guilts, especially Bradley Meyers, a violence-prone Vietnam veteran unable to forget his war experiences, and Jim Callendar, a former school bus driver who may, in a moment of panic, have inadvertently caused the death of several children, including his own son. A disturbing, original ghost story with exceptional characterization and provocative thematic implications. Compare Maxim's *Platforms* [4-222].

4-329. Soulstorm. Tor, 1986.
Five people—a dying millionaire, his wife, an unemployed mercenary, an ex-police officer and a shady businessman—are sealed into The Pines, a huge stone mansion atop a mountain in northern Pennsylvania, where they encounter, not conventional ghosts, but the souls of all the damned from the beginning of time. This ingenious, if not overly subtle, variation on the psychic-investigators-locked-in-a-haunted-house motif is exciting and visceral, and offers several neat twists and a rousing finale. Characterization is superficial except for the hero, George McNeely, a war-weary mercenary, who convincingly outwits an entity that represents all mankind's combined evil. Compare *The Haunting of Hill House* [4-155] and *Hell House* [4-216].

Wilson, Colin (U.K.), 1931- .

ABOUT: WW, F, CA, NE, SFE, SFFL, TCSF, PE, ESF

4-330. The Mind Parasites. Arkham House, 1967.
Probing the reasons behind a close friend's suicide, archeologist Gilbert Austin discovers the existence of "mind parasites," ostensibly products of an ancient

race, that inhibit man's creativity and drain his psychic vitality. At great personal risk, Austin and his colleagues probe within themselves to find and release their own potential, while discovering the true nature and vulnerability of the mind parasites. Mankind's final victory is rather far-fetched and the characters are often little more than animated ideas, but Wilson's imaginative harnessing of Lovecraftian imagery to his philosophy of human possibility is challenging and stimulating. Compare Erik Frank Russell's more science fictional *Sinister Barrier* (1943).

4-331. The Philosopher's Stone. Arthur Barker, 1969.
After an operation on their prefrontal lobes gives them extraordinary mental powers, including the ability to time travel mentally, scientists Lester and Littleway learn the truth about the Old Ones, human evolution and the terrible threats and glorious possibilities that await mankind. Wilson's second philosophical science fiction story again successfully reinvents the Lovecraft mythos to illuminate a personal vision. Cerebrally stimulating and imaginative, if more philosophical diatribe than conventional novel.

4-332. The Space Vampires. Random, 1976.
Another science fiction variation on Wilson's notion that hostile psychic entities drain man's potential unless he fights back to transcend his mundane self. A derelict ship unleashes hostile outlaw aliens, who feed off human energy. Good aliens appear and guide Captain Carlson in his struggle against the space vampires, whom he can vanquish only if he accepts and fulfills his own heroic destiny. Wilson's third SF/horror novel is the most polished as a fictional narrative, but the least interesting as a philosophical statement. Sensationalized and stripped of its ideas, the novel was filmed by Tobe Hooper as *Lifeforce* (1985).

Wilson, F(rancis) Paul, 1946- .
ABOUT: NE, H, TCSF, PE

4-333. The Keep. Morrow, 1981.
When the Nazis invade Ploiesti, Romania, they take over the "keep," a huge fortress-castle in the middle of the city, to house their troops. Very soon an ancient evil begins to destroy them systematically. This malevolent force—called Rasalom—then attempts to coax an old Jew, Theodore Cuza, into releasing him to destroy the Nazis en masse. To counter the creature comes the mysterious Glaeken, a man in his needs and desires, but much more than that in his relationship to Rasalom. An original, ambitious variation on the vampire novel that poses some interesting moral questions, while offering a very entertaining mix of horror, adventure and romance. Michael Mann's 1983 film adaptation started well, with some excellent performances and special effects, but the rationale of the Rasalom-Glaeken relationship was never mentioned and the final confrontation resembled a Saturday morning cartoon climax.

4-334. The Tomb. Berkley, 1984.
Repairman Jack, a deliberately unknown soldier-of-fortune, accepts two jobs, one from an ex-lover and another from a member of the Indian delegation, which dovetail to immerse him in a complicated revenge plot complete with the "ra-

kosh," unstoppable demonic Indian creatures. *The Tomb* lacks the atmospheric density and serious ideas of *The Keep*, but as a fast-moving adventure yarn with interesting characters it is first rate.

Wood, Bari, 1936- .

ABOUT: CA

4-335. The Killing Gift. Putnam, 1975.
Dr. Jennifer List Gilbert discovers that she can kill by wishing it, and this terrible gift isolates her from lovers, friends and even herself. David Stavitsky, chief of homicide, suspects the truth and becomes obsessed with Jennifer, not as a criminal, but as a person and, perhaps, even more than that. An ingenious, upsetting book, although the ending is a bit thin. Jennifer can be seen as an adult version of King's *Carrie* [4-162]. *The Killing Gift* won Putnam's first-novel award.

4-336. The Tribe. Signet, 1981.
From Blezec, a Nazi death camp, to a Minnesota suburb, the Jacob Levy family is followed by a dark force that protects them from harm or rights injustices done to their tribe—but once loosed, can the force be controlled? And who is responsible for its destructiveness? Of all the major monsters of literature and legend, perhaps the Golem has been the most neglected. Woods fills this gap with a large novel that explores the practical and moral implications of such a creature. She is especially good at delineating Jewish culture and the relationship between the "pogrom mentality" and the Golem's evil. The cabalistic rituals and Golem lore are also handled most effectively. An impressive novel.

Wright, T. M., 1947- .

ABOUT: CA, PE

4-337. Strange Seed. Everest House, 1978.
Strange Seed is a fascinating surrealistic novel in which the horror is shown but not explained, its origin hinted at but not revealed. A couple move back to the husband's childhood home in downstate New York, a heavily wooded, scarcely populated region where the forest is inhabited by strange, wild children. Against the advice of their lone neighbor, the couple take in a wild boy, to whom the wife soon becomes sexually attracted. Their relationship deteriorates rapidly as the forest seems to become increasingly sentient. Wright is a fine writer, and he uses awkward time transitions, a limited omniscience and unattributed dialogue to bring a hallucinatory quality to the work and to make the reader as disoriented as the characters. Similar in many ways to Raucher's *Maynard's House* [4-247], *Strange Seed* is an excellent, unforgettable book. Wright continued his story of "The Children of Earth" in *Nursery Tale* (1982) and *The Children of the Island* (1983). (B.L.)

Wyndham, John (pseud. of **John Benyon Harris**), 1903–1969.

ABOUT: GSF, CA, NE, SFE, MF, SFFL, RG, TCSF

4-338. The Midwich Cuckoos. M. Joseph, 1957.
During a mysterious "sleep," all the females of Midwich, a small English town,

are simultaneously impregnated by an alien force and, nine months later, give birth to near-identical golden-eyed children. As they grow up, the children exhibit extraordinary powers, particularly their group mind, which pose an increasing threat to mankind, a threat recognized only by the narrator, a writer, and George Zellaby, local squire, teacher and philosopher. A provocative early science fiction/horror story variation on the evil child theme. Compare Wright's *Strange Seed* [4-337]. The "cuckoo" metaphor is also used effectively by Bernard Taylor in *The Godsend* [4-295]. Wolf Rilla's faithful 1960 film adaptation, retitled *Village of the Damned*, with George Sanders as Zellaby, is a minor classic.

Yarbro, Chelsea Quinn, 1942- .

ABOUT: CA, NE, SFE, MF, SFFL, RG, TCSF, PE

4-339. The Godforsaken. Warner, 1983.
During the Spanish Inquisition, a curse falls on the house of King Alonzo in general and on his heir apparent, Rolon, in particular—the curse of the werewolf. In *The Godforsaken*, Yarbro tries to do for werewolves what she does for vampires in the Saint Germain series. A large, rich book, filled with rounded characters and period detail, if somewhat slow-moving at times.

***4-340. Hotel Transylvania**. St. Martin's, 1978; **The Palace**. St. Martin's, 1978; **Blood Games**. St. Martin's, 1979; **Path of the Eclipse**. St. Martin's, 1981; **Tempting Fate**. St. Martin's, 1982; **The Saint-Germain Chronicles**. Pocket Books, 1983.
Five novels and one collection featuring François Rgoczy, Count de Saint Germain, a noble, sympathetic vampire. In *Hotel Transylvania*, against a background of eighteenth-century Parisian decadence, Saint Germain clashes with Saint Sebastian, leader of a satanic cult, who plans to sacrifice the Count's lover, Madelaine de Montalia. Saint Germain travels to Renaissance Florence in *The Palace*, where the art and culture of Lorenzo de Medici gradually give way to the fanaticism and suppression of Savonarola. The Count and his friends are threatened by the flames of the *auto-da-fé*. Nero's Rome is the setting for *Blood Games*, in which Saint Germain again attempts to save a woman he loves, Octavia, who has been framed for attempted murder by her ambitious, sadistic husband. Risking his life for her, Saint Germain faces final death in the Colosseum. *Path of the Eclipse* is a more open novel, as Saint Germain moves from China, where he helps a female warlord defend her people against the Mongol hordes, to travel through Tibet to India, where he clashes with a blood-mad high priestess of the Goddess Kali. During the Tibetan interlude we learn something of Saint Germain's history and initiation into vampirism. *Tempting Fate* brings Saint Germain into the twentieth century. As a result of rescuing a young girl from the Russian Revolution, Saint Germain is slowly drawn into the political, social and moral chaos that swept Europe in the years between World War I and the rise of Nazism. *The Saint-Germain Chronicles* contains five stories that take Saint Germain from seventeenth-century Antwerp to the modern world, where he encounters such phenomena as American teenagers, Hollywood and Senator Joseph McCarthy's 1950s Red Hunt. An impressive, entertaining series that blends the historical romance with the horror story—the horror coming from the human villains. Saint Germain is a superhero with just enough vulnerability to

be believable. Most impressive is Yarbro's ability to convey a sense, not only of the look of a historical era, but even of how it felt to live each day in such a world. A very interesting genre mix, although, despite some scenes of very graphic violence, hard-core horror fans may feel that the "historical romance" has overwhelmed the horror. Compare to Daniels's Don Sebastian series [4-92], Kast's *The Vampires of Alfama* [4-159] and Saberhagen's Dracula series [4-258].

[For other works of this author, see the companion guide to fantasy.]

Anthologies

by Mike Ashley

During the 1960s and 1970s the paperback anthology to a large degree superseded the magazine as the main source of short horror fiction. Nevertheless, the modern age has yet to rival the status of the 1920s and 1930s as the Golden Age of horror anthologies, especially in Britain. Despite a number of good original volumes, especially those edited by August Derleth and Charles L. Grant, the majority of the anthologies are still retrospective selections picked from magazines and books. The following annotated entries cover the most representative of both types of anthology produced in the last forty years. WFA means World Fantasy Award (see chapter 13).

***4-341. The Arbor House Treasury of Horror and the Supernatural**. Ed. by Bill Pronzini, Barry Malzberg and Martin H. Greenberg. Arbor House, 1981.
A 600-page omnibus of forty-one stories, divided into two sections, "Grandmasters" and "Modern Masters," although with no explanation for the division. We are left to presume that since only one year separates the Leiber and Brown stories in the first section from the Kornbluth story in the second, the division means no more than pre- and post-1950. The first section contains seventeen stories, all acknowledged classics, including works by Poe, Hawthorne, Le Fanu, Stoker, Bierce and Lovecraft, most of which will be known to even the newest reader, although Truman Capote's "Shut a Final Door" may be a surprise. The second section demonstrates the wide variety of themes in modern horror fiction, ranging from the science fiction base of Robert Silverberg's "Passengers," through the violence of military conflict in Jack Dann's "Camps," to the updated traditional horrors of Joyce Carol Oates's "The Doll" and the unrelenting terror of Stephen King's "The Crate." This section contains a good selection of less-well-known stories that nevertheless represent the state of modern horror fiction. Stephen King provides an elucidating and infectious introduction that clearly and authoritatively states the case for the defense of horror stories. Compare Hartwell [4-345].

***4-342. The Architecture of Fear**. Ed. by Kathryn Cramer and Peter D. Pautz. Arbor House, 1987.
Fourteen stories written to demonstrate that true horror comes when one's own private refuge is invaded or betrayed and there is nowhere to turn for safety or security. The stories, all but two new, are thus set in houses or similar retreats and explore the invasion or denial of privacy. All have a powerful impact, attacking most of the emotions relentlessly. Authors include Gene Wolfe, Ramsey Camp-

bell, Charles L. Grant, Karl Edward Wagner, Robert Aickman, Dean R. Koontz, John M. Ford, Jessica Amanda Salmonson, John Skipp and Craig Spector and Michael Bishop, all writing at their best. The anthology and two of its contents were nominated for the 1988 WFA, and was co-winner.

4-343. The Best Horror Stories from The Magazine of Fantasy and Science Fiction. Ed. by Edward L. Ferman and Anne Jordan. St. Martin's, 1988.
Despite the absence of the word from the title of *The Magazine of Fantasy and Science Fiction* [11-13], horror has formed an integral part of its content, and this selection of twenty-four stories ranging from 1951 to 1987 demonstrates the depth and variety available. Authors include Charles Beaumont, Stephen King, Robert Bloch, Richard Matheson, Charles L. Grant, Robert Aickman, Russell Kirk, Lucius Shepard and Michael Shea, with stories that are as freshly horrifying as the day they were first published.

4-344. Cutting Edge. Ed. by Dennis Etchison. Doubleday, 1986.
Twenty stories, all but one original, intended to show the state of the art of modern horror fiction; this volume has come to be hailed as one of the harbingers of the new wave "splatterpunk" movement. Not all the stories have the raging violence and graphic descriptions associated with the new fiction, but the works by even the elder writers like Robert Bloch, William F. Nolan and George Clayton Johnson are less subtle than usual for them. Clive Barker, one of the progenitors of the movement, contributes a comparatively mild story. While not to everyone's taste, this volume is required reading for anyone tracing the current evolution of horror fiction. The anthology and two of its stories were nominated for the 1987 WFA.

***4-345. The Dark Descent**. Ed. by David G. Hartwell. Tor, 1987.
A massive thousand-page volume containing fifty-six stories intended to show the evolution of the horror short story from its origins to the present, when its purpose has, to a large degree, been eclipsed by the novel. Hartwell provides a thoughtful and literate introduction evaluating this thesis. Though not presented in chronological order, the stories range from Poe's "The Fall of the House of Usher" and Le Fanu's "Schalken the Painter," through classics like Oliver Onions's "The Beckoning Fair One," Algernon Blackwood's "The Willows" and Robert Hichens's "How Love Came to Professor Guildea," to a variety of modern stories from authors including Stephen King, Russell Kirk, Harlan Ellison, Michael Shea, Robert Aickman, Clive Barker, Ramsey Campbell and Philip K. Dick with a selective diversity in between. In scale, scope and quality this must rank as one of the most important anthologies of the last half-century. Essential for all libraries.

***4-346. Dark Forces**. Ed. by Kirby McCauley. Viking, 1980.
A landmark volume designed to bring together revolutionary new tales of terror and fantasy as Harlan Ellison's *Dangerous Visions* (1967) did for speculative fiction. It includes twenty-three new stories by most of the modern masters of horror and fantasy, including Robert Aickman, Joyce Carol Oates, T. E. D. Klein, Ramsey Campbell, Theodore Sturgeon, Robert Bloch, Russell Kirk, Ray Bradbury and Stephen King, the latter represented by his short novel *The Mist* [4-174]. The stories themselves are not necessarily so revolutionary as the overall mood of

the anthology, which demonstrates the immense variety of treatment and concept within the fields of fantasy and horror fiction. One of the stories was nominated for the 1981 WFA, and *Dark Forces* went on to win.

4-347. Dark Mind, Dark Heart. Ed. by August Derleth. Arkham House, 1962.
Derleth was always a better anthologist than a writer. Although his best anthologies assemble reprinted stories such as *Sleep No More* (1944), his anthologies of new material still have a special fascination. They contain not only new stories by modern writers, such as Joseph Payne Brennan, Robert Bloch and Ramsey Campbell (who made his first appearance here), but previously unpublished stories by past masters, including William Hope Hodgson, Robert E. Howard and H. P. Lovecraft (the latter story written almost wholly by Derleth). In addition, there were new stories by writers generally no longer active such as David H. Keller, John Metcalfe and H. Russell Wakefield. This format was repeated in Derleth's remaining original anthologies, *Over the Edge* (1964), *Travellers by Night* (1967) and *Dark Things* (1971).

***4-348. Dodd, Mead Gallery of Horror**. Ed. by Charles L. Grant. Dodd, Mead, 1983.
A collection of twenty stories, fourteen of them new, with no particular theme or framework other than to assemble work by some of the best writers of the day, including William F. Nolan, Stephen R. Donaldson, Robert Bloch, T. E. D. Klein, Ramsey Campbell, Michael Bishop, David Morrell, Tanith Lee and Stephen King. The result is a solid, diverse volume of stories. Lee's "Nunc Dimittis" and the anthology were both nominated for the 1984 WFA.

***4-349. Frights**. Ed. by Kirby McCauley. St. Martin's, 1976.
The forerunner to *Dark Forces* [4-346], *Frights* presents fourteen new stories designed to explore the modern shape of fear and to give a new twist to old themes. The result is a powerful collection with authors Russell Kirk, R. A. Lafferty, Davis Grubb, Ramsey Campbell, Dennis Etchison and Robert Bloch, in particular, writing at their best. Three of the stories were nominated for the 1977 WFA, with Kirk's "There's a Long, Long Trail A-Winding" and the anthology itself both winners. There is a useful introduction by Fritz Leiber on the nature of fear.

4-350. The Ghost Book series. Ed. by Cynthia Asquith (U.K.) and others. Various publishers, 1952–77.
Twenty-five years after the first *Ghost Book* [3-6], Cynthia Asquith brought out a second volume concentrating on modern ghosts. The result, as Elizabeth Bowen highlights in her introduction, is an obsession with obsession, the driving force of the spirit that causes it to linger after death. The contributors were all British members of the literati not necessarily noted for their ghost stories (with the possible exceptions of L. P. Hartley, Lord Dunsany and Walter De la Mare) but all having produced a significant body of work. With the success of the second volume the series continued. *The Third Ghost Book* (1955) was introduced by L. P. Hartley and contained twenty-seven stories by many of the same writers but also included Robert Aickman. Following Cynthia Asquith's death, the series was revived by others. *The Fourth Ghost Book* (1965) was edited by James Turner, who suggested that the interest in ghost stories was due to a decline in organized

religion. His volume of twenty-three stories continued the trend of selecting new stories by establishment, nongenre writers. Rosemary Timperley edited *The Fifth, Sixth, Seventh, Eighth* and *Ninth Ghost Books* (1969–73), now an annual, with the ghosts becoming increasingly psychological and ethereal. Aidan Chambers edited *The Tenth* and *Eleventh Ghost Books* (1974 and 1975), Polly Parkin *The Twelfth* (1976) and James Hale *The Thirteenth* (1977) before the series ended. The quality of the later volumes is not as consistently high as the earlier ones, but these later volumes are especially valuable in tracing the treatment of the ghost story through the postwar years to the modern era. The spirit of the *Ghost Books* was continued by James Hale in subsequent anthologies, *The Midnight Ghost Book* (1978), *The After Midnight Ghost Book* (1980) and *The Twilight Book* (1981).

4-351. In the Field of Fire. Ed. by Jeanne Van Buren Dann and Jack Dann. Tor, 1987.
A collection of twenty-two stories and free-form poetry inspired by the horrors of the Vietnam War and intended to explore the fears and traumas engendered by the conflict in an attempt to transform "the terrifying chaos of war into meaning." Some of the items are science fiction, though only in its technological trappings. All the stories are nightmares, the majority of a fantastic nature, including powerful stories by Lucius Shepard, Dave Smeds, Richard Paul Russo and Lewis Shiner. All but five of the stories were written especially for the volume, which was nominated for the WFA in 1988. Encapsulates more than any other recent anthology the true horrors of the late twentieth century.

4-352. Masters of Darkness. Ed. by Dennis Etchison. 2 vols. Tor Books, 1986; 1988.
Two revealing volumes of stories selected by the authors themselves as examples of their personal favorites of their work. The authors made textual revisions in some cases and added commentaries. Each volume contains fifteen authors; the first includes Ray Bradbury, Robert Bloch, Richard Matheson, Ramsey Campbell, Ray Russell (who chose two poems) and William F. Nolan; the second includes Frank Belknap Long, Kate Wilhelm, Fritz Leiber and Tanith Lee, and two stories by dead authors, Manly Wade Wellman and Richard McKenna. All the stories are good, but the anthologies are most useful for the authors' own revelations about their work and their selections.

4-353. New Tales of the Cthulhu Mythos. Ed. by Ramsey Campbell (U.K.). Arkham House, 1980.
In the years since Lovecraft's death, the Cthulhu framework that he devised has been imitated and enlarged to a point where in the 1970s it was rapidly becoming a parody of itself. Campbell's anthology, a reaction to this trend, encouraged writers to rethink the Mythos and to create authentic modern treatments of the genuine article. The result is one of the best modern anthologies of Lovecraftian derivatives. It includes strong stories by Stephen King, A. A. Attanasio, Brian Lumley, Basil Copper and Ramsey Campbell and the especially powerful "Black Man with a Horn" by T. E. D. Klein.

4-354. New Terrors. Ed. by Ramsey Campbell (U.K.). 2 vols. Pan Books, 1980.
A showcase anthology of contemporary terrors, with thirty-seven new stories spread through the two paperback volumes. The anthology is really a British

Dark Forces [4-346], but it has never received the credit it deserves. Except for Robert Aickman's "The Stains," few of its stories have survived as memorable classics, even though every one of them is a powerful treatment of modern-day horrors and nightmares, ranging from a traditional approach in Russell Kirk's "Watchers at the Strait Gate" to the enigmatic approaches of Charles L. Grant and Kathleen Resch. It was nominated for the WFA in 1981.

4-355. Night Chills. Ed. by Kirby McCauley. Avon, 1975.
A collection of eighteen stories selected because they have not previously been easily accessible in mass-market paperbacks. Three of the stories, including Ramsey Campbell's now classic "Call First," are new. The remainder are a fine cross-section of twentieth-century weird fiction, with the emphasis on the strange and the frightening rather than on the gruesome. Included are lesser-known stories by Ray Bradbury, Robert Bloch, Manly Wade Wellman and Marjorie Bowen along with the first paperback printing of Karl Edward Wagner's "Sticks." Six of the stories were written before 1950, but none is dated.

***4-356. Night Visions**. Ed. by Alan Ryan and others. Dark Harvest, 1984- .
This annual series has rapidly established itself as one of the best quality markets of weird and fantasy fiction. Originally conceived by Paul Mikol of Dark Harvest Books along with Alan Ryan, the basic concept is for each volume to contain 30,000 words of new fiction by each of three writers. The authors could write one long novella or several short stories. The first volume contained eighteen stories by Charles L. Grant, Steve Rasnic Tem and Tanith Lee. Volume 2 (1985), edited by Charles L. Grant, contained twelve stories by David Morrell, Joseph Payne Brennan and Karl Edward Wagner, of which Morrell's "Dead Image" was nominated for the WFA. Volume 3 (1986), edited by George R. R. Martin, contained eleven stories by Clive Barker, Ramsey Campbell and Lisa Tuttle, of which Barker's "The Hellbound Heart" was nominated for the WFA. Volume 4 (1987), edited by Clive Barker, had twelve stories by Dean R. Koontz, Edward Bryant and Robert R. McCammon, with McCammon's "Best Friends" nominated for the WFA while his "The Deep End" won the 1988 Bram Stoker Award. Volume 5 (1988), edited by Douglas E. Winter, contains ten stories by Stephen King, Dan Simmons and George R. R. Martin. The first four volumes were all nominated for the WFA. Each volume contains some of the writers' very best works, and these remain showcase anthologies.

4-357. Pan Book of Horror Stories. Ed. by Herbert van Thal (U.K.). Pan Books, 1959–84. Ed. by Clarence Paget (U.K.). Vol. 26- , 1985- .
This long-running British series has, in its thirty years, purportedly sold in excess of four million copies. The series has been consistent in quality—though the measure of quality is very subjective—with the emphasis on corporeal rather than supernatural horror, though ghost stories do still occasionally appear and were more prevalent in the early volumes. The early volumes were also predominantly reprinted stories from both British and American sources, but the stories are now chiefly original with an occasional reprint by Stephen King. Perhaps the series' greatest service was in reprinting the stories by David Case and providing new ones. It has also run debut stories by a number of writers seeking to establish

themselves in the field. In the light of the recent "splatterpunk" movement, the *Pan Horror* series stands clearly as a precursor. For library holdings of this title, see chapter 11.

***4-358. Prime Evil**. Ed. by Douglas E. Winter. New American Library, 1988.
Given the publishing hype and high advances, this anthology had much to live up to. Winter, well known as a critic and analyst of the horror field, gave thirteen writers complete freedom to write their best and the results are variable. All, however, demonstrate the power of horror fiction in the 1980s, and, when properly handled, the stories raise penetrating questions in line with Winter's introductory thesis that horror is not a fiction genre but an emotion. The stories are thus designed to explore and release emotions, not simply to entertain. This assembly of stories by Stephen King, Clive Barker, David Morrell, Ramsey Campbell, Charles L. Grant, Whitley Strieber and others does just that. There is a rare professional appearance by Thomas Ligotti.

***4-359. Shadows**. Ed. by Charles L. Grant. 10 vols. Doubleday, 1978–87.
The *Shadows* series rapidly established a yardstick for quality in the field and included some of the best original horror fiction published in the last ten years. Grant's judgment is consistently reliable, and he has, for the most part, avoided visceral horror to concentrate on stories of unease and the uncanny that evoke fear rather than revulsion. The first volume won the WFA in 1979, and volumes 2 to 6 were all nominated for the WFA. Eight stories have also been nominated for the WFA over the years; they include "Naples" by Avram Davidson (#1), "Mackintosh Willy" by Ramsey Campbell (#2) and "The Gorgon" by Tanith Lee (#5), which won in 1979, 1980 and 1983 respectively. *The Best of Shadows* (1988) collected thirteen stories from vols. 1–10 and included an author/title index to these volumes. For library holdings of this title, see chapter 11.

4-360. 13 Short Horror Novels. Ed. by Charles G. Waugh and Martin H. Greenberg. Bonanza Books, 1987.
One of the few anthologies to give space to longer works of horror fiction, although the description "short novel" (normally considered to be between 30,000 and 40,000 words) is used here with a certain editorial license (in fact only three of the stories qualify). The stories range from Victorian (Arthur Conan Doyle's "The Parasite") to topical (T. E. D. Klein's "Children of the Kingdom") to pulp (Frank Belknap Long's "The Horror from the Hills" and Manly Wade Wellman's "Fearful Rock") to quasi-science fiction (Theodore Sturgeon's "Killdozer" and H. P. Lovecraft's "The Shadow Out of Time") to slick (Ray Russell's "Sardonicus") and the uneasily strange (Robert Aickman's "The Strains"), and each is a good example of its type. Compare Mike Ashley's *The Mammoth Book of Short Horror Novels* (1988), which selects ten generally longer items and duplicates only Doyle's "The Parasite."

***4-361. Whispers**. Ed. by Stuart David Schiff. Doubleday, 1977– .
A spin-off from the editor's *Whispers* magazine [11-21], the series has included both selections from the magazine and new stories. The volumes appear in alternate years, the editor carefully selecting stories out of the ordinary in both the horror and fantasy fields. Volumes 1, 2, 3 and 5 were each nominated for the

WFA, and "The Chimney" by Ramsey Campbell (#1) and "Elle Est Trois, (La Mort)" by Tanith Lee (#4) won the WFA in their respective years. For library holdings of this title, see chapter 11.

4-362. The World Fantasy Awards. Ed. by Gahan Wilson. Doubleday, 1977.
The first volume, properly titled *First World Fantasy Awards,* commemorated the first World Fantasy Convention and Awards, organized by Gahan Wilson, and includes both fiction and essays, reprinting winners, nominees and other representative fiction. A second volume, edited by Stuart David Schiff and Fritz Leiber (1980), offered a further selection. Also annotated as [F4A-291].

***4-363. The Year's Best Horror Stories**. DAW, 1973- .
This series has had a confusing chronology due to its genesis in Britain under editor Richard Davis prior to its continuation by DAW Books in America under editor Gerald W. Page after the original British series ceased publication. For many years the only annual collection of the year's best stories, the series has varied both in quality and content with the editors' own idiosyncratic and subjective selections. Under Davis (vols. 1-3) the series reflected chiefly the lackluster image of horror fiction in Britain in the early 1970s. Under Page (vols. 4-7) the series widened its scope to include new fiction and to reflect Page's own fondness for polished pulp-style fiction with a more fantastic element. The current editor, Karl Edward Wagner (vols. 8-), is a master at combing diverse publications for obscure weird stories that usually possess a more trenchant and powerful bite than those selected by his predecessors. The series to date is a good barometer of the fall and rise of popularity in weird and horror fiction. Volumes 5, 6 and 15 were nominated for the WFA. For library holdings of this title, see chapter 11.

5

Fantasy and Horror Fiction and Libraries

Neil Barron

Fantasy and horror fiction has been regularly published since at least the eighteenth century, and most major writers have written some "fantastic" fiction. As chapters 6–9 indicate, it is only in recent years that fantastic fiction and film have been the subject of sustained scholarship. By contrast, science fiction's creation and publication were at least partially dependent on the development of science and technology. Although science fiction was also published fairly widely in general periodicals from the nineteenth century on, beginning in the mid-1920s the shorter fiction tended to move into the American pulp magazines, beginning with *Amazing* in 1926. This also happened, but to a much lesser degree, to fantasy and horror fiction, as chapter 11 indicates. *Weird Tales* [11-20] began in 1923 and is—for older readers at least—easily the best known of the pulps which emphasized fantastic fiction, mostly with supernatural/horror themes but occasionally SF themes as well, especially in the earlier years.

Almost every trade publisher has issued an occasional work of fantasy or horror fiction, but it was only relatively recently that such fiction became a distinct form of category fiction, like SF, mysteries, westerns or romances. Fantasy and sometimes horror are usually shelved with SF in chain bookstores, particularly mass-market paperbacks. With the notable exception of Arkham House, which was founded in 1938 to preserve and publicize the work of H. P. Lovecraft, few publishers have specialized in fantasy and horror fiction. The specialty publishers active in the decade following World War II, which failed as the major trade publishers entered the field, usually emphasized science fiction. (A brief summary of specialty SF publishers is provided by Robert Weinberg in his chapter in Hall's *Science/Fiction Collections* [6-37].) Only in the 1980s have publishers specialized in fantasy or horror fiction. Tables 5-1, 5-2 and 5-3 list the principal U.S. and British general and specialty publishers of fantasy and horror fiction and the related secondary literature.

The most detailed and accurate statistics for U.S. and U.K. fantastic fiction publishing are compiled by *Locus* [11-40], which provides an annual summary in each February issue and in its annual hardbound bibliographies [6-6]. Clear distinctions between science fiction, fantasy and horror fiction are sometimes difficult to make, but the figures in table 5-4 provide a reasonably accurate summary and show the relative magnitude of each type of fiction. Figures refer to books published or distributed in the U.S. and exclude British and other foreign books not distributed in the U.S. Thus the figures shown understate total publication of English-language fantastic fiction.

For all types of fantastic fiction, reprints and reissues have totaled about 40% to 47% of all titles in the 1980s. For hardcover books, the figure is about 20%. For mass-market paperbacks, the most common format, the figure has varied from about 50% to 60%. There are a large number of mass-market originals, which libraries that systematically acquire fantasy and horror fiction should acquire in prebound format and catalog like any other book. The public library practice of dumping paperbacks on spinner racks or shelves with no cataloging to make users aware of their existence is not a satisfactory policy for any library desiring to provide anything more than a quickly expendable popular fiction collection. Prebinding mass-market copies adds about $3–4 to their original modest wholesale cost ($2–3) and results in a volume likely to outlast most trade hardcovers.

Currently roughly 300 original works of fantasy in English—novels, collections and anthologies—are published in the U.S. and U.K. each year. The figure for horror is about 200, a figure which has grown rapidly in the 1980s. Because of the large number of books published, particularly in recent years, contributors to this guide were asked to be extremely selective and to choose only the best or better works for consideration by libraries and interested readers.

Table 5-1. Principal U.S. General Publishers of Fantasy and Horror Fiction

Publishers or imprints in boldface issue the largest number of titles. Paperback publishers are primarily mass market, but those which issue occasional trade paperbacks are marked by an asterisk.

Paperbacks	*Hardcover*	*Secondary Literature*
*Academy Chicago	**Ace/Putnam**	Advent: Publishers
Ace	**Arbor House**	Borgo Press
Archway	Argo *see* Atheneum	Bowling Green State Univ. Popular Press
Avon	Arkham House	Crossroad/Continuum
Baen	**Atheneum**	Gale Research
***Ballantine/Del Rey**	**Ballantine/Del Rey**	Garland Publishing
Bantam/Spectra	**Bantam/Spectra**	Greenwood Press
Bart Books	Congdon & Weed	G. K. Hall
Berkley	Crown	Indiana Univ. Press
Carroll & Graf	**DAW**	

Table 5-1. (continued)

Charter
Critic's Choice
DAW
*Delacorte
Dell
Del Rey *see* Ballantine
*Donning/Starblaze
Fawcett
*Harvest
Jove
Leisure
Pageant
Paperjacks
Pinnacle
*Plume
Pocket Books
Popular Library/ Questar
Questar *see* Popular Library
Signet/NAL
Spectra *see* Bantam
Starblaze *see* Donning
TOR
Warner
Worldwide Library
Zebra

Delacorte
Del Rey *see* Ballantine
Donning
Doubleday/Foundation
E. P. Dutton
Easton Press
Farrar
Donald Fine
Foundation *see* Doubleday
Greenwillow
Harcourt
Harper & Row
Houghton Mifflin
Maclay & Associates
Macmillan
Millennium *see* Walker
William Morrow
New American Library
Poseidon Press
Putnam
St. Martin's
SF Book Club
Simon & Schuster
Spectra *see* Bantam
Tor
Viking Penguin
Walker/Millennium
Warner
Franklin Watts

Kent State Univ. Press
Locus Press
McFarland & Co.
Meckler
Oxford Univ. Press
Scarecrow Press
Scribner's
Serconia Press
Southern Illinois Univ. Press
Starmont House
Twayne
UMI Research Press

Table 5-2. Principal U.K. General Publishers of Fantasy and Horror Fiction

See note to table 5-1. My thanks to Mike Ashley for much of the information in this table.

Paperbacks
*Abacus
Arrow
Bantam
Beaver
*Black Swan
*Chatto & Windus

Hardcover
W. H. Allen
Bantam Press
Jonathan Cape
Cassell
Century Hutchinson
Chatto & Windus

Secondary Literature
See table 5-3 under Dragon's World and Ferret Fantasy

Table 5-2. (continued)

Corgi	Collins
Coronet	**Equation**
*Equation	**Gollancz**
Fontana	**Grafton**
Futura/Orbit	**Headline**
Grafton	**Hodder & Stoughton**
Headline	Michael Joseph
Kestrel	**William Kimber**
Magnet	**MacDonald Futura**
New English Library	Macmillan
Orbit	**Methuen**
Pan	Piatkus
***Penguin**	Robinson Publishing
*Picador	Robson Books
Piccolo	**Severn House**
Puffin	Simon & Schuster
Robinson	**Unwin Hyman**
Sphere	Viking
*Titan	Virago
Unwin Paperbacks	Women's Press
VGSF (Gollancz)	
Virago	
Women's Press	

Table 5-3. Specialty U.S. and U.K. Publishers of Fantasy and Horror Fiction and Related Criticism

These publishers specialize in fantastic fiction, primarily fantasy and horror but sometimes science fiction as well (publishers specializing almost exclusively in SF are omitted; see list in chapter 7 of my *Anatomy of Wonder*, 1987). These publishers typically issue no more than one or two titles per year, often less. A limited, signed, numbered, often slipcased edition is marketed to collectors, and a trade edition to a slightly larger market. Total print runs rarely exceed 2,000 copies. Co-publishing with nonspecialty trade publishers has occasionally occurred.

Advent: Publishers, Box A3228, Chicago, IL 60690. History and criticism, emphasizing SF

Arkham House, Box 546, Sauk City, WI 53583. Mostly supernatural fiction; Lovecraft's principal publisher

Axolotl Press, c/o Pulphouse, Box 1227, Eugene, OR 97440

Cheap St., Rt. 2, Box 293, New Castle, VA 24127. Original fiction handset in very fine quality editions

Corroboree Press, 2729 Bloomington Ave. S, Minneapolis, MN 55407. Emphasizes work of R. A. Lafferty

Dark Harvest, Box 941, Arlington Heights, IL 60006. Mostly horror fiction

Table 5-3. (continued)

Dragon's World/Paper Tiger, 19 Hereford Square, London SW7 4TS. Mostly illustrated books, heavily fantasy and SF
Chris Drumm, Box 445, Polk City, IA 50226. Pamphlet author bibliographies plus original pamphlet short stories
Ferret Fantasy, 27 Beechcroft Rd., Upper Tooting, London SW17 7BX. Bibliographies by George Locke of fantastic literature
Footsteps Press, Box 75, Round Top, NY 12473
W. Paul Ganley/Weirdbook Press, Box 149, Buffalo, NY 14226
Donald M. Grant, Box 187, Hampton Falls, NH 03844. Long established, emphasizing reprints from the pulps
Hypatia Press, 86501 Central Rd., Eugene, OR 97402. Prints *SFRA Newsletter*
Kerosina Publications, 27 Hampton Rd., Worcester Park, Surrey KT4 8EU, U.K.
Kinnell Pubs. Ltd., 43 Kingsfield Ave., N. Harrow, Middlesex HA2 6AO, UK
Land of Enchantment, Box 5360, Plymouth, MI 48170
Locus Press, Box 13305, Oakland, CA 94661. Bibliographies
Lord John Press, 19073, Los Alimos St., Northridge, CA 91326
Maclay & Associates, Box 16253, Baltimore, MD 21210
Morrigan Publications, 5 Mythop Ave., Lytham St. Annes, Lancashire FY8 4HZ, U.K.
Necronomicon Press, 101 Lockwood St., West Warwick, RI 02893. Lovecraft and related writers
Nemo Press, 1205 Harney St., Omaha, NE 68102. Ellison books
NESFA Press, Box G, MIT Branch PO, Cambridge, MA 02139. Indexes plus books by convention guests of honor
Outland Publishers, Box 1104, Englewood Cliffs, NJ 07632
Owlswick Press, Box 8243, Philadelphia, PA 19101
Phantasia Press, 5536 Crispin Way, West Bloomfield, MI 48033 Both fantasy and SF
Philtrum Press, Box 1186, Bangor, ME 04401. Stephen King material
Pulphouse Publishing, Box 1227, Eugene, OR 97440
Scream/Press, Box 481146, Los Angeles, CA 90048. Horror fiction
Serconia Press, Box 1786, Seattle, WA 98111. Essay collections
Soft Books, 89 Marion St., Toronto M6R 1E6, Canada
Space & Time Press, 138 W. 70th St., #4B, New York, NY 10023
SteelDragon Press, Box 7253, Powderhorn Sta., Minneapolis, MN 55407
Strange Co., Box 864, Madison, WI 53701. Mostly horror fiction
2AM Publications, Box 6754, Rockford, IL 61125-1754
Ultramarine Pub. Co., Box 303, Hastings-on-Hudson, NY 10706
Underwood-Miller, 708 Westover Dr., Lancaster, PA 17601. Fiction and occasional nonfiction, originally emphasizing work of Jack Vance
United Mythologies Press, Box 390, Station A, Weston, Ontario M9N 3N1, Canada. Lafferty booklets
Ursus Imprints, 5539 Jackson, Dept. 0, Kansas City, MO 64130. Illustration
Weird Tales Library, Box 13418, Philadelphia, PA 19101
Whispers Press, 70 Highland Ave., Binghamton, NY 13905. Horror fiction, notably in the irregular serial *Whispers* [11-21]
Xanadu, 5 Uplands Rd, London N8 9NN. Criticism
Mark V. Ziesing, Box 76, Shingletown, CA 96088

Table 5-4. Original Fantastic Fiction Published/Distributed in U.S.

1988 [volumes]	Category	1988	1987	1986 [percent]	1985	1984	1983
317	SF novels	26.7	29.0	34.7	31.6	32.4	32.4
264	Fantasy novels	22.2	24.9	23.9	30.2	25.3	22.0
182	Horror novels	15.3	9.4	7.2	1.4	2.8	3.5
98	Anthologies	8.3	9.4	8.5	8.1	9.3	9.2
77	Collections	6.5	7.4	7.9	6.1	8.8	7.0
64	Novelizations	5.4	7.0	2.6	4.9	4.9	6.4
134	Nonfiction	11.3	9.7	11.6	13.0	13.6	11.3
19	Omnibus	1.6	2.4	2.6	2.5	1.8	3.1
31	Miscellaneous	2.6	0.7	0.9	2.2	1.1	5.1

Source: *Locus,* February 1989

Reviewing and Selection

All reviewing media are necessarily very selective in choosing to review a small fraction of the more than 30,000 original books published each year in the U.S., of which perhaps 15% is fiction, 3%+ is fantastic fiction, and 1.5% fantasy or horror fiction. Original mass-market paperbacks are, like their pulp predecessors, heavily formulaic and are usually designated category fiction—the principal categories being science fiction (with fantasy usually included), horror fiction (sometimes included with SF and fantasy), westerns, mystery/detective, romances, men's adventure and a miscellany of smaller categories.

Space limitations and a natural desire to review the more "significant" books mean that little category fiction is reviewed in the general or library-oriented media. Table 5-5 shows the principal review media for fantasy and horror fiction, in hardcover and paperback. The general media review mostly hardcovers, especially books not designated category fiction by their publishers. The specialty journals, published by and for fans, review both formats. Of the specialty magazines, only *Locus* provides prepublication reviews with any consistency. This is important since mass-market paperbacks have shelf lives not much longer than those of monthly magazines, although wholesalers and specialty dealers can provide such paperbacks for some months after publication. *Library Journal* reviews most fantasy under the heading science fiction; horror fiction is reviewed much more selectively. *Science Fiction Chronicle,* which, like *Locus* [11-40], devotes space to fantasy and horror fiction and film, prints more reviews than any other specialty magazine, many of them of SF. All are written by one reviewer, who consistently devotes about 100 words to every book, good or bad. His lack of selectivity is combined with a frequent failure to identify rubbish as such. *Locus* includes detailed monthly listings of U.S. and British books received, hardcovers and paperbacks, original and reprints, with brief notes for most. A knowledgeable librarian or other reader can often use these listings for selection.

Table 5-5. Fantasy and Horror Fiction Reviewing

Magazine	Issues/Year	Est. No. of Fantasy/ Horror Books (including nonfiction) Reviewed Annually
General/Library		
Booklist	26	60
Choice	11	20
Horn Book	4	8
Kirkus	24	20
Kliatt YA Paperback Guide	8	25
Library Journal	26	45
Publishers Weekly	52	125
VOYA (Voice of Youth Advocates)	4	25
Specialty		
American Fantasy	4	90
Isaac Asimov's SF Magazine	13	25
British Fantasy Society Newsletter	4	150
Ghosts and Scholars	1	10
Gothic	1	5
The Horror Show	4	36
Locus	12	150
Lovecraft Studies	2	5
Magazine of Fantasy & SF	12	50
Science Fiction Chronicle	12	200–250
Studies in Weird Fiction	1	4
Weird Tales	4	40*

*projected figure, based on first two issues
Source: information from Hal Hall and Mike Ashley

Acquisitions

Standard library wholesalers are probably the best source for in-print trade and mass-market editions. Specialty press books are better ordered directly from the publisher (see table 5-3) or from dealers specializing in fantastic literature. Two of the more reliable and long established are:

Robert and Phyllis Weinberg Books, 1515 Oxford Drive, Oak Forest, IL 60452. A monthly catalog lists new and forthcoming books and fanzines, SF, fantasy and horror, domestic and some imports. Strong on paperbacks and the specialty presses.

L. W. Currey, Elizabethtown, NY 12933. Generally regarded as the foremost antiquarian dealer specializing in fantastic literature, he carries new original hardcover and selective paperback fiction and much nonfiction as well, including the many short-discount titles often purchased by libraries. His frequent catalogs of both in- and out-of-print materials are valuable and authoritative.

The classified and display ads in *Locus* list many dealers, as do those in the annual fantasy and SF issues of *AB Bookman's Weekly*, published each October since 1983 and distributed at the World Fantasy Conventions. The many conventions listed in each issue of *Locus* usually have dealer exhibits. Specialty retail bookstores are found in many metropolitan areas.

The selection criteria for this guide exclude rarity, scarcity or collectibility. But fantasy and horror fiction is avidly collected by fans, as science fiction has been collected for many years. There have been several price guides published in recent years, most of them not merely valueless but frequently very misleading. Few discuss the points necessary to identify first editions or issues (for this, see Currey [6-2]). The crucial importance of condition is often ignored, even though a merely very good copy might command half the price of a fine copy. And in a rapidly changing market, even a reliable guide would date quickly. The most reliable guides remain the catalogs of established and reliable dealers like Currey.

Cataloging

Cataloging and classification of fantasy and horror fiction vary widely. Hardcover books are usually cataloged and typically shelved with science fiction, since relatively few librarians are concerned with making distinctions among different types of fantastic literature. Academic libraries commonly use the Library of Congress classification system and classify either in the PS (American) or PR (British) literature classes or sometimes in the catchall PZ fiction classes. The revised guide by Burgess [6-35] provides a thorough, current explanation of LC policies of classification and subject indexing of fantastic literature, film and art.

6

General Reference Works

Neil Barron

Almost every reference book discussed here was published in the past decade, one measure of the growing interest in fantasy and horror literature. Many of these books are also annotated in chapter 8 of my *Anatomy of Wonder* (3rd ed., 1987). The annotations have been revised to stress their usefulness to the reader of fantasy and horror fiction. See also chapters 9, 10 and 11 for discussion of specialized reference books. Not annotated here are more general library reference works, notably *Contemporary Authors,* one of the works to which reference is made in the fiction chapters (see preface). Several H. W. Wilson publications, such as the *Fiction Catalog, Junior High School Catalog* and others, are of some value in selecting fantasy and horror fiction.

Bibliographies and Indexes

6-1. Bleiler, Everett F. **The Checklist of Science-Fiction and Supernatural Fiction**. Firebell Books, 1978.

Few knowledgeable readers doubt Bleiler's preeminence in the field of fantastic fiction scholarship, for which he was belatedly recognized by the Science Fiction Research Association's Pilgrim award. *The Checklist of Fantastic Literature* (1948) was the standard for many years. This carefully revised edition adds about 1,150 titles, drops about 600 borderline books, corrects entries and adds an index by ninety-two thematic/subject matter categories, thoroughly explained in a twelve-page chapter. First editions of about 5,000 English-language works of fantastic fiction, including translations, from 1800 to 1948 are listed by author with a title index. Entries include author, including cross-references from pseudonyms, title, place of publication, publisher, year, pagination and subject code(s). The introduction and afterword explain the ground rules more fully. Bleiler says approximately one thousand of his listings are improperly omitted from Reginald [6-3], as does Currey [6-2], the only one of the three to include points of interest to the collector. An essential work for the collector and bibliographer.

6-2. Currey, L. W., comp. **Science Fiction and Fantasy Authors: A Bibliography of First Printings of Their Fiction and Selected Nonfiction**. G. K. Hall, 1979 (now available only from the compiler; see chapter 5).
A comprehensive and authoritative listing of more than 6,200 printings and editions of works published through June 1977 by 215 authors, from Wells to contemporary writers. Nonfantastic books by the authors are also listed, along with significant reference material published through mid-1979. This is the principal bibliography listing the points necessary to identify first editions or printings. Currey is continuing this bibliography in the form of interim author bibliographies in the *The New York Review of Science Fiction* (1988-). A work emphasizing scarce works published in the nineteenth and early twentieth centuries, with fuller notes, is George Locke's *A Spectrum of Fantasy* (Ferret Fantasy, 1980).

6-3. Reginald, R. **Science Fiction and Fantasy Literature: A Checklist, 1700–1974, with Contemporary Science Fiction Authors II**. 2 vols. Gale Research, 1979.
This work lists 15,884 books published in English from 1700 through 1974, excluding drama, verse and most children's books. Volume 2 is a biographical directory of 1,443 modern SF and fantasy authors, replacing the author's *Stella Nova* (1970). Books listed were examined and, if necessary, read to determine if they fell within the work's relatively elastic limits. More than 4,000 titles were rejected as unsuitable (see comment in Bleiler [6-1]). Biographical information was compiled from questionnaires from the authors or their estates whenever possible. The bibliographic entries are cross-referenced to the biographies. A series index by series title occupies thirty-four pages (largely superseded by Cottrill et al. [6-8]). Dated and very incomplete awards index. Title index. A supplement covering the 1975–86 period is in preparation, and will list more than 10,000 titles (this in little more than a decade), corrections and additions to earlier listings, and revisions and additions to the biographies. For large libraries. Compare Bleiler [6-1] and Currey [6-2].

***6-4**. Tuck, Donald H(enry) (Australia). **The Encyclopedia of Science Fiction and Fantasy through 1968**. Advent, vol. 1, 1974; vol. 2, 1978; vol. 3, 1983.
Although increasingly dated, this is still a major bibliography, an outgrowth of the compiler's earlier works. The first two volumes include a who's who and works, listing contents of collections and anthologies, and frequently those of original magazine sources as well; fifty-two-page book title index. Volume 3 provides magazine checklists, extensive paperback information, pseudonyms, series and other information. Descriptive, sometimes evaluative comment accompanies all book listings. Although quite different from Bleiler [6-1], whose historical scope is wider, it represented a major advance in bibliographic control over fantastic literature, and credit is due its publisher for issuing it and keeping it in print.

6-5. Schlobin, Roger C. **The Literature of Fantasy: A Comprehensive Annotated Bibliography of Modern Fantasy**. Garland, 1979.

The nominal scope of this book is 1858 through mid-1979, although a few earlier titles are listed. The coverage is "restricted to adult fantasy and juvenile fantasy with strong adult appeal . . . primarily limited to prose works originally published in book form in the English language." A few foreign authors who have "conspicuously contributed to the Anglo-American literary tradition" are included, such as Calvino, Hoffmann and Singer. Horror literature is excluded "unless it contains material that would be of particular interest to the fantasy reader," which leaves a wide opening. The entries include a plot summary, but there is relatively little evaluation except that implied by the book's inclusion. Complete contents of 244 collections and 101 anthologies are listed, supplementing Contento [6-7]. Of the 800 authors of about 1,000 novels and collections, approximately a fifth have a bibliography cited. Series are annotated as a unit. Thorough author and title indexes. Moderately useful as a descriptive bibliography, but of little value as a critical guide for readers or libraries. Compare the far superior guide by Waggoner [6-34].

***6-6**. Brown, Charles N., and William G. Contento, comps. **Science Fiction in Print: 1985**. Locus Press, 1986; **Science Fiction, Fantasy, & Horror: 1986, 1987, 1988**. Locus Press, 1987, 1988, 1989.

Locus [11-40] is the closest thing to a journal of record that English-language fantastic fiction has. These clothbound 8½×11-inch volumes cumulate and revise the Books Received listings in each issue, including both originals and reprints. The author list includes complete contents of collections, anthologies and fiction magazine issues, with pagination shown, and with original sources of publication if reprinted. A subject list divides the books into a variety of categories. Title index. The volume covering 1985 appeared first, followed by 1986, 1987, and 1988. The 1984 retrospective volume will fill the gap between Contento [6-7] and the 1985 volume. Each successive volume has increased in size and thoroughness and introduced improvements in general layout. Surveys of the year and *Locus* reader poll results supplement the bibliography/indexes. An important, current bibliography.

***6-7**. Contento, William G. **Index to Science Fiction Anthologies and Collections**. G. K. Hall, 1978; **Index to Science Fiction Anthologies and Collections 1977–1983**. G. K. Hall, 1984.

The first volume, which indexes 12,000 English-language stories by 2,500 authors in more than 1,900 anthologies and collections published through June 1977, is largely limited to SF. The supplement indexes about 8,550 short stories, 348 introductions, 506 poems and 22 plays. Some pre-1978 books and some weird, horror and suspense books are indexed. Although future supplements may appear, the indexing is continued in Brown and Contento [6-6]. Mike Ashley is working on an index to about 1,100 anthologies (no collections) of fantasy/supernatural short fiction. Schlobin [6-5] indexes 244 collections and 101 anthologies containing 3,610 stories. Bleiler [6-19] indexes 1,775 books, novels and collections, totaling about 7,200 individual stories, and provides the most detailed index.

6-8. Cottrill, Tim; Martin H. Greenberg; and Charles G. Waugh. **Science Fiction and Fantasy Series and Sequels: A Bibliography, Volume 1: Books**. Garland, 1986.
Building on works such as Reginald [6-3] and Tuck [6-4], this lists about 1,160 series and 6,600 books, mostly published from 1900 to 1985, by which time series had become extremely common, especially in mass-market paperbacks. Author, title, year, publisher and sequence in series are shown, with series and book title indexes. The series index in chapter 13 was built on this bibliography. Useful for larger libraries and specialty booksellers. Volume 2, which may never appear, is to be devoted to short fiction in series.

6-9. Hall, H. W. **Science Fiction Book Review Index, 1923–1973**. Gale Research, 1975; **Science Fiction Book Review Index, 1974–1979**. Gale Research, 1981; **Science Fiction and Fantasy Book Review Index, 1980–1984**. Gale Research, 1985.
Preceding Hall's companion secondary bibliography [6-10] were his valuable book review indexes, three cumulations of which have been published to date. The 1980–84 volume includes 16,000 author and subject citations to more than 4,700 books and articles, whose inclusion added considerably to the volume's cost and which were later included in the reference index. Hall publishes annual supplements (3608 Meadow Oaks Lane, Bryan, TX 77802), which are likely to be cumulated. Standard library book review indexes do not index the many specialty magazines Hall includes, and such reviews are often the only critical commentary available. For large libraries.

6-10. Hall, H. W. **Science Fiction and Fantasy Reference Index, 1878–1985**. 2 vols. Gale Research, 1987.
This is the most comprehensive single bibliography of the secondary literature devoted to SF and fantasy, including horror. About 19,000 books, articles, theses, interviews and audio-visual items are indexed by author (16,000 citations in vol. 1) and subject (27,000 citations in vol. 2). Approximately 1,400 entries are for non-English-language items. The emphasis is on SF, but fantasy and horror are not neglected. Most entries are from the post-1945 period, and probably 75% from the last two decades. Hall estimates that he has indexed only 50–60% of the material within his scope. Principal omissions are hundreds of fugitive fanzines, newspapers and out-of-the-way sources. (Some of the index's limitations are discussed in the review by Robert Philmus, *Science-Fiction Studies*, 15 [November 1988], 383–4.) A good starting point for the serious reader, but the set's high price will limit it to large libraries. Compare Tymn and Schlobin [6-11], which includes a number of citations not in Hall. Annual hardcover supplements to this set are compiled by Hall and issued by Borgo Press. Volume 7, 1988, was the first and covers 1986 publications. Annuals covering 1988 and later publications will be included in Brown and Contento [6-6].

6-11. Tymn, Marshall B., and Roger C. Schlobin, eds. **The Year's Scholarship in Science Fiction and Fantasy: 1972–1975**. Kent State, 1979.
This begins where Thomas Clareson's *Science Fiction Criticism* (Kent State, 1972) ended. Coverage is limited to American and British journals, selected fanzines, books and doctoral and master's theses. Supplements cover 1976–79 (1983), and 1980, 1981 and 1982 annuals, with 1983–88 bibliographies in *Extrapolation*, an academic quarterly devoted to SF, and 1989 and later bibliogra-

phies in the *Journal of the Fantastic in the Arts* [11-39]. The pre-journal listings are briefly annotated. Heavily overlaps Hall [6-10], but there are enough unique entries to make consultation of both necessary.

Gothic Literature

*6-12. Frank, Frederick S. **Guide to the Gothic: An Annotated Bibliography of Criticism**. Scarecrow, 1984.
Frank is one of the foremost scholars of the Gothic, whose literature is vast. He focuses on nineteenth- and twentieth-century authors in the 2,508 numbered citations (38 of them for earlier guides), each usefully annotated, mostly descriptively, occasionally critically. Although he emphasizes the classic Gothic period, he treats late nineteenth-century and twentieth-century authors as well. A very useful starting point, continued in his 1988 bibliography [6-13]. Also annotated as [H7-81].

6-13. Frank, Frederick S. **Gothic Fiction: A Master List of Twentieth Century Criticism and Research**. Meckler, 1988.
This unannotated bibliography cites 2,491 articles, dissertations and books, most of them published in the last twenty years. Academic interest is strong—almost one-fourth of the entries are dissertations. The citations are grouped into thirteen categories, with the four chapters devoted to English Gothic fiction containing 1,497 citations. American Gothic citations total 600, including contemporary authors such as King. Other chapters survey European Gothics, werewolves and vampires and books about Gothic (horror) films. Index of critics and of authors and artists. The listing is current but necessarily selective, since entire books have been devoted to some of the subject authors, from Walpole and Shelley to Lovecraft and King. This newest listing adds about 200 citations to the 1984 work. Gothic specialists will want both books, but most libraries will find the annotated guide sufficient. Also annotated as [H7-83].

*6-14. Frank, Frederick S. **The First Gothics: A Critical Guide to the English Gothic Novel**. Garland, 1987.
From the 4,500 to 5,000 Gothic novels and chapbooks published between 1764 and 1820 Frank has selected 500 which meet several criteria: contemporary availability, artistic uniqueness or historical importance or popularity, and value in showing the development of Gothic fiction. Entries are by author with first edition shown, modern reprints (if any), type of Gothic, secondary sources and a 100 to 500 word critical synopsis. Appendixes include a useful glossary of Gothic terms, a selected bibliography of criticism and a chronology. Indexes by author, title and critic. Fourteen reproductions of engravings and woodcuts add a period feel. Titles annotated in the horror volume of this set are keyed to the fuller discussions in *The First Gothics* (see preface). Frank's chapter in Tymn [6-33] annotated 422 novels. A valuable guide for the serious student and larger library.

6-15. McNutt, Dan J. **The Eighteenth-Century Gothic Novel: An Annotated Bibliography of Criticism and Selected Texts**. Garland, 1975.
A useful guide, albeit growing dated, to the huge literature of the Gothic. Chapters include bibliographies and research guides; literary, psychological, social and scientific backgrounds; general and specific studies; and chapters on

such authors as Horace Walpole, Clara Reeve and Charlotte Smith. The approximately 1,000 entries are succinctly annotated. Compare the more current Frank bibliographies [6-12–6-13] and the more recent bibliographic guide by Fisher [H7-81].

6-16. Radcliffe, Elsa J. **Gothic Novels of the Twentieth Century: An Annotated Bibliography**. Scarecrow, 1979.
Only about one-fourth of the nearly 2,000 titles in this checklist are annotated. Many titles are fantasy, SF or straight mysteries, and others are doubtful as Gothics. Biographical data are often dated, and unreliable secondary sources were often used to compile bibliographic data. Many suitable titles were omitted. Used cautiously, this can be of use to the more knowledgeable reader exploring this relatively unmapped region of Gothic fiction.

6-17. Tracy, Anne B. **The Gothic Novel, 1790–1830: Plot Summaries and Index to Motifs**. Univ. Press of Kentucky, 1981.
Plot summaries of 208 works, motif index, index of characters, title index. Apparently derived from a 1974 doctoral thesis. Less useful and less knowledgeable than Frank's much more comprehensive chapter in Tymn [6-33] or his *The First Gothics* [6-14].

Biocritical Works

6-18. Ashley, Mike. **Who's Who in Horror and Fantasy Fiction**. Elm Tree Press, 1977.
Approximately 400 authors are briefly profiled, from Antoine Galland (1646–1715), translator of the *Arabian Nights* [1-23] to writers who had achieved moderate prominence by the 1970s, such as Stephen King. The entries range from a short paragraph to a bit more than a page and blend biographical details with descriptive and evaluative comments about key novels, collections and individual stories. Pseudonyms and cross-references are included. Supplementing the 171 pages of biocritical entries are a chronology (*Gilgamesh* to 1977), keyed to the main entries, a title index to key novels and stories, a selective listing with partial contents of weird fiction anthologies, brief profiles of U.S. and British pulp magazines (greatly expanded in the authoritative volume co-edited by Tymn [11-54], a few awards and a bibliography. One of the earlier such works, anticipated by the more comprehensive Tuck [6-4] and followed by the recent work by Sullivan [6-31].

***6-19**. Bleiler, Everett F. **The Guide to Supernatural Fiction**. Kent State, 1983.
This comprehensive guide (732 8½x11-inch pages) represents more than twenty-five years of reading and reflection. In a sense it is an expansion of his checklist [6-1], excluding science fiction, the subject of a forthcoming companion guide. The subtitle reads "A full description of 1,775 books from 1750 to 1960, including ghost stories, weird fiction, stories of supernatural horror, fantasy, Gothic novels, occult fiction, and similar literature." The 1960 date includes stories published by that year in magazines but later in books. Novels and short fiction total about 7,200 individual stories. An individual story is described and evaluated, often

acerbically, only once, although cited each time it appears. Arrangement is by author, then chronologically. Biographical notes precede the numbered entries. In addition to the author and book story title indexes is a fifty-three-page motif index to what Bleiler prefers to call contranatural (rather than supernatural) fiction. This could be very valuable to librarians seeking to identify a half-remembered tale, or to anyone wishing to explore an evolving theme. A major reference work to which references are made for fiction authors (see preface).

***6-20**. Bleiler, Everett F., ed. **Supernatural Fiction Writers: Fantasy and Horror**. 2 vols. Scribner, 1985.
A major reference work which provides a comprehensive overview of the works of 148 authors, from Apuleius (AD second century) to Arthurian romances to today's writers. The expertise of sixty-one contributors has been carefully edited to provide clear, balanced essays including biography, description and evaluation of major works, and an assessment of the author's historical position. The essays are arranged roughly chronologically or by nationality (American, French, British, German), and each contains a selective primary and secondary bibliography. Many essays treat writers rarely or never discussed in such detail. Coverage is limited to selected Western literatures, excluding Italian, Spanish, Russian and Asian. Its scope is still wide and it is an essential contribution to its subject. Thoroughly indexed. Cross-referenced in this guide (see preface).

6-21. Cawthorn, James, and Michael Moorcock (U.K.). **Fantasy: The 100 Best Books**. Xanadu; Carroll & Graf, 1988.

6-22. Jones, Stephen, and Kim Newman. (U.K.), eds. **Horror: 100 Best Books**. Xanadu; Carroll & Graf, 1988.

6-23. Pringle, David (U.K.). **Modern Fantasy: The Hundred Best Novels, an English-Language Selection, 1946–1987**. Grafton, 1988; Peter Bedrick, 1989.
The "100 best" series began in 1985 with Pringle's excellent volume on post-World War II SF. The quality is sustained in the fantasy guide, most of whose works were also selected for evaluation in this guide. Only twenty-four of Pringle's choices are discussed in Cawthorn's equivalent years. The two-page essays average 600–700 words in Pringle, sometimes reaching 800–1,000 words in the other volumes. Most essays include plot summary and varying amounts of biocritical comment, with Pringle including quotations to suggest the novel's tone and the author's skill with language. Cawthorn, who wrote most of the entries, has selected from a much larger historical sample than Pringle, and the average quality of his selections may be judged better. Most of his selections are evaluated in this guide. The three guides largely exclude translated works, although Jones has four. Most young adult works are excluded save for a few by key authors like Le Guin and Garner. The essays in Jones are interesting, even when one's interest is in the critic as much as the work. The horror volume evaluations were written by 100 individual authors, almost all currently active writers. All critics are profiled, each entry has a headnote, a list of recommended books beyond the basic 100 is provided, but there is no author or title index. Within their self-imposed limitations, of which the most serious is a bias toward books of the last forty

years, these are useful guides which many libraries should acquire. All three are cross-referenced to the fiction authors in this guide (see preface). Pringle is also annotated as [F7-46].

***6-24**. Magill, Frank N., ed. **Survey of Modern Fantasy Literature**. 5 vols. Salem Press, 1983.
This is a companion to the 1979 set devoted to SF. It contains about 500 essays on books by 341 authors of fantasy and horror literature. Lesser titles receive about 1,000 words, most titles about 2,000, with series, trilogies and major works 3,000–10,000. Each essay has a bibliography. Volume 5 contains nineteen topical essays (theories of fantasy, witchcraft, nineteenth-century religious fantasy, fantasy games as folk literature, etc.), a chronology from 1764 to 1981, an annotated bibliography of secondary book-length literature, a list of anthologies and a detailed index. Cross-referenced to the fiction authors in this guide (see preface). A major reference work whose price will limit it to the largest libraries.

6-25. Cowart, David, and Thomas L. Wymer, eds. **Twentieth-Century American Science-Fiction Writers**. 2 vols. Gale Research, 1981. Dictionary of Literary Biography, vol. 8.
Of the ninety biocritical essays about authors who began writing after 1900 and before 1970, a number also write fantasy, such as Anthony, Bradbury, Bradley, Burroughs, de Camp, Disch, Ellison, Farmer, Jack Finney, Kuttner, Lafferty, Le Guin, Leiber, Matheson, C. L. Moore, Norton, Saberhagen, Silverberg, Sturgeon, Vance, Williamson and Zelazny. The emphasis of each three- to sixteen-page essay is on the SF, but there is brief discussion of fantasy writings. Compare the much more comprehensive compilation by Smith [6-30]. Cross-referenced to the fiction authors in this guide (see preface).

6-26. Gunn, James, ed. **The New Encyclopedia of Science Fiction**. Viking, 1988.

6-27. Nicholls, Peter (U.K.), general ed. **The Science Fiction Encyclopedia**. Doubleday, 1979. U.K. title: *The Encyclopedia of Science Fiction*. Granada, 1979.
These encyclopedias have hundreds of author entries (Nicholls has 3.5 times as many, about 1,800), and many of these authors write fantasy and sometimes horror fiction as well as SF. The Nicholls volume has 1.7 times the text of Gunn, more entries in almost every category, and equivalent entries are more detailed, as well as being more evaluative rather than simply descriptive. Gunn has almost as many film entries as Nicholls, a grotesque imbalance given Gunn's length. Gunn's greatest merit is its currency, and the inclusion of a number of significant contemporary authors. It is attractively designed on good paper and should be acquired by most libraries, but it isn't the pioneering work Nicholls was, nor is its scope or critical rigor equal to that of its Hugo-winning predecessor. Both are cross-referenced to the fiction author entries (see preface).

6-28. Rosenberg, Betty. **Genreflecting: A Guide to Reading Interests in Genre Fiction**. 2d ed. Libraries Unlimited, 1986.
Chapter 1 gives an overview of genre fiction and libraries' responsibilities in reader advisory services. The remaining six chapters survey westerns, thrillers, romances, SF, fantasy and horror. The genre chapters list books under Themes and Types, then by topic—anthologies, bibliographies, encyclopedias, history

and criticism, background, awards, etc. Many of the nonfiction books are descriptively, sometimes critically annotated, but often too briefly to judge their relative merit. Some weak books receive extraordinarily long listings, e.g., J. B. Post's *An Atlas of Fantasy* (see [6-39]). Indexes to genre authors, to genre themes and to secondary materials. The revised edition emphasizes books available in hardcover. A very uneven guide with many gaps.

6-29. Searles, Baird; Beth Meacham; and Michael Franklin. **A Reader's Guide to Fantasy**. Avon, 1982.
Three former staff members of New York's The Science Fiction Shop prepared two guides, one to SF, one to fantasy, designed for buyers or browsers at the shop and for any interested reader. The author profiles, from Richard Adams to Roger Zelazny, occupy 145 of the 216 pages. The emphasis is mostly on fantasy rather than horror fiction, but King, Stoker and a few other primarily horror writers are included. Readers who like more of the same will find useful the twenty-two-page series listing, as well as the division of books into six broad thematic categories. A best books list and a list of winners of three awards conclude the book. An original paperback, now out of print, it was useful for several years, although it includes far too many minor authors, lacks critical rigor and is growing increasingly dated.

6-30. Smith, Curtis C., ed. **Twentieth-Century Science-Fiction Writers**. 2d ed. St. James Press, 1986.
A number of the 614 SF writers profiled here also write fantasy, and this compilation is therefore cross-referenced to this guide (see preface). A supplement profiles five "major fantasy writers"—Dunsany, Eddison, Morris, Peake and Tolkien. Coverage of authors specializing in YA fiction is weak. The bibliographies must be used with caution; inaccuracies and errors are common. A valuable biocritical guide to SF writers but, like Cowart and Wymer [6-25] and the two encyclopedias [6-26, 6-27], marginal for fantasy.

***6-31**. Sullivan, Jack, ed. **The Penguin Encyclopedia of Horror and the Supernatural**. Viking, 1986.
This is the first such encyclopedia, a measure of the increasingly widespread popularity of the literature of fear, supernatural or psychological. Sullivan, who has capably written about ghost stories and related topics, and his sixty-five contributors have provided a comprehensive, readable, accurate survey, enlivened by 300 black-and-white illustrations. The 600 signed entries cover approximately 405 individuals (writers, artists/illustrators, actors, directors, composers, etc.), about 150 films and fifty-four thematic entries, such as books into film, *femme fatale*, horror and science fiction, mad doctors, opera, possession, the supernatural and writers of today (this last entry mentions many dozens of writers in addition to those who are subjects of the individual entries). Abundant cross-references enhance reference use.

6-32. Tymn, Marshall B.; Kenneth J. Zahorski; and Robert H. Boyer. **Fantasy Literature: A Core Collection and Reference Guide**. Bowker, 1979.
Boyer and Zahorski explain the rationale for their selections in a thirty-six-page chapter. They favor "high" fantasy, the creation of self-contained Secondary Worlds in which the dominant emotions for the reader are awe and wonder, and

the style is "elevated." Various subdivisions are examined, such as myth and fairy tale fantasy, Gothic fantasy (low and high), science fantasy, and sword-and-sorcery/heroic fantasy. The core collection consists of 208 novels and collections, 1858–1978, and sixteen anthologies, many of them original paperbacks published since 1960. The annotations vary from a short paragraph to about one page and mix plot summary (often excessive) with generally favorable evaluation (this core collection is by definition recommended). The restrictive selection criteria used by Boyer and Zahorski were explicitly rejected for these guides, although many of their selections will also be found here, and cross-references to this guide are made in the fiction author entries (see preface). The chapters by Tymn are badly dated. Articles as well as books are briefly annotated. Organizations, awards and library collections are described briefly.

6-33. Tymn, Marshall B., ed. **Horror Literature: A Core Collection and Reference Guide**. Bowker, 1981.
Four chapters, from Gothic works to 1980, survey almost 1,100 novels, collections and anthologies. Robert Weinberg surveys the horror pulps, 1933–40, excluding *Weird Tales* [11-20], the best and best known of such pulps. Supernatural verse in English is analyzed in detail, in a thirty-five-page introduction preceding sixty-four annotations. Other chapters survey author studies, reference works, criticism, with lists of periodicals, societies, awards and library collections. Core collection checklist selected by contributors only; no outside readers were used.

This guide, patterned after my *Anatomy of Wonder*, lacked careful editorial guidance and thus critical rigor and balance. There are seventeen Blackwood collections, heavily overlapping, all starred as core titles. The anthology annotations merely list contents and lack any critical comment. The chapter on Gothic fiction, 173 pages, 422 annotations, is almost twice the length of the chapter on the modern masters (1920–80), 94 pages, 310 annotations, a gross imbalance which ill serves readers and libraries. The guide you are reading and its companion were partly designed to avoid the deficiencies of this and of *Fantasy Literature* [6-32].

***6-34**. Waggoner, Diana. **The Hills of Faraway: A Guide to Fantasy**. Atheneum, 1978.
Although only a decade old, one of the earliest relatively comprehensive studies of fantasy, adult and children's, generally excluding horror. Her touchstones are Tolkien's long essay, "On Fairy-Stories" (see [F7-62]), and Northrop Frye's influential *Anatomy of Criticism* (1957), which provide her theoretical framework and vocabulary, outlined in chapter 1. Chapter 2 discusses "eight major trends or strains" in fantasy: mythopoeic, heroic, adventurous, ironic, comic, nostalgic, sentimental and horrific, with many examples cited. A different arrangement is later presented in which subgenres of fantasy are outlined and in which all books later annotated are discussed. The 178-page bibliographic guide is arranged by author, with each of the 996 entries numbered and used in the various indexes. Citations to secondary literature about many authors follow the fiction annotations. Indexes to names, terms, illustrators and titles.

Adult and nominally children's fantasy is included, with most picture books excluded. The annotations are vigorously and clearly written, often acerbic, and effectively blend plot summary and intelligent evaluation. There are some bibliographic inaccuracies and omissions, but these are more than offset by the work's scope, clarity and forceful writing. A first-rate guide, far better than Schlobin [6-5] and Tymn et al [6-32].

Other Works

6-35. Burgess, Michael. **A Guide to Science Fiction and Fantasy in the Library of Congress Classification Scheme**. 2d ed., rev. & exp. Borgo Press, 1988.
Burgess, whose bibliographic alter ego is R. Reginald [6-3], is a cataloger. This second edition is considerably revised from the 1984 first edition, notably in the ninety-two-page list of authors (almost twice as many) and literature class numbers, when assigned (about 40% lack such numbers, mostly authors who have written only original paperbacks, which LC only infrequently catalogs). Also revised is the list of SF and fantasy/horror subject headings, the classification schedules (not only literature but art, film, etc.) with an alphabetical index to the class numbers. The introductions to each chapter note the inconsistencies which have developed over the years. Companion volumes to mystery/detective and western fiction are also available. Mostly of interest to a few catalogers and to those using large LC-classed collections of fantastic literature.

6-36. Collins, Robert A., and Robert Latham, eds. **Science Fiction & Fantasy Book Review Annual 1988**. Meckler, 1988.
When Meckler folded *Fantasy Review* [11-32] they decided to continue with an annual, reprinting most of the reviews in the *SFRA Newsletter* (see chapter 13) along with many previously unpublished reviews. The first annual includes reviews of 441 books of adult fiction, 33 YA titles, and 73 nonfiction works, almost all originals. Also included is a profile of Orson Scott Card and critical surveys of SF, fantasy, horror and nonfiction. Title index. Too many poor books were reviewed, many of them original paperbacks which were out of print by the time this annual appeared. Future volumes may have a different mix more useful to libraries. Compare the bibliographic surveys issued by *Locus* [6-6].

6-37. Hall, H. W., ed. **Science/Fiction Collections: Fantasy, Supernatural and Weird Tales**. Haworth Press, 1983.
Hall was the guest editor of this issue of *Special Collections* (vol. 2, no. 1/2), available separately as an overpriced hardcover. Chapters are devoted to seven public collections (see chapter 12, whose pertinent entries are cross-referenced to these descriptions), two large private collections, a short history of SF specialty publishers, a dated essay on the bibliographic control of fantastic literature, an essay on the cataloging and classification of SF and a dated list of specialty dealers. Most valuable for the detailed descriptions of the public collections. Libraries receiving the journal will have received this on subscription; others can safely ignore.

6-38. Inge, M. Thomas, ed. **Handbook of American Popular Literature**. Greenwood, 1988.
This spinoff from Inge's *Handbook of American Popular Culture* (3 vols., 1979–81, second ed., 1989) includes revisions of ten chapters in the earlier work plus five new essays. Each chapter includes a brief introduction, historical outline, discus-

sion of key reference works, a description of major library collections, a critical and descriptive survey of the principal historical and critical works, and a bibliography of books, articles, indexes and key periodicals. Roger Schlobin's chapter on fantasy literature excludes horror, which is also largely ignored in Kay Mussell's chapter on Gothic novels, an oversight which should be corrected in a future edition. The survey is broad, current, often fascinating, although it's peripheral to the study of fantasy and horror fiction.

6-39. Manguel, Alberto, and Gianni Guadalupi. **The Dictionary of Imaginary Places**. Macmillan, 1980. Rev. ed., Harvest/Harcourt, 1987.
Some of the approximately 1,250 entries in this dictionary compiled by two European scholars will be familiar—Oz, Shangri-La, Narnia—but more will not. The alphabetical entries range from a short paragraph to almost three large three-column pages (Peake's Gormenghast, for example). Many cross-references link entries, and the author, title and year of the source book are cited at the end of each entry. Illustrations by Graham Greenfield and excellent maps and charts complement the text, which is clearly and interestingly written. There is a relatively heavy emphasis on traditional European literature, and many works are esoteric indeed. Most SF is excluded, since works set on other planets are excluded. Lovecraft's sinister towns are here, but no locales from Dunsany or Clark Ashton Smith, which may have been judged too unearthly. The expanded edition, a trade paperback, adds fourteen pages and several dozen entries. Index by author, title and locale. An interesting, inevitably incomplete compilation which rewards casual browsing. Vastly superior to the only comparable work, J. B. Post's *An Atlas of Fantasy* (1973; rev. ed., 1979).

***6-40**. Wolfe, Gary K. **Critical Terms for Science Fiction and Fantasy: A Glossary and Guide to Scholarship**. Greenwood, 1986.
Academics from various disciplines entered the critical ranks of fantastic literature beginning in the 1950s, bringing their special vocabularies and backgrounds. A valuable introduction traces the historical development of fantasy and SF critical discourse. Approximately three-fourths of this book is devoted to a glossary of almost 500 terms and concepts, ranging from brief definitions to short essays, keyed to a secondary bibliography and to authors of cited fiction. Most of the specialized terms used by this guide's contributors are included. Clear and concise and a most welcome and long overdue work that all libraries should consider.

7

History and Criticism

Michael A. Morrison

The transition from the vapid sentimentality of the novel of 50 years ago to the goblin horrors of the last 20 is so strong and sudden that it almost puzzles us to find a connecting link.

—*Charles Robert Maturin in* The British Review (*1818*)

The denizens of Grub Street, ever busily agog, have from time to time attempted to scribble something on sorcery, on the invisible world, on occult crafts, and of late they seem to have been especially pretentious and prolific.

—*Montague Summers in* The Vampire: His Kith and Kin (*1928*)

Since the publication of Mike Ashley's chapters on reference sources in Tymn [6-33] in 1981, the secondary literature on Gothic, ghostly, horror and supernatural fiction has grown enormously. One need not dig far before one is awash in popularizations, amateur criticism, specialized studies and fan and academic essays. A glance at the list of books in this and the next chapter will reveal that nearly every major university press and several major commercial houses now regularly publish books in this field. More than a hundred books read in the course of preparing chapters 7 and 8 were not annotated, usually because they were too specialized, too marginal or valueless. I have, however, annotated a few widely available, often cited books that seemed to me misleading or in some other way seriously flawed.

Structure of This Chapter and the Next

To help the reader, I have grouped titles under these headings: **Historical and Critical Surveys, Gothicism: General Studies, British and German Gothic, North American Gothic and the American Weird Tale, Extra-Generic Studies, Vampires, Werewolves and Doppelgängers, Other Studies** (i.e., books that did not fit into the other categories) and **Bibliographic Aids**.

A few items in some of these groups reflect my conviction that horror, supernatural, ghostly and Gothic fiction can profitably be considered from a critical vantage point well outside "the genre"—whether that word is defined by the fiction, as in late eighteenth-century England, or by the marketplace, as in America today. In particular, some of the books in **Extra-Generic Studies** extend this guide into various mainstreams of fiction via critical works that either directly discuss (e.g., Kawin) or directly relate to (e.g., Sadoff) supernatural and horror fiction—especially modern fiction—even when, in the latter cases, that fiction is not the thrust of the work.

Within each group the reader will find three levels of reference. To those seeking an introduction or overview, I recommend the items marked with asterisks; these are the best references I could find. The second, deeper level is the collection of annotated titles in the group. To get to the third level (not present in every annotation), follow the cross-references to other annotations and/or the brief descriptions of additional books, those I considered too specialized to warrant a full annotation but too useful to omit. Cross-references indicate only works that significantly expand upon an annotated book. To help the reader decide whether to follow the cross-reference, I have (except where the connection seemed obvious) briefly indicated what is to be found at the other end.

At the third level only a handful of essays are noted. I am uncomfortable about this: much important criticism on horror and supernatural fiction has not made the transition from essay to book. But there are simply too many essays to make practical the mention of even the major ones. So within an annotation I have referred only to articles of singular importance or influence that treat topics not adequately addressed in the annotated book. This is not that great a deficiency—most essays are necessarily specialized, and the excellent bibliographies noted here and in chapters 6 and 8 will direct the reader to them.

Three reference guides were so valuable to me in preparing these chapters that I recommend them to all readers, scholars or libraries with serious interest in this field: Bleiler's *Supernatural Fiction Writers* [6-20], Sullivan's *The Penguin Encyclopedia of Horror and the Supernatural* [6-31] and Frank's *Guide to the Gothic* [6-12].

Editorial policy precluded the inclusion of foreign works not available in English, which I regret. Critics writing in English seem to have given rather little attention thus far to the work of their colleagues outside the United States and Britain. There are signs, however, that this is changing. The recent translation of Lévy's excellent critical book on H. P. Lovecraft [8-70] whets one's appetite for translations of other important studies, especially Roger Caillois's *Au coeur du fantastique* (Paris, 1965) and *Images, images: Essais sur le rôle et les purvoirs de l'imagination* (Paris, 1966) and Lévy's history of the British Gothic novel, *Le Roman "gothique" anglais, 1764-1824* (Toulouse, 1968), a work many critics consider the best of its kind.

An Overview and a Few Reflections

The surge of horror criticism since the early 1970s is evident both here and in chapter 8. Less immediately apparent are the major changes in critical attitudes and approaches that have taken place since early in the century. Early critics of the novel such as David Daiches, E. M. Forster and J. M. S. Tompkins seem at times to be writing from the apparent premise that horror fiction in general—and the British Gothic novel in particular—is *inherently* flawed, a point of view that would seem to obviate the possibility of useful criticism. Hence the importance of the early historical studies of Birkhead, Summers, Railo and Varma. Although often marred by defensiveness and a tendency to hyperbole, these surveys contain much to inform and delight reader and scholar alike. Still, considerable work needs to be done to bring these overviews up to date and to refine their critical judgments in light of subsequent scholarship. All emphasize Gothic fiction—as others included in **Historical and Critical Surveys** emphasize one or another necessarily narrow collection of texts. But Dorothy Scarborough's lament—"the mass of fiction itself introducing ghostly or psychic motifs is simply enormous. It is manifestly impossible to discuss, or even to mention, all of it"—is far truer today than when she wrote it in 1917. Particularly needed are further looks at the American horror story: the weird tale of the 1930s and 1940s and its seemingly unrelated and far more problematic modern heir.

More recent critics have applied a range of analytical methods, some quite sophisticated, to various types of horror fiction and to a few largely canonical texts (see, for example, the section in chapter 8 on book-length studies of *Frankenstein*). Thus, Robert Kiely has applied formalist theory to several Gothic novels, David Ketterer has probed philosophical and thematic issues in *Frankenstein* and the works of Edgar Allan Poe, Jerrold E. Hogle and others have brought deconstruction to the field, and Norman Holland and Leona Sherman have employed reader-response theory.

Other criticism of the past three decades has opened up the texts and subtexts of horror in unexpected, fruitful ways—especially feminist criticism by Ellen Moers and by the team of Sandra Gilbert and Susan Gubar and Marxist criticism by David Punter, Rosemary Jackson and others. As this brief and incomplete list attests, the thinking of major literary theorists—from Jacques Lacan to Michel Foucault—has begun to inform horror criticism.

But perhaps no thinker since Freud has so impacted criticism in this field as has Tzvetan Todorov. Whatever one's opinion of Todorov's structuralist approach to literature as laid out in *The Fantastic* (1975)—and thoughtful critiques have been mounted by Stanislaw Lem, Tobin Siebers and others—his influence is unmistakable. Rosemary Jackson, for example, criticizes Todorov for slighting metaphysics, overlooking the social and political implications of the literary structures he describes and rejecting Freudian theories, then proceeds to build on his work in ways that open up new areas of inquiry into the fantastic. And Terry Heller, blending structuralism and reader-response theory, devises insightful readings of such overanalyzed works as Poe's "The Fall of the House of Usher" and James's "The Turn of the Screw."

At a far remove from the rarefied air of structuralist analyses one finds Les Daniels, James B. Twitchell, Louis S. Gross, Gregory A. Waller and Stephen King examining horror fiction in the context of popular culture, arguably where it belongs. For while it is useful to consider this fiction from a position well outside its genre, one must always keep a keen eye on the fecund myth pool of popular culture.

Gothic Studies

In at least one area—Gothic studies—the secondary literature is fast approaching critical mass, a phenomenon that parallels the explosive growth of the fiction Gothic critics study. During its heyday (1764–1820) roughly one-third of the novels published in Great Britain were Gothics. The form vanished soon thereafter, but not without continuing influence: on the English Romantic novel, as Robert Kiely shows, and on the "classic" nineteenth-century English novel of manners, as Joseph Wiesenfarth shows in his fine book *Gothic Manners and the Classic English Novel* (Univ. of Wisconsin Press, 1988).

Some time in the recent past the British Gothic novel became academically respectable. There followed a torrent of essays, books and dissertations. Writing in 1988, the Gothic bibliographer Frederick S. Frank noted that of the approximately 2,500 entries in his *Gothic Fiction* [6-13, 7-83], nearly one-quarter "are doctoral dissertations on the Gothic" and roughly a third of these "stud[y] the form from a feminist perspective." The Gothic novel, academically speaking, is "in."

Such has not always been the case, and the roller coaster of Gothic studies since the appearance in 1938 of Montague Summers's vast *The Gothic Quest* [7-33] would be a ride in itself. Suffice it to note that prior to the 1960s most criticism of the Gothic novel was patronizing, deprecatory or (at best) dismissive. More recently, the pendulum has swung the other way, and hyperbolic excess colors otherwise fine studies by Varma, Penzoldt and others.

Today critics still disagree, even over the definition and expanse of British literary Gothicism. But nearly all acknowledge its historical importance. The most recent advance in Gothic studies comes in books by Elizabeth R. Napier, Eve Kosofsky Sedgwick and Coral Ann Howells and in a number of excellent essays that reconsider earlier enthusiastic claims for the merit of the mode. Napier's tightly reasoned work, in particular, seems to demand a thoughtful response if the Gothic critical establishment is to continue arguing for the literary value and psychological depth of the British Gothic.

So even now the quality and curious power of the British Gothic novel remain at issue. Late in his study of the form, Robert I. Le Tellier poses the unanswered questions: "In the end, just how is the Gothic novel to be assessed? Is it trivial, a collection of risible conventions, or is it profound, reflecting some primordial instinct, literary mystery, or surreal question?"

On American Gothicism little more need be said than to note Leslie Fiedler's widely accepted view, no less true today than when he published it in 1960, that the entire tradition of American fiction has been and remains *essentially* Gothic. Still, the American Gothic tradition needs careful definition, examination of the affective response its texts generate in its readers, a synthesis of the periods examined in works by Fiedler, Malin and others, and an in-depth look at the recent variants noted by King and Gross.

Beyond the Gothic

Far less attention has been given to the British ghost story, although Sullivan and Briggs have made important contributions in this direction, and even less to the American weird tale. But if Gothic studies have recently become academically respectable and the ghost story only a bit less so, no such fate has befallen the modern horror story. Widely perceived by mainstream critics as subliterary trash, the horror story languishes on the margins of literary culture.

It is, of course, true that Stephen King, Peter Straub, Ramsey Campbell and all the rest write avowedly *popular* literature, a form the establishment dislikes. But popular literature, whether serious or trivial, does portray social, economic, political and (increasingly as this century comes to a close) scientific attitudes contemporary to the culture in which it is written, published and read. Such works thus define an essential dimension of that culture. Horror fiction, with its ability to expose unacknowledged anxieties that course beneath the veneer of society, would seem to warrant serious attention even were it devoid of literary merit. The obviousness of these remarks makes the continuing abuse of some critics all the more incomprehensible.

Looking at the publishers and critics whose works appear in these chapters might lead one to think that the literature of fear has indeed been accepted as worthy of critical attention, either for its own (literary) sake or as an important index to popular culture. But even in 1989 horror fiction is often subjected to the same prejudicial, presumptive criticism that bedeviled it in earlier days. Indeed, the critic—presuming himself or herself to be serious, reasonably objective and honestly excited about the inquiry—may hardly know what to think when he or she finds critic Roger C. Schlobin writing in an article published in *The Journal of the Fantastic in the Arts* (1 [1988]: 25–50), "Obviously, those who are fascinated with deep horror harbor deadly and potentially explosive and debilitating mentalities. . . . Its great and rising popularity points to serious emotional problems, frustrations, and anger. . . . At worst, it identifies repressed sadism and masochism."

But more pernicious, I think, than such overt attacks, which at least generate healthy discussion, are efforts by mainstream and academic critics to forcibly marginalize horror fiction—efforts infused with a zeal that makes one all the more curious about what it is about this fiction that provokes so fervid a response.

Still other critical issues emerge from my reading of the books and essays here noted. As Sullivan has remarked about the English ghost story, horror fiction in the broad sense needs a critical language appropriate to its place in literature as mediator between popular culture and serious art. Genre considerations remain confused: for example, while a superficial analysis might distinguish horror from fantasy by its simple lack of faerie, the conflation of these two genres and their recent eruption in such "mainstream" novels as Clive Barker's *Weaveworld* [F4A-18, 4-23] pose new challenges to genre criticism.

The Death of Ghost and Horror Fiction?

So in spite of the impressive scholarship discussed in these chapters, the status of horror fiction in 1989 remains ambiguous and anomalous—and perhaps rightly so. But horror fiction and the critical issues it raises are likely to be around for the foreseeable future. Critics have been lamenting the demise of the ghostly tale since the turn of the century. Thus Olivia Howard Dunbar, writing in *The*

Dial (38 [1905]: 377-380), noted that "for approximately a generation, the ghost has been missing from fiction." Philip Van Doren Stern, introducing his 1942 anthology *The Midnight Reader: Great Stories of Haunting and Horror*, bemoaned the "dark" outlook for ghost stories: "No commercial market exists for good ones, and a debased product is lowering the whole genre in public esteem." Pamela Search declared in her introduction to *The Supernatural in the English Short Story* (1959) that "the horror tale is unlikely to survive except as a crime story," and a year later Leslie Fiedler wrote in *Love and Death in the American Novel* that "the classic ghost story seems now an obsolescent sub-genre." And as recently as 1977, Julia Briggs put the subtitle *The Rise and Fall of the English Ghost Story* on her critical survey *Night Visitors*.

These lamentations to the contrary, the form lives on—in traditional modern works by Thomas Owen, Ramsey Campbell, Thomas Ligotti and others, and transmogrified into post-modernism by Italo Calvino, Dino Buzzati, John Fowles, Donald Barthelme and many others. Indeed, horror fiction in the 1980s has undergone explosive growth, appalling degeneration and unexpected mutation. One hopes this renaissance will continue, that horror fiction won't become *too* respectable, and that serious criticism of it will no longer have the effect, attributed by Tobin Siebers to even a casual mention of supernaturalism, of "casting one's intentions and scholarship in doubt."

Acknowledgments

No one gets through a project like this without incurring significant debts. First and foremost, I want to thank my wife, Mary, for her professionalism and generosity in the seemingly endless library research and proofreading that went into preparing these two chapters. At the University of Oklahoma I am indebted to my colleagues Professors Ronald Schleifer and Robert Con Davis of the English Department and to Dean Robert E. Hemenway for sharing their expertise in American and contemporary fiction and to Carolyn Mahin and the staff of Bizzell Library for tracking down a host of otherwise unavailable items. Several other colleagues and friends took the time to read preliminary drafts, loan me precious books from their personal collections or respond to pleas for help and advice: S. T. Joshi, Steve Behrends, Marc Michaud, Frederick S. Frank, Mike Ashley, Walter Albert, Rob Latham, Gary William Crawford and especially Stephan Dziemianowicz, whose kindness in response to my requests for assistance went well beyond the call of duty. Finally, Neil Barron has provided more than the usual editorial guidance and patience and deserves more than the usual acknowledgment.

Bibliography

Note: because many of the same works of fiction are repeatedly cited, I have omitted references to entry numbers. Consult the indexes.

Historical and Critical Surveys

7-1. Barclay, Glen St. John (U.K.). **Anatomy of Horror: The Masters of Occult Fiction**. St. Martin's, 1978.

Perhaps Glen St. John Barclay meant his subtitle ironically; evidently he considers most of the writers he discusses anything but masters. Bram Stoker is "a worse writer than one would have believed possible"; H. P. Lovecraft's "only real contribution to literature might be to serve as a contrast to Poe"; Charles Williams was "totally unsuited to the craft of fiction"; and Dennis Wheatley is "the greatest living master of the cliché." Barclay is more appreciative of Sheridan Le Fanu, William Peter Blatty and (in his best chapter) H. Rider Haggard. But his treatment of this hodgepodge of writers is filled with misinterpretations, overstatements and wild generalizations. Worse, Barclay persists in interpreting horror in fiction as repressed authorial sexuality. Oblivious to prior scholarship on the supernatural, Barclay apparently lacks a coherent critical perspective of his own—other than condescension toward most authors. Notes, brief bibliography, index.

7-2. Birkhead, Edith (U.K.). **The Tale of Terror: A Study of the Gothic Romance**. Constable, 1921.

In this comprehensive critical history Birkhead follows the evolution of the British Gothic novel into American and British short fiction of the early twentieth century. Birkhead writes lucid, sometimes witty prose, and her evaluations are well considered, although some seem naive and dated by today's standards. Readers will profit from her sections on the fictions of Sir Walter Scott, Nathaniel Hawthorne and Edgar Allan Poe as well as her commentary on less well-known works: Nathan Drake's Gothic fictions, William Harrison Ainsworth's novels, Percy Shelley's zestful Gothic romances and (especially) satires on the Gothic by Eaton Stannard Barrett, Regina Maria Roche and others. But as a survey of the terror tale this book has been superseded by those of Varma [7-34] and Punter [7-10]. Moreover, her treatment of the short tale of terror is too brief to be of value (e.g., she relegates Sheridan Le Fanu, E. F. Benson, Algernon Blackwood and other important writers to a perfunctory concluding chapter); see instead Scarborough [7-12] and, more recently, Briggs [7-3] and Sullivan [7-15]. Index.

***7-3.** Briggs, Julia (U.K.). **Night Visitors: The Rise and Fall of the English Ghost Story**. Faber, 1977.

Beginning with ancient epics and myths, Briggs traces the British ghost story through the heyday of the Gothic novel into the early twentieth century—when, she claims, it entered a period of decline from which it has not recovered. Like Jack Sullivan [7-15], Briggs stresses the importance of Sheridan Le Fanu, "one of the finest ghost story writers of all time." But she also treats works by a host of other authors, notably Arthur Machen, M. R. James, Walter De la Mare, Vernon

Lee, W. W. Jacobs and Oscar Wilde, and, in a brief epilogue, supernatural verse. She emphasizes three features of the evolution of the ghost story: the omnipresence of the double as "a powerful symbol of unresolved inner conflict"; the use of the supernatural to reintegrate an increasingly dislocated sense of the past; and the problem of how to render evil convincingly in fiction. But Briggs exaggerates the presumed demise of the ghost story. Dating its decline from 1914, she asserts that post-World War I writers have lost commitment to the mode. More important, she argues that the growing influence of science and technology after World War I led to the gradual replacement of the ghost story by SF "as the central expression of the predicament of modern man." Primary bibliography emphasizing anthologies, index. Compare Sullivan [7-15] and Punter [7-10].

***7-4.** Daniels, Les. **Living in Fear: A History of Horror in the Mass Media**. Scribner's, 1975.
Novelist Les Daniels here surveys horror in British and American mass media from the late eighteenth century to the early 1970s. Proceeding chronologically, he begins with major Gothic novels, plays and poems, then moves through early American terror tales and Victorian ghost stories into the early twentieth century. More ambitious is this book's second half, which encompasses recent manifestations of horror in fiction, films, radio dramas, horror comics, the pulps, television anthologies, monster magazines, paperback originals, rock music, TV movies and cartoons. As an introduction and overview, Daniels' popular history is successful in spite of its brevity (many of its 248 pages are consumed by eighty illustrations and seven reprints of classic horror stories). Well-written and well-researched, *Living in Fear* is less penetrating but more comprehensive than King's *Danse Macabre* [7-6], which highlights horror in mass media after the 1950s. Strongly recommended for readers and all libraries. Index. Also annotated as [9-14].

7-5. Davis, Richard (U.K.), ed. **The Octopus Encyclopedia of Horror**. Octopus, 1981.
Not an encyclopedia but a collection of essays, this coffee table overview of horror in fact, fiction and film embraces SF, the supernatural and fantasy as well as the myths and legends behind these forms. Appropriately, Michael Parry's essay on the Frankenstein monster emphasizes its film appearances, while Mike Ashley's overview of the ghostly tale emphasizes fiction. The other five articles balance factual background with descriptions of film and both classic and popular fictions. Basil Copper synthesizes his books on the vampire [7-56] and werewolf [7-57] in a single essay; Richard Davis reviews zombies and mummies; and Richard Cavendish discusses Satanism, black magic and witchcraft. Of particular interest is Douglas Hill's survey of the interface of SF and horror. Although introductory, all seven essays are interesting and valuable, and this book is recommended to newcomers to the field and to all libraries. Extensively illustrated, not only with the obligatory stills but also with drawings, paintings and woodcuts. An appendix—"the catalogue"—lists horror comics and films. Index.

***7-6.** King, Stephen. **Danse Macabre**. Everest House, 1981; Berkley (corrected), 1982.
King's long, loving look at horror in fiction and the mass media from the 1950s to

the 1980s may be the most widely read book of literary criticism ever. It's as chatty and discursive as King's novels, but King's style belies the depth of his insights. And this book offers gems on the allegorical function of The Monster, as exemplified by the major horror icons the vampire, the werewolf and "the Thing without a Name" (Frankenstein's monster, King Kong, etc.); on scare tactics and subtexts in the American horror film; on the craft of evoking terror, horror and revulsion (the "gross-out"); and many other topics. In his long chapter on horror fiction King enthusiastically and intelligently analyzes works by largely neglected writers such as James Herbert and Ramsey Campbell. This chapter contains the best criticism to date on several major modern novels: Peter Straub's *Ghost Story*, Jack Finney's *The Body Snatchers*, Richard Matheson's *The Shrinking Man*, Anne Rivers Siddons's *The House Next Door* and Shirley Jackson's *The Haunting of Hill House*. King also updates the concept of the New American Gothic, as expounded by Fiedler [7-36], Ringe [7-44] and Malin [7-42]. Appendices list King's choices for the best hundred (or so) films and books produced since the 1950s. Along with Daniels [7-4], this book is essential for any library of horror fiction. Index. Also annotated as [9-15].

***7-7**. Lovecraft, H. P. **Supernatural Horror in Literature**. Ben Abramson, 1945; Dover, 1973.
Written during 1924–27 at the request of Lovecraft's friend Paul W. Cook, this survey first appeared in Cook's magazine *The Recluse*. Lovecraft subsequently revised his essay, and it was that revision that was published in the classic (posthumous) collection *The Outsider and Others* [3-132]. Lovecraft's lively and opinionated historical essay follows the supernatural tale from folktales, ballads and myths of the Middle Ages through the Gothic novel (an extended treatment) to the turn-of-the-century British ghost story. Lovecraft provides only cursory coverage of many writers and omits others (e.g., Mark Twain, Oliver Onions and Herman Melville). But his more lengthy discussions of Poe, Hawthorne, Machen and Hodgson are among the best available. For all its value this essay must be used with care—Lovecraft's superb plot summaries and subjective assessments are permeated by his aesthetic precepts and artistic credo—and should be supplemented by reading Penzoldt [7-9], Briggs [7-3] and Sullivan [7-15]. Useful perspectives on Lovecraft's essay are J. Vernon Shea's "On the Literary Influences Which Shaped Lovecraft's Works" in S. T. Joshi's collection of Lovecraft criticism [8-66] and E. F. Bleiler's introduction to the 1973 Dover reprint. A corrected text with a new index (both prepared by S. T. Joshi) appears in the sixth printing of Lovecraft's *Dagon and Other Macabre Tales* (Arkham House, 1986).

7-8. Messent, Peter B., ed. **Literature and the Occult: A Collection of Critical Essays**. Prentice-Hall, 1981.
Messent situates "the literature of the occult" at the junction of the material and supernatural worlds and argues that its power derives from the "dislocatory thrill" that results when these worlds collide. This collection is dominated by well-chosen excerpts from well-known books by Todorov [7-76], Thompson [7-20], Varma [7-34], Lovecraft [7-7], Kerr et al. [7-39], Scarborough [7-12], Shreffler [8-71] and Sullivan [7-15]. Messent also reprints essays on the numinous in Gothic literature (an essay by S. L. Varnado that he later expanded into his book *Haunted Presence* [7-22]), late Victorian occult literature, the works of

Carlos Casteneda, and the rival epistemologies embedded in *Dracula*. Because so much of its contents are familiar, this collection is recommended only as an introduction to the field. Chronology, select bibliography.

7-9. Penzoldt, Peter (U.K.). **The Supernatural in Fiction**. Peter Nevill, 1952.
This well-written though sometimes labored doctoral thesis on British supernatural short fiction underscores structural and psychological concerns. Penzoldt considers this field to lie "on the borderline between literary criticism and medical psychology," so it's no surprise that his work is heavily informed by Freudian and Jungian theories. A long, methodical introduction dealing with structural aspects proposes that the ghost story is fundamentally different from the mimetic short story and thus "not subject to the same rules." Penzoldt then traces major supernatural motifs from literal appearances in primitive tales through myriad psychological, scientific and allegorical transformations in the modern ghost story. All this lays the groundwork for historical/psychological discussions of works by Sheridan Le Fanu, Charles Dickens, Robert Louis Stevenson, Walter De la Mare and other major authors. Penzoldt is at his best on M. R. James and Algernon Blackwood (with whom he corresponded extensively) and at his most provocative on authors of "the pure tale of horror"—Arthur Machen, F. Marion Crawford, H. P. Lovecraft and others—who, he argues, "brought some discredit on . . . the short story of the supernatural." Pamela Search's introduction to her excellent anthology *The Supernatural in the English Short Story* (1959) amounts to a concise summary of Penzoldt's main points. See also comparable studies by Sullivan [7-15], Briggs [7-3] and Scarborough [7-12]. Extensive notes, but, regrettably, no index.

***7-10.** Punter, David (U.K.). **The Literature of Terror: A History of Gothic Fiction from 1765 to the Present Day**. Longman, 1980.
Because this book is arranged chronologically, it seems at first glance just another history of the Gothic in American and British literature. In this ambitious, largely successful book, Punter in fact attempts to redefine literary Gothicism so as to encompass fantastic fiction (and film) of the past 200 years and to demonstrate the continuity of language and symbol that derives from this fiction's preoccupation with fear. To these ends, Punter laces textual analyses of individual works with accounts of philosophical, psychological, social, economic and political forces that continually reshaped the Gothic mode. He identifies interconnections among the thematic preoccupations and stylistic peculiarities of a wide variety of texts to support his argument that the Gothic is "a literature of alienation" which consistently "defines itself on the borderland of [bourgeois] culture." Even readers who object to Punter's extremely broad definition of Gothic or his reliance on Marxist and Freudian theories are likely to find fascinating the cross-connections he establishes, especially in chapters on the modern horror film and on modern works by Mervyn Peake, Isak Dinesen, William Burroughs, Thomas Pynchon, J. G. Ballard, Angela Carter and others. Scholars and students will find useful Punter's description of the multiplex meanings of "Gothic" and the origins of literary Gothicism in graveyard poetry, the sentimental novel, the theory of the sublime and the impulse to recapture England's cultural past. All, however, should consult Napier [7-31] for an alternative signification

of the Gothic and supplement Punter's discussion of American Gothic with Ringe [7-44] and Fiedler [7-36]. Primary and secondary bibliographies. Index.

7-11. Rottensteiner, Franz (Austria). **The Fantasy Book: An Illustrated History from Dracula to Tolkien**. Thames & Hudson; Collier Books, 1978.
Over half of this "succinct [160-page] overview of the variety of literary fantasy" is devoted to supernatural fiction. His selection of texts and critical commentary is informed by the definition of fantasy Lars Gustafsson presented in his 1969 essay "On the Fantastic in Literature": fantasy is a mode that "[shows] the world as opaque, as inaccessible to reason on principle." Rottensteiner's best sections are those on German Romanticism, the Russian horror fantasies of Nicolai Gogol, Cthulhu Mythos tales by H. P. Lovecraft and others, Latin American magic realists, and French, Austrian, Belgian, Polish and Japanese writers. But, like the rest of this book, these sections are too cursory and superficial to serve even as an introduction; for this purpose, Daniels [7-4] and King [7-6] are recommended instead. And Rottensteiner's coverage of British and American works is marred by condescending asides about English-language fantasists and critics. The large and uncommonly good selection of illustrations in this book includes rarely seen dust jackets of foreign editions. Secondary bibliography, index. Also annotated as [F7-48] and [10-30].

7-12. Scarborough, Dorothy. **The Supernatural in Modern English Fiction**. Putnam, 1917.
One of the goals of this, the first major critical overview of occult fiction, was the identification of influences that shaped the early twentieth-century ghost story—particularly those of folklore and late nineteenth-century science. So she organized her book around major motifs of the supernatural: ghosts, Satan and his minions, beings that live beyond death, etc. Of course, this study is now dated: some works Scarborough discusses at length have since faded into insignificance. But her chapter showing how German Romanticism, French supernaturalism, Russian literature, science, dreams, folklore and spiritualism link the late eighteenth-century Gothic novel to the early twentieth-century ghost story remains of great interest. On balance, this well-written overview of the major themes and motifs of supernatural fiction should be in all libraries on the subject. Detailed index.

7-13. Schweitzer, Darrell, ed. **Discovering Modern Horror Fiction**. Starmont House, 1985.

7-14. ———, ed. **Discovering Modern Horror Fiction: II**. Starmont House, 1988.
Schweitzer designed these collections of essays "to introduce the reader to the broad range of modern horror fiction," which he defines as "post pulp-era writing"—in particular, "post-Lovecraftian fiction." This they do, providing brief surveys of works by important modern writers who have been largely ignored by critics. But both volumes are wildly uneven: their contents range from excellent, insightful overviews to tedious catalogues of plot summaries punctuated by superficial, effusive commentary. The best essays in Volume I are an analysis of the style and subtexts of T. E. D. Klein's works, an even-handed appraisal of Jonathan Carroll's first two novels, and articles on Manly Wade

Wellman, Karl Edward Wagner and Shirley Jackson. Volume II, the better of the two, includes excellent articles by Ramsey Campbell on James Herbert's novels, by Schweitzer on Bradbury's horror tales and by Klein on Campbell's short fiction, the latter reprinted from Ashley's collection of pieces on Campbell's horror fiction [8-13]. Moreover, Volume II contains new essays on Peter Straub, Chelsea Quinn Yarbro, Fritz Leiber, Robert Aickman, Michael McDowell, David Case and Joseph Payne Brennan. But its standout is Steve Eng's essay on the supernatural poetry of Richard L. Tierney, G. Sutton Breiding and Joseph Payne Brennan. Both volumes contain sufficient useful material to justify purchase by libraries of horror fiction. Both are indexed, and Volume I contains a secondary bibliography by Marshall B. Tymn.

***7-15.** Sullivan, Jack. **Elegant Nightmares: The English Ghost Story from Le Fanu to Blackwood**. Ohio Univ. Press, 1978.
In this brief book, Sullivan covers less ground than Briggs [7-3], Penzoldt [7-9], or Punter [7-10], eschewing breadth in favor of depth in examinations of several early twentieth-century English ghost stories, examples of the form he considers seminal for modern short fiction. Thus he begins with a long analysis of the work he considers archetypal: Le Fanu's "Green Tea" (1869). Essentially, Sullivan sees the modern ghost story evoking loss and helplessness in the face of a random and uncaring universe that can, without warning or provocation, disrupt man's "rationally and morally ordered world." As such, he contends, this form is fundamentally opposed to the aesthetic of Gothicism. From this vantage point, Sullivan examines the language, style and technique of early twentieth-century British writers, classifying them as antiquarians (e.g., M. R. James) or visionaries (e.g., Algernon Blackwood). Especially valuable are Sullivan's commentaries on James's successors E. G. Swain, R. H. Malden, L. P. Hartley, Walter De la Mare and H. R. Wakefield; less so are his disparaging remarks on Gothicism and the works of Poe. Readers interested in Sullivan's explication of the differences between Le Fanu's and James's ghost stories should also consider (as Sullivan does not) the alternative perspective of Jack P. Franzetti in *A Study of the Preternatural Fiction of Sheridan Le Fanu and Its Impact upon the Tales of Montague Rhodes James* (St. John's Univ., 1956). And all should consult Sullivan's companion (edited) volume *Lost Souls: A Collection of English Ghost Stories* (Ohio Univ. Press, 1983), which contains erudite introductions to stories by writers considered in the present book. G. R. Thompson disputes Sullivan's views in an essay on Washington Irving and the American ghost story in *The Haunted Dusk* [7-39]. Notes, primary and secondary bibliographies, index.

Gothicism: General Studies

***7-16.** Bayer-Berenbaum, Linda. **The Gothic Imagination: Expansion in Gothic Literature and Art**. Fairleigh Dickinson Univ. Press, 1982.
The introductory chapters of this valuable interdisciplinary study discuss the paraphernalia and preoccupations of Gothic fiction and relate its aesthetic and philosophical tenets to those of Gothic art. In her chapter on Gothic architecture, Bayer-Berenbaum illustrates with carefully selected photographs such commonalities as the replacement of symmetry by repetition as an organizing principle.

She presents as the primary motive forces behind the Gothic aesthetic the "compulsive expansionism" of consciousness and the pursuit of intensification of reality and perception. These drives, in turn, led to the Gothic's characteristic inclusiveness and juxtaposition of extremes. She elaborates these points by unpacking the imagery, structure and themes of a range of representative texts: *Frankenstein, Melmoth the Wanderer,* "The Haunter and the Haunted" by Edward Bulwer-Lytton, *Uncle Silas* by Le Fanu and *On the Night of the Seventh Moon* by Victoria Holt. Bibliography, index. For more on the relation of Gothic literature and architecture see *Le Roman "gothique" anglais, 1764–1824* by Maurice Lévy (Université de Toulouse, 1968).

7-17. Day, William Patrick. **In the Circles of Fear and Desire: A Study of Gothic Fantasy**. Univ. of Chicago Press, 1985.
This stimulating psychological and historical analysis of Gothic fantasy ranges from the origins of Gothicism in the late eighteenth-century British novel through incarnations in nineteenth-century fiction to recent renderings in twentieth-century film. Day views Gothic fantasy from several perspectives: as a "dynamic literary system" defined by rigid conventions, as an elaboration of fears concerning the family and as a historical and cultural search for selfhood. The latter context leads to fascinating connections of the Gothic hero/villain to the contemporary detective, of Gothicism to the "apocalyptic vision" of Modernism and of Gothic parody to Freudian psychology. Day shows the Gothic form to be subversive of heroic possibility, of realism, of the numinous—a view quite different from that of Varnado [7-22]—and of its own mythography. Although ostensibly escapist, the Gothic also subverts its readers' expectations, forcing them to confront their anxiety of sexual identity, which is made manifest in the Gothic's many sadomasochistic scenarios of imprisonment, violence and incest. Essential reading for students of Gothicism. Notes, index. An important counterpoint to Day's view is offered by Daniel Cottom in *The Civilized Imagination: A Study of Ann Radcliffe, Jane Austen, and Sir Walter Scott* (Cambridge Univ. Press, 1985).

7-18. MacAndrew, Elizabeth. **The Gothic Tradition in Fiction**. Columbia Univ. Press, 1979.
Unlike most studies of Gothic fiction, MacAndrew's book focuses on the conventions of the mode. By delineating interconnections among Gothic and borderline Gothic texts written during the late eighteenth and nineteenth centuries, she shows how these conventions changed as writers gained insight into human psychology and how the tradition came to "present new views of human nature ambiguously." In her analyses of the ideas and aesthetics of these works MacAndrew underlines their symbolism, which she sees as "almost . . . allegorical." Part One begins with an elaborate psychological reading of Horace Walpole's *The Castle of Otranto.* This leads to the eighteenth-century Sentimental novel, a precursor to which MacAndrew returns in chapters on character (the "reflected self" and the "split personality"), narrative structure and setting. Part Two takes up Victorian supernatural stories, the tales of Edgar Allan Poe, mystery and detective fiction, the supernatural fiction of Nathaniel Hawthorne, Henry James's "Turn of the Screw," and many other works. A cursory epilogue surveys the Gothic in the twentieth century. The usefulness of this study is limited by a number of inadequately supported generalizations and its awkward structure,

which forces MacAndrew to circle around rather than directly engage some important texts. The comparable book by Punter [7-10] is preferable. Notes, bibliography, index.

7-19. Sedgwick, Eve Kosofsky. **The Coherence of Gothic Conventions**. Methuen, 1986.
While acknowledging "the tendentiousness of examining thematic conventions," Eve Sedgwick here applies phenomenological, psychoanalytic and structuralist critical methods to Gothic texts in order to discover how their conventions interact. Drawing on the "continuous, reiterative stream of explicitly thematic language" in Gothic novels, she first identifies and names such major themes as the unspeakable, live burial and sleep-like states. Around these she constructs a veritable topology of the Gothic, a spatial model of the congruences between conventions quite different from the prevailing "spatial metaphor of interiority" found in, for example, *The Divided Self* by Masao Miyoshi (New York Univ. Press, 1969). Although often pedantic and occasionally opaque, this revision of Sedgwick's 1975 dissertation (a reprint of the Arno Press 1980 version) has much to offer on specific works: e.g., its comparison of the structure of Charlotte Brontë's *Villette* to that of sister Emily Brontë's *Wuthering Heights* and its argument that the essays of Thomas De Quincey justify declaring him "a great Gothic novelist." Sedgwick's chapter on the mode's near obsession with superficial, formulaic emotionalism introduces an important dimension to Gothic criticism; see also Howells [7-27] and Napier [7-31]. Notes, but no bibliography or index. For a less theoretical treatment of Gothic conventions see Railo [7-32] and MacAndrew [7-18].

7-20. Thompson, Gary Richard, ed. **The Gothic Imagination: Essays in Dark Romanticism**. Washington State Univ. Press, 1974.
The nine original essays in this splendidly unified collection explore aspects of Gothicism from before the thirteenth century to the twentieth. Drawing on both Gothic art and diabolist literature, they depict the Gothic romance as metaphysical quest literature in which a "lonely, self-divided hero" pursues the Absolute and finds instead destruction. The collection itself is a kind of intellectual quest for "a Gothic monomyth": a definition of the mode that can account for its impact and continuing popularity. Many of these essays are relevant to modern horror fiction: Thompson's syncretic introduction, Nicolas Kiessling's essay on the meanings embodied in the recurrent icon of the Incubus; Joel Porte's on the Calvinist conception of man in works by Ann Radcliffe, Matthew Gregory Lewis and others; and Virginia M. Hyde's on Gothic iconography in Franz Kafka's *The Trial* and *The Castle*. Although somewhat specialized and aimed at scholars, this book should be in all but the smallest libraries of Gothic studies. See also Lowry Nelson, Jr.'s influential related 1963 essay "Night Thoughts on the Gothic Novel," which is reprinted in Harwell [7-26] and in *Pastoral and Romance*, ed. by Eleanor Terry Lincoln (Prentice-Hall, 1969).

***7-21.** ———, ed. **Romantic Gothic Tales 1790–1840**. Harper, 1979.
To introduce this anthology, Thompson extensively revised his essay in *The Gothic Imagination* [7-20] and produced an excellent primer on literary Gothi-

cism. Within a carefully defined historical context—the Gothic as "the dark counterforce to optimistic Romanticism"—he identifies two major modes: "low" (e.g., shilling shockers) and "high" (e.g., *Frankenstein*). He then partitions high Gothic into historical, explained, supernatural and ambiguous submodes and illustrates each with succinct, insightful discussions of works by British and American writers. While this categorization may seem to elide certain subtleties, it is certainly helpful to the newcomer. This long essay comes complete with a wide-ranging bibliography and commentaries on a thoughtful selection of illustrative tales.

7-22. Varnado, S. L. **Haunted Presence: The Numinous in Gothic Fiction**. Univ. of Alabama, 1987.
Varnado's chronological survey of the aesthetics and ontology of Gothic literature is informed throughout by the concept of the numinous as articulated by theologian Rudolf Otto (1860–1937) in *The Idea of the Holy* (1923; Oxford Univ. Press, 1958). The foundation of this book, an expansion of Varnado's essay in *The Gothic Imagination* [7-20], is an explication of Otto's theory of the "numinous," an affective state of consciousness in which sensations of awe, mystery and fascination induce an awareness of objective nonrational experience. Varnado's intent in identifying the numinous in supernatural fiction from the eighteenth to the twentieth centuries is to demonstrate its "high seriousness and moral purpose." Varnado probes representative (mainly familiar) works by Horace Walpole, Ann Radcliffe, Matthew Gregory Lewis, Charles Maturin, Mary Shelley, Edgar Allan Poe, Henry James, Bram Stoker, Arthur Machen, Algernon Blackwood and H. P. Lovecraft and a host of other writers. But this book is frustrating in its brevity (160 pages) and in the consequent superficiality of Varnado's comments on specific texts. Still, it does illuminate the curious fascination of tales of supernatural dread. Notes, bibliography, index.

British and German Gothic

***7-23.** Carter, Margaret L. **Specter or Delusion? The Supernatural in Gothic Fiction**. UMI Research Press, 1987.
In this well-written, insightful book (a revision of her 1986 Ph.D. thesis) Carter studies the narrative structure of eighteenth- and nineteenth-century Gothic tales. Building on theoretical work by Tzvetan Todorov and Clayton Koelb, she explores how writers use "mediated narrative" ("narration . . . that comes to the reader's knowledge through indirect means rather than through the voice of the primary third-person or first-person narrator") to induce in their readers a state of (sometimes radical) doubt about the reality of the supernatural. To illustrate this thesis, she examines the romances of Radcliffe, the Germanic Gothics *Horrid Mysteries* by Karl Grosse (1797) and *The Necromancer* by Karl Friedrich Kahlert (writing as Lawrence Flammenberg) (1794), Shelley's *Frankenstein*, Maturin's *Melmoth the Wanderer*, Bulwer-Lytton's *A Strange Story*, three "Dr. Hesselius" tales from Le Fanu's *In a Glass Darkly* and *Dracula*. To broaden the context of her study, Carter relates these authors' attitudes toward the ontology of the supernatural to their worldviews and the philosophical concerns of their society. Bibliography, index.

For more on the occult fiction of Bulwer-Lytton see the long essay in *Strange Stories and Other Explorations in Victorian Fiction* by Robert Lee Wolff (Gambit, 1971).

7-24. Coleman, William Emmet. **On the Discrimination of Gothicisms**. Arno Press, 1980.
Arguably the best of Arno's "Gothic Studies and Dissertations" series, this book reprints Coleman's 1979 Ph.D. dissertation. Following the obligatory review of prior criticism, Coleman classifies eighteenth-century British Gothic novels, poems and dramas according to their style, theme and worldview as Enlightenment Gothic (Walpole, Scott, Reeve), Gothicism of sensibility (Radcliffe, Lewis, Godwin, Byron, Maturin) or Romantic Gothicism (Percy Bysshe and Mary Shelley, Wordsworth, Keats, Coleridge). He then explicates the aesthetic, psychological and philosophical content of Gothicism and tracks its evolution, carefully relating its developing tradition to the transformation of English literature at the turn of the century. The adaptability of the Gothic mode, Coleman argues, enabled it to provide literature with a coherence and continuity vital to the birth throes of Romanticism. Coleman's treatment of Romantic Gothicism is too cursory, and his identification of Gothic texts by the presence of Malin's [7-42] three "essential characteristics, . . . the haunted castle, the voyage into the forest, and the reflection" seems a bit mechanical. And this printing is filled with typos. Still, this insightful, accessible book is recommended to newcomers to Gothic studies. Bibliography, index.

7-25. Hadley, Michael. **The Undiscovered Genre: A Search for the German Gothic Novel**. Peter Lang, 1978.
Hadley preceded this book with *Romanverzeichnis: Bibliographie der zweischen 1750–1800 erschienenen Erstausgaben* (Lang Verlag, 1977), a bibliography of over 5,000 German novels published during the last half of the eighteenth century. In the present book he draws upon this bibliography and his prior study, *The German Novel in 1790: A Descriptive Account and Critical Bibliography* (Bern, 1973), as well as a multitude of rare primary texts and materials from a contemporary review journal to attack two critical assumptions: first, that during the late eighteenth century, German commercial fiction was dominated by the *Schauerroman* (i.e., novels emphasizing horror themes and motifs) and second, that German Gothics were heavily influenced by (and, in turn, influenced) British Gothics. Exponents of these views include Birkhead [7-2], Summers [7-33] and Varma [7-34]. To the contrary, Hadley shows that the *Schauerroman* did not even exist until very near the end of the century, at which time it appeared as an offshoot of the chivalric romance and the historical novel. He further shows that historical and cultural forces (e.g., judicial practices) influenced the nineteenth-century German Gothic far more than did its British counterpart. Hadley's case is persuasive and important, and his book suggests numerous directions for future scholarship. Its secondary bibliography is invaluable, but it lacks an index, and its many long excerpts from German novels are not translated into English.

7-26. Harwell, Thomas Meade, ed. **The English Gothic Novel: A Miscellany in Four Volumes**. Universität Salzburg, 1986.
The excerpts and essays in this vast compilation embrace a range of attitudes toward the eighteenth-century British Gothic novel and its successors. Vols. I

("Contexts") and II ("Texts") focus on the period from 1764 to 1824, the heyday of British Gothicism; Vols. III and IV ("Collateral Gothic") treat works before and after these dates. About half of the 1,266 pages in these four volumes consist of intelligently chosen excerpts from well-known studies by MacAndrew [7-18], Summers [7-33], Railo [7-32], Thompson [7-20], Birkhead [7-2], Fiedler [7-36], and several excerpts by Varma [7-34]. But even libraries and scholars that own these books may be interested in the many essays Harwell includes. For example, in Vol. I we find Robert D. Hume's genre study "Gothic versus Romantic: A Reevaluation of the Gothic Novel," Lowry Nelson, Jr.'s "Night Thoughts on the Gothic Novel," Archibald Bolling Shepperson's witty look at the satiric legacy of Gothicism, and a selection from J. H. Matthews's important book *Surrealism and the Novel* (Univ. of Michigan Press, 1966). Essays in Vol. IV consider the influence of British Gothicism on Charles Brockden Brown, Samuel Taylor Coleridge and others, and include an excellent essay by Robert B. Heilman on Charlotte Brontë. Reprints of valuable bibliographies by Jakob Brauchli (in Vol. I) and Maurice Lévy (in Vol. II) make these volumes important for all medium-to-large libraries. Several essays appear (untranslated) in French or German with headnotes by Harwell (in English) that summarize their contents. Available only in paperback.

***7-27.** Howells, Coral Ann (U.K.). **Love, Mystery, and Misery: Feeling in Gothic Fiction**. Athlone Press; Humanities Press, 1978.

The distinctive element of the British Gothic novel was its presentation of nonrational experience. Early Gothic novelists, trying to free themselves from conventional Christian morality but fearful of the consequences of doing so, fell into irreconcilable ambiguities of form and substance, producing subjective, moralistic romances that oscillate wildly between fantasy and realism. Unable to come to terms with these feelings and values, these books offer instead displays of extreme, superficial emotional states. This critique raises a host of critical issues: e.g., the dread of sex that permeates early Gothics, their authors' attempts to unify feeling and reason, and the influence of eighteenth-century Shakespearean drama and performance tradition. Howells supports her critique with analyses of the rhetoric, imagery and technique of Ann Radcliffe's *The Mysteries of Udolpho*, Matthew Gregory Lewis's *The Monk*, Jane Austen's *Northanger Abbey* and two Minerva Press novels: Regina Maria Roche's *The Children of the Abbey* (1796) and Mary-Anne Radcliffe's *Manfroné* (1809). In later chapters, she shows how the Gothic fused with Romanticism in Charles Robert Maturin's *Melmoth the Wanderer* and merged with the mainstream in Charlotte Brontë's *Jane Eyre*. Although Howells neglects the historical relevance of literary Gothicism, her critique should be considered by readers and scholars of the Gothics, ideally together with that of Napier [7-31]. Notes, selective list of Gothic novels, index. On the transformation of the Gothic in *Jane Eyre* see also R. B. Heilman, "Charlotte Brontë's 'New Gothic,'" reprinted in Harwell [7-26] and in *Victorian Literature: Modern Essays in Criticism*, ed. by Austin Wright (Oxford Univ. Press, 1961). For a closer look at the Gothic and supernatural in drama see *Gothic Drama from Walpole to Shelley* by Bertrand Evans (Univ. of California Press, 1947) and *Witchcraft and Magic in Seventeenth Century English Drama* by Anthony Harris (Manchester Univ. Press, 1980).

7-28. Jarrett, David. (U.K.). **The Gothic Form in Fiction and Its Relation to History**. King Alfred's College, 1980.

In this extended essay, Jarrett takes issue with the conventional critical wisdom concerning the eighteenth-century British Gothic novel. Defining the mode in terms of structure rather than mood, Jarrett identifies it with "the directness of the ballad rather than with Ariostan romantic complication." Essential but often overlooked in Gothic studies, he claims, are the ironic character of the Gothic novel and its relationship to contemporary social and historical realities. Indeed, Jarrett suggests that by shaping Gothic conventions, novelists of the period creatively engaged the problem of history itself. He supports these views with concise comments on a large number of English and American works from the 1760s to the present. His discussions of Sir Walter Scott, Charles Dickens, Nathaniel Hawthorne and William Faulkner, although brief, are penetrating. In an excellent longer section he shows that Ann Radcliffe's Gothicism "dramatizes a long-standing social and historical crisis that involves the opposition of . . . the inner life of a woman and her outer social role." Although Jarrett's somewhat revisionist ideas deserve more elaboration than this pamphlet allows, even this brief treatment is recommended as background to the past 200 years of horror fiction. Notes but no index.

***7-29.** Kiely, Robert. **The Romantic Novel in England**. Harvard Univ. Press, 1972.

Robert Kiely portrays the Gothic novel as "a battleground" between the forces of "imagination and the supremacy of the self" (the romance) and those of "reason and the public welfare" (the realistic novel). Out of this unresolved struggle was born a form intrinsically flawed by juxtapositions of radically different styles, structures and themes. Following an excellent introduction contrasting the aesthetics of the romantic novel to those of its nineteenth-century predecessors, Kiely illustrates the form's main thematic innovations in close reconsiderations of twelve texts, including *The Castle of Otranto, Vathek, The Mysteries of Udolpho, Melmoth the Wanderer, The Monk, Frankenstein* and *Wuthering Heights*. This level-headed, well-written book, one of the first of several recent reappraisals of literary Gothicism, is highly recommended to readers interested in the British novel or Gothic studies. Notes, bibliography, index. For a different slant on the issues Kiely engages, see *The Realistic Imagination: English Fiction from Frankenstein to Lady Chatterley* by George Levine (Univ. of Chicago Press, 1981).

7-30. Le Tellier, Robert I. **An Intensifying Vision of Evil: The Gothic Novel (1764–1820) as a Self-Contained Literary Cycle**. Institut für Anglistik & Amerikanistik, 1980.

Le Tellier conceives of the late eighteenth-century British Gothic novel as a prototype for fiction itself. He argues that the elements of fiction—character, setting, plot, worldview, etc.—are brought into play in the Gothic novel with singular clarity. Consistent with this view, Le Tellier organizes his close readings of major texts not around the works themselves but around those elements, showing in great detail how they are "linked and characterized by a common inspiration that progressively intensifies in detail, lucidity, and symbolic resonance." The lack of original insights in this book should not deter the newcomer to Gothic studies, who will benefit from its description of the evolution of the rudiments of fiction during the late eighteenth century, from its lengthy quotations from primary texts and from its clear, coherent picture of the Gothic vision of evil. In particular, this book is a useful precursor to the more sophisticated studies of Kiely [7-29] or Coleman [7-24]. Primary and secondary bibliographies, but no index.

***7-31.** Napier, Elizabeth R. (U.K.). **The Failure of Gothic: Problems of Disjunction in an Eighteenth-Century Literary Form**. Oxford Univ. Press, 1987.
In this clear-headed reevaluation of British Gothicism, Elizabeth Napier challenges its importance and viability as a fictional form. Focusing on novels published from 1764 to 1820, she effectively refutes the critical view (prevalent since the 1960s) that the Gothic is a Romantic genre marked by rich coherence and psychological complexity—a view propounded by, for example, MacAndrew [7-18], Wilt [7-80], Varma [7-34] and Punter [7-10]. For Napier the Gothic is, rather, "a genre of imbalance" irreparably flawed by tension between a conservative, stabilizing tendency toward moral, structural and generic closure and a contrary destabilizing tendency toward fragmentation, excess and moral ambivalence. Following analyses of the disorienting narrative techniques and stylistic disjunctions of the Gothic, Napier critiques four major works. In her first of two chapters on Ann Radcliffe, Napier shows *The Mysteries of Udolpho* to be riven by internal contradictions and marred by Radcliffe's misunderstanding of "the relationship of female feeling to female action." In a later chapter she demonstrates that in *The Italian,* Radcliffe failed to develop the potential complexity of its hero-villain, Schedoni. Napier also displays major flaws in characterization, tone and morality in *The Monk* and tonal instabilities, discords and evasions that undercut *The Castle of Otranto.* This tightly reasoned, ultimately persuasive book is sure to raise hackles among Gothic scholars, but it should not be ignored. Bibliography, index.

7-32. Railo, Eino. **The Haunted Castle: A Study of the Elements of English Romanticism**. Dutton, 1927.
Railo was a pioneer in Gothic studies, but today his book is of minimal value. Essentially a catalogue of literary Gothicism, it is organized around central themes and images: "The Criminal Monk," "The Byronic Hero," "Ghosts and Demonic Beings," "Incest and Romantic Eroticism," etc. This structure inevitably introduces some repetitiveness. But the book's main flaws are its inclusiveness and lack of perspective: like Summers [7-33], Railo exerts too little control over too much material. For example, his often-noted fifty-three-page chapter on Lewis and *The Monk,* which he considered the apotheosis of the Gothic, is marred by biographical errors pointed out by Peck [8-59] and others. Copious references appear in notes, but the book lacks both a bibliography and (more seriously) an index. Readers seeking a contextual study of Gothicism should go to Birkhead [7-2] or (if they know French) to *Le Roman "gothique" anglais, 1764–1824* by Maurice Lévy (Université de Toulouse, 1968). For an introduction to the Gothic novel, see Varma [7-34]. On Gothic conventions, see MacAndrew [7-18] and Le Tellier [7-30].

7-33. Summers, Montague (U.K.). **The Gothic Quest: A History of the Gothic Novel**. Fortune Press, 1938.

Summers was a controversial and contentious scholar of Restoration drama, witchcraft and mysticism, and Gothic literature (see [7-84]). Even today his erudite but partisan books are singularly comprehensive—one of the qualities that makes them difficult to use. This pioneering literary history embraces an enormous number of obscure Gothic writers but excludes major figures such as Maturin and Radcliffe, who were slated for a projected sequel left uncompleted at Summers's death in 1948. Indomitably discursive, filled with gossip, and all but useless as literary criticism, this book is nevertheless notable for its coverage of minor writers and for its long chapter on Matthew Gregory Lewis—which, however, is often bewildering in its detail and inaccurate in its biography; see Peck [8-59]. General index and index of novels. Summers's remarks on surrealism are particularly misleading; readers should consult *Surrealism and the Novel* by J. H. Matthews (Univ. of Michigan Press, 1966).

7-34. Varma, Devendra P. (U.K.). **The Gothic Flame: Being a History of the Gothic Novel in England: Its Origins, Efflorescence, Disintegration, and Residuary Influences**. Arthur Barker, 1957.
In this history of the rise and fall of British Gothicism, Devendra P. Varma seeks to demonstrate the long-term importance of its philosophies, atmospherics and conventions to nineteenth-century fiction. Against a backdrop of developments in art, architecture and Freudian psychology, he tracks the form through its major variants: the Historical Gothic (e.g., Clara Reeve), the School of Terror (Ann Radcliffe) and the *Schauerromantik* (Matthew Gregory Lewis). Many of Varma's critical insights derive from earlier work, especially that of Birkhead [7-2]. Nevertheless, his insights into the disintegration of the Gothic in the nineteenth century—its decline in popularity, victimization by parodists and corruption into "shilling shockers"—are fascinating. Less compendious than Summers [7-33] and better organized than Railo [7-32], this book is enlivened by Varma's enthusiasm and by excerpts from contemporary reviews of the works he discusses. Appendixes relate Gothicism in literature to art and to the detective thriller. Extensive classified bibliography, index. To balance Varma's partisanship, readers should also consult the broad contextual discussions in *The Popular Novel in England, 1770-1800* by J. M. S. Tompkins (1932) and *History of the Pre-Romantic Novel in England* by James R. Foster (MLA, 1949).

7-35. Watt, William Whyte. **Shilling Shockers of the Gothic School: A Study of the Chapbook Gothic Romances**. Harvard Univ. Press, 1932.
By studying the shilling shocker, argues William Watt, "we [can] study the unadorned elements of English Gothicism on which the novels were actually based, and [can] appreciate the absurd extent to which the Gothic vogue was carried in the declining years of its life." These chapbooks of thirty to seventy pages published during the first two decades of the nineteenth century contained either hackneyed Gothic pastiches or plagiarized abridgments of classic novels. By exaggerating and trivializing the already rather ludicrous characteristics of the Gothic hero, heroine, villain and plot, these little books helped bring about the death of the form in the early nineteenth century. Watt groups these mini-Gothics according to locale—the monastery or convent and the ruined castle and environs—then discusses their props and characters. This affectionate, witty and

appropriately brief book also makes a persuasive case for the shilling shockers as progenitor of the short horror story of the nineteenth and twentieth centuries. See also *The Shilling Shockers* by Peter Haining (St. Martin's, 1979).

North American Gothic and the American Weird Tale

***7-36.** Fiedler, Leslie. **Love and Death in the American Novel.** Criterion, 1960; reprinted, Stein & Day, 1966.

Perhaps the most famous quotation from Leslie Fiedler's huge essay on the American novel from 1789 to 1959 is his description of classic American fiction as "a literature of horror for boys." Fiedler considers the American novel, with its essential antirealism and irrationalism, a thematic and symbolic adaptation of the British Gothic. In analyses based on the theories of Freud and Jung (with a sprinkling of Marx and D. H. Lawrence) of a huge number of books—sentimental novels, westerns, historical fictions, novels of seduction, horror-pornography and more—he develops his thesis: that the American Gothic, an avant-garde, antibourgeois blend of the analytic and projective modes of the novel, was from the beginning obsessed by unconventional forms of love and death: brother-sister incest, necrophilia and homosexuality. Note especially Fiedler's long chapter on Poe and his arguments that classic works by Twain, Hawthorne and Melville are actually Gothic in theme and atmosphere. Brilliantly argued, rich with speculations on issues literary and cultural, and readable throughout, this comparative study—itself "a kind of Gothic novel (complete with touches of black humor) whose subject is the American experience as recorded in our classic fiction"—is simply essential. See also Levin [7-41] and Malin [7-42]. Index.

7-37. Gross, Louis S. **Redefining the American Gothic: From *Wieland* to *Day of the Dead*.** UMI Research Press, 1988.

A major strength of this brief but intriguing book is its range. Louis Gross takes up the entire tradition of American Gothicism from 1798 to the 1980s, applying historical and psychoanalytic methods to fiction and to "the natural heirs to the Gothic tradition," American horror films. Gross defines the Gothic as a literature of demonic quest narratives that examine the causes and effects of fear—a definition broad enough to admit several unusual novels: e.g., James Fenimore Cooper's *Lionel Lincoln* (1825), Oliver Wendell Holmes's *Elsie Venner* (1861) and John Rechy's *The City of Night* (1963). Gross shows that American Gothics portrayed a view of the American experience quite different from that found in such mainstream texts as the Constitution, a view shot through with images of terror, institutional oppression and perversity. Thus the Gothic offered its readers a haven where they could confront the cultural anxieties of a newly industrialized America about the power of women, the bisexual impulse and the presence of blacks and Indians. Most creators of American Gothics, Gross notes—"women, gays, and colonials"—lived on the margins of American culture. For more detail on the precursors to late twentieth-century American Gothic, see Fiedler [7-36], then Malin [7-42]. Notes, primary and secondary bibliographies, index.

7-38. Kerr, Howard. **Mediums, and Spirit-Rappers, and Roaring Radicals: Spiritualism in American Literature, 1850–1900.** Univ. of Illinois Press, 1972.
In late nineteenth-century America spiritualists united mesmerism and belief in poltergeist phenomena into a widely popular social and religious movement. Although only a few ghost stories incorporated the occult machinery of spiritualism *per se,* the mood of millennial expectancy in spiritualist tracts of the time persisted in American supernatural fiction for years. In this competent history Kerr shows how the movement focused public attention on the supernatural and influenced Hawthorne, Twain, Melville and other important writers. He treats at length Henry James's *The Bostonians* (1886), William Dean Howell's *The Undiscovered Country* (1880) and the stories of Fitz-James O'Brien, one writer who did successfully use spiritualism in tales of supernatural horror. Bibliography of cited sources, index. For a briefer synthesis of the ideas in this book, see Kerr's essay in *The Haunted Dusk* [7-39]. Also annotated as [F7-26].

7-39. ———, John W. Crowley; and Charles W. Crow, eds. **The Haunted Dusk: American Supernatural Fiction, 1820–1920.** Univ. of Georgia Press, 1983.
The ten essays in this collection "chart the course of [the American ghost story] from its emergence out of Gothicism to its merger with psychologism early in this century." Together, they clarify the importance of the supernatural, not just to familiar exponents such as Poe and Henry James but also to Mark Twain, Jack London, Herman Melville, Orestes Brownson, William Dean Howells and others. Several essays consider the impact on American writers of early nineteenth-century supernaturalist movements, a subject treated at greater length by Kerr [7-38]. Also important are G. R. Thompson's essay on the origin of the American "inconclusive psychological ghost story" in Washington Irving's tales and Cruce Stark's study of the impact on American fiction and its philosophy of advances in psychology and the physical sciences. The essays in this book address social and psychological concerns rather than close textual analysis and usefully supplement the in-depth studies of Fiedler [7-36] and Ringe [7-44]. Notes, index.

7-40. Jones, Robert K. **The Shudder Pulps: A History of the Weird Menace Magazines of the 1930's.** FAX Collectors' Edition, 1975.
Like some bizarre trash transmutation of eighteenth-century Radcliffean explained Gothic, the "weird menace" story thrived in America during the 1930s. Unlike the pulp horrors of *Weird Tales,* the weird menace story was "a form of mystery story in which the villain perpetrated seemingly supernatural deviltries, which were logically explained at the end." In this entertaining, well-illustrated history, derived from a series of articles, Robert Jones sensibly eschews analysis and offers instead a lively tour of these mass-produced throwaway thrillers. Recommended to libraries of American cultural studies and to students of the modern American horror story. Index. For a look at the true supernatural tale in 1930s pulp fiction, see Weinberg [7-45]. Also annotated as [11-53].

7-41. Levin, Harry. **The Power of Blackness: Hawthorne, Poe, Melville.** Knopf, 1958.
This impressionistic study of "the workings of the imaginative faculty, particularly in what may be called fabulation" investigates symbols of darkness in the

tragic visions of three visionary writers who exemplify nineteenth-century American Gothic. Particularly noteworthy are Levin's chapters on Poe's "cult of blackness," with its excellent discussions of *The Narrative of Arthur Gordon Pym* (1837–38) and his tales of M. Auguste Dupin. Levin is one of the few critics to note the centrality of horror to the tradition of mainstream American fiction. Bibliography, chronology, index. See also Fiedler [7-36] and Ringe [7-44].

7-42. Malin, Irving. **New American Gothic**. Southern Illinois Univ. Press, 1962. Malin focuses on Truman Capote, James Purdy, Flannery O'Connor, John Hawkes, Carson McCullers and J. D. Salinger, authors who, while obviously writing within the tradition of Poe, Hawthorne and Henry James, were also "the inheritors of [the] old Gothic" of Walpole, Lewis and Radcliffe. Malin shows how the symbolic use of images derived from Gothicism ("the haunted castle, the voyage into the forest, and the reflection") empowers the nonsupernatural stories typical of twentieth-century American Gothic. These intensely psychological stories about isolation and narcissism, hostility to community, obsessive love and the breakdown of order into chaos "image the terrors of the buried self." Malin sometimes seems to confuse the Gothic with the grotesque—see "Gothic Fiction and the Grotesque" by Maximillian E. Novak (*Novel* 13 [1979]: 50–67) and Kayser [7-52]—and has been criticized for his very broad definition of Gothicism. But his book remains important to students of American fiction, horror fiction and later exponents of New American Gothic such as Michael McDowell, Fred Chappell and Anne Rivers Siddons. Notes, index. See also chapter 9 of King [7-6].

7-43. Northey, Margot. **The Haunted Wilderness: The Gothic and Grotesque in Canadian Fiction**. Univ. of Toronto Press, 1976.
This engaging look at selected nineteenth- and twentieth-century Canadian novels builds on Leslie Fiedler's analysis of American Gothic [7-36] and on Wolfgang Kayser's theory of the grotesque [7-52]. But Northey establishes Canadian Gothic as a distinct mode whose major themes are domination and the dual fears of nature and civilization. After an introductory sketch of the genesis of Canadian Gothic in early French- and English-Canadian folk tales and legends, she examines four nineteenth-century novels that show how the British Gothic tradition was adapted to Canadian literature. Subsequent discussions of seven twentieth-century works, including Margaret Atwood's *Surfacing* (1972) and Mordecai Richler's *Cocksure* (1968), demonstrate the increasingly grotesque character of the mode in this century. Happily, Northey is no polemicist, and she carefully notes the weaknesses of these novels: e.g., their uneasy juxtapositions of Gothicism and sentimentality, Gothicism and didacticism, or Gothicism and sociology. Of special relevance to modern horror fiction (outside Canada) is the moral/philosophical distinction Northey draws between "disruptive" versus "directed" grotesque. Excerpts from one work, *Le Chercheur de trésors* (1837) by Philippe Aubert de Gaspé, appear only in French. Notes, primary and secondary bibliographies, index. For a closer look at the Gothic novels of Margaret Atwood, see "Atwood Gothic" by Eli Mandel and "Margaret Atwood's *Lady Oracle*: Fantasy and the Modern Gothic Novel" by Susan J. Rosowski, both in *Critical Essays on Margaret Atwood*, ed. by Judith McCombs (G. K. Hall, 1988).

7-44. Ringe, Donald A. **American Gothic: Imagination and Reason in Nineteenth-Century Fiction**. Univ. Press of Kentucky, 1982.
Ringe's critical history traces the development of American literary Gothicism during the nineteenth century, a period (paradoxically) of relentless rationalism and literary realism. Abjuring the psychological approach adopted by Leslie Fiedler [7-36], Ringe prefers "to examine the historical development that took place from one writer to another, and determine the various influences, both native and foreign, that over a period of years were exerted on all of them." To frame his readings, Ringe identifies two strains of American Gothicism. The more important, derived from British and German Gothics imported to America during the early eighteenth century, took root in the psychologically oriented novels of "the father of American fiction," Charles Brockden Brown; the other germinated in the rationalistic, psychological tales of Washington Irving. Ringe then shows that as later writers adapted the Gothic mode and its motifs to the American context, they transformed its epistemological function. These changes culminate in the works of Nathaniel Hawthorne and Edgar Allan Poe, whose stories get extended but problematical and sometimes oversimplified readings. Ringe ends his study in 1860, arguing that soon thereafter the resurgence of realism marginalized American Gothicism for nearly a century. Notes, index. While this book contains much of value to students of American horror fiction, it never clearly defines the effect of works in the American Gothic tradition, and readers should supplement it with Fiedler [7-36], Malin [7-42] and Gross [7-37], who show the recrudescence of the Gothic in the twentieth-century psychological tale. Also important are the essays in the collection edited by Kerr, Crowley and Crow [7-39] and the excellent essays in the two-issue symposium on American Gothic in *ESQ* (1972): 1-123. On American Southern Gothic, see also Chester E. Eisinger's "The Gothic Spirit in the Forties," in *Pastoral and Romance: Modern Essays in Criticism*, ed. by Eleanor Terry Lincoln (Prentice-Hall, 1969).

***7-45.** Weinberg, Robert. **The Weird Tales Story**. FAX Collector's Edition, 1977.
In this anecdotal history Weinberg sets out to confute the many rumors and legends that have grown up around *Weird Tales* [11-20], the most important American pulp of the 1930s and 40s. The core of his book narrates the magazine's rise and fall in sequential discussions of every issue from the first (March 1923) to the last (September 1954). Although heavy on plot summary, this book is invaluable for its biographical information about editors and authors and for its coverage of important but offbeat and little-known stories by H. Warner Munn, Eli Colter and H. F. Arnold and many other neglected writers. Weinberg also describes *Weird Tales*'s physical appearance and its cover and interior art (and includes a wonderful selection of illustrations). Finally, he reprints reminiscences by many major authors, a famous editorial that includes a (partisan) capsule history of the weird tale, and excerpts from its famous letters column, The Eyrie. Regrettably, no index. For complete bibliographical data see *The Collector's Index to Weird Tales* by Sheldon R. Jaffrey and Fred Cook (Bowling Green Univ. Popular Press, 1985). Also annotated as [11-55].

Extra-Generic Studies

7-46. Auerbach, Nina. **Woman and the Demon: The Life of a Victorian Myth**. Harvard Univ. Press, 1982.
In this feminist critique, Auerbach reconstructs the Victorian myth of woman: "a myth that was never quite formulated but that recurs incessantly in [popular and classical] literature and art, a myth crowning a disobedient woman in her many guises as heir of the ages and demonic savior of the race." She examines illustrations of prevalent myths and monsters of the era and fiction by Wilkie Collins, Robert Louis Stevenson, Sheridan Le Fanu, Bram Stoker, Oscar Wilde and others. Illustrated. Notes, index. For a broad, informal look at the contributions of Victorian authors of supernatural fiction, see the articles in *Mainly Victorians* by Stewart M. Ellis (Hutchinson, 1925).

7-47. Bataille, Georges (France). **Literature and Evil**. Calder & Boyars, 1973. Tr. by Alastair Hamilton of *La Littérature et la mal,* 1957.
The intimate tone of parts of this "attempt to extract the essence of literature" may put off some readers, but Bataille raises issues that are central to twentieth-century psychological horror fiction. In addition to an excellent chapter on Franz Kafka, Bataille discusses two other particularly relevant writers: Emily Brontë, whose *Wuthering Heights* renders evil through its depiction of "the horror of atonement," and the Marquis de Sade, whose works make evil appear desirable as they strive for "the clear consciousness of suppression of the difference between subject and object." Notes but no index.

7-48. Gilbert, Sandra M., and Susan Gubar. **The Madwoman in the Attic: The Woman Writer and the Nineteenth-Century Literary Imagination**. Yale Univ. Press, 1979.
In this imaginative, ideological 719-page critical inquiry into nineteenth-century poetry and prose, Gilbert and Gubar dig beneath the surface of a host of texts to discover surprising feminist subtexts, which (they postulate) grew out of women writers' "anxiety of authorship." The immediate relevance of this book to supernatural and horror fiction is its readings of novels in the "Gothic/Satanic mode": *Jane Eyre* (1847), *Wuthering Heights* (1847) and (especially) *Frankenstein* (1818). But the feminist poetics articulated by Gilbert and Gubar carries implications for modern horror fiction as well, especially the sexist hack-and-slash school. Notes, index. See also Auerbach [7-46] and Ellen Moers's *Literary Women* (Doubleday, 1974). In a related study focused on supernatural fiction, *Demon-Lovers and Their Victims in British Fiction* (Univ. Press of Kentucky, 1988), Toni Reed exposes the essentially patriarchal assumptions underlying British fiction. Reed applies historical and psychoanalytic criticism to fictions about the archetypal figure of the supernaturally endowed demon-lover: nineteenth-century works such as *Dracula* (1897) and *Wuthering Heights* (1847), and modern stories such as Elizabeth Bowen's "The Demon Lover."

7-49. Grossvogel, David I. **Mystery and Its Fictions: From Oedipus to Agatha Christie**. Johns Hopkins Univ. Press, 1979.
In this book, which has little to do with mystery or detective fiction, Grossvogel undertakes close textual analyses of selected "metaphysical mysteries": modern

fictions that "convey a sense of the mystery rather than its analysis." Among these mysteries are Poe's "The Purloined Letter," Kafka's *The Trial* and several short stories by Jorge Luis Borges. Grossvogel seems unaware of a great deal of modern crime fiction, but this does not detract from his book's value to students of modern horror fiction, for it is filled with insights relevant to exponents of the open-ended horror story: writers, such as Steve Rasnic Tem and M. John Harrison, who seek to evoke metaphysical anxiety by turning the reading of their fiction into an encounter with the ineffable. Bibliography, index.

7-50. Hughes, Winifred. **The Maniac in the Cellar: Sensation Novels of the 1860s**. Princeton Univ. Press, 1980.
As lurid and formulaic as their Gothic and Romantic antecedents, the sensation novels dominated the British literary scene during the 1860s. These melodramatic, densely plotted fusions of realism and romanticism (but not Gothic supernaturalism) evolved from the tales of terror published in *Blackwood's Edinburgh Magazine* in the 1820s and 1830s and attained their apotheosis in the novels of Wilkie Collins. In this well-written survey, Hughes exposes the inherently subversive nature of works by Collins and other Victorian writers. Although now of minor importance, the sensation genre remains significant as a bridge between the British Gothic and the English ghost story of Sheridan Le Fanu and others. Notes, bibliography, index. For more on the sensation novel, see chapter 8 of Punter [7-10]. A comprehensive summary of precursors can be found in J. M. S. Tompkins's important survey *The Popular Novel in England, 1770–1800* (Constable, 1932). Finally, two guides to literature on Collins's works are *Wilkie Collins: A Critical Survey of His Prose Fiction with a Bibliography* by R. V. Andrew (Garland, 1979) and *Wilkie Collins: An Annotated Bibliography, 1889–1976* by Kirk H. Beetz (Scarecrow, 1978).

***7-51.** Kawin, Bruce F. **The Mind of the Novel: Reflexive Fiction and the Ineffable**. Princeton Univ. Press, 1982.
Kawin brings an impressive arsenal of sophisticated analytical techniques to bear on a host of stories and novels in this attempt to discuss the literature of the ineffable: "that which, by definition, cannot be adequately verbalized." At the outset, he establishes a correspondence between these fictions and human consciousness. Out of this correspondence there arises in the fiction a sense of metaphysical mystery akin to that of supernatural fiction. Kawin considers horror "a major category within . . . the literature of the ineffable," and his interest in narrative devices for dealing with the unnameable leads him to such works as *Frankenstein, Dracula,* "The Turn of the Screw" and—most interestingly—Thomas Pynchon's *Gravity's Rainbow,* "one of the greatest and perhaps most optimistic horror stories of our time." The ineffable became cosmic in the works of Poe, Robert W. Chambers and Lovecraft, each of whom Kawin considers at length, and it remains so in the writings of their many successors. Although Kawin's long book is at times as hard to comprehend as the fictions he discusses, it is recommended to readers concerned with modern supernatural and horror fiction. Notes, selected bibliography, index.

***7-52.** Kayser, Wolfgang (Germany). **The Grotesque in Art and Literature**. Tr. by Ulrich Weisstein. Indiana Univ. Press, 1963.
In this synoptic study of art and literature from the end of the fifteenth century to the present, Kayser sets out to define and delineate the phenomenon of the grotesque. His end point is an interpretation that has become highly influential: in literature, the grotesque is an expression of man's sense of disorientation in an estranged world, a form in which writers use the absurd in an "attempt to invoke and subdue the demonic aspects of [that] world." Although Kayser emphasizes European writers—e.g., E. T. A. Hoffmann and Franz Kafka—and early twentieth-century German writers of *Schauerliteratur* (the literature of horror) such as H. W. Ewers and Gustav Meyrink, his observations are relevant to modern horror writers: Stephen King, Thomas Tessier and others. Notes, index. To balance Kayser's emphasis, see also *The Grotesque in English Literature* by Arthur Clayborough (Oxford Univ. Press, 1965) and the title essay in *The Grotesque: An American Genre and Other Essays* (Southern Illinois Press, 1962), in which editor William Van O'Connor surveys the American grotesque of Nathanael West, Nelson Algren and William Faulkner. See also Muller's book on Flannery O'Connor [8-79] and *The Ludicrous Demon: Aspects of the Grotesque in German Post-Romantic Prose* by Lee Byron Jennings (Univ. of California Press, 1963).

7-53. Sadoff, Dianne F. **Monsters of Affection: Dickens, Eliot & Brontë on Fatherhood**. Johns Hopkins Univ. Press, 1982.
This stimulating book explores the mythology of the father as symbol, character and ideological representative in the works of three mid-nineteenth-century writers. Sadoff uses Freud's notion of childhood fantasies (the primal scene, seduction and castration) as "metaphor[s] in literary criticism which facilitate interpretation of certain recurring problems in a novelist's work"—an approach that might fruitfully be applied to the works of several twentieth-century horror writers. And the resulting blend of feminist discourse, psychoanalytic interpretation and structuralist criticism yields acute observations on, for example, Charlotte Brontë's *Jane Eyre* (1847). Notes, index.

7-54. Senior, John. **The Way Down and Out: The Occult in Symbolist Literature**. Cornell Univ. Press, 1959.
In its day, occultism was "the world view of the romantic movement." Here Senior shows its influence on Edward Bulwer-Lytton, Henry James and the symbolist poets that are his focus. His first five chapters contain a wealth of anthropological, archeological, philosophical and historical background on the occult "sciences." Bibliography, index.

Vampires, Werewolves and Doppelgängers

7-55. Carter, Margaret L. **Shadow of a Shade: A Survey of Vampirism in Literature**. Gordon Press, 1975.
Carter's fine study of vampirism "as a literary phenomenon" in English-language fiction is less well known than it ought to be—probably because it's available in a book of 176 poorly reproduced typewritten pages that sells for $250. Carter begins with a chronological track of the vampire in eighteenth-century

German literature, pre-Romantic folklore and ballads, and Gothic novels through *Dracula*. She then shifts to a thematic organization, devoting chapters to psychic vampirism, the lamia, the afterlife as effected by magic, elemental and extradimensional (SF) vampires, the "explained vampire" and other topics. Carter considers the essence of the myth to be the vampire's simultaneous capacity for divine creation and diabolical destruction, a view that positions this Byronic hero/victim firmly in the Gothic tradition. But her survey ranges far beyond British Gothicism, encompassing Victorian ghost stories by Sheridan Le Fanu, F. Marion Crawford and others, and modern works by Basil Copper, Frank Belknap Long and Charles Beaumont, and other largely neglected authors. With its exhaustive annotated bibliography of vampire stories published prior to 1973, extensive notes, secondary bibliography and index, this work is an important addition to libraries on horror fiction. Carter's *Vampirism in Literature: A Critical Bibliography* (UMI Research Press 1989) largely supersedes the 1975 study but was received too late to annotate.

7-56. Copper, Basil (U.K.). **The Vampire in Legend, Fact, and Art**. Robert Hale, 1973.

7-57 ———. **The Werewolf in Legend, Fact, and Art**. Robert Hale, 1977.
Avowedly popular studies "not intended to be read as [works] of solemn scholarship," these books survey the high points in the histories of two great mythic figures of fiction, film, theater, legend and life. The most useful section in either book is Copper's survey of werewolf literature, although as he notes, "the whole of werewolf fiction of any importance can be contained within . . . the past hundred and fifty years and during that period relatively few works of lasting quality have been produced." And as elsewhere, these chapters are clotted with plot summaries. Throughout both books, Copper adopts an irritatingly condescending tone toward earlier writers such as John Polidori, Charles Robert Maturin and Bram Stoker, as though they should have been writing for a twentieth-century audience. Irrelevant asides, careless writing, pointless pseudo-fictive passages, poor judgment concerning emphasis on individual works and many factual errors further limit their value for libraries. Both contain bibliographies and indexes. Preferable popular introductions are those of Daniels [7-4] and King [7-6] and, for readers interested primarily in film, *Horror!* by Drake Douglas (Collier-Macmillan, 1969).

7-58. Frayling, Christopher (U.K.), ed. **The Vampyre: Lord Ruthven to Count Dracula**. Gollancz, 1978.
Much of this collection consists of intelligently chosen pre-twentieth-century vampire fiction with long scholarly headnotes. But students of the genre will want to consult Frayling's seventy-two-page introduction, which traces "the family tree of the card-carrying vampire of modern European fiction." Frayling organizes his introduction around two distinct subgenres that emerged during the nineteenth century: one focused on the Byronic figure derived from John Polidori's *The Vampyre* (1819), the other on the *femme fatale*. Within this frame he delineates and (through fictional excerpts) illustrates four archetypal vampire figures in European fiction. Frayling also identifies recurring motifs and structures in a valuable twenty-page tabulation of vampires in folklore, prose and

poetry from 1687 to 1913. A section entitled "Haemosexuality" reprints nonfiction material by Richard van Krafft-Ebing and Ernest Jones on the sexual aspect of the vampire's relationship to his victim. Annotated bibliography. Frayling's introduction is broader in coverage but less deep than the book-length studies by Twitchell [7-67] and Senf [7-63], and is more reliable (and far less discursive) than the volumes by Summers [7-64, 7-65]

7-59. Keppler, Carl F. **The Literature of the Second Self**. Univ. of Arizona Press, 1972.
Keppler, author of the novel *The Other* (Houghton Mifflin, 1964), here anatomizes the *doppelgänger* motif by viewing the second self from multiple angles: as pursuer, as tempter, as figure of horror, etc. Emphasizing the unified but dual nature of the double and the quality of uncanniness that both separates and bonds the first and second selves, Keppler advances the thesis that the second self is "an always contradictory being, a paradox of simultaneous outwardness and inwardness, of difference from and identity with the first self." Although he begins with pre-literary traditions, in which the second self appears as the Twin Brother, Keppler devotes most of this book to Romantic and post-Romantic European and American literature. He discusses works of terror by Edgar Allan Poe, Guy de Maupassant, E. T. A. Hoffman, H. H. Ewers, Nathaniel Hawthorne, Oscar Wilde and others. Bibliography of works cited, notes, index. For a sociologically oriented critical look at the double in Gothic and Victorian supernatural fiction see *The Divided Self: A Perspective on the Literature of the Victorians* by Masao Miyoshi (New York Univ. Press, 1969); for a psychological perspective on this literature, see *A Psychoanalytic Study of the Double in Literature* by Robert Rogers (Wayne State Univ. Press, 1970).

7-60. Miller, Karl. **Doubles: Studies in Literary History**. Oxford Univ. Press, 1985.
This long (468-page) study of *doppelgängers,* multiple selves and dualistic thought explores literature from the Romantic period to the present. Of special interest are Miller's acute commentaries on Stevenson's *Strange Case of Dr. Jekyll and Mr. Hyde,* Wilde's *Picture of Dorian Gray,* Henry James's "The Jolly Corner" and Poe's stories "William Wilson" and "The Unparalleled Adventures of One Hans Pfaall." In these and other discussions of the "dynamic metaphor" of the second self, Miller integrates psychological speculation, biographical reportage and textual criticism. In spite of his concentration on literary texts, Miller also recounts personal experiences of duality, mostly by individuals he interviewed. Although his book is flawed in minor ways—imprecise use of terminology, a lack of historical background on some subjects and occasional flippancy—its protean scope and acute insights justify a recommendation as a complement to Keppler's introductory book [7-59]. Notes, index.

7-61. Otten, Charlotte F., ed. **A Lycanthropy Reader: Werewolves in Western Culture**. Syracuse Univ. Press, 1986.
Easily the best sourcebook on the werewolf *outside* literature, this collection reprints documents from the ancient world, the Middle Ages, the Renaissance and the modern world. In her preliminary essay, Otten first clarifies the important distinction between *werewolf,* "a non-medical term for a fantasy or criminal

state," and *lycanthrope*, "a professional term for a pathological condition." She then sketches the entire history of lycanthropy as a medical, social and metaphysical issue. There follow sections on Medical Cases, Diagnoses, Descriptions; Trial Records, Historical Accounts, Sightings; Philosophical and Theological Approaches to Metamorphosis; Critical Essays on Lycanthropy; Myths and Legends; Allegory, each prefaced by an authoritative introduction. In the last section, Otten reprints and comments upon Clemence Housman's classic nineteenth-century allegory *The Were-Wolf* (1896). An essential resource for students of werewolves as well as of lycanthropes. Illustrated. Bibliography, index.

***7-62.** Riccardo, Martin V. **Vampires Unearthed: The Complete Multi-Media Vampire and Dracula Bibliography**. Garland, 1983.
This comprehensive, fully cross-indexed bibliography and filmography updates Glut's *The Dracula Book* [8-110] and extends its coverage to "the vampire mythos" in the mass media through 1982. Organized into twenty-five sections, each with an insightful (though brief) introduction, this book contains unannotated bibliographic data on anthologies, editions of *Dracula*, stand-alone and series novels, short stories, poetry, songs, etc., as well as appearances of vampires in children's literature, comics, and on stage, screen and television. Riccardo also includes lists of secondary literature about vampires in fact and fiction, lists of alternate and foreign film titles, and indexes of authors and editors and of subjects and characters.

***7-63.** Senf, Carol A. **The Vampire in Nineteenth-Century English Literature**. Bowling Green State Univ. Popular Press, 1988.
Senf begins this book on the literary vampire with the campy, oddly attractive figure that stalks through twentieth-century fiction and film. But her real subject is the motif as used by nineteenth-century writers to explore questions of human identity and sexual roles. After describing the origins and characteristics of tales of overt vampirism (e.g., *Varney the Vampyre* and *Dracula*), Senf turns to works in which vampirism is ambiguous (e.g., Bram Stoker's *The Lady of the Shroud*) or solely metaphoric (e.g., Charlotte Brontë's *Jane Eyre*). At each stage, she treats a few major works in ways that carefully connect the ever-changing vampire motif to broad developments in English fiction during the nineteenth century. The most important such development was, of course, the rise of realistic treatments of setting and character. And the most important part of Senf's book is her explication of aspects of Gothicism in works that manifest this development: from Emily Brontë's *Wuthering Heights* (1847), which preserves the Gothic awe and mystery of the vampire while leaving its nature uncertain; to Charles Dickens's *Bleak House* (1853), which uses the vampire as a social metaphor for exploitation; to even so realistic a novel as George Eliot's *Middlemarch* (1871–72). In a final chapter, Senf speculates that changes in the literary vampire during the nineteenth and twentieth centuries were driven by attitudinal changes toward women and sexual identity. Although a bit repetitive, this well-researched study is recommended for its breadth, acuity and persuasiveness. Bibliography, extensive notes, but no index. Compare to Twitchell [7-67] and the discussion of supernaturalism in nineteenth-century English fiction by Kiely [7-29].

7-64. Summers, Montague (U.K.). **The Vampire, His Kith and Kin**. Kegan Paul, 1928.

7-65. ———. **The Vampire in Europe**. Kegan Paul, 1929.

7-66. ———. **The Werewolf**. Kegan Paul, 1933.
As Frank's fine bibliographical portrait [7-84] shows, Montague Summers was a profoundly strange man. These erudite, purportedly factual books read at times as though written by a crazed antiquarian anthropologist whose skepticism had been blown away by one too many case histories. Still, they offer a wealth of obscure information to readers who can get past Summers's fervid prose style, affinity for archaisms and apparent credulity. His vampire books should be considered as one. The exhaustively researched *The Vampire, His Kith and Kin*, which contains Summers's "philosophy of vampirism," focuses on the basis of the legend and includes case histories, ancient accounts, a survey of the habits of the vampire, a long chapter on Victorian and Gothic vampire tales, a bibliography and an index. Its sequel, based on on-site investigations by the author, recounts incidents of vampirism throughout the world. Index. *The Werewolf*, although good on the cultural background of the legend of the lycanthrope, is less readable, less discriminating and, in its "Note on the Werewolf in Literature," less comprehensive than the vampire books. Bibliography, index, appendix on witch ointments. For sources on werewolfery, see Otten [7-61]. Summers also wrote three books on the demonological roots of Gothic horror, the most authoritative of which is *The History of Witchcraft and Demonology* (Knopf, 1926).

7-67. Twitchell, James B. **The Living Dead: A Study of the Vampire in Romantic Literature**. Duke Univ. Press, 1981.
Twitchell's invigorating look at nineteenth-century English Romantic prose and poetry treats the vampire mythopoetically, as "an analogy for aberrant energy transfer" in interpersonal relationships. Following a survey of origins in early folklore and elaborations in pre-Romantic art and literature, Twitchell discusses male and female vampires in poetry by Samuel Taylor Coleridge, John Keats, Edgar Allan Poe, Lord Byron and Percy Bysshe Shelley; and in prose by Charlotte and Emily Brontë, John Polidori, Byron, Poe and Sheridan Le Fanu. He is best on *Dracula* and *Varney the Vampyre*—a useful appendix summarizes the plot of *Varney*, eliminating the need for most to read it. But Twitchell seems to lose control of his main metaphor. "Vampirism as energy dynamic" is so vague a concept that it admits problematical works in which the vampire is (at best) marginal. Twitchell's further abstraction of vampirism to the relationship between the artist, text and reader projects his coverage to such works as William Wordsworth's "Resolution and Independence" and Henry James's *The Sacred Fount*. An epilogue generalizes the metaphor further still, to D. H. Lawrence's *The Rainbow* and *Women in Love*. Ultimately, this increasingly diffuse focus leads to the untenable inference that *all* nineteenth-century poetry and prose is about vampires. (Twitchell cursorily dismisses virtually all twentieth-century vampire fiction.) So although his book offers stimulating insights into the changing nature of Romanticism during the early nineteenth century, as a study of the vampire it is less useful than Waller [7-68] or Senf [7-63]. Index.

***7-68.** Waller, Gregory A. **The Living and the Undead: From Stoker's *Dracula* to Romero's *Dawn of the Dead*.** Univ. of Illinois Press, 1986.
In this unique genre study, Waller explicates "the play of repetition and difference" in myriad versions of *Dracula* on stage and television and in film and fiction. His foundational chapter on Stoker's novel concentrates on its ideological structure, Freudian underpinnings and relationship to other texts of the period. He then addresses the "countless retellings of this story that have appeared in the last eighty-five years" in four chapters on film adaptations and a long chapter on American vampire novels. The latter includes King's *'Salem's Lot* (1976), Robert R. McCammon's vampire epic *They Thirst* (1981) and Richard Matheson's *I Am Legend* (1954), which Waller sees as the progenitor of George Romero's film *Night of the Living Dead* (1968). Throughout this fascinating book Waller develops several key cultural themes: the formation and preservation of community, the possibility of heroic action, the nature and function of violence. He also raises issues related to the nature of genre: self-consciousness versus uncritical texts, strategies of closure and repetition, etc. Unlike Twitchell [7-67], Waller treats at length twentieth-century renderings of the vampire story. Essential for anyone interested in modern horror or cultural studies. Illustrated, notes, index. Also annotated as [9-50].

Other Studies

***7-69.** Büssing, Sabine. **Aliens in the Home: The Child in Horror Fiction.** Greenwood, 1987.
Not only is this the first extended work on the motif of the child in horror fiction, it is also one of the few critical books to consider modern novels and stories. Concentrating on the function and significance of the child from the post-Gothic era to the present, Büssing treats generational conflicts, brother/sister doubling, social contexts, images of the beast and the doll, connections to mainstream literature of the New American Gothic school and to the Theater of the Absurd, and other topics. Her most interesting speculation is that children perform functions in contemporary horror fiction that in the Gothic novel were accomplished by adults. The scope of this fine book is suggested by the spectrum of writers it considers: Stephen King, Guy de Maupassant, John Wyndham, John Saul, Brian Lumley, Henry James, D. H. Lawrence, etc. Still, there are omissions: e.g., Bernard Taylor and Ramsey Campbell. Büssing also treats a few non-English-language works, plays and poems and, in an appendix, child-monsters and child-victims in horror films. Notes, primary and secondary bibliography, index.

7-70. Fleenor, Juliann E., ed. **The Female Gothic.** Eden Press, 1983.
The term "Female Gothic" was coined by Ellen Moers in her influential 1976 book *Literary Women*, but the form has existed since the late eighteenth century. Moers showed how women writers expressed via Gothic structures and conventions otherwise inarticulable perceptions of feminine reality. This collection of essays extends this idea to the whole subgenre of works from the late eighteenth-century Gothics to Ann Radcliffe to twentieth-century Harlequin Romances. In four sections—Mystique, Madness, Monsters and Maternity—feminist critics explore aspects of the Female Gothic: e.g., its implicit dread of female sexuality, its

reflection of the dominant patriarchal paradigm, its rendering of the primal identity conflict between daughter and "all-powerful, devouring mother." Readers should note particularly the essays on the Gothic heroine; on connections between setting and sexuality in *The Monk, Mysteries of Udolpho* and *Jane Eyre*; on the autobiographical use of Gothic by Charlotte Perkins Gilman in "The Yellow Wallpaper" and other stories; and on the transformation of nineteenth-century Gothic characteristics in twentieth-century works by Isak Dinesen, Flannery O'Connor and Margaret Atwood. Throughout these essays, nearly all of which are accessible to the nonspecialist, one finds provocative, divergent speculations on why the Female Gothic was (and remains) so popular with women readers. Recommended to libraries of popular culture and Gothic studies. Notes.

***7-71.** Heller, Terry. **The Delights of Terror: An Aesthetics of the Tale of Terror**. Univ. of Illinois Press, 1987.
This theoretical study of the mechanisms by which authors induce fear in their readers is based on the reader-response theories of Wolfgang Iser, psychoanalytic ideas of Jacques Lacan and descriptive poetics of Todorov [7-76]. Heller introduces a useful typology of terror texts—e.g., the uncanny horror story, the horror thriller, the terror fantasy—then within each category analyzes representative works, ranging from H. P. Lovecraft's *At the Mountains of Madness* (1931) to William Faulkner's *Sanctuary* (1931) and Jerzy Kosinski's *The Painted Bird* (1972). By clarifying the relationship between implied reader, protagonist and real reader, Heller shows how authors control the protective aesthetic distance between the (real) reader and the text—a distance vital to the evocation of terror. Somehow, Heller manages to come up with original insights even on fictions one would think have been analyzed to death: Poe's "Ligeia" and "The Fall of the House of Usher" and James's "The Turn of the Screw" (1898). Moreover, his syncretic view of horror fiction indirectly sheds light on works of modern writers (not considered here) such as Robert Aickman, Ramsey Campbell and Dennis Etchison, whose literary strategies open radical gaps in the experience of their readers. Essential for even the smallest collections about the tale of terror. Primary and secondary bibliographies, index.

***7-72.** Jackson, Rosemary. **Fantasy: The Literature of Subversion**. Methuen, 1981.
Rosemary Jackson expands Tzvetan Todorov's structuralist approach to the fantastic [7-76] by considering psychological, social and political aspects of the form. Her original, penetrating application of psychoanalysis to this "literature of desire" in the first, theoretical part of her book is based on theories of Freud and Jacques Lacan. In the second part she treats individual stories and novels, including tales of horror and the supernatural by Lovecraft, Hoffmann, Poe and Wells, as well as fantastic works by Kafka, Dickens, Emily Brontë, Conrad and Dostoyevsky. Jackson's chapter on Gothic fiction explicates the "rhetoric of fantasy" these works established for future fictions. Although her prose is sometimes a bit convoluted and abstract and she devotes fewer than twenty pages to twentieth-century literature, Jackson's book is essential for students of dark fantasy. Notes, bibliography, subject and name indexes. Also annotated as [F7-25].

7-73. Riffaterre, Hermine, ed. **The Occult in Language and Literature**. New York Literary Forum, 1980.
This special volume of *New York Literary Forum* (vol. 4) draws together a disparate group of essays on the occult as a traditional supernatural motif and as a dimension of language. Writers examined range from Apuleius to Victor Hugo. Most useful are the many essays on occult drama and poetry—notably "Ghosts, Spirits, and Force: Samuel Taylor Coleridge" by Anya Taylor. The epilogue is a one-act play "portraying man in the clutches of unseen diabolic forces." This collection complements Messent [7-8], which focuses on fiction. Illustrated. Bibliography, index.

7-74. Siebers, Tobin. **The Romantic Fantastic**. Cornell Univ. Press, 1984.
In this successor to his study of superstition, *The Mirror of Medusa* (Univ. of California Press, 1983), Siebers uses anthropology, history, aesthetics and textual analysis in his search for the literary strategies by which Romantic fantastics dealt with the problem of belief in an age where superstition still carried the Enlightenment stigma of untruth. He develops his thesis—that "the Romantic fantastic . . . reveals more boldly than other literary forms the role of superstition in all artistic representation"—in analyses of stories by Baudelaire, E. T. A. Hoffmann, Nikolai Gogol, Guy de Maupassant, Prosper Merimée and others. His discourse with prior work by Freud, Michel Foucault, Tzvetan Todorov and Paul de Man yields valuable insights on the role of violence in fantastic literature; the use of ironic, allegorical and symbolic language in supernatural fiction; the reasons for Hawthorne's avoidance of the fantastic; and the myth of the mad Romantic artist. Index. Readers interested in the latter topic should consult *The Romantic Agony* by Mario Praz (reprinted 1978), which presents the Romantic artist as characteristic of the period's focus on attaining sexual pleasure through pain.

7-75. Spacks, Patricia Myer. **The Insistence of Horror: Aspects of the Supernatural in Eighteenth Century Poetry**. Harvard Univ. Press, 1962.
Spacks's examination of supernaturalism in eighteenth-century poetry is likely to revise her readers' preconceptions about that century's attitude toward the ghostly and ghastly. Her long chapter on the intellectual and religious bases of eighteenth-century beliefs about the supernatural will be of interest also to students of the fiction of that era. Unfortunately, Spacks does not consider the macabre verse that writers of Gothic fiction such as Matthew Gregory Lewis interpolated into their novels. Extensive bibliography, notes, index. Somewhat narrower in focus but also useful is Sukumar Dutt's *The Supernatural in English Romantic Poetry, 1780–1830* (Folcroft Library, 1972). The best and most comprehensive treatment of supernatural poetry is Steve Eng's trail-blazing essay "Supernatural Verse in English" in *Horror Literature* [6-33].

***7-76.** Todorov, Tzvetan (France).**The Fantastic: A Structural Approach to a Literary Genre**. Cornell Univ. Press, 1975. Tr. by Richard Howard of *Introduction à la littérature fantastique*, 1970.
Todorov's definition of the fantastic in literature—"that hesitation experienced by a person who knows only the laws of nature, confronting an apparently supernatural event"—admits only a handful of works. But the value of this book

for students of supernatural horror is the frame Todorov erects around this definition: the relationship of the fantastic to neighboring genres such as poetry, allegory, the uncanny and the marvelous and to allied subgenres. Also valuable is the clear, coherent theory of genres that opens the book. Todorov's approach to literary texts as systems leads to insights both general and specific about three dimensions of the fantastic: verbal, syntactical and semantic (i.e., thematic). Todorov develops the latter aspect into a typology of themes, either "themes of the self" (the relationship between the psychic and physical worlds) or "themes of the other" (the relationship between consciousness and sexual desire). What is most remarkable about this stimulating and challenging book is that, except for the odd paragraph, it is lucid and accessible. Essential for all serious readers and scholars in the field. Bibliography, index. A briefer exposition of Todorov's ideas can be found in his "The Fantastic in Fiction," tr. by Vivienne Mylne (*Twentieth Century Studies* 3 [1970]: 76–92) and in a clear introduction to structuralism in his brief book *Introduction to Poetics*, tr. by Richard Howard (Univ. of Minnesota, 1981). For important extensions to Todorov's ideas see Jackson [7-72] and Heller [7-71]. Finally, note the critique of Todorov's work, Stanislaw Lem's "Todorov's Fantastic Theory of Literature," in *Microworlds: Writings on Science Fiction and Fantasy* [F7-29]. Also annotated as [F7-61].

7-77. Twitchell, James B. **Dreadful Pleasures: An Anatomy of Modern Horror**. Oxford Univ. Press, 1985.

Twitchell presents an interpretation of horror from eighteenth-century Romantic fiction to present-day schlock films in psychosexual terms—as "fables of adolescent identity" that "prepare the teenager for the anxieties of reproduction" by transmitting coded messages that detail "the 'do's' and 'don't's' of breeding, especially as they pertain to incest." The problem is Twitchell's determination to apply this interpretation to all "horror art." To do so he must summarily discard *all* modern prose horror fiction and nearly all modern films—the latter on the curious grounds either that they are not "real horror stories" [e.g., Alfred Hitchcock's *Psycho* (1960)] or that they are "art renditions" [e.g., Tod Browning's *Dracula* (1933)]. What's left Twitchell analyzes in long chapters on three major archetypes: the vampire, the "hulk with no name" (e.g., Frankenstein's monster) and the "transformation monster" (e.g., the Wolf Man). He is erudite and witty as he tracks these icons from their original appearances in prose through stage and early film incarnations to their final resting places in parodies and vacuous exploitation films. But the whole exercise is ultimately reductive; it ignores, for example, the deeper fear of death encoded in these icons. Extensive notes, select bibliography, index. Waller [7-68], though narrower in scope, is preferable. Also annotated as [9-16].

7-78. Williamson, J. N., ed. **How to Write Tales of Horror, Fantasy, & Science Fiction**. Writer's Digest Books, 1987.

These twenty-eight essays range from theoretical disquisitions on the function of fantasy to solid chapters on the use of elements of fiction, and from autobiographical reminiscences to practical articles on manuscript preparation. Of special interest are Williamson's appendix of publishers of genre fictions, inventories of favorite works by critics and writers, and a huge recommended reading list. Unfortunately, a number of superficial, platitude-laden essays significantly depreciate the value of this collection. Prospective writers of horror fiction are advised to turn instead to T. E. D. Klein's *Raising Goosebumps for Fun and Profit* (Footsteps Press, 1988). Current information about book and magazine markets appears several times a year in *Science Fiction Chronicle* (see [11-40]).

7-79. Wilson, Colin (U.K.). **The Strength to Dream: Literature and the Imagination**. Houghton Mifflin, 1962.
Wilson, a British literary critic and philosopher, was stimulated to write this exploration of "the problem of imagination" by his accidental discovery at a friend's farm of H. P. Lovecraft's *The Outsider and Others.* Wilson's book infuriated Lovecraft's fans—not surprisingly: he characterizes Lovecraft as "a sick recluse" and "a very bad writer" whose closest relation is "with Peter Kürten, the Düsseldorf murderer." Wilson later recanted this description in the introduction to his own Cthulhu Mythos novel *The Mind Parasites* (Arkham House, 1967)—which he followed with a second, even better Mythos novel, *The Philosopher's Stone* (Crown, 1969). This book, however, explores in some depth "the horror story and the type of imagination that produces it" and deserves attention not so much for its commentary on Lovecraft as for its concern with values, which anticipates John Gardner's celebrated *On Moral Fiction* (Basic Books, 1978), and for its discussions of the ghostly fiction of E. T. A. Hoffmann, Nikolai Gogol, Sheridan Le Fanu, M. R. James and others. Index. Also annotated as [F7-63].

7-80. Wilt, Judith. **Ghosts of the Gothic: Austen, Eliot, and Lawrence**. Princeton Univ. Press, 1980.
Judith Wilt argues that eighteenth-century British Gothicism provided later "subtle architects of the great 'serious' tradition of English fiction" (Jane Austen, George Eliot and D. H. Lawrence) with "tools" of imagery, plot and narrative strategy which they used to represent the subconscious and to reassert the primacy of community. For Wilt, the purpose of Gothicism is essentially religious: "to affirm an ontology, a structure of being governed by mystery." Unfortunately, her explanation of this interesting thesis is wildly uneven. Her early chapters on classic Gothic novels are marked by wit, clarity and insight. But the heart of her book—discussions of Austen's *Northanger Abbey* and *Emma,* Eliot's *Middlemarch* and Lawrence's *Sons and Lovers* (and other novels)—is loaded with imprecise, unsupported assertions in muddied, prolix prose. Wilt has a propensity for weird geometrical metaphors that obscure meaning more often than they clarify it, and she often lapses into an impressionistic style that leads her to misrepresent some aspects of works she discusses. But ultimately, this well-intentioned study founders on a conception of the Gothic that is so all-encompassing and malleable as to be almost useless. Illustrated. Brief index. Readers can find better treatments of the Gothic influence on Jane Austen in Michael Sadleir's *The Northanger Novels: A Footnote to Jane Austen* (English Association Pamphlet Number 68, November 1927) and Daniel Cottom's *The Civilized Imagination: A Study of Ann Radcliffe, Jane Austen, and Sir Walter Scott* (Cambridge Univ. Press, 1985). The importance of the *absence* of the monster in works of this period is demonstrated by George Levine in *The Realistic Imagination: English Fiction from Frankenstein to Lady Chatterley* (Univ. of Chicago Press, 1981).

Bibliographic Aids

7-81. Fisher, Benjamin Franklin IV. **The Gothic's Gothic: Study Aids to the Tradition of the Tale of Terror**. Garland, 1988.

Fisher has organized this bibliography into sections on author studies and special topics. He aspires to comprehensiveness, including—in addition to major and minor British, American and Continental Gothic novels—drama, the "Newgate" and sensation novels, SF, film, anti-Gothicism and parodies, architecture and many other byways of Gothicism. And he admits a multitude of items not found in other bibliographies: essays, fictional texts, biographies, a huge number of doctoral dissertations, early press notices and reviews in literary magazines. But many of these seem irrelevant even under a broad definition of Gothic. And this is but one of the serious flaws of this book. Although published in 1988, it includes few entries after 1977. Fisher justifies this feature by citing the bibliographies Gary W. Crawford began publishing in *Gothic* [11-36] in the late 1970s; but the last such bibliography covered 1980. So the 80s—a major decade for Gothic criticism—is missing from Fisher's work. Finding one's way through what is included is made difficult by Fisher's propensity for chronological ordering, and his choppy annotations are too brief to be of real value. Finally—and, considering Fisher's claim to inclusiveness, most peculiarly—he simply omits several major works by Railo [7-32], Malin [7-42] and many other critics. Indexes of critics; (primary) titles; authors, artists and subjects. This bibliography serves at best as a supplement to Frank's more comprehensive and better annotated *Guide* [7-82].

***7-82.** Frank, Frederick S. **Guide to the Gothic: An Annotated Bibliography of Criticism**. Scarecrow, 1984.

7-83. ———. **Gothic Fiction: A Master List of Twentieth Century Criticism and Research**. Meckler, 1988.

Far broader in scope than McNutt's earlier guide [6-15], Frank's book embraces post-1900 criticism of Gothicism from around the world. Organized by nationality, author and subject area into 126 sections, it covers secondary works published through 1982. Many of the twenty-one topic sections are especially useful: e.g., those on Continental Gothics, criticism of horror films, "Death by Spontaneous Combustion"; "The Gothic Revival in Architecture, Gardening, and Landscape Design"; and "Special Collections of Gothic Literature." Although this book is not truly comprehensive (especially on American Gothic), its excellent annotations, which truly enable the reader to decide which references are worth tracking down, make this the guide to buy if you're buying only one. List of journals and collections referenced; indexes of critics and of authors, artists and actors. Like the *Guide*, Frank's 1988 checklist of about 2,500 secondary works published through 1987 is useful for its international scope and coverage of special subject areas, themes and motifs, and film. But it is not annotated and therefore is recommended only to completists or libraries that must have bibliographic information on the few hundred additional items Frank has added to the more recent volume. On some topics (e.g., American writers), its usefulness is further limited by the unfortunate decision to lump together some writers who in the *Guide* were accorded separate sections. Introduction, indexes of critics and of authors and artists. Also annotated as [6-12, 6-13].

7-84. ———. **Montague Summers: A Bibliographical Portrait**. Scarecrow, 1988.
Summers was one of the first and certainly the most controversial partisan for Gothic fiction. In addition to his writings on Gothicism, this tribute covers his contributions to the study of theology, demonology and Restoration drama. Prefaced by a memoir of Summers and essays evaluating (favorably) his scholarship—including an ardent tribute by Devendra P. Varma, considered by many to be Summers's literary heir—the heart of this book consists of excerpts from Summers's bibliographies, letters and essays, and a complete annotated bibliography of writings by and about him. Recommended for large libraries and anybody who is curious about this most enigmatic and eccentric scholar. Chronology, indexes of names and of titles.

***7-85.** Spector, Robert Donald. **The English Gothic: A Bibliographic Guide to Writers from Horace Walpole to Mary Shelley**. Greenwood, 1984.
More than an annotated bibliography, Spector has written extended critical essays on a vast but carefully selected range of secondary literature (excluding unpublished dissertations) pertaining to the eighteenth-century British Gothic. The introduction grapples with the problem of defining the Gothic and summarizes the contributions of major writers. Following a chapter on general histories and other bibliographies, Spector pairs significant authors—Horace Walpole and Clara Reeve, Charlotte Smith and Ann Radcliffe, Matthew Gregory Lewis and William Beckford, Charles Robert Maturin and Mary Shelley—in chapters that include biographical sketches, early reviews of their works and extensive bibliographies (with in-depth evaluations) of relevant secondary literature. Blunt and opinionated, Spector's guide is invaluable for those new to Gothic studies. Readers should beware, however, of typos, a number of minor errors and mismatches between index and text. The many important writers and secondary works not included here are more briefly annotated in Frank [7-82].

7-86. Summers, Montague (U.K.). **A Gothic Bibliography**. Fortune Press, 1940.
Summers's vast bibliography of works from 1728 to 1916, a companion to his vast history of the British Gothic novel [7-33], is of limited value at best. Its long section of author's works omits important writers such as Sheridan Le Fanu, and the subsequent title index is irregularly annotated and lists innumerable works that are in no way Gothic. Addenda, list of circulating libraries. Frank's study [7-84] provides fascinating background on Summers's curious bibliographical practices. Better organized (though less complete) alternatives to Summers's bibliography are Frank's *The First Gothics* [6-14], Tracy's *The Gothic Novel: 1790–1830* [6-17]. Jakob Brauchli's *Der englische Schauerroman um 1800 un der Berücksichtigung der untbekannten Bücher* (Garland, 1979) and Maurice Lévy's bibliography in *Le Roman "gothique" anglais, 1764–1824* (Université de Toulouse, 1968). Brauchli's most useful lists are reprinted in Vol. 1 of Harwell [7-26], and Lévy's chronological bibliography, alphabetical list of titles and author index appear in Vol. II.

8

Author Studies

Michael A. Morrison

"Literary criticism"? Images of desiccation creak to mind: dry leaves aflutter in the carrel, dry bones aclacking in the charnel houses of Western literature, where the only good writer is a dead one.
The common reader shudders.

—Frances Taliaferro, Harper's, *December 1979*

I fear I am but a little way on the road I would travel.

—Count Dracula to Jonathan Harker in Dracula *(1897) by Bram Stoker*

Researching this chapter was an exasperating experience. Rather naively, I set out to try to find at least one worthwhile critical work on every major (and many an interesting minor) writer of supernatural and horror fiction. Bibliographical excavation turned up a promising working list of well over 200 titles. But as I read these books, I realized that my quest was doomed. Over half I have either jettisoned or relegated to mere mention in annotations of other books. Many turned out to be solely biographical, others fannish puff jobs, still others highly specialized jargon-laden works on overanalyzed fictions such as *Frankenstein* and "The Turn of the Screw." So if nothing else, this chapter shows striking imbalances in the critical literature on individual authors of supernatural and horror fiction.

I hope that readers who have not already done so will read the introduction to chapter 7. Nearly everything I say there—about the structure of these annotations and about criticism of this field—pertains to this chapter as well. This is especially true of the acknowledgments: this chapter incorporates suggestions and advice from a number of experts.

What Is and Isn't in This Chapter—and Why

Space limitations and uneven coverage in the secondary literature have resulted in a chapter that emphasizes American and British authors whose works appeared after the luminous date of 1764 when Horace Walpole presented the world with *The Castle of Otranto.* Commentary on writers from Germany, France, Canada and elsewhere can be found in many books annotated in chapter 7 and in Sullivan [6-31] and Bleiler [6-20]; further sources are annotated in the bibliographies by Frank [7-82, 7-83].

Not *every* writer who contributed to the literature of supernatural horror is present here; that's what encyclopedias are for. Indeed, many writers whose works I cherish are not here because their impact seems comparatively minimal or has not been clarified in books devoted to them (e.g., Colin Wilson, Theodore Sturgeon, Sir Arthur Conan Doyle, Rudyard Kipling). Several others aren't included simply because I could not find even a single book on their work that I could recommend (e.g., E. F. and A. C. Benson, Robert Aickman, John Buchan, Edward Bulwer-Lytton). A further imbalance has resulted from the policy of including only authors about whom full-length books have been written.

Happily, many writers excluded from the entries in this chapter are included in the various histories, surveys and topic studies in chapter 7. In order to provide readers with some guidance to criticism on these authors, I have appended to this introduction a table of *selected* books from chapter 7 that contain substantive commentary and/or useful bibliographies on their works. Not *every* book that mentions these writers is referenced; that's what indexes are for. This table will also guide readers to discussions of a few writers (e.g., Horace Walpole and Ann Radcliffe) whose importance *outside of their subgenre* (e.g., the British Gothic novel) seems best appreciated in the context of a critical survey; I have relegated writers to this limbo only if excellent bibliographic guides to their fiction exists.

Readers interested in any of these writers should consult the essays in Bleiler's excellent collection [6-20] and Magill's survey [6-24]. Bleiler's book, along with Sullivan's encyclopedia [6-31] and the bibliographies by Frank [7-82] and (on the British Gothic novel) by Spector [7-85] were enormously valuable in the preparation of this chapter.

Sadly, even these valuable reference works give short shrift to important modern writers: Dennis Etchison, Peter Straub, Clive Barker, T. E. D. Klein, Karl Edward Wagner, Lisa Tuttle, Charles L. Grant, Bernard Taylor and many more. One can find interviews with many of these writers in Douglas E. Winter's collection [8-112], essays on some in Darrell Schweitzer's collections on modern horror fiction [7-13, 7-14] and insights into a few of their works in Stephen King's *Danse Macabre* [7-6]. But that's about it.

King, of course, has recently been subjected to endless critical analysis. Which brings me to the other extreme: King, H. P. Lovecraft, Edgar Allan Poe, Mary Shelley and Bram Stoker—writers about whom there is so *much* criticism that I have had to break their sections into subsections such as *Biographical and Bibliographical Studies, Essay Collections* and *Full-Length Studies,* or individual works. Within these subsections I have used the various levels of reference described in the introduction to chapter 7 to suggest the relative value of books I did not eliminate altogether.

Yet another group of writers requires comment. Most critics do not associate Charles Dickens, William Faulkner, Flannery O'Connor, Nathaniel Hawthorne and Sir Walter Scott with supernatural terror. But each made important contributions to this literature, and each belongs in this chapter. My annotations on these "cross-over" writers, however, *exclude* an enormous amount of fine critical work that deemphasizes or ignores those contributions. And in at least one case, Herman Melville, I could find no critical work that satisfactorily treated this dimension of his fiction.

Similarly, my annotations on Robert Louis Stevenson, Henry James, Edgar Allan Poe, Washington Irving and L. P. Hartley ignore nearly all books that concentrate on their nonsupernatural, nonhorrific work—although in a few cases I had to broaden this simple exclusionary gambit. In any case, readers need look no further than a nearby university library to find excellent bibliographic guides to scholarship on these writers.

For each writer who made it through all this into the present chapter, I have (subject to availability!) annotated at least one biography (preferably critical), at least one bibliography and those critical books that seemed to me substantive, unique and apprehensible. Other meritorious books I have relegated to brief mentions within annotations. And, as in chapter 7, a few sections include remarks on an essay or two that treat significant aspects of the writer's works.

Finally, readers interested in writers who wrote horror fiction but whose work is predominantly fantasy (e.g., Charles Williams, H. Rider Haggard, G. K. Chesterton, David Lindsay, Sax Rohmer, Franz Kafka, James Branch Cabell, E. H. Visak, C. S. Lewis, E. T. A. Hoffmann, Lafcadio Hearn, Jonathan Carroll, Robert E. Howard, John Collier, Ray Bradbury) should consult the companion fantasy guide.

A Final Thought

During the writing of these annotations, I found myself jotting many vexed notes about the lack of substantive critical attention to this author or the excess of writing on that one. Readers who pursue my suggestions will find that even annotated writers often want for criticism of their supernatural fiction. Examples from all eras abound: M. R. James, L. P. Hartley, William Hope Hodgson, Ramsey Campbell, Algernon Blackwood, Vernon Lee, Fritz Leiber, Fitz-James O'Brien. The list goes on.

None of this is intended to disparage the fine critical work that *has* been done on writers of horror fiction; readers will find in the books annotated in this chapter a wealth of fascinating scholarship. It is, rather, to plead for a greater diffusion of attention: for perhaps one less book on *Frankenstein* or the tales of Edgar Allan Poe and one more on the ghostly tales of M. R. James, the short stories of Dennis Etchison, the prose poems of Clark Ashton Smith, or others of the myriad unexplored works that constitute the literature of fear.

A Guide to Author Studies in Chapter 7

Author	**Reference(s)**
Aickman, Robert	Sullivan [7-15]
Beckford, William	Kiely [7-29]; Day [7-17]; Punter [7-10]; Birkhead [7-2]; Varma [7-34]
Benson, E. F.	Sullivan [7-15]; Briggs [7-3]; Carter [7-55]

Blatty, William Peter	King [7-6]; Büssing [7-69]
Bowen, Elizabeth	Reed, noted in [7-48]; Briggs [7-3]
Brontë, Charlotte	Sadoff [7-53]; Heilman, in Harwell [7-26]; Gilbert and Gubar [7-48]
Brontë, Emily	Kiely [7-29]; Sedgwick [7-19]; Bataille [7-47]; Gilbert and Gubar [7-48]
Bulwer-Lytton, Edward	Bayer-Berenbaum [7-16]; Senior [7-54]; Carter [7-23]; Briggs [7-3]; Punter [7-10]
Chambers, Robert W.	Lovecraft [7-7]; Kawin [7-51]; Sullivan [7-15]; Punter [7-10]
Collins, Wilkie	Auerbach [7-46] and works noted; Hughes [7-50]; Briggs [7-3]; Punter [7-10]
Conrad, Joseph	Day [7-17]; Jackson [7-72]; Wilt [7-80]
Doyle, Sir Arthur Conan	Day [7-17]; Punter [7-10]
Gilman, Charlotte Perkins	Fleenor [7-70]; Briggs [7-3]
Godwin, William	Day [7-17]; Birkhead [7-2]; Jackson [7-72]; Punter [7-10]; Varma [7-34]
Harvey, W. F.	Sullivan [7-15]; Penzoldt [7-9]
Hoffmann, E. T. A.	Kayser [7-52]; Keppler [7-59]; Jackson [7-72]; Siebers [7-74]; Wilson [7-79]
Hogg, James	Day [7-17]; Kiely [7-29]; Punter [7-10]; Wilt [7-80]
Jacobs, W. F.	Briggs [7-3]
Kafka, Franz	Hyde, in Kayser [7-52]; Thompson [7-20]; Grossvogel [7-49]; Jackson [7-72]
Kipling, Rudyard	Briggs [7-3]; Jackson [7-72]; Penzoldt [7-9]
Malden, R. H.	Sullivan [7-15]
Matheson, Richard	King [7-6]; Waller [7-68]; Büssing [7-69]
Maupassant, Guy de	Keppler [7-59]; Büssing [7-69]; Siebers [7-74]
Melville, Herman	Fiedler [7-36]; Kerr [7-38]; Levin [7-41]
Onions, Oliver	Sullivan [7-15]; Briggs [7-3]; Carter [7-55]
Peake, Mervyn	Punter [7-10]; Jackson [7-72]
Radcliffe, Ann	Carter [7-23]; Jarrett [7-28]; Napier [7-31]; Kiely [7-29]; Spector [7-85] (bib)
Reeve, Clara	Coleman [7-24]; Varma [7-34]; Spector [7-85] (bib)
Riddell, Mrs. J. H.	Briggs [7-3]
Shiel, M. P.	Lovecraft [7-7]
Straub, Peter	King [7-6]; Bosky, in Schweitzer [7-14]
Wakefield, H. R.	Sullivan [7-15]
Walpole, Horace	Varma [7-34]; MacAndrew [7-18]; Kiely [7-29]; Spector [7-85] (bib)
Wellman, Manly Wade	Schweitzer [7-13]
Wharton, Edith	Ringe [7-44]; Scarborough [7-12]
Wilde, Oscar	Briggs [7-3]; Auerbach [7-46]; Miller [7-60]

Beaumont, Charles, 1929-1967.

8-1. Nolan, William F. **The Work of Charles Beaumont: An Annotated Bibliography and Guide**. Borgo Press, 1986.
Though his career as a writer was tragically cut short by Alzheimer's disease, Beaumont's contributions—his psychologically informed stories of everyday horrors and his excellent scripts for *The Twilight Zone*—significantly influenced the current generation of horror writers. This useful bibliography begins with a biographical introduction by Nolan and continues with checklists of Beaumont's fiction (with brief plot summaries of his novels), nonfiction, comic scripts, screenplays and teleplays. Index of titles. For a survey of Beaumont's career and contributions, see Roger Anker's introduction to *Charles Beaumont: Selected Stories* [4-27].

Bierce, Ambrose, 1842-1914?

8-2. Davidson, Cathy N., ed. **Critical Essays on Ambrose Bierce**. G. K. Hall, 1982.

***8-3.** ———. **The Experimental Fictions of Ambrose Bierce: Structuring the Ineffable**. Univ. of Nebraska Press, 1984.

8-4. Fatout, Paul. **Ambrose Bierce: The Devil's Lexicographer**. Univ. of Oklahoma Press, 1951.

8-5. Gaer, Joseph, ed. **Ambrose Gwinett Bierce: Bibliography and Biographical Data**. Burt Franklin, 1935.

***8-6.** Grenander, M. E. **Ambrose Bierce**. Twayne, 1971.
Since the still-unexplained disappearance in 1914 of this American antirealist writer, would-be biographers have written a great deal of myth-tinged nonsense about his life. And critics have written a morass of wrong-headed, simplistic commentary on his fiction. As a full biography, though, Paul Fatout's book—which should be read with its successor, *Ambrose Bierce and the Black Hills* (Univ. of Oklahoma Press, 1956)—is reliable and balanced. Readers may wish to supplement Fatout's books with Richard Saunders's *Ambrose Bierce: The Making of a Misanthrope* (Chronicle, 1985), which argues that Bierce's years in San Francisco (1866-1900) "hold the key to his exceedingly complex character." Spiced with quotations from Bierce's writings, this book sheds indirect light on his deeply pessimistic philosophy, the dark heart of his tales of horror and the supernatural. The influence of those tales, with their potent combination of Gothicism, black humor and cynical irony, on the American short horror story has persisted throughout the century—in spite of the effort by early critics to paint Bierce as just another Poe. M. E. Grenander neatly demolishes this misperception in her well-written, often witty overview of Bierce's life and works. Grenander contributes one of several major essays to Cathy Davidson's collection. Most of the critics in this book spend a good deal of time correcting misinformation promulgated by earlier critics. Two of these essays focus on Bierce's major tales of horror: "The Death of Halpin Frayser," which W. B. Stein properly places in the tradition of American Gothicism; and "An Occurrence at Owl Creek Bridge," which F. J. Logan shows to be more subtle than its conventional reading

as merely a grisly war story with a trick ending. Valuable as these essays are, the most important critical work to date on Bierce is Davidson's full-length study. She develops a fascinating parallel between Bierce's approach to fiction and the contemporary semiotician C. S. Peirce's approach to signification. This stratagem radically but convincingly repositions Bierce in American literature as "the premodern precursor of postmodern fiction." Davidson's insights are critical to those modern horror writers who, like Bierce, use innovative linguistic and narrative techniques to explore the nature and failure of human perception of reality. As if to prove the point, Davidson, in a remarkable afterword, links Bierce's tales to works by Jorge Luis Borges, Julio Cortázar and Ryunosuke Akutagawa. Notes, bibliography, index. Both of Davidson's books and Grenander's contain useful secondary bibliographies (the latter with excellent annotations); readers needing a more complete primary bibliography should consult Joseph Gaer's book, which also includes a biographical sketch, brief critical evaluations of Bierce's works and a (now dated) list of secondary commentaries.

Blackwood, Algernon (U.K.), 1869–1951.

***8-7.** Ashley, Mike. **Algernon Blackwood: A Bio-Bibliography**. Greenwood, 1987.
Algernon Blackwood was an important mystical, visionary British writer. Ashley calls him "one of the major forces in the shaping and development of modern supernatural fiction." Ashley has overcome the enormous problems posed by Blackwood's personal habits to assemble a truly definitive guide to all relevant primary and secondary literature. The principal part of this book consists of annotated listings of Blackwood's fiction and its appearances and adaptations (together with unpublished works), and his nonfiction, reviews, poetry and songs, plays and broadcasts on radio and television. But this exhaustively complete, extensively cross-indexed bibliography also includes an index to locales and themes of Blackwood's works, lists of library and archival holdings, and chronologies of his life and of first publications of his works. Readers should also consult Ashley's long and invaluable prefatory biographical essay, sections on Blackwood in Sullivan [7-15] and Penzoldt [7-9], and David Punter's essay in Bleiler [6-20] and Bleiler's introduction to *Best Ghost Stories of Algernon Blackwood* (Dover, 1973).

Bloch, Robert, 1917– .

8-8. Larson, Randall D. **The Complete Robert Bloch: An Illustrated International Bibliography**. Fandom Unlimited (Box 70868, Sunnyvale, CA 94086), 1986.

8-9. ———. **Robert Bloch**. Starmont House, 1986.
In spite of his long, prolific career, Robert Bloch has been the subject of little critical attention. In his brief Starmont House survey, Randall Larson has, with Bloch's help, partly redressed this imbalance. Larson skillfully and coherently organizes Bloch's vast *oeuvre* by theme and period. Then, within this frame, he tracks Bloch's evolution through thematic shifts in his fiction: from early tales of cosmic (Lovecraftian) horrors to post-1940s stories and novels of psychological terror—works that, with their emphasis on everyday human evil, echo through-

out modern horror fiction by Peter Straub, Stephen King, Charles L. Grant and many others. More descriptive than analytical, Larson occasionally supplements plot summaries by a few critical observations, quotations from less-accessible secondary material and excerpts from letters from and interviews with Bloch. Chronology, primary and secondary bibliographies, index. A great deal more information appears in Larson's complementary book-length list of Bloch's professional and amateur appearances; these include fiction (in print, radio, television, film, comics) and nonfiction (e.g., essays and introductions). This book is extensively illustrated with photos of magazine covers, advertisements, opening pages of stories and film stills and also includes specialized lists of first appearances; unanthologized, collaborative and pseudonymous stories; works organized by magazine, etc. Both books are recommended for moderate-to-large libraries of modern American horror fiction.

Brown, Charles Brockden, 1771-1810.

8-10. Axelrod, Alan. **Charles Brockden Brown: An American Tale**. Univ. of Texas Press, 1983.

***8-11.** Parker, Patricia. **Charles Brockden Brown: A Reference Guide**. G. K. Hall, 1980.

8-12. Ringe, Donald E. **Charles Brockden Brown**. Twayne, 1966.
Charles Brockden Brown innovatively appropriated devices of British Gothicism to peculiarly American ends and focused the nascent American novel on exaggeration and grotesquerie. But his main contribution to American horror fiction was an intense concentration on the psychodynamics of fear: this emphasis significantly influenced Poe and prefigured themes of modern writers such as Stephen King and David Morrell. Brown's uncertain literary reputation, the flawed nature of his novels and his myth-enshrouded biography have stimulated a huge amount of criticism. Patricia Parker's annotated guide blazes a trail through this critical maze, and Bernard Rosenthal's introduction to his edited collection of *Critical Essays on Charles Brockden Brown* (G. K. Hall, 1981) surveys its high points. Much of this criticism has concentrated on Brown's Gothic novel *Wieland* (1798) [1-9]. In his fine overview, Donald Ringe summarizes various interpretations of this novel and situates it in relation to the rest of Brown's writings. Note that here and in *American Gothic* [7-44], Ringe stresses the influence on Brown of British and German Gothic writers; by contrast, Robert D. Hume, in "Charles Brockden Brown and the Uses of Gothicism: A Reassessment" (*Emerson Society Quarterly* 17 [1972]: 10–18), minimizes the influence of British Gothicism on the form of Brown's novels. Ringe's survey also provides a chronology, annotated secondary bibliography and index. Since Ringe emphasizes criticism over biography, readers in search of the latter should consult Harry R. Warfel's *Charles Brockden Brown: American Gothic Novelist* (Florida Univ. Press, 1949), which includes a chapter on the plots and themes of Brown's major novels. The best book-length study of those novels is Alan Axelrod's well-documented, in-depth analysis. What makes this book of more than specialized interest are Axelrod's skillful positioning of Brown's major novels in the broad cultural context of turn-of-the-century America and his identification of their distinctively American qualities. In this

regard, see also Fiedler [7-36], who elucidates Brown's position as heir to the Gothic and Sentimental traditions and discusses his problematic status in American fiction.

Campbell, Ramsey (U.K.), 1946- .

8-13. Ashley, Mike. **Fantasy Reader's Guide #2: Ramsey Campbell**. Cosmos, 1980; Borgo Press, 1984.

8-14. Crawford, Gary William. **Ramsey Campbell**. Starmont House, 1988.

The ambiguous, intensely subjective narratives of this most stylish of modern writers of dark fantasy warrant more critical attention than they have received. The one book-length study is Crawford's perfunctory, disappointing sixty-two-page essay. In his determination to portray Campbell as a Gothic writer, Crawford passes over much of his subject's subtlety (e.g., transformation in Campbell's later works of Lovecraftian themes that dominated his earlier stories) and complexity (e.g., the decidedly non-Gothic characterizations in many of Campbell's novels). Chronology, (incomplete) primary and secondary bibliographies, index. No biography of Campbell yet exists, but he has written an extraordinary autobiographical introduction to the Scream/Press edition of his novel *The Face That Must Die* (1983) [4-66] and a less substantive autobiographical essay for Mike Ashley's collection. The critical high points of Ashley's collection are excellent essays by T. E. D. Klein and Jack Sullivan on Campbell's short fiction. See also Crawford's essay on Campbell's short stories in *Survey of Modern Fantasy Literature* [6-24]. Ashley also provides a complete bibliography of works through 1980. On Campbell's novels, the best critical essays are Kenneth Jurkiewicz's survey in Bleiler [6-20] and Joel Lane's "Negatives in Print: The Novels of Ramsey Campbell" (*Foundation*, no. 36 [1986]: 35–44).

Cave, Hugh B., 1910- .

8-15. Parente, Audrey. **Pulp Man's Odyssey: The Hugh B. Cave Story**. Starmont House, 1988.

During his sixty-year career as a writer of popular fiction, Cave has produced several novels, myriad stories and a nonfiction book about voodoo entitled *Haiti: Highroad to Adventure* (1952). Cave's best weird tales, selected from well over a thousand short stories he has published in pulp and slick magazines, can be found in the collection *Murgunstrumm and Others* [3-48]. The only book about Cave is Audrey Parente's well-written literary biography, which draws on Cave's personal library, correspondence and review files as well as extensive personal correspondence and interviews with him. Although it contains little analysis of Cave's fiction *per se*, Parente's book is filled with anecdotes and valuable historical information about the American pulps, a genre that prefigured the American horror story as the eighteenth-century Gothic did the British ghostly tale. In addition to a foreword by Cave and an introduction by Robert Bloch, this book reprints a selection of letters from Cave to his long-time friend and correspondent Carl Jacobi, who also contributes an afterword, and contains a huge primary bibliography. Index. For more on the American pulps, see Jones [7-40] and Weinberg [7-45].

Crawford, F. Marion, 1854-1909.

8-16. Moran, John C. **An F. Marion Crawford Companion**. Greenwood, 1981. Although supernatural tales formed only a small fraction of the output of this prolific American historian and Romantic novelist, those tales have endured long after Crawford's other works have sunk into oblivion. Echoes of the short stories in Crawford's famous collection *Wandering Ghosts* (1911) [2-17]—especially "For the Blood Is the Life," "The Dead Smile" and "The Upper Berth"—resound through fiction by later writers such as E. F. Benson, William Hope Hodgson and H. P. Lovecraft. Moran's vast compilation touches on matters biographical, bibliographical and critical and includes a chronology, detailed publication histories and concordances to geographical references and characters in Crawford's works. Ghost story enthusiasts will find particularly interesting the prefatory appreciations by Russell Kirk and Donald Sydney-Fryer. Indexes of authors, subjects, titles. For critical and biographical information, see *Francis Marion Crawford* by John Pilkington, Jr. (Twayne, 1964).

De la Mare, Walter (U.K.), 1873-1956.

***8-17.** McCrosson, Doris Ross. **Walter De la Mare**. Twayne, 1966.

8-18. Mégroz, R. L. **Walter De la Mare: A Biographical and Critical Study**. Hodder and Stoughton, 1924.

8-19. Reid, Forest. **Walter De la Mare: A Critical Study**. Faber and Faber, 1929. De la Mare's deeply felt awe at the beauty and strangeness of existence often led him to the spirit world, to ghosts and witchcraft and magic. These themes he rendered in original, subtle stories and poems, many of which seem obsessed with death and the possibilities thereafter. The best general overview of De la Mare's career is Kenneth Hopkins's brief book *Walter De la Mare* (Longmans, 1953; rev. 1957), which also includes a useful bibliography. The more detailed volumes by Mégroz and Reid emphasize De la Mare's early writings. Mégroz's book, published midway through his subject's career, contains a notable discussion of De la Mare's fairy play *Crossings* (1921) and an interesting comparison of "Out of the Deep" to Henry James's "Turn of the Screw" (1898). An appendix by William Thompson analyzes De la Mare's famous poem "The Listeners." Reid's critical work, written in a charming personal tone emphasizes both De la Mare's use of realism and the dream-like fabrics he wove into his supernatural tales and poems. Reid analyzes at length De la Mare's novel of possession, *The Return* (1910) [3-58], and ghost stories such as "Seaton's Aunt" and "The Green Room." The best critical book to date on De la Mare is McCrosson's. In discussions of the novels, McCrosson elucidates three concepts central to De la Mare's fiction: the human imagination, the nature of dreams and the quality of children's perception. Her close look at his "ghost-ridden" stories shows how he used credible characterizations and realistic settings to force suspension of disbelief. Chronology, index, complete annotated secondary bibliography. Note also John Clute's acute essay in Bleiler [6-20], which argues that De la Mare's works prefigure the ghost stories of Robert Aickman, and discussions of De la Mare in Sullivan [7-15], Briggs [7-3] and Penzoldt [7-9].

Derleth, August, 1909-1971.

8-20. Wilson, Alison M. **August Derleth: A Bibliography**. Scarecrow, 1983.
Best known within the genre as co-founder (with Donald Wandrei) of Arkham House and its publisher until his death in 1971, August Derleth also has a place in mainstream American literature: as a minor regionalist, the creator of the Sac Prairie Saga of Wisconsin. But, as Wilson's excellent bibliography shows, Derleth was also an accomplished poet, essayist, biographer, historian and critic. Over half of Wilson's book concerns Derleth's contributions to the weird tale: his traditional ghost stories, the best of which were published in the 1940s under the pen name Stephen Grendon; the influential anthologies he edited in the 1940s and 60s; and his Holmesian pastiches about the Praed Street detective Solar Pons and his companion Lyndon Parker. Wilson also annotates Derleth's posthumous "Lovecraft collaborations" and Derleth's own Lovecraft pastiches. Supplementing Wilson's well-annotated bibliographic entries are a thoughtful introduction assessing Derleth's failure to attain national recognition and a biographical sketch of Derleth as seen through the eyes of contemporary news stories from his native Wisconsin. Index of titles. For additional biographical information on Derleth, see *Remembering Derleth*, ed. by Bill Dyke (August Derleth Society, 1988). Derleth's *Thirty Years of Arkham House 1939–1969: A History and Bibliography* (Arkham House, 1970) provides insight into his influential publishing venture. The issue of Derleth's appropriation and alteration of Lovecraft's ideas is essential to an evaluation of his horror fiction: scholars now deprecate Derleth's Lovecraftian works for their revision of the Cthulhu Mythos into a pallid parallel of Christian mythology; see Richard L. Tierney's essay in Schweitzer [8-67] and (the best writing on the subject) Dirk W. Mosig's "H.P. Lovecraft: Myth-Maker" in Joshi's collection of Lovecraft criticism [8-66].

Dickens, Charles (U.K.), 1812–1870.

8-21. Frank, Lawrence. **Charles Dickens and the Romantic Self**. Univ. of Nebraska Press, 1984.

8-22. Stone, Harry. **Dickens and the Invisible World: Fairy Tales, Fantasy, and Novel-Making**. Indiana Univ. Press, 1979.
The intense realism of Dickens's stories obscures, for many readers, their supernaturalism. Dickens imbued the supernatural tale with moral substance and thus influenced many a future writer. He also stimulated Bulwer-Lytton, Wilkie Collins and others to write ghost stories and thus advanced the British ghostly tradition. Readers can find succinct overviews of this aspect of Dickens's writings in Peter Haining's enthusiastic introduction to *The Complete Ghost Stories of Charles Dickens* (Franklin Watts, 1983) and in Brian M. Stableford's fine essay in

Bleiler [6-20]. A far more detailed look at Dickens's supernaturalism forms the substance of Harry Stone's engagingly written blend of biography, critical analysis and psychological speculation. Stone explores why fairy tales and fairyland carried "surcharged meanings for Dickens [and] shaped the nature of his imagination." Stone treats mythic images and themes in many of Dickens's works—notably *David Copperfield* (1849-50) and *Great Expectations* (1860-62)—and is especially good on Dickens's best-known ghost story, *A Christmas Carol* (1843) [2-19]. Index. Lawrence Frank's psychoanalytic study incorporates ideas from Sigmund Freud, Jean-Jacques Rousseau, Michel Foucault, Friedrich Nietzsche, Roland Barthes and many many others—all in order to show how Dickens used Romantic paradigms to construct voyages of self-discovery and self-creation for his characters. Although specialized, this book is notable for its third part, "Dickens' Urban Gothic," which treats *Our Mutual Friend* (1865) and *The Mystery of Edwin Drood* (1870) [2-19]. Notes, index. Of the myriad other specialized studies of Dickens, readers should consider *Dickens, Reade, and Collins: Sensation Novelists: A Study of the Conditions and Theories of Novel Writing in Victorian England* (Columbia Univ. Press, 1919), in which Walter C. Phillips illustrates Dickens's adaptation of devices from horror fiction. Finally, Rosemary Jackson unfolds the ideological subtext underlying Dickens's "complex reworking of a Gothic mode" in her valuable essay, "The Silenced Text: Shades of Gothic in Victorian Fiction" (*Minnesota Review* 13 [1979]: 98–112).

Faulkner, William, 1897-1962.

8-23. Kerr, Elizabeth M. **William Faulkner's Gothic Domain**. Kennikat Press, 1979. Kerr here discovers Gothic elements not only in Faulkner's predominantly (and obviously) Gothic works such as "A Rose for Emily," *Sanctuary* (1931) and *Absalom, Absalom!* (1936), but also in many other novels. This demonstration rests on a very broad definition of Gothicism which Kerr has derived, like much of this book, from ideas of Northrop Frye, Irving Malin [7-42] and Leslie Fiedler [7-36]. She identifies Faulkner's use of the Gothic as distinctly Southern: "the South provided William Faulkner . . . with a reality which could be depicted with the strong contrasts of the Gothic genre to reveal social and psychological truths less accessible to purely objective and realistic treatment." While Kerr sternly chastises previous critics for their failure to note Gothicism in Faulkner's work, she errs in the other direction, labeling as "Gothic" virtually any work with *any* elements in common with the British Gothic tradition. But the Gothic elements in, say, *The Sound and the Fury* (1929) and *Sartoris* (1929) are secondary to the overriding tone, structure and intent of these novels. Focusing so intently on these elements is more misleading than insightful. Kerr's treatment of the influence of Faulkner's Gothicism on later writers is far too cursory. And her eccentric and awkward "Notes/Bibliography/Index" makes tracking down primary and secondary references difficult. See instead the introduction and essays in *American Dreams, American Nightmares*, ed. by David Madden (Southern Illinois Univ. Press, 1970). On *Absalom, Absalom!*, see *Doubling and Incest/Repetition and Revenge: A Speculative Reading of Faulkner* by John T. Irwin (Johns Hopkins Univ. Press, 1975).

Hartley, L. P. (U.K.), 1895-1972.

8-24. Bien, Peter. **L. P. Hartley**. Pennsylvania State Univ. Press, 1963.

8-25. Jones, Edward T. **L. P. Hartley**. Twayne, 1978.

***8-26.** Mulkeen, Anne. **Wild Thyme, Winter Lightning: The Symbolic Novels of L. P. Hartley**. Wayne State Univ. Press, 1974.
Most critical writings on this twentieth-century British author stress his themes of English rural life and class conflict. But Hartley's best novels, *The Go-Between* (1953) [4-138] and the trilogy *Eustace and Hilda* (1944-47), contain significant fantastical elements, and his *Facial Justice* (1960) is Orwellian science fiction. These novels are symbolically and thematically linked to Hartley's elegant, often witty ghost stories, Poesque Gothic sketches, and experiments with ambiguous supernaturalism; and it is a misrepresentation to dismiss the latter, as does Paul Bloomfield in his otherwise fine overview, *L. P. Hartley* (Longmans, 1970). Like many critics, Bloomfield sees Hartley as a social realist. Peter Bien and Anne Mulkeen, however, show him to be a symbolist who incorporated into modern British fiction American traditions of Nathaniel Hawthorne and Henry James—particularly their use of fantasy. Like Bloomfield, Bien deemphasizes Hartley's short fiction, but he does compare his ghostly tales to those of Elizabeth Bowen, M. R. James and Edith Wharton. While Bien interprets Hartley's symbols as moral and psychological, Mulkeen, whose book is the best so far on Hartley, sees them as mythic and metaphysical. Stressing the need for close attention in reading Hartley, she teases out the myth of "the cosmic beneath the commonplace" in his writings and, by identifying their symbolic patterns, reveals them to be metaphorical quests for selfhood. Somewhere between Bien's and Mulkeen's approaches lies Edward Jones's less sophisticated introduction to Hartley. Unfortunately, Jones deprecates Hartley's supernatural stories, calling them "examples of craft rather than art" akin to Lovecraft's in intent but sadistic, repetitive and unsuccessful in execution. Notes, references, annotated secondary bibliography. See also sections on Hartley in Sullivan [7-15] and Briggs [7-3] and Giorgio Melchiori's important essay "The English Novelist and the American Tradition" (*Sewanee Review* 18 [1960]: 502-515).

Hawthorne, Nathaniel, 1804-1864.

8-27. Lundblad, Jane. **Nathaniel Hawthorne and the European Literary Tradition**. Harvard Univ. Press, 1947.
The first major phase of American Gothicism ended, according to Donald Ringe [7-44], with the publication in 1860 of Nathaniel Hawthorne's *The Marble Faun*. In this and other works, Hawthorne adapted the structures and conventions of British Gothicism in ways that elevated American Gothic to new heights of functionality and sophistication. Jane Lundblad concentrates on this dimension of Hawthorne's fiction in the first half of her book, a revision of her 1946 monograph *Nathaniel Hawthorne and the Tradition of Gothic Romance*. She specifies twelve signatures of Gothicism, then proceeds systematically to note their presence in fifteen short stories and several novels. Although rather mechan-

ical, this analysis, when applied to "Young Goodman Brown" (1828–29) and *The House of the Seven Gables* (1851) [2-38], clearly suggests how Hawthorne rationalized the supernatural by juxtaposing it to historical elements. But Lundblad's book, although well researched, gives only an incomplete picture of supernaturalism in Hawthorne's fiction. Readers should also consult *Hawthorne's Faust: A Study of the Devil Archetype* (Univ. of Florida Press, 1953), in which William Bysshe Stein explores Hawthorne's use of myth, and *Hawthorne's Mad Scientists: Pseudoscience and Social Science in Nineteenth-Century Life and Letters* (Archon, 1978), in which Taylor Stoehr discusses Hawthorne's interest in mysticism, spiritualism and mesmerism. The implications of these -isms on Hawthorne are elaborated by Kerr [7-38]. Ringe [7-44] and Fiedler [7-36] relate Hawthorne to the tradition of American Gothicism, and Levin [7-41] relates his work to that of two other great American nineteenth-century Gothicists, Poe and Melville.

Hodgson, William Hope (U.K.), 1877–1918.

8-28. Bell, Ian, ed. **William Hope Hodgson: Voyage and Visions**. Bell: 5 The Meadows, Watlington, Oxford OX9 5JN, 1987.

8-29. Bell, Joseph. **William Hope Hodgson: Night Pirate, Volume 1: An Annotated Bibliography of Published Works, 1902–1987**. Soft Books, 1987.

8-30. Everts, R. Alain. **Some Facts in the Case of William Hope Hodgson: Master of Phantasy**. Soft Books, 1987.
William Hope Hodgson's powerful tales of terror at sea, intense visionary horror novels and (less successful) stories about an occult detective named Carnacki continue to entertain enthusiasts and influence writers. Underappreciated by critics now as he was by readers during his lifetime, Hodgson has yet to be the subject of a full biography or critical study. On the biographical front, we have Sam Moskowitz's 109-page essay, first published in a 1973 reincarnation of *Weird Tales* and reprinted as the introduction to *Out of the Storm: Uncollected Fantasies of William Hope Hodgson* [3-90], which includes plot summaries of Hodgson's major works along with details of their publication and reception. Equally valuable is R. Alain Everts's more detailed (though still brief) reminiscence. Revised from its 1971 appearance in *Shadow* and supplemented with new photographs, this book excerpts rare articles and letters by and about Hodgson and recollections by many who knew him. On the critical front, we have Lovecraft's section on Hodgson in *Supernatural Horror in Literature* [7-7], E. F. Bleiler's essay in his *Supernatural Fiction Writers* [6-20] and seven fine essays in Ian Bell's invaluable book. Although these essays touch many bases, the most important are those about Hodgson's novels, two of which are so imbued with visionary intensity and ineffable cosmic malignancy as to be near-classics. Brian Stableford examines the structure and philosophy of one of these, *The House on the Borderland* (1908) [3-92], and Ian Bell, Roger Dobson and Andy Sawyer take on the other, *The Night Land* (1912) [F3-178], whose strange, baroque style continues to generate controversy. Also useful are Mark Valentine's spirited defense of the Carnacki stories and a secondary bibliography by Mike Ashley. The primary bibliography by Joseph Bell lists the contents, physical descriptions and,

as available, price and print run of Hodgson's books and indexes the appearances of his tales in magazines and anthologies. For a detailed look at Carnacki as well as other psychic detectives of the pulps, see chapter 2 of *Strange Days*, Vol. II of Robert Sampson's remarkable multi-volume account of pulp series characters, *Yesterday's Faces* (Bowling Green Univ. Popular Press, 1984).

Irving, Washington, 1783-1859.

8-31. Hedges, William L. **Washington Irving: An American Study, 1802-1832**. Johns Hopkins Univ. Press, 1965.
Washington Irving, a noted American diplomat and historian, was also the country's first successful professional author. Although best known for "The Legend of Sleepy Hollow" and "Rip Van Winkle," both of which appeared in *The Sketch Book of Geoffrey Crayon* (1819-20), Irving also wrote more horrific supernatural tales—notably, the ghost stories in *Tales of a Traveller* (1824). In his detailed, penetrating analysis, William Hedges compares these and other stories to works by Poe, Nathaniel Hawthorne and various Gothic forerunners and clarifies Irving's place in nineteenth-century American literature and culture. Hedges does not, however, fully explore certain influential aspects of Irving's supernatural fiction: his mixture of humor, irony and terror; and his psychological rationalization of the supernatural as his characters' misconception of reality. See instead sections on Irving in Ringe [7-44] and Fiedler [7-36] and G. R. Thompson's essay in Kerr, Crowley and Crow [7-39].

Jackson, Shirley, 1919-1965.

8-32. Friedman, Lenemaja. **Shirley Jackson**. Twayne, 1975.

8-33. Oppenheimer, Judy. **Private Demons: The Life of Shirley Jackson**. Putnam, 1988.
In many of Shirley Jackson's subtle tales of terror, supernatural powers fuse with characters' mental aberrations to breed uniquely domestic horrors that variously haunt and bedevil those characters, their placid houses and their charming rural communities. Jackson was, that is to say, far more complex and interesting a writer than the mere "born teller of tales" portrayed in Friedman's book. Friedman plods through catalogues of themes, characteristics of style and so forth without ever really coming to grips with her subject's strengths or weaknesses. Nor does she connect Jackson to the Gothic predecessors who clearly influenced her or to the modern writers whom she influenced. Particularly disappointing is the chapter on Jackson's three great novels, *The Haunting of Hill House* (1959) [4-155], *We Have Always Lived in the Castle* (1962) [4-157] and *The Sundial* (1958) [4-156]: heavily padded with plot summary and quotations, this chapter, like the rest of Friedman's book, offers as analysis little more than simplistic commentary and excerpts from contemporary reviews. Notes, bibliography, index. Jackson's complexity as a person does emerge from Judy Oppenheimer's popular biography, which she based on extensive original research into Jackson's private papers and on interviews and correspondence with friends and family. Unfortunately, though, Oppenheimer's splendid portrait of this multi-faceted woman offers only

brief insights into her works. The best critical writings on Jackson are the brief essay by Jack Sullivan in Bleiler [6-20] and "Chambers of Yearning: Shirley Jackson's Use of the Gothic" by John G. Parks (*Twentieth-Century Literature*, 30 [1984]: 15–29).

Jacobi, Carl, 1908- .

8-34. Smith, R. Dixon. **Lost in the Rentharpian Hills: Spanning the Decades with Carl Jacobi**. Bowling Green State Univ. Popular Press, 1985.

The many short stories of this prolific pulp fictioneer include such powerful tales as "Portrait in Moonlight" and "Revelations in Black." A host of details concerning the publication of these and other stories (as well as illustrations from their magazine appearances) fill the bibliography of R. Dixon Smith's anecdotal, adulatory book on Jacobi. Apart from a 1977 chapbook edited by William H. Pugmire, this is the only study of Jacobi and so is noteworthy in spite of its lack of critical balance or apparatus. Photos, index and an appendix of letters to Jacobi from publishers and other writers.

James, Henry, 1843–1916.

Overviews of James's Supernatural Fiction

8-35. Banta, Martha. **Henry James and the Occult: The Great Extension**. Indiana Univ. Press, 1972.

***8-36**. Edel, Leon, ed. **The Ghostly Tales of Henry James**. Rutgers Univ. Press, 1948.

Although Henry James's primary importance to literature was his impact on American modernism and such writers as Virginia Woolf and Edith Wharton, his "ghostly tales" have had their influence as well—e.g., on Peter Straub's *Ghost Story* (1979) [4-286]. As a writer of supernatural fiction, James is identified in most readers' minds with "The Turn of the Screw" (1898). But, as Leon Edel points out in a long introduction to his collection of James's ghost stories, this short novel "is not the isolated work most critics have believed it to be." This introduction and the long essays that preface each tale are packed with insights into their sources, primary among which (in Edel's view) were James's childhood experiences and his exposure to the spiritualist movement in late nineteenth-century America. The only book on James's supernatural fiction is Martha Banta's readable, well-researched study. In chapters on psychic vampirism, ghosts, self-haunting and other topics, Banta shows how a "new psychological gothicism" evolved out of James's "manipulation of the tradition of literary supernaturalism." Of particular interest is her witty survey of prior criticism on "The Turn of the Screw" and a speculative final chapter that shows how James applied narrative strategies worked out in his ghostly tales to such realistic fictions as *The Portrait of a Lady* (1876) and *The Bostonians* (1886). Extensive notes, index. Note also that the explosion of James criticism since 1984, with its increasing emphasis on psychoanalytic interpretations, has produced a host of good articles—far too many to list here—that comment on his ghostly tales.

On "The Turn of the Screw"

*8-37. Kimbrough, Robert, ed. **The Turn of the Screw (Norton Critical Edition).** W. W. Norton, 1966.

8-38. Willen, Gerald, ed. **A Casebook on James' "The Turn of the Screw."** Crowell, 1960.

During the 1890s James was increasingly preoccupied with perception and consciousness. This absorption led him to present in this, his greatest ghost story, ambiguities that opened vast spaces for interpretation—spaces critics have rushed to fill. The amount of ensuing nonsense written about "The Turn of the Screw" almost makes one question the value of literary criticism. Still, the true believer can find much of value. Gerald Willen's *Casebook* reprints the text, brief comments by James and fifteen essays, among them a fascinating radio symposium in which Katherine Anne Porter, Allen Tate and Mark Van Doren discuss the story. The Norton Critical Edition, edited by Robert Kimbrough, offers a superb selection of James's writings about ghost stories in general and "The Turn of the Screw" in particular as well as initial reviews and reactions (1898–1923), influential critical essays (1924–57) and selected recent commentaries. Kimbrough's skillful design elucidates major shifts in critical thinking that occurred after open warfare broke out when, in 1934, Edmund Wilson published his notorious non-supernatural interpretation (sex-repressed governess projects "ghosts" as hallucinations). Kimbrough also reprints a high point in James criticism: a hilarious take-off on critical exegesis entitled "The Return of the Screw," in which Eric Solomon uses Holmesian deduction to prove that the governess, the children, Peter Quint and Miss Jessel are all victims of "that most clever and desperate of Victorian villainesses, the evil [housekeeper] Mrs. Grose." Detailed annotated bibliography. This short novel has also spawned (at least) four full-length studies, of which E. A. Sheppard's *Henry James and The Turn of the Screw* (Oxford Univ. Press, 1974) is the most accessible. This exhaustively researched book, based on public lectures Sheppard gave in 1970 at the University of Auckland, situates James's story in appropriate literary, cultural and personal contexts, discusses its composition and initial reception and convincingly justifies a pro-supernatural interpretation. Extensive notes, index. Readers should also note the articulate, highly negative critique leveled by Charles Thomas Samuels in *The Ambiguity of Henry James* (Univ. of Illinois Press, 1971). Even all this criticism leaves untapped a few important points. Heller [7-71] and Tobin Siebers, in "Hesitation, History, and Reading: Henry James' *The Turn of the Screw*" (*Texas Studies in Literature and Language* 25 [1983]: 558–573), profitably apply Todorov's theory of the fantastic [7-76] to James's narrative. On its Gothic and supernatural elements, see the essays by Jay Martin and Howard Kerr in *The Haunted Dusk* [7-39] and "The Turns in *The Turn of the Screw*" by Hans-Joachim Lang (*Jahrbuch für Amerikanstudien* IX [1964]: 110–128), and also "The Trap of Imagination: The Gothic Tradition, Fiction, and 'The Turn of the Screw,'" (*Criticism* 22 [1981]: 297–319), in which Ronald Schleifer provocatively juxtaposes James's novel to *Dracula*. Finally, see "Turning the Screw of Interpretation" by Shoshana Felman in her (edited) book, *Literature and Psychoanalysis* (Johns Hopkins Univ. Press, 1983).

James, M. R. (U.K.), 1862–1936.

***8-39**. Cox, Michael. **M. R. James: An Informal Portrait**. Oxford Univ. Press, 1983.

8-40. Haining, Peter, ed. **M. R. James Book of the Supernatural**. Foulsham, 1978. U.S. title: *The Book of Ghost Stories*. Stein and Day, 1982.
The elegant, formal ghost stories M. R. James wrote in the 1890s influenced a whole school of later writers, including H. R. Wakefield, R. H. Malden and E. G. Swain. Yet no substantive critical work on James's ghostly fiction exists. R. W. Pfaff's highly regarded book *Montague Rhodes James* (Scolar Press, 1980) emphasizes James's biblical and medieval studies and includes a vast bibliography of his scholarly writings but mentions only briefly the genesis of his ghost stories. Similarly, S. G. Lubbock's impressionistic "purely personal sketch," *A Memoir of Montague Rhodes James* (Cambridge Univ. Press, 1939), notes the ghost stories only in passing. But Michael Cox's fine biography contains considerable anecdotal information on the writing, publication and reception of these stories—and of James's well-known fantasy *The Five Jars* (1922) [F3-192]. In fact, Cox argues, James's ghost stories are important precisely because they exemplify a specific (nineteenth-century) literary form: a form Jack Sullivan dubbed "the antiquarian ghost story." Cox also excerpts a little-known but important essay on ghostly fiction that James wrote for a 1929 issue of *The Bookman*. The latter essay is reprinted in Peter Haining's illustrated miscellany along with marginalia, a few stories not in James's *Collected Ghost Stories* (1931) and the text of James's lecture on Sheridan Le Fanu, whose ghost stories were an important influence. Readers should also consult the chapter on James in *Connections* by Austin Warren (Univ. of Michigan Press, 1970) and relevant chapters in the historical and critical surveys annotated in chapter 7. See especially Penzoldt [7-9] and Briggs [7-3]; the latter usefully illuminates the basic patterns of James's tales as "'Bluebeard,' 'Faust,' or the spirits of revenge." Michael Cox's introduction to his recent selection of *The Ghost Stories of M. R. James* (Oxford Univ. Press, 1986) neatly summarizes his longer biography. Those interested in Le Fanu's influence should consult Sullivan [7-15] (the best critical work so far on James) and Jack P. Franzetti's *A Study of the Preternatural Fiction of Sheridan Le Fanu and Its Impact upon the Tales of Montague Rhodes James* (St. John's Univ., 1956). The Jamesian tradition lives on today in the magazine *Ghosts & Scholars* [11-35], and readers can sample works by James's heirs in *Ghosts and Scholars: Ghost Stories in the Tradition of M. R. James*, ed. by Richard Dalby and Rosemary Pardoe (Crucible, 1987).

King, Stephen, 1947– .

Biographical and Bibliographical Works

8-41. Collings, Michael R. **The Annotated Guide to Stephen King: A Primary and Secondary Bibliography of the Works of America's Premier Horror Writer**. Starmont House, 1986.

***8-42**. Winter, Douglas E. **Stephen King: The Art of Darkness**. NAL, 1984; Plume (expanded and updated version), 1986.
More than a writer, Stephen King is a major phenomenon of late twentieth-century American popular culture. Although one of the most widely read writers

ever, King has yet to be the subject of a full biography. Douglas E. Winter's "critical appreciation," an extensive revision of his pioneering 1982 Starmont House guide, contains sufficient personal history, anecdotes and quotations from interviews to join King's *Danse Macabre* [7-6] as a primary biographical source. Winter positions King in the Romantic/naturalistic tradition of American fiction, and in discussions of works from *Carrie* (1974) [4-162] to the collaborative novel (with Peter Straub) *The Talisman* (1984) [4-178] shows that the social, political and economic subtexts of King's work posit an "intrinsically subversive" critique of late twentieth-century America—an insight elaborated by Magistrale [8-46] and Reino [8-47]. Appendices summarize the plots of King's short fiction and list credits of film and TV adaptations; more on these adaptations can be found in *The Films of Stephen King* by Michael R. Collings (Starmont, 1986) and *Stephen King at the Movies* by Jessie Horsting (Starlog Press, 1986). Notes, chronology, primary and secondary bibliographies, index. Michael Collings's *Annotated Guide* offers the most complete King bibliography to date. Annotating over 1,000 items from fan, review and academic sources (including foreign publications), this valuable research tool gives a fascinating perspective on what Collings rightly calls, in the title of one of his many books on the subject, *The Stephen King Phenomenon* (Starmont House, 1987).

Essay Collections

8-43. Underwood, Tim, and Chuck Miller, eds. **Fear Itself: The Horror Fiction of Stephen King**. Underwood-Miller, 1982.

8-44. ——, eds. **Kingdom of Fear: The World of Stephen King**. Underwood-Miller, 1986.

The bulk of commentary on King threatens to equal that of his fiction. King's output, its peculiar unevenness and his extensive and extravagant borrowing of themes, images, plot devices and even characters from traditional horror literature and film make unusual demands on critics. These demands, along with King's enormous popularity, may account for the superficiality of much of this commentary. Essays and books alike are so clotted with commendations that King's strengths get lost along with his weaknesses in the torrents of praise. Most collections of academic and fan essays to date are wholly negligible, and even the best are uneven. Thus, Darrell Schweitzer's wide-ranging *Discovering Stephen King* (Starmont, 1985) includes some excellent articles: by Michael R. Collings on "generic fluidity" in *The Stand* (1978) [4-175], by Robert M. Price on King's use of Lovecraft's Cthulhu Mythos and by Bernadette Bosky on the mutual influences of King and Peter Straub. But much of the rest is given over to an article about collecting King, yet another selected bibliography, and a long, extraneous batch of plot synopses of King's novels and short stories. *Fear Itself,* the first major collection of essays on King, contains thoughtful appreciations by Fritz Leiber and Charles L. Grant as well as excellent essays by Chelsea Quinn Yarbro on King's use of material from myths and fairy tales, by Alan Ryan on *'Salem's Lot* (1975) [4-172], and by Don Herron on social realism as a source of King's literary horror. Herron also contributed a devastating article on King's derivativeness to Underwood and Miller's second collection, *Kingdom of Fear*. This book—the only one I know with two forewords and five introductions—also includes outstanding essays by Harlan Ellison on why film adaptations of King's works are so dreadful, by Michael McDowell on King's use of rhythm in his narrative design and by Bosky on the psychology of King's characters.

Full-Length Studies

8-45. Collings, Michael R. **The Many Facets of Stephen King**. Starmont House, 1985.

*8-46. Magistrale, Tony. **Landscape of Fear: Stephen King's American Gothic**. Bowling Green State Univ. Popular Press, 1988.

8-47. Reino, Joseph. **Stephen King: The First Decade, Carrie to Pet Sematary**. Twayne, 1988.
Of Collings's *seven* Starmont House books on King, two offer specialized information. *Stephen King as Richard Bachman* (1985) addresses the birth and death of King's pseudonym and the five novels he produced before King laid him to rest. And *The Shorter Works of Stephen King* (1985), written with David A. Engebretson, synopsizes and discusses King's poetry and short fiction, including *The Dark Tower: The Gunslinger* (1982) [4-164]. While all Collings's books contain much that is of value, they are also fragmentary, repetitive and marred by occasional awkward writing and superficial analysis. His *Many Facets*, a thematic approach to King's work (including the Bachman novels), hints at the fine single critical book struggling to find its way out of these many volumes. The best book so far on King's work as serious social fiction is Tony Magistrale's well-written study. Aggressively digging beneath the surface of King's novels, Magistrale explores major themes, patterns and motifs in order to identify King's major sociopolitical concerns, the subtexts beneath the monsters. Magistrale also relates King to his American Gothic predecessors Poe, Hawthorne and Melville and to late nineteenth-century naturalists such as Stephen Crane and Frank Norris. Best of all, Magistrale unpacks the moral implications of King's work, which emerges as a devastating critique of "the contemporary strain on American social institutions." Index, selected bibliography. Joseph Reino's book is, he says, a "preliminary study . . . not intended to be definitive." But Reino takes King seriously as a subtle craftsman, and he treats several aspects of King's fiction: cultural references, Gothic devices, symbolism, mythic dimensions, use of fairy tales and more. Although his discussions of *'Salem's Lot* (1975) [4-172], *Apt Pupil* and *The Body* (both 1982) [4-166] are convincing, Reino sometimes stretches, as when linking King to canonical authors such as Randall Jarrell and T. S. Eliot, and his book is marred by typos and an occasionally pretentious tone. Still, this book, like Magistrale's, is a significant step toward a coherent critical perspective on the Charles Dickens of our day. Chronology, notes, brief annotated secondary bibliography, index.

Koontz, Dean R., 1945- .

8-48. Munster, Bill, ed. **Sudden Fear: The Horror and Dark Suspense Fiction of Dean Koontz**. Starmont House, 1988.
Although typecast early in his career as an SF writer, Dean R. Koontz has long

since broken into the mainstream. His recent works—long novels with multiple plots and heavy measures of suspense and horror—exhibit a growing feel for characterization and a skill at pacing worthy of John D. MacDonald. This book combines a long interview, informal appreciations and more substantive essays on Koontz's SF works, his treatment of women in his novels, the interplay of art and text in the Land of Enchantment edition of *Twilight Eyes* (1985) [4-191], and his reflexive use of generic icons as monsters. Chronology, bibliography, selected index of names and titles.

Lee, Vernon (U.K.), 1856-1935.

8-49. Gunn, Peter. **Vernon Lee: Violet Paget, 1856-1935**. Oxford Univ. Press, 1964.
In the preface to her collection *Hauntings* (1890) [2-48], Violet Paget, writing as Vernon Lee, described her spirits as "spurious ghosts (according to me the only genuine ones)." The little-known supernatural tales of this poet, novelist, polemicist and historian of Italian culture exhibit a remarkable range of themes and styles and show affinities with works by Henry James (a friend of Paget) and Virginia Woolf. Horace Gregory discusses these literary connections, among other matters, in his overview of Lee's life and supernatural fiction; this essay appears as the introduction to another collection, *The Snake Lady and Other Stories* (Grove, 1954). Peter Gunn's full biography, based in part on Lee's letters and private papers, makes clear the importance to her of Victorian ideals, even well into the twentieth century. Bibliography, index. The publication in 1987 of Lee's *Supernatural Tales: Excursions into Fantasy* (Peter Owen) should bring her work the attention it deserves.

Le Fanu, J. Sheridan, (Ireland), 1814-1873.

8-50. Begnal, Michael H. **Joseph Sheridan Le Fanu**. Bucknell Univ. Press, 1971.

8-51. Browne, Nelson. **Sheridan Le Fanu**. Barker, 1951.

***8-52**. McCormack, W. J. **Sheridan Le Fanu and Victorian Ireland**. Clarendon Press, 1980.
Sheridan Le Fanu's strategy for creating ghostly fear, described by E. F. Benson as "the quiet cumulative method leading up to intolerable terror," influenced heirs in both British and American supernatural fiction and finds exponents today in the school of "quiet horror" championed by Charles L. Grant. Readers new to Le Fanu will find Michael Begnal and Nelson Browne useful guides to his fiction. Both summarize Le Fanu's life and discuss his novels and stories. Browne deftly balances plot summary and critique (not inappropriately, considering the limited accessibility and uneven quality of much of Le Fanu's writings) and shows a fine sensitivity to Le Fanu's achievements, noting his "melancholy cast of mind, bordering upon a morbid obsession." Unlike Browne, Begnal considers Le Fanu's most valuable works to be his nonsupernatural stories and novels, which he considers vital to the tradition of Irish literature. Both writers, discussing Le Fanu's ghost stories, inaccurately situate him "firmly within the 19th-century Gothic tradition"—missing Sullivan's point that in his best works, Le Fanu replaced Gothic props by the familiar and let his absurdist horrors

emerge unbidden from everyday surroundings. The most recent book on Le Fanu, Ivan Melada's *Sheridan Le Fanu* (Twayne, 1987), adds little to these earlier studies. When Melada does consider Le Fanu's ghost stories, his superficial readings (e.g., "Green Tea" [1872] is "an allegory whose theme is the pain of the creative process") belie their skill and subtlety. Browne includes a primary bibliography and index, Begnal a chronology and select bibliography, Melada a useful annotated bibliography. In his extensive, authoritative work, W. J. McCormack emphasizes the influence of Le Fanu's early life experiences, such as his family's involvement in the Tithe Wars, on his later fiction. As much a history of early Victorian Ireland as a literary biography, this book reveals Le Fanu to be a writer "raised in a crisis of which he saw himself as a constituent, later composing fiction in which incident and emptiness virtually exclude the creation of character." The major critical focus of this book is Le Fanu's novel *Uncle Silas* (1864) [2-51], which McCormack reads "first as the intelligent layman's tale of terror and mystery, and then as a symbolic pattern in which metaphor transforms landscape and characterization into a symmetrical order." In this chapter he relates the ideology underlying Le Fanu's plots to the theological writings of the radical mystic Emanuel Swedenborg and establishes connections to later works by William Butler Yeats and Oscar Wilde. Index, bibliography, checklist of primary works and an appendix on anonymous fiction published in *Dublin University Magazine*, Le Fanu's main venue, that may be attributable to him. For all the merits of McCormack's book, the best critical analysis of Le Fanu's ghost stories remains Sullivan's delineation in *Elegant Nightmares* [7-15] of his essential modernity, use of irony and humor and experiments with narrative structure. On Le Fanu's important vampire novella *Carmilla* (1871), see also Carter [7-55], Waller [7-68] and Senf [7-63]. Note also the delightful anecdotal account of Le Fanu's life and the useful primary bibliography in S. M. Ellis's collection of literary portraits, *Wilkie Collins, Le Fanu, and Others* (Constable, 1931).

Leiber, Fritz, 1910- .

8-53. Frane, Jeff. **Fritz Leiber**. Starmont House, 1980.

8-54. Morgan, Chris. **Fritz Leiber: A Bibliography 1934–1979**. Morgenstern, 1979.

8-55. Staicar, Tom. **Fritz Leiber**. Ungar, 1983.

Leiber is a remarkably diverse and stylish writer who virtually invented the postindustrial urban horror story. His (semi-autobiographical) novels of occult forces impinging on modern rationalist man, *Conjure Wife* (1943) [3-125] and *Our Lady of Darkness* (1977) [4-203], prefigure works by many a modern writer. Readers in search of insights into Leiber's horror fiction should start with Leiber's essays and introductions to his many collections. This literature (through mid-1979) is surveyed in Chris Morgan's bibliography. The most useful of these is Leiber's long introduction to *The Ghost Light* [4-201], "Not Much Disorder and Not So Early Sex: An Autobiographical Essay." Neither book-length study is satisfactory: both Jeff Frane and Tom Staicar try to deal with Leiber's entire *ouevre,* which includes SF, a disaster novel, heroic fantasy, horror and more, in books too brief to do it justice. Frane devotes most of the sixty-four pages of his guide to plot summaries and comments that relate Leiber's works to one another; at best his essay is useful as an introduction. Incomplete primary bibliography (annotated with plot summaries) of first edition titles and library editions, secondary bibliography, index. Like Frane, Staicar devotes too much space to plot summary. And, although he provides useful readings of Leiber's horror novels, his discussions of short fiction are incomplete and perfunctory. Notes, primary and secondary bibliographies, index.

Levin, Ira, 1929- .

8-56. Fowler, Douglas. **Ira Levin**. Starmont House, 1988.
Ira Levin's brilliant 1967 novel, *Rosemary's Baby* [4-206], made the best-seller list safe for horror fiction. Even so, Douglas Fowler exaggerates Levin's importance. Following a perfunctory biographical chapter, Fowler takes up each of Levin's novels in chapters freighted with plot summaries and cavils at prior reviews and critics who failed to appreciate Levin's genius. Worse, this brief book is awkwardly written, irritatingly cute and condescending to Levin's predecessors (such as Arthur Machen and H. P. Lovecraft). Far better than such superficial analyses as one finds here are Stephen King's discussion of Levin in *Danse Macabre* [7-6], from which Fowler quotes extensively. Chronology, primary and secondary bibliography, index.

Lewis, Matthew Gregory (U.K.), 1775–1818.

8-57. Irwin, Joseph James. **M. G. "Monk" Lewis**. Twayne, 1976.

8-58. Parreaux, André. **The Publication of "The Monk": A Literary Event 1796-1798**. Marcel Didier, 1960.

***8-59**. Peck, Louis F. **A Life of Matthew G. Lewis**. Harvard Univ. Press, 1961.
Matthew Gregory Lewis was no innovator. But his sensational, morbid, hugely popular novel *The Monk* (1796) [1-58] so powerfully synthesized and summarized British literary Gothicism that its influence on English literature persisted through the nineteenth century—and, as Joseph Irwin shows in his thoughtful overview of Lewis's life and works, continues even today. Lewis was also a playwright and poet, and Irwin surveys his Gothic ballads and plays as well as his other novels. Useful annotated secondary bibliography. Irwin's necessarily sketchy biographical chapter should be supplemented by L. F. Peck's scrupulously researched full-length life study, about a third of which consists of reprints of Lewis's fascinating letters. Extensive notes, index, secondary bibliography and a list of Lewis's works, including many that have been spuriously attributed to him. The importance of Lewis and *The Monk* extends beyond the biographical and literary: the publication of this novel was, according to André Parreaux, "an episode in the momentous changes in morals and manners which took place [in England] between 1780 and 1840." Parreaux, who along with the Marquis de Sade considers *The Monk* "the master work of all Gothic fiction," concentrates on the unprecedented impact its publication had on late eighteenth-century readers. In so doing, he exposes the religious, moral, social and political undercurrents that surged through the public, critical and legal controversies over the book. Although specialized, Parreaux's fascinating literary history is recom-

mended to those interested in the Gothic novel, its successors and the social dimension of writing horror. Extensive notes, valuable bibliography, indexes of names and titles. Readers interested in Lewis's plays should consult (in addition to Irwin's chapter) *Gothic Drama from Walpole to Shelley* by Bertrand Evans (Univ. of California Press, 1947). A great deal of material on Lewis appears in Summers [7-33] and in Railo [7-32], but readers should note Peck's critique of these chapters. Birkhead [7-2] positions Lewis in the tradition of British horror fiction, and Kiely [7-29] discusses his importance to nineteenth-century English fiction. Readers curious about Lewis's depiction of Roman Catholicism should consult Sister Mary Muriel Tarr's *Catholicism in Gothic Fiction* (Catholic Univ. of America Press, 1946).

Lovecraft, Howard Phillips, 1890-1937.

Bibliographical Works

***8-60**. Joshi, S. T. **H. P. Lovecraft and Lovecraft Criticism: An Annotated Bibliography**. Kent State Univ. Press, 1981.

8-61. ——, and L. D. Blackmore. **H. P. Lovecraft and Lovecraft Criticism: An Annotated Bibliography, Supplement, 1980-1984**. Necronomicon, 1985.
Lovecraft, whom Barton Levi St. Armand called "the Aristotle of the horror tale," was the most important American writer of weird fiction since Poe. Yet Lovecraft's fiction attracted a mass readership only in the 1960s and 70s, with Ballantine's paperback reprints of his works. And Lovecraft scholarship is, in the words of its primary exponent, S. T. Joshi, "at an amazingly backward stage." Although critics in France, Italy and Spain have long considered Lovecraft the equal or superior of Poe, his work received only fitful attention from American and British critics until the 1980s. Early in that decade there appeared Joshi's indispensable bibliography of magazine, book and anthology appearances of Lovecraft's fiction, translations and foreign editions, critical works, Lovecraft apocrypha and works thought to have been destroyed. Joshi's 1985 supplement updates this bibliography through 1984 and corrects a few errors. Joseph Bell has further updated Lovecraft's growing bibliography in *Howard Phillips Lovecraft: The Books (4) 1915-1986* (Soft Books, 1986). And Robert E. Weinberg and E. P. Berglund have provided a different kind of bibliographical compilation in *Reader's Guide to the Cthulhu Mythos* (Silver Scarab Press, 2d rev. ed., 1973), which lists (chronologically and alphabetically) the torrent of amateur fiction and nonfiction about Lovecraft's Cthulhu Mythos published from his death in 1937 to 1973.

Biographical Works

8-62. de Camp, L. Sprague. **Lovecraft: A Biography**. Doubleday, 1975.

8-63. Long, Frank Belknap. **Howard Phillips Lovecraft: Dreamer on the Nightside**. Arkham House, 1975.
Most curious considering the amount of research and writing on Lovecraft is the still problematical nature of his biography. Of many existing memoirs, one of the

best is W. Paul Cook's *In Memoriam Howard Phillips Lovecraft: Recollections, Appreciations, Estimates* (The Driftwind Press, 1941). Cook—Lovecraft's friend of twenty years and publisher, both of his weird fiction, in the magazine *The Vagrant*, and of his essay *Supernatural Horror in Literature* [7-7] in *The Recluse*—wrote this memoir without access to documentation or data. The result, as Cook describes it, is "very, very random, discursive, and disconnected." Of all Lovecraft's chroniclers, the one who probably knew him best was Frank Belknap Long. Long's affectionate "portrait of HPL" includes a wealth of anecdotal material and reconstructed conversations with Lovecraft, but it makes no pretense at formal biography. The first book-length biographical (and critical) study, August Derleth's *H. P. L.: A Memoir* (Ben Abramson, 1945), must be noted, for it contains material unavailable elsewhere; but it remains inadequate. The sole serious biography, de Camp's lengthy book, has been criticized for its lack of objectivity, superficial literary analysis and attempts to posthumously psychoanalyze Lovecraft. Still, de Camp's remains the most comprehensive and factual look to date at this strange, multi-faceted writer. Ballantine's 1976 paperback edition is abridged and omits the notes, bibliography, index and several photos published in the Doubleday hardcover.

***8-64** Lovecraft, Howard Phillips. **Selected Letters, Vol. I: 1911-1924; Vol. II: 1925-1929; Vol. III: 1929-1931; Vol. IV: 1932-1934; Vol. V: 1934-1937,** ed. by August Derleth and Donald Wandrei (Vols. I-III), by August Derleth and James Turner (Vols. IV-V). Arkham House, 1965-76.

8-65. Lovecraft, Howard Phillips. **H. P. Lovecraft: Commonplace Book, Vols. I-II**, ed. by David E. Schultz. Necronomicon, 1987.

Lovecraft was an incredibly prolific letter writer who "viewed letters in the same way that the average person uses conversation." The five volumes of his *Selected Letters* provide essential insights into his psychology, philosophy and writing techniques. Each is illustrated and includes a preface placing the letters in the context of Lovecraft's life and career. Yet even these compendious volumes contain but a fraction of Lovecraft's estimated 100,000 letters, and more continue to appear—in, for example, *Uncollected Letters*, ed. by S. T. Joshi (Necronomicon, 1986). Additional insights into Lovecraft's fictions are sprinkled throughout the *Commonplace Book*, his collection of "ideas and images for subsequent use in fiction." This "repository of gruesome and fantastick [sic] thoughts" has appeared in four different versions—three of which are seriously corrupted: the original Futile Press edition (Lakeport, Ca., 1938); the one in *Beyond the Wall of Sleep* (Arkham House, 1943); and the one in *The Shuttered Room and Other Pieces* (Arkham House, 1959). Only Schultz's edition restores and extensively annotates the complete text, which emerges as an essential resource for anyone interested in the genesis of Lovecraft's stories and the infamous Derleth-Lovecraft "posthumous collaborations," most of which originated in a line or two in this book. Bibliography, index.

Essay Collections

***8-66**. Joshi, S. T. **H. P. Lovecraft: Four Decades of Criticism**. Ohio Univ. Press, 1980.

8-67. Schweitzer, Darrell, ed. **Discovering H. P. Lovecraft**. Starmont House, 1987.
Joshi's superb collection of critical essays provides a coherent picture of "the astoundingly ambivalent interpretations [that have been] imposed upon Lovecraft's work" since his death. Of greatest consequence for nonspecialists will be Joshi's chronology of Lovecraft's fiction, nonfiction and poetry and his critical survey of the secondary literature. Joshi also reprints (and extensively annotates) in-depth essays on works from various periods of Lovecraft's career. Among the most important of these are two by Fritz Leiber that explore Lovecraft's use of science and of science fictional motifs and one by Richard Tierney that shows how Lovecraft created the mood of cosmic horror that typifies his best work. Other essays by Paul Buhle and J. Vernon Shea situate Lovecraft in political, cultural and literary contexts, and articles by George Wetzel and Dirk Mosig examine the Cthulhu Mythos and its distortion and trivialization by August Derleth and Brian Lumley. Index. Darrell Schweitzer's collection, a revision and expansion of his earlier *Essays Lovecraftian* (T-K Graphics, 1976), is intended as "an introduction to Lovecraft studies." But as such it's far less useful than Joshi's Starmont guide [8-69]. Apart from an essay by Leiber (also available in Joshi's collection), the most valuable item in Schweitzer's book is a detailed comparison of five distinct readings of Lovecraft's important story "The Outsider." Short reading list, index. Readers in search of overviews of Lovecraft's works should consult the introductions to the three (corrected) Arkham House editions of his fiction, especially T. E. D. Klein's essay "A Dreamer's Tales" in *Dagon and Other Macabre Tales* (Arkham House, 1986).

Full-Length Studies

8-68. Burleson, Donald. **H. P. Lovecraft: A Critical Study**. Greenwood, 1983.

***8-69**. Joshi, S. T. **H. P. Lovecraft**. Starmont House, 1982.

***8-70**. Lévy, Maurice. **Lovecraft: A Study in the Fantastic**. Wayne State Univ. Press, 1988. Tr. by S. T. Joshi of *Lovecraft, ou, Du fantastique*, 1972.

8-71. Shreffler, Philip A. **The H. P. Lovecraft Companion**. Greenwood, 1977.
Although Lin Carter's 1972 paperback *Lovecraft: A Look behind the "Cthulhu Mythos"* (Ballantine) brought Lovecraft (and other Mythos writers) to the attention of many readers, this book is filled with errors and misinterpretations, many deriving from Carter's wholesale adoption of Derleth's version of the Mythos, and has long since been superseded by Joshi and Burleson. Joshi packs an amazing amount of analysis and acumen into his brief guide and gives coherence to his discussions of myriad Lovecraft texts (including, briefly, essays and poems) by his overarching insights into Lovecraft's mechanistic materialist philosophy. He links this philosophy to Lovecraft's life in a preliminary biographical chapter, then ties it to Lovecraft's style and themes in a succinct concluding overview. Readers should note especially Joshi's discussions of the influences of Poe, Lord Dunsany and Hawthorne and his excellent annotated primary and secondary bibliographies. Notes, chronology, index. Donald Burleson's book, although

longer than Joshi's, is disappointingly thin. Proceeding chronologically, Burleson provides a plot summary for each major story along with relevant comments from Lovecraft's letters, occasional critical asides, a brief paragraph of interpretation and (generally positive) evaluation. Although Burleson occasionally illuminates, as in his discussions of the hero monomyth in "The Dunwich Horror," his book is more introductory than analytical. Notes, index, selected bibliography. Shreffler's *Lovecraft Companion* is useful primarily as a secondary resource for readers of Lovecraft's fiction. Following an interesting introductory essay that relates Lovecraft to the American and British literary traditions, Shreffler moves to the heart of his book: an alphabetical index of plot summaries of both juvenilia and mature fiction. Some of these entries contain supplemental information on sources of selected stories. Shreffler also provides a concordance to Lovecraft's characters and creatures and a description of the pantheon of Mythos monsters. Illustrated, with index and annotated selected bibliography. By far the best critical work to date on Lovecraft is Maurice Lévy's revision of his 1969 dissertation. This engaging book is both a penetrating look at Lovecraft and his fiction and a useful commentary on the American fantastic tradition; its final chapter, a briefly elaborated theory of the fantastic in literature, is worthy of consideration alongside Todorov [7-76]. Lévy begins with a problem of American history: that its brevity precluded those mythic dimensions so important to the fantastic. This feature, in turn, undercut the development in America of a unified, substantive fantastic tradition. But Lovecraft got around this problem by *dreaming* an archaic mythic tradition into the imagined topography of his beloved New England, contributing to the American weird tale an "intimate fusion of oneiric vision and mythic elaboration." Lévy relates this thesis to Lovecraft's imagery and to the "bestiary" of repugnant monsters that in his fiction is hybridized from the human through the action of heredity. The notes and bibliography were prepared in large part by the translator, S. T. Joshi. Index. Of the many more specialized studies of Lovecraft's work, two by Barton Levi St. Armand are especially noteworthy. In *H. P. Lovecraft: New England Decadent* (Silver Scarab Press, 1979) he relates Lovecraft to the late nineteenth-century European aesthetes and decadents, explores the role of the Puritan ethos in his writings and discusses the influence of Poe and Wilde. In *The Roots of Horror in the Fiction of H. P. Lovecraft* (Dragon Press, 1977), St. Armand uses Ann Radcliffe's differentiation between terror and horror, Rudolf Otto's notion of religious awe, which Varnado has applied to Gothic fiction in *Haunted Presence* [7-22], and Carl Jung's theories of psychological process in a close thematic reading of Lovecraft's "The Rats in the Walls." This reading clarifies more than any other critical work the paradoxical "spiritual terror" at work in most of Lovecraft's fiction. In addition to Lévy's book and Joshi's collection and bibliography, libraries with medium or large collections on American horror fiction should add St. Armand's books and the journal *Lovecraft Studies* [11-41], the primary outlet for serious Lovecraft criticism. Readers interested in Lovecraft's monsters should supplement Shreffler with Lin Carter's "H. P. Lovecraft: The Gods" in *The Shuttered Room and Other Pieces* (Arkham House, 1959) and Peter Cannon's temporal chart of "the modern Lovecraftian age, from Abdul Alhazred and the *Necronomicon* . . . [to] 1935," *The Chronology Out of Time: Dates in the Fiction of H. P. Lovecraft* (Necronomicon, 1986).

Machen, Arthur (U.K.), 1863-1947.

***8-72**. Goldstone, Adrian, and Wesley Sweetser. **A Bibliography of Arthur Machen**. Univ. of Texas Press, 1964.

8-73. Reynolds, Aidan, and William Charlton. **Arthur Machen: A Short Account of His Life and Work**. The Richards Press, 1963.

***8-74**. Sweetser, Wesley D. **Arthur Machen**. Twayne, 1964.

8-75. Valentine, Mark, and Roger Dobson, eds. **Arthur Machen: Apostle of Wonder**. Caermaen Books, 1985.

Arthur Machen's large but uneven output includes several brilliant psychological tales of the transcendental occult—including the once notorious "The Great God Pan." Machen's best works, visionary stories written late in the nineteenth century, draw on his knowledge of occultism and Celtic folklore and his keen sensitivity to the enchantment of nature; these stories evoke ancient evil and spiritual terror in ways that prefigure works by H. P. Lovecraft and Ray Bradbury. Moreover, Machen's desire to render ineffable mystery in fiction anticipates later modernist writers, as explored by Kawin [7-51]. Machen laid a trap for seekers after his life story, for, as D. P. M. Michael remarks in his brief overview *Arthur Machen* (Univ. of Wales Press, 1971), Machen's autobiographical books *Far Off Things* (1922), *Things Near and Far* (1923) and *The London Adventure* (1924) "conceal as many facts as they reveal." Quite trustworthy, though, is the literary biography by Reynolds and Charlton. This book both considers Machen's literary fortunes and defines a literary and philosophical context for his work. In Machen's weird fiction, Reynolds and Charlton argue, "horror is elevated to the intellectual plane without losing its nauseousness." This remark notwithstanding, these authors are thoughtful and even-handed; e.g., they note the deleterious effects of Machen's gift for literary imitation and the compensating effect of his life-long devotion to great literature. Far less impartial is William Francis Gekle's often-referenced book *Arthur Machen: Weaver of Fantasy* (Round Table Press, 1949). Filled with fervent paeans to the "uncanny genius" of "that wonderful Welshman," Gekle's book leaves one thinking Machen had no weaknesses as a man or as a writer. Still, in spite of its arch, self-consciously quaint, irrepressibly discursive style and complete lack of critical perspective, Gekle's book is useful on the reception Machen's works received when, in the 1920s, Knopf began reprinting them in America. Gekle's bibliography of Machen's essays, tales, translations and miscellaneous writings has been superseded by that of Goldstone and Sweetser. In addition to detailed lists of writings by and about Machen (including dissertations but excluding reviews), this bibliography also includes a concise introduction by Sweetser, something of a condensation of his thorough, authoritative 1964 book on Machen. Although this book-length study includes considerable biographical information, it concentrates on Machen's writings and ideas. Working from essays and letters, Sweetser first defines his philosophical context. He then builds a complementary literary context out of the literary traditions in which Machen wrote (Romanticism, Symbolism and Mysticism, and the weird and occult) and the dominant influences on him (e.g., Edgar Allan Poe, Sir Richard Burton and Robert Louis Stevenson). Sweetser concludes that Machen's fiction postulates that "the hieroglyphs of man's heritage[,] . . . to those who read them aright reveal awful, unspeakable, and inexpungable forces of nature which the bodies of organized knowledge . . . tend to de-emphasize." Chronology, annotated bibliography, index. An excellent prelude to reading Machen is the overview by Mark Valentine in his collection of tributes and critical essays. This short book also includes a perceptive essay by Andy Sawyer on Machen's greatest work, the experimental symbolist novel *The Hill of Dreams* (1907). The best contextual discussions of Machen's place in the tradition of the weird tale are to be found in Lovecraft [7-7] and Scarborough [7-12].

Maturin, Charles Robert (U.K.), 1780–1824.

8-76. Kramer, Dale. **Charles Robert Maturin**. Twayne, 1973.

***8-77**. Lougy, Robert E. **Charles Robert Maturin**. Bucknell Univ. Press, 1975.
This Irish priest, author and dramatist created what many consider the apotheosis of British Gothicism. *Melmoth the Wanderer* (1820) [1-64], a fusion of the legends of Faust and the Wandering Jew, influenced numerous later Romantic and Symbolist authors; Honoré de Balzac considered Melmoth one of the four supreme allegorical figures in modern European literature (along with Molière's Don Juan, Goethe's Faust and Byron's Manfred). Robert Lougy's brief overview contains all most readers will want to know about Maturin. His account, well written and leavened by occasional wit, of Maturin's brief and unhappy life provides a frame for his acute analyses of Maturin's major works. Readers wanting more should consult Dale Kramer's fine study, which underscores Maturin's relation to the late eighteenth-century British Gothic novel and drama. Indeed, Kramer's first chapter is an admirable, concise summary of the development of the mode. Following this foundation, Kramer discusses Maturin's novels and plays, including his first Gothic novel, *Fatal Revenge* (1807), his successful Gothic play *Bertram* (1816) and, of course, his "marred masterpiece" *Melmoth*. Kramer skillfully unpacks the "stories, stories within stories, and stories within stories within stories" that comprise *Melmoth* and shows that Maturin was hamstrung by a form more limited than his powers of invention. Chronology, annotated bibliography, index. Large libraries will also want Niilo Idman's pioneering study *Charles Robert Maturin: His Life and Works* (Constable, 1923) for its extensive plot summaries, glimpses of contemporary reviews and useful bibliography. An invaluable related resource is *The Legend of the Wandering Jew* by George K. Anderson (Brown Univ. Press, 1965). Compare Kramer's discussion of *Melmoth* to those of Kiely [7-29] and Napier [7-31].

O'Brien, Fitz-James, 1828–1862.

8-78. Wolle, Francis. **Fitz-James O'Brien: A Literary Bohemian of the Eighteen-Fifties**. Univ. of Colorado Press, 1944.
Introducing the first volume of *The Supernatural Tales of Fitz-James O'Brien* (Doubleday, 1988), Jessica Amanda Salmonson described O'Brien as "the most important figure after Poe and before Lovecraft in modern horror literature." Certainly O'Brien was one of the best American storytellers of the mid-nineteenth century; his major contribution to the American weird tale was probably his

insistence on a (pseudo)scientific basis for the supernatural. But he also introduced new motifs in, for example, "What Was It? A Mystery" (1859) which later appeared transformed in works by Guy de Maupassant, Ambrose Bierce, H. G. Wells and others. Francis Wolle's exhaustively researched biography summarizes contemporary reviews and early twentieth-century assessments of O'Brien's stories and includes an invaluable primary bibliography. But for critical work focused on his fiction, readers must go elsewhere. The place to start is probably Thomas D. Clareson's essay in Bleiler [6-20], which surveys O'Brien's major stories. His contributions to supernatural fiction are (briefly) discussed in context in Lovecraft [7-7] and Scarborough [7-12]. Salmonson's introductions to Vols. I ("Macabre Tales") and II ("Dream Stories and Fantasies") of her edited collection summarize O'Brien's life and show his place in nineteenth-century American literature. And both volumes include fascinating critical and historical notes on each story. Finally, Howard Kerr et al. [7-39] explores O'Brien's adaptation to supernatural fiction of the spiritualist movement that was rampant in 1850s America.

O'Connor, Flannery, 1925-1964.

8-79. Muller, Gilbert H. **Nightmares and Visions: Flannery O'Connor and the Catholic Grotesque**. Univ. of Georgia Press, 1972.

In "Rural Gothic: The Stories of Flannery O'Connor" (*Modern Fiction Studies* 28 [1982]: 475-485), Ronald Schleifer ties the problem of the Gothic to the problem Flannery O'Connor faced in her fiction: how to make the supernatural ("the Sacred") credible to readers whose world seems to admit at most the metaphorical supernatural. O'Connor solved this problem, Schleifer argues, by bringing her "good country people" face to face with metaphors made literal. Like the Gothic novel, O'Connor's fictions juxtapose extremes and are permeated by an atmosphere of eschatological immanence. Complicating this relationship are O'Connor's particular concern for ethical and theological questions. In his fascinating book Gilbert Muller examines structural, thematic and tonal aspects of her use of violence and the grotesque and of Gothic conventions and the supernatural. Elaborating the premise that "Miss O'Connor wrote Christian, explicitly Catholic stories about the grotesque in which men are activated in obscure, seemingly demonic ways," Muller begins by surveying the grotesque aesthetic in literature. O'Connor's protagonists, for Muller, often manifest the influence of the devil and invariably turn to the demonic. Her plots are either mystic quests or literal voyages through which these protagonists enter a chaotic, absurd world against which they perpetually rage. This metaphysical frame illuminates not only O'Connor's fiction but also works by her successors in the American psychological horror story. Notes, index. Additional important works on O'Connor's Gothicism include *Flannery O'Connor's Religion of the Grotesque* by Marshall Bruce Gentry (Univ. of Mississippi Press, 1986), "The Functional Gothic of Flannery O'Connor" by Ollye Tine Snow (*Southern Review* 50 [1965]: 286-299) and articles noted in the bibliographies of *The Added Dimension: The Mind and Art of Flannery O'Connor*, ed. by M. J. Friedman and L. A. Lawson (Fordham Univ. Press, 1966) and *Critical Essays on Flannery O'Connor*, ed. by M. J. Friedman and B. L. Clark (G. K. Hall, 1985).

Poe, Edgar Allan, 1809-1849.

Full-Length Studies

***8-80**. Buranelli, Vincent. **Edgar Allan Poe**. 2nd ed. Twayne, 1977.

8-81. Ketterer, David (Canada). **The Rationale of Deception in Poe**. Louisiana State Univ. Press, 1979.

***8-82**. Saliba, David R. **A Psychology of Fear: The Nightmare Formula of Edgar Allan Poe**. Univ. Press of America, 1980.

Poe's *Tales of the Grotesque and Arabesque* (1840) [2-77] spawned the American horror story and influenced authors from H. P. Lovecraft and Jorge Luis Borges to Ishmael Reed. But Poe's literary reputation remains anomalous, and, perhaps in consequence, Poe scholarship is as uneven as it is vast. Since before Poe's death, reactions to his works have ranged from contempt and dismissal (e.g., Henry James's famous crack, "an enthusiasm for Poe is the mark of a decidedly primitive stage of reflection") to adulation and hyperbole (e.g., the writings of French critics)—as the reader can discover in the reviews and critiques in *Edgar Allan Poe: The Critical Heritage*, ed. by I. M. Walker (Routledge & Kegan Paul, 1986). In the 1980s, much of Poe criticism has degenerated into arguments between literary historians and pure theorists. At issue is the latter's contention that the actual subjects of Poe's fiction are language and writing and the relationship of these issues to the self. Readers interested in this theoretical approach to Poe will find that an accessible and useful example is *A World of Words: Language and Displacement in the Fiction of Edgar Allan Poe* by Michael J. S. Williams (Duke Univ. Press, 1988). Readers seeking a coherent introductory book on Poe's writings should try Vincent Buranelli's critical synthesis. Like the critics in Regan's collection [8-85], Buranelli stresses Poe's diversity, presenting him as poet, hoaxer, critic, fantasist, dreamer, rationalist, ironist, etc. Buranelli also shows the influence on Poe's fiction of a host of factors: Romanticism, Gothicism, pseudo-Oriental ideas, the occultism boom in early nineteenth-century America, the multiple tragedies of Poe's life. In his excellent final chapter, Buranelli addresses the vagaries of Poe criticism and his influence on American and British successors. Chronology, useful and witty annotated bibliography, index. Buranelli acknowledges the emphasis in Poe's doom-laden horror romances on apocalyptic terror. But many critics write as though Poe was not *really* writing horror stories; e.g., David Ketterer [8-81] suggests that "he used the horror format largely for market considerations." Not so says David R. Saliba in his book on Poe's psychology of fear. Based on circumstantial evidence in the tales, Saliba speculates that Poe *deliberately* wrote according to a formula derived from the structure of nightmare, his intent being to deceive and traumatize his readers. Saliba's assumption that Poe, well known to be an articulate critic and literary theorist, never communicated such a recipe is a little hard to credit. And the rigidity with which Saliba applies his thesis to "all" Poe's tales makes that thesis seem ultimately reductive. But his blend of Jungian psychology, dream theory and Gothicism does lead to some fascinating readings. Notes, extensive bibliography, index. Almost as important to Poe's tales as fear is his use of irony, an aspect G. R. Thompson addresses in his extended study *Poe's Fiction: Romantic Irony in the*

Gothic Tales (Univ. of Wisconsin Press, 1973). Thompson argues that what unifies Poe's disparate tales is a blend of skepticism and trickery, the latter derived from German Romantics such as Ludwig Tieck and E. T. A. Hoffmann, that Poe used to hoax gullible readers. But this exhaustively documented book, however stimulating for the specialist, overstates the importance of irony and contains misleading readings of several stories, including two of Poe's best, "Ligeia" and "The Fall of the House of Usher." A different slant on these and other stories is offered by David Ketterer, who represents them as examples of Poe's transcendentalism. Indeed, Ketterer considers Poe an essentially visionary writer. And, like Thompson, Ketterer considers him essentially duplicitous. In the course of making this case, Ketterer clarifies Poe's essential concepts of the grotesque and the arabesque. But the latter half of his book lacks the clarity of its early chapters, and his determination to cover all of Poe's writings results in some cursory treatments. On balance, Ketterer's largely successful effort to reveal the "concerns disguised, like the image of Red Death, in the accoutrements of horror" usefully broadens the view one gains from general critical histories.

Essay Collections

***8-83.** Carlson, Eric W., ed. **Critical Essays on Edgar Allan Poe**. G. K. Hall, 1987.

8-84. Howarth, William L., ed. **Twentieth-Century Interpretations of Poe's Tales**. Prentice-Hall, 1971.

***8-85.** Regan, Robert. **Poe: A Collection of Critical Essays**. Prentice-Hall, 1967. Much of the best Poe criticism is in essay form, and there are several collections ideal for specialist and nonspecialist alike. The place to start is David B. Kesterson's *Critics on Poe* (Univ. of Miami, 1973); its format—bite-sized excerpts from critiques from Poe's era to the present plus longer excerpts from essays on specific topics or works—affords an accessible (albeit superficial) overview of the perplexing panoply of Poe criticism. More depth and breadth is offered by Regan's collection, probably the best single such volume. The essays in it represent varying assessments (pro and con) of Poe's poetry, criticism and fiction, many of which reveal the multiplicity of meanings that emerge from close scrutiny of the tales. Especially noteworthy is Sidney Kaplan's sketch of the history and reception of Poe's romance *The Narrative of Arthur Gordon Pym* (1838). The critics in Howarth's more focused collection concentrate on Poe's major works of horror fiction, adopting historical, theoretical and technical perspectives. Howarth's long introduction is one of the two best overviews of Poe's works, the other being E. F. Bleiler's essay in his *Supernatural Fiction Writers* [6-20]. Howarth clarifies the confusing relationship of Poe's fiction to the Romantic tradition, juxtaposes his critical theories to his stories and explicates the structure, characterizations, style and modes of the tales. Chronology, brief bibliography, index of tales discussed. More focused still is Thomas Woodson's collection on what is probably the most analyzed of Poe's tales: *Twentieth-Century Interpretations of "The Fall of the House of Usher"* (Prentice-Hall, 1969). In brief commentaries and longer essays critics explore symbolism, the *doppelgänger*, Gothic vampirism and other topics related to "Usher," illustrating along the way the ambivalence of twentieth-century criticism toward Poe's work and Romanticism itself. Two more recent collections, however, are to be avoided. Harold Bloom's entries in his "Modern Critical Views" series, *Edgar Allan Poe* (Chelsea House, 1985) and *The Tales of Poe* (Chelsea House, 1987), are uneven in quality, difficulty and degree of specialization. The former contains five well-known essays published prior to 1954, three excerpts from recent books and, in lieu of an introduction, a reprint of a 1984 book review by Bloom. The latter, in which Bloom deprecates Poe's poetry and criticism and only grudgingly acknowledges his status as "a great fantasist," seems singularly out of place. Bloom's other collection contains two important works: Walter Stepp's fascinating essay on the ironic double in "The Cask of Amontillado" and J. Gerald Kennedy's consideration of Poe's conception of death. Still, this volume is hardly "a representative selection of the most useful criticism available on Poe's tales." That description more properly applies to Eric Carlson's *Critical Essays*, a companion to his *The Recognition of Edgar Allan Poe: Selected Criticism since 1829* (Univ. of Michigan, 1966). Carlson collects contemporary reviews, essays by other writers and modern critiques and, in his introduction, deftly surveys trends in Poe criticism from 1829 to 1985.

Biographical and Bibliographical Works

***8-86**. Hyneman, Esther F. **Edgar Allan Poe: Annotated Bibliography of Books and Articles in English, 1827–1973**. G. K. Hall, 1974.

***8-87**. Wagenknecht, Edward. **Edgar Allan Poe: The Man behind the Legend**. Oxford, 1963.
Readers new to Poe biography should be wary; a great deal of claptrap has been written about his life. But Edward Wagenknecht's readable book is reliable, as is Arthur Hobson Quinn's more detailed *Edgar Allan Poe: A Critical Biography* (Appleton-Century-Crofts, 1941). Esther Hyneman's guide to the secondary literature (and to other bibliographies) is valuable for its detailed annotations but should be supplemented by the (briefly annotated) lists of critical articles in *Edgar Allan Poe: A Bibliography of Criticism 1827–1967* by J. Lesley Dameron and Irby B. Cauthen, Jr. (Univ. of Virginia Press, 1974). Libraries and specialists should note the journal *Poe Studies* [11-47], which regularly publishes essays, notes, reviews and wide-ranging bibliographies.

Scott, Sir Walter (U.K.), 1771–1832.

8-88. Parsons, Coleman O. **Witchcraft and Demonology in Scott's Fiction**. Oliver & Boyd, 1964.
Scott's narrative poems are steeped in the supernatural and in folk traditions of the Scottish highlands. Even in his better-known historical novels, one finds important supernatural episodes inserted into their texts. Scott was also an important critic of supernatural fiction and promoted authors such as Matthew "Monk" Lewis and Charles Robert Maturin. Coleman Parsons's scholarly study concentrates on the Waverley novels, showing Scott's use in them of legends, ghosts, haunted places, witchcraft and other supernatural motifs. Parsons also sketches Scott's view of his Gothic predecessors and shows his influence on successors such as Robert Louis Stevenson. Extensive bibliography and indexes.

Shelley, Mary (U.K.), 1797–1851.

Biographical and Bibliographical Works

***8-89**. Lyles, W. H. **Mary Shelley: An Annotated Bibliography**. Garland, 1975.

***8-90**. Nitchie, Elizabeth. **Mary Shelley: Author of Frankenstein**. Rutgers Univ. Press, 1953.

8-91. Spark, Muriel. **Mary Shelley: A Biography**. Dutton, 1987.
Something about Mary Shelley seems to inspire biographers. There have been over twenty full biographies, the latest of which is Emily W. Sunstein's detailed *Mary Shelley: Romance and Reality* (Little, Brown, 1989). Elizabeth Nitchie's is the best critical biography. Well written and filled with thoughtful comments about the style and structure of Shelley's novels, this book also includes a full bibliography (to 1952), a character concordance and detailed listings of Shelley's works and their stage adaptations. Readers wanting a more focused biography should seek out R. Glynn Grylls's *Mary Shelley: A Biography* (Oxford, 1938). Also recommended is the biography section of Muriel Spark's revision of her *Child of Light: A Reassessment of Mary Wollstonecraft Shelley* (Tower Bridge, 1951). Sparks focuses sympathetically on the conflicts, contrasts and contradictions of Shelley's life. These problems began in childhood and continued through Mary's troubled relationship with Percy Bysshe Shelley and in them Spark discerns the seeds of her fiction. Her longer critical section explores, among other topics, Mary Shelley's literary kinship with Edgar Allan Poe and sheds indirect light on Spark's own novels. Little light is shed on Shelley's fiction by her letters. Although numerous, her letters, which have been published in several volumes edited by Betty T. Bennett (Johns Hopkins Univ. Press, 1980–), are less interesting and less illuminating than, say, Lovecraft's. Turning from biography to bibliography, we find W. H. Lyles's definitive (though now dated) volume. This bibliography contains detailed annotations of biographical and critical books, articles and reviews, foreign-language works, M.A. and Ph.D. theses and even fictional works in which Shelley appears as a character. Useful appendices enumerate her works chronologically; reprint the legend of "the heroic George of Frankenstein" (on which she may have based her novel); and list cast and plot information for major theater, film and television adaptations through 1973. Extensive index. A more current though less complete annotated list appears in Frank's *Guide to the Gothic* [7-82] and its update, *Gothic Fiction* [7-83].

Full-Length Critical Studies

8-92. Phy, Allene Stuart. **Mary Shelley**. Starmont House, 1988.

***8-93**. Walling, William A. **Mary Shelley**. Twayne, 1972.
Unfortunately, the best single critical work on Shelley is as yet untranslated. In *Mary Shelley dans son oeuvre: Contribution aux études Shelleyennes* (Klincksieck, 1969), Jean de Palacio applies historical and psychological critical methods to Mary's complete works and clarifies the literary reciprocity between her, her husband, Percy Bysshe Shelley, and other figures in their literary circle such as Lord

Byron and John Polidori. The best critical overview in English is Walling's succinct survey. While acknowledging Shelley's ultimate failure to fulfill the early promise of *Frankenstein* (1818), Walling argues persuasively for the excellence of her next two novels, *Valperga: or, the Life and Adventures of Castruccio, Prince of Lucca* (1823) and the apocalyptic *The Last Man* (1826). Chronology, notes, annotated bibliography, index. General readers whose primary interest is fantasy and science fiction may find Phy's well-written introduction more to their taste. Seeking to rescue Mary Shelley from the shadow of her most famous novel and its pop culture adaptations, Phy summarizes Shelley's biography, situates her in the English Romantic movement and comments intelligently on all her writings. Her chapter on *Frankenstein* summarizes initial reactions to the novel as well as major subsequent criticism. Detailed chronology, excellent annotated bibliography, index.

Essay Collections

***8-94**. Levine, George, and V. C. Knoepflmacher, eds. **The Endurance of Frankenstein: Essays on Mary Shelley's Novel**. Univ. of California Press, 1979.

It is a testament to the power of the myth currents Mary Shelley tapped in *Frankenstein* that so flawed a novel by so minor a literary figure has had so powerful and pervasive an influence. In Levine and Knoepflmacher's seminal collection, critics explore this apparent paradox in eleven original essays and one reprint. Arguing that *Frankenstein* demands multiple, sometimes conflicting interpretations, the editors have skillfully assembled essays on the novel's literary context, biographical origins, political overtones, language and structure, and adaptations on stage and in film. Of special value is Levine's introduction to its mythic origins, its technique, subsequent influence and implications for popular culture. Also noteworthy are Philip Stevick's look at comic incongruities in the novel and Ellen Moers's interpretation, reprinted from her important book *Literary Women* (Doubleday, 1974), of *Frankenstein* as a female "birth myth." Because of the diversity of approaches represented, the readability of its essays and the internal discourses in which they engage, this collection is the best single book on *Frankenstein*. A detailed chronology, annotated bibliography, index and fascinating appendix relating *Frankenstein* to T. H. Huxley's *Man's Place in Nature* (1863) round out this volume. Far less valuable are Harold Bloom's more recent collections, *Mary Shelley*, Modern Critical Views (Chelsea House, 1985) and *Mary Shelley's Frankenstein*, Modern Critical Interpretations (Chelsea House, 1987). Bloom reprints his important 1965 article on *Frankenstein* as the introductions to *both* collections. Each does include a few important works, but both are uneven, spotty in their coverage and overpriced. Neither, unfortunately, makes available M. A. Goldberg's influential essay on the themes of isolation and knowledge in the novel, "Moral and Myths in Mrs. Shelley's 'Frankenstein'" (*Keats-Shelley Journal* 8 [1959]: 27–38).

On Frankenstein

8-95. Baldick, Chris. **In Frankenstein's Shadow: Myth, Monstrosity, and Nineteenth-Century Writing**. Clarendon Press, 1987.

8-96. Ketterer, David. **Frankenstein's Creation: The Book, the Monster, and Human Reality**. Univ. of Victoria, 1979.

***8-97**. Thornburg, Mary K. Patterson. **The Monster in the Mirror: Gender and the Sentimental/Gothic Myth in Frankenstein**. UMI Research Press, 1987.
The resurgence of *Frankenstein* criticism in the 1980s has led to a host of fine books, the best of which is Thornburg's. In relating sentimental and Gothic fiction, Thornburg has identified a myth that is central to Western society. The "sentimental/Gothic myth" is a secular, ostensibly realistic middle-class myth that integrates a multitude of dualities. In essentially sexual terms, it elaborates the tension between two views of reality: the sentimental (secure and rational) and the Gothic (threatening and irrational). Thornburg explains that Shelley's "Gothic parable of the self" novel has retained so firm a grip on the popular imagination because it exposes this myth. Wide-ranging, well researched and wonderfully free of jargon, Thornburg's book is as exciting for what it implies about the past 200 years of Western culture as for what it has to say about Mary Shelley's novel. Bibliography and index. Readers can find additional information on sentimental writers of the period in Wilt [7-80]. Myth is also Chris Baldick's concern in his illuminating study. Specifically, Baldick tracks the apparently anomalous *modern myth* consisting of "that series of adaptations, allusions, accretions, analogues, parodies, and plain misreadings which follows upon Mary Shelley's novel" through works from 1789 to 1917. His most interesting insights derive from his application of historical criticism and the myth theories of Claude Lévi-Strauss to *Frankenstein*. Note that Gregory A. Waller has similarly tracked the Dracula myth in *The Living and the Undead* [7-68]. Index. Three other recent studies contain much of interest. An early examination of the mythic and metaphoric dimensions of *Frankenstein* is Christopher Small's *Ariel Like a Harpy: Shelley, Mary, and Frankenstein* (Gollancz, 1972), which was reprinted as *Mary Shelley's "Frankenstein": Tracing the Myth* (Univ. of Pittsburgh Press, 1973). Underscoring Mary Shelley's biography, Small contends that the novel reflects her attitude toward her marriage. Thus, the dualism she perceived in her husband appears in both monster and creator, but the latter is doomed by his obliviousness to his true nature. A related premise informs the most detailed and controversial book yet on the novel, William Veeder's *Mary Shelley & Frankenstein: The Fate of Androgyny* (Univ. of Chicago Press, 1986). Veeder fragments the text of *Frankenstein*, then applies to the shards psychological critical methods in order to present the novel as a story of "the self divided"—the self being Mary's husband, the androgynous Percy, who becomes both the "[psychologically] hermaphroditic" Victor and his friend Henry Clerval. Veeder's book is interesting and exhaustively documented, but it is far too long and, in its reliance on linguistic coincidences, often strains toward the ludicrous. Unlike Veeder, David Ketterer starts with "the proposition that [Frankenstein's] monster symbolizes [Mary Shelley's novel]." Ketterer disentangles the novel's sources, thematic and metaphoric content and philosophical character. His book, although sometimes obscured by involuted prose, is consistently interesting, especially on Shelley's use of the double, the novel's sexual undercurrents and its relevance to science fiction. On this relevance, see also Brian W. Aldiss's *Trillion Year Spree: The History of Science Fiction* (Atheneum, 1986) and Lowry Nelson, Jr.'s essay "Night Thoughts on the

Gothic Novel," which is reprinted in Harwell [7-26]. Finally, Samuel Holmes Vasbinder examines the structure, setting and the psychologies of Victor and the monster in order to ascertain the *Scientific Attitudes in Mary Shelley's Frankenstein* (UMI Research Press, 1984). Vasbinder's book is useful for its (rather plodding) summary of criticism prior to 1975. But he overstates his thesis that science is more important to *Frankenstein* than magic and alchemy. And readers should compare his speculations on Mary Shelley's knowledge of science at the time she wrote the novel to Small's *Ariel Like a Harpy* and Robert M. Philmus's *Into the Unknown* (Univ. of California Press, 1983). Anyone wanting still more about *Frankenstein* may wish to consult *In Search of Frankenstein* by Radu Florescu (New York Graphic Society, 1975) for historical and geographical background.

Frankenstein in Popular Culture

8-98. Glut, Donald F. **The Frankenstein Catalogue: Being a Comprehensive Listing of Novels, Translations, Adaptations, Stories, Critical Works, Popular Articles, Series, Fumetti, Verse, Stage Plays, Films, Cartoons, Puppetry, Radio & Television Programs, Comics, Satire & Humor, Spoken & Musical Recordings, Tapes, and Sheet Music Featuring Frankenstein's Monster and/or Descended from Mary Shelley's Novel.** McFarland, 1984.

***8-99**. Tropp, Martin. **Mary Shelley's Monster: The Story of Frankenstein**. Houghton Mifflin, 1977.

It is precisely *Frankenstein*'s status as modern myth that makes imperative the study of its transformations in the myriad media of modern culture. Any reader who doubts the omnipresence of the myth in Western culture should spend a couple of hours with Glut's *Catalogue*. The subtitle tells it all: this bibliography of 2,666 items in forty-one categories encompasses every imaginable allusion to the monster or its creator in every conceivable medium—although amazingly, Glut misses such well-known scholarly works as Birkhead [7-2] and Punter [7-10]. Glut's earlier book, *The Frankenstein Legend: A Tribute to Mary Shelley and Boris Karloff* (Scarecrow, 1973), is structured like his *The Dracula Book*. After a cursory chapter on Mary Shelley and her novel, Glut presents a wealth of facts on Frankenstein and his thematic progeny in all media. Sample oddities include sections on Frankenstein films that were never made, underground and X-rated films, films in which the image of the monster is merely glimpsed, and occurrences of the motif in masks, wax museums and coffee houses. Comprehensive to a fault, both volumes are copiously illustrated. More serious and substantive is Martin Tropp's lively book. Bridging the gap between serious literary study and investigation of pop culture, Tropp provocatively discusses the novel's background, dream imagery, technological meaning and use of the *dopplegänger* motif, then segues into several chapters on its stage and film adaptations. Thorough notes, a chronology of Frankenstein films, careful index and a well-organized bibliography. Glut and Tropp are also annotated as [9-45].

Smith, Clark Ashton, 1893-1961.

***8-100**. Sidney-Fryer, Donald. **Emperor of Dreams: A Clark Ashton Smith Bibliography**. Donald M. Grant, 1978.

8-101. ———. **The Last of the Great Romantic Poets.** Silver Scarab Press, 1973. Considering the brilliance of the poetry and prose of Clark Ashton Smith, his critical neglect is a minor scandal. Smith's works—more than 100 exquisite, phantasmagorical, baroque weird tales and prose poems—influenced writers as diverse as Ray Bradbury, Harlan Ellison and Jack London. Donald Sidney-Fryer's oddly organized "textual bibliography" is reliable (though out of date) on Smith's published verse and prose but not on his unpublished works. This book also includes a biographical sketch, a memoir by Smith's friend Eric Baker, letters from acquaintances and a critical essay by Marvin R. Hiemstra. Joseph Bell has brought Smith's primary bibliography up to date in *The Books of Clark Ashton Smith* (Soft Books, 1987). Sidney-Fryer's other book is a strange, extended review-essay on Smith's place in the romantic tradition. In this learned but awkwardly written book, Sidney-Fryer tries to show that "[Smith's] romanticism and . . . prosody . . . are the ultimate flowering . . . of the great romantic-psychological-ethical-mythological-aesthetic synthesis effected by Edmund Spenser." An addendum reviews a recording of the Fourth Symphony by Franz Schmidt (1874–1939), an Austrian composer whose "position in the world of music is roughly analogous to that of Clark Ashton Smith in the world of poetry." Other biographical and critical sources are few, far between and incomplete. For the former, readers can consult chapter 8 of *Literary Swordsmen and Sorcerers* by L. Sprague de Camp [F8-118], essays in *In Memoriam: Clark Ashton Smith*, ed. by Jack L. Chalker (Anthem, 1963) and *Clark Ashton Smith: Letters to H. P. Lovecraft* (Necronomicon, 1987). For the latter, see Charles K. Wolfe's introduction to his edited *Planets and Dimensions: Collected Essays of Clark Ashton Smith* (Mirage, 1973); Brian Stableford's essay in *Survey of Modern Fantasy Literature* [6-24]; and "The Song of the Necromancer: 'Loss' in Clark Ashton Smith's Fiction" by Steven Behrends (*Studies in Weird Fiction* 1 [1986]: 3–12).

Stevenson, Robert Louis (U.K.), 1850–1894.

8-102. Eigner, Edwin M. **Robert Louis Stevenson and the Romantic Tradition.** Princeton Univ. Press, 1966.

8-103. Geduld, Harry M., ed. **The Definitive Dr Jekyll and Mr Hyde Companion.** Garland, 1983.

***8-104.** Veeder, William, and Gordon Hirsch, eds. **Dr. Jekyll and Mr. Hyde after One Hundred Years.** Univ. of Chicago Press, 1988.
Although Stevenson wrote a handful of supernatural tales and fantasies, his major contribution to horror fiction was *The Strange Case of Dr. Jekyll and Mr. Hyde* [2-93]. From its initial publication as a "shilling shocker" in 1886, Stevenson's novella, the prototype of the transformation myth as realized by science, has given rise to a whole subgenre of psychological terror tales about man's inherent moral dichotomy. In the essays collected by Geduld and by Veeder and Hirsch, critics offer various responses to the problematic nature of the novella: as Henry James put it two years after the novella was published, "Is *Dr. Jekyll and Mr. Hyde* a work of high philosophic intention, or simply the most ingenious and irresponsible of fictions?" Geduld's book, the more introductory of the two, reprints the text of Stevenson's story; sequels and parodies; and selected excerpts and essays written from various historical and psychological perspectives. Geduld's

fine opening essay assays the novella's sources, contexts and themes. The most useful of his reprints, an excerpt from Ralph Tymms's *Doubles in Literary Psychology* (Bowes and Bowes, 1971), exhibits a parallel between Stevenson's concept of moral dualism and contemporary theories of (pre-Freudian) experimental psychology on the alteration of personality. Tymms also places *Jekyll and Hyde* in the tradition of allegorical and realistic treatments of the *doppelgänger*, making connections to works by Fyodor Dostoyevsky, Oscar Wilde, H. G. Wells and others that are also explored by Miller [7-60]. But the most useful critical piece in Geduld's collection is an excerpt from Irving S. Saposnik's fine book-length study *Robert Louis Stevenson* (Twayne, 1974). Saposnik restores the structural and thematic dualism that has been leached from Stevenson's fable by its simplistic film adaptations. Geduld does not neglect these adaptations: he reprints descriptions and reviews of early stage and cinema renderings and a fascinating interview with Rouben Mamoulian, who directed the 1932 film version. Geduld's primary bibliography lists main editions; parodies, sequels and stories inspired by Stevenson's novella; and adaptations for stage, film, radio and television through 1973. The critics in the collection by Veeder and Hirsch apply sophisticated critical methods to Stevenson's novella. In addition to their stimulating, largely accessible essays, Veeder and Hirsch include a carefully chosen selection of illustrations and film stills and a collation of extant fragments of Stevenson's two manuscript drafts. Two essays are particularly provocative: in an openly subversive reading, Peter Garret questions "whether any conception of *Jekyll and Hyde*'s moral purpose can contain and stabilize its tensions." And in a related essay Ronald Thomas argues that in its withdrawal of the author and consequent autonomy of the text, Stevenson's story anticipates the modernist novels of Samuel Beckett, Joseph Conrad and James Joyce. Other essays discuss the relationship of *Jekyll and Hyde* to detective fiction and SF, unveil its expression of rage against the failures of Victorian patriarchy and portray it as an "unconscious 'allegory' about the commercialization of literature and the emergence of a mass consumer society in the late-Victorian period." This volume's secondary bibliography is thorough but unannotated. Edwin Eigner discusses Stevenson's ghost and horror stories, situates his works in the tradition of nineteenth-century prose romance and compares his fiction to stories by a number of other writers, including late eighteenth-century Gothicists. Index. A fine recent biography of Stevenson is Jennie Calder's *Robert Louis Stevenson: A Life Study* (Oxford Univ. Press, 1980), which readers may wish to supplement with the wide-ranging overview of his fiction contained in David Daiches's *Robert Louis Stevenson* (New Directions, 1947). Important perspectives on the place of *Jekyll and Hyde* in horror fiction can be found in Briggs [7-3], Punter [7-10], Day [7-17] and Jackson [7-72]. Finally, Beth Kalikoff situates *Jekyll and Hyde* amid a host of late nineteenth-century crime fiction in which men and women descend to amoral animality in *Murder and Moral Decay in Victorian Popular Culture* (UMI Research Press, 1986). Geduld is also annotated in [9-36].

Stoker, Bram (U.K.), 1847–1912.

Biographical and Critical Studies

***8-105**. Carter, Margaret L., ed. **Dracula: The Vampire and the Critics**. UMI Research Press, 1988.

8-106. Leatherdale, Clive. **Dracula: The Novel & the Legend: A Study of Bram Stoker's Masterpiece**. Aquarian Press, 1985.

***8-107**. Roth, Phyllis A. **Bram Stoker**. Twayne, 1982.
Considering the intense critical and popular interest in *Dracula* (1897) since 1970, it is surprising to find no satisfactory biography of its creator. The canonical *A Biography of Dracula: The Life Story of Bram Stoker* by Harry Ludlum (Foulsham, 1962) is tedious, filled with (minor) errors, and offers as literary commentary only plot summaries and superficial asides. *The Man Who Wrote Dracula: A Biography of Bram Stoker* (St. Martin's, 1976) should have been better, for Daniel Farson is Stoker's grand-nephew. But, although he introduces some materials from the Stoker family, Farson relies too heavily upon Ludlum, perpetuates some of the latter's errors and further mars his book with unpleasant speculations that the perverse (sexual) aspects of Stoker's fiction reflect their author's psyche. Fortunately, Phyllis Roth's thorough, thoughtful literary biography begins with a fine capsule biography. Roth portrays both sides of Stoker: "the prolific if not major author and . . . acting manager of Britain's first knighted actor [Henry Irving]." Organizing the rest of her book around the genres in which Stoker wrote—romance, fairy stories, tales of mystery and horror—Roth identifies major themes such as sentimentality and blurring of identity, offers well-balanced accounts of lesser-known works and builds a convincing case that unresolved Oedipal rivalry and "marked ambivalence towards the mother figure" animate all of Stoker's fiction. In her chapter on *Dracula,* which she considers the apotheosis of the Gothic tradition as defined by MacAndrew [7-18], Roth lays out sources, context, history and details of composition, then presents a fascinating psychoanalytic reading of the novel as a pre-Oedipal fantasy of ambivalent sexuality and repressive orality. Chronology, index, excellent annotated secondary bibliography. Roth's reading is but one of several Clive Leatherdale canvasses in his retrospective survey. After introductory chapters on the vampire in European literature and folklore, Stoker's life and the genesis of *Dracula,* Leatherdale looks closely at the novel's major characters, effectively refuting the often-leveled charge—see, for example, Barclay [7-1]—that Stoker was unwilling or unable to create mortals as credible as his monster. Leatherdale then presents five distinct analyses of *Dracula*: in addition to psychoanalytic and sociopolitical interpretations, he considers the novel as manifestation of Victorian sexual repression, as Christian parody and as Arthurian, medieval occult myth. Notes, useful selected bibliography, index. Leatherdale's book, in turn, whets the appetite for Margaret Carter's major collection of critical essays. Although consisting solely of reprints, this book is as important for *Dracula* scholarship as the collection by Veeder and Hirsch [8-104] is for *Dr. Jekyll and Mr. Hyde* and that by Levine and Knoepflmacher [8-94] is for *Frankenstein.* These twenty critics view *Dracula* from various perspectives: psychoanalytic, feminist, formalist, structural, metaphysical, historical and psychosexual. Not surprisingly, the psychosexual approach generates some provocative essays: by Christopher Bentley on sexual symbolism, by Thomas Byers on male dependency and by Christopher Craft on homoeroticism. Less provocative but no less valuable are essays by Carol Senf and David Seed on the narrative structure of *Dracula* and by Mark Hennelley, Jr. on *Dracula* as "a drama of conflicting [Victorian] epistemologies." Although some of these

essays are rather specialized, Carter's collection is notable for its breadth and accessibility, and her introductory survey of *Dracula* scholarship should be consulted by all. Index and useful (but unannotated) bibliography. See also the discussions of *Dracula* in Senf [7-63] and Jackson [7-72], and Leonard Wolf's application of Jungian psychology to vampirism in his eccentric book *A Dream of Dracula: In Search of the Living Dead* (Little, Brown, 1972).

Background on Dracula

8-108. Haining, Peter. **The Dracula Centenary Book.** Souvenir Press, 1987.

8-109. Leatherdale, Clive. **The Origins of Dracula: The Background to Bram Stoker's Gothic Masterpiece.** William Kimber, 1987.
Two recent findings have greatly augmented our knowledge of the writing of *Dracula*. One was the discovery in the mid-1970s of Stoker's research notes: seventy-eight pages of charts, clippings, outlines, etc., that now reside in the Rosenbach Museum and Library in Philadelphia. From these notes, Clive Leatherdale has chosen seventeen nonfiction sources that Stoker used in preparing his novel. Leatherdale's excellent introduction summarizes the contents of Stoker's notes and sketches various critical approaches to his novel. Even more extraordinary was the discovery in the early 1980s of the original manuscript of Stoker's novel, which had been stuffed in a trunk and stored in a barn on a farm in Pennsylvania. In the first half of his heavily illustrated book, Haining recounts this story and describes the manuscript, which bore Stoker's original title, *The Un-Dead*. Haining also surveys Dracula's historical antecedents: Vlad Tepes, the sadistic prince of Wallachia in the fifteenth century, and Elisabeth Bathory, a blood-loving Countess in Hungary in the sixteenth century. But the rest of his book, yet another look at vampire films and the actors who play in them, is of minimal interest. Appendixes list selected case histories of vampirism from the thirteenth century to the present and major Dracula films through 1981. Readers interested in Vlad should consult the more complete book by Radu Florescu and Raymond T. McNally, *Dracula: A Biography of Vlad the Impaler, 1431–1476* (Hawthorn Books, 1973). Those seeking background on vampirism should also consult the general studies by Summers [7-64] and [7-65] and Frayling [7-58], and the introductions and annotations by Leonard Wolf in *The Annotated Dracula* (Potter, 1975) and by McNally and Florescu in *The Essential Dracula* (Mayflower, 1979).

Dracula *in Popular Culture*

8-110. Glut, Donald F. **The Dracula Book.** Scarecrow, 1975.

8-111. Haining, Peter, ed. **The Dracula Scrapbook.** Bramhall House, 1976.
Haining reprints a wealth of hitherto unavailable vampire lore, including articles, movie stills, ancient drawings, reviews, newspaper clippings, maps, poems and memorabilia, as well as overviews of Dracula on film and television—all of which manifest the veritable cult that has grown up since Stoker's Count first stalked into the myth pool of Western culture. Glut's exhaustive look at the Dracula industry reveals the scale of that cult. Vastly comprehensive (though rather undiscriminating) this book surveys the vampire (and Dracula in particular) in history, legend and fiction before and after Stoker; in comics, plays, operas;

on radio and television; and—at great length—in films from around the world. Although Glut's commentary rarely rises above fan level, his book remains an invaluable resource. Scholars and libraries will also want Riccardo's more broadly based bibliography of vampirism [7-62] and Richard Dalby's valuable *Bram Stoker: A Bibliography of First Editions* (Dracula Press, 1983).

Collective Biography

***8-112**. Winter, Douglas E. **Faces of Fear: Encounters with the Creators of Modern Horror**. Berkley, 1985.

Stimulated by the paucity of adequate sources of biographical information on writers of contemporary horror fiction, Winter interviewed seventeen of "the best and the best-selling of modern horror" for this collection. He then reworked transcripts of his interviews into profiles like those in Charles Platt's *Dream Makers: Science Fiction and Fantasy Writers at Work* (Ungar, 1987). Winter eschews commentary and analysis, preferring to let the authors speak for themselves. But he is a fine interviewer—knowledgeable about contemporary horror fiction and conversant with these authors' works—and has elicited from his subjects fascinating and provocative observations on the craft of writing horror as well as about their personal lives and views. The writers interviewed are V. C. Andrews, Clive Barker, William Peter Blatty, Robert Bloch, Ramsey Campbell, John Coyne, Dennis Etchison, Charles L. Grant, James Herbert, Stephen King, T. E. D. Klein, Michael McDowell, Richard Matheson, David Morrell, Alan Ryan, Whitley Strieber and Peter Straub. (Winter's interview with Strieber is particularly interesting in light of the latter's revelations in *Communion* [Wilson & Neff, 1987].) Recurrent themes include religious beliefs and work habits, the trend in the 1980s toward graphic violence, and constraints imposed on writers by commercial considerations. Winter also provides useful guides to reference books, news sources and specialty booksellers who deal in horror fiction; and eclectic (often eccentric) lists of "the best of horror fiction and film" from 1951 to 1985. Reviews of novels and stories by many of the writers interviewed in this book and essays on Campbell, Morrell and Etchison appear in Winter's *Shadowings: The Reader's Guide to Horror Fiction, 1981–1982* (Starmont, 1983).

9

Horror on Film and Television

Michael Klossner

Horror [9-5], edited by Phil Hardy, lists a mere 28 horror films made prior to 1920; 50 made in the 1920s; 65 in the 1930s; 93 in the 1940s; 106 in the 1950s; 306 in the 1960s; 470 in the 1970s; and 210 from 1980 through 1984. This growing appetite for horror was interrupted only in the late 1940s and the early 1950s when horror and SF themes merged in films about monsters which arrived from outer space or were created by radiation. (The best source of information on these hybrid horror-SF films is *Keep Watching the Skies!: American Science Fiction of the Fifties*, vol. 1, 1950–57, by Bill Warren and Bill Thomas [1982].)

The early fifties was an interregnum period between two very distinct phases in the history of the horror film. The period from 1919 (*Cabinet of Dr. Caligari*) to 1946 (the last of the suggestive horror films produced at RKO by Val Lewton) is preferred by traditionalist critics who agree with William K. Everson [9-28, p. 3] that "the best horror films have always been those that relied more on suggestion than on outright statement." Besides Everson, traditionalists include Butler [9-12], Clarens [9-13], Prawer [9-19], Soren [9-20] and Halliwell [9-39]. The modern period, which began in 1957 with the controversial productions of Hammer Films in England and continues to this day, has been characterized by pessimism, cynicism and, above all, explicit violence. Critics who accept the validity of this trend include Nicholls [9-18], Derry [9-25], Pirie [9-32], Hoberman and Rosenbaum [9-41], Newman [9-48], Waller [9-54] and Wood [9-57]. These two schools agree on little but the importance of their subject. Traditionalist Clarens [9-13, p. 33] writes that "Science fiction ages fast and horror remains timeless," and modernist Nicholls [9-18, p. 34] adds that "Fantastic cinema has always been better able to cope with horror, to which imagery and atmosphere are central, than with science fiction, which in its literary form relies on quite complex intellectual structures." In the filmography of Nicholls's *The World of Fantastic Films* [9-18], four critics rate 700 horror, fantasy and SF films on an equal footing. Of the 136 films which received the three highest ratings (4, 4.5 or 5) 57 were horror, 46 fantasy and 33 science fiction. (The count of excellent horror films would have been even higher had not Nicholls excluded horror films without supernatural content, such as *Psycho.*)

Most horror films continue to be cheap productions whose stars and directors are either unknown or famous mainly for horror work. However, since *The Exorcist* (1973) and *Jaws* (1975) showed that even big-budget horror films could make enormous profits, Hollywood has made a steady stream of expensive genre films, often with mainstream directors and stars. Unhappily, one of these films became the focus of a major scandal, when an actor and two child extras were accidentally killed during the filming of *Twilight Zone–The Movie* (1983). A well-known director was tried and acquitted of manslaughter; the case was chronicled in two 1988 books, *Outrageous Conduct* by Stephen Farber and Mark Green and *Special Effects* by Ron LaBrecque.

In the 1980s, the growth of videocassette rentals and of uncensored movie channels on cable TV have made horror films of all periods and types available to a wide audience. However, several disadvantages have accompanied this increased access. The television screen is the wrong size and shape for viewing films. The bad tends to drive out the good in the undiscriminating cable and video markets. Plans were announced late in 1988 to colorize *King Kong* and *Night of the Living Dead* for video release; *Psycho* and the Universal classics of the 1930s will probably be subjected to the same defacement. The easy profits of video and cable have encouraged the production of dozens of cheap and usually terrible horror films which cannot earn back even their small budgets in theatrical release. Libraries should take advantage of the videocassette boom by collecting cassettes of the best films (Table 9-1) in unaltered versions.

Books about the production of specific films can be valuable, and often make nonsense of the theories of critics who have seen the films but have not studied the conditions of their production. Examples of such books in this chapter are Gagne [9-33], Russo [9-34], Goldner and Turner [9-37], Mank [9-45], McGee [9-46] and Siegel [9-53]. Gerald Gardner's *The Censorship Papers* (1987) casts light on an important constraint imposed on filmmakers of the classic period, reprinting letters from the Hays Office which ordered cuts in *Bride of Frankenstein* (1935) and *Dr. Jekyll and Mr. Hyde* (1941). In the 1970s, Richard J. Anobile edited several books, each devoted to a single film, each with hundreds of stills in sequential order showing every scene, with captions for every word of dialogue. The Anobile books were hailed as the next best thing to seeing the film, until home video made them commercially unviable. Serious students will still find Anobile's books on *Frankenstein* (1931), *Dr. Jekyll and Mr. Hyde* (1932), *Psycho* (1960) and *Alien* (1979) valuable.

Jack Sullivan's *Penguin Encyclopedia of Horror and the Supernatural* [6-31] has critical essays on B-movies, books into film, cinema, Dracula in films, Hammer Films, Japanese films, "the pits of horror" (bad horror films), radio, slasher movies, special effects and television; shorter entries on 129 films, one television series (*The Twilight Zone*) and forty-three persons associated with horror films; as well as mentions of films in essays on werewolves, zombies, etc. This chapter is confined to books in English, but readers of French should note that David Pirie, in his *Vampire Cinema* (9-49), calls Gérard Lenne's *Le Cinema fantastique et ses mythologies* (1970) "probably the most perspicacious book about horror films anyone has written." Leonard Wolf annotates 192 theatrical films and two made-for-TV films in his *Horror: A Connoisseur's Guide to Literature and Film* (1989). Some of his choices are outlandish, but his criticism is well worth consulting.

Horror films have always been a popular topic for authors. I rejected about as many books as I selected for this chapter, many of them coffee-table picture books with fan-oriented texts. I wish to thank Milton Subotsky for his help in planning this chapter.

Boundaries between genres are frequently artificial and murky; fantastic films of different types often appeal to the same audience. Readers interested in the books in this chapter should also consult the film and television chapters in *Anatomy of Wonder: A Critical Guide to Science Fiction* (3d ed., 1987) and *Fantasy Literature: A Reader's Guide* (1990), both edited by Neil Barron.

Table 9-1. Best and Most Significant Horror Films and Television Programs

1919 The Cabinet of Dr. Caligari (2)
1922 Nosferatu (2)
1927 The Unknown (1)
1929 Un Chien Andalu (1)
1931 Frankenstein (1)
1932 Dr. Jekyll and Mr. Hyde (1)
1932 Freaks (3)
1932 Island of Lost Souls (1)
1932 Mask of Fu Manchu (1)
1932 The Most Dangerous Game (1)
1932 Vampyr (5)
1933 King Kong (3)
1934 The Black Cat (1)
1935 Bride of Frankenstein (4)
1935 Mad Love (1)
1936 The Walking Dead (1)
1941 Dr. Jekyll and Mr. Hyde (1)
1942 Cat People (3)
1943 I Walked with a Zombie (2)
1944 The Lodger (1)
1944 The Uninvited (1)
1945 Dead of Night (2)
1946 The Beast with Five Fingers (1)
1953 Ugetsu (2)
1954 Them! (1)
1955 Les Diaboliques (2)
1956 Invasion of the Body Snatchers (1)
1957 Enemy from Space (2)
1958 Curse of the Demon (2)
1959 The Tingler (1)
1966 Plague of the Zombies (1)
1967 The Devil Rides Out (1)
1967 The Fearless Vampire Killers (1)
1967 Sorcerers (1)
1967 Wait until Dark (1)
1968 Night of the Living Dead (4)
1968 Oh, Whistle and I'll Come to You My Lad (TV film) (1)
1968 Rosemary's Baby (2)
1968 Witchfinder General (3)
1969 Scream and Scream Again (1)
1969 Taste the Blood of Dracula (1)
1971 Blood from the Mummy's Tomb (1)
1971 Daughters of Darkness (1)
1971 Duel (TV film) (1)
1971 The Night Stalker (TV film) (1)
1972 Death Line (1)
1972 Sisters (3)
1972 The Stone Tapes (TV film) (1)
1973 Don't Look Now (2)
1973 It's Alive (1)
1973 The Wicker Man (3)
1974 Shivers (1)
1974 The Texas Chainsaw Massacre (2)
1975 Jaws (2)
1976 Carrie (1)
1976 Communion (1)
1976 Demon (1)

Table 9-1. *(continued)*

1959–64 The Twilight Zone (TV series) (1)
1959 Les Yeux Sans Visage (5)
1960 Black Sunday (1)
1960 Little Shop of Horrors (2)
1960 Peeping Tom (7)
1960 Psycho (7)
1961 The Innocents (1)
1961 Night of the Eagle (1)
1962 Carnival of Souls (1)
1962 The Premature Burial (1)
1963 The Birds (1)
1963 Dementia 13 (1)
1964 Kwaidan (1)
1964 The Masque of the Red Death (1)
1965 Repulsion (1)
1965 The Tomb of Ligeia (1)
1976 Eraserhead (5)
1977 Count Dracula (TV film) (1)
1978 The Fury (1)
1978 Halloween (4)
1979 Alien (2)
1979 The Brood (2)
1979 Driller Killer (1)
1979 Nosferatu the Vampyr (2)
1980 Scanners (1)
1980 The Shining (1)
1981 An American Werewolf in London (2)
1981 The Howling (1)
1982 Christine (1)
1982 The Thing (2)
1982 Videodrome (1)
1984 A Nightmare on Elm Street (1)
1987 Near Dark (1)

Votes (in parentheses) from Hardy [9-5]; nine critics' lists, pp. 397–399; films with five-star ratings (averaging four critics' ratings) in Nicholls [9-18]; and Michael Klossner.

Table 9-2. Top Horror Rental Films

Title, Year	**$ (thousands)**
Ghostbusters, 1984	130,211
Jaws, 1975	129,549
The Exorcist, 1973	89,000
Gremlins, 1984	79,500
Jaws II, 1978	50,431
Young Frankenstein, 1974	38,823
Poltergeist, 1982	38,248
King Kong, 1976	36,915
The Amityville Horror, 1979	35,000
Beetlejuice, 1988	33,200
The Witches of Eastwick, 1987	31,800
The Shining, 1980	30,900
The Omen, 1976	28,544
Jaws 3-D, 1983	27,035
The Rocky Horror Picture Show, 1975	26,000
A Nightmare on Elm Street, Part 4: The Dream Master, 1988	22,000
A Nightmare on Elm Street, Part 3: Dream Warriors, 1987	21,345
Love at First Bite, 1979	20,600
Poltergeist 2, 1986	20,482

Table 9-2. *(continued)*

Title, Year	$ (thousands)
Little Shop of Horrors, 1986	19,300
Halloween, 1978	18,500
The Fly, 1986	17,500
Friday the 13th, 1980	17,113
A Clockwork Orange, 1971	17,000
Friday the 13th, Part 3, 1982	16,500
Twilight Zone—The Movie, 1983	16,400
Friday the 13th, Final Chapter, 1984	16,000
Psycho II, 1983	15,910
Carrie, 1976	15,207
Dressed to Kill, 1980	15,000
Rosemary's Baby, 1968	15,000
Coma, 1978	14,538
The Texas Chainsaw Massacre, 1974	14,221
The Lost Boys, 1987	14,100
Child's Play, 1988	14,000
Exorcist II: The Heretic, 1977	13,900
An American Werewolf in London, 1981	13,763
A Nightmare on Elm Street, Part 2: Freddy's Revenge, 1985	13,500
Magic, 1978	13,268
Teen Wolf, 1985	12,950
Altered States, 1980	12,500
Omen II: Damien, 1978	12,100
The Elephant Man, 1980	12,010
Halloween II, 1981	11,919
Jaws, the Revenge, 1987	11,282
Psycho, 1960	11,200
Ghost Story, 1981	11,136
The Fury, 1978	11,100
Fright Night, 1985	10,840
When a Stranger Calls, 1979	10,828

Source: *Variety*, January 11, 1989. The figures are rentals paid to the studios, not box-office receipts, for the U.S. and Canada only, not adjusted for inflation.

Table 9-3. Horror Films and Their Literary Sources

This list is selective, especially for books such as *Frankenstein* and *Dracula*, which have been filmed often. Anthology films, short films and made-for-TV films and miniseries are excluded, as are sequel films, which usually bear little resemblance to the original novel. Arrangement is by film title. Titles of literary sources are given only if different from the film title. Titles of novels are in italics, titles of shorter fiction in quotes. Consult author index for entry numbers of annotated fiction.

Table 9-3. *(continued)*

Film title, year(s)	Author, title (if different)
Altered States, 1980	Chayefsky, Paddy
The Amityville Horror, 1979	Anson, Jay (nonfiction)
And Now the Screaming Starts, 1973	Case, David. *Fengriffen*
Angel Heart, 1987	Hjortsberg, William. *Falling Angel*
Audrey Rose, 1977	de Felitta, Frank
The Awakening, 1980	Stoker, Bram. *The Jewel of Seven Stars*
The Bad Seed, 1956	March, William (novel); Anderson, Maxwell (play)
The Beast from 20,000 Fathoms, 1953	Bradbury, Ray. "The Foghorn"
The Beast with Five Fingers, 1946	Harvey, William F. "The Beast"
The Believers, 1987	Conde, Nicholas. *The Religion*
The Birds, 1963	du Maurier, Daphne
Black Sunday, 1960	Gogol, Nikolai. "The Vij"
Blood and Roses, 1961	Le Fanu, Sheridan. "Carmilla"
Blood from the Mummy's Tomb, 1972	Stoker, Bram. *The Jewel of Seven Stars*
The Body Snatcher, 1945	Stevenson, Robert Louis
Bug, 1975	Page, Thomas. *The Hephaestus Plague*
Burnt Offerings, 1976	Marasco, Robert
Cameron's Closet, 1989	Brandner, Gary
Carrie, 1976	King, Stephen
Children of the Corn, 1984	King, Stephen
Christine, 1983	King, Stephen
A Clockwork Orange, 1971	Burgess, Anthony
Coma, 1978	Cook, Robin
Communion, 1989	Strieber, Whitley (nonfiction)
The Company of Wolves, 1984	Carter, Angela. *The Bloody Chamber*
Consuming Passions, 1988	Palin, Michael, and Terry Jones. *Secrets* (play)
Countess Dracula, 1970	Penrose, Valentine. *The Bloody Countess* (nonfiction)
Cujo, 1983	King, Stephen
The Curse of Frankenstein, 1957	Shelley, Mary. *Frankenstein*
Curse of the Demon, 1958	James, M. R. "Casting the Runes"
Curse of the Werewolf, 1961	Endore, Guy. *The Werewolf of Paris*
Dead Calm, 1989	Williams, Charles
The Dead Zone, 1983	King, Stephen
Deadly Friend, 1986	Henstall, Diana. *Friend*
The Devil Bat, 1936	Merritt, Abraham. *Burn Witch Burn!*
The Devils, 1971	Huxley, Aldous. *The Devils of London* (nonfiction)
Die, Monster, Die, 1965	Lovecraft, H. P. "The Colour Out of Space"

Table 9-3. *(continued)*

Film title, year(s)	Author, title (if different)
Dr. Jekyll and Mr. Hyde, 1920, 1932, 1941	Stevenson, Robert Louis
Dr. Jekyll and Sister Hyde, 1972	Stevenson, Robert Louis. *The Strange Case of Dr Jekyll and Mr Hyde*
Don't Look Now, 1973	du Maurier, Daphne
Dracula, 1931, 1958, 1979	Stoker, Bram
The Dunwich Horror, 1970	Lovecraft, H. P.
The Entity, 1983	de Felitta, Frank
The Evil Mind, 1935	Lothar, Ernst. *The Clairvoyant*
The Exorcist, 1973	Blatty, William Peter
The Face of Fu Manchu, 1965	Rohmer, Sax. Fu Manchu series
Fanatic, 1965	Blaisdell, Anne. *Nightmare*
Firestarter, 1984	King, Stephen
Flowers in the Attic, 1987	Andrews, V. C.
The Fly, 1958, 1986	Langelaan, George
Frankenstein, 1931	Shelley, Mary
Freaks, 1932	Robbins, Tod. "Spurs"
Full Circle, 1976	Straub, Peter. *Julia*
The Fury, 1978	Farris, John
Ghost Story, 1981	Straub, Peter
The Godsend, 1979	Taylor, Bernard
The Golem, 1920, 1936	Meyrinck, Gustav
The Hand, 1981	Brandel, Marc. *The Lizard's Tail*
The Hands of Orlac, 1924, 1960	Renard, Maurice
The Haunted Palace, 1963	Lovecraft, H. P. "The Case of Charles Dexter Ward"
The Haunting, 1963	Jackson, Shirley. *The Haunting of Hill House*
Hellraiser, 1987	Barker, Clive. "The Hellbound Heart"
The Hound of the Baskervilles, 1939, 1959	Doyle, Arthur Conan
House of Usher, 1960	Poe, Edgar Allan. "The Fall of the House of Usher"
The Howling, 1981	Brandner, Gary
The Hunchback of Notre Dame, 1923, 1939, 1957	Hugo, Victor
The Hunger, 1983	Strieber, Whitley
I, Monster, 1972	Stevenson, R. L. *The Strange Case of Dr Jekyll and Mr Hyde*
I Walked With a Zombie, 1943	Brontë, Charlotte. *Jane Eyre*
The Incredible Shrinking Man, 1957	Matheson, Richard. *The Shrinking Man*
Incubus, 1982	Russell, Ray
The Inheritance, 1947	Le Fanu, Sheridan. *Uncle Silas*

Table 9-3. *(continued)*

Film title, year(s)	Author, title (if different)
The Innocents, 1961	James, Henry. "The Turn of the Screw"
Invasion of the Body Snatchers, 1955, 1973	Finney, Jack. *The Body Snatchers*
The Invisible Man, 1933	Wells, H. G.
The Island of Dr. Moreau, 1977	Wells, H. G.
The Island of Lost Souls, 1933	Wells, H. G. *The Island of Dr. Moreau*
Jaws, 1975	Benchley, Peter
The Keep, 1983	Wilson, F. Paul
The Lair of the White Worm, 1988	Stoker, Bram
The Last Man on Earth, 1964	Matheson, Richard. *I Am Legend*
The Legend of Hell House, 1973	Matheson, Richard. *Hell House*
The Leopard Man, 1943	Woolrich, Cornell. *Black Alibi*
Lifeforce, 1985	Wilson, Colin. *The Space Vampires*
Lord of the Flies, 1963	Golding, William
Mad Love, 1935	Renard, Maurice. *The Hands of Orlac*
Magic, 1978	Goldman, William
Manhunter, 1986	Harris, Thomas. *Red Dragon*
The Manitou, 1978	Masterson, Graham
The Mask of Fu Manchu, 1932	Rohmer, Sax
The Masque of the Red Death, 1964	Poe, Edgar Allan
Maximum Overdrive, 1986	King, Stephen. "Trucks"
The Medusa Touch, 1978	Van Greenaway, Peter
The Mephisto Waltz, 1971	Stewart, Fred Mustard
The Monkey's Paw, 1923, 1933, 1948	Jacobs, W. W.
The Most Dangerous Game, 1932	Connell, Richard
The Naked Jungle, 1954	Stephenson, Carl. "Leiningen vs. the Ants"
The Nanny, 1965	Piper, Evelyn
Night of the Demon, 1958	James, M. R. "Casting the Runes"
Night of the Eagle, 1962	Leiber, Fritz. *Conjure Wife*
Night of the Hunter, 1955	Grubb, Davis
The Nightcomers, 1972	James, Henry. "The Turn of the Screw"
Nightwing, 1979	Smith, Martin Cruz
The Ninth Configuration, 1981	Blatty, William Peter
Nosferatu, 1922, 1979	Stoker, Bram. *Dracula*
The Old Dark House, 1932, 1963	Priestley, J. B. *Benighted*
The Omega Man, 1971	Matheson, Richard. *I Am Legend*
The Other, 1972	Tryon, Thomas
Pet Sematary, 1989	King, Stephen
The Phantom of the Opera, 1925, 1943, 1962	Leroux, Gaston

Table 9-3. *(continued)*

Film title, year(s)	Author, title (if different)
The Phantom of the Paradise, 1974	Leroux, Gaston. *The Phantom of the Opera*
The Picture of Dorian Gray, 1945	Wilde, Oscar
The Pit and the Pendulum, 1961	Poe, Edgar Allan
The Possession of Joel Delaney, 1972	Stewart, Ramona
The Power, 1968	Robinson, Frank M.
The Premature Burial, 1962	Poe, Edgar Allan
Psycho, 1960	Bloch, Robert
The Queen of Spades, 1949	Pushkin, Alexander
The Re-Animator, 1985	Lovecraft, H. P. "Herbert West—Re-Animator"
The Reincarnation of Peter Proud, 1975	Ehrlich, Max
Rosemary's Baby, 1968	Levin, Ira
Scream and Scream Again, 1970	Saxon, Peter. *The Disoriented Man*
Seconds, 1966	Ely, David
The Sentinel, 1976	Konvitz, Jeffrey
The Serpent and the Rainbow, 1988	Davis, Wade (nonfiction)
Seven Keys to Baldpate, 1930, 1935, 1947	Biggers, Earl Derr
The Shining, 1980	King, Stephen
Silver Bullet, 1985	King, Stephen. *Cycle of the Werewolf*
The Skull, 1965	Bloch, Robert. "The Skull of the Marquis de Sade"
Something Wicked This Way Comes, 1983	Bradbury, Ray
The Spiral Staircase, 1946, 1975	White, Ethel Lina. *Some Must Watch*
The Stepford Wives, 1975	Levin, Ira
The Strange Door, 1951	Stevenson, R. L. "The Sire de Maletroit's Door"
The Student of Prague, 1926	Poe, Edgar Allan. "William Wilson"
The Survivor, 1980	Herbert, James
The Tell-Tale Heart, 1963	Poe, Edgar Allan
The Tenant, 1976	Topor, Roland. *Le Locataire chimérique*
Terror in the Crypt, 1963	Le Fanu, Sheridan. "Carmilla"
To the Devil a Daughter, 1976	Wheatley, Dennis
The Tomb of Ligeia, 1965	Poe, Edgar Allan
The Two Faces of Dr. Jekyll, 1961	Stevenson, R. L. *The Strange Case of Dr Jekyll and Mr Hyde*
Ugetsu, 1953	Ueda, Akinari. 2 stories
The Uninvited, 1944	Macardle, Dorothy. *Uneasy Freehold*
The Vampire Lovers, 1970	Le Fanu, Sheridan. "Carmilla"

Table 9-3. *(continued)*

Film title, year(s)	Author, title (if different)
Village of the Damned, 1960	Wyndham, John. *The Midwich Cuckoos*
Wait Until Dark, 1967	Knott, Frederick (play)
Watcher in the Woods, 1980	Randall, Florence E.
What Ever Happened to Baby Jane?, 1962	Farrell, Henry
White Zombie, 1932	Seabrook, William. *The Magic Island* (nonfiction)
Willard, 1971	Gilbert, Stephen. *Ratman's Notebook*
The Witches, 1966	Lofts, Norah. *The Devil's Own*
The Witches of Eastwick, 1987	Updike, John
Witchfinder General, 1968	Bassett, Ronald
The Wolfen, 1981	Strieber, Whitley
Les Yeux sans visage, 1959	Redon, Jean

Reference Works

9-1. Halliwell, Leslie (U.K.). **Halliwell's Film and Video Guide.** 6th ed. Scribner's, 1987.

Halliwell's views are often old-fashioned, but his *Guide* is the most sophisticated of three popular, one-volume, annotated guides to most English-language and selected foreign films. Most of the 16,000 entries include date, length, color or black-and-white, credits (production company, producer, director, actors, writer, literary source, photographer, composer, art director), a rating of from zero to four, a brief synopsis and critique and any alternate titles or important awards. Halliwell's rivals, Leonard Maltin's *TV Movies and Video Guide* and Steven H. Scheuer's *Movies on TV* (both annuals) include less information and generally more lenient ratings.

9-2. Nash, Jay Robert, and Stanley Ralph Ross, eds. **The Motion Picture Guide**. 12 vols. Cinebooks, dist. Bowker, 1985–87.

9-3. Variety Film Reviews. 16 vols. Garland, 1983.

Each of these two expensive sets covers almost all English-language films and many silent and foreign films. Nash provides credits (including actors and names of characters portrayed), descriptions and criticism for about 35,000 sound films and 3,500 silents, and credits only for 2,000 minor sound films and 10,000 silents. The main set covers films through 1984; annual supplements for 1985, 1986, 1987 and 1988 releases have appeared to date. The *Variety* set has credits, descriptions and reviews for over 40,000 films from 1907 to 1980, with biennial updates for 1981–82, 1983–84, 1985–86, and 1987–88 so far. Nash's annotations are new and reflect up-to-date attitudes, while the reprinted *Variety* reviews, contemporary with the films, are often quaint. The Nash set is several hundred dollars cheaper, includes 10,000 more films and is more consistent in format and treatment, but *Variety*'s reviews are generally shrewder, wittier and more erudite. *Variety* is written by and for hard-headed film industry professionals; the Nash set is typical of film buff criticism. Since neither set is indexed by genre, students of fantastic films must use them in conjunction with the specialized reference works annotated below. (Many of the approximately 1,000 reviews reprinted in *Variety's Complete Science Fiction Reviews* (1985), edited by Donald Willis and covering 1907 to 1984, are borderline horror or fantasy.)

9-4. Scheuer, Steven H., ed. **The Complete Guide to Videocassette Movies.** Holt, 1987.
Horror films are one of the mainstays of the videocassette rental market. With over 5,000 entries, Scheuer's *Guide* is the best and most complete of many guides to films on video, although some of the unsigned, one-paragraph reviews are supercilious about acceptable popular films. Entries are in alphabetical order by title and include date, running time, country of origin, MPAA rating, director, cast, a genre symbol and a rating of from one to four. A genre index identifies horror and SF titles. The eleven-inch paperback is not designed for heavy use and should be prebound.

***9-5.** Hardy, Phil (U.K.), ed. **Horror**. Aurum, 1985. (Reprinted as *The Encyclopedia of Horror Movies*. Harper, 1986.)
The entries for more than 1,300 films, arranged chronologically from 1896 to 1985, include variant titles (which are common among horror films), studios, running time, color or black-and-white, principal credits and from 100 to 1,000 words of synopsis and clear, terse, well-informed evaluation. The title index, in very small print, includes all variant titles. Hundreds of black-and-white and dozens of color stills are well chosen and well reproduced. (The color illustrations are omitted from the U.S. reprint.) Appendixes include box office champions, best film lists by nine critics (used in Table 9-1), Oscar nominees and winners and a selective bibliography. Especially valuable is the inclusion of dozens of silent films and hundreds of films from Germany, France, Italy, Spain, Mexico, Japan and several other countries; many books in the field concentrate parochially on U.S. and British sound films. The third volume in the Aurum Film Encyclopedia series, *Horror* is the best reference work devoted to horror films. Hardy also edited *Science Fiction* (1984), the equally important second volume in the Aurum series.

9-6. Lee, Walt. **Reference Guide to Fantastic Films: Science Fiction, Fantasy and Horror.** 3 vols. Chelsea-Lee Books, 1972–74.
Many well-spent years of fan scholarship lie behind this remarkable compilation. About 15,000 films are arranged by title in three sturdy eleven-inch paperbacks. Many entries are incomplete; complete entries include date, country, length, credits (including casts but not names of characters), a brief, nonevaluative note describing the film's fantastic elements (not a complete synopsis) and references to information (not necessarily reviews) found in hundreds of sources listed in the bibliography. About 5,000 more films are listed briefly as "exclusions" (films which appear to have fantastic elements but do not) and "problems" (for which sufficient information could not be found). The approximately 150 illustrations are mainly unfamiliar and interesting. This is by far the most complete filmography of fantastic films made before the 1970s.

9-7. Lentz, Harris M. **Science Fiction, Horror and Fantasy Film and Television Credits.** 2 vols. McFarland, 1983.
Lentz lists credits in genre films and TV programs for more than 10,000 actors, directors, producers, writers, cinematographers, special effects and makeup artists and composers of film scores. Birth and death dates are given in many but not all cases. Entries for actors include the names of characters portrayed. Vol. 2 is arranged by titles of films and TV series. For films, only the director and actors are listed; it is necessary to look in other works to find who performed other functions on a film. Lentz provides the most complete information anywhere on fantastic TV series, including title, actors, character names and broadcast dates for each episode. This very complete work has been updated by a 1989 supplement, current through 1987.

9-8. Weldon, Michael. **The Psychotronic Encyclopedia of Film.** Ballantine, 1983.
Weldon includes art films and expensive productions and ranges from the 1930s to the 1980s, but B-movies of the 1950s and 1960s are his first love. Many of the over 3,000 films listed are nonfantastic exploitation movies, such as juvenile delinquent and prison films. Except for the very good and the very bad, Weldon describes but does not evaluate most films, recognizing that B-movie fans are attracted by plot elements and stars, not by conventional dramatic and cinematic values. He has something interesting to say about almost every film. As a fan critic, Weldon is superior to John Stanley, whose *Revenge of the Creature Features Movie Guide* (3d ed., 1988) has more films (almost 4,000) but less wit. Joe Bob Briggs's *Joe Bob Goes to the Drive-In* (1987) humorously describes several dozen exploitation films of the early 1980s, about half of them horror or sword-and-sorcery, throwing light on the psychology and simple needs of B-movie fans. For a much more analytical study of such films, see Hoberman and Rosenbaum [9-41] and Danny Peary's *Cult Movies* (1981), *Cult Movies 2* (1983) and *Cult Movies 3* (1988).

9-9. Willis, Donald. **Horror and Science Fiction Films.** Scarecrow, vol. I, 1972; vol. II, 1982; vol. III, 1984.
Entries include the usual information (year, country, running time, production company, credits, cast, variant titles) as well as citations to reviews and sources of more complete information. Vol. I has about 4,400 films, Vol. II about 2,350 and Vol. III, 760, but many entries in Vols. II and III are critical commentaries for films listed briefly in a previous volume. As the number of films in each volume has decreased, the length of Willis's commentaries has increased. His Vol. I is comparable to but much less complete than Lee's *Reference Guide* [9-6]. Willis's critical annotations are respectable, but less authoritative than those in Hardy's *Horror* [9-5] and *Science Fiction.*

Periodicals

***9-10. Cinefantastique.** ISSN 0145-6032. 1970– . 5 issues per year. Frederick S. Clarke, ed. Box 270, Oak Park, IL 60303. Circulation: 20,000.

9-11. Fangoria. ISSN 0164-2111. 1979– . 10 issues per year. Anthony Timpone, ed. Starlog Group, Inc., 475 Park Ave. S, New York, NY 10016. Circulation: 150,000.
Cinefantastique is the highest-quality English-language magazine on fantastic cinema, covering horror, fantasy and SF films and TV. Issues range from sixty to

ninety pages, with in-depth articles and excellent illustrations. Short pieces profile forthcoming releases. Current films and TV programs are reviewed with independence and sophistication. *Cinefantastique*'s irreverence has led to a lengthy feud with the Lucas-Spielberg empire, which has curtailed the periodical's ability to cover many major productions in depth. *Fangoria* is aimed squarely at young fans of gory horror movies. Issues are usually seventy pages long and heavily illustrated, with informative but uncritical articles. *Fangoria* maintains friendly relations with studios by not reviewing current films. Videocassettes of older films are reviewed. Both *Cinefantastique* and *Fangoria* carry major articles on historically important films from past decades. *Fangoria* frequently interviews filmmakers, including actors; *Cinefantastique* interviews film workers but usually eschews actors, an unjustified and snobbish policy. *Cinefantastique* is essential for students of fantastic films; *Fangoria*, with its abundance of facts and paucity of analysis, is useful for large collections. Comments on forthcoming films appear regularly in *Locus* [11-40] and *Science Fiction Chronicle* [11-40]. Gahan Wilson's lively reviews in *Twilight Zone* [11-15] are worthwhile, but Harlan Ellison's rambling pieces on films in *Magazine of Fantasy and Science Fiction* [11-13], collected in *Harlan Ellison's Watching* (1989), are more often harangues against the iniquities of Hollywood than critiques of specific films. Special issues of three mainstream film periodicals—vol. 19 of *Photon*, vol. 2 (no. 2) of *Film Journal* and Vol. 6 (no. 1) of *Film Criticism*—have been devoted exclusively to horror films. Two annuals, *International Index to Film Periodicals* and *Film Literature Index*, index articles and reviews in film magazines. *Film Review Index* (2 vols., 1986, 1987), edited by Patricia King Hanson and Stephen L. Hanson, indexes both reviews in periodicals and discussions in hundreds of books of over 7,000 significant films from the silents to 1985. Lee [9-6] and Willis [9-9] provide citations to periodical literature.

Critical Studies

9-12. Butler, Ivan (U.K.). **Horror in the Cinema.** A. S. Barnes. 3d ed., 1979.
Butler discusses only a few dozen films, mostly well-known classics. His analyses of individual films are often excellent, but his insistence that subtlety and restraint are the only legitimate tactics for a horror film is outdated.

***9-13.** Clarens, Carlos. **An Illustrated History of the Horror Film.** Putnam, 1967. (*Horror Movies: An Illustrated Survey*. 2d ed. Secker and Warburg, 1968.)
Peter Nicholls [9-18] calls Clarens "the most respected critic of horror films but a frightful snob." Despite his title, Clarens discusses many fantasy and SF films, from Georges Meliès's trick films and *Metropolis* to 1950s alien invasion films and *Alphaville*. Writing in 1967, he covers only about fifty years of horror cinema. As the premiere traditionalist critic of horror films, he prefers suggestion to violence and dislikes films that dabble in psychology and politics, but he is surprisingly sympathetic to many European shockers of the 1950s, such as *Les Yeux sans visage* and the works of Mario Bava and Ricardo Freda. Despite his austere reputation, Clarens approaches his subject with enthusiasm and his insights are exciting as well as elegant.

9-14. Daniels, Les. **Living in Fear: A History of Horror in the Mass Media.** Scribner's, 1975.

9-15. King, Stephen. **Danse Macabre.** Everest House, 1981.

9-16. Twitchell, James. **Dreadful Pleasures: An Anatomy of Modern Horror.** Oxford Univ. Press, 1985.
All three books fruitfully consider both literature and film. Daniels has the widest scope, examining horror in the pulps, comics, radio, TV and even rock music, as well as fiction and films. His comments on individual works are necessarily terse, and he does not take time to defend his more controversial opinions. King on the other hand is leisurely, loquacious and level-headed, with a sharp eye for detail, as he addresses several questions. How do horror films scare people? Why do some intelligent viewers enjoy bad horror movies? Why is TV usually a hopeless medium for horror? Why is radio superior to visual media? King lists about 100 of his favorite films in an appendix. The most insightful of the three, Twitchell maintains that horror has changed little since the eighteenth century and is an essentially conservative part of the sexual initiation of adolescents, "the morality plays of our time." Daniels is also annotated as [7-4], King as [7-6] and Twitchell as [7-77].

9-17. Huss, Roy, and T. J. Ross, eds. **Focus on the Horror Film.** Prentice-Hall, 1972.
Most of the twenty-four essays collected here are from 1960s film journals. Even in 1972 they must have seemed old-fashioned; there is little mention of the profound changes wrought in horror films by relaxation of censorship and by such films as *Night of the Living Dead* (1968), and inadequate attention is paid to foreign films. Most of the essays examine only one film. Almost all are sophisticated and jargon-free. One is by a film director, Curtis Harrington; two are by writers—Jack Kerouac on *Nosferatu* and Ray Bradbury on *Rosemary's Baby.*

***9-18.** Nicholls, Peter (U.K.). **The World of Fantastic Films: An Illustrated Survey.** Dodd, Mead, 1984. U.K. title: *Fantastic Cinema.* Ebury, 1984.
Nicholls's survey of fantastic films of all kinds, horror, fantasy and SF, has an exceptional critical text, illustrations carefully selected to represent many periods and types of films, and reference information. The latter is found in a filmography of 700 titles; each entry includes country, date, length, color or black-and-white, production company, principal credits and cast and a rating based on the average of four critics' opinions. Recent horror films have an additional rating system to indicate explicit horrific material. The filmography briefly annotates 400 films; the other 300 are discussed at greater length in the well-organized text. In a field where many books omit important films or delve deeply into trivia, Nicholls includes almost all significant titles and none of interest only to completists. He can be faulted only for omitting horror films without supernatural content, such as *Psycho* and *Peeping Tom,* and for rushing through several decades; 44 pages cover films from the 1890s to 1967, while 120 pages are devoted to works from 1968 to 1983. Coverage of foreign films is strong. *The World of Fantastic Films* is the best one-volume critical work covering all kinds of fantastic cinema. Baird Searles discusses a few dozen horror films in his heavily illustrated *Films of Science Fiction and Fantasy* (1988), but he omits several important titles and is rarely as insightful as Nicholls.

9-19. Prawer, S. S. **Caligari's Children: The Film as Tale of Terror.** Oxford Univ. Press, 1980.
Prawer discusses only five films at length. *Caligari, Vampyr, Frankenstein* and *Dr. Jekyll and Mr. Hyde* all date from 1919 to 1932; the fifth, *Dracula Prince of Darkness,* is a mediocre Hammer film chosen as a horrible example. The author carries old-fashioned dislike of sensation and violence to the extreme of smug derision of all but the most securely recognized art. He even disapproves of the original *King Kong*. Prawer should be consulted as an example of ultra-traditionalism, but also for his admirable knowledge of how filmmakers have used their arsenal of techniques (lighting, sound, music, camera angles, editing) to create unease.

9-20. Soren, David. **The Rise and Fall of the Horror Film: An Art Historical Approach to Fantasy Cinema.** Lucas Bros., 1977.
Soren examines the influence of mainstream art movements, especially Expressionism and Surrealism, on horror films, with examples from the works of Meliès, Lang, Murnau, Cocteau, Jean Vigo, Dreyer, Czech animator Karel Zeman and others. Some of the films cited are only marginally horror or fantasy, such as the surreal musicals of Busby Berkeley. As his title suggests, Soren prefers older films. Although his perspective is unique and illuminating, Soren's book is unindexed and the vital illustrations, which include art works as well as film stills, are black and white and very small. Compare Eisner [9-27].

Specialized Studies

9-21. Adler, Alan. **Science Fiction and Horror Movie Posters in Full Color.** Dover, 1977.
Most of the forty-six posters reproduced here promoted schlock films of the 1950s, when the posters were frequently more thrilling than the movies. Almost all reproductions are a generous 13 × 9 inches. Adler's brief annotations are informative about both the films and the poster art.

9-22. Bouzereau, Laurent. **The De Palma Cut: The Films of America's Most Controversial Director.** Dembner Books, 1988.
In addition to supernatural films (*Carrie, The Fog*), Brian De Palma has made violent thrillers (*Sisters, Phantom of the Paradise, Dressed to Kill, Body Double*), which are usually considered horror films. Admitting that De Palma's works are "my obsession," Bouzereau defends the director against charges of plagiarism, misogyny and sensationalism; argues that De Palma is a genius misunderstood by studios, critics and audiences; and finds De Palma's preference for "visual concepts over a substantial plot" perfectly legitimate. Although Bouzereau is often effusive about his idol, his analysis of De Palma's themes and techniques is thorough. Susan Dworkin's *Double De Palma* (1984) concentrates on the film *Body Double.*

9-23. Brosnan, John (U.K.), **The Horror People.** St. Martin's, 1976.
Brosnan's sprightly sketches of seven directors, seven actors, four producers, two writers (Matheson and Bloch), three production organizations (Val Lewton's RKO horror unit, AIP and Hammer) and one fan (Forrest Ackerman) associated

with horror films rely heavily on quotations from the subjects and their colleagues. Sometimes interviewees contradict each other interestingly. An appendix devotes a paragraph to each of forty-nine lesser figures. Michael Pitts's *Horror Film Stars* (1981) covers fifteen stars and twenty-eight supporting players, but his profiles are scarcely more than filmographies padded by very brief comments on individual films. Brosnan's work provides a historical overview of trends in U.S. and British horror films from the 1920s to the 1970s. Pitts is needed only for the people he covers who are not in Brosnan. Compare Weaver [9-55].

9-24. Collings, Michael R. **The Films of Stephen King.** Starmont House, 1986. Collings's critiques of eleven feature films and four short films based on novels and stories by King are detailed and persuasive but repetitious. The reader's familiarity with both the fiction and the films is assumed, although only perhaps four of the films are important enough to warrant study. Collings includes a substantial bibliography, mostly of magazine articles and reviews. Jeff Conner's *Stephen King Goes to the Movies* (1987) is more current but less analytical than Collings, with many quotations from King about his experiences with filmmakers. King also discusses the films made from his works in a chapter in *Bare Bones: Conversations with Stephen King* (1988), ed. by Tim Underwood and Chuck Miller. Other books on films based on a single author's works include Rose London's heavily illustrated *Cinema of Mystery* (1975), which identifies many films based on Poe but provides only terse, idiosyncratic commentary; Gary Morris's *Roger Corman* (1985), with fifty pages on Corman's six Poe films; and Darrell Schweitzer's outdated, sophomoric twenty-two-page booklet *Lovecraft in the Cinema* (1975), which describes only three feature films and two TV episodes. Each of three essays in *The English Novel and the Movies* (1981), ed. by Michael Klein and Gillian Parker, examines one major film based on a classic novel—*Dracula, Frankenstein* and *Dr. Jekyll and Mr. Hyde.*

9-25. Derry, Charles. **Dark Dreams: A Psychological History of the Modern Horror Film.** A. S. Barnes, 1977.
After the decline of both the classic Gothic horror cinema and the horror-SF of the 1950s, and before the rise of the slasher film, the 1960s and the early 1970s saw a surprising number of interesting horror films with ambitious psychological themes. Major titles included *Psycho, The Birds, Rosemary's Baby, Don't Look Now, The Innocents* and *Jaws.* Derry's succinct, sensible criticism demonstrates that these and dozens of minor films of the period shared the same concerns and tactics. Heavily illustrated, with a few pages of surprising praise for Japanese monster movies. Updated by Derry's essay in Waller's *American Horrors* [9-54].

9-26. Dillard, R. H. W. **Horror Films.** Monarch Press, 1976.
Provocative, chapter-length examinations of four films Dillard believes are "of real and serious value to the individual moral consciousness." Attempting to rehabilitate two films of the classic Hollywood era which have recently fallen in critical esteem, he makes great claims for *Frankenstein* (1931) and modest claims for *The Wolf Man* (1941). Considering two much more recent and explicit films, he finds *Night of the Living Dead* (1968) to be a work of utter nihilism and calls *Fellini Satyricon* (1969), a controversial work often omitted from surveys of fantastic films, the "greatest and most perfect of horror films."

***9-27.** Eisner, Lotte (Germany). **The Haunted Screen: Expressionism in the German Cinema and the Influence of Max Reinhardt.** Univ. of California Press, 1969. Tr. of *L'Écran démoniaque,* 1952.

The German film renaissance of the 1920s, influenced by Expressionism, Surrealism and the experiments of theater director Max Reinhardt, was characterized by bizarre costumes, sets and even (often artificial) landscapes, nonnaturalistic acting and an obsession with light and shadow. Most of the significant films were horror, fantasy, SF or horrific mysteries and had an immense influence on the Hollywood horror classics of the 1930s. Eisner, an art historian who knew many of the important German filmmakers of the time, brings a thorough knowledge of the social, cultural and intellectual background to her brilliant analyses of the films. Many striking illustrations complement the text.

9-28. Everson, William K. **Classics of the Horror Film.** Citadel Press, 1974.

9-29. ———. **More Classics of the Horror Film.** Citadel Press, 1986.

9-30. Turner, George E., and Michael H. Price. **Forgotten Horrors: Early Talkie Chillers from Poverty Row.** A. S. Barnes, 1979.

Although he includes some silents and a few recent films, most of the several dozen films discussed by Everson in his two volumes are little-remembered films of the 1930s and 1940s which he believes deserve more attention. Despite his titles, Everson admits that most of the films were not "classics." Several are only marginal horror; there is even a chapter in the second volume on horror in nonhorror films. Everson may be too tolerant of some of these old films, but he has a good appreciation of the importance of art direction, music, cinematography and editing. Turner and Price give credits, synopses and well-informed criticism of 115 films and serials made very cheaply by independent producers from 1929 to 1937, during the heyday of the Universal horror classics. Most were mysteries, westerns or jungle movies with horrific or occult elements; several were horror comedies; and some were real horror films. The authors claim that several were worthwhile and even innovative, such as *White Zombie* (1932) and the SF film *Deluge* (1933), which exists only in a recently discovered Italian-dubbed print. All three books describe many films rarely discussed elsewhere.

9-31. Eyles, Allen; Robert Adkinson; and Nicholas Fry (U.K.). **The House of Horror: The Complete Story of Hammer Films.** 2d ed. Lorrimer, 1984.

9-32. Pirie, David (U.K.). **A Heritage of Horror: The English Gothic Cinema, 1946–1972.** Avon, 1973. (British ed.: Gordon Fraser, 1973.)

From 1957 to 1976, Hammer Films in Britain made dozens of popular Gothic horror films, many of them based on Universal classics of the 1930s, but in color and with as much violence and sexuality as changing censorship standards would allow. Traditionalist critics consider the Hammer films lurid and sensationalist; progressives scorn them as reactionary and sexist. Nobody likes them much except the public and David Pirie. Pirie's detailed and eloquent if not entirely persuasive defense of Hammer relates the films to the long British Gothic literary heritage and contrasts them with the excessively genteel tradition of mainstream British films. Pirie also praises several little-known films made by Hammer's smaller British rivals. *A Heritage of Horror* is a serious, important alternate point of view on a series of very popular and, for a time, influential films. *The House of Horror* is an uncritical short history of Hammer Films, useful for interviews with Hammer executive Michael Carreras and controversial director Terence Fisher and for an excellent selection of stills which display Hammer's distinctive visual style.

9-33. Gagne, Paul R. **The Zombies That Ate Pittsburgh: The Films of George A. Romero.** Dodd, Mead, 1987.

9-34. Russo, John. **The Complete Night of the Living Dead Filmbook.** Harmony Books, 1985.

Russo, screenwriter of *Night of the Living Dead,* tells how a small, talented company led by director George Romero made the immensely profitable and influential film on a tiny budget in rural Pennsylvania in 1968. His account of ingenuity in planning, filming, postproduction work and marketing is a primer and an inspiration for independent filmmakers. Gagne describes the production of all of Romero's films through 1985. Insisting on independence from the major studios, Romero ran into perennial money problems as he made several horror films which proved much less lucrative than his debut film. Gagne considers almost all of Romero's films important and fills his book with immodest quotations from Romero and his associates. Although *Zombies* is almost adulatory, it does present a fuller and grimmer picture than Russo's *Filmbook* of the long-term difficulties facing regional filmmakers.

9-35. Gaiman, Neil, and Kim Newman (U.K.). **Ghastly beyond Belief.** Arrow, 1985.

This collection of delightfully awful genre quotations draws on both fiction and films. The fiction section is based mostly on SF rather than horror works, but horror movies contribute much more than SF films to the movie section. The wisecracks, clichés, pseudo-profound philosophy, scientific gobbledygook and dumbfounding chauvinism, sexism and racism from the mouths of mad doctors, hunchbacked assistants, know-it-all scientists, malicious aliens and hysterical peasants are almost always hilarious ("For this one, Father, I suggest a slower death"; "Gamera is headed this way with a spaceship in his mouth!") and often revealing (strong-jawed hero to babbling scientist: "Don't tell me how you created it. Tell me how to destroy it.").

9-36. Glut, Donald F. **Classic Movie Monsters.** Scarecrow, 1978.

Glut, who considers many minor films "classics," offers wordy synopses and bland criticism of films, TV programs, plays, fiction and comics featuring the Wolf Man, Dr. Jekyll and Mr. Hyde, the Invisible Man, the Mummy, the Hunchback of Notre Dame, the Phantom of the Opera, the Creature from the Black Lagoon and King Kong. Aside from an entertaining and informative survey of the Japanese giant monster movies, Glut's book is of value only as a complete list of the works dealing with each monster. Glut's *The Frankenstein Legend* (1973) is a similar catalogue of works about both the Frankenstein monster and the Golem, the creature based on Jewish folk tradition. Essays on the most celebrated film of *Dr. Jekyll and Mr. Hyde,* directed in 1932 by Rouben Mamoulian, are found in

Dr Jekyll and Mr Hyde after One Hundred Years [8-104], ed. by William Veeder and Gordon Hirsch and in *The English Novel and the Movies* (1981), ed. by Michael Klein and Gillian Parker. *The Definitive Dr. Jekyll and Mr. Hyde Companion* (1983), ed. by Harry M. Geduld, includes an interesting interview with Mamoulian and a very complete filmography of films and TV programs. (Geduld is also annotated as [8-103].) George Perry's *The Complete Phantom of the Opera* (1988) has two critical chapters on film and TV versions of the *Phantom*, as well as extensive uncritical material on the stage musical by Andrew Lloyd Webber. *The Great Book of Movie Monsters* (1983) by Jan Stacy and Ryder Syvertsen treats dozens of minor monsters, most of which appeared in only one film.

9-37. Goldner, Orville, and George E. Turner. **The Making of King Kong.** A. S. Barnes, 1975.
Goldner worked as a technician on *King Kong* (1933). His account of the production of the classic is detailed, enthusiastic and almost reverential. Most illustrations are of the filmmakers at work, not stills from the film. *The Making of King Kong* is a more valuable study of the development of the stop-motion animation technique than *Film Fantasy Scrapbook* (3d ed., 1981) by Ray Harryhausen, a more famous practitioner who made fantasy but not horror films. The essays in *The Girl in the Hairy Paw* (1976), ed. by Ronald Gottesman and Harry Geduld, vary widely in quality. Several pieces describe the film's production in less detail than Goldner; others discuss *King Kong*'s folkloric, literary and cinematic antecedents and the controversy over the authorship of the screenplay. *Kong* fiction and parodies and a great variety of *Kong*-inspired art are included. An important essay on *Kong* is included in Grant's *Planks of Reason* [9-38]. Goldner is the first choice.

9-38. Grant, Barry Keith, ed. **Planks of Reason: Essays on the Horror Film.** Scarecrow, 1984.
Most of the twenty-one essays collected by Grant suffer from the jargon typical of academic film studies, but only three are impenetrable. All are concerned with the political and psychological subtexts hidden in horror films, not with the films' entertainment value or the skills of the filmmakers. The nine pieces which examine individual films in detail are generally more useful than the twelve survey articles. The most influential essay in the collection is Robin Wood's outline of Freudian-Marxist film interpretation and its application to horror films, reprinted from his *American Nightmare* [9-57]. Perhaps the best essay is by Noel Carroll on the literary roots of the apparentaly rootless *King Kong*. Also of special interest are feminist critiques of two usually sexist subgenres, the witchcraft film and the lesbian vampire film. Needed by academic collections.

9-39. Halliwell, Leslie (U.K.). **The Dead That Walk.** Continuum, 1988.
A well-known author of film reference books [9-1] compares the Universal and Hammer series of films featuring Dracula, Frankenstein and the Mummy, always to Hammer's disadvantage. Although he claims a special interest in horror films, of all those he discusses Halliwell admires only the first two Universal Frankenstein movies. Halliwell is witty and perceptive, but he seems happiest when detailing the absurdities of a minor bad film. Less a labor of love than one of affectionate contempt. Compare Glut [9-36].

9-40. Handling, Piers, ed. **The Shape of Rage: The Films of David Cronenberg.** New York Zoetrope, 1983.
Cronenberg is perhaps the most respected film director associated with graphic horror; since this book appeared in 1983, he has graduated to bigger budgets. A seventy-nine-page analysis of his early films by William Beard is marred by heavy academese but makes a strong case for Cronenberg as a serious filmmaker of growing thematic maturity. Handling includes a much shorter essay by Robin Wood, who is strongly critical of Cronenberg, a long interview with Cronenberg and four other pieces.

9-41. Hoberman, J., and Jonathan Rosenbaum. **Midnight Movies.** Harper, 1983.
With great erudition, the authors explore the roots of major cult films—*El Topo, Night of the Living Dead, Eraserhead, Rocky Horror Picture Show* and the deliberately disgusting films of John Waters—in both popular culture (rock, comics, AIP movies) and the counterculture (gays, hippies, underground films). Hoberman and Rosenbaum are as interested in the audiences for these films as in the films themselves, and convincingly demonstrate that cult films are a quasi-religious experience for their devotees. A serious examination of a unique phenomenon. Compare Weldon [9-8].

9-42. Hogan, David. **Dark Romance: Sexuality in the Horror Film.** McFarland, 1986.
Hogan's brief critiques of hundreds of films from all periods are clear, well written and intelligent but not profound and sometimes marred by adolescent humor. His special interest is not really sex but the sociological subtexts of the films. Hogan is better at analyzing individual films than at generalizing about historical trends. With chapters on Alfred Hitchcock, Roger Corman and revered cult actress Barbara Steele and ten pages with everything anyone would ever need to know about the lamentable Edward D. Wood, Jr. (*Plan 9 from Outer Space*). *Eros in the Mind's Eye: Sexuality and the Fantastic in Art and Film* (1986), ed. by Donald Palumbo, includes essays on erotic painting and illustration as well as sex in SF, fantasy and horror films. Some of the essays on films are either obvious or farfetched, but four are worthwhile—one on actress Fay Wray as the perfect heroine-victim, two on *Rocky Horror Picture Show*, a happy hunting ground of sexual imagery, and a particularly good chapter by Sam Unland claiming that recent genre films are anti-sex.

9-43. Kinnard, Roy. **Beasts and Behemoths: Prehistoric Creatures in the Movies.** Scarecrow, 1988.
Kinnard is a reliable guide to which of the low-budget American films of the 1950s about city-stomping dinosaurs are still watchable, and he is well informed about special effects, the main attraction of most of these movies. However, he neglects both the Japanese monster movies (covered in Glut's *Classic Movie Monsters* [9-36]) and prehistoric caveman-vs.-dinosaur fantasies (covered in Glut's *Dinosaur Scrapbook*, 1980).

9-44. Larson, Randall D. **Musique Fantastique: A Survey of Film Music in the Fantastic Cinema.** Scarecrow, 1985.
Larson discusses the scores of hundreds of fantasy, horror and SF films from the 1930s to the 1980s, with special chapters on TV scoring, electronic music, classical

music, British, Japanese and other foreign films, and on four major composers; over 200 pages of filmography and discography and many quotations from composers and critics. An enormous amount of information is gathered, but Larson's criticism is suspect; he comments favorably about the vast majority of the scores, in keeping with his enthusiastic conclusion that "music has always seemed to be at its best in fantastic films."

9-45. Mank, Gregory William. **It's Alive!: The Classic Cinema of Frankenstein.** A. S. Barnes, 1981.
Mank's detailed accounts of the production of the eight Frankenstein films made by Universal from 1931 to 1948 may concentrate too much on studio politics, but the fascinating anecdotes, hundreds of quotations from veterans of the films and dozens of illustrations make *It's Alive!* essential for the study of these films, despite the lack of an index. *James Whale* (1982) by James Curtis, a biography of the director of the first two of Universal's Frankenstein movies, includes many quotations which are alarmingly at odds with those cited by Mank. More comprehensive and more analytical than either Mank or Curtis are the four chapters on film and TV versions from 1910 to 1974 in *Mary Shelley's Monster* (1976) [8-99] by Martin Tropp; many of Tropp's insights are not found elsewhere. *The Endurance of Frankenstein* (1979) [8-94], ed. by George Levine and U. C. Knoepflmacher, includes a useful survey of "The Stage and Film Children of Frankenstein" by Albert J. Lavalley. Donald Glut's *The Frankenstein Legend* (1973) combines amateurish criticism with complete filmographic information on every film and TV version. Glut's *Frankenstein Catalog* (1984) [8-98] is even more obsessively complete but wisely dispenses with attempts at criticism. Halliwell [9-39] also discusses Frankenstein films at length.

9-46. McGee, Mark Francis. **Roger Corman: The Best of the Cheap Acts.** McFarland, 1988.
Neither a biography nor a critical work, McGee's *Corman* is the most up to date of several anecdotal accounts of Corman's colorful career as director and producer of both art and exploitation films. Often hilarious stories about Corman's cut-rate filmmaking can be found here, in Ed Naha's *The Films of Roger Corman* (1982) and in McGee's *Fast and Furious* (1984), a history of the early years of AIP. Gary Morris's *Roger Corman* (1985) is a serious but rather theoretical work which studies Corman's series of Poe films and his *X—The Man with the X-Ray Eyes* but neglects his other horror films.

9-47. Meyers, Richard. **For One Week Only: The World of Exploitation Films.** New Century, 1983.
Although he includes a few important movies (*Eraserhead, Night of the Living Dead* and *Texas Chainsaw Massacre*), Meyers admits that most of the 200 low-grade horror, sex and violence films described here are dedicated to the message that "women are fodder, there's no use in trying, and people are less than garbage." Meyers wisely judges these films on their own terms, giving high marks for outrageousness and to films which live up to their lurid titles and posters. *For One Week Only* is a goldmine of information for anyone interested in this unpleasant subject, which is made palatable by Meyers's sense of humor.

9-48. Newman, Kim (U.K.). **Nightmare Movies: Wide Screen Horror since 1968.** Proteus, 1984.

Despite many stylistic differences, most of the hundreds of post-1968 films considered here share a tendency to bleakness and strong violence. Newman is sympathetic to this trend, but he has no illusions about the general level of quality. Nevertheless, he finds much to praise, including several works usually considered minor. British, Australian, Italian and Spanish movies are thoroughly covered, as are U.S. TV films. Newman's criticism is witty, perceptive and vastly knowledgeable, but the book is marred by several disgusting illustrations. A revised edition, *Nightmare Movies: A Critical History of the Horror Film, 1968–1988,* was published by Bloomsbury Publishing in late 1988, too late to annotate.

9-49. Pirie, David (U.K.). **The Vampire Cinema.** Crescent Books, 1977.

***9-50.** Waller, Gregory A. **The Living and the Undead.** Univ. of Illinois Press, 1986.

Although he may overstate the cultural importance of the theme of warfare between the living and the violent dead, the careful distinctions Waller makes among twelve key works (Stoker's novel *Dracula*; a play, six theatrical films and two TV films based on Stoker; and George Romero's first two *Living Dead* films) are exceptionally revealing. The amazing diversity among versions of the same story is an object lesson in the power of artists to transform a familiar legend for their own artistic, commercial and political purposes. Pirie's heavily illustrated *Vampire Cinema* provides brief but serious critiques of dozens of films not in Waller, including French, Spanish and Italian works. A chapter on the lesbian vampire subgenre finds some value in a few of those notorious films. Michael Murphy's *The Celluloid Vampires* (1979) and Donald Glut's *The Dracula Book* (1975) both aspire to be complete filmographies but offer only the shallowest criticism. Also annotated as [7-68].

9-51. Savini, Tom. **Bizarro.** Harmony Books, 1983.

9-52. Taylor, Al and Sue Roy. **Making a Monster: The Creation of Screen Characters by the Great Makeup Artists.** Crown, 1980.

Makeup is often as important to horror films as special effects are to SF films. Taylor's *Making a Monster* is clumsily written and anecdotal but rich in facts about the ingenuity with which twenty-eight American and British makeup artists met the endlessly varied challenges they found in hundreds of films from the silents to the 1970s. Mainstream, SF and fantasy films as well as horror works are discussed. Although historically important, Taylor's book is outdated by advances made in the 1980s, some of which were the work of Savini, a specialist in gory makeup for violent horror movies. Savini's heavily illustrated *Bizarro* (also published as *Grande Illusions*) is a how-to-do-it book with a proper emphasis on safety, of interest to both filmmakers and fans. Both books make clear how much the development of genre films has been influenced by advances in technology and by the ingenuity of technical specialists.

9-53. Siegel, Joel E. **Val Lewton: The Reality of Terror.** Viking, 1983.

Producer-writer Val Lewton headed the RKO unit which made nine subtle, poetic low-budget horror and fantasy films from 1942 to 1946, beginning with *Cat People*. Siegel devotes about 100 revealing pages to the planning and production of the series, plus a few pages of synopsis and cogent criticism of each film. J. P. Telotte's *Dreams of Darkness: Fantasy and the Films of Val Lewton* (1985) is more detailed on each film but suffers from excessive psychoanalytic jargon.

9-54. Waller, Gregory A., ed. **American Horrors: Essays on the Modern American Horror Film.** Univ. of Illinois Press, 1987.
Half the twelve essays collected here are rather dry reprints from film journals, but all are serious and make clear the diversity and importance of U.S. horror films since 1968. Charles Derry's essay explicitly updates his book *Dark Dreams* [9-25]. Four contributors examine slasher films and identify three good films in that disreputable subgenre. An essay by Waller finds that made-for-TV films are the last refuge of optimistic, suggestive horror.

9-55. Weaver, Tom. **Interviews with B Science Fiction and Horror Movie Makers: Writers, Producers, Directors, Actors, Moguls and Makeup.** McFarland, 1988.
Most of the twenty-nine film workers interviewed by Weaver will be known only to ardent fans of 1950s low-budget films. There is little overlap between Weaver's work and either Brosnan's *Horror People* [9-23] or Pitts's *Horror Film Stars.* Weaver's well-informed questions elicit articulate, nostalgic, anecdotal responses which throw light on a colorful period in the history of genre filmmaking.

9-56. Wexman, Virginia Wright. **Roman Polanski.** Twayne, 1985.
Polanski has made important films both within and outside the horror genre. Wexman's book, in the Twayne Filmmakers Series, is detailed and sophisticated but rather theoretical. Wexman finds pessimism and despair in all of Polanski's horror films—*Repulsion, Rosemary's Baby, The Tenant,* his gory *Macbeth* and even the comedy *The Fearless Vampire Killers.*

9-57. Wood, Robin, and Richard Lippe, eds. **American Nightmare: Essays on the Horror Film.** Festival of Festivals, Toronto, 1979.
Wood, who wrote half this obscurely published but influential book and edited three other contributors, is a Marxist Freudian for whom sexual liberation is more important than traditional left-wing concerns. He sees modern horror films as a particularly important battleground between opponents and defenders of a disintegrating bourgeois society and of his *bête noire,* the nuclear family. Most of the films discussed date from the 1970s. Although his ideology is uncompromising and his writing graceless, the value of Wood's insights has been acknowledged by more accessible critics, including Nicholls [9-18]. Wood's long, theoretical introduction to *American Nightmare* (the title is to be taken literally) is reprinted in Grant's *Planks of Reason* [9-38] and with changes in Wood's *Hollywood from Vietnam to Reagan* (1986), which has additional chapters on horror films of the 1980s and on directors George Romero and Larry Cohen. Other psychoanalytic approaches to horror films are found in Will H. Rockett's Jungian *Devouring Whirlwind: Terror and Transcendence in the Arena of Cruelty* (1989); in Frank McConnell's *The Spoken Seen* (1975), which makes plausible claims for the importance of *The Creature from the Black Lagoon*; and in Harvey R. Greenberg's *The Movies on Your Mind* (1975), with its admirably clear analyses of *Psycho, King Kong* and Frankenstein and Dracula films.

9-58. Zicree, Marc Scott. **The Twilight Zone Companion.** Bantam, 1982.
Science fiction and comedy have predominated over horror in fantastic television. Most horror TV series have been anthologies, of which *The Twilight Zone* was the most popular. For each of the 156 episodes Zicree provides a synopsis, credits, at least one illustration, every word of Rod Serling's opening and closing narrations, an anecdotal account of production and a genuinely critical commentary. The *Companion* also includes biographical profiles of Serling, Richard Matheson and Charles Beaumont, the principal writers of the series. Zicree may overvalue the series as a whole, but he is objective about individual episodes. Lentz [9-7] has the most complete reference information on fantastic TV. Gary Gerani's and Paul H. Schulman's *Fantastic Television* (1977) has critical commentary and brief episode synopses for five horror series: *The Twilight Zone, One Step Beyond, Thriller, Night Gallery* and *Kolchak. The Outer Limits: The Official Companion* (1986) by David J. Schow and Jeffrey Frentzen is a detailed guide to a series which combined SF and horror. *Alfred Hitchcock Presents* (1985) by John McCarty and Brian Kelleher covers a mystery series with frequent horror elements. Waller [9-54] and Newman [9-48] examine the made-for-TV horror film. Glut [9-36] describes many TV programs. A second revised edition of Zicree was published in late 1989 by Bantam.

10

Fantastic Art and Illustration

Walter Albert

Diana Waggoner, in her note on fantasy illustration in *The Hills of Faraway* [6-34], claims that "fantasy art and fantasy illustration are not the same thing. . . . Fantasy art is untroubled by considerations of internal logic [while] fantasy illustration is, or should be, the servant of literary fantasy and should conform to the same rules of logic and order that a narrative does" (p. 70). She also sees fantasy illustration as deriving from two principal sources, pulp magazines and children's books. Yet, curiously, she includes among fantasy artists Randolph Caldecott, Arthur Rackham and Kate Greenaway—all of them illustrators of children's books—and implicitly excludes them from fantasy illustration, as she defines it.

If Waggoner has some difficulty in establishing precise boundaries to distinguish fantasy art from fantasy illustration, it may be because fantasy in art has been a problematic area for critics. While the fantastic has often been associated with religious and mythological subjects, it is only in the twentieth century that a major artistic movement has made the "marvelous" a key tenet of its aesthetics. Surrealism, with its belief in the inherent creative energy of dreams and the unconscious, began as a revolution in avant-garde aesthetics but has, ironically, become a part of the establishment it intended to alter. Surrealist fantasy is so prevalent in modern advertising and, more recently, music videos, as well as in fantasy illustration that it may almost be considered an accepted "norm." Surrealism, then, has accomplished its goal of altering human consciousness even if it appears to be at the expense of the domestication of the movement.

However, if the post-World War I phenomenon of Surrealism is a major influence on contemporary fantasy illustration, the roots of fantasy illustration lie in the nineteenth century. Victoria's utilitarian society was entertained by a variety of leisure arts, many of them deriving from a fascination with fairy pictures and fairy tales—often derived from German or Oriental sources—accompanied by an obsession with the occult and the supernatural. The Victorians seemed to delight in the playful, inventive forms of an art that surprised and enchanted as they turned away from the restraints of realism and naturalism.

This flourishing of fantasy art as an infatuation with the nonutilitarian is evident in the "first generation" illustrators who consistently exploited fantasy motifs. Richard Doyle's *In Fairyland* (1870), the illustrations by the gifted Arthur Boyd Houghton for the Dalziel Brothers edition of the *Arabian Nights* (1867), and the children's books designed and illustrated by Kate Greenaway, Walter Crane and Randolph Caldecott were enormously popular. They drew on diverse traditions: the fairy tale, Oriental tales and German Romantic myths and legends. The Mother Goose rhymes were still popular and the penny dreadfuls—ancestors of the American dime novel and pulp magazines—were decorated with horrific, crude line drawings.

While popular illustration mined the twilight world of faerie fantasy, more disturbing fantasies, reflections of a darker sensibility, could be seen in France in the work of French Symbolist artists, including the jewel-adorned, highly ornate oils of Gustave Moreau and the nightmarish black-and-white lithographic series by Odilon Redon. In England this new spirit was echoed in the work of the Decadent writers and artists and in publications like *The Yellow Book*. The erotic fantasies of Aubrey Beardsley, characterized, like the work of Redon, by a highly personal use of the possibilities of line and chiaroscuro, gave expression to the spirit of an age and defined an aesthetic attitude and style.

In the 1890s, in England, France and America, a generation of artists, drawing on the French Symbolists and English Decadents, revolutionized poster and magazine design. Art Nouveau, which also introduced innovations in furniture and fabric design, could not only be identified on the magazine covers and interior illustrations and advertising layouts but would also coincide with an age of book illustration and design.

Internationally, this was the period of the ascendance of British fantasy illustrator Arthur Rackham. Rackham's vision of the world of faerie, in contrast to the Victorian idyllic pastoral, was often dark. His illustrations for Grimm, Irving's *Rip Van Winkle* and Barrie's *Peter Pan in Kensington Gardens* [F3-18] still convey something of the cozy, familial Victorian view, but there is often a sullen undercurrent that threatens that world, and it is this darker side that can be seen in the nightmarish flight of Snow White from the huntsman in Disney's *Snow White and the Seven Dwarfs*, where the forest background is clearly inspired by Rackham's early work.

Other illustrators of note were the Beardsley-influenced Harry Clarke (illustrator of Goethe's *Faust* and of Poe), the Oriental fantasist Edmund Dulac and Kay Nielsen, creator of highly sylized, allegorical theatrical vignettes, as well as the less well-known Danish artist Gustav Tenggren, who was later to make significant contributions to Disney's *Snow White* and *Pinocchio*. In addition, Nielsen's contribution to the Walpurgis-night episode of *Fantasia* is well known, and this continuity with the work of the European illustrators in American animation art is worthy of note.

If the lavish signed, limited editions of British illustrated books found a significant audience in this country, the age of British illustrators had a counterpart in great American illustrators, whose work was widely used in both magazines and books. While fantasy was not as important an element in their work as it was in the work of the British illustrators, the period from the early 1880s to the early years of World War I is often referred to as the Golden Age of American Illustration. Howard Pyle dominated much of this period, influential both as a practicing illustrator and teacher, while the illustrated book of the post-World War I period was dominated by N. C. Wyeth and his students, as well as by the enormously popular Maxfield Parrish. Wyeth is best known for his contributions to the Scribner Classics series with their predominance of adventure rather than fantasy titles. Wyeth's original work is ill served in the books by the much-reduced reproductions, but there is no question of the importance of the influence of his romantically heroic style in this period. In his later years Wyeth was to become increasingly unhappy with his designation as an illustrator rather than an artist, a distinction that has always plagued the practitioners of popular art. And Wyeth's unhappy final years are echoed in the fate of one of the most gifted illustrators of this period, W. W. Denslow, today most readily identified as the illustrator of L. Frank Baum's first Oz book, *The Wonderful Wizard of Oz* [F3-20].

Denslow's career would not parallel the successful later career of Baum, but his illustrations for such books as *Father Goose: His Book, The Pearl and the Pumpkin, The Jewelled Toad* and a series of classic children's fairy stories constitutes an impressive body of work focusing on fantasy literature. Denslow was, however, only one of a group of gifted contemporaries, which included Palmer Cox (creator of the "Brownies"), Peter Newell and, in newspaper comic strips and film animation, the prodigiously talented Winsor McCay. Many of these artists also published in the long-lived *St. Nicholas Magazine,* which was a showcase of black-and-white artwork for children's literature.

Fantasy art continued to flourish in the children's book field, but another kind of popular fantasy art would make its mark in the American pulp magazine where fantasy writing was to reach a wide audience. The most important of the magazines for fantasy literature, and one noted in the 1930s for the quality of its cover art and interior drawings, was *Weird Tales* [11-20], whose first issue was dated March 1923. This issue featured "Ooze," an "extraordinary novelette" by Anthony M. Rud, and sported a horrific cover illustration for the story, as an octopus-like creature with inappropriately mild eyes encircles a damsel-in-distress while a pop-eyed man threatens the creature with a knife and gun. The artwork was similar to the blunt, tawdry cover art of the nineteenth-century dime novel. Matters improved somewhat in 1927 when the magazine's editorial office was moved to Chicago and a local artist, C. C. Senf, began doing covers. Interestingly, Senf's work bears a strong resemblance to that of Gino Starace, illustrator of the popular French *feuilleton* series, Fantômas, but, as was the case with Starace, Senf's work, although more skillful than that of the other cover artists of the magazine's early years, tended more toward the grotesque than the fantastic.

Hugh Rankin brought an Art Deco style to the covers, and his strong sense of design and color may have resulted in the most attractive cover art to be seen on pulp magazines in the late 1920s. However, the 1930s were the most notable decade for fantasy cover art, dominated by the work of Margaret Brundage and, later in the decade, the influential Virgil Finlay, whose magazine work set the standard by which pulp magazine fantasy illustration was judged for at least a decade.

Readers of pulp magazines of the 1930s and 1940s remember with particular fondness Finlay's illustrations of the work of American fantasist A. Merritt, in *Fantastic Novels* and *Famous Fantastic Mysteries* [11-4]. Also, Finlay was as gifted at interior black-and-white drawings as he was at cover illustrations, and his work gained acceptance so quickly that in many of the late 1930s issues of *Weird Tales*—whose interior work had not previously been of the quality of its covers—all or most of the interior illustrations were by Finlay.

In addition to Finlay (and his contemporaries on *FFM* and *FN*, Hannes Bok and Lawrence), the witty, accomplished line drawings of Edd Cartier in *Unknown* [11-18], the fantasy companion to Street and Smith's hard science fiction magazine, *Astounding Science Fiction*, attracted the attention of readers while the fantastic exploits of heroes like Doc Savage and The Shadow were celebrated on covers by talented illustrators like Walter Baumhofer and Jerome Rozen. The stylized, boldly colored covers of scores of pulps showed a skill in color and line that was superior to much of the prose style inside the magazine and, indeed, probably drew attention away from the slick magazines whose idealized American scenes have often dated in ways that the pulp art has not. One of the features of paperback publishing of the 1980s has been the resurgence of the pulp-style magazine cover, reflecting both the nostalgic rediscovery of popular art of the 1930s and a writing style celebrated in the reissue of pulp fiction. (Paperback cover art is the subject of two useful books. Thomas L. Bonn's *Under Cover: An Illustrated History of American Mass Market Paperbacks* [Penguin, 1982] provides intelligent commentary and hundreds of reproductions in color and black and white. Somewhat similar is Piet Schreuders's *Paperbacks, U.S.A.: A Graphic History* [Blue Dolphin Enterprises, 1981].)

The massive paper drives of World War II were responsible for the destruction of thousands of issues of pulp magazines, but the great days of the pulps had passed, and in the wake of the paper drives and with the increasing popularity of a new medium for fantasy fiction, the paperback, the vast numbers of pulp magazines on the stands shrank dramatically. By the mid-1950s they were replaced by the digest magazines that were to provide a much reduced market for fiction. The best artists of the 1930s and early 1940s had left the field or had greatly reduced their contributions to it. Virgil Finlay's work in the 1950s for *Astrology Magazine* was as fine as much of his earlier work, but he no longer dominated the field. Indeed, no fantasy artist comparable to Finlay in stylistic recognizability and popularity was to surface until Frank Frazetta established himself as the most influential fantasy artist of the 1960s, in the wake of a revival of the work of Edgar Rice Burroughs, published in paperback by Ace Books.

For a time, Frazetta and his stylistic look-alikes dominated paperback cover art. In the 1970s Frazetta's by-now classic status was confirmed by a series of trade art books [10-81, 10-82], published by Ballantine Books, that also presaged the development of a market for fantasy art that shows no signs of diminishing today.

Although a number of small presses had published hardback editions of fantasy and science fiction in the 1950s, with dust jackets featuring the work of prominent artists of the period, this phenomenon was to be greatly outdistanced by the proliferation of small press editions in the 1970s and 1980s. Pulp writer

Robert E. Howard was one of the first to be celebrated in this fashion, with the limited editions published by Don Grant distinguished for a time by the use of artists of the quality of Jeff Jones, George Barr and Alicia Austin, but Grant was less successful in choosing artists of comparable quality for later publications. However, by this time (the mid-1970s) a number of other small presses (see chapter 5) were turning out signed, limited and trade editions of works featuring original artwork, as well as portfolios of illustrations, although relatively few contemporary illustrators have had entire books devoted to their work.

Virgil Finlay's work was once again available, in books published by Don Grant and Gerry de la Ree, a collector and now inactive publisher, but a new style was emerging and a new, post-Frazetta generation of artists. The style was dominated—in contrast to the heroic romanticism of Frazetta in which one could see the influence of Wyeth and his generation—by a hyperrealism based on the work of Surrealist artists like Dalí and Magritte. The work of the Brothers Hildebrandt for a series of annual calendars based on the Tolkien cycle was typical of the new style which, in the 1980s, has been continued by the very popular illustrator Michael Whelan.

It is too early to characterize definitively the work of this generation, but the artists are technically proficient and given to pristine, emotionally restrained, even cold treatments of fantasy subjects. On the other hand, there has also emerged a new generation of artists drawing on artists of the classic age (like Clarke, Rackham, Charles Robinson, Dulac) who are reinterpreting works illustrated by those artists. Many of these artists who have more recently come to fantasy book illustration are comic book artists, and among the most prominent—and gifted—are Michael Kaluta, Berni Wrightson, Barry Windsor-Smith and Charles Vess, whose illustrations for Shakespeare's *Midsummer Night's Dream* (Donning, 1988) are almost a textbook example of stylistic influences at work in an artist who has yet to develop in his book illustrations an individual, distinctive style. (Comic strip and comic book illustration are excluded from consideration in this critical survey, as is the so-called graphic novel, which has become moderately popular in recent years. For guidance in this area, see Inge's chapter on comic books in his *Handbook of American Popular Literature* [6-38].) Also of note, in the generation of the very popular, somewhat arid Michael Whelan, is the highly ornate work of Don Maitz, in whom the distinctive work of Edmund Dulac is fused with a more contemporary style.

Thus, the 1980s would appear to be a period of great technical competence as well as of the rediscovery of the illustrators of earlier generations in an apparent attempt to forge a new style for the age. It is a period of great diversity with artists working in animated film, music videos, paperback and hardcover book illustrations, and exhibiting original works that are bought by an avid generation of new collectors willing to pay prices for popular art that fall short of the astronomical figures of mainstream and avant-garde artists yet are symptomatic of an escalating market. It is a market that, like most new and many old markets, is susceptible to trends and fashions not always wedded to work of unusual quality, but it is a phenomenon of great vitality and even greater potential.

The adjective in the chapter title includes both fantasy and horror illustration and art. Although the emphasis in this chapter has been on fantasy, illustration or art designed to provoke fear, terror or unease is not absent. See especially entries [10-9], [10-12] and the work of Doré, some of Finlay and Giger. The work of many contemporary horror illustrators, such as J. K. Potter, has not yet been collected in books.

Bibliography

The author wishes to express his appreciation for the assistance of Robert E. Briney and Neil Barron in compiling this bibliography. Their contributions are identified as (REB) and (NB).

Unlike volumes reproducing the works of "fine" artists, relatively few of the books annotated show medium, size of original or present location. Most original illustrations for pulp magazines were discarded (see Weinberg, [10-35], for the unhappy details).

General and Multi-Subject Entries

***10-1.** Best, James J. **American Popular Illustration: A Reference Guide.** Greenwood, 1984.
After a brief historical overview of the subject, the chapters focus on such topics as history and aesthetics, illustrators and illustrated works, and social and artistic contexts. Bibliographic citations for the books he discusses are given at the end of each chapter. Best is particularly good on the period up to 1920. His primary interest is in illustrative material published in the slick magazines and in books; dime novel, pulp and paperback illustration receive only cursory treatment. This undoubtedly reflects the relative paucity of secondary material on popular art of the post-1920 period and the richness of material on the "great age" of popular illustration, 1880–1920. Index of names and some subjects. Regrettably lacks illustrations.

10-2. Blashfield, Jean, ed. **The Art of Dragon Magazine**. TSR, 1988.
Includes all of the cover art from the first ten years of *Dragon* Magazine, plus color and black-and-white interior artwork, by sixty-six artists, including Larry Elmore, Clyde Caldwell, Jeff Easley and Dean Morrissey. There are a couple of covers each by Tim Hildebrandt and Carl Lundgren, plus single contributions from George Barr and Boris Vallejo. (REB)

10-3. Canham, Stephen. "**What Manner of Beast? Illustrations of 'Beauty and the Beast.'**" In *Image & Maker: An Annual Dedicated to the Consideration of Book Publication*, pp. 13–25. Green Tiger, 1984.
The last of the Green Tiger Press publications dedicated to classic illustrations for children's books, and what was intended to be the first of a series of annual publications. Canham, in his beautifully illustrated essay, discusses the ways artists have depicted the beast—and his Beauty—in the classic fairy tale.

10-4. Cochran, Russ, ed. **The Edgar Rice Burroughs Library of Illustration**. 3 vols. Cochran, 1976, 1977, 1984.
Volume 1 is dedicated to J. Allen St. John and is an impressive tribute to the artist

many consider to be the quintessential Burroughs illustrator. In Volume 2, much of which is devoted to comic strip art by Hal Foster and John Coleman Burroughs, there is also cover and interior art for the books by St. John, and by Studley and John Coleman Burroughs. Volume 3 includes comic strip and comic book art by Burne Hogarth, Russ Manning, Rex Maxon and Jesse Marsh as well as book and paperback art by St. John, Schoonover, Reed Crandall, Roy Krenkel and Frank Frazetta. There is also a perfectly dreadful illustration by Mahlon Blaine for the Canaveral Press edition of *Pellucidar*. Whatever one may think of Blaine's other work, his pairing with Burroughs was most unfortunate. Volume 3 also includes interviews with Roy Krenkel and Frazetta. This was clearly a labor of love for publisher Cochran, and the production meets very high standards.

10-5. Comini, Alessandra. **The Fantastic Art of Vienna**. Ballantine, 1978.
Twenty-five-page essay, plus fifty-nine plates (forty of them in color) and twenty-six additional illustrations. Artists range from the early sixteenth century to the mid-twentieth: Albrecht Altdorfer, Alfred Kubin, Klimt, Kokoschka, Egon Schiele, Arnold Schönberg, Friedrich Hundertwasser, etc. Grim, satirical, often self-mocking works, with an occasional flash of color or beauty. (REB)

10-6. Dean, Martyn. **The Guide to Fantasy Art Techniques.** Text by Chris Evans. Paper Tiger & Arco, 1984.
Interviews between Dean and the following artists: Jim Burns, Ian Miller, Patrick Woodroffe, Philip Castle, Syd Mead, Chris Foss, Martin Bower and Boris Vallejo. Fantasy is used rather broadly since some of the artists (Mead, Foss, Bower) work in a medium closer to science fiction hardware art. Sketches as well as examples of finished work. The artists talk about influences on their work, techniques, working habits and ways they research their illustrations.

10-7. Dean, Martyn and Roger. **The Flights of Icarus**. Paper Tiger & A & W Visual Library, 1977.
A verse cycle by Donald Lehmkuhl is used as the excuse for displaying more than 120 paintings by thirty-two British and U.S. artists, including Jim Burns, Roger Dean, Jim FitzPatrick, Jeff Jones, Michael W. Kaluta, Alan Lee, Ian Miller, Patrick Woodroffe and Berni Wrightson. Brief biographical and career notes on each artist. (REB)

10-8. de la Ree, Gerry, ed. **The Art of the Fantastic.** Gerry de la Ree, 1978.
Brief general introduction, with notes on the artists included, plus a short discussion of Lynd Ward's illustrations for the *Haunted Omnibus*, fifty-four of which are included in this compilation. Other artists included are Hannes Bok (11), Virgil Finlay (7), Lawrence (5), Frank R. Paul (7), Stephen E. Fabian (12), Edd Cartier (3), Ed Emsh, Tim Kirk, Frank Kelly Freas, Mahlon Blaine, Roy Krenkel, Frank Utpatel, Ronald Clyne, Clark Ashton Smith, Harry Clarke, Roy Hunt and such uncommon artists as G. Watson David (for *Tanglewood Tales* and John Ruskin's "The King of the Golden River") and J. R. Weguelin (for Haggard's *Montezuma's Daughter*). Thirty-three artists are represented, some by illustrations not previously published (including seven by Lynd Ward). All illustrations are reproduced from originals in the editor's collection. (REB)

10-9. Durie, Alison (U.K.). **Weird Tales**. Jupiter Books, 1979.
An anthology of cover art for this popular pulp magazine. A few of the plates are in color, but most of the reproductions are in black and white or monochromatic tints. The earliest color examples are for 1933 (J. Allen St. John and Margaret Brundage). The reproduction is particularly damaging to the covers of Hugh Rankin and C. C. Senf, most of whose work was done in the 1920s. In spite of this defect, the book is a generous sampling of the cover art of this important and influential magazine.

10-10. Edwards, Malcolm, and Robert Holdstock (U.K.). **Realms of Fantasy**. Doubleday & Dragon's World, 1983.
A successor to *Alien Landscapes* (1979), which emphasized SF worlds, this survey explores ten fictional fantasy worlds, such as Middle-earth, Le Guin's Earthsea, Peake's Gormenghast and Gene Wolfe's Urth. Approximately seventy illustrations by various British hands, forty in color. A later, similar work by the same authors is *Lost Realms* (1984). Compare the somewhat different dictionary by Manguel and Guadalupi [6-39]. (NB)

10-11. Gaunt, William, ed. **Painters of Fantasy: From Hieronymus Bosch to Salvador Dali.** Phaidon, 1974.
The short introduction is superficial and the high point is a statement that "[the fantastic] has appealed to the sense of wonder in every age. . . ." Of interest for the 104 reproductions.

10-12. Haining, Peter. **Terror! A History of Horror Illustrations from the Pulp Magazines**. Souvenir Press & A & W Visual Library, 1976. Reprinted as *The Art of Horror Stories*. Chartwell Books, 1986.
Examples of illustrations for pulp fiction, broadly defined as Gothic/penny dreadful/dime novel/pulp fiction. Several color plates, but most of the reproductions are in black and white. Captions for the illustrations contain some information on the illustrators; short chapter introductions. Fine for browsing and for a noncritical introduction to pulp illustrations, most of which have some fantasy elements.

10-13. Hammacher, Abraham Marie. **Phantoms of the Imagination: Fantasy in Art & Literature from Blake to Dali**. Abrams, 1981.
Hammacher attempts a study of the fantastic in eighteenth- through twentieth-century art, with chapters on Blake, Fuseli, the Gothic, French Symbolism and Surrealism, to which almost a third of the book is devoted.

***10-14.** Johnson, Diana L. **Fantastic Illustration and Design in Britain, 1850–1930**. Museum of Art, Rhode Island School of Design, 1979. Also published as *Bulletin of Rhode Island School of Design Museum Notes*, 65:5 (April 1979).
This handsome 239-page exhibition catalog includes examples of work by artists of the great period of book and magazine illustration in England. There are substantial notes on the artists and the works exhibited, an extensive bibliography of secondary sources and two fine essays, a title essay by Johnson, and George P. Landow's "And the World Became Strange: Realms of Literary Fantasy," which includes commentary on British and American horror fiction and which was reprinted in Schlobin [F7-51].

10-15. Jones, Bruce, and Armand Eisen, eds. **Sorcerers: A Collection of Fantasy Art**. Ariel/Ballantine, 1978.
A collection of color and black-and-white work by eleven fantasy artists: Tim Conrad, Alex Nino, Steve Hickman, Michael Hague, Kenneth Smith, Brad Johannsen, Bruce Jones, Jack Kirby, George Barr, Jim Steranko and Michael Whelan. Photo and brief statement by each contributor. (REB)

10-16. Kirchoff, Mary, ed. **The Art of the Dragon Lance Saga**. TSR, 1987.
Preliminary drawings, black-and-white and color art for the Dragon Lance Saga fantasy game. A world and its inhabitants are depicted by Larry Elmore, Clyde Caldwell, Denis Beauvais, Dave Sutherland, Tom Yeates, Diana Magnuson, Keith Parkinson, Jeff Butler and Jeff Easley. Parkinson's color illustrations and Elmore's ink drawings occasionally rise above the prevailing mediocrity.

10-17. Larkin, David, ed. **Fantastic Art.** Ballantine, 1973.
Forty color illustrations by artists of the fifteenth to the twentieth century, including Bosch, Pieter Brueghel (the Younger), Turner, Richard Dadd, Gustave Moreau, Odilon Redon, Max Ernst and Ivan Albright. The introduction provides brief career biographies.

10-18. Larkin, David, ed. **The Fantastic Kingdom: A Collection of Illustrations from the Golden Days of Storytelling**. Ballantine, 1974.
Color plates of illustrations of Jessie Willcox Smith, Howard Pyle, Arthur Rackham, Charles Robinson, Maxfield Parrish, W. Heath Robinson, Jean de Bosschère, Edmund Dulac, E. J. Detmold, Paul Bransom, Kay Nielsen, Harry Clarke, Dorothy P. Lathrop and the "elusive" T. Mackenzie. Larkin gives short biographies of the artists.

10-19. Larkin, David, ed. **Once Upon a Time: Some Contemporary Illustrators of Fantasy**. Peacock Press/Bantam, 1976.
Anthology of works by a group of British illustrators, with short biographies. Includes Frank Bellamy, Pauline Ellison (with a stunning fold-out illustration for Le Guin's Earthsea trilogy), Chris McEwan, Tony Meeuwissen, Nicola Bayley, Peter Le Vasseur, Alan Lee, Reg Cartwright, Ian Miller, James Marsh, Peter Barrett, Owen Wood, Ken Laidlaw and Brian Froud.

10-20. Meyer, Susan E. **America's Great Illustrators.** Abrams, 1978.
Includes, among others, Howard Pyle, N. C. Wyeth and Maxfield Parrish. Biocritical essays with numerous examples of the artists' work. One of the essential reference works for the Golden Age of American illustration.

***10-21.** Meyer, Susan E. **A Treasury of the Great Children's Book Illustrators**. Abrams, 1983.
Short but substantial essays, copiously illustrated, on Lear, Tenniel, Crane, Caldecott, Kate Greenaway, Beatrix Potter, E. H. Shepherd, Rackham, Dulac, Nielsen, Pyle, Wyeth and Denslow. Bibliography and index.

10-22. Page, Michael, and Robert Ingpen (U.K.). **Encyclopedia of Things That Never Were**. Dragon's World, 1985; Viking, 1987.
Page wrote the text of this book exploring myths, legends and other fantastic and supernatural topics. Chapters deal with broad topics, such as things of the night,

with entries alphabetical within each chapter, with a master index. Ingpen's color illustrations—for which he won the 1986 Hans Christian Andersen Award—are imaginative and plentiful. (NB)

10-23. Palumbo, Donald, ed. **Eros in the Mind's Eye: Sexuality and the Fantastic in Art and Film**. Greenwood, 1986.
About half the eighteen original essays in this collection claim to deal with sexuality and the fantastic but they often—particularly in the early essays on medieval and Renaissance artists—have only slight fantasy content. Two essays are of particular interest: Sylvie Pantalacci's "Surrealistic Female Monsters" and Gwendolyn Layne's "Subliminal Seduction in Fantasy Illustration." However, Layne's "Mum's the Word: Sexuality in Victorian Fantasy Illustration (and Beyond)" (pp. 59–74) is disappointing and leans heavily on unsupported quotations from Brigid Peppin's *Fantasy* [10-24] for a cursory overview of this seminal period for modern illustration. And the substantial use of female nudes in Rackham's post-1916 work does not support Layne's statement that his work was "pure of [sexual] content." Sarah Clemens's essay, "And Now, This Brief Commercial Message: Sex Sells Fantasy!," is also of interest. Illustrations chosen are almost exclusively of color works and the darkish reproduction—along with the absence of color—obscures the detail to which the reader is referred. Still, given the lack of serious discussion of modern fantasy illustration, the best things here are of some importance.

10-24. Peppin, Brigid (U.K.). **Fantasy: The Golden Age of Fantastic Illustration**. Watson-Guptill, 1975.
On fantasy illustration in England in the Victorian and Edwardian periods (1860–1920), historically rather than critically oriented. Less probing than Johnson [10-14] but with more color-plate examples of artists' work.

***10-25.** Peppin, Brigid (U.K.), and Lucy Micklethwait (U.K.), eds. **Book Illustrators of the Twentieth Century**. Arco, 1984.
More than 800 British illustrators working in the twentieth century are covered in this encyclopedia. The biographical entries contain a selected list of book and periodical illustrations, as well as a short bibliography of secondary sources. There are also several hundred well-chosen black-and-white illustrations. A major reference text that complements Simon Houfe's *Dictionary of British Book Illustrators and Caricaturists 1800–1914* (Antique Collectors' Club, 1978).

10-26. Petaja, Emil, comp. and ed. **The Hannes Bok Memorial Showcase of Fantasy Art**. SISU Publishers, 1974.
Examples of early twentieth-century magazine illustrations, as well as of work by a score of modern illustrators, mostly in black and white, but with color plates of illustrations by Alicia Austin, George Barr, Jack Gaughan and Tim Kirk. The artists also profile themselves and their work.

10-27. Petersen, Sandy; Tom Sullivan; and Lynn Willis, eds. **Petersen's Field Guide to Cthulhu Monsters**. Chaosium, 1988.
Dictionary entries on twenty-seven "terrors of the hyper-geometrical realms," drawn from the writings of H. P. Lovecraft and featuring color and black-and-

white illustrations by Tom Sullivan. A sense of fun lurks in the pages of this book, published by a firm well known in the fantasy game market.

10-28. Poltarnees, Welleran. **All Mirrors Are Magic Mirrors: Reflections on Pictures Found in Children's Books.** Green Tiger, 1972.
The Green Tiger Press Rackham calendars of the 1970s are notable for the splendor of the reproductions and are among the handsomest examples of the recent calendar revival, while the Press's annual apointment books are copiously illustrated with black-and-white and color children's book illustrations by nineteenth- and twentieth-century book illustrators. Poltarnees's observations on what he sees in illustrations are evidence of a first-rate critical eye. Highly recommended. The author's pseudonym is derived from Dunsany's fictions.

10-29. Robertson, Bruce (U.K.). **Fantasy Art.** North Light Books, 1988.
Numerous examples from fine art, illustrations for books and magazines, and advertising graphics dramatically highlight Robertson's text. Much of the book is a practical guide to techniques for creating fantasy art.

10-30. Rottensteiner, Franz (Austria). **The Fantasy Book: An Illustrated History from Dracula to Tolkien.** Collier, 1978.
A superficial study of fantasy in literature. Although the 202 illustrations, 40 in color, are not always identified by artist, they constitute something of an anthology of fantasy illustration, with many examples of pulp and paperback cover artwork, including European work seldom seen in North America. Also annotated as [H7-11] and [F7-48].

10-31. Sackmann, Eckart. **Great Masters of Fantasy Art.** Berlin: Taco, 1986. Tr. by Hugh Beyer.
Collection of forty-four paintings by sixteen fantasy artists. Apart from two European artists (Oliviero Berni and Vincente Segrelles), the artists are American and British: Frazetta, Boris Vallejo, Rowena, Greg Hildebrandt, Carl Lundgren, Freas, Corben, Barclay Shaw, Rodney Matthews, Paul Lehr, Richard Hescox, Tim White, Michael Whelan and Don Maitz. General introduction, plus photo and short article on each contributor. (REB)

10-32. Schlobin, Roger O., ed. **The Aesthetics of Fantasy Literature and Art.** Univ. of Notre Dame Press, 1982.
The first of the two articles on fantasy illustration in this collection of essays, by Landow, was originally published in Johnson [10-14]. Terry Reece Hackford's "Fantastic Visions: British Illustration of the *Arabian Nights*," is an original, detailed comparative study of illustrations by four illustrators (Arthur Boyd Houghton, J. D. Batten, H. J. Ford and Edmund Dulac) for editions of the *Arabian Nights*. Hackford points out that all four artists "share a reliance upon the pictorial conventions associated with realism" but develop "distinctive means" for "manipulating, intensifying or departing" from those conventions. The illustrations are well chosen, although the black-and-white reproduction of the Dulac color originals inevitably betrays the points the author is trying to make. Also annotated as [7-51].

10-33. The Studio: Jeffrey Jones, Michael Kaluta, Barry Windsor-Smith and Berni Wrightson. Dragon's Dream, 1979.
The four artists are interviewed in their Manhattan loft studio where they talk about their careers and their *fin-de-siècle* roots. The interviews are illustrated with photographs of the artists and examples of their recent work. Grimmer Graphics has announced publication of *The Michael Wm. Kaluta Treasury*, which will feature more recent work by the artist.

10-34. Summers, Ian, ed. **Tomorrow and Beyond: Masterpieces of Science Fiction Art**. Workman, 1978.
The former art director of Ballantine has assembled over 300 color reproductions from sixty-seven illustrators, primarily American. Much of the work depicted appeared on mass-market paperback covers of the 1970s, as well as on LP jackets, in articles and the like. No biographical information on the illustrators is provided nor are medium and size of original shown. Yet the survey is a broad one and is valuable for larger collections devoted to contemporary book illustration. (NB)

***10-35.** Weinberg, Robert. **A Biographical Dictionary of Science Fiction and Fantasy Artists.** Greenwood, 1988. Don Grant, 1978.
In addition to the more than 250 entries, there are an introduction providing a historical overview, an essay on the collecting of original art, a list of major awards for science fiction/fantasy artists, a bibliography and an index. Each of the entries is a mini-essay with biographical and critical information and a bibliography of the artist's work. The bibliographies are in themselves a major feature of the book since they show appearances in magazines and hardback and paperback artwork. Entries are based where possible on information supplied by the artists. Inevitably, there will be complaints about omissions (the prolific Michael Hague is one notable omission), but this is a major addition to the short list of references on genre artists.

10-36. Weinberg, Robert. **The Weird Tales Story**. Fax, 1977.
See especially chapters 6 ("Cover Art") and 7 ("Interior Art") for numerous examples of the artwork accompanied by a running commentary by Weinberg on the art and artists. A frustrating aspect of the book is the lack of an index and the separation of the reproductions from the appropriate commentary. Durie [10-9], with its more numerous and larger-format reproductions, is a valuable complement to this volume. Also annotated as [11-55] and [H7-45].

10-37. Weis, Margaret, ed. **The Art of the Dungeons & Dragons Fantasy Game**. TSR 1985.
Color and black-and-white art by fifteen artists, principally Clyde Caldwell, Jeff Easley and Larry Elmore. A few items are reprinted from *Amazing Stories*, including a George Barr cover. Lots of dash and color, with little subtlety except in two quiet paintings by Dean Morrissey. (REB)

Individual Artists

Achilleos, Chris (Cyprus), 1947- .

10-38. Achilleos, Chris. **Beauty and the Beast.** Dragon's World, 1978.

10-39. Achilleos, Chris. **Medusa.** Dragon's World, 1988.

10-40. Achilleos, Chris. **Sirens.** Dragon's World, 1986.
These three volumes provide a comprehensive survey of Achilleos's work in advertising and for paperbacks, film posters and even (in *Medusa*) for tattoo designs. In *Medusa,* some of the artist's work is traced from concept through sketches to the finished version. His style, with its heroic, dramatic figures, seems particularly well suited to movie posters. As with other artists of his generation, the influence of Frazetta is obvious, but the figures lack that artist's romantic dash; in their warrior armor, both men and women seem more inclined to set forth to battle than to dally in amorous interludes.

Artzybasheff, Boris (U.S.S.R.), 1899–1965

10-41. Artzybasheff, Boris. **As I See.** Dodd, Mead, 1954.
The only collection of this artist's book and magazine illustrations (including those for Finney's *The Circus of Dr. Lao* [F3-137]) and his editorial depictions of the machines of industry and war, all reproduced in superb gravure printing. Artist's commentary, in an oblique and philosophical style, reveals general social attitudes, but no specific commentary on the drawings. (REB)

Austin, Alicia, 1942- .

10-42. Austin, Alicia. **Alicia Austin's Age of Dreams**. Introduction by George Barr; Afterword by Austin. Don Grant, 1978.
An anthology of her color and line work, printed on fine stock and elegantly produced. Austin's hieratic, sumptuously robed figures and the decorative nature of her design recall the English Decadents, particularly Aubrey Beardsley and Harry Clarke.

Barr, George, 1937- .

10-43. Barr, George. **Upon the Winds of Yesterday and Other Explorations: The Paintings of George Barr**. Don Grant, 1976.
Numerous examples of Barr's color and black-and-white artwork. Barr works in several styles, ranging from a cockeyed whimsy to neoromantic treatments of mythological subjects. Thus, there is not the impression—so common with many contemporary fantasy artists—of a single style imposed upon every project.

Beardsley, Aubrey (U.K.), 1872–1898.

***10-44.** Reade, Brian (U.K.). **Aubrey Beardsley**. Studio Vista, Macmillan, 1967.
Beardsley's decorative, frank treatment of subjects his contemporaries found obscene revolutionized the concept of line drawing. Reade's book is considered by many critics to be the definitive study of his work. See also Brigid Brophy's *Black and White: A Portrait of Aubrey Beardsley* (Cape, 1968).

Blaine, Mahlon, 1894–1970.

10-45. Legman, G. **The Art of Mahlon Blaine.** Peregrine Books, 1982.
Introduction by artist Robert Arrington, "The Art of Mahlon Blaine" by G. Legman, "A Mahlon Blaine Bibliography" compiled by Roland Trenary and over eighty pages of Blaine drawings and paintings, including four pages in color. Much of Blaine's work was strongly influenced by Beardsley in both style and content. His subjects range from fantastic erotica (the 1929 portfolio *Venus Sardonica* and work for Olympia Press) to Apache and Hopi Indian legends. His elaborately detailed and macabre drawings for Burke's *Limehouse Nights,* Ewers's *The Sorcerer's Apprentice* and *Alraune,* Beckford's *Vathek* and Flaubert's *Salammbô* constitute his best work. (REB)

Bok, Hannes, 1914–1964

10-46. Bok, Hannes. **Beauty and the Beasts: The Art of Hannes Bok**. Gerry de la Ree, 1978.

10-47. Brooks, C. W. **The Revised Hannes Bok Checklist.** T-K Graphics, 1974.

10-48. de la Ree, Gerry, ed. **Bok**. Gerry de la Ree, 1974.

10-49. de la Ree, Gerry, and Gene Nigra, eds. **A Hannes Bok Sketchbook**. Gerry de la Ree, 1976.

10-50. Petaja, Emil. **And Flights of Angels: The Life and Legend of Hannes Bok**. Bokanalia Memorial Foundation, 1968.
Bok was largely self-taught and developed a style heavily influenced by the work of Maxfield Parrish. His precise and polished drawings and paintings feature age-softened landscapes, preternaturally limber human figures and monsters both grotesque and comic. In the science fiction magazine world of the 1940s, Bok's work was equaled only by that of Virgil Finlay [10-70–10-77] and Edd Cartier [10-53] for stylistic distinctiveness. In the 1950s, unlike Finlay, whose principal market continued to be magazines, Bok illustrated dust jackets for the new small press market and did some of his finest work in this field. The major work devoted to his art (*Beauty and the Beasts*) unfortunately contains none of his color illustrations, but does provide a generous sampling of his work for the science fiction and fantasy pulps. The *Sketchbook* contains work dating back to his high-school days, while the Petaja biography and de la Ree *Bok* include essays by artist and writer contemporaries, which offer multiple perspectives on his career. (REB/WA)

Booth, Franklin, 1874–1948.

10-51. Booth, Franklin. **The Art of Franklin Booth.** Nostalgia Press, 1976.
Reprint of a 1925 tribute to Booth, with an introduction by Meredith Nicholson, an appreciation by Earnest Elmo Calkins and sixty plates: scenes from classical antiquity, dream images, fantastic architecture, biblical scenes, etc. Booth was one of the finest pen-and-ink craftsmen of the early twentieth century, his fine-lined work often looking like steel engraving. His most characteristic drawings

convey an impression of vastness: small foreground figures dominated by huge vaulted ceilings, impossibly tall buildings, looming walls or cliffs. (REB)

Burns, Jim (U.K.), 1948- .

10-52. Burns, Jim. **Lightship.** Text by Chris Evans. Dragon's World, 1985.
125 color and 9 black-and-white illustrations, including preliminary studies and alternative versions. Book jackets and paperback covers for many works by Robert Silverberg, C. L. Moore, Frank Herbert, Philip José Farmer, etc.; space scenes, futuristic vehicles, alien landscapes, imaginary beasts. (REB)

Cartier, Edd, 1914- .

10-53. Cartier, Edd. **Edd Cartier: The Known and the Unknown.** Ed. by Dean Cartier. Gerry de la Ree, 1977.
Cartier withdrew from science fiction/fantasy illustration in the 1950s; this book is an anthology of his work. Examples are drawn from his illustrations for *Unknown* and for *Astounding Science Fiction*, and for fantasy calendars for the years 1949 and 1950. Cartier's precise, humorous but wry drawings have not aged and are among the most distinctive, accomplished work for pulp magazines of the era. And, as Cartier's son Dean notes in his dedication, Cartier's gnomes are a particular delight.

Cherry, David A., 1949- .

10-54. Cherry, David A. **Imagination: The Art & Technique of David A. Cherry.** Donning, 1987.
Forty-one paintings, most done for book jackets and paperback covers, with individual commentary on each painting, covering both subject and technique, plus a general preface by the artist and a biographical afterword. The inclusion of much journeyman work dilutes the impact of the more accomplished paintings. (REB)

Clarke, Harry (U.K.), 1889-1931.

***10-55.** Bowe, Nicola Gordon (U.K.). **Harry Clarke: His Graphic Art.** The Dolmen Press, 1983. Distributed in North America by H. Keith Burns, Los Angeles.
Clarke's illustrations for *Faust* are thought to be his finest work, but it is his drawings for Poe's *Tales of Mystery and Imagination* that are his most popular, with numerous reprints since their first publication in 1919. Bowe's fine biocritical study is illustrated by numerous black-and-white reproductions (Clarke's most distinctive medium), including a number of drawings published here for the first time.

Coll, Joseph Clement, 1881-1921.

***10-56.** Coll, Joseph Clement. **The Magic Pen of Joseph Clement Coll.** Ed. by Walt Reed. Don Grant, 1970.
Pen-and-ink illustrations from books and magazine serials by A. Conan Doyle,

Sax Rohmer, Talbot Mundy, Edgar Wallace and others, including some preliminary studies and unfinished drawings. Text includes a short article, "How Coll Worked," by the compiler. Much of Coll's early work appeared in the pages of the *Associated Sunday Magazine* from 1903 to 1913 and is largely forgotten, but his work for *Collier's Weekly Magazine* from 1911 to his death is more accessible. In addition, his influence can be seen clearly in the work of the talented but almost completely forgotten *Blue Book* artist of the 1930s and 1940s, John Richard Flanagan (1895-1964). Coll was in the tradition of Howard Pyle [10-110] and thus links "mainstream" popular art (books and the slick magazines) with newspaper supplements and the pulps. This collection is a significant contribution to the history of modern American illustration. (REB/WA)

Corben, Richard, 1940- .

10-57. Bharucha, Fershid. **Richard Corben: Flights into Fantasy.** Thumb Tack Books, 1981.
Paintings, drawings and comic strips from all stages of Corben's career, from underground comics to book jackets and paperback covers. Extensive commentary by Bharucha, including photos and biographical information, plus comments by several of Corben's fellow illustrators (Eisner, Wrightson, Moebius, etc.). (REB)

Crane, Walter (U.K.), 1845-1915.

***10-58.** Spencer, Isobel (U.K.). **Walter Crane.** Studio Vista, Macmillan, 1975.
Spencer shows how Crane continued the "transformation of narrative illustration begun by the pre-Raphaelites." Crane belonged to the generation immediately preceding that of Rackham [10-111-10-113], and it is clear that Rackham was greatly indebted to him. Crane's work appeared in *St. Nicholas,* and meetings with Denslow [10-60] and Pyle [10-110] during a visit to America confirm a crucial link between the British and American Arts & Crafts movements.

Dean, Roger (U.K.), 1944- .

10-59. Dean, Roger. **Views.** Text by Dominy Hamilton and Carla Capalbo in association with Roger Dean. Dragon's Dream, 1975.
Paintings, record jackets, posters and other commercial art, characterized by the artist's distinctive combination of the ethereal and the grotesque; biographical and career summary, with notes on sources and techniques. Dean's work on jazz and rock record jackets and on related posters and stage designs left its mark on a generation of consumers, as well as on other artists. *Magnetic Storm* (Paper Tiger, 1984) illustrates the varied work of Roger and his brother, Martyn, in architecture, film TV, album covers, posters and video games. (REB/NB)

Denslow, W. W., 1856-1915.

***10-60.** Greene, Douglas G., and Michael Patrick Hearn. **W. W. Denslow.** Central Michigan Univ.: Clarke Historical Library, 1976.
The authors note that Denslow was "the first American to create picture books in

the aesthetic tradition of Walter Crane, Kate Greenaway, and Randolph Caldecott." An ironic commentary on the career of this great popular illustrator who is now remembered only as the illustrator of *The Wonderful Wizard of Oz* [F3-20]. Some of the best scholarship on American popular literature is written by Baum enthusiasts, and the Baum Society magazine, *The Baum Bugle* [11-26], contains much illustrated material as well as articles on illustration. This splendid biography, with a comprehensive bibliography of Denslow's work, is in that tradition for its scholarship, although it is regrettable that this plainly produced, sparsely illustrated book could not have been published in a format more suitable for the creator of the modern American picture book.

Detmold, Charles Maurice (U.K.), 1883–1908, and **Edward Julius Detmold** (U.K.), 1883–1957.

10-61. Larkin, David. **The Fantastic Creatures of Edward Julius Detmold.** Scribner, 1976.

Fantastic is used rather loosely here since the Detmolds' bestiary consists of uncommonly detailed and imaginatively designed portraits of animals and insects. However, there is no question about the fantastic elements in Edward's illustrations for the *Arabian Nights,* and several of the color plates for this edition rank among the finest fantastic illustrations of the modern period.

Dillon, Leo, and **Diane Dillon,** both 1933– .

10-62. Dillon, Leo and Diane. **The Art of Leo and Diane Dillon**. Ed. by Byron Preiss. Ballantine, 1981.

Numerous color plates, examples of the Dillons' work for various media: album covers, paperbacks, magazines. Impressive work in a variety of styles, drawing on artistic sources from Renaissance oils to expressionist woodcuts, but not always fantastic in content. As Harlan Ellison points out in his preface, the Dillons are perfectionists who may not be appreciated by editors facing imminent deadlines but are greatly respected by their peers for their skill and graphic imagination. With a long critical introduction by Preiss.

Donahey, William, 1883–1970.

10-63. Cahn, Joseph M. **The Teenie Weenies Book: The Life and Art of William Donahey**. Green Tiger, 1986.

Donahey was a Cleveland artist whose comic strip, the *Teenie Weenies,* was a national success for more than fifty years and spawned a number of book editions. Of special interest is a chapter by Welleran Poltarnees on the graphic ancestors of Donahey's little people and on the phenomenon of the fascination many people have with the "miniature." As is customary with Green Tiger Press books, the choice of color and black-and-white illustrations is superb, with color work that should put more prestigious publishers to shame.

Doré, Gustave (France), 1832–1883.

***10-64.** Gosling, Nigel. **Gustave Doré**. Praeger, 1973.

The well-written, informative text by Gosling is accompanied by an impressive gallery of drawings by Doré, arranged by subject (satire, adventure, horror, etc.). His magnificent, awesome illustrations for Dante are represented, as well as some wonderful drawings for Perrault's *Contes* that must have given nightmares to generations of children. One can understand, on seeing an illustration for *Paradise Lost* of a winged Satan plummeting in a starlit sky toward a clouded globe, why Dunsany thought of Doré for his stories of gods and men, and it is a measure of Sime's success [10-122–10-123] that he captures some of Doré's grandeur without imitating him.

Doyle, Richard (U.K.), 1824–1883.

***10-65**. Engen, Rodney (U.K.) **Richard Doyle**. Catalpa Press, 1983.
Uncle of Arthur Conan Doyle and best known for the color illustrations for *In Fairyland* (1870) and the posthumously published *Jack the Giant-Killer*, Doyle was on the staff of *Punch*. Numerous examples of fantasy black-and-white illustrations but very little of the fine color work. The Victorians loved books about fairies and Doyle's unsentimental work is among the finest examples of fairy art.

Dulac, Edmund (France/U.K.), 1882–1953.

***10-66**. White, Colin. **Edmund Dulac**. Scribner, 1976.
Dulac and Rackham were contemporaries whose lavish signed, limited editions were—and still are—much prized by collectors. Dulac's work was influenced by Persian miniatures and even his illustrations for Andersen have a distinctly Oriental cast. His illustrations for the *Arabian Nights* have set a standard by which all other renderings are judged. Colin White's sensible biography is flawed only by inferior color reproductions (181 reproductions in all, 39 in color) and a bibliography that lists only first editions and does not always succeed in describing the first trade issues in such a way that they can be readily distinguished from the numerous successive printings. White does not disparage Dulac's later work, and his discussion is always nicely judged in its handling of biographical and artistic detail. A more recent, less ambitious book that provides a good introduction to Dulac's art is the Peacock Press/Bantam Books *Edmund Dulac*, edited by David Larkin, with an introduction by Brian Sanders, and forty color plates.

Escher, M(aurits) C(ornelis) (Netherlands), 1898–1972.

10-67. Escher, M. C. **The World of M. C. Escher**. Ed. by J. L. Locher. Abrams, 1971.
In addition to the 300 reproductions, eight in color, there are five essays on Escher's work, plus a bibliography and list of exhibitions of the artist's work. Much of his work is based on mathematics and geometry, and much of it is overly didactic in intent. But even in the geometric prints there are fantastic beasts and

monsters, and one of the most pervasive themes in his work is the transformation of one kind of life into another, one of the most basic fantasy concepts. (REB)

Fabian, Stephen E., 1930- .

10-68. Fabian, Stephen E. **Fantasy by Fabian: The Art of Stephen E. Fabian**. Ed. by Gerry de la Ree. Gerry de la Ree, 1978.

10-69. Fabian, Stephen E. **More Fantasy by Fabian: The Art of Stephen E. Fabian**. Ed. by Gerry de la Ree. Gerry de la Ree, 1979.
Fabian is a prolific magazine and book illustrator of science fiction and fantasy, strongly influenced by Virgil Finlay. The two de la Ree books include work originally published by de la Ree as well as illustrations done for books and magazines. At least half a dozen portfolios of Fabian's work have been published, including *Fabian in Color* (Starmont, 1980), which contains eight color plates and includes a separate eight-page booklet of the artist's "comments and reflections" on the paintings. (WA/REB)

Finlay, Virgil, 1914–1971.

10-70. de la Ree, Gerry, ed. **Virgil Finlay Remembered**. Gerry de la Ree, 1981.

10-71. Finlay, Virgil. **The Book of Virgil Finlay**. Ed. by Gerry de la Ree. Gerry de la Ree, 1975.

10-72. Finlay, Virgil. **Finlay's Lost Drawings**. Ed. by Gerry de la Ree. Gerry de la Ree, 1975.

10-73. Finlay, Virgil. **The Second/Third/Fourth/Fifth/Sixth Books of Virgil Finlay**. Ed. by Gerry de la Ree. Gerry de la Ree, 1975, 1978, 1979, 1979, 1980.

***10-74**. Finlay, Virgil. **Virgil Finlay**. Ed. by Don Grant. Don Grant, 1971. Introduction by Sam Moskowitz; checklist of Finlay's work compiled by Gerry de la Ree.

10-75. Finlay, Virgil. **Virgil Finlay: An Astrology Sketchbook**. Ed. by Don Grant. Don Grant, 1975.

10-76. Finlay, Virgil. **Virgil Finlay in The American Weekly**. Nova, 1977.

10-77. Finlay, Virgil. **Virgil Finlay: 1914–1971**. Ed. by Gerry de la Ree. Gerry de la Ree, 1971.
In the 1970s there were an unprecedented number of books devoted to Virgil Finlay, who began his extensive career as a magazine illustrator in *Weird Tales* in the mid-1930s. Farnsworth Wright, the legendary editor of the magazine, was so taken with Finlay's work that he published, in 1935, an illustrated edition of Shakespeare's *Midsummer Night's Dream*, which was to initiate a series of inexpensive popular editions of the classics. The intended series was a failure, but Finlay's reputation as the finest of American pulp illustrators was unchallenged for at least a decade. After his return from military service in World War II, Finlay continued to work in the declining pulp market, still meticulous about detail and still the master of pen-and-ink drawing. Several portfolios of Finlay's work for the

pulps were published as early as the late 1940s, but it was not until 1971, and after his death, that there would be an outpouring of tributes to his work, celebrating the black-and-white work (except for four color plates in the first Don Grant publication). Throughout the decade the tributes continued to appear, most often under the imprint of Gerry de la Ree, an enterprising collector of popular art. Frazetta and his successors may currently be more honored, but when the definitive history of the artists of the pulp years is written, Virgil Finlay will be seen as the professional who raised standards and created a model of excellence that honors him and the field.

FitzPatrick, Jim (Ireland), 1948- .

10-78. FitzPatrick, Jim. **The Book of Conquests**. Paper Tiger, 1978.

10-79. FitzPatrick, Jim. **Érinsaga. The Mythological Paintings of Jim FitzPatrick**. De Danann Press, 1985.

10-80. FitzPatrick, Jim. **The Silver Arm**. Paper Tiger, 1981.
FitzPatrick's subject, in both text and artwork, is the legendary history of pre-Celtic and Celtic Ireland. His intricately detailed drawings, paintings and decorations form a unique body of work, incorporating and building upon traditional Irish motifs. *Érinsaga* contains an illustrated retrospective of the artist's work, plus detailed commentary on the more than 100 drawings and paintings included. The printing quality in the Paper Tiger books does not do complete justice to the artwork, but the fine detail and glowing colors are faithfully reproduced in several portfolios and in a 1986 *Érin-saga* wall calendar published in West Germany. (REB)

Frazetta, Frank, 1928- .

***10-81**. Frazetta, Frank. **The Fantastic Art of Frank Frazetta**. Scribner, 1975.

10-82. Frazetta, Frank. **Frank Frazetta, Book One–Book Five**. Ed. by Betty Ballantine. Peacock Press, 1977, 1978, 1980, 1985.
Undoubtedly the most influential of contemporary fantasy book illustrators. After a two-decade career as a comic book and magazine artist, Frazetta did a series of covers for Ace reprints of Edgar Rice Burroughs that established him as the finest Burroughs illustrator since J. Allen St. John. This series was so successful that Frazetta embarked on a new career as a creator of paperback covers. The collections of his artwork marked a new phase in the acceptance of his work and of modern fantasy illustration as an art form. Elements of his distinctive style can be seen in the work of illustrators such as Boris Vallejo, Rowena and Michael Whelan, and it is probably safe to say that no single illustrator has influenced the field since the 1960s in the way that he has.

Freas, Frank Kelly, 1922- .

10-83. Freas, Frank Kelly. **The Art of Science Fiction**. Donning, 1977.

10-84. Freas, Frank Kelly. **The Astounding Fifties: A Portfolio of Illustrations**. Freas, 1971.

10-85. Freas, Frank Kelly. **A Separate Star**. Greenswamp, 1984.
The Astounding Fifties, the second Freas portfolio (the first was issued by Advent in 1957), is devoted to interior illustrations for *Astounding Science Fiction,* 1953-59. In the introduction Freas mentions that he illustrated over 160 stories in *Astounding* during this period, and that the eighty-four drawings included here represent "both some of the best and some of the worst of my work." (REB)

Freas, winner of ten Hugos, is probably the best known of all science fiction illustrators since the early 1950s. People are the center of his art, in contrast to the hardware emphasis of other illustrators. His anecdotal text in *The Art of Science Fiction* clearly explains the development of each illustration. The self-published *A Separate Star* collects more recent work, from preliminary sketches to finished work. His commentary might be useful to aspiring illustrators. (NB)

Froud, Brian (U.K.), 1948- .

10-86. Froud, Brian. **The Land of Froud**. Ed. by David Larkin. Introduction by Brian Sanders. Peacock Press/Ballantine, 1974.

10-87. Froud, Brian. **The World of the Dark Crystal**. Knopf, 1982.
Froud is best known for his gnomic book illustrations for *Fairies* and his designs for the 1983 Jim Henson/Frank Oz film *The Dark Crystal,* but his art—as the examples in this collection show—is markedly influenced by British illustrators like W. Heath and Charles Robinson, Dulac, S. H. Sime and, especially, Arthur Rackham.

Gallardo, Gervasio (Spain), 1934- .

10-88. Gallardo, Gervasio. **The Fantastic World of Gervasio Gallardo**. Peacock Press/Bantam, 1976.
Born in Spain in 1934, Gallardo has worked in Europe and the U.S. His commercial and fine art shows his debt to Surrealism, especially Magritte, but has a more playful quality. He did many covers for Ballantine's Adult Fantasy paperback series in the 1970s. This ninety-six-page paperback collects reproductions of many of these book covers as well as his other work in a variety of media. (NB)

Giger, H. R. (Switzerland), 1940- .

10-89. Giger, H. R. **H. R. Giger's Necronomicon**. Big O, 1978.

10-90. Giger, H. R. **H. R. Giger's Necronomicon 2**. Editions C, 1985.
Giger is a Swiss artist and illustrator who achieved prominence with his set designs for the 1979 film *Alien,* for which he and others won an Academy Award for visual effects. The autobiographical account in the 1978 volume reveals a preoccupation with death, the fantastic and the morbid, evident in all his work. He strikingly juxtaposes or blends the human figure with mechanical structures to create biomechanoid images of great power, in which a decadent eroticism is

prevalent. The 1985 collection is more of the same, unsettling and visceral in its impact. Giger is one of the more important artists working in nongenre fantastic art, and libraries with large art collections should consider one of his oversized collections. (NB)

Gorey, Edward, 1925- .

***10-91**. Gorey, Edward. **Amphigorey**. Putnam, 1972.

10-92. Gorey, Edward. **Amphigorey Also**. Congdon & Weed, 1983.

10-93. Gorey, Edward. **Amphigorey Too**. Putnam, 1975.
Many of Gorey's early books, small volumes long out of print, are included in these three collections. Gorey has created a neo-Victorian world in books which he both writes and illustrates. His witty, menacing line drawings bring to deliciously chilling life the texts of books that are graced by titles such as *The Doubtful Guest, The Gashlycrumb Tinies* and *The Deranged Cousins.* Gorey has also edited and illustrated collections of ghost stories and designed the sets and costumes for a notable modern stage production of *Dracula,* starring Frank Langella. These stage designs have been preserved in *Dracula: A Toy Theater* (Scribner, 1979). (WA/REB)

Hildebrandt, Tim and **Greg**, both 1939- .

10-94. Hildebrandt, Greg. **From Tolkien to Oz: The Art of Greg Hildebrandt**. Ed. by William McGuire. Unicorn Publishing House, 1985.

10-95. Hildebrandt, Tim and Greg. **The Art of the Brothers Hildebrandt**. Ed. by Ian Summers. Ballantine, 1979.

10-96. Hildebrandt, Tim and Greg. **The Brothers Hildebrandt**. Catalog of an exhibition of their work at the Maryland Funnybook Festival, 1978.
The Hildebrandt brothers speak of an early enthusiasm for Johnny Gruelle and for Pyle, Wyeth and Parrish, later wedded to an interest in Surrealists like Dalí and Magritte. Their characteristic lighting effects are based on photos, but used only as references. Recently the two artists have worked separately, with Greg illustrating fantasy classics such as *Dracula* and *The Wizard of Oz* while Tim has returned to the illustration of children's books. The exhibition catalog includes—in addition to sketches and preliminary drawings, finished color work and photographs—an interview with the artists. (WA/REB)

Jones, Jeffrey (U.K.), 1944- .

10-97. Jones, Jeffrey. **Yesterday's Lily**. Dragon's Dream, 1980.
Biographical sketch, interview with Jones, critical essay by Irma Kurtz and more than sixty pages of color paintings and black-and-white artwork by Jones. Not only SF and fantasy book covers, but western paintings and some very impressive portraits and delicate pencil drawings. (REB)

Jones, Peter (U.K.), 1951- .

10-98. Jones, Peter. **Solar Wind**. Perigee/Paper Tiger, 1980.
Ninety-five paintings, mostly for paperback and book covers. Biographical sketch, notes on technique, some commentary on subject matter. The first half of the book consists of fantasy paintings, principally sword and sorcery, in which the influences of Frazetta and Jeff Jones are clearly evident. Even amid the spaceships and futuristic war machines in the remainder of the book, Frazetta-ish figures are prominent participants. The paintings give the impression of barely arrested motion; there is scarcely a static composition in the lot. (REB)

Kirk, Tim, 1947- .

10-99. Beahm, George, ed. **Kirk's Works: An Index of the Art of Tim Kirk**. Heresy Press, 1980.
The major portion of this book is an index of Kirk's work, accompanied by numerous examples. Only the wraparound cover illustration is in color; all of the interior reproductions are in black and white. However, much of Kirk's best work is in the witty interiors he has done for magazines and books, and this essential text gives a broad picture of his talents. Kirk's illustrations of Dunsany are as attractive as those of Sime, who has surely been a major influence on him.

Krenkel, Roy G., 1918-1983.

10-100. Krenkel, Roy G. **Cities and Scenes from the Ancient World**. Owlswick Press, 1974.
Krenkel's illustrations for L. Sprague de Camp's *Great Cities of the Ancient World* (Doubleday, 1974), together with many additional drawings and a color frontispiece. Preface by Sanford Zane Meschkow and introductory essay by Krenkel. Many of these drawings show Krenkel's debt to Franklin Booth [10-51], to whom the book is dedicated. (REB)

Lawson, Robert, 1892-1957.

10-101. Lawson, Robert. **Robert Lawson, Illustrator: A Selection of His Characteristic Illustrations**. Ed. by Helen L. Jones. Little, Brown, 1971.
Includes an index of titles and a checklist of books illustrated by Lawson. Jones was his editor at Little, Brown and she includes comments from the artist's correspondence on his work. His first published work was fantasy and shows the influence of both Arthur Rackham and Charles Robinson, as well as Hugh Lofting and Dorothy Lathrop. A delightful sense of humor helped make Lawson one of the finest, and least dated, illustrators of children's books of his period.

Maitz, Don, 1953- .

10-102. Maitz, Don. **First Maitz: Selected Works by Don Maitz**. Ursus Imprints, 1988.
This collection of Maitz's work consists largely of paperback cover art, not

surprising for an artist who has painted over 150 covers since his professional debut in 1975. Ron Walotsky comments that Maitz's style has the "feeling and look of the old master illustrators like Arthur Rackham or N. C. Wyeth." To that short list, one could also add Edmund Dulac, Maxfield Parrish, Sulamith Wülfing and Frank Frazetta. This is not to disparage Maitz, who is a very accomplished illustrator, but the accompanying text is not very enlightening except when Maitz talks about his working methods.

Mathews, Rodney (U.K.), 1945- .

10-103. Mathews, Rodney. **In Search of Forever**. Paper Tiger, 1985.
Mathews early developed an interest in nature and still prefers drawing animals—often very fantastic animals—to people. Some of his work has a playful quality. It has been featured in several calendars and on many posters, and has illustrated many works of Michael Moorcock. He uses various media—ink, ink and gouache, and watercolor—for his books, LP jackets and posters, logos and alphabets. The text by Mathews and Nigel Suckling provides interesting details about Mathews's work, which heavily favors the fantastic, with typical science fiction icons uncommon. (NB)

Morrill, Rowena *see* **Rowena**

Mugnaini, Joseph A., 1912- .

10-104. Mugnaini, Joseph A. **Joseph Mugnaini: Drawings and Graphics**. Scarecrow, 1982.
Italian born, U.S. educated, Mugnaini is best known to fantasy readers for his book jackets and interiors for several of Ray Bradbury's books. He works in various media, and many samples of his work are included, some of them from his many Limited Editions Club books. This collection's major weakness is the absence of any color reproductions, but it is otherwise strongly recommended. (NB)

Nielsen, Kay, 1886-1957.

***10-105**. Nielsen, Kay. **Kay Nielsen**. Ed. by David Larkin. Introduction by Keith Nicholson. Peacock Press/Bantam, 1975.
Nielsen, a Danish expatriate who settled first in London and later in California, was younger than Dulac and Rackham, his great contemporaries, but his illustrations of classic fairy tales are in no way inferior to theirs, and two of his books, *In Powder and Crinoline* (1913) and *East of the Sun and West of the Moon* (1914), are among the finest of the Golden Age of British illustration. Some of the perversity of Beardsley and Clarke is evident in his elegant aristocrats, but there are also an innocence and naiveté that contrast strangely with the Decadent strain. In the absence of a major study on Nielsen, the Bantam trade paperback is a good introduction to his work. It should, however, be supplemented by *The Unknown Kay Nielsen* (Peacock Press/Bantam, 1977), introduced by a moving tribute by

Hildegarde Flanner, who knew the Nielsens in California, and, especially, by another fine Green Tiger Press tribute, Welleran Poltarnees's *Kay Nielsen: An Appreciation* (1976). Here, the color reproductions approach the quality of the original publications and the drawings, printed on heavy tinted stock, are particularly well served.

Parrish, Maxfield, 1870–1966.

***10-106**. Ludwig, Coy. **Maxfield Parrish**. Watson-Guptill, 1973.
Much of Parrish's work is not fantasy, but some of his best-known work is, including illustrations for Kenneth Grahame's *Dream Days* and *The Golden Age*, and the *Arabian Nights*. In addition, Parrish's techniques presage those of later illustrators, and his use of color has been widely imitated.

Peake, Mervyn (U.K.), 1911–1968.

10-107. Gilmore, Maeve, and Shelagh Johnson. **Mervyn Peake: Writings and Drawings**. Academy Editions and St. Martin's, 1974.
Not a formal biography, but a retrospective account of Peake's life and career as author, poet, playwright and illustrator. The 200 illustrations include twelve color plates. Bibliography of books by and about Peake, list of books he illustrated (including Lewis Carroll, Grimm, Coleridge and Robert Louis Stevenson) and a list of his principal exhibitions. (REB)

Pitz, Henry C., 1895–1976.

10-108. Likos, Patricia. **Henry C. Pitz 1895–1976: The Art of the Book**. Brandywine River Museum, 1988.
Catalog of a 1988 exhibition. Henry Pitz is well known to students of modern illustration for his many books on Howard Pyle and his successors. What has been lost sight of is the illustrative work of Pitz, himself an artist, and his crucial role in the history of the illustrated book in America. This catalog attempts to correct some of this, and the well-chosen examples of his work show his skill at fantastic illustration. His line drawings are particularly fine, and the examples of his work from the 1920s and 1930s show him maintaining a high standard of pictorial design in the manner of the Brandywine school, with some elements of Nielsen and Rackham.

Powers, Richard, 1921– .

10-109. Powers, Richard. **Spacetimewarp**. Nelson Doubleday, 1983.
This portfolio of sixteen loose plates, thirteen of them book covers, was a premium of the Science Fiction Book Club. Powers was one of the most prolific illustrators of paperback covers and hardcover jackets in the 1950s and 1960s. Robert Weinberg [10-35] considers him to be, with Finlay and Frazetta, one of the major influences on the field and to have "changed the perception of science fiction from space opera to real literature." Powers's background was in "fine" art at a time when science fiction and fantasy illustrators typically had begun their

career in the pulps. His images tend toward the abstract/surrealistic, unlike the hard-edged photographic realism favored by many science fiction illustrators. (NB)

Pyle, Howard, 1853-1911.

***10-110**. Pitz, Henry C. **Howard Pyle: Writer, Illustrator, Founder of the Brandywine School**. Clarkson N. Potter, 1975.
Pyle wielded enormous influence as an illustrator and as a teacher and he may be said to have founded the modern American illustrative style, with his influence extending to N. C. Wyeth and his students. Pitz's study is a model of its kind, by a practicing illustrator who understood Pyle's art and aims. A bibliography of Pyle's work for books and magazines is included.

Rackham, Arthur, 1867-1939.

***10-111**. Gittings, Fred. **Arthur Rackham**. Macmillan, 1975.

10-112. Hudson, Derek. **Arthur Rackham: His Life and Work**. Scribner, 1960.

10-113. Latimore, Sarah Briggs, and Grace Clark Haskell. **Arthur Rackham: A Bibliography**. San Marco Bookstore (Jacksonville, FL), 1987 (first published London, 1936).
Rackham was, for many people, the finest illustrator of his generation and his vision of the classic world of Andersen, Grimm and Barrie the definitive visualization of that world. His influence extends to the present generation of fantasy illustrators (Froud, Hildebrandt, Maitz, among many) and a number of books are still in print, albeit in pale copies of their original splendor. Hudson's biography is painstaking and uninspired, and he finds himself unable to respond to much of the later work. However, the first edition was lavishly produced with tipped-in color plates, heavy stock for the text paper, and illustrated endpapers. Gittings's study was more economically produced, but its strengths are an abundance of wonderful line drawings, a more balanced evaluation of Rackham's career and a reasonable attempt at recording magazine appearances. Both Hudson and Gittings describe only the limited and first trade editions of the books illustrated by Rackham, and there are no comments on the quality of the reproduction of the color originals, which does vary, particularly between the American and British editions. The Lattimore/Haskell bibliography includes books published only through 1935, but the descriptions are more detailed than in either Hudson or Gittings.

Robinson, Charles (U.K.), 1870-1937.

10-114. de Freitas, Leo. **Charles Robinson**. Academy Editions, St. Martin's, 1976.
Charles Robinson is not as generally admired as his brother, W. Heath Robinson, but his fantasy line drawings and color illustrations are among the most charming of the period and, perhaps, among the most influential for contemporary fantasy artists. The illustrations for his *Bee: The Princess of the Dwarfs* (1912) are strikingly modern and would not look out of place on a 1980s fantasy paperback

cover. See especially the work of Craig Russell and Michael W. Kaluta, both of whom appear to be familiar with Robinson's work. De Freitas provides a critical introduction and numerous examples of Robinson's work in color and black and white.

Robinson, W. Heath (U.K.), 1872–1944.

10-115. Beare, Geoffrey. **The Illustrations of W. Heath Robinson**. Werner Shaw, 1983.

10-116. Robinson, W. Heath. **The Fantastic Paintings of Charles & William Heath Robinson**. Ed. by David Larkin. Peacock Press/Bantam, 1976.
W. Heath Robinson was noted for his versatility; after early successes as the illustrator of Poe, Shakespeare and De la Mare, he became noted for his comic drawings in which he satirized the contraptions of the machine age. Charles seems never to have lost a certain Romantic lyricism that turned, in W. Heath's later work, to humor. The biography by Beare includes an excellent bibliography. There are, however, only three examples of Robinson's color illustrations and, for this reason, the Peacock Press collection is a useful supplement.

Rowena (Rowena Morrill), 1944– .

10-117. Morrill, Rowena. **The Fantastic Art of Rowena**. Introduction by Boris Vallejo; Foreword by Theodore Sturgeon. Pocket Books, 1983.
Photo and biographical sketch of the artist. "Description of painting technique," illustrated with progressive stages of one of the plates. Twenty-six plates with individual commentary by the artist. The most immediately noticeable feature of almost any Rowena painting is the incredible satiny texture of flesh and clothing. She confesses to "a real weakness" for this effect, and no one does it better. Many of her paintings feature muscular males or lush females, sometimes caught in static and seemingly uncomfortable poses. In quite a different vein is her fine portrait of the young hero of Theodore Sturgeon's *The Dreaming Jewels*. (REB)

Salomoni, Tito (Italy), 1928– .

10-118. Salomoni, Tito. **The Surrealistic World of Tito Salomoni**. Prestige Art Galleries (Skokie, IL), 1984.
Salomoni has done cover work for a number of paperback publishers and magazines, and his work has been published extensively in this country and abroad. Most of the illustrations appear to be nonillustrative work, and Salomoni appends comments to a number of them. An accomplished artist in the Surrealist tradition with Chirico, Escher, Magritte and Dalí evoked as influences in the short preface.

Schomburg, Alex, 1905– .

10-119. Gustafson, Jon. **Chroma: The Art of Alex Schomburg**. Father Tree Press, 1986.
Introductions and appreciations by Harlan Ellison, Stan Lee, Frank Kelly Freas,

Vincent Di Fate, Brian Aldiss, George Barr. Extensive biographical and critical commentary by Gustafson, with interpolated comments by Schomburg. More than eighty reproductions of science fiction magazine and book covers, comic book covers and fine art, plus a generous sampling of black-and-white work; the non-science fiction material ranges from advertising work in the 1920s to landscapes and architectural renderings. Individual commentary on most of the pieces reproduced. (REB)

Segrelles, Vicente (Spain), 1940- .

10-120. Segrelles, Vicente. **The Art of Segrelles**. NBM, 1987.
After an early career alternating between advertising and illustration, Segrelles left advertising in 1970 to concentrate on paperback cover artwork in England and the United States. In 1980, he began the series of *Mercenary* graphic novels, which is published in fourteen countries. The twenty-nine color plates include several double-page spreads. The illustrations are primarily fantastic and romantic-historical in subject. Segrelles is particularly effective in the creation of fantastic beasts and monsters. The cover illustration, with its evocative melancholy background, is representative of his best work.

Sendak, Maurice, 1928- .

***10-121**. Lanes, Selma G. **The Art of Maurice Sendak**. Abradale/Abrams, 1980.
Sendak, the most popular and honored children's book artist of this generation, is the subject of this detailed study. His illustrations are grounded in the work of the great nineteenth-century illustrators such as Crane and Caldecott, as well as the early twentieth-century American comic strip artist Winsor McCay. His illustrations also show his affection for the movies, but the diverse influences have been integrated into a highly accomplished style in which the fantastic is as appealing to adults as to children. A recently published book of essays by Sendak on illustrators and illustration (*Caldecott & Co.*, Farrar, Straus, 1988) is an ideal complement to Lanes's detailed study, whose numerous color examples of Sendak's color and black-and-white work enhance the pleasure of a well-written text.

Sime, S(idney) H(erbert) (U.K.), 1867-1941.

10-122. Heneage, Simon, and Henry Ford. **Sidney Sime: Master of the Mysterious**. Thames & Hudson, 1980.

10-123. Skeeters, Paul W. **Sidney H. Sime: Master of Fantasy**. Ward Ritchie, 1978.
Sime is now known principally as the illustrator of many of Dunsany's collections of fantastic tales, but his early work is of almost as much interest. His fantastic creatures may have influenced Dr. Seuss, and his satirical drawings are as fine as the work of the great French nineteenth-century magazine illustrators. Sime worked largely in black and white, but the drawings have much of the richness and range one normally associates with color. Sime is well served in both these books, and although many of the Dunsany illustrations appear in both works, Sime was so prolific in his earlier years that many striking examples of his

work are not duplicated. Skeeters also includes some rare examples of Sime's color work, including some delicious monochrome illustrations from Sime's *From An Ultima Dim Thule* and *Beasts That Might Have Been.*

Vallejo, Boris (Peru), 1941- .

10-124. Vallejo, Boris. **The Fantastic Art of Boris Vallejo**. Ballantine, 1978.

10-125. Vallejo, Boris. **Fantasy Art Techniques**. Dragon's Dream, 1985.

10-126. Vallejo, Boris. **Mirage**. Ballantine, 1982.
Peruvian-born Boris, as he signs his paintings, is one of the more popular illustrators (a three-time Hugo nominee), especially in the field of heroic fantasy/sword and sorcery. His first collection includes forty color plates, along with early paintings, pen-and-ink drawings and cartoons. *Mirage* assembles eleven black-and-white drawings with commentary by Boris, and twenty-nine color plates with bad poetry by his wife, Doris, on the facing page. The techniques volume, while nominally aimed at would-be art students, collects many examples of Vallejo's work, preliminary sketches, Polaroid photos of models, and finished paintings. Boris was, for a time, the most successful emulator of Frazetta's heroic style, although he quite outdid the master in creating steatopygian females. (NB)

Whelan, Michael, 1950- .

10-127. Whelan, Michael. **Michael Whelan's Works of Wonder**. Ballantine, 1987.

10-128. Whelan, Michael. **Wonderworks: Science Fiction and Fantasy Art**. Ed. by Polly and Frank Kelly Freas. Donning, 1979.
Whelan is one of the most accomplished of today's illustrators, and these two retrospective collections reproduce both working sketches and the finished art, usually much larger than the American paperback covers it adorned. In the Ballantine collection, there is extensive commentary by the artist on the individual works and on his painting technique. Hugo Award winner, 1988. (NB/REB)

White, Tim (U.K.), 1952- .

10-129. White, Tim. **The Science Fiction and Fantasy World of Tim White**. New English Library, 1981; Paper Tiger, 1988.
Most of the examples of White's work—he is an artist who has worked in a number of media—are of his paperback cover art. The earliest examples, from 1973, are of science fiction hardware, gleaming ships against the backgrounds of deep space or settled in peaceful fields. Increasingly, fantasy creatures invade his futuristic settings, but human figures, only intermittently seen, are distant from the viewer, too small for detail to register, turned away or moving away from the foreground or, in the occasional startling closeup, offering up an untroubled profile, as pure of emotion as the ships and fantastic creatures. The illustrations were commissioned for English publications, and his work deserves to be better known in this country.

Wood, Robin

10-130. Wood, Robin. **The People of Pern**. Donning, 1988.
A gallery of color portraits for Anne McCaffrey's Dragon series [F4A-179]. Wood is best known for her drawings of children and animals in fantasy settings. McCaffrey wrote the introduction and accompanying text. Also annotated as [8-59].

Woodroffe, Patrick (U.K.), 1940- .

10-131. Woodroffe, Patrick. **A Closer Look: The Art Techniques of Patrick Woodroffe**. Dragon's Dream & Harmony Books, 1986.
An indispensable complement/supplement to *Mythopoeikon*. Woodroffe discusses his techniques in a variety of mediums. There is a fine sequence of drawings for "The Hunting of the Snark," and in addition to numerous color reproductions, there are many examples of his black-and-white pen work. The Dalí influence is less evident but the influence of the crowded canvases of Bosch is, if anything, more pervasive than in his earlier work.

10-132. Woodroffe, Patrick. **Hallelujah Anyway**. Dragon's World, 1984.
This is a collection of illustrated lyrics, billed as an "exploration of the border between reality and imagination." Most of the illustrations are tomographs, which blend painting with photographs of backgrounds and of intricate cut-outs and models built by the artist. (REB)

10-133. Woodroffe, Patrick. **Mythopoeikon: Fantasies, Monsters, Daydreams**. Dragon's World, 1976.
A kaleidoscopic collection of Woodroffe's work, with a running commentary by the artist. Woodroffe speaks of his early infatuation with Dalí, the Flemish and Dutch "primitives" and Hieronymus Bosch. A number of his early pen-and-ink drawings are included, and this work is as virtuosic as his color paintings. His work is all fantastic in treatment—even when the subject, like Dashiell Hammett, is not fantastic—and his paperback cover illustrations for reprints of A. Merritt's novels are particularly successful. Woodroffe is a self-taught artist of great versatility.

10-134. Woodroffe, Patrick. **The Second Earth: The Pentateuch Re-Told**. Dragon's World, 1987.
A "very much enlarged" edition of *The Pentateuch of the Cosmogony* (Dragon's World, 1979). The paintings, drawings, calligraphy and text are integrated into a seamless whole, portraying the birth, life-cycle and apocalyptic fate of a manlike race on another planet, as revealed by five books of alien scripture found on a derelict spacecraft in the twenty-fourth century. Artwork from the original edition has been extensively rearranged and sometimes reduced or cropped (not always to its advantage), with much new material added. (REB)

Wrightson, Berni, 1948- .

10-135. Wrightson, Berni. **A Look Back**. Ed. by Christopher Zavisa. Land of Enchantment, 1979.
Wrightson created *Swamp Thing* for DC Comics and some distinctive horror

adaptations and original stories for Warren Publications, but has also done posters, book illustrations (for *Frankenstein* and Stephen King's *Silver Bullet*) and, with Michael Kaluta, greatly influenced younger artists. His gallery of grotesques is unmistakable and this elaborate tribute was well deserved. The text includes comments by the artist on his work.

11

Fantasy and Horror Magazines

Mike Ashley

Fantasy and Horror have formed a part of the magazine scene for as long as magazines have featured fiction. As magazines began to take shape in the seventeenth and eighteenth centuries, they were predominantly political broadsheets with little to distinguish a magazine from a newspaper or a political tract. When fiction appeared, it was often of a political or satirical nature, though one exception was *The Adventurer* (1752–54), edited by John Hawkesworth, which contained, in addition to its essays and political sermonizing, a number of the editor's own stories, many in the then current vogue for Oriental fiction, mostly fantasy.

The earliest regular publication to devote itself to the weird and wonderful was an Irish periodical, *The Marvellous Magazine* (1822). It ran for only thirteen weekly issues but featured much that was, in its own words, "spicy, sensational, curious, strange, eccentric, extraordinary, surprising, supernatural, comical and whimsical." It ran many abridgments of Gothic novels and stories along with retellings of legends and folklore. These were to become standard fare in many popular magazines, but few let them dominate the contents. One early exception was *The Romancist and Novelist's Library* (1839–42), edited by William Hazlitt the Younger. Collecting Gothic and Romantic stories and novellas, it was originally issued as a weekly magazine, but after two years Hazlitt converted it to a part-work collection issued serially. At that time it was common for forthcoming novels to be issued as serial part-works before being bound as the final volume. The same thing happened to Hazlitt's magazine and collection, and there is little to distinguish between the bound volumes of a magazine and an anthology (a situation that has recurred in recent years).

By the nineteenth century magazines were published in profusion throughout Europe and America and those featuring fiction regularly carried fantasy and horror. *Bentley's Magazine* (1837–68), for instance, carried Richard Barham's popular *Ingoldsby Legends* as well as reprints of Poe's stories. *The Dublin University Magazine* (1833–77) carried many of J. Sheridan Le Fanu's ghost stories and, during his period as editor (1861–70), heavily emphasized the supernatural. One of the best known, longest-lived and most influential of the Victorian magazines was *Blackwood's* (1817–1980), published in Scotland, which featured many ghost stories including the best known of them all, "The Haunted and the Haunters" by Lord Bulwer Lytton (1859). Selections of weird stories have been assembled as *Strange Tales from Blackwood* (1950) and *Ghost Tales from Blackwood* (1969). *Blackwood's* and other leading Victorian magazines and reviews are indexed in *The Wellesley Index to Victorian Periodicals, 1824–1900*, edited by Walter E. Houghton (4 vols., 1966); American magazines are indexed in *Poole's Index to Periodical Literature, 1802–1906* (6 vols., 1882–1908).

An often overlooked publishing feature of the last century was the Christmas Annual and Giftbook. The most influential of the early ones was *The Keepsake* (1828–57), edited by Frederick Reynolds, which published most of the supernatural stories by Mary W. Shelley and Sir Walter Scott. Charles Dickens, who added impetus to the vogue for ghost stories at Christmas, frequently published special Christmas issues of his own magazines, *Household Words* (1850–59) and *All The Year Round* (1859–95), and by the latter half of the century these special issues and annuals had become a significant source for supernatural stories. For instance, Fisher Unwin's annual for 1886, *The Witching Hour*, edited by Henry Norman, contained all supernatural stories. Routledge's Christmas annual for 1877 featured Mrs. Riddell's novel *The Haunted River* [H2-83]; in fact, Mrs. Riddell's stories became a regular Christmas feature for the annuals. These volumes have not been adequately indexed or assessed.

The heyday of the popular periodical began in 1891 with the publication of *The Strand Magazine* (1891–1950; see *Index to the "Strand Magazine"* by Geraldine Beare, 1982). This, and such imitators as *The Idler* (1892–1911), *Pall Mall* (1893–1937), *Pearson's* (1896–1939) and *The Royal* (1898–1939), regularly carried supernatural stories. *The Novel Magazine* (1905–37) developed its use of weird fiction as a marketing feature, publishing at least one "uncanny story" each issue from 1913 to 1921. Several of these were later collected in book form (see omnibus *Ghost Stories and Other Queer Tales* [1931]). Sam Moskowitz has surveyed this period in the introduction to his anthology *Science Fiction by Gaslight* (1968), but his emphasis is necessarily on SF and the full import of horror and fantasy fiction in these magazines has yet to be documented adequately.

The same is true for the United States, where magazines like *Harper's* (1850–) and *Atlantic Monthly* (1871–) regularly carried weird fiction. This is still true today, more so in the United States, where fiction has remained a stronger feature of magazines than in Britain. Popular periodicals like *The Saturday Evening Post* and *Playboy* became strong markets for stories of the bizarre and grotesque. (For representative anthologies see *Shapes That Haunt the Dark* [1907], edited by William Dean Howells and Henry Mills Alden from *Harper's*; *The Saturday Evening Post Fantasy Stories* [1951], edited by Barthold Fles; and *The Playboy Book of Horror and the Supernatural* [1967] and other selections anonymously edited by Ray Russell.)

The development of fantastic fiction in nineteenth-century American magazines has been chronicled by Sam Moskowitz in his introduction to *The Crystal Man* (1973) by Edward Page Mitchell and in *Science Fiction in Old San Francisco: Vol. 1, History of the Movement from 1854 to 1890* (1980). He has also surveyed its development in the pulp magazines of the first decades of this century in his anthology *Under the Moons of Mars* (1970). It was through the pulp magazines, pioneered by Frank A. Munsey's *Argosy* (1882–), that the true specialist fiction magazine evolved.

The Specialist Publications

Despite the false reputation given *The Black Cat* (1895–1923), which was a general magazine with a penchant for the offbeat story, the first specialist weird fiction magazine was not American or English but German. *Der Orchideengarten* (1919–21) selected material from a wide variety of European authors and was beautifully illustrated and decorated. In America *The Thrill Book* (1919) verged on being a fantasy magazine, but gave too great an emphasis to adventure fiction. The first regular English-language fantasy magazine was *Weird Tales* [11-20]. It has also proved the most durable, for although it ceased publication in 1954 it has had four subsequent revivals. *Weird Tales* was never a major financial success but was sufficiently popular to encourage imitators, of which *Strange Tales* [11-17] was the best. Other lesser magazines from this period were *Ghost Stories* (1926–31), *Tales of Magic and Mystery* (1927–28) and *Mind Magic* (1931), which catered more to the gullible believer than the fantasy fan.

It was not until *Unknown* [11-18] that a new slant was brought to fantasy and horror fiction in the pioneering hands of editor John W. Campbell, Jr. The legacy of *Unknown* was later inherited by *Beyond* [11-2] and *The Magazine of Fantasy and Science Fiction* [11-13], which, through a series of highly capable editors, has become the leading fantasy publication available today.

In the heyday of the pulps, during the 1920s and 1930s, there were many specialist magazines of borderline fantasy/horror interest. There were the weird menace pulps such as *Terror Tales* (1934–41) and *Horror Stories* (1935–41), where the menace was usually directed by madmen and maniacs rather than the supernatural. Their history is well documented in Robert K. Jones's *The Shudder Pulps* [11-53]. There were also the character/hero-villain pulps, of which *Doc Savage* (1933–49) and *The Shadow* (1931–49) are the best known. These often included fantastic or supernatural episodes, although the only title character to have exclusively supernatural powers was featured in *Doctor Death* (1935). There are a growing number of specialist books about the pulps, and the hero pulps in particular, the best of which is the four-volume series *Yesterday's Faces* by Robert Sampson (1983–87). More general, though personalized, pulp histories are available in *The Fiction Factory* (1955) by Quentin Reynolds about the firm of Street & Smith, *Pulpwood Editor* (1937) by pulp editor and publisher Harold Hersey and *The Pulp Jungle* (1967) by prolific writer Frank Gruber. A useful basic overview of the pulps is Ron Goulart's *Cheap Thrills: An Informal History of the Pulp Magazines* (1972), which includes coverage of the hero, terror and weird fiction titles. Tony Goodstone's *The Pulps: 50 Years of American Pop Culture* (1970) is a good sampler of pulp fiction with a chapter on supernatural fiction and a colorful selection of covers. Another representative selection will be found in Peter Haining's *The Fantastic Pulps* (1975). Bill Blackbeard's chapter "Pulps and Dime Novels" in Inge's *Handbook of American Popular Literature* [6-38] provides a useful, current overview of pulp magazines of all types.

Today only a limited number of professional fantasy and horror magazines survive, the best of the new ones being *Rod Serling's "The Twilight Zone" Magazine* [11-15], which ceased publication as this guide was being written. There has been a trend toward serial anthologies such as the *Shadows* [H4-359] series, but the greatest growth in magazine fantasy and horror fiction has been in the small press field. There has always been a healthy amateur press field, pioneered and promoted by H. P. Lovecraft among others. The first specialist fantasy small press magazine, *The Recluse* (1927), came from within the Lovecraft circle of epistolarians. The specialist fantasy amateur magazines (or "fanzines") came into their own in the 1930s allied to the burgeoning SF fan field. The leading fan magazines of the day, *The Fantasy Fan* [11-31] and *The Phantagraph* (1935–46), have their more sophisticated counterparts today in *Whispers* [11-21], *Weirdbook* [11-19], *The Horror Show* [11-10], *Fantasy Book* [11-7], *Shayol* (1977–85), *Argonaut* (1972-) and *Eldritch Tales* [11-3]. Even the recently revived *Weird Tales* is an outgrowth of the small press movement. Jessica Amanda Salmonson's anthology series, *Tales by Moonlight* (1983 and 1988), has presented stories by small press writers, the second volume specifically selecting the best from small press magazines.

The small press field is also noted for its critical and academic magazines which study, review and analyze fantasy fiction. Many of these are dedicated to the works of a particular author, most significantly H. P. Lovecraft (see *The Acolyte* [11-22], *Crypt of Cthulhu* [11-27], *Lovecraft Studies* [11-41] and *Nyctalops* [11-45]), but also covering such diverse authors as L. Frank Baum (*The Baum Bugle* [11-26]), Edgar Rice Burroughs (*Erbania* [11-29]), F. Marion Crawford (*The Romantist* [11-48]), Robert E. Howard (*Amra* [11-24], *The Howard Collector* [11-38] and the recent *Cromlech* [1985-]), M. R. James (*Ghosts & Scholars* [11-35]), Mervyn Peake (*Peake Studies* [11-46]), Edgar Allan Poe (*Poe Studies* [11-47]), Clark Ashton Smith (*Nyctalops* [11-45] and the new *Klarkash-Ton* [1988-]), and J. R. R. Tolkien (*Mythlore* [11-43] and *Niekas* [11-44]). These magazines usually feature the author as a pivot around which is balanced a view of that author's influence on weird or fantasy fiction and a study of associational aspects. More general studies of the field are less common but include *American Fantasy* [11-23], *Dark Horizons* [11-28] and *Horrorstruck* [11-37] plus the new *Midnight Graffiti* (1988-).

The fan field also provides the medium for spreading news, information and reviews. The leading news magazine is *Locus* [11-40], which emphasizes SF but also provides good coverage of the fantasy and horror fields. Other specialist news magazines include *American Fantasy* [11-23], which is too irregular to be topical, *Mystery Scene* [11-42], which has rather divided loyalties, and the defunct *Fantasy Review* [11-32], which until its recent demise was the best in a limited field. There are also many magazines devoted to the pulp field; the best of the current titles are *Echoes* (1982-) and *The Pulp Collector* (1985-), while former titles of note were *The Pulp Era* (1959–76) and *Xenophile* (1974–78).

Studies and Indexes

The first source of reference for study of all of the fiction titles included in this section is *Science Fiction, Fantasy, and Weird Fiction Magazines* [11-54] by Marshall B. Tymn and Mike Ashley, which is the only complete work on these specialist magazines. Few other detailed studies of the field have been written, although Robert Weinberg's *The Weird Tales Story* [11-55] is an affectionate memoir of this leading title.

The primary index to all weird fiction and fantasy magazines is *Monthly Terrors* [11-68] by Frank H. Parnell and Mike Ashley, which indexes all titles to the end of 1983. All other indexes are either related directly to the SF field (such as Day [11-60] and Metcalf [11-64]) or the pulp field in general. *The Pulp Magazine Index* (1989) by Leonard Robbins indexes 198 titles by issue, author, artist, title and character, but covers only a few magazines of fantasy interest. The index overlaps to a degree a larger-scale series, started by the late Michael L. Cook and assisted by Stephen T. Miller, to index all pulps. Volume 1 covers *Mystery, Detective, and Espionage Fiction, 1915–1974* (1988), Volume 2, *Adventure, War and Sports Fiction* (forthcoming) and Volume 3, *Science Fiction, Fantasy, and Weird Fiction Magazines* (forthcoming). The best index to all current titles is the annual *Science Fiction, Fantasy, & Horror*, compiled by Charles N. Brown and William G. Contento [6-6], which covers all publications, including magazines, from 1984 to date. Considerable scholarly work has been carried out on modern writers of horror and fantasy as well as those who wrote primarily for the pulps, but little bibliographic work has been done on the weird and fantastic in the popular magazines, especially in Britain, which is almost virgin territory for the dedicated bibliophile.

Bibliography

Magazines Featuring Fiction

Annotated below are selected past and current magazines featuring horror and fantasy fiction. Publication addresses are given for current magazines only but subscription details are omitted due to frequency of changes. Information is current as of January 1989. Abbreviations for awards: HN, HW = Hugo nominee, winner; WFA = World Fantasy Award (see chapter 13).

Holdings information for selected magazines was obtained by Randall Scott, who compiled chapter 12. To conserve space, the holding library is designated by a number corresponding to the item number of the library in chapter 12. The letter in parentheses following the library number denotes A (all), M (most) or S (some). In a few instances holdings are on microfilm or microfiche, and these are designated mf after the letter. "All" denotes a complete run, and a current subscription if the magazine is currently published. "Most" denotes ownership of at least half and, in many cases, almost all issues published. "Some" denotes that fewer than half the published issues were held, or that the library simply designated its holdings as "incomplete."

***11-1. Avon Fantasy Reader**. 1947-52 (18 issues). Irregular. Donald A. Wollheim, ed. Avon Books, New York. Indexed in Day, Metcalf, Parnell, Strauss.
Although designed as a regular anthology series, *AFR* has become closely identified as a magazine. It concentrated on reprinting fiction selected widely from the pulps, especially *Weird Tales* [11-20], and from classic literature. Authors most represented include William Hope Hodgson, Robert E. Howard, Ray Bradbury and Lord Dunsany. Essential for its key selection of primary material. *AFR* had a companion *Avon Science Fiction Reader* (1951-52), which also published fantasy. Two representative anthologies were edited by George Ernsberger as *Avon Fantasy Reader* and *2nd Avon Fantasy Reader* (both 1968). Compare *Magazine of Horror* [11-14].
Holdings: 1 (A), 2 (A), 4 (A), 6 (A), 9 (M), 11 (A), 12 (A), 14 (A), 16 (A), 17 (A), 19 (A), 21 (A), 23 (A), 27 (A), 35 (A), 36 (A), 38 (S), 39 (A), 40 (S), 42 (S)

11-2. Beyond Fantasy Fiction. 1953-55 (10 issues). Bi-monthly. Horace L. Gold, ed. Galaxy Publishing, New York. Indexed in Metcalf, Strauss, Parnell.
A literary fantasy magazine that published more classic stories than are generally remembered despite the turn of the tide against fantasy in the 1950s. The best stories are more in the vein of science fantasy, with Gold treating *Beyond* as a fantasy companion to the SF magazine *Galaxy*, much as John W. Campbell had created *Unknown* [11-18] as a fantasy equivalent to *Astounding SF*. Authors include Robert Sheckley, Theodore Sturgeon and Damon Knight, with the best-known story being "The Wall around the World" by Theodore Cogswell. Selective anthology, *Beyond* (1963), published anonymously. Compare *Unknown* and *The Magazine of Fantasy and Science Fiction* [11-13].
Holdings: 1 (A), 2 (A), 4 (A), 6 (A), 9 (M), 11 (A), 12 (S), 13 (M), 14 (A), 15 (A), 16 (A), 17 (M), 19 (A), 21 (A), 23 (A), 27 (A), 28 (A), 35 (S), 36 (A), 38 (M), 39 (A), 41 (A), 42 (S)

11-3. Eldritch Tales. No ISSN. 1975- . Quarterly. Crispin Burnham, ed. 1051 Wellington Rd., Lawrence, KS 66044. Circulation: 1,000. Indexed in Parnell.
Subtitled "A Magazine in the Weird Tales Tradition," *ET* (titled *The Dark Messenger Reader* for issue #1) has until recently concentrated more on the Lovecraftian influence rather than the true *Weird Tales* tradition of the off-beat and bizarre. It has matured gradually and is now one of the more regular and reliable small press magazines. In addition to fiction and verse each issue carries news and reviews (film and book). Compare *Weirdbook* [11-19].
Holdings: 23 (M), 26 (M), 28 (S)

11-4. Famous Fantastic Mysteries. 1939-53 (81 issues). Monthly/Quarterly/Bi-monthly. Mary Gnaedinger, ed. Frank A. Munsey Co./Popular Publications, New York. Indexed in Day, Metcalf, Parnell, Strauss.
A pulp magazine highly prized today for its artwork by Virgil Finlay and Lawrence Stevens. Initially reprinted lead novels and stories from the early Munsey pulp magazines, selecting scientific romances or fantastic adventures (especially lost race) but including many weird fantasies. Later reprints were selected from book sources generally unavailable in the U.S. at the time. Authors selected included A. Merritt, William Hope Hodgson, Philip M. Fisher and Francis Stevens. Companion titles *Fantastic Novels* (1940-41, 1948-51) and *A. Merritt's Fan-*

tasy Magazine (1949–50) had same policy. Compare *Avon Fantasy Reader* [11-1]. Holdings: 1 (M), 2 (A), 6 (A), 9 (M), 11 (M), 12 (A), 13 (S), 14 (A), 16 (A), 17 (M), 19 (A), 21 (A), 23 (A), 26 (S), 27 (A), 28 (S), 29 (S), 35 (A), 36 (A), 38 (S), 39 (A), 41 (A), 42 (S)

11-5. Fantastic. 1952–80 (208 issues). Monthly/Bi-monthly. Now merged with *Amazing SF Stories* (ISSN 0279-1706), Patrick L. Price, ed. Box 110, Lake Geneva, WI 53147. Indexed in Boyajian, Metcalf, NESFA, Parnell, Strauss.
A digest magazine, uneven in quality, which for much of its life published formula SF and later reprinted lesser material. It had three major periods, however. First from 1952 to 1954, under editor Howard Browne, who endeavored to produce a literary magazine with quality fantasy by Ray Bradbury, Fritz Leiber, Theodore Sturgeon and Richard Matheson and new and reprinted fiction by such establishment names as E. M. Forster, Raymond Chandler and Stephen Vincent Benét. From 1960 to 1965, Cele Goldsmith Lalli encouraged new and innovative fantasy. Under her, new writers like Roger Zelazny, Piers Anthony and Thomas M. Disch emerged, and established writers like Fritz Leiber and Edmond Hamilton reemerged. *Fantastic* did much to lay the foundations for a revival of interest in fantasy, especially sword and sorcery, in the mid-1960s. From 1970 to 1978, under Ted White, *Fantastic* became a major source for sword and sorcery and also a vehicle for supernatural and innovative fiction by writers like Barry Malzberg, Jack Dann, Gordon Eklund and Avram Davidson. *Fantastic* was a HN in 1963 and 1972 and White was HN as best editor from 1974 to 1977. Had a short-lived fantasy companion, *Dream World* (1957), which printed "wish-fulfillment" stories. Selective anthologies are *The Best from Fantastic* (1970), edited by Ted White, and *Fantastic Stories: Tales of the Weird and Wondrous* (1987), edited by Martin H. Greenberg and Patrick L. Price.
Holdings: 1 (S), 2 (A), 4 (M-mf), 6 (A), 9 (S), 11 (S), 12 (S), 13 (S), 14 (A), 15 (A), 16 (A), 17 (M), 18 (S), 19 (A), 21 (A), 23 (M), 27 (A), 28 (S), 29 (S), 35 (M), 36 (M), 38 (A), 39 (A), 42 (S)

11-6. Fantastic Adventures. 1939–53 (129 issues). Monthly/Bi-monthly. Raymond A. Palmer, Howard Browne, eds. Ziff-Davis, Chicago. Indexed in Day, Gallagher, Metcalf, Strauss.
Pulp magazine which initially provided formula sensational adventure stories, mostly SF/lost race, aimed at the younger reader. During the war years it shifted to humorous lighthearted fantasies by Nelson S. Bond, Robert Bloch and David Wright O'Brien. After World War II, and especially under Browne, it improved in quality and became an important source for weird fantasies by Theodore Sturgeon, Fritz Leiber, Walter M. Miller, Jr., William Tenn and L. Sprague de Camp. It was later merged with *Fantastic* [11-5]. See *Guide* by Gallagher [11-52].
Holdings: 2 (A), 4 (A-mf), 6 (A), 9 (A), 11 (A), 12 (S), 13 (S), 14 (A), 15 (A), 16 (S), 17 (M), 19 (A), 21 (A), 23 (S), 27 (A), 28 (S), 29 (A), 35 (A), 36 (A), 37 (A-mf), 38 (M), 39 (A), 40 (S-mf), 41 (S), 42 (S)

11-7. Fantasy Book. ISSN 0277-0717. 1981– . Quarterly. Dennis Mallonee, ed. Heroic Publishing, 6433 California Ave., Long Beach, CA 90805. Circulation: 5,000. Indexed in Boyajian, Brown, Parnell.

Small press magazine, attractively illustrated, with the emphasis on high fantasy though also including humorous and dark fantasy. Each issue contains ten to twelve stories, the occasional classic reprint, two or three poems and a serial. The magazine suspended publication in 1987 due to publishing commitments but was to be relaunched in 1989 with the same policy and format but with the addition of interior full-color graphic story material. Its format has been closely imitated by the new *Marion Zimmer Bradley's Fantasy Magazine* (1988- , ISSN 0897-9286, quarterly, PO Box 72, Berkeley, CA 94701).
Holdings: 1 (S), 2 (A), 4 (S), 6 (A), 13 (S), 15 (A), 16 (S), 17 (A), 27 (A), 28 (S), 38 (S), 39 (A), 41 (S)

11-8. Fantasy Fiction. 1953 (4 issues). Bi-monthly. Lester del Rey, ed. Future Publications, New York. Indexed in Metcalf, Parnell, Strauss.
High-quality digest magazine, short-lived only due to the whims of the publisher. Maturely edited by Lester del Rey, it carried a mixture of dark fantasy and humor, successfully blending the twin traditions of *Weird Tales* [11-20] and *Unknown* [11-18]. Leading contributors were Robert Sheckley, L. Sprague de Camp, Poul Anderson and Philip K. Dick, with collectible covers by Hannes Bok. Compare *Beyond* [11-2].
Holdings: 1 (A), 4 (A), 6 (A), 9 (M), 11 (M), 13 (A), 14 (A), 17 (A), 19 (A), 21 (A), 23 (A), 27 (A), 35 (A), 36 (A), 39 (A)

11-9. Fantasy Tales. No ISSN. 1977- . Semi-annual. David A. Sutton and Stephen Jones, eds. Robinson Publishing, 11 Shepherd House, Shepherd Street, London W1Y 7LD. Circulation: 10,000. Indexed in Brown, Parnell.
Small press publication issued in emulation of *Weird Tales* [11-20]. Despite the title it concentrates on weird fiction, featuring both new and established writers from Britain and America. In 1988 *FT* received a professional boost when publication was taken over by a national British publisher with distribution on a "paperback magazine" basis. Quarterly publication and U.S. distribution are goals in 1990. Issues contain eight to ten stories plus verse and editorial features. Anthology, *The Best from Fantasy Tales* (1988), edited by Jones and Sutton. *FT* was a WFA nominee in 1981, 1982, 1983 and 1987 and winner in 1984.
Holdings: 27 (M), 35 (S), 39 (A), 41 (S)

11-10. The Horror Show. ISSN 0748-2914. 1982- . Quarterly. David B. Silva, ed. Phantasm Press, 14848 Misty Springs Lane, Oak Run, CA 96069. Circulation: 44,000.
A large-format small press magazine concentrating on horror and terror stories by the new generation of writers in the wake of Stephen King. A mature and professional approach by editor/publisher Silva has made it one of the leading small press publications. Each issue includes eight to ten stories, an interview, book and film reviews and a variety of other features. A few special issues have concentrated on Dean R. Koontz, Steve Rasnic Tem, J. K. Potter, Robert McCammon and Dennis Etchison. A representative anthology, *Best of the Horrow Show* (1987), edited by Silva, and including an index to the first nineteen issues, was published by another small press which publishes *2 AM* (1986- , ISSN 0886-8743, quarterly, PO Box 6754, Rockford, IL 61125), a magazine of similar content though of lesser quality in production. *THS* was nominated for WFA in 1986

and 1987 and was co-winner in 1988. The editor announced in summer 1989 that publication would cease by year's end.
Holdings: 27 (S)

11-11. Interzone. No ISSN. 1982- . Bi-monthly. David Pringle, ed. 124 Osborne Rd., Brighton BN1 6LU, England. Circulation: 15,000. Indexed in Boyajian, Brown.
A small press magazine that has steadily grown in stature since its early experimental issues and now has national distribution. *IZ* owes much of its initial inspiration to the Michael Moorcock issues of *New Worlds*, though there is a greater emphasis on surreal, dark and technophobic fantasy and SF. *IZ* has developed several new writers including Scott Bradfield and Alex Stewart. In addition to the fiction, each issue carries news, perceptive reviews and interviews and the occasional illustrated feature. Selective annual anthologies have appeared from three different publishers in 1985, 1987 and 1988, edited by John Clute, Simon Ounsley and David Pringle. *IZ* was a HN in 1986, 1987 and 1988.
Holdings: 4 (S), 15 (A), 27 (S), 28 (S), 38 (A), 39 (A), 41 (A), 42 (S)

***11-12. Isaac Asimov's Science Fiction Magazine**. ISSN 0162-2188. 1977- . 13 issues per year. Gardner Dozois, ed. Davis Publications, 380 Lexington Ave., New York, NY 10017. Circulation: 82,000. Indexed in Boyajian, Brown, NESFA; self-indexed at end of each annual volume.
Although marketed as a science fiction magazine, in recent years *IAsfM* has published the whole range of fantastic fiction including light and dark fantasy but avoiding straight sword and sorcery. *IAsfM* is a particularly good source for a new treatment of the *Unknown*-style fantasy, a policy developed by initial editor George Scithers, who also enjoyed the occasional light, humorous spoof. Stories from *IAsfM* have been regularly nominated for and won awards. Scithers was HW for best editor in 1978 and 1980 and later editor Shawna McCarthy was HW in 1984. The magazine also runs book reviews and other nonfiction features. There have been many derivative anthologies but only *Isaac Asimov's Fantasy* (1985), edited by Shawna McCarthy, is wholly fantasy.
Holdings: 2 (M), 4 (A), 5 (A), 6 (A), 13 (M), 14 (S), 15 (A), 16 (S), 17 (M), 21 (S), 23 (A), 27 (A), 28 (S), 29 (M), 35 (S), 38 (A), 39 (A), 41 (A), 42 (S)

***11-13. The Magazine of Fantasy and Science Fiction**. ISSN 0024-984X. 1949- . Monthly. Edward L. Ferman, ed. Mercury Press, Box 56, Cornwall, CT 06753. Circulation: 60,000. Indexed in Boyajian, Brown, Day, Metcalf, NESFA and Strauss; self-indexed at end of each six-issue volume.
The premier magazine featuring fantasy and weird fiction, which has retained a consistent quality of literary and mature fiction over a succession of editors. It was founded by Anthony Boucher and J. Francis McComas with the intention of being wholly fantasy-based, following the success of *Avon Fantasy Reader* [11-1]. SF has always been a strong feature but has seldom dominated the fantasy content. Each issue carries a selection of long and short stories, a book review column by Algis Budrys, a media column by Harlan Ellison and a science column by Isaac Asimov. *F&SF* is unique in its lack of interior art, aside from a few cartoons. More stories from *F&SF* have been nominated for and won awards than from any other fantasy magazine. *F&SF* was a HN for every year from 1957 to 1971

and a HW eight times. Ferman has likewise been HN as best editor for every year from 1972 and HW three times. Ferman also won the WFA for Professional Achievement in 1979. There have been many anthologies selecting from *F&SF* including twenty-four annual selections and three major retrospectives. Three especially useful volumes are *The Eureka Years* (1982), edited by Annette McComas, which looks at the magazine's formative years, and the two omnibuses, *The Best Fantasy Stories from Fantasy and Science Fiction* (1985), edited by Edward L. Ferman, and *The Best Horror Stories from Fantasy & Science Fiction* (1988), edited by Edward Ferman and Anne Jordan.
Holdings: 1 (S), 2 (A), 3 (M), 4 (A), 5 (M), 6 (A), 9 (M), 11 (M), 12 (A), 13 (M), 14 (A), 15 (A), 16 (M), 17 (A), 18 (S), 19 (A), 21 (A), 23 (A), 27 (A), 28 (M), 29 (M), 35 (M), 36 (M), 37 (A), 38 (A), 39 (A), 41 (M), 42 (S)

11-14. Magazine of Horror. 1963–71 (36 issues). Bi-monthly/Quarterly. Robert A. W. Lowndes, ed. Health Knowledge, New York. Indexed in Cook, Metcalf, NESFA, Parnell, Strauss.
Primarily a reprint magazine selecting fiction from the pulps, especially *Weird Tales* [11-20] and *Strange Tales* [11-17], and from earlier as well as scarcer sources. Printed both old and new stories by David H. Keller and Robert E. Howard and featured many new stories in the traditional style. *MoH* had three fantasy companions: *Weird Terror Tales* (1969–70) and *Bizarre Fantasy Tales* (1970–71) were almost identical in policy, and *Startling Mystery Stories* (1966–71) featured weird mysteries. Compare *Avon Fantasy Reader* [11-1].
Holdings: 4 (S), 13 (S), 14 (M), 21 (M), 23 (A), 27 (A), 28 (S), 35 (M), 36 (A), 38 (M), 39 (M)

***11-15. Rod Serling's "The Twilight Zone" Magazine**. ISSN 0279-6090. 1981–1989. Bi-monthly. Tappan King, ed. Montcalm Publishing, New York. Indexed in Boyajian, Brown, Parnell.
A large-format ninety-six-page magazine inspired by Rod Serling's innovative television series, in keeping with which *TZ* usually published offbeat stories of odd things happening to everyday people. Each issue carried seven or eight stories plus a number of illustrated media features, book, film and video reviews and news. Liberally illustrated, the magazine offered a good range of fiction from traditional to experimental. Ceased publication with June 1989 issue. A digest reprint of stories from *TZ*, *Night Cry* (1984), became a regular quarterly companion magazine which, though it lasted only eleven issues, carried a strong selection of horror stories beyond the normal pale of *TZ*.
Holdings: 1 (M), 2 (M), 3 (M), 4 (M), 5 (A), 15 (M), 17 (A), 19 (A), 27 (S), 28 (S), 38 (A), 39 (M), 41 (S)

11-16. Science Fantasy. 1950–67 (93 issues). Bi-monthly. John Carnell, Kyril Bonfiglioli, eds. Nova Publications/Roberts & Vinter, London. Indexed in Metcalf, NESFA, Parnell, Strauss.
Originally a digest-sized SF companion to *New Worlds*, edited by Walter Gillings, *SF* developed its own distinct character under Carnell during the mid-1950s and early 1960s. Each issue featured a lead novella, often by John Brunner or Kenneth Bulmer, and five or six short stories. *SF* was one of the few magazines to feature fantasy in the 1950s and is noted for publishing the early historical

fantasies by Thomas Burnett Swann and the Elric stories by Michael Moorcock. From 1964 to 1966 new editor Bonfiglioli dramatically changed the character of the magazine, now in pocketbook format, and introduced author Keith Roberts. Retitled *Impulse* from 1966 to 1967, and primarily edited by Roberts, it featured his "Pavane" series. *SF* was HN in 1962 and 1964.
Holdings: 1 (S), 4 (A), 11 (M), 14 (A), 15 (M), 16 (S), 17 (M), 19 (A), 21 (S), 23 (M), 27 (A), 28 (S), 35 (A), 36 (A), 38 (S), 39 (A), 41 (M). *Impulse*: 16 (S), 17 (A), 21 (A), 23 (A), 35 (A), 38 (A), 39 (A), 41 (A), 42 (S)

11-17. Strange Tales. 1931–33 (7 issues). Bi-monthly. Harry Bates, ed. Clayton Magazines, New York. Indexed in Cockcroft, Cook/Miller, Parnell.
The only serious rival pulp magazine to *Weird Tales* [11-20], and although short-lived it had an immediate impact. Although written by many of *WT*'s regular authors the stories were stronger in action, more formula-based and less offbeat and thus more digestible by the majority of readers. Issues of *ST* are now highly prized by collectors. Most of the stories were reprinted in *Magazine of Horror* [11-14] and its companions and in the facsimile anthology *Strange Tales* (1976) from Odyssey Publications.
Holdings: 1 (A), 4 (S), 14 (A), 23 (A), 27 (A), 36 (A)

***11-18. Unknown** (later **Unknown Worlds**). 1939–43 (39 issues). Monthly/Bi-monthly. John W. Campbell, Jr., ed. Street & Smith, New York. Indexed in Day, Hoffman, Metzger, Parnell.
The most innovative of the fantasy pulps presenting a more mature and logical face to weird fiction than earlier titles. Editor Campbell asked authors to project a rational sequence of events from a "what-if?" fantasy situation, thereby turning the supernatural into a quasi-science. *Unknown* carried a strong selection of short fiction but is best remembered for its lead novels, which included work by Eric Frank Russell, L. Ron Hubbard, L. Sprague de Camp, Jack Williamson, Robert A. Heinlein, Fritz Leiber and Cleve Cartmill. *Unknown* had a long-running British reprint edition (1939–49). Campbell assembled a pulp sampler, *From Unknown Worlds* (1948), prior to a planned but aborted revival of the magazine. Likewise, Stanley Schmidt (editor of *Analog* [formerly *Astounding SF*], the former companion to *Unknown*) has also recently edited a selective anthology, *Unknown* (1988), prior to a possible revival. Other representative anthologies include *The Unknown* (1963) and *The Unknown Five* (1964), both edited by D. R. Bensen [F3-28], and *Hell Hath Fury* (1963), edited by George Hay.
Holdings: 1 (M), 2 (A), 4 (A), 6 (A), 9 (M), 11 (A), 14 (A), 15 (A), 16 (A), 17 (M), 18 (A), 21 (A), 23 (A), 27 (A), 35 (A), 36 (A), 38 (M), 39 (A), 41 (S), 42 (S)

11-19. Weirdbook. ISSN 8755-7452. 1968– . Irregular. W. Paul Ganley, ed. Box 149, Amherst Branch, Buffalo, NY 14226. Circulation: 1,000. Indexed in Boyajian, Brown, Parnell.
A small press magazine that over the twenty years of its twenty-three issues has maintained a standard of enjoyable diversity. It is less sophisticated than other leading small press titles, being produced solely as a hobby, and the fiction is not always of a high quality—though it has improved in recent years—but it does provide a healthy selection of offbeat stories much in the tradition of *Weird Tales*

[11-20]. Recent issues have presented longer stories with an increasing bias toward fantasy over horror. *Weirdbook* is very much a "fan's" magazine. It was nominated for the WFA in 1979, 1982, 1983, 1985 and 1986 and won in 1987. Ganley publishes an irregular companion magazine, *Weirdbook Encores* (formerly *Eerie Country* [1976-]).
Holdings: 4 (S), 14 (A), 23 (S), 26 (S), 39 (A)

***11-20. Weird Tales**. ISSN 0898-5073. 1923- . Quarterly. Darrell Schweitzer, John Betancourt, George H. Scithers, eds. Terminus Publishing, PO Box 13418, Philadelphia, PA 19101. Circulation: 10,000. Indexed in Cockcroft, Jaffery, Parnell.
In its first incarnation, 1923–54, *WT* was the leading pulp magazine of horror and fantasy, though its heyday was 1929–40, under editor Farnsworth Wright. *WT* was subtitled "the Unique Magazine," a soubriquet well earned through its publication of many offbeat stories for which there was no other market. *WT* is best remembered as the primary market for H. P. Lovecraft's fiction (the Cthulhu mythos began to take shape in its pages) and Robert E. Howard's fantasies (including the Conan stories, which gave birth to the sword-and-sorcery subgenre), but in addition *WT* was a leading market for many fantasy authors including Clark Ashton Smith, Edmond Hamilton, August Derleth, Seabury Quinn, Frank Owen, Henry Kuttner, Manly Wade Wellman, Robert Bloch and Ray Bradbury, many of whom made their first or early sales to the magazine. It has seen four revivals (in 1973, 1981, 1985 and 1988) of which the latest is the most faithful to the magazine's original intent. It contains seven to eight stories of fantasy and horror, up to ten items of verse, plus nonfiction features, interviews, reviews and a good selection of interior art. *WT* has been well-mined by anthologists and a good selection of stories will be found in *The Unexpected* (1961), *The Ghoul Keepers* (1961), *Weird Tales* (1964) and *Worlds of Weird* (1965), all edited by Leo Margulies; *Weird Tales* (1976), edited by Peter Haining and reproduced in facsimile; and *Weird Tales: 32 Unearthed Terrors* (1988), edited by Stefan R. Dziemianowicz, Robert Weinberg and Martin H. Greenberg, which selects one story from each year of the magazine's original run.
Holdings: 1 (M), 3 (M), 4 (M), 5 (S), 6 (S), 11 (M), 12 (S), 13 (S), 14 (M), 15 (S), 16 (S), 17 (M), 19 (M), 21 (M), 23 (M), 24 (A), 26 (S), 27 (A), 29 (S), 35 (S), 36 (A), 37 (S), 38 (M), 39 (S), 41 (S-British edition), 42 (S)

***11-21. Whispers**. No ISSN. 1973- . Irregular. Stuart David Schiff, ed. Whispers Press, 70 Highland Ave., Binghamton, NY 13905. Circulation: 3,000. Indexed in Boyajian, Brown, Parnell.
Originally intended to follow on from *The Arkham Collector* (see under [11-25]) after Derleth's death, *Whispers* has now established itself as the leading small press magazine of weird fiction. Its publication schedule has become irregular of late, but each issue is an impressive production in digest format, 176 pages. Past issues have included special author features including Manly Wade Wellman, Ramsey Campbell and Stephen King. Most issues contain between fifteen and twenty stories, news and review features, poetry and art portfolios. A series of anthologies has evolved, also called *Whispers* [H4-361], containing both reprints from the magazine and new material. Both magazine and anthology series place an emphasis on nontraditional treatments of horror and fantasy themes. Schiff

won the WFA in the Non-Professional category in 1975, 1977, 1983 and 1985, was a HN in 1984 and 1985 and won the 1984 British Fantasy Award.
Holdings: 3 (M), 4 (A),14 (A), 15 (M), 21 (S), 23 (S), 27 (S), 28 (M), 35 (S), 38 (A), 39 (A), 41 (M)

Magazines about Fantasy and Horror

Annotated below are selected past and current magazines which provide discussion, analysis and criticism of fantasy and horror fiction. Some of the titles also include fiction but are included in this section because the fiction is secondary.

11-22. The Acolyte. 1942–46 (14 issues). Quarterly. Francis T. Laney and Duane W. Rimel, eds.
One of the most popular fanzines of the 1940s, *The Acolyte* was started by two devotees of H. P. Lovecraft and became an organ for Lovecraft discussion, though that had not been its prime purpose. It did cover a variety of topics in weird fiction and also published fiction and verse. Regular contributors included Forrest J. Ackerman, Sam Moskowitz, Fritz Leiber and Anthony Boucher. *The Acolyte* was mimeographed, with issues of thirty to thirty-two pages each. Compare *Crypt of Cthulhu* [11-27] and *Lovecraft Studies* [11-41].
Holdings: 4 (A), 12 (S), 21 (M), 23 (S), 28 (S)

11-23. American Fantasy. No ISSN. 1982- . Quarterly. Robert and Nancy Garcia, eds. PO Box 41714, Chicago, IL 60641. Circulation: 3,500. Indexed in Brown.
A slick, quality production with an emphasis on articles, interviews, news and reviews but with two or three stories per issue, all profusely and attractively illustrated and packaged. *AF* evolved from the much smaller *Chicago Fantasy Newsletter* (1979–81), which concentrated on news and reviews. The first two issues of *AF* were almost the last, but the magazine was relaunched on a firmer financial basis in 1986, though issues have still been irregular. It is the leading review magazine in the fantasy field. The Garcias were nominated for the WFA in 1983 and won in 1988.
Holdings: 12 (S), 13 (S), 27 (S), 28 (S), 38 (S), 39 (S)

11-24. Amra. No ISSN. 1956- . Irregular. George R. Heap/George Scithers, eds. Box 8243, Philadelphia, PA 19101. Circulation: 1,000. Self-indexed every tenth issue.
Originally the newsletter of the Hyborian League and dedicated to the works of Robert E. Howard, under Scithers *Amra* expanded to cover all aspects of "swordplay & sorcery." It was in its pages that the term "sword and sorcery" was coined. Regular contributors of essays, verses, fiction and reviews include Fritz Leiber, L. Sprague de Camp, Poul Anderson and Lin Carter, and the neatly multilithed magazine was noted for its illustrations by Roy Krenkel and George Barr. *Amra* is moribund, with issue #72 ready but awaiting publication. HN 1962, HW 1964, 1968. Compare *Erbania* [11-29] and *The Howard Collector* [11-38]. Collections of essays from *Amra* have been published as *The Conan Reader* (1968) and *The Spell of Conan* (1980), both edited by L. Sprague de Camp.
Holdings: 4 (S), 12 (S), 14 (S), 17 (S), 21 (M-early), 23 (S), 27 (S), 28 (M), 38 (M), 39 (M), 41 (S)

11-25. The Arkham Sampler. 1948–49 (8 issues). Quarterly. August Derleth, ed. Arkham House, Sauk City, WI. Indexed in Parnell.
A literary quarterly issued primarily as a vehicle to show the type of fiction published by Arkham House, this soon became one of the earliest scholarly publications with extensive reviews and comment on fantasy and weird fiction. Noted for its first printing of new fiction by H. Russell Wakefield and John Beynon Harris, it also reprinted lesser-known stories. There was an inevitable emphasis on the life and works of H. P. Lovecraft, which enhances the magazine's collector's value today. Derleth repeated the concept on a lesser scale with *The Arkham Collector* (1967–71), which featured fiction, verse, news and reviews. Compare *Whispers* [11-21]. The name *The Arkham Sampler* survives today in a series of chapbooks issued annually by The Strange Company, Madison, WI, with individual issues featuring fiction, verse, photographs or artwork.
Holdings: 1 (M), 3 (M), 4 (A), 5 (M), 9 (M), 11 (A), 14 (A), 15 (A), 19 (A), 21 (S), 23 (A), 27 (M), 28 (S), 29 (A), 33 (A), 35 (A), 36 (A), 38 (M), 42 (S)

11-26. The Baum Bugle. ISSN 005-6677. 1957– . Three times a year. Michael Gessel, ed. International Wizard of Oz Club, PO Box 748, Arlington, VA 22216. Circulation: 2,000.
An attractive glossy magazine, specializing in popular and scholarly articles about Oz, its creator L. Frank Baum and other authors and artists, with biographical and critical studies and first edition checklists. Research into the people and places within the Oz books appears frequently and there are features on the Oz films and other media adaptations. Fiction appears rarely and is usually by Baum. A specialist magazine with a dedicated treatment of its subject. For large libraries only or those with a specialist Baum collection.
Holdings: 3 (M), 5 (M), 11 (A), 13 (S), 16 (M), 17 (S), 23 (S), 28 (S)

Cinefantastique *See* [F9-9; H9-10] for annotation.
Holdings: 3 (M), 4 (S), 5 (A), 10 (S), 14 (S), 17 (M), 21 (S), 23 (M), 27 (M), 28 (S), 29 (S), 36 (M), 37 (S), 38 (A), 41 (S), 42 (S)

11-27. Crypt of Cthulhu. No ISSN. 1981– . Every six weeks. Robert M. Price, ed. Cryptic Publications, 216 Fernwood Ave, Upper Montclair, NJ 07043. Circulation: 550. Index to first 50 issues in issue #55.
Crypt is one of the leading current small press magazines dedicated to studying the life and works of H. P. Lovecraft in particular and the *Weird Tales* school in general. Articles vary from the studious to the humorous and cover a wide variety of themes and topics despite the apparent limitations. *Crypt* also publishes Lovecraftian fiction by or associated with the *Weird Tales* fraternity. Compare *Lovecraft Studies* [11-41] and *Nyctalops* [11-45].
Holdings: 13 (S), 23 (S)

11-28. Dark Horizons. No ISSN. 1971– . Irregular. Jon Harvey, ed. British Fantasy Society, 15 Stanley Road, Morden, Surrey, SM4 5DE, England. Circulation: 350. Indexed in Holland, Parnell.
The official journal of the British Fantasy Society (see chapter 13), *DH* has had an irregular and uneven history with its best issues under editors Stephen Jones (#9–15) and David Sutton (#23–30). Issues are predominantly nonfiction with analyses

of fantasy themes or authors' works, but usually a story and poetry are also included and occasional special fiction issues appear. The BFS also publishes a *Newsletter* and two fiction annuals, *Winter Chills* and *Mystique.*
Holdings: 38 (S), 39 (M)

11-29. Erbania. No ISSN. 1956- . Twice yearly. D. Peter Ogden, ed. 8001 Fernview Lane, Tampa, FL 33615. Circulation: 350.
The longest running of the magazines dedicated to the memory of Edgar Rice Burroughs. Contains essays on every aspect of his life and work in all media, as well as on such Burroughs-associated writers as Otis Adelbert Kline, Robert E. Howard, John Norman and Philip José Farmer. Issued in large format with from fifteen to twenty pages. Compare *Amra* [11-24].
Holdings: information not collected

11-30. Fantasiae. 1973–80. Monthly. Ian M. Slater, ed. Fantasy Association, Los Angeles, CA.
The monthly newsletter of the defunct Fantasy Association, aimed at coverage of all writers in the fantasy field, but especially those at the literary end of the spectrum, exemplified by the mythographic works of Tolkien and Lewis. Contents included news, reviews and author features with issue sizes varying between eight and twenty-four pages.
Holdings: 3 (M), 4 (A), 15 (A), 27 (A), 28 (M), 36 (A), 38 (M), 39 (A)

11-31. The Fantasy Fan. 1933–35. (18 issues). Monthly. Charles D. Hornig, ed. Elizabeth, NJ.
The first regular amateur magazine devoted to weird fiction, containing stories, news and reviews, plus nonfiction features. It is most noted for its stories by H. P. Lovecraft, Clark Ashton Smith, David H. Keller and Robert Bloch and for running the revised version of Lovecraft's essay "Supernatural Horror in Literature" (incomplete) [H8-7]. Especially useful for its interviews and behind-the-scenes news by Mort Weisinger and Julius Schwartz.
Holdings: 4 (S), 12 (S), 14 (S), 21 (S), 28 (S)

***11-32. Fantasy Review** [formerly **Fantasy Newsletter**]. 1978–87 (103 issues). Monthly. Paul Allen, later Robert A. Collins, eds. Meckler Publishing, Westport, CT.
Initially a newsletter on current and forthcoming publications, *FN* rapidly expanded under both editors into an intelligent review of the fantasy field with regular columns by Fritz Leiber, Karl Wagner, Jack Chalker and Somtow Sucharitkul, plus news, interviews, critical and analytical essays and, after a merger with Neil Barron's *Science Fiction and Fantasy Book Review* in 1984, the most extensive review section of any small press magazine. It ceased publication through lack of financial support and has been converted into an annual volume [6-36]. HN, 1983, 1984, 1985, 1986, 1987. WFA nominee 1979, WFA winner 1980, 1982.
Holdings: 4 (A), 10 (M), 11 (A), 13 (S), 15 (A), 17 (A), 19 (S), 26 (A), 27 (A), 29 (S), 36 (S), 38 (A), 39 (A), 41 (S)

11-33. Fear. ISSN 0954-8017. 1988- . Monthly. John Gilbert, ed. Newsfield Ltd., PO Box 20, Ludlow, Shropshire, SY8 1D8, England. Circulation: 100,000.
A heavily illustrated, visual magazine strongly influenced by the film and televi-

sion media, reflected in its contents coverage of visual events. Early issues emphasized horror fiction, but from the third issue there was a slight increase in the coverage of fantasy fiction. Each issue carries short fiction and serializations of novels and nonfiction, and the magazine is especially strong in author interviews and profiles as well as in media news and reviews.
Holdings: information not collected

11-34. The Ghost. 1943–47 (4 issues). Annual. W. Paul Cook, ed. Driftwind Press, N. Montpelier, VT.
A noted fanzine of the 1940s which, despite its primary interest in the works of H. P. Lovecraft, published a variety of useful scholarly and reflective essays on fantasy personalities and works, including E. Hoffman Price's series "The Book of the Dead," August Derleth's "The Weird Tale in English since 1890" and bibliophilic columns by Rheinhart Kleiner and H. C. Koenig. For the specialist collector and library; issues are now rare. Compare *The Acolyte* [11-22].
Holdings: 3 (M), 21 (A)

11-35. Ghosts & Scholars. No ISSN. 1979– . Annual. Rosemary Pardoe, ed. Haunted Library, Flat 1, 36 Hamilton St., Hoole, Chester, CH2 3JQ, England. Circulation: 500. Indexed in Holland, Parnell.
A small press magazine dedicated to the ghost stories of M. R. James and his imitators. Each issue contains two or three stories, articles about James's works and studies of fellow writers. A much respected magazine, with stories selected for annual "year's best" anthologies, it has also generated its own anthology, *Ghosts & Scholars* (1987), edited by Richard Dalby and Rosemary Pardoe.
Holdings: 26 (S)

11-36. Gothic. ISSN 0193-0184. 1979–80 (first series), 1986–1988. Annual. Gary W. Crawford, ed. PO Box 80051, Baton Rouge, LA 70898. Circulation: 100. First series indexed in Parnell.
A scholarly annual devoted to studies of all aspects of Gothicism in literature with an emphasis on prose fiction. The first series included fiction and was issued in large format. The second series was in a smaller format with around forty pages, unillustrated, and included four or five critical analyses of Gothic themes and a number of detailed reviews of related books. An essential reference source for all Gothic collections that died from lack of support. Compare *Poe Studies* [11-47].
Holdings: 5 (M), 15 (S), 17 (M), 26 (A), 31 (S), 41 (S)

11-37. Horrorstruck. 1987–88 (9 issues). Bi-monthly. Paul F. Olson, ed. Carruth Bay Press, Glen Ellyn, IL.
In its short run *Horrorstruck* showed considerable promise as a leading study of horror fiction. It contained regular columns on various features of the field, interviews, analyses and reviews. The emphasis was on modern horror but classic horror was not ignored. Contributing editors included Charles de Lint, Gordon Linzner, Dean R. Koontz, Thomas F. Monteleone, William F. Nolan, J. K. Potter and Robert Weinberg.
Holdings: none reported.

11-38. The Howard Collector. 1961–73 (18 issues). Irregular. Glenn Lord, ed.
A small press magazine dedicated to the memory of Robert E. Howard. Each issue averaged thirty-six pages, was professionally printed and brought into print a wealth of items by Howard himself (almost 100) plus many items of memorabilia, essays, reviews and letters. Although Howard almost single-handedly created the sword-and-sorcery field, the magazine concentrated more on Howard's life and works and not solely on the fantasy field. A representative sample of the editor's selection of the best from the magazine was published as *The Howard Collector* (1979). Compare *Amra* [11-24].
Holdings: 4 (A), 21 (S), 23 (S), 27 (A), 35 (M), 38 (M), 39 (S)

11-39. Journal of the Fantastic in the Arts. ISSN 0897-0521. 1988- . Quarterly. Carl B. Yoke, executive ed. Orion Publishing, 1401 N. Salina St., Syracuse, NY 13208. Circulation: 300.
Sponsored by the International Association for the Fantastic in the Arts (see chapter 13), which provides this journal as a membership benefit, this is the most recent of the academic journals devoted to its subject. The scope is broad, including fantastic literature, film, painting and the performing arts. Some articles are revised from papers presented at the IAFA's annual conference. Special issues are planned dealing with individual authors, film and other topics. The authors are mostly academics writing for other academics, which often makes for rather heavy going. Articles will be supplemented by interviews, reviews and commentary. Primarily for university libraries.
Holdings: 17 (A), 38 (A), 39 (A)

***11-40. Locus**. ISSN 0047-4959. 1968- . Monthly. Charles N. Brown, ed. Locus Publications, PO Box 13305, Oakland, CA 94661. Circulation: 8,200. Indexed annually.
The "newspaper" of the SF field, *Locus* also gives wide news coverage to all developments in the fantasy and horror fields as well as extensive reviews. *Locus* presents an annual Locus Award based on readers' votes in categories including Best Fantasy Novel. The annual readers' survey shows that over 50% of the readers read both SF and fantasy. *Locus* is especially useful for its monthly listing of books and magazines received, which forms the basis for the annual *Science Fiction, Fantasy & Horror* [6-6] bibliography. *Locus* has been a HN every year since 1970 and a HW thirteen times. *Science Fiction Chronicle* (ISSN 0195-5365, 1979- , monthly, Andrew Porter, ed., Box 2730, Brooklyn, NY 11202-0056) is the field's other news magazine with considerable duplication of the major news in *Locus*. Regular columns cover fantastic films and British publications, with Frederik Pohl's irregular Pohlemic column a highlight. Each issue includes a list of next month's books by publisher. A summary of book and magazine markets is included several times yearly. There are many reviews, all by Don D'Ammassa, almost all a short paragraph long, regardless of the book's importance, and lacking much critical rigor. As in *Locus*, coverage of fantasy and horror is secondary. A second choice for libraries. Compare also *Fantasy Review* [11-32] and *Mystery Scene* [11-42].
Holdings: 1 (A), 3 (M), 4 (A), 5 (S), 12 (S), 13 (A), 14 (M), 15 (A), 17 (A), 21 (A), 23 (A), 27 (A), 28 (M), 29 (A), 36 (S), 38 (M), 39 (A), 41 (A), 42 (S)

11-41. Lovecraft Studies. No ISSN. 1979– . Twice yearly. S. T. Joshi, ed. Necronomicon Press, 101 Lockwood St., West Warwick, RI 02893. Circulation: 500. Indexed in *Fubar* #6, Soft Books, Toronto.
A scholarly small press magazine dedicated to the study of the life and works of H. P. Lovecraft. Unlike *Crypt of Cthulhu* [11-27], its nearest rival, *LS* is wholly studious with detailed analyses of Lovecraft's writings. Each forty-page issue usually contains four to six articles or bibliographies plus a selection of critical reviews. The text is unleavened by any artwork.
Holdings: 17 (S), 26 (M), 38 (S), 39 (M)

11-42. Mystery Scene. No ISSN. 1985– . Bi-monthly. Ed Gorman, Bob Randisi, eds. Mystery Enterprises, 3840 Clark Rd. SE, Cedar Rapids, IA 52403.
Despite the title and the fact that it also covers western fiction, *MS* devotes a large portion of its news, reviews and interviews to horror fiction. The related fields of horror and mystery fiction share many writers, and this magazine is a useful guide to that common ground and helps put horror fiction into perspective with other popular genre fiction. Compare *Fantasy Review* [11-32] and *Locus* [11-40].
Holdings: information not collected

11-43. Mythlore. ISSN 0163-8246. 1969– . Quarterly. The Mythopoeic Society, Box 6707, Altadena, CA 91001. Circulation: 1,000. Submissions to Glen H. GoodKnight, ed., 740 S. Hobart Blvd., Los Angeles, CA 90005.
The journal received by members of the Mythopoeic Society (see chapter 13), its subtitle indicates its content: "a journal of J. R. R. Tolkien, C. S. Lewis, Charles Williams and the genres of myth and fantasy studies." Articles, reviews, letters, columns on current fantasy and Middle-earth linguistics. Intermediate between a fanzine and an academic journal and a good choice for any library or reader with a strong interest in the Inklings, as this trio of writers is informally known.
Holdings: 3 (M), 4 (S), 5 (M), 15 (A), 17 (S), 19 (S), 21 (M), 27 (M), 28 (S), 31 (A), 35 (S), 37 (S), 38 (A)

11-44. Niekas. No ISSN. 1962–69, 1977– . Irregular. Ed Meskys, ed. RFD 1, Box 63, Center Harbor, NH 03226. Circulation: 750.
Originally a small amateur press magazine of SF interest, *Niekas* changed considerably in 1965 with the editor's reading of *Lord of the Rings* [F3-340] and became, for a period, the leading Tolkien-based magazine, featuring Robert Foster's detailed glossary and guide to Middle-earth [F8-89]. *Niekas*, in its revived form, is a highly professional-style magazine, slickly produced but retaining the fannish touches. It still emphasizes fantasy but has broadened its coverage from Tolkien to all areas of high/heroic fantasy and SF, including a special issue on Arthurian fiction. HN 1966, HW 1967.
Holdings: information not collected

***11-45. Nyctalops**. No ISSN. 1970– . Irregular. Harry O. Morris, ed. Silver Scarab Press, 502 Elm St. SE, Albuquerque, NM 87102. Circulation: 500. Indexed in Parnell. Inquire about subscriptions.
An amateur magazine originally dedicated to the memories of H. P. Lovecraft and Clark Ashton Smith (issue #7, August 1972, is an especially important Smith issue). While this basis remains, recent issues have expanded to cover all areas of dark fantasy with a growing emphasis on what might be termed "decadent"

fantasy with the outré artwork of J. K. Potter and Morris himself, the surreal fiction of Thomas Ligotti and the obscure verse by Sutton Breiding and Neal Wilgus. One final issue was planned for 1989. Compare *Crypt of Cthulhu* [11-27] and *The Romantist* [11-48].
Holdings: 4 (S), 14 (S), 17 (M), 21 (A), 23 (S), 26 (S), 28 (S), 39 (S)

11-46. Peake Studies. ISSN 1013-1191. 1988- . Irregular. G. Peter Winnington, ed. Les 3 Chasseurs, 1413 Orzens, Vaud, Switzerland.
PS is a new, independent journal intended to complement and possibly even supersede the *Mervyn Peake Review* published by the Peake Society (see chapter 13), which has become primarily a newsletter in recent, irregular issues. *PS* covers the same territory as a forum for criticism and debate on all aspects of Peake's career as a novelist, artist, poet and playwright. It contains articles, reviews, news and comment.
Holdings: information not collected

11-47. Poe Studies [formerly **Poe Newsletter**]. ISSN 0032-1877. 1968- . Twice yearly. Alex Hammond, ed. Washington State Univ. Press, Pullman, WA 99164. Circulation: 550.
A scholarly journal of sixty-four pages, dedicated to the study of Poe's work and the broader issues of Gothic fiction and the influence of Poe on mystery and horror fiction. Compare *Gothic* [11-36].
Holdings: 1 (A), 3 (M), 4 (S), 5 (A), 15 (A), 19 (A), 28 (S), 29 (A), 31 (A), 35 (A)

11-48. The Romantist. 1977- . Annual. John C. Moran, Jesse F. Knight, Steve Eng, eds. F. Marion Crawford Memorial Society, Saracinesca House, 3610 Meadowbrook Ave., Nashville, TN 37205. Circulation limited to 300.
Although issued by the F. Marion Crawford Memorial Society, and thus regularly featuring aspects of his life and work, *The Romantist* explores the wider Romantic literary tradition, especially in weird and fantasy fiction and verse. The five irregular issues published to date (one double and one triple issue strive to follow the "annual" schedule) have stretched this realm to include essays about M. P. Shiel, Arthur Machen, Algernon Blackwood, H. Warner Munn, George Sterling, John Gawsworth, Clark Ashton Smith, Leslie Barringer and even Lew Wallace, as well as coverage of composer Erich Korngold and Irish singer John McCormack. Each issue is attractively printed, runs to eighty pages or more, and carries ten to twelve essays and comment, plus reviews, poetry and related features. Compare *Nyctalops* [11-45].
Holdings: 10 (A), 15 (A), 26 (A), 37 (S)

11-49. Shadow. 1968–74 (21 issues). Irregular. David A. Sutton, ed. Birmingham, England.
In its time *Shadow* was Britain's only serious magazine devoted to the study of supernatural fiction. Although early issues were poorly duplicated, the magazine contained a variety of well-researched articles on a wide range of topics. It remains one of the few magazines to have given any serious coverage to European horror writers, like Jean Ray. It is best remembered today for R. Alain Everts's primary study of the life of William Hope Hodgson.
Holdings: 16 (S), 27 (S)

11-50. Studies in Weird Fiction. No ISSN. 1986- . Twice yearly. S. T. Joshi, ed. Necronomicon Press, 101 Lockwood Street, West Warwick, RI 02893. Circulation: 500.
A scholarly magazine, fan-based, designed to promote the criticism of fantasy, horror and supernatural fiction, after Poe. Issues to date have evaluated aspects of the works of Clark Ashton Smith, William Hope Hodgson, Arthur Machen, T. E. D. Klein and Donald Wandrei. There is a distinct bias toward classic writers and the *Weird Tales* school even though studies of modern writers are not discouraged. A moderately produced publication of around forty pages, each issue includes five or six essays and a similar number of reviews. Suitable for libraries with a large collection of weird fiction.
Holdings: 4 (S)

Serial Anthologies

This information regarding holdings of selected serial anthologies was collected by Randall Scott. The second and third titles were not annotated. Cross-references from the annotated anthologies were made to this holdings list.

The Best from Fantasy and Science Fiction, 1952- [11-13]
Holdings: 1 (M), 3 (M), 4 (S), 9 (S), 13 (S), 17 (S), 19 (S), 23 (M), 27 (A), 28 (S), 31 (S), 35 (S), 36 (M), 37 (S), 38 (A), 39 (A), 40 (S)

The Fontana Book of Great Ghost Stories, 1964–80
Holdings: 17 (S), 23 (M), 36 (M), 39 (M)

The Fontana Book of Great Horror Stories, 1966–74
Holdings: 17 (S), 23 (M), 27 (S), 36 (A), 39 (M)

New Worlds of Fantasy, 1967- [F4A-299]
Holdings: 4 (S), 13 (S), 17 (S), 23 (M), 27 (S), 35 (S), 38 (S)

The Pan Book of Horror Stories, 1959- [H4-357]
Holdings: 4 (S), 17 (M), 19 (S), 23 (M), 36 (M), 39 (M)

Shadows, 1978–87 [H4-359]
Holdings: 4 (S), 14 (A), 17 (A), 19 (S), 23 (M), 28 (M), 38 (A), 39 (S)

Whispers, 1977- [H4-361]
Holdings: 4 (S), 9 (S), 13 (S), 14 (S), 15 (A), 17 (S), 23 (M), 28 (S), 37 (S), 38 (A), 39 (S)

The Year's Best Fantasy Stories, 1975- [F4A-305]
Holdings: 4 (S), 13 (M), 15 (S), 17 (S), 19 (S), 23 (M), 28 (S), 36 (S), 38 (A), 39 (M)

The Year's Best Horror Stories, 1971- [H4-363]
Holdings: 4 (S), 13 (S), 15 (S), 17 (S), 23 (M), 28 (S), 36 (M), 38 (A), 39 (S)

The Year's Finest Fantasy/Fantasy Annual, 1978–82 [F4A-299]
Holdings: 4 (S), 5 (S), 10 (A), 14 (S), 17 (S), 22 (M), 27 (S), 28 (S), 29 (S), 38 (A), 39 (A)

Studies

Few serious studies of fantasy and horror fiction have considered the contribution made by magazine and serial publications. Most coverage has been superficial and part of general studies of the field. The following titles are primary reference sources.

11-51. Cook, Michael L. **Mystery, Detective, and Espionage Magazines**. Greenwood, 1983.
In the same format as Tymn and Ashley's *Science Fiction, Fantasy, and Weird Fiction Magazines* [11-54] with a useful, though too brief, historical introduction by Cook, a long section on English-language magazines, an overview of foreign magazines and coverage of book clubs. There are seven appendixes listing magazines by category, key writers, a magazine chronology from 1882 to 1982, American and Canadian true detective magazines, Sherlock Holmes-related material and other periodicals of interest. Despite its title this book contains entries on many fantasy magazines (forty-seven entries overlap with Tymn/Ashley, sometimes with conflicting data) and is useful for its coverage of borderline mystery/terror/horror magazines and as a guide to the many writers who have sold to the related fields. The entries are not as comprehensive as in Tymn/Ashley but contain much data not readily available elsewhere.

11-52. Gallagher, Edward J. **The Annotated Guide to Fantastic Adventures**. Starmont, 1985.
A useful annotated story index to one of the less important fantasy titles [see 11-6]. Gives plot outlines for all 852 stories and serials in chronological order. Also has a seventeen-page historical survey useful for its grouping of stories by type and style; plus appendixes listing editorial departments, artists, story motifs and author biographies. Indexes stories by author and title.

11-53. Jones, Robert Kenneth. **The Shudder Pulps: A History of the Weird Menace Magazines of the 1930's**. FAX, 1975.
The only book-length survey and analysis of that group of magazines that emphasized sex and sadism and the mildly erotic, concentrating on unsophisticated terror with little, if any, supernatural connection. A well-written history drawing on many contemporary sources and recent interviews with the leading writers of the day. Jones shows the evolution (or degeneration) from Gothic fiction and traces the influence of the terror pulps on the associated mystery, fantasy and SF fields.

***11-54**. Tymn, Marshall B., and Mike Ashley. **Science Fiction, Fantasy, and Weird Fiction Magazines**. Greenwood, 1985.
The definitive volume on fantasy magazines in all their forms. Divided into four sections plus a historical introduction by Thomas Clareson. The main section covers 279 English-language magazines, with the other sections covering 15 associational English-language anthologies, 78 academic periodicals and major fanzines and 178 non-English-language magazines. There are two appendixes covering major cover artists plus a chronology of magazines from 1882 to 1983. Entries vary in length and there is the inevitable emphasis on SF magazines

which have dominated the "fantasy" field. All significant fantasy and weird fiction magazines are covered, with each entry containing an informative and occasionally critical essay plus a bibliography and reference to index, reprint and location sources. There is also a detailed publication history. A basic reference work. Note also Cook's *Mystery, Detective, and Espionage Magazines* [11-51].

***11-55**. Weinberg, Robert. **The Weird Tales Story**. FAX, 1977.

11-56. Weinberg, Robert. **WT50**. Weinberg, 1973.
The Weird Tales Story is a loving tribute to the leading weird pulp magazine [11-20] and is the only complete history of the title. This volume is valuable for its historical coverage of the magazine and its survey of the major stories and artwork, plus its personalized memoirs by some of the leading contributors. It reproduces many of the covers, though for more complete coverage see Durie's *Weird Tales* [10-9]. The book drew to some degree from Weinberg's earlier *WT50*, which was a more idiosyncratic tribute to the magazine and contains additional retrospectives and appraisals plus some fiction. Also annotated as [H7-45] and [10-36].

Indexes and Checklists

For most of their history fantasy and horror magazines have remained secondary to the science fiction field and have been indexed only when grouped with their SF companions. As a result, until the appearance of *Monthly Terrors* [11-68] no comprehensive index existed to all weird and fantasy titles. The following annotated entries cover all of the specialist indexes including those for predominantly SF titles.

***11-57**. Boyajian, Jerry, and Kenneth R. Johnson. **Index to the Science Fiction Magazines**. 8 vols., 1977–84. Twaci Press, 1981–86.
Reliable and neat annual index covering contents by issue, author, title and artist with a useful appendix of "SF in Miscellaneous Magazines." Duplicates much that is in NESFA [11-67] but is easier to read. Covers many titles of fantasy interest. Two useful supplements were *Index to the Semi-Professional Fantasy Magazines 1982* and *1983*, covering lesser-known titles of fantasy interest.

***11-58**. Cockcroft, T[homas] G. L. **Index to the Weird Fiction Magazines**. Originally published by the author, 2 vols.: 1. Title, 1962; 2. Author, 1964. Rev. ed., Arno Press, 1975.
Index to eight English-language magazines: *Weird Tales, Strange Tales, Strange Stories, The Thrill Book, Strange Tales* (British), *Oriental Stories, Magic Carpet Magazine* and *Golden Fleece*, the latter three of only borderline fantasy interest. Largely superseded by Parnell [11-68] but still valuable for its index by story title as well as its useful notes and appendixes. Lacks an issue-by-issue contents listing.

11-59. Cook, Michael L. **Monthly Murders: A Checklist and Chronological Listing of Fiction in the Digest-Size Mystery Magazines in the United States and England**. Greenwood, 1982.
A massive 1,167-page index concentrating on mystery magazines but with some overlap with Parnell [11-68], though generally less detailed. Indexed by issue

contents and by author but not by story title. Contains a few titles of fantasy interest not indexed by Parnell, especially *Alfred Hitchcock's Mystery Magazine, Doc Savage* (from 1944 only), *London Mystery Magazine, The Man from U.N.C.L.E. Magazine, Shock Mystery Tales, Strange* and *Web Terror Stories.* Cook also completed, just before his death, his companion index to the mystery pulp magazines: *Mystery, Detective and Espionage Fiction: A Checklist of Fiction in the U.S. Pulp Magazines, 1915–1974* (Garland, 1988), compiled with Stephen T. Miller. It indexes several magazines of fantasy interest (some also covered by Parnell) including *Ace Mystery, Book of Terror, Captain Hazzard, Captain Satan, Captain Zero, Detective Tales* (the companion to *Weird Tales*), *Dime Mystery, Doc Savage, Doctor Death, Dr. Yen Sin, Dusty Ayres and His Battle Birds, Eerie Mysteries, Eerie Stories, G-8 and His Battle Aces, Horror Stories, Jungle Stories, Mind Magic, The Mysterious Wu Fang, The Shadow, Strange Stories, Strange Tales, Tales of Magic and Mystery, Terror Tales, Uncanny Stories* and *Uncanny Tales.*

***11-60**. Day, Donald B. **Index to the Science Fiction Magazines, 1926–1950**. Perri Press, 1952. Rev. ed., G. K. Hall, 1982.
Pioneering index to major SF titles, which also covers titles of fantasy interest: *Avon Fantasy Reader, Famous Fantastic Mysteries, Fantastic Novels, Fantasy Fiction, Magazine of Fantasy & Science Fiction, A. Merritt's Fantasy* and *Unknown.* Indexes by author and story title but not by issue. The revised edition includes Day's corrections but is otherwise not updated. Index continued by Metcalf [11-64] and Strauss [11-69].

11-61. Hoffman, Stuart. **An Index to Unknown and Unknown Worlds by Author and by Title**. Sirius Press, 1955.
An idiosyncratic index by author, story title and principal characters. The title index provides a sublist of locale and characters. Introduction by Robert Bloch. Preferable to Metzger [11-65].

11-62. Holland, Steve. **Fantasy Fanzine Index**. British Fantasy Society, 1987.
A neat thirty-six-page booklet indexing contents of thirty-one British small press publications running to eighty-five separate issues. Contents indexed by issue and author. Useful for monitoring growth in British fantasy publications.

11-63. Jaffery, Sheldon, and Fred Cook. **Collector's Index to Weird Tales**. Bowling Green Univ. Popular Press, 1985.
Indexes *Weird Tales* [11-20] only, so does not supersede Cockcroft [11-58] or Parnell [11-68] but does complement them as the author index lists stories in chronological rather than alphabetical order. Also indexes contents by issue and title with separate indexes to poetry and cover artists. Also annotated as [H7-45].

***11-64**. Metcalf, Norm. **The Index of Science Fiction Magazines 1951–1965**. J. Ben Stark, 1968.
A continuation of Day [11-60] with additional errata on that volume. Concentrates on SF magazines but has titles of fantasy interest: *Avon Fantasy Reader, Beyond Fantasy Fiction, Bizarre Mystery, Fantastic, Fantastic Adventures, Fear!, Magazine of Fantasy & Science Fiction, Magazine of Horror* and *Science Fantasy.* Index was published in haste and contains some erroneous data on pen names but

is otherwise more readable and reliable than Strauss [11-69]. Indexes by author, story title, artist and editor, but not by issue.

11-65. Metzger, Arthur. **An Index and Short History of Unknown**. T-K Graphics, 1976.
A twenty-eight-page booklet containing a brief history of *Unknown* [11-18] followed by an index by author and by title, a note on important reprints and a list of cover artists. Has little advantage over Day [11-60], Parnell [11-68] or Hoffman [11-61].

***11-66**. New England Science Fiction Association. **Index to the Science Fiction Magazines, 1966–1970**. NESFA, 1971.

***11-67**. New England Science Fiction Association. **The NESFA Index: Science Fiction Magazines and Original Anthologies**. NESFA, 11 vol., 1973–84, covering 1971–72, 1973, 1974, 1975, 1976, 1977, 1978, 1979–80, 1981, 1982, 1983.
Reliable and accurate continuation of Strauss [11-69] with computer print-out format indexing by issue, author and title. The subsequent annual volumes also cover anthologies with original material. Covers both SF magazines and titles of fantasy interest. Duplicates to a large degree the work by Boyajian and Johnson [11-57]. Later years now indexed by Brown and Contento [6-6].

***11-68**. Parnell, Frank H., and Mike Ashley. **Monthly Terrors: An Index to the Weird Fantasy Magazines Published in the United States and Great Britain**. Greenwood, 1985.
Indexes 1,733 issues of 168 English-language magazines containing more than 50% weird fantasy. Main indexes are by issue and author, with artist and editor indexes and appendixes on series and connected stories, honorable mentions (thirty magazines that almost qualified for entry), chronological listing of magazines and geographical listing. Has a foreword by Peter Haining plus a short historical survey by the compilers of the weird fantasy magazines from 1919 to 1983. This is the major index to all weird fiction magazines, particularly important for its coverage of small press publications and rare titles not normally included in the standard indexes. Author index contains brief biographical details plus much information on pseudonyms not available elsewhere. No title index. Note also Cockcroft [11-58].

11-69. Strauss, Irwin S. **The MIT Science Fiction Society's Index to the SF Magazines, 1951–1965**. MIT Science Fiction Society, 1965.
Covers same period as Metcalf [11-64] but is generally less reliable or accurate and is poorly printed despite its computer print-out format. Has the advantage of an issue-by-issue index in addition to the author and story title indexes. Covers more titles than Metcalf, of which *Weird Tales* and *Phantom* are of fantasy interest. Continued by NESFA [11-66].

12

Library Collections

Randall W. Scott

Producing this section on library special collections of horror and fantasy literature has been a cooperative venture involving at least fifty librarians around the world. A few collections, like those built around the works of H. P. Lovecraft or J. R. R Tolkien, can be easily and accurately described, but it has been difficult for the typical "fantasy and horror librarian" to produce precise statements about his or her collection. Most of the materials form parts of larger collections normally thought of as science fiction collections. Much of the task has therefore been to focus on hidden specialties. The procedure leaves suspicions that a slight twist of thought might have illuminated still more interesting facets of some of these collections.

The emphasis has been on research collections, and usually special, noncirculating collections with holdings that can be counted upon to remain stable. Although most public libraries collect and circulate fantasy and horror fiction, such collections are difficult for out-of-town researchers to use. The collections listed here are those most likely to be available in full at all times. Libraries whose collections, when described in published accounts or in response to questionnaires, do not seem to offer fantasy or horror materials at a level beyond that which could be expected from any research library have not been included in this listing.

The prospective library user should be aware that any national library, university library or metropolitan public library will have at least a few of the important texts and reference books in horror and fantasy. National libraries, such as the British Library and the national libraries of Canada and Australia, typically receive materials through copyright deposit arrangements, and thus do not automatically arrange them in the logical categories that result from a more intentional acquisitions program. It is always worth asking at any large nearby library before deciding to buy an expensive item, or deciding to make a voyage.

This directory is intended primarily to aid prospective researchers to identify possible sources of material to study. It will also serve to help prospective donors and sellers of horror and fantasy material to find suitable depositories or customers. In this way the flow of information both into and out of these libraries should be expedited.

The researcher/librarian relationship can sometimes be fragile when materials of a quasi-recreational nature are involved. It is important, therefore, that users who are traveling to any of these collections call ahead, identify themselves and make sure of the schedule of open hours. This level of seriousness will almost certainly motivate the librarian in charge to provide the best possible service.

Most of the libraries listed have said that they will provide photocopies, and some will loan materials through interlibrary loan (ILL). In every case, however, libraries will not photocopy materials if they believe that to do so would violate copyright or privacy (in the case of personal letters or papers), of if the act of photocopying would endanger fragile materials. Similar restrictions apply to ILL, of course.

One tool of potential practical value to researchers is the OCLC (Online Computer Library Center) network, which links several thousand libraries worldwide, including many of those listed here. Access to an OCLC terminal at a library anywhere (or through CompuServe) means access in some detail to the holdings records of other libraries. These holdings records are rarely complete, however, since OCLC became widely used only in the mid-1970s, and earlier cataloging is only gradually being added to the database. OCLC libraries have been identified in this directory in most cases.

In the course of putting together this directory, I compiled a union list of horror and fantasy serials (pulps, journals, magazines and serial anthologies). The libraries with the best serial collections have been designated as in the top ten (or twenty) for completeness in serial holdings. Those libraries not so designated either have significantly smaller collections or chose not to represent themselves here. Holdings of specific journals and serial anthologies are shown in chapter 11.

Private libraries routinely open to the public have been included in the main listing, but four private collections not included there should be noted. Since private collections usually have very small or inconsistent staffing, they often have little time for such activities as answering mail inquiries, and may therefore present special problems to their prospective users. The four collections are:

The Count Dracula Permanent Collection of Vampire Memorabilia. 29 Washington Square West, Penthouse North, New York, NY 10011. 212-533-5018. Maintained by the Count Dracula Fan Club and the International Frankenstein Society. Viewing by appointment.

The Los Angeles Science Fantasy Society Library. 11513 Burbank Blvd., North Hollywood, CA 91601. 818-760-9234. A club collection primarily for members' use, with 7,000 volumes and over 120 magazine titles. Public use by appointment.

The MIT Science Fiction Society Library. MIT Student Center, Room W20-473, Cambridge, MA 02139. 617-258-5126. A club collection with a long history and reputation as one of the most complete science fiction magazine collections in North America. Hours irregular, mostly evenings. Some material circulates to members, room-use only for the public.

The San Francisco Academy of Comic Art. 2850 Ulloa St., San Francisco, CA 94116. 415-681-1737. A collection of over 4.5 million newspaper comic strips; also includes horror and fantasy fiction and pulp magazines. Call for appointment.

Please send corrections or additions to this compilation to the editor (see list of contributors).

The arrangement of this directory is alphabetical by state for the United States, followed by other countries in alphabetical order.

Directory

Arizona

12-1. University of Arizona Library. Special Collections, Tucson, AZ 85721. 602-621-6423.
A science fiction collection of 18,000 volumes, with current acquisitions restricted to science fiction, rather than fantasy and horror. In spite of current policy, the extensive older holdings make this a valuable resource. The periodicals held put this collection in the top twenty for library collections of fantasy and horror serials, and they are supplemented by some microfilm. This is a noncirculating collection, and is 90% cataloged. The University of Arizona is an OCLC library, so many of its holdings can be checked remotely on the OCLC network. Photocopies are sometimes available, but materials are not released for interlibrary loan.

California

12-2. San Francisco Public Library. McComas Collection of Fantasy and Science Fiction, Civic Center, San Francisco, CA 94102. 415-558-3511.
A science fiction and fantasy collection of 2,900 volumes including approximately 760 fantasy volumes. The fantasy periodical collection is excellent, ranking in the top twenty libraries surveyed. The collection is active, adding a few volumes regularly by purchase. The materials do not circulate, either locally or through interlibrary loan.

12-3. University of California, Los Angeles. Special Collections, University Library, 405 Hilgard Avenue, Los Angeles, CA 90024. 213-825-4988.
A fantastic fiction collection of over 10,000 volumes that does not separate science fiction from fantasy. Ray Bradbury manuscripts, 1.5 linear feet, and a collection of over 400 early editions of H. Rider Haggard. An extensive magazine and pulp collection ranks this collection among the top twenty for fantasy and horror serials. The collection is cataloged, but has limited staff to answer written information requests. Limited photocopying is available, but not interlibrary loan.

12-4. University of California, Riverside. Eaton Collection, University Library, P.O. Box 5900, Riverside, CA 92517. 714-787-3233.
A science fiction collection with over 50,000 items, comprehensive enough to include something of most fantasy and horror authors. Fantasy and horror are not treated separately. Includes over 200 sound recordings, nearly 500 films, over 200 shooting scripts and over 2,000 comic books, all with something like 50% horror/fantasy content. The fantasy and horror periodical collection is one of the ten most complete. Over 60 linear feet of fanzines. Uncorrected proofs of Terry Brooks, Nancy Springer; manuscripts and letters of Colin Wilson. The collection grows by 5,000 to 10,000 items yearly, through purchases, gifts and exchanges. The collection is fully catalogued on OCLC, noncirculating, and provides photocopies and restricted interlibrary loan. An occasional newsletter is published.

Bibliography: *Dictionary Catalog of the J. Lloyd Eaton Collection.* 3 vols. Boston: G. K. Hall, 1983.

"The J. Lloyd Eaton Collection." *Special Collections* II, 1/2 (Fall–Winter 1982), 25–38.

District of Columbia

12-5. Library of Congress. Washington, DC 20540. 202-707-5000.
The nature and extent of this library's holdings of fantastic literature and related materials do not lend themselves to concise or tabular descriptions. The Library of Congress does not maintain a special collection of fantasy or horror literature, nor does it make special efforts to collect such materials. Publications received under the copyright law are added to the general collections, while foreign publications are purchased. No statistics are kept on the library's holdings or annual receipts of fantastic literature.

The Manuscript Division (phone: 202-707-5383) holds the papers of Shirley Jackson (approximately 4,400 items) and the George M. Gould collection of Lafcadio Hearn (approximately 2,700 items). It also holds letters and other manuscripts of a number of other horror or fantasy authors, but does not consider these holdings to be significant. In addition, the Manuscript Division holds collections of radio scripts and playscripts, some of which would classify as horror and suspense, but material in these collections is not retrievable by subject. Original materials in the Manuscript Division are not available on interlibrary loan but may be examined (preferably by advance appointment) in the Manuscript Reading Room.

The Rare Book and Special Collections Division (phone: 202-707-5434) collects comprehensively the works of Kingsley Amis, Donald Barthelme, Ray Bradbury, Roald Dahl, Stephen King, Robert Nathan, Joyce Carol Oates and Colin Wilson, and maintains significant holdings of the published works of Ambrose Bierce, Wilkie Collins, Walter De la Mare, Nathaniel Hawthorne, Lafcadio Hearn, Shirley Jackson, William Morris, Edgar Allan Poe and James Thurber. Custody of a Pulp Fiction Collection is divided between the Rare Book and Special Collections Division and the Serial and Government Publications Division (phone: 202-707-5467). The fantasy and horror content of the pulp and periodical collection ranks it in the top twenty of collections surveyed.

The Motion Picture, Broadcasting and Recorded Sound Division (phone: 202-707-5840) holds more than 125,000 films and television programs, and over 1,500,000 audio recordings, but neither collection is currently accessible by genre or subject. Interlibrary loan for recorded materials is not available, and copying of records is not permitted. Questions concerning access should be directed to the division.

Illinois

12-6. Northern Illinois University. Founders Library, DeKalb, IL 60115. 815-753-0255.
Over 100 volumes of horror and fantasy fiction, plus a few letters of H. P. Lovecraft, and published works of Lord Dunsany and August Derleth. Complete holdings of several fantasy magazines puts this collection in the top twenty for serial fantasy. The collection is growing by twenty volumes per year through gift and purchase, and has been a Science Fiction Writers of America depository since 1983. The collection is fully cataloged, and may be used by appointment only. Photocopies are available.

12-7. Wheaton College. Marion E. Wade Center, Buswell Memorial Library, Wheaton, IL 60187-5593. 312-260-5908.
Over 700 volumes of the fiction of C. S. Lewis, George MacDonald, J. R. R. Tolkien and Charles Williams, plus 60 critical books and 188 dissertations; 945 letters, mostly of Williams; and 199 sound recordings, many of them oral history interviews. The collection is growing through purchase and gift at a rate of about 200 items per year. The collection is 50% cataloged, and noncirculating. Unpublished material may not be photocopied.

12-8. Wheaton College. Special Collections, Buswell Memorial Library, Wheaton, IL 60187-5593. 312-260-5705.
The library holds 160 published volumes, and over 60 linear feet of manuscripts and letters, by Madeleine L'Engle. Also included are thirty-six sound recordings, six videotapes and a filmstrip. The L'Engle collection is increased regularly by gift and purchase. A collection of Lewis Carroll material totals eighty-five volumes and is not currently growing. Most published material is cataloged; all is noncirculating. Unpublished material in the L'Engle collection is available only with her written permission.

Indiana

12-9. Indiana University. Lilly Library, Bloomington, IN 47405. 812-855-2452.
The Lilly Library has no separate fantasy or horror collection, but has significant holdings in these areas. The collection holds papers of August Derleth, Robert Bloch and Fritz Leiber, and first edition collections of Derleth, H. Rider Haggard and H. P. Lovecraft. The Lilly Library houses the Elisabeth Ball and Andrew Lang fairy tale collections, and holds fantasy and horror periodicals that rank it in the top twenty of collections surveyed. These are active collections, with new materials acquired regularly through gift and purchase, and the holdings are fully cataloged on OCLC.

Iowa

12-10. University of Iowa Libraries. Special Collections Department, Iowa City, IA 52242. 319-335-5921.
The library collects film and TV scripts, plus popular fiction by Iowa authors, but does not have an estimate of the fantasy/horror content of the collection. Works by Thomas M. Disch and Edgar Allan Poe are included, plus some R. A. Lafferty manuscript material. The collection includes some fantasy magazines. The materials are cataloged on OCLC, with photocopies available but not interlibrary loan.

Kentucky

12-11. University of Louisville Library. Rare Books and Special Collections, Louisville, KY 40292. 502-588-6762.
An Edgar Rice Burroughs collection of 20,000 items, plus special collections of Ambrose Bierce, L. Frank Baum, Isak Dinesen, Lafcadio Hearn and Ursula Le Guin, and some published work by most horror and fantasy authors. A fantasy and horror pulp collection ranks among the top twenty of collections surveyed. The five author collections listed above are fully cataloged, and the Burroughs and pulp collections are partially cataloged. The collection is active, added to regularly through purchase and gifts. Materials are for room use only. Photocopies can be provided, but not interlibrary loan.

Bibliography: Goddin, Geoffrey. "Lafcadio Hearn." *Library Review* 32 (March 1982).

McWhorter, G. T. "Edgar Rice Burroughs." *Library Review* 30 (May 1980).

McWhorter, G. T. "Karen Blixen/Isak Dinesen." *Library Review* 36 (Sept. 1986).

Maryland

12-12. University of Maryland, Baltimore County. Special Collections, Albin O. Kuhn Library & Gallery, Baltimore, MD 21228. 301-455-2353.
Primarily a science fiction collection of 5,500 volumes, with a fanzine collection containing over 15,000 items. Many fantasy and horror authors are represented, with manuscripts by Roger Zelazny. The collection is growing by 300 volumes per year through purchase and gifts. The magazine collection includes more titles than most libraries ranked in the top twenty for fantasy and horror serials, but they are mostly incomplete runs. The hardcover fiction (2,500 volumes) is fully cataloged; the paperbacks (3,000 volumes) are listed only. The collection is noncirculating, with photocopies available.

Michigan

12-13. Michigan State University Library. Special Collections, East Lansing, MI 48824-1048. 517-355-3770.
Approximately 1,500 volumes of horror and fantasy fiction within a larger science fiction and fantasy collection. Special interest in Robert Bloch and A. Conan

Doyle (vertical files) and Jorge Luis Borges and Edward Gorey (published works); also includes representative published works of almost all horror and fantasy authors. The magazines held would place this collection in the top ten for fantasy and horror periodicals if they were complete runs. This collection is active, but growing only slowly through donations. MSU has been a Science Fiction Writers of America depository since 1982. All books and magazines are cataloged on OCLC, and are noncirculating. Photocopies are available, but not interlibrary loan.

New Mexico

12-14. Eastern New Mexico University. Golden Library, Jack Williamson Science Fiction Library, Portales, NM 88130. 505-562-2636.
A total of nearly 10,000 volumes of science fiction, fantasy and horror are not inventoried separately by these categories, but the collection holds published material by most fantasy and horror authors. Manuscript material of Brian W. Aldiss, Poul Anderson and Piers Anthony is held. The fantasy and horror periodical collection is one of the ten most complete. Through local recording and from the Science Fiction Oral History Association the collection has sound recordings of Anderson, Peter Beagle, Robert Bloch, Ray Bradbury, Marion Zimmer Bradley, Jack Chalker, C. J. Cherryh, Harlan Ellison, Stephen King, Katherine Kurtz, Richard Matheson, Ray Russell and Roger Zelazny. The library has been a Science Fiction Writers of America depository since 1970. The overall collection is growing at about 200 volumes per year. The collection is fully cataloged. Photocopies are available, and 30% of the fiction books circulate with one-week interlibrary loan available.

New York

12-15. New York Public Library. General Research Division, Microforms Division, Fifth Avenue and 42nd Street, New York, NY 10018. 212-930-0838.
The General Research Division has over 5,000 volumes of science fiction in closed stacks, of which an estimated 40% are fantasy and horror. Paperbacks are being filmed routinely in the Microforms Division, and currently over 2,000 are on film with a similar estimate of 40% fantasy and horror. The most unusual aspect of this library collection is its commitment to preservation through microfilming of both paperbacks and magazines. An effort is being made by the Microforms Division to acquire science fiction, fantasy and horror literature not owned on paper, and thus the Microforms Division is in the unusual position of keeping track of the General Research Division's holdings. The magazine collection as combined in film and in hard copy is a good one, ranking in the top ten of those surveyed. The collection is growing actively and is completely cataloged. The materials do not circulate, but are available for use by the general public. Photocopies are available.

The library's Pforzheimer Collection contains materials relating to Mary W. Shelley. Access to this collection is by appointment only (phone: 212-930-0740).

Bibliography: Dowd, Alice. "The Science Fiction Microfilming Project at the New York Public Library," *Microform Review* XIV, 1 (Winter 1985), 15–20.

12-16. Syracuse University. George Arents Research Library. 600 E. S. Bird Library, Syracuse, NY 13244-2010. 315-443-2697.
The Rare Books Division holds a science fiction collection of about 3,000 volumes, of which only an estimated 10% are fantasy or horror. The Manuscripts Division has manuscripts by fantasy authors Piers Anthony, Anne McCaffrey, Andre Norton and Roger Zelazny, and has a large collection of Forrest Ackerman papers. Fantasy and horror periodicals are represented by a few complete runs and some partial runs. The collection is uncataloged and noncirculating. Acquisitions by gift amount to about twenty-five volumes and 3 linear feet of manuscripts per year. Photocopies are available, but not interlibrary loan.

Bibliography: Lerner, Fred. "Syracuse University," *Special Collections* II, 1/2 (Fall–Winter 1982), 59–62.

Ohio

12-17. Bowling Green State University. Jerome Library, Popular Culture Library, Bowling Green, OH 43403. 419-372-2450.
The science fiction collection of about 10,000 volumes, plus 23 linear feet of manuscripts and letters, includes fantasy and horror, but no separate counts are available. Extensive holdings of the published works of all fantasy and horror authors are included. Manuscript material of Robert Bloch, Charles L. Grant and Carl Jacobi is held. One of the ten most complete collections of fantasy and horror periodicals. This is an active collection, growing rapidly through gift and purchase. The collection is 75% cataloged, with holdings available on OCLC. Photocopies are available, but not interlibrary loan.

The Rare Books Division of the Center for Archival Collections (phone: 419-372-2411) in the Jerome Library has an extensive Robert Aickman collection, including forty manuscripts, correspondence, etc., and Aickman's personal library of over 3,000 volumes. An extensive Ray Bradbury manuscript collection is also housed in the Rare Books Division.

12-18. Kent State University Library. Special Collections, Kent, OH 44242. 216-672-2270.
A Stephen Donaldson collection of books and manuscripts, with works of several other fantasy and horror authors, makes up a science fiction and fantasy collection of about 1,000 volumes. An exhibit in 1981, "Ohio's Contribution to Science Fiction & Fantasy," featured authors born in Ohio. The collection is active, growing by gifts and purchase, and is noncirculating. Cataloging is on OCLC.

12-19. Ohio State University Libraries. Division of Rare Books and Manuscripts, 1858 Neil Ave. Mall, Columbus, OH 43210. 614-268-5725.
A very extensive American fiction collection includes thousands of volumes of fantasy and horror, but there is no practical way to sort them and count by these categories. Under the designation "The William Charvat Collection of American Fiction," Ohio State has been working for years to assemble a complete American fiction collection up to the year 1926, and has been collecting new fiction comprehensively since 1986. The intervening years are substantially represented as well, and the goal is to fill them in where possible. A computer search of 173 fantasy and horror authors' names in the OSU computer produced about 4,400 volumes.

The library holds an especially large James Thurber collection, including 22 linear feet of Thurber's papers. The horror and fantasy periodical collection is one of the twenty most complete. The library reports a near-complete Arkham House collection. The collection is growing through gifts and purchases. Part of it is circulating through interlibrary loan. Cataloging is on OCLC. Photocopies are available.

Oklahoma

12-20. University of Tulsa. McFarlin Library. Special Collections Department, 600 S. College Ave., Tulsa, OK 74104. 918-631-2496.
Works by a handful of fantasy and horror authors are included in the science fiction collection, which is not a primary focus of the library. Books by M. P. Shiel, James Thurber and R. A. Lafferty, and some Arkham House editions of H. P. Lovecraft, are held. A large collection of Lafferty manuscripts is the most significant relevant holding. Cataloging is on OCLC, and photocopies are available.

Oregon

12-21. American Private Press Association Library. 112 E. Burnett St., Stayton, OR 97383. 503-769-6088.
A collection of over 200,000 fanzines, 1,000 books and 3,000 letters, including both science fiction and fantasy. Separate counts are not kept by genre. The collection is strongest in 1960s and 1970s fanzines, and includes extensive fantasy periodicals, one of the ten most complete fantasy periodical collections. Open to the public. An internal catalog covers all books, and 70% of the fanzines. Photocopies are available, but not interlibrary loan.

Pennsylvania

12-22. Pennsylvania State University. Pattee Library, Special Collections Department, University Park, PA 16802. 814-865-1793.
A fiction collection of 1,600 volumes. The library collects utopias, science fiction, H. P. Lovecraft, Robert E. Howard and Arkham House. Several fantasy and horror authors are included as science fiction, with manuscripts of August Derleth and Talbot Mundy. Aside from Lovecraft, utopias are the only fantasy-related material being actively purchased, though the other collections are growing through gifts. Horror and fantasy represent 20% or less of the collection. The collection is two-thirds cataloged, and some holdings are on OCLC. Photocopies are available.

12-23. Temple University Libraries. Rare Book Collection, Science Fiction & Fantasy Collection, Philadelphia, PA 19122. 215-787-8230.
Until 1984 the collection of 8,000 books and 5,000 periodical issues excluded fantasy. Since then, 10,000 new and unsorted volumes have arrived, which do include fantasy, but exact figures are unavailable. Perhaps 20% are horror or fantasy. Over 1,000 fanzines also have undetermined fantasy content. The fantasy

and horror part of the collection is growing by purchase and gift at the rate of about seventy-five volumes per year. The library has significant holdings of almost all fantasy and horror authors, with manuscripts of James Blish, Marion Zimmer Bradley, Walter De la Mare and John Cowper Powys. Gothic horror is collected outside the SF&F collection, but still in the Rare Book Collection, with strong holdings of Mervyn Peake, Monk Lewis, Horace Walpole, George MacDonald, H. P. Lovecraft and Robert E. Howard, and a complete or nearly complete Arkham House collection. The collection of fantasy and horror periodicals is one of the ten most complete. The collection is 65% cataloged, and holdings are on OCLC. Photocopies are available.

Rhode Island

12-24. Brown University. John Hay Library, Providence, RI 02912. 401-863-2146. The definitive H. P. Lovecraft collection, with over 700 printed and over 5,000 manuscript items, half by Lovecraft himself and half by Lovecraft correspondents such as August Derleth, Frank Belknap Long, C. L. Moore, E. Hoffmann Price and Clark Ashton Smith. A separate Clark Ashton Smith collection includes over 5,000 manuscripts and 5,000 letters, and a separate John Buchan collection is maintained. A complete run of *Weird Tales* is held. Publisher collections include the complete works of Arkham House including most ephemera, and complete Donald W. Grant and Necronomicon Press collections. Psychic science, the occult, conjuring and magic are also collecting specialties. The collection is active, and cataloged. The Lovecraft collection is cataloged on the Research Libraries Information Network (RLIN).

South Carolina

12-25. University of South Carolina. Thomas Cooper Library, Special Collections, Columbia, SC 29208. 803-777-8154.
The result of an isolated purchase, this library has a complete set of Arkham House publications as of 1975, plus a collection of H. P. Lovecraft first editions. The collection is not being added to, but is being preserved as a noncirculating resource, cataloged on OCLC.

Tennessee

12-26. Bibliotheca Crawfordiana. F. Marion Crawford Memorial Society, Saracinesca House, 3610 Meadowbrook Ave., Nashville, TN 37205. 615-226-1890.
A fiction collection of about 1,225 volumes contains books by F. Marion Crawford and about thirty other mostly contemporary (late nineteenth-, early twentieth-century) horror and fantasy authors. The collection also includes 500 letters, 25 pieces of art and diverse related items, including 200 articles about Crawford. The collection holds some fantasy and horror periodicals. The collection is growing (at about forty items per year) through purchase, gifts and exchanges. The holdings may be used by appointment only. Photocopies are available, but not interlibrary loan.

Texas

12-27. Texas A&M University. Evans Library, Special Collections Division, College Station, TX 77843-5000. 409-845-1951.
A science fiction collection of 21,000 volumes, including an unknown percentage of horror and fantasy material. Includes 20 linear feet of manuscripts and letters, 115 videotapes and 15 films. Horror has not been a collecting emphasis. The collection of horror and fantasy periodicals is one of the ten most complete. This is a very active collection, adding about 2,000 volumes per year through purchase, gifts and exchanges. The books are about 70% cataloged; manuscripts are uncataloged. Photocopies are available, but not interlibrary loan.

12-28. University of Texas at Austin. Harry Ransom Humanities Research Center, Box 7219, Austin, TX 78713. 512-471-9119.
The Harry Ransom Humanities Research Center has nearly 7,000 volumes of fiction and hundreds of magazines, manuscripts and letters organized into several distinct collections of interest to the student of fantasy and/or horror: The I. R. Brussel Bibliography Collection of James Branch Cabell, the Dan Laurence Collection of Robert Nathan and the Adrian Homer Goldstone Collection of Arthur Machen. The Ellery Queen Collection has an extensive "psychic detective" section and many Bram Stoker, William Hope Hodgson and Edgar Allan Poe titles. Also available is the Dorothy Sayers Wilkie Collins Collection, Arthur Conan Doyle's Spiritualism Library, M. P. Shiel's and John Gawsworth's Realm of Redondo Collection, the George Matthew Adams Lafcadio Hearn Collection and the library and archive of T. H. White. In all, the Center holds substantial manuscripts or letters of nearly fifty fantasy authors. The publisher holdings include complete sets of Kelmscott Press, Arkham House, Carcosa, Dark Harvest and Roy Squires.

In 1982 the Center acquired the L. W. Currey Science Fiction and Fantasy Collection, essentially his bibliography collection. While primarily utopias and science fiction, it contains comprehensive fantasy holdings, both high and dark. The H. P. Lovecraft, Ray Bradbury, David H. Keller, David Lindsay and Clark Ashton Smith holdings are particularly noteworthy. Holdings are also strong in promotional, script and other materials related to fantastic film.

The periodical collection, in number of titles, is one of the most extensive. In terms of completeness it is in the top twenty of the libraries surveyed. The collection is developing along the lines of established strength through purchase and regular gifts. Most of its books are cataloged. Photocopies are available, but not interlibrary loan.

Utah

12-29. Brigham Young University. Lee Library, Provo, UT 84602. 801-378-6730.
This collection holds an estimated 4,000 volumes of fantasy and horror fiction, within a larger science fiction/fantasy collection. Some fantasy and horror magazines are held. The collection is active, adding about fifty volumes annually. It is a circulating collection except for a small percentage held in the Rare Book Collection and vault. The books are fully cataloged, and available through interlibrary loan, as are photocopies.

Virginia

12-30. University of Virginia. Alderman Library, Special Collections Department, Charlottesville, VA 22903-2498. 804-924-3025.
The Sadleir-Black Collection of Gothic Fiction contains over 1,000 titles published mainly between 1765 and 1830. Focusing on English writers and imprints, it is unique in its coverage of minor authors writing in this genre and its holdings of original and subsequent editions of their works. Along with the English editions are American, French and German editions dating from the same period. The University of Virginia Library also holds manuscript material of Ambrose Bierce, Jorge Luis Borges, Chas. Brockden Brown, James Branch Cabell (extensive), Robert W. Chambers, Nathaniel Hawthorne, Lafcadio Hearn, Jack London and Edgar Allan Poe. The collection is noncirculating and growing.

Wisconsin

12-31. Marquette University Libraries. Department of Special Collections, 1415 W. Wisconsin Ave., Milwaukee, WI 53233. 414-224-7256.
The J. R. R. Tolkien Collection includes 6.4 cubic feet of original manuscripts of *The Hobbit, Farmer Giles of Ham, The Lord of the Rings* and *Mr. Bliss*; copies of books by Tolkien; and books, periodicals, art, games and other secondary material relating to Tolkien. The manuscripts are available for use on microfilm only in the Department of Special Collections; all Tolkien holdings are noncirculating. A brochure, "JRR Tolkien Collection, an Inventory to the Manuscripts at Marquette University" (typescript, thirty-nine pages, revised 1987) is available by mail for $4.00. An estimated 500 volumes of related interest are available in the general circulating collection. The Tolkien collection is fully cataloged, and photocopies are available.

12-32. State Historical Society of Wisconsin. 816 State St., Madison, WI 53706. 608-262-3266.
The August Derleth papers include fantasy pulps (issues that include Derleth contributions) and most Arkham House books, as well as Derleth's manuscripts and personal papers. Manuscripts or letters by Stephen Vincent Benét, Algernon Blackwood, Robert Bloch, Ray Bradbury, Arthur Conan Doyle, H. P. Lovecraft, Donald Wandrei and Colin Wilson are also part of the collection, which is noncirculating.

12-33. University of Wisconsin, La Crosse. Murphy Library, La Crosse, WI 54601. 608-785-8511.
The Paul W. Skeeters Collection of fantasy, science fiction and horror literature holds 1,100 volumes, primarily first editions, and an Arkham House collection of about 100 titles. Among the authors collected are Joan Aiken, Algernon Blackwood, James Branch Cabell, A. Conan Doyle, Lord Dunsany, H. Rider Haggard, Talbot Mundy, Sax Rohmer, M. P. Shiel and Bram Stoker. The collection grows by purchase of five volumes per year on the average. The books are fully cataloged on OCLC, and noncirculating. Photocopies are available, but not interlibrary loan.

Wyoming

12-34. University of Wyoming. Coe Library, Box 3924, Laramie, WY 82071. 307-766-6385.
A collection of science fiction and fantasy, including extensive manuscripts. Of note in the horror genre is the Robert Bloch collection, which consists primarily of materials from 1947 to date, and includes publications by and about Bloch, and manuscripts, fanzines, contracts, scripts, videotapes, correspondence and uncorrected proofs. This library reports its holdings in cubic feet: the overall collection takes up 275 cubic feet, to which 10–15 cubic feet per year are added through gifts. Catalogs and finding aids are available on site. The collection may be used in-house only, and interlibrary loan is not offered. Photocopies are available.

Australia

12-35. University of Queensland Library. Special Collections, St. Lucia, Queensland 4067, Australia. Phone: Brisbane 3773249.
This library holds the Donald Tuck collection of science fiction and fantasy, used to compile his *The Encyclopedia of Science Fiction and Fantasy through 1968* [6-4]. Most fantasy and horror authors are represented by published books. Most fantasy and horror primary magazines are in the collection, placing this periodical collection in the top twenty of those surveyed. The collection is actively growing through purchase of materials, and is fully cataloged. Hardcover books circulate and are available for interlibrary loan. Photocopies are available.

12-36. University of Sydney Library. Rare Books and Special Collections, Science Fiction and Fantasy Collection, Sydney, N.S.W. 2006, Australia. 02-692-4162.
Of a science fiction and fantasy collection of over 44,000 volumes, an estimated 50 to 60% are fantasy and horror. Manuscript material by Brian Aldiss, Lloyd Alexander, Harlan Ellison, H. P. Lovecraft and Clark Ashton Smith is included. The library has holdings of all fantasy and horror authors, with significant amounts (over two-thirds of their output) of at least ninety authors, plus a half-dozen each of sound recordings and filmstrips, and seven pieces of Virgil Finlay art. The collection of fantasy and horror periodicals is one of the ten most complete. There are 12,000 science fiction (including horror and fantasy) comic books of related interest. The collection grows by 250 to 300 volumes per year through purchases and donations. A Science Fiction Writers of America depository since 1980. The books are 20% fully cataloged; another 40% can be located by a title list on cards. Photocopies are available, but this is a noncirculating collection; no interlibrary loan.

Canada

12-37. Queen's University. Special Collections, Douglas Library, Kingston, Ontario, Canada K7L 5C4. 613-545-2528.
This library holds a science fiction collection of 1,600 books and 2,500 magazines, with a Gothic-fantasy orientation, and a 6-inch pile of H. P. Lovecraft manuscript material. The magazines are in Special Collections, but the novels are in

the main stacks. Most fantasy and horror authors are represented. The collection is fully cataloged, but not growing. Photocopies are available, but not interlibrary loan.

12-38. Toronto Public Library. Spaced Out Library, 40 St. George Street, Toronto, Ontario, Canada M5S 2E4. 416-393-7748.
A collection of nearly 18,000 volumes of science fiction and fantasy, plus over 15,000 periodicals, for which separate fantasy and horror statistics are not maintained. The collection policy defines the Spaced Out Library as an adult research collection of science fiction and fantasy, and the curator estimates that the collection may be 50% fantasy. There is very little dark fantasy, except for writers like Stephen King and Peter Straub for whom there is a current demand. The fantasy and horror periodical collection is one of the ten most complete. The collection is actively growing through purchases and gifts, and is fully cataloged. There is a circulating library of 6,000 paperbacks in addition to the noncirculating main collection listed above. Photocopies can be supplied, but not interlibrary loan. An occasional newsletter is published.

Bibliography: Aylward, David. "Spaced Out Library: Toronto Public Library's Spaced Out Collection," *Special Collections* II, 1/2 (Fall–Winter 1982) 63–67.

12-39. University of New Brunswick. Science Fiction and Fantasy Collection, Ward Chipman Library, Box 5050, St. John, New Brunswick, Canada E2L 4L5. 506-648-5703.
A science fiction collection of over 15,000 items, which includes fantasy materials but excludes most strictly horror or Gothic material. An extensive periodical collection includes complete runs of most fantasy fiction pulps and magazines, and is one of the ten most complete fantasy periodical collections. This is an active collection, adding regularly through gifts and purchase. The books are fully cataloged, and items that are not rare circulate locally and through interlibrary loan. Photocopies are available.

12-40. University of Winnipeg Library. 515 Portage Ave., Winnipeg, Manitoba, Canada R3B 2E9. 204-786-9805.
A science fiction collection of 2,425 volumes (plus 140 volumes of reference and critical works) includes detective, horror, weird, ghost and fantasy fiction. Of this total, 161 volumes are considered fantasy, and 45 horror. The collection includes works by nearly all horror and fantasy authors. Only a few fantasy and horror periodicals are held, with *Fantastic Adventures*, 1939–45, on microfilm. The overall collection is active, adding fifty volumes annually. The books are fully cataloged. This is a circulating collection, but with closed stacks. Interlibrary loan and photocopies are available.

England

12-41. Science Fiction Foundation. North East London Polytechnic, Longbridge Road, Dagenham, Essex, RM8 2AS, England. 01-590-7722.
A collection of fiction, manuscripts, microfilm, audio recordings and videotapes, numbering over 13,000 total items. Books by many fantasy and horror authors are

included, but are not sorted as fantasy and/or horror. The periodical collection has some holdings of most fantasy magazines, with enough complete runs to rank in the top twenty of collections surveyed. An internal catalog is available, as are photocopies.

Switzerland

12-42. Maison d'Ailleurs. Musée de l'Utopie, des Voyages Extraordinaires et de la Science-Fiction, Rue du Four 5, CH-1400 Yverdon-les-Bains. Switzerland. 024-216438.

Fantasy and horror are not counted separately in this 25,000-volume collection of science fiction, fantastic voyages and utopian novels. Fantasy and horror are ordinarily collected only when they overlap with the collection's three main areas of interest, but most fantasy authors are represented, and there is some manuscript material from H. P. Lovecraft. The collection has extensive correspondence files, and some manuscripts, sound and video recordings and artworks. The Maison holds growing collections of most fantasy magazines. The collections are 15–20% cataloged, and noncirculating (duplicates are circulated as a separate library). Photocopies are available, but not interlibrary loan (to date). The collection is active, growing by 400–450 volumes per year through gifts and purchases.

13

Core Collection, Awards, Organizations, Series

Neil Barron

Core Collection

Librarians desiring to evaluate or strengthen their collections should begin with the first-purchase recommendations in this listing, particularly those books with multiple recommendations. Readers, especially those relatively unfamiliar with fantasy or horror fiction, should probably begin with this listing, then let their developing interests guide them.

This core collection best books listing is derived from several sources:

1. First-purchase recommendations by this guide's contributors, which are denoted by an asterisk preceding the entry number in the bibliographies above and preceding the surname in this listing.

2. Books selected by these knowledgeable outside readers, whose initials follow the book titles:

DH–David Hartwell, respected editor of fantasy and SF, editor of several excellent anthologies, Ph.D. in comparative literature, Columbia University;

SM–Sam Moskowitz, editor and author of many books and articles, with a special interest in the early history of SF; Pilgrim Award winner, 1981;

RR–R. Reginald, best known for his authoritative bibliography of fantastic literature [6-3]; owner of Borgo Press;

DW–Diana Waggoner, author of *The Hills of Faraway* [6-34], one of the best earlier surveys of fantasy.

A few of their selections were not annotated in the bibliographies. Readers were not equally familiar with all annotated books, and the absence of their initials does not necessarily mean they thought the book less meritorious, but simply that they were not sufficiently familiar with it to judge it.

3. Three 100 best books guides by Cawthorn and Moorcock [6-21], Jones and Newman [6-22] and Pringle [6-23], designated F, H and MF, respectively.

4. The thirty-three titles in the *Locus* all-time best fantasy listing (see under Locus Awards in this chapter), designated L.

5. The 208 novels and collections and 16 anthologies in Tymn's *Fantasy Literature* [6-32], designated F.

All books are listed in the sequence in which they appear in this guide. Consult the indexes for entry numbers of annotated books. Titles followed by a year of publication were not annotated, although in some cases portions of their contents are included in books which are annotated. Recommendations of best films (as distinct from books about films) will be found in chapter 9.

The Early Gothic, 1762–1824

*Austen, Jane. *Northanger Abbey* (DH, SM, RR, H)
*Beckford, William. *Vathek* (DH, SM, RR, F)
*Brown, Charles Brockden. *Wieland* (DH, SM, RR)
*Dacre, Charlotte. *Zofloya* (SM)
*Godwin, William. *Things As They Are* (DH, SM, H)
———. *St. Leon* (SM, RR)
Hazlitt, William, ed. *The Romancist, and Novelist's Library* (4 vols., 1839–40) (DH)
*Hoffmann, E. T. A. *Die Elixiere des Teufels* (DH, SM, RR)
———. *Nachtstücke* (RR)
———. *The Best Tales of E. T. A. Hoffmann* (H, FL)
*Hogg, James. *The Private Memoirs and Confessions of a Justified Sinner* (DH, SM, H)
*Irving, Washington. "Adventure of the German Student" (RR)
*Lee, Sophia. *The Recess*
*Leland, Thomas. *Longsword, Earl of Salisbury*
*Lewis, Matthew G. *The Monk* (DH, SM, RR, F, H)
*Maturin, Charles R. *Melmoth the Wanderer* (DH, SM, RR, F, H)
*Peacock, Thomas Love. *Nightmare Abbey* (DH, SM, RR)
Peake, R. B. *Presumption* (SM)
*Polidori, John. *The Vampyre* (DH, SM, RR)
*Radcliffe, Ann. *The Mysteries of Udolpho* (DH, SM, RR, DW)
*———. *The Italian* (DH, SM)
*Reeve, Clara. *The Old English Baron* (DH, SM)
*Sade, Marquis de. *Justine* (DH, SM)
*Shelley, Mary W. *Frankenstein* (DH, SM, RR, F, H)
Shelley, Percy. *Zastrozzi* (RR)
*Smollett, Tobias. *The Adventures of Ferdinand Count Fathom* (SM)
*Walpole, Horace. *The Castle of Otranto* (DH, SM, RR, F)
Webster, John. *The White Devil* (1612) (H)

The Later Gothic Tradition, 1825–96

*Ainsworth, W. H. *The Lancashire Witches* (SM)
*Balzac, Honoré de. *The Magic Skin* (DH, SM, RR)
*Bierce, Ambrose. *Tales of Soldiers and Civilians/Can Such Things Be?* (DH, SM, RR, H)
Bleiler, Everett F., ed. *Classic Ghost Stories by Charles Dickens and Others* (1975) (DH)
———. *Five Victorian Ghost Novels* (1971) (DH)
———. *Three Supernatural Novels of the Victorian Period* (1975) (DH)
———. *A Treasury of Victorian Ghost Stories* (1981) (DH)
Brontë, Emily. *Wuthering Heights* (RR, F)
*Chambers, Robert W. *The King in Yellow* (DH, SM, RR, H)
Collins, Wilkie. *The Woman in White* (RR)
Crawford, F. Marion. *Wandering Ghosts* (DH)
Dickens, Charles. *The Complete Ghost Stories* (DH, RR)
*Dumas, Alexandre. *The Wolf-Leader* (SM, RR)
*Falkner, John Meade. *The Lost Stradivarius* (SM)
Gilman, Charlotte Perkins. *The Yellow Wallpaper* (DH, RR)
Gotthelf, Jeremias. *The Black Spider* (H)
Hawthorne, Nathaniel. *The House of the Seven Gables* (DH)
*———. *Mosses from an Old Manse* (DH, SM, RR, H)
*———. *The Scarlet Letter* (DH, SM)
*Housman, Clemence. *The Were-Wolf* (SM)
*Huysmans, Joris-Karl. *Là-Bas* (SM, RR)
James, Henry. *The Ghostly Tales* (DH)
Lamb, Hugh, ed. *Victorian Tales of Terror* (DH)
———. *Terror by Gaslight* (DH)
———. *Victorian Nightmares* (DH)
———. *Forgotten Tales of Terror* (DH)
———. *Tales from a Gaslit Graveyard* (DH)
*Lee, Vernon. *Hauntings* (SM, RR)
*Le Fanu, J. Sheridan. *In a Glass Darkly* (DH, SM, RR)
———. *A Stable for Nightmares* (1896) (DH)
———. *Uncle Silas* (F, H)
*Lytton, Edward Bulwer. *The Haunters and the Haunted* (SM, RR)
*———. *A Strange Story* (SM)
*Machen, Arthur. *The Great God Pan* (DH, SM, RR)
*———. *The Three Imposters* (DH, SM)
Melville, Herman. *The Confidence Man* (1857) (H)
Mérimée, Prosper. *Tales* (DH)
Nesbit, E. *Grim Tales* (DH, RR)
*Oliphant, Margaret. *A Beleaguered City* (SM)
*———. *Stories of the Seen and Unseen* (SM, RR)
*Poe, Edgar Allan. *The Narrative of Arthur Gordon Pym* (DH, SM, RR, F)
*———. *Tales of the Grotesque and Arabesque* (DH, SM, RR, H)
Reynolds, G. W. M. *Wagner, the Wehr-Wolf* (RR)

*Riddell, Mrs. J. H. *The Uninhabited House* (DH, SM)
Shelley, Mary W. *Tales and Stories* (RR)
Shiel, M. P. *Shapes in the Fire* (DH)
*Stevenson, Robert Louis. *The Strange Case of Dr Jekyll and Mr Hyde* (DH, SM, RR, DW, F, H)
Sullivan, Jack, ed. *Lost Souls* (1983) (DH)
Wells, H. G. *The Island of Dr. Moreau* (1896) (H)
*Wilde, Oscar. *The Picture of Dorian Gray* (SM, RR, DW, F)

Early Modern Horror Fiction, 1897–1949

Aickman, Robert, and R. Chetwynd-Hayes, eds. *The Fontana Book of Great Ghost Stories* (1964–84) (DH)
Andreyev, Leonid. *Lazarus* (DH)
Arlen, Michael. *Ghost Stories* (RR)
Asquith, Cynthia, ed. *The Ghost Book* (DH, RR)
Bailey, Paul. *Deliver Me from Eva* (1946) (H)
*Benson, E. F. *The Room in the Tower* (DH, SM, RR, H)
Benson, R. H. *The Necromancers* (RR)
Birkin, Charles, ed. *Creeps* (DH)
*Blackwood, Algernon. *The Empty House* [and others] (SM, RR)
*———. *John Silence* (DH, SM, RR, H)
Blayre, Christopher. *The Purple Sapphire* (RR)
Bloch, Robert. *The Opener of the Way* (RR)
*Bowen, Marjorie. *Black Magic* (SM, RR, F)
*———. *The Last Bouquet* (DH, SM, H)
*Bradbury, Ray. *Dark Carnival* (DH, SM, RR)
*Briussof, Valeri. *The Fiery Angel*
Buchan, John. *The Watcher by the Threshold/The Mood Endureth* (FL)
———. *Witch Wood* (RR, F)
Burrage, A. M. *Some Ghost Stories* (RR)
*Busson, Paul. *The Man Who Was Born Again*
Cave, Hugh B. *Murgunstrumm and Others* (H)
Clark, Walter van Tilburg. *Track of the Cat* (1949) (H)
*Conrad, Joseph. *Heart of Darkness* (DH, SM, H)
Cox, Michael, and R. A. Gilbert, eds. *The Oxford Book of English Ghost Stories* (1986) (DH)
Cuddon, J. A., ed. *The Penguin Book of Ghost Stories* (1984) (DH)
———. *The Penguin Book of Horror Stories* (1984) (DH)
*De la Mare, Walter. *The Return* (SM, RR)
*———. *The Riddle/On the Edge* (DH, SM, RR)
Derleth, August. *The Lurker at the Threshold* (H)
———. *Someone in the Dark* (RR)
———, ed. *The Night Side* (1947) (DH)
———, ed. *Sleep No More* (1944) (DH)
———, ed. *Who Knocks?* (1946) (DH)
———, ed. *The Sleeping and the Dead* (1947) (DH, H)
Dinesen, Isak. *Seven Gothic Tales* (DH, RR)

*Endore, Guy. *The Werewolf of Paris* (SM, RR, F, H)
*Ewers, Hanns Heinz. *The Sorcerer's Apprentice/Alraune/Vampire* (SM, RR)
Hammett, Dashiell, ed. *Creeps by Night* (1931) (DH)
Hartley, L. P. *Night Fears* (DH)
Harvey, W. F. *Midnight Tales* (RR)
Heard, H. F. *The Great Fog* (RR)
Heinlein, Robert A. *The Unpleasant Profession of Jonathan Hoag* (MF)
*Hichens, Robert. *Tongues of Conscience* (DH, SM)
Hodgson, William Hope. *The Boats of the Glen Carrig* (FL)
———. *Carnacki the Ghost-Finder* (RR)
*———. *The Ghost Pirates* (SM, RR)
*———. *The House on the Borderland* (DH, SM, RR, F, H, FL)
*Hubbard, L. Ron. "Fear" (F)
Ingram, Eleanor. *The Thing from the Lake* (RR)
Jackson, Shirley. *The Lottery* (DH, RR)
*James, Henry. *The Two Magics/The Turn of the Screw* (DH, SM, F, H)
*James, M. R. *Ghost Stories of an Antiquary* (DH, SM, RR, H)
Kafka, Franz. *The Castle* (1926) (F)
———. *Metamorphosis* (DH, SM, RR)
———. *The Trial* (F, H)
Karloff, Boris, ed. *And the Darkness Falls* (DH, H)
Kersh, Gerald. *The Horrible Dummy* (RR)
Laing, Alexander. *The Cadaver of Gideon Wyck* (H)
———, ed. *The Haunted Omnibus* (1937) (DH)
*Lee-Hamilton, Eugene. *The Lord of the Dark Red Star* (SM)
*Leiber, Fritz. *Conjure Wife* (DH, SM, RR, F, H, MF, L)
*———. *Night's Black Agents* (DH, RR)
*Lovecraft, H. P. *The Outsider and Others* (DH, SM, RR, F, H)
Machen, Arthur. *The House of Souls* (RR, H)
*Mann, Jack. *Grey Shapes/Nightmare Farm/Maker of Shadows/The Ninth Life/ Her Ways Are Death* (SM, RR)
Merritt, A. *Burn, Witch, Burn!* (RR)
*Meyrink, Gustav. *The Golem* (SM)
*Onions, Oliver. *Widdershins* (DH, SM, RR, H)
Pain, Barry. *Stories in the Dark* (RR)
Quinn, Seabury. *Is the Devil a Gentleman?* (RR)
*Robbins, Tod. *Who Wants a Green Bottle?* (SM)
Rohmer, Sax. *Brood of the Witch-Queen* (RR)
Saki. *The Complete Short Stories* (RR)
Sayers, Dorothy L., ed. *Great Short Stories of Detection, Mystery and Horror* (DH)
Scarborough, Dorothy, ed. *Famous Modern Ghost Stories* (1921) (DH)
Shiel, M. P. *The Pale Ape* (RR)
*Sinclair, May. *Uncanny Stories* (SM)
Sloane, William. *To Walk the Night* (1937) (F)
Smith, Clark Ashton. *The Abominations of Yondo* (FL)
———. *Out of Space and Time* (DH, RR, F, H)
*Stoker, Bram. *Dracula* (SM, RR, F, H, L)
———. *The Jewel of Seven Stars* (H)

———. *The Lair of the White Worm* (RR)
Sturgeon, Theodore. *Without Sorcery* (DH, RR)
Thomson, Christine C., ed. *Not at Night* series (DH, RR)
Trumbo, Dalton. *Johnny Got His Gun* (1939) (H)
Wagenknecht, Edward, ed. *The Fireside Book of Ghost Stories* (1947) (DH)
———. *Six Novels of the Supernatural* (1944) (DH)
*Wakefield, H. Russell. *They Return at Evening* (DH, SM, RR)
Walpole, Hugh, ed. *A Second Century of Creepy Stories* (1937) (H)
Walton, Evangeline. *Witch House* (RR)
Wellman, Manly Wade. *Worse Things Waiting* (DH, RR, H)
*Wharton, Edith. *Ghosts* (DH, SM)
*Williamson, Jack. *Darker Than You Think* (SM, RR, F, MF)
Wise, Herbert A., and Phyllis Fraser, eds. *Great Tales of Terror and the Supernatural* (1944) (DH)
Wollheim, Donald A., ed. *Terror in the Modern Vein* (1955) (DH)
Woolrich, Cornell. *Night Has a Thousand Eyes* (1945) (H)

Contemporary Horror Fiction, 1950–88

Aickman, Robert. *Cold Hand in Mine* (RR)
———. *Powers of Darkness* (RR)
*———. *Sub Rosa* (DH, SM, H)
———. *The Wine-Dark Sea* (1988) (DH)
Aldiss, Brian W. *Frankenstein Unbound* (RR)
Amis, Kingsley. *The Green Man* (DW, F, H, MF)
Baker, Scott. *Dhampire* (1982) (DH)
Ballard, J. G. *Crash* (DH)
———. *The Crystal World* (RR, F, H)
*———. *High-Rise* (DH, SM)
Banks, Iain. *The Bridge* (1986) (MF)
———. *The Wasp Factory* (H)
*Barker, Clive. *Books of Blood* I–VI (DH, SM, RR)
———. *The Damnation Game* (H)
Beagle, Peter. *A Fine and Private Place* (DW, MF, FL)
Beaumont, Charles. *Best of Beaumont* (RR)
*———. *Charles Beaumont: Selected Stories* (DH, SM, RR)
*Birkin, Charles. *My Name Is Death* (DH, SM)
Bishop, Michael. *Who Made Stevie Crye?* (H, MF)
*Blackburn, John F. *For Fear of Little Men* (DH, SM)
*Blatty, William Peter. *The Exorcist* (DH, SM, RR, H)
*Bloch, Robert. *Psycho* (DH, SM, RR, H)
*———. *The Selected Stories* (DH, SM, RR)
Bradbury, Ray. *The October Country* (1985) (H)
*———. *Something Wicked This Way Comes* (DH, SM, DW, L)
*———. *The Stories of Ray Bradbury* (DH, SM, RR)
Brennan, Joseph Payne. *Nine Horrors and a Dream* (H)
Brunner, John. *The Sheep Look Up* (1972) (H)
*Cady, Jack. *The Well* (DH, SM)

*Campbell, Ramsey. *Dark Companions* (DH, SM)
———. *Dark Feasts* (1987) (H)
———. *The Hungry Moon* (MF)
*———. *To Wake the Dead* (DH, SM)
Carr, John Dickson. *The Devil in Velvet* (1951) (F)
*Case, David. *The Cell, and Other Tales of Horror* (DH, SM)
Charnas, Suzy McKee. *The Vampire Tapestry* (MF)
Demijohn, Thom. *Black Alice* (1968) (RR)
Dick, Philip K. *Collected Stories* (1987) (DH)
———. *The Three Stigmata of Palmer Eldritch* (DH, H)
Disch, Thomas M. *The Businessman* (F, MF)
*du Maurier, Daphne. *Echoes from the Macabre* (DH, SM, RR)
———. *The House on the Strand* (RR)
*Ellison, Harlan. *The Essential Ellison* (RR, SM, H)
Etchison, Dennis. *The Dark Country* (H)
Farris, John. *All Heads Turn When the Hunt Goes By* (H)
*———. *The Fury* (DH, SM)
*Finney, Jack. *The Body Snatchers* (DH, SM, RR)
Fowles, John. *The Magus* (DH)
Golding, William. *Lord of the Flies* (H)
Grant, Charles L. *The Pet* (H)
Grubb, Davis. *The Night of the Hunter* (DH)
*Harris, Thomas. *Red Dragon* (DH, SM)
*Herbert, James. *The Fog* (DH, SM)
*Hjorstberg, William. *Falling Angel* (DH, SM, RR, H)
Honeycombe, Gordon. *Neither the Sea Nor the Sand* (1969) (F)
Household, Geoffrey. *The Sending* (F)
Irwin, Robert. *The Arabian Nightmare* (1983) (H)
*Jackson, Shirley. *The Haunting of Hill House* (DH, SM, RR, F, H, MF)
*———. *We Have Always Lived in the Castle* (DH, SM)
Jeter, K. W. *Soul Eater* (MF)
*Kast, Pierre. *The Vampires of Alfama* (DH, SM)
*Kersh, Gerald. *Men without Bones* (DH, SM)
King, Stephen. *Carrie* (RR)
———. *The Dead Zone* (RR)
*———. *Night Shift* (DH, SM, RR)
*———. *Pet Sematary* (DH, SM, RR)
*———. *'Salem's Lot* (DH, SM, H, MF, L)
*———. *The Shining* (DH, SM, RR, H, MF, L)
*———. *Skeleton Crew* (DH, SM, RR)
*———. *The Stand* (DH, SM, L)
Kirk, Russell. *Old House of Fear* (RR)
———. *The Princess of All Lands* (DH)
Klein, T. E. D. *The Ceremonies* (H)
———. *The Dark Gods* (DH)
Kneale, Nigel. *Quatermass and the Pit* (1959) (H)
*Koontz, Dean R. *Watchers* (DH, SM, RR)
Kosinski, Jerzy. *The Painted Bird* (H)

Laski, Marganhita. *The Victorian Chaise Longue* (RR)
Laymon, Richard. *The Cellar* (H)
Leiber, Fritz. *The Best of Fritz Leiber* (RR)
*———. *Our Lady of Darkness* (DH, SM, F, MF, FL)
*———. *The Sinful Ones/You're All Alone* (DH, SM, RR, F, MF)
*Levin, Ira. *Rosemary's Baby* (DH, SM, RR, F, MF)
Lewis, C. S. *The Dark Tower* (1977) (H)
Marasco, Robert. *Burnt Offerings* (H)
March, William. *The Bad Seed* (DH)
Martin, George R. R. *Fevre Dream* (RR)
Matheson, Richard. *Hell House* (RR)
*———. *I Am Legend* (DH, SM, RR, H)
*———. *Shock I, II, III, Shock Waves* (DH, SM)
———. *The Shrinking Man* (H)
*McCammon, Robert R. *Swan Song* (DH, SM, H)
*———. *Usher's Passing* (DH, SM)
*McDowell, Michael. *Blackwater* series (SM)
Morrell, David. *The Totem* (H)
*Oates, Joyce Carol. *Bellefleur*
———. *Night-Side* (DH)
Raven, Simon. *Doctors Wear Scarlet* (DH)
*Rice, Anne. *Interview with a Vampire* (DH, SM, RR)
*Russell, Ray. *Haunted Castles* (DH, SM, RR)
*Ryan, Alan. *Cast a Cold Eye* (SM)
*Saberhagen, Fred. *The Dracula Tape* (DH, SM)
*Samson, Joan. *The Auctioneer* (DH, SM)
Sarban. *The Sound of His Horn* (RR, H, MF)
*Siddons, Anne Rivers. *The House Next Door* (DH, SM)
Simmons, Dan. *Song of Kali* (H)
Singer, Isaac B. *Collected Stories* (DH, RR)
*Somtow, S. P. *Vampire Junction* (DH, SM)
Stallman, Robert. *The Orphan* (DH)
*Straub, Peter. *Ghost Story* (DH, SM, RR, H)
———. *Shadowland* (DH, RR)
*Strieber, Whitley. *The Wolfen* (DH, SM, H)
Sturgeon, Theodore. *Some of Your Blood* (RR)
Taylor, Bernard. *Sweetheart, Sweetheart* (H)
*Tessier, Thomas. *The Nightwalker* (DH, SM)
*Tryon, Thomas. *Harvest Home* (DH, SM, RR)
*———. *The Other* (DH, SM)
Tuttle, Lisa. *A Nest of Nightmares* (H)
Tutuola, Amos. *My Life in the Bush of Ghosts* (1954) (RR)
Updike, John. *The Witches of Eastwick* (RR, MF)
Wagner, Karl Edward. *In a Lonely Place* (H)
Wellman, Manly Wade. *John the Balladeer* (RR)
*Wheatley, Dennis. *They Used Dark Forces* (DH, SM)
Williamson, Chet. *Ash Wednesday* (DH)
Wilson, Colin. *The Philosopher,s Stone* (F)

Wilson, F. Paul. *The Keep* (H)
*Yarbro, Chelsea Quinn. *Hotel Transylvania* (DH, SM)

Anthologies

**The Arbor House Treasury of Horror and the Supernatural*, ed. by Bill Pronzini et al. (DH)
**The Architecture of Fear*, ed. by Kathryn Cramer and Peter D. Pautz (DH)
The Best Horror Stories from the Magazine of Fantasy and Science Fiction, ed. by Edward Ferman and Anne Jordan (DH)
**The Dark Descent*, ed. by David Hartwell (DH, SM)
**Dark Forces*, ed. by Kirby McCauley (DH, SM)
Dark Mind, Dark Heart, ed. by August Derleth (DH)
Dark Things, ed. by August Derleth (1971) (DH)
**Dodd, Mead Gallery of Horror*, ed. by Charles Grant
**Frights*, ed. by Kirby McCauley (DH, SM)
Ghost Books, ed. by Cynthia Asquith et al. (DH)
New Terrors, ed. by Ramsey Campbell (DH)
Night Chills, ed. by Kirby McCauley (DH)
**Night Visions*, ed. by Alan Ryan et al. (DH, SM)
Over the Edge, ed. by August Derleth (1964) (DH)
**Prime Evil*, ed. by Douglas Winter (DH, SM)
**Shadows*, ed. by Charles L. Grant
13 Short Horror Novels, ed. by Charles G. Waugh and Martin H. Greenberg (DH)
Travellers by Night, ed. by August Derleth (1967) (DH)
**Whispers*, ed. by Stuart Schiff (DH, SM)
The World Fantasy Awards, ed. by Gahan Wilson (DH)
**The Year's Best Horror Stories* (DH, SM)

General Reference Works

Bleiler, Everett F. *The Checklist of Science-Fiction and Supernatural Fiction* (RR)
Currey, L. W., comp. *Science Fiction and Fantasy Authors* (RR)
Reginald, R. *Science Fiction and Fantasy Literature* (RR)
*Tuck, Donald H. *The Encyclopedia of Science Fiction and Fantasy through 1968* (DH, SM, RR, DW)
Schlobin, Roger C. *The Literature of Fantasy* (RR)
*Brown, Charles N., and William G. Contento, comps. *Science Fiction in Print: 1985/Science Fiction, Fantasy, & Horror* (SM)
*Contento, William G. *Index to Science Fiction Anthologies and Collections* and supplement (DH, SM)
*Frank, Frederick S. *Guide to the Gothic*
*Frank, Frederick S. *The First Gothics* (DH, SM)
Ashley, Mike. *Who's Who in Horror and Fantasy Fiction* (RR)
*Bleiler, Everett F. *The Guide to Supernatural Fiction* (DH, SM)
*Bleiler, Everett F. *Supernatural Fiction Writers* (DH, SM, DW)
Pringle, David. *Modern Fantasy* (RR)
*Magill, Frank N. *Survey of Modern Fantasy Literature* (DH, SM, RR)

Nicholls, Peter. *The Science Fiction Encyclopedia* (RR, DW)
Rosenberg, Betty. *Genreflecting* (DW)
*Sullivan, Jack, ed. *The Penguin Encyclopedia of Horror and the Supernatural* (DH, SM)
Tymn, Marshall, et al. *Fantasy Literature* (RR, DW)
*Waggoner, Diana. *The Hills of Faraway* (SM, RR, DW)
Inge, M. Thomas, ed. *Handbook of American Popular Literature* (DW)
*Wolfe, Gary K. *Critical Terms for Science Fiction and Fantasy*

History and Criticism

Birkhead, Edith. *The Tale of Terror* (RR)
*Briggs, Julia. *Night Visitors*
*Daniels, Les. *Living in Fear*
*King, Stephen. *Danse Macabre* (RR)
*Lovecraft, H. P. *Supernatural Horror in Literature* (RR)
*Punter, David. *The Literature of Terror*
*Sullivan, Jack. *Elegant Nightmares* (RR)
*Bayer-Berenbaum, Linda. *The Gothic Imagination*
*Thompson, G. Richard, ed. *Romantic Gothic Tales 1790–1840*
*Carter, Margaret L. *Specter or Delusion?*
*Howells, Coral Ann. *Love, Mystery, and Misery*
*Kiely, Robert. *The Romantic Novel in England*
*Napier, Elizabeth R. *The Failure of Gothic*
Summers, Montague. *The Gothic Quest* (RR)
Varma, Devendra P. *The Gothic Flame* (RR)
*Fiedler, Leslie. *Love and Death in the American Novel*
*Weinberg, Robert. *The Weird Tales Story* (RR)
*Kawin, Bruce F. *The Mind of the Novel*
*Kayser, Wolfgang. *The Grotesque in Art and Literature*
*Riccardo, Martin V. *Vampires Unearthed*
*Senf, Carol A. *The Vampire in Nineteenth-Century English Literature*
*Waller, Gregory A. *The Living and the Undead*
*Büssing, Sabine. *Aliens in the Home*
*Heller, Terry. *The Delights of Terror*
*Jackson, Rosemary. *Fantasy: The Literature of Subversion*
*Todorov, Tzvetan. *The Fantastic* (RR)
Wilson, Colin. *The Strength to Dream* (RR)
*Frank, Frederick S. *Guide to the Gothic*
*Spector, Robert Donald. *The English Gothic*
Summers, Montague. *A Gothic Bibliography* (RR)

Author Studies

Castro, Albert D. *Portrait of Ambrose Bierce* (1929) (SM)
*Davidson, Cathy N. *The Experimental Fictions of Ambrose Bierce*
*Grenander, M. E. *Ambrose Bierce*
Neale, Walter. *Life of Ambrose Bierce* (1939) (SM)

*Ashley, Mike. *Algernon Blackwood* (RR)
*Parker, Patricia. *Charles Brockden Brown*
*McCrosson, Doris Ross. *Walter de la Mare*
*Mulkeen, Anne. *Wild Thyme, Winter Lightning*
*Edel, Leon, ed. *The Ghostly Tales of Henry James*
*Kimbrough, Robert, ed. *The Turn of the Screw*
*Cox, Michael. *M. R. James*
*Winter, Douglas E. *Stephen King*
*Magistrale, Tony. *Landscape of Fear*
*McCormack, W. J. *Sheridan Le Fanu and Victorian Ireland*
*Peck, Louis F. *A Life of Matthew G. Lewis*
*Joshi, S. T. *H. P. Lovecraft and Lovecraft Criticism*
*Lovecraft, Howard Phillips. *Selected Letters. Vols. 1–5*
*Joshi, S. T. *H. P. Lovecraft: Four Decades of Criticism*
*———. *H. P. Lovecraft*
*Lévy, Maurice. *Lovecraft: A Study in the Fantastic*
*Goldstone, Adrian, and Wesley Sweetser. *A Bibliography of Arthur Machen*
*Sweetser, Wesley D. *Arthur Machen*
*Lougy, Robert E. *Charles Robert Maturin*
*Buranelli, Vincent. *Edgar Allan Poe*
*Saliba, David R. *A Psychology of Fear*
*Carlson, Eric W., ed. *Critical Essays on Edgar Allan Poe*
*Regan, Robert. *Poe: A Collection of Critical Essays*
*Hyneman, Esther F. *Edgar Allan Poe: Annotated Bibliography of Books and Articles in English, 1827–1973*
*Wagenknecht, Edward. *Edgar Allan Poe: The Man behind the Legend*
*Lyles, W. H. *Mary Shelley: An Annotated Bibliography*
*Nitchie, Elizabeth. *Mary Shelley, Author of Frankenstein*
*Walling, William A. *Mary Shelley*
*Levine, George, and V. C. Knoepflmacher, eds. *The Endurance of Frankenstein*
*Thornburg, Mary K. Patterson. *The Monster in the Mirror*
*Tropp, Martin. *Mary Shelley's Monster: The Story of Frankenstein*
*Sidney-Fryer, Donald. *Emperor of Dreams: A Clark Ashton Smith Bibliography*
*Veeder, William, and Gordon Hirsch, eds. *Dr Jekyll and Mr Hyde after One Hundred Years*
*Carter, Margaret L., ed. *Dracula: The Vampire and the Critics*
*Roth, Phyllis A. *Bram Stoker*
*Winter, Douglas E. *Faces of Fear*

Horror in Film and TV

*Hardy, Phil. *Horror*
Lee, Walt. *Reference Guide to Fantastic Films* (RR)
Lentz, Harris M. *Science Fiction, Horror and Fantasy Film and Television Credits* (RR)
Willis, Donald. *Horror and Science Fiction Films* (RR)
**Cinefantastique*
*Clarens, Carlos. *An Illustrated History of the Horror Film*

*Nicholls, Peter. *The World of Fantastic Films*
*Eisner, Lotte. *The Haunted Screen*
*Waller, Gregory A. *The Living and the Undead*

Fantastic Art and Illustration

*Best, James J. *American Popular Illustration*
Dean, Martyn. *The Guide to Fantasy Art Techniques* (RR)
Haining, Peter. *Terror!* (RR)
*Johnson, Diana L. *Fantastic Illustration and Design in Britain, 1850-1930* (DW)
Larkin, David, ed. *The Fantastic Kingdom* (RR, DW)
*Meyer, Susan E. *A Treasury of the Great Children's Book Illustrators* (DW)
Page, Michael, and Robert Ingpen. *Encyclopedia of Things That Never Were* (DW)
*Peppin, Brigid, and Lucy Micklethwait. *Book Illustrators of the Twentieth Century*
Petaja, Emil, comp. and ed. *The Hannes Bok Memorial Showcase of Fantasy Art* (RR)
Rottensteiner, Franz. *The Fantasy Book* (RR, DW)
Summers, Ian, ed. *Tomorrow and Beyond* (RR)
*Weinberg, Robert. *A Bibliographical Dictionary of Science Fiction and Fantasy Artists* (RR)
*Reade, Brian. *Aubrey Beardsley*
Bok, Hannes. *Beauty and the Beasts* (DW)
*Bowe, Nicola G. *Harry Clarke*
*Coll, Joseph Clement. *The Magic Pen of Joseph Clement Coll*
*Spencer, Isobel. *Walter Crane* (DW)
*Greene, Douglas G., and Michael Patrick Hearn. *W. W. Denslow* (DW)
Dillon, Leo and Diane. *The Art of Leo and Diane Dillon* (DW)
*Gosling, Nigel. *Gustave Doré*
*Engen, Rodney. *Richard Doyle*
*White, Colin. *Edmund Dulac*
*Finlay, Virgil. *Virgil Finlay*, ed. by Don Grant (DW)
———. *The [Second-Fifth] Books of Virgil Finlay* (RR)
*Frazetta, Frank. *The Fantastic Art of Frank Frazetta* (DW)
———. *Frank Frazetta, Book One-Book Five* (RR)
Freas, Frank Kelly. *The Art of Science Fiction* (RR)
———. *The Astounding Fifties* (DW)
Gallardo, Gervasio. *The Fantastic World of Gervasio Gallardo* (DW)
*Gorey, Edward. *Amphigorey* (DW)
Lawson, Robert. *Robert Lawson, Illustrator* (DW)
*Nielsen, Kay. *Kay Nielson* (DW)
*Ludwig, Coy. *Maxfield Parrish* (RR, DW)
Gilmore, Maeve, and Shelagh Johnson. *Mervyn Peake* (DW)
**Howard Pyle* (DW)
*Gittings, Fred. *Arthur Rackham* (DW)
*Lanes, Selma G. *The Art of Maurice Sendak* (DW)

Skeeters, Paul W. *Sidney H. Sime* (RR)
Whelan, Michael. *Wonderworks* (RR)

Fantasy and Horror Magazines

**Avon Fantasy Reader*
**Beyond Fantasy Fiction*
Famous Fantastic Mysteries (DH, RR)
**Isaac Asimov's Science Fiction Magazine*
**The Magazine of Fantasy and Science Fiction* (RR)
**Rod Serling's "The Twilight Zone" Magazine*
**Unknown/Unknown Worlds* (RR)
Weirdbook (RR)
**Weird Tales* (RR)
**Whispers* (RR)
Amra (RR)
The Arkham Collector (RR)
Fantasy Commentator (1943-) (SM)
**Fantasy Newsletter/Review* (RR)
The Golden Atom (1939-43) (SM)
**Locus* (RR)
**Nyctalops*
The Phantagraph (ca. 1935-46) (SM)
Science Fiction Chronicle (RR)
*Tymn, Marshall B., and Mike Ashley. *Science Fiction, Fantasy and Weird Fiction Magazines*
*Weinberg, Robert. *The Weird Tales Story* (RR)
*Boyajian, Jerry, and Kenneth R. Johnson. *Index to the Science Fiction Magazines, 1977-84*
*Cockcroft, T. G. L. *Index to the Weird Fiction Magazines* (RR)
Day, Bradford M. *An Index of the Weird & Fantastica in Magazines* (1953) (SM)
*Day, Donald B. *Index to the Science Fiction Magazines, 1926-1950*
*Metcalf, Norm. *The Index to the Science Fiction Magazines, 1951-1965*
*NESFA. *Index to the Science Fiction Magazines, 1966-1970*
*———. *The NESFA Index*
*Parnell, Frank H., and Mike Ashley. *Monthly Terrors* (RR)

Awards

Works of popular literature are rarely considered for prestigious awards, which is why most of the following awards are unknown outside the narrow confines of category fiction readers. The numbers voting for the awards range from a presumably knowledgeable committee to a few hundred readers, often members of an organization which sponsors the award.

The listings which follow are selective and are largely limited to fantasy and horror literature and films (and some science fiction) or to individuals associated with these fields. See also the organizations listing for additional details about selected awards. Foreign-language awards are excluded from these listings. Consult the index for entry numbers of annotated books.

The American Book Award (TABA)

Sponsored by the Association of American Publishers, the awards are given for books written by U.S. authors and published by U.S. publishers. A successor to the National Book Awards (see following), they have been presented since 1980 in various categories. Science fiction was among the original categories but was eliminated when the categories were revised.

1983	Goldstein, Lisa. *The Red Magician* (best original paperback)
1980	Pohl, Frederik. *JEM* (best hardcover science fiction)
	Wangerin, Walter, Jr. *The Book of the Dun Cow*
	L'Engle, Madeleine. *A Swiftly Tilting Planet* (best children's paperback; reprint of 1978 edition; science fiction)

Balrog Award

Named for a Tolkien creature and awarded at various local conventions but voted on by anyone who requested a ballot. Both SF and fantasy were included. Year of award shown. Categories include novel, short story, collection, anthology, poet, artist, amateur publication, professional publication, amateur and professional achievement, SF film, fantasy film, occasionally a special judges award. The award is a statuette with a balrog crouching above the base. 1985 was the last year of the award.

1985	Brin, David. *The Practice Effect* (SF novel)
	Donaldson, Stephen. *Daughter of Regals* (collection)
	E.T. and *Starman* (SF films)
	Raiders of the Lost Ark (fantasy film)
1984	Martin, George R. R. *Armageddon Rag* (novel)
	Zelazny, Roger. *Unicorn Variations* (collection)
1983	Donaldson, Stephen. *The One Tree* (novel)
	Asprin, Robert, ed. *Storm Season* (anthology)
1982	Kurtz, Katherine. *Camber the Heretic* (novel)
	Asprin, Robert, ed. *Shadows of Sanctuary* (anthology)
	Forbidden Planet (SF film, 1956)
	King Kong (fantasy film, 1933)

British Fantasy Award

Presented by the British Fantasy Society (see organizations) and called the August Derleth Award from 1972 through 1976; given to the best novel of the preceding year. Derleth co-founded Arkham House, the oldest surviving fantastic fiction specialty publisher. From 1977 to date the Derleth award has been given only to the best novel; winners in other categories receive the British Fantasy Award. A scroll was presented from 1972 through 1975, a statuette thereafter. Categories have varied over the years and currently include novel, film, short fiction, small press publication, artist and a special award to an individual. Only winners in the first two categories are shown. Year of award shown.

1988 Campbell, Ramsey. *The Hungry Moon*
Hellraiser
1987 King, Stephen. *It*
Aliens
1986 Klein, T. E. D. *The Ceremonies*
A Nightmare on Elm Street
1985 Campbell, Ramsey. *Incarnate*
1984 Straub, Peter. *Floating Dragon*
Videodrome
1983 Wolfe, Gene. *The Sword of the Lictor*
Blade Runner
1982 King, Stephen. *Cujo*
Raiders of the Lost Ark
1981 Campbell, Ramsey. *To Wake the Dead*
The Empire Strikes Back
1980 Lee, Tanith. *Death's Master*
Alien
1979 Donaldson, Stephen. *The Chronicles of Thomas Covenant the Unbeliever* (trilogy)
Close Encounters of the Third Kind
1978 Anthony, Piers. *A Spell for Chameleon*
Carrie
1977 Dickson, Gordon R. *The Dragon and the George*
The Omen
1976 Moorcock, Michael. *The Hollow Lands*
Monty Python and the Holy Grail
1975 Moorcock, Michael. *The Sword and the Stallion*
The Exorcist
1974 Anderson, Poul. *Hrolf Kraki's Saga*
The Legend of Hell House
1973 Moorcock, Michael. *The King of the Swords*
Tales from the Crypt
1972 Moorcock, Michael. *Knight of the Swords*

Canadian Science Fiction and Fantasy Award

Called the Casper, this is presented at an annual Canadian national convention to English- or French-speaking Canadian writers. Trophies have varied over the years, and the number of categories has grown. Only English-language novels or individuals are shown.

1988 de Lint, Charles. *Jack the Giant Killer*
1987 Kay, Guy Gavriel. *The Wandering Fire*
1986 Merril, Judith. For lifetime editing
1985 Kernaghan, Eileen. *Songs from the Drowned Land*
1984 no award

1983	Merril, Judith. For lifetime contributions
1982	Gotlieb, Phyllis. *Judgment of Dragons* and lifetime achievement
1981	Wood, Susan. For lifetime contributions (posthumous)
1980	van Vogt, A. E. For lifetime contributions

Carnegie Medal

This is the British equivalent of the Newbery Medal (see following) and is awarded to the outstanding book for children written in English and published in the U.K. A Library Association committee selects from members' lists. Nonfiction as well as fiction is eligible. Only fantasy winners are listed.

1988	Price, Susan. *The Ghost Drum*
1985	Mahy, Margaret. *The Changeover*
1983	Mahy, Margaret. *The Haunting*
1974	Lively, Penelope. *The Ghost of Thomas Kempe*
1972	Adams, Richard. *Watership Down*
1969	Harris, Rosemary. *The Moon in the Cloud*
1968	Garner, Alan. *The Owl Service*
1963	Clarke, Pauline. *The Twelve and the Genii*
1962	Boston, Lucy Maria. *A Stranger at Green Knowe*
1959	Pearce, Philippa. *Tom's Midnight Garden*
1957	Lewis, C. S. *The Last Battle*
1956	Farjeon, Eleanor. *The Little Bookroom*
1953	Norton, Mary. *The Borrowers*
1948	De la Mare, Walter. *Collected Stories*
1946	Goudge, Elizabeth. *The Little White Horse*

Crawford Award

Named for William L. Crawford (1911–1984), who founded and edited one of the earliest semi-professional magazines (*Marvel Tales*, 1933), the award is given to the outstanding new writer of fantasy fiction. It is announced at the annual International Conference for the Fantastic in the Arts by the IAFA (see organizations).

1989	Michaela Roessner
1988	Elizabeth Marshall Thomas
1987	Judith Tarr
1986	Nancy Willard
1985	Charles de Lint

August Derleth Fantasy Award

Named for the co-founder of Arkham House, this award was presented annually by the British Fantasy Society (see above) in several categories, but since 1977 has been given only for the novel, with the BFS award given in all other categories. See under British Fantasy Society for awards.

J. Lloyd Eaton Award

Named after a San Francisco–area physician and SF collector, this is awarded to the author of the best work of criticism of SF or fantasy published two years prior to the year of the award shown below. Winners are selected by the curator of the Eaton Collection [12-4], George Slusser, and his conference co-directors. The award consists of a plaque.

1989	Alkon, Paul K. *Origins of Futuristic Fiction*
1988	Aldiss, Brian W. *Trillion Year Spree*
1987	Clareson, Thomas D. *Some Kind of Paradise*
	Stableford, Brian. *Scientific Romance in Britain*
1986	Hume, Kathryn. *Fantasy and Mimesis*
1985	Greenland, Colin. *The Entropy Exhibition*
1984	Huntington, John. *The Logic of Fantasy: H. G. Wells and Science Fiction*
1983	Rose, Mark. *Alien Encounters*
1982	Franklin, H. Bruce. *Robert A. Heinlein: America as Science Fiction*
1981	Wolfe, Gary K. *The Known and the Unknown*
1980	Brosnan, John. *Future Tense*
1979	Carter, Paul A. *The Creation of Tomorrow*

Gandalf Award

Named for a Tolkien creature like the Balrog, this is officially known as the Grand Master of Fantasy award. It was presented as part of the world SF convention (Hugo) award ceremonies for a writer's lifetime contribution to fantasy literature. Lin Carter (1930–1988) was the principal person responsible for selecting the winner and presenting the statuettes, which he personally paid for.

1981	C. L. Moore
1980	Ray Bradbury
1979	Ursula K. Le Guin
1978	Poul Anderson
1977	Andre Norton
1976	L. Sprague de Camp
1975	Fritz Leiber
1974	J. R. R. Tolkien

A special Gandalf award for book-length fantasy was given for two years:

1979	McCaffrey, Anne. *The White Dragon*
1978	Tolkien, J. R. R. *The Silmarillion*

IAFA Distinguished Scholarship Award

A panel of judges of the International Association for the Fantastic in the Arts (see organizations) presents this award at the annual ICFA meetings late each winter in Florida. A cash prize of $500 and a plaque are given the winner for total contributions to the study of fantastic literature or film.

1989 C. N. Manlove
1988 Kathryn Hume
1987 Brian Stableford
1986 Brian W. Aldiss

International Fantasy Award

Established by four British fans for a 1951 British convention and given to fiction and nonfiction judged of interest by a panel of American and British judges. Only fiction is listed.

1957 Tolkien, J. R. R. *Lord of the Rings*
1955 Pangborn, Edgar. *A Mirror for Observers*
1954 Sturgeon, Theodore. *More Than Human*
1953 Simak, Clifford D. *City*
1952 Collier, John. *Fancies and Goodnights*
1951 Stewart, George R. *Earth Abides*

Locus Award

Begun in 1971 and voted by readers. More than 1,000 people voted for the 1988 awards, many more than those voting for any other single award. Categories have varied over the years. Only best fantasy novel is listed. Year of award shown.

1989 Card, Orson Scott. *Red Prophet*
1988 Card, Orson Scott. *Seventh Son*
1987 Wolfe, Gene. *Soldier of the Mist*
1986 Zelazny, Roger. *Trumps of Doom*
1985 Heinlein, Robert. *Job: A Comedy of Justice*
1984 Bradley, Marion Zimmer. *The Mists of Avalon*
1983 Wolfe, Gene. *The Sword of the Lictor*
1982 Wolfe, Gene. *The Claw of the Conciliator*
1981 Silverberg, Robert. *Lord Valentine's Castle*
1980 McKillip, Patricia. *Harpist in the Wind*
1979 McIntyre, Vonda. *Dreamsnake*
1978 Tolkien, J. R. R. *The Silmarillion*
[Earlier awards were for SF novels only]

Approximately 600 *Locus* readers voted their all-time best fantasy novels, tabulated in the August 1987 issue. Here are the thirty-three titles in descending rank order:

Tolkien, J. R. R. *The Lord of the Rings*
Tolkien, J. R. R. *The Hobbit*
Le Guin, Ursula K. *A Wizard of Earthsea*
Wolfe, Gene. *The Shadow of the Torturer*
Beagle, Peter S. *The Last Unicorn*
White, T. H. *The Once and Future King*
Zelazny, Roger. *Nine Princes in Amber*

Donaldson, Stephen R. *The Chronicles of Thomas Covenant*
McCaffrey, Anne. *Dragonflight*
Crowley, John. *Little, Big*
Carroll, Lewis. *Alice's Adventures in Wonderland*
Peake, Mervyn. *The Gormenghast Trilogy*
McKillip, Patricia. *The Riddlemaster of Hed*
Pratt, Fletcher, and L. Sprague de Camp. *The Incomplete Enchanter*
Adams, Richard. *Watership Down*
Vance, Jack. *The Dying Earth*
Heinlein, Robert A. *Glory Road*
Anthony, Piers. *A Spell for Chameleon*
Stoker, Bram. *Dracula*
Baum, L. Frank. *The Wizard of Oz*
Myers, John Myers. *Silverlock*
Bradbury, Ray. *Something Wicked This Way Comes*
McCaffrey, Anne. *The White Dragon*
King, Stephen. *The Stand*
Silverberg, Robert. *Lord Valentine's Castle*
Lewis, C. S. The Chronicles of Narnia
King, Stephen. *The Shining*
Leiber, Fritz. *Conjure Wife*
Kurtz, Katherine. *Deryni Rising*
Eddison, E. R. *The Worm Ouroboros*
Norton, Andre. *Witch World*
King, Stephen. *Salem's Lot*
L'Engle, Madeleine. *A Wrinkle in Time*

Milford Award

Awarded by the Borgo Press its first year, this is now awarded at and by the Eaton conference each spring for lifetime contributions to the publishing and editing of SF and fantasy literature. The award consists of a plaque.

1989 Martin H. Greenberg
1988 Lloyd Arthur Eshbach
1987 H. L. Gold
1986 Harlan Ellison
1985 T. E. Dikty
1984 Edward L. Ferman
1983 Terry Carr
1982 Lester and Judy-Lynn del Rey
1981 Robert Silverberg
1980 Donald A. Wollheim

Mythopoeic Award

Chosen each year by volunteer members of the Mythopoeic Society (see organizations) and presented at the annual Mythcon. The Fantasy award is for a book-length work of fantasy in the spirit of the Inklings (Tolkien, Lewis, Williams) and published the preceding year. The Scholarship award is for a work on the Inklings published during the preceding three years. No awards were made in the years not listed.

Fantasy Award

1989	Bishop, Michael C. *Unicorn Mountain*
1988	Card, Orson Scott. *Seventh Son*
1987	Beagle, Peter. *The Folk of the Air*
1986	Hughart, Barry. *Bridge of Birds*
1985	Yolen, Jane. *Cards of Grief*
1984	Chant, Joy. *When Voiha Wakes*
1983	Kendall, Carol. *The Firelings*
1982	Crowley, John. *Little, Big*
1981	Tolkien, J. R. R. *Unfinished Tales*
1975	Anderson, Poul. *A Midsummer Tempest*
1974	Stewart, Mary. *The Hollow Hills*
1973	Walton, Evangeline. *The Song of Rhiannon*
1972	Chant, Joy. *Red Moon and Black Mountain*
1971	Stewart, Mary. *The Crystal Cave*

Scholarship Award

1989	Tolkien, Christopher. *Return of the Shadow*
1988	Christopher, Joe R. *C. S. Lewis*
1987	Purtill, Richard. *J. R. R. Tolkien: Myth, Morality and Religion*
1986	Cavaliero, Glen. *Charles Williams, Poet of Theology*
1985	Schakel, Peter J. *Reason and Imagination in C. S. Lewis*
1984	Shippey, T. A. *The Road to Middle-earth*
1983	Ford, Paul F. *Companion to Narnia*
1982	Carpenter, Humphrey. *The Inklings*
1976	West, Richard C. *Tolkien Criticism*
	Christopher, Joe R., and Joan K. Ostling. *C. S. Lewis: An Annotated Checklist*
	Glenn, Lois. *Charles W. S. Williams: A Checklist*
1974	Lindskoog, Kathryn. *C. S. Lewis, Mere Christian*
1973	Kocher, Paul H. *Master of Middle-earth*
1972	Walter Hooper
1971	C. S. Kilby, Mary McDermott Shideler

National Book Award

Begun in 1950 by U.S. book publishers, booksellers and book manufacturers, selections were made by members of the National Institute of Arts and Letters. Awards were given in a number of categories, including adult and children's fiction. Superseded by the American Book Award (see above).

1974	Cameron, Eleanor. *The Court of the Stone Children*
	Pynchon, Thomas. *Gravity's Rainbow*

1973 Le Guin, Ursula K. *The Farthest Shore*
Barth, John. *Chimera*
1971 Alexander, Lloyd. *The Marvelous Misadventures of Sebastian*
1969 Le Guin, Ursula K. *A Wizard of Earthsea*
1964 Updike, John. *The Centaur*

John Newbery Medal

Awarded since 1922 by the Children's Literature Division of the American Library Association for the most distinguished contribution to American literature for children. The bronze medal, given at the summer ALA conference, is named for John Newbery (1713-1767), a London bookseller who first conceived the idea of publishing books especially for children.

1985 McKinley, Robin. *The Hero and the Crown*
1983 McKinley, Robin. *The Blue Sword* (honor book, not winner)
1976 Cooper, Susan. *The Grey King*
1972 O'Brien, Robert C. *Mrs. Frisby and the Rats of NIMH*
1969 Alexander, Lloyd. *The High King*
1963 L'Engle, Madeleine. *A Wrinkle in Time*
1948 DuBois, William Pene. *The Twenty-One Balloons*
1947 Bailey, Carolyn Sherwin. *Miss Hickory*
1945 Lawson, Robert. *Rabbit Hill*
1923 Lofting, Hugh. *The Voyages of Doctor Dolittle*

Pilgrim Award

Judges from the Science Fiction Research Association (see organizations) select the winner, who is given the award at the summer convention. The award, a framed certificate, is given to the individual judged to have contributed most to the study of fantastic literature or film. The award is very similar to the IAFA Distinguished Scholarship award described above. The Pilgrim is named for the book by the first recipient, *Pilgrims through Space and Time.*

1989 Ursula K. Le Guin
1988 Joanna Russ
1987 Gary K. Wolfe
1986 George E. Slusser
1985 Samuel R. Delany
1984 Everett F. Bleiler
1983 H. Bruce Franklin
1982 Neil Barron
1981 Sam Moskowitz
1980 Peter Nicholls
1979 Darko Suvin
1978 Brian W. Aldiss
1977 Thomas D. Clareson
1976 James Gunn
1975 Damon Knight

1974	I. F. Clarke
1973	Jack Williamson
1972	Julius Kagarlitski
1971	Marjorie Hope Nicolson
1970	J. O. Bailey

Mrs. Ann Radcliffe Award

Given annually for outstanding achievements in television, film and literature. The award, a scroll and a medal, is presented at a dinner held each April in Los Angeles. This is one of three awards given by the Count Dracula Society (see organizations) to honor outstanding achievement in Gothic literature and film.

1988–77	Information unavailable
1976	Leonard Wolf
1975	Arthur Lenig
1974	Thomas Tryon
1973	Devendra P. Varma
1972	Henry Eichner
1971	Ray Bradbury
1970	Fritz Leiber
1969	Robert Bloch
1968	A. E. van Vogt
1967	August Derleth
1966	Forrest J. Ackerman
1965	Ray Bradbury
1964	Russell Kirk, Donald A. Reed
1963	Forrest J. Ackerman

Saturn Award

Presented annually by the Academy of Science Fiction, Fantasy and Horror Films (see organizations) in Los Angeles. Awards are given to both films and individuals. Members vote for the best films, and committees select the acting and technical awards. Only those for best fantasy and horror films, in that order, are shown, by year of film release.

1987	*The Princess Bride*
	The Lost Boys
1986	*The Boy Who Could Fly*
	The Fly
1985	*Ladyhawke*
	Fright Night
1984	*Ghostbusters*
	Gremlins
1983	*Something Wicked This Way Comes*
	The Dead Zone

1982	*The Dark Crystal*
	Poltergeist
1981	*Raiders of the Lost Ark*
	American Werewolf in London
1980	*Somewhere in Time*
	The Howling
1979	*The Muppet Movie*
	Dracula
1978	*Heaven Can Wait*
	The Wicker Man
1977	*Oh, God*
	The Little Girl Who Lives Down the Lane
1976	*The Holes*
	Burnt Offerings
1975	*Doc Savage*
	Young Frankenstein
1973	*The Golden Voyage of Sinbad*
	The Exorcist
1972	*Blacula* [no fantasy film award first year]

Bram Stoker Award

Awarded by the 300 members of the Horror Writers of America (see organizations) for the best novel, first novel, short fiction and nonfiction work, and life achievement. The award consists of a sculpture of a Gothic castle designed by Disney artist Steve Kirk. It is analogous to the Nebula Award given by the Science Fiction Writers of America. The award was first given in 1988.

1989	Harris, Thomas. *The Silence of the Lambs* (novel)
	Wilde, Kelley. *The Suiting* (first novel)
	Charles Beaumont: Selected Stories (collection)
	Ray Bradbury, Ronald Chetwyn-Hayes (life achievement)
1988	King, Stephen. *Misery* (novel)
	McCammon, Robert. *Swan Song* (novel)
	Cantrell, Lisa. *The Manse* (first novel)
	Ellison, Harlan. *The Essential Ellison* (collection)
	Spark, Muriel. *Mary Shelley* (nonfiction)
	Fritz Leiber, Clifford Simak, Frank Belknap Long (life achievement)

Reverend Dr. Montague Summers Memorial Award

Given annually for outstanding achievement in Gothic literature. The gold trophy is presented at the Mrs. Ann Radcliffe awards dinner in Los Angeles. Summers was one of the foremost scholars of Gothic literature (see chapter 8 of the companion guide to horror).

1988–77 Information unavailable

1976 Don Glut
1975 Raymond McNally
1974 E. B. Murray
1973 Bob Clampett
1972 William Crawford
1971 Devendra P. Varma
1970 Frank H. Cunningham
1969 Donald A. Reed

Twilight Zone Dimension Awards

A one-shot given for the best book and film as judged by readers of *Rod Serling's "The Twilight Zone" Magazine* [11-15]. The award was a curved lucite slab with a light in the base.

1985 King, Stephen, and Peter Straub. *The Talisman*
Indiana Jones and the Temple of Doom
Ghostbusters

Horace Walpole Gold Medal

Given annually for achievements in fantasy, horror, terror or science fiction literature or film. The gold medal is presented at the Mrs. Ann Radcliffe awards dinner in Los Angeles. The award is named for the author of one of the first and best known of all Gothic novels [F1-92, H1-108].

1988–77 Information unavailable
1976 Margaret L. Carter
1975 Devendra P. Varma
1974 W. S. Lewis, Manuel Weltman
1973 Radu Florescu, Raymond McNally
1972 Christopher Lee, Rod Serling
1971 George Pal, Barbara Steele
1970 Rouben Mamoulian, Devendra P. Varma
1969 Vincent Price
1968 Donald A. Reed

World Fantasy Award

Given each fall at the World Fantasy convention and selected by a panel of judges, the award is nicknamed the Howard after Howard Phillips Lovecraft and Robert E. Howard. The statuette by Gahan Wilson is modeled approximately on Lovecraft and is none too flattering. Only winning novels, anthologies/collections and recipients of Life Achievement awards are shown, in that order.

1988 Grimwood, Ken. *Replay*
Shepherd, Lucius. *The Jaguar Hunter*
Cramer, Kathryn, and Peter D. Pautz, eds. *The Architecture of Fear*

	Hartwell, David G., ed. *The Dark Descent*
	Everett F. Bleiler
1987	Süskind, Patrick. *Perfume*
	Tiptree, James, Jr. *Tales of the Quintana Roo*
	Jack Finney
1986	Simmons, Dan. *Song of Kali*
	McKinley, Robin, ed. *Imaginary Lands*
	Avram Davidson
1985	Holdstock, Robert. *Mythago Wood*
	Hughart, Barry. *Bridge of Birds*
	Barker, Clive. *Books of Blood*, vols. 1–3
	Theodore Sturgeon
1984	Ford, John M. *The Dragon Waiting*
	Davies, Robertson. *High Spirits*
	Jack Vance, L. Sprague de Camp, Richard Matheson, E. Hoffmann Price and Donald Wandrei
1983	Shea, Michael. *Nifft the Lean*
	Grant, Charles L., ed. *Nightmare Seasons*
	Roald Dahl
1982	Crowley, John. *Little, Big*
	Windling, Terry, and Mark Arnold, eds. *Elsewhere*
	Italo Calvino
1981	Wolfe, Gene. *The Shadow of the Torturer*
	McCauley, Kirby, ed. *Dark Forces*
	C. L. Moore
1980	Lynn, Elizabeth A. *Watchtower*
	Salmonson, Jessica Amanda, ed. *Amazons!*
	Manly Wade Wellman
1979	Moorcock, Michael. *Gloriana*
	Grant, Charles L., ed. *Shadows*
	Jorge Luis Borges
1978	Leiber, Fritz. *Our Lady of Darkness*
	Cave, Hugh B. *Murgunstrumm and Others*
	Frank Belknap Long
1977	Kotzwinkle, William. *Doctor Rat*
	McCauley, Kirby, ed. *Frights*
	Ray Bradbury
1976	Matheson, Richard. *Bid Time Return*
	Davidson, Avram. *The Enquiries of Dr. Esterhazy*
	Fritz Leiber
1975	McKillip, Patricia. *The Forgotten Beasts of Eld*
	Wellman, Manly Wade. *Worse Things Waiting*
	Robert Bloch

Organizations

Just as fans of science fiction have formed clubs and other organizations in support of their hobby, so have fans of fantasy/horror fiction and film. Some organizations have relatively broad interests, such as the British Fantasy Society; others are very specialized, such as those devoted to the works of a single writer. Membership ranges from a few dozen to a few hundred, and some exist more on paper than as active, functioning organizations. Because they are staffed exclusively by volunteers, responses to queries are often slow, as I discovered. Some organizations to which I wrote may exist, but repeated queries produced no responses, and I have therefore omitted them from this listing. If an organization would like to be listed in future editions of this guide, please write the editor (see list of contributors for address). Information in this section is current as of early 1989. Listed individuals will usually forward queries to their successors if they don't respond directly.

When an organization gives an award for a book or film or to an individual, such awards are listed in the awards section. Some publications are listed in chapter 11 and are cross-referenced by entry number. The date the organization was founded is given following its name.

Academy of Science Fiction, Fantasy and Horror Films. 1972
334 W. 54th St., Los Angeles, CA 90037. Donald A. Reed, President.

Founded to give recognition to fantastic cinema. Reed claims a membership of about 3,000, many of them associated with the film industry. The Saturn Awards are given annually for outstanding achievements. Some award ceremonies have been televised over independent stations. A monthly newsletter, *Saturn*, lists the many free screenings for members and contains related news.

Association of Science Fiction & Fantasy Artists. Late 1970s.
Ms. Robin Brunner, Box 55188, Indianapolis, IN 46205.

A professional organization of about 350 members, most of them illustrators/artists or art directors. The *ASFA Quarterly* has how-to articles, convention and gallery art show reports, interviews and market news. Awards called Chesleys (after Chesley Bonestell, 1888–1986) are given each year in a variety of categories.

British Fantasy Society. 1971.
Di Wathen, 15 Stanley Rd., Morden, Surrey, SM4 5DE, U.K.

Devoted to the study of fantasy and horror literature, film and art. Publishes the *British Fantasy Society Newsletter* (1971–), quarterly; *Winter Chills* (1986–), annually; and *Dark Horizons* [11-28] and occasional booklets about or by authors. Presents the BFS and August Derleth awards (see awards).

Count Dracula Society. 1962.
Donald A. Reed, 334 W. 54th St., Los Angeles, CA 90037.

An organization whose 500 members overlap those of the Academy of Science Fiction, Fantasy and Horror Films, also run by Reed. Three awards are given at a dinner each April: Mrs. Ann Radcliffe, a scroll and a medal, for outstanding achievements in TV, film or literature; Horace Walpole Gold Medal for achievement in fantasy, horror or SF literature or film; and the Dr. Montague Summers Memorial Award, a gold trophy, for outstanding achievement in Gothic literature.

F. Marion Crawford Memorial Society. 1977.
Saracinesca House, 3610 Meadowbrook Ave., Nashville, TN 37206.

Crawford (1854-1909) was a prolific writer, but it is mostly for his horror fiction, notably "The Upper Berth," that he is best known. The society publishes an annual, *The Romantist* [11-48].

August Derleth Society. 1977.
Dr. Frank Attix, 3333 Westview Lane, Madison, WI 53713.
The August Derleth Society Newsletter is published three to four times yearly. Derleth (1909-1971) was the co-founder of Arkham House (see chapter 5) and a prolific regional writer. The society gives an annual creative writing award to the University of Wisconsin English Department. The British Fantasy Society gives the August Derleth Award each year (see awards).

Horror Writers of America. 1987.
Lisa Cantrell, Secretary, Box 655, Madison, NC 27025.

A professional organization analogous to the Science Fiction Writers of America and, like the SFWA, not limited to American writers. Affiliate members receive all publications and services, including the right to recommend works for the Bram Stoker Awards, but may not vote for awards or officers. Active members must have sold short fiction, articles or filmscripts. The society's newsletter, *Transfusions*, six issues yearly, has member news, articles, market information, etc. Annual membership directory. An annual convention is held at which the Bram Stoker Awards for superior achievement are given (see awards).

International Association for the Fantastic in the Arts. 1982.
Olena H. Saciuk, Call Box 5100, Caja 2 Universidad Interamericano, San German, PR 00753.

Similar to the Science Fiction Research Association but with a broader scope. Members receive the quarterly *IAFA Newsletter*, an annual membership directory and the *Journal of the Fantastic in the Arts* [11-39]. An annual conference is held in Florida each winter at which the William L. Crawford Award, IAFA Distinguished Scholarship Award and (irregularly) the Robert A. Collins Service Award are given. Most members are academics, but academic affiliation is not a requirement for membership.

International Wizard of Oz Club. 1957.
Box 95, Kinderhook, IL 62345.

L. Frank Baum is still one of the most popular children's authors, mostly for the Oz books, of which he wrote fourteen. *The Baum Bugle* [11-26] is for the Oz enthusiast, and the club sells many Oz-related magazines, books and other items.

C. S. Lewis Societies

Lewis has had a devoted following for many years. The New York C. S. Lewis Society was founded in 1969 and has about 525 members. Its current secretary is Mrs. John Kirkpatrick, 466 Orange St., New Haven, CT 06511. A monthly bulletin, *CSL*, contains reports of meetings, short articles, essays, reviews, letters and notices. A monthly meeting is held in New York, open to all without charge. The Southern California C. S. Lewis Society, Box 533, Pasadena, CA 91102, publishes *The Lamp-Post*, a quarterly, and holds meetings in the southern California area.

The Mythopoeic Society. 1967.
Box 6707, Altadena, CA 91001.

Founded to study and discuss fantasy and mythopoeic literature, particularly the works of the Inklings—J. R. R. Tolkien, C. S. Lewis and Charles Williams. Publishes *Mythlore* [11-43], a quarterly; *Mythprint* (1980-), a monthly newsletter; and *The Mythic Circle* (1987-), a quarterly fiction and poetry magazine. The society sponsors the annual summer Mythopoeic conference, Mythcon, at which the Mythopoeic Awards are given, one for the best fantasy novel "in the spirit of the Inklings," the other for scholarship about the Inklings; see awards.

Although I did not receive direct replies from many Inkling-related societies, Joe R. Christopher, a scholar who is very knowledgeable in this area, supplied some information which I summarize here for anyone interested. Unrelated to the Mythopoeic Society but with similar interests is The Inner Ring: The Mythopoeic Literature Society of Australia, which publishes a quarterly, *The Ring Bearer*; write Managing Editor, *The Ring Bearer*, University of Queensland, St. Lucia, Queensland 4068, Australia.

A somewhat fan-oriented group is the American Tolkien Society, Box 373, Highland, MI 48031-0373, which publishes a quarterly journal, *Minas Tirith Evening-Star*. This is not related to the Tolkien Society of America, which merged with the Mythopoeic Society. Charles Williams enthusiasts may wish to investigate The Charles Williams Society, Richard Wallis, Treasurer, 6 Matlock Ct., Kensington Park Rd., London W11 3BS, which issues a quarterly newsletter and apparently has an American branch. The Tolkien Society appears to be located at 12 Madeley Rd., Earling, London W5 2LH. It publishes a newsletter, *Amon Hen*, a journal, *Mallorn*, and a linguistic journal. Local British clubs, called "smials," often issue their own fan publications.

The Mervyn Peake Society. 1975.
John Watney, Flat 36, 5 Elm Park Gardens, London SW10 9QQ.

Peake is best known for his remarkable Gormenghast trilogy [3-285]. A skilled artist, he illustrated many books, including a number of his own. The society publishes the *Mervyn Peake Newsletter* about three times yearly and the annual *Mervyn Peake Review* [11-46].

Science Fiction Research Association. 1970.
Thomas J. Remington, Treasurer, English Department, University of Northern Iowa, Cedar Falls, IA 50614.

The oldest organization devoted to the study and teaching of fantastic literature and film, its members include academics, editors, publishers, libraries and interested readers. The *SFRA Newsletter*, ten issues yearly, contains reviews, announcements of forthcoming books, work in progress, organization news, etc. Members also receive *Extrapolation* (quarterly) and *Science-Fiction Studies* (three issues yearly) and an annual membership directory. The Pilgrim Award for lifetime contribution to the study of fantastic literature (see awards) is presented at an annual summer conference.

Science Fiction Writers of America. 1965.
Peter D. Pautz, Box 4236, West Columbia, SC 29171.

Although the majority of the 1,035 members are probably more interested in

SF than in fantasy or horror fiction, many authors write both. Like the recently founded Horror Writers of America, both affiliate and active memberships are available. Members receive the quarterly *SFWA Bulletin* (market reports, how-to articles, etc.), the bi-monthly *SFWA Forum* (for active members only; information on markets, contracts, etc.) and an annual directory, which lists the agents of the members. At the annual conventions, usually held on either the east or west coast, the Nebula Awards are presented. Because most awards are for SF, they are not listed in this guide.

Series

Listed here are series of three or more books, at least one of which is annotated in this guide. Some books require or at least benefit from a knowledge of preceding books in the series. Books are therefore listed in their internal reading sequence or by year of publication if the sequence is unimportant. Included here are prequels, works "describing earlier events involving characters or settings from a previous work" (Wolfe, [6-40]). Series may be organized around a continuing character (Don Sebastian), a place (Oxrun Station) or an implied world (Cthulhu), with the last inspiring fiction by many other authors, an example of the "shared world" which became popular in the 1980s.

Following the author listing is an index by keywords of the series title cross-referenced to the author. Thus, Chronicles of the Vampires is also listed as Vampires, Chronicles of the. Series titles are sometimes not fixed; I have therefore used the "standard" title, if any, or the publisher's title. Most series are in the fantasy guide; relatively few are in this horror guide. Consult the index for entry numbers.

Andrews, V. C. Dollanganger Family
Flowers in the Attic, 1979
Petals in the Wind, 1980
If There Be Thorns, 1981
Seeds of Yesterday, 1984
Garden of Shadows, 1987

Burke, John. Dr. Alexander Caspian
The Devil's Footsteps, 1976
The Black Charade, 1977
Ladygrove, 1978

Daniels, Les. Don Sebastian
The Silver Skull, 1979
Citizen Vampire, 1981
The Black Castle, 1978
Yellow Fog, 1986

Eulo, Ken. Brownstone
The Brownstone, 1980
The Bloodstone, 1981
The Deathstone, 1982

Grant, Charles L. Oxrun Station
The Hour of the Oxrun Dead, 1977

The Sound of Midnight, 1978
The Last Call of Mourning, 1979
The Grave, 1981
A Glow of Candles, 1981*
Tales from the Nightside, 1981*
Nightmare Seasons, 1982*
The Bloodwind, 1982
The Soft Whisper of the Dead, 1982
The Dark Cry of the Moon, 1986
The Long Night of the Grave, 1986
The Orchard, 1986

*Short fiction, not all set in Oxrun Station

Herbert, James. Rats
The Rats, 1974
Lair, 1979
Domain, 1984
Lovecraft, H. P. Cthulhu Mythos

Many of Lovecraft's tales describe a pantheon of "monsters" which collectively have come to be called the Cthulhu Mythos, although the god Cthulhu appears only in "The Call of Cthulhu" (1926, published 1928). For an explanation of this unholy pantheon see Shreffler [8-71], chapter 4. Listed below is a selection of books in which the mythos is explicit. See also the studies of Lovecraft in chapter 8 and Robert E. Weinberg's *A Reader's Guide to the Cthulhu Mythos* (1983). See index for annotated titles.

Lovecraft, H. P. *The Outsider and Others*, 1939
———. *Beyond the Wall of Sleep*, 1943
———, and August Derleth. *The Lurker at the Threshold*, 1945
Bloch, Robert. *The Opener of the Way*, 1945
Wandrei, Donald. *The Web of Easter Island*, 1948
Derleth, August. *The Mask of Cthulhu*, 1958
Derleth, August. *The Trail of Cthulhu*, 1962
Wilson, Colin. *The Mind Parasites*, 1967
———. *The Philosopher's Stone*, 1969
Chappell, Fred. *Dagon*, 1968
Derleth, August, ed. *Tales of the Cthulhu Mythos*, 1969
Carter, Lin, ed. *The Spawn of Cthulhu*, 1971
Lumley, Brian. *The Burrowers Beneath*, 1974
Bloch, Robert. *Strange Eons*, 1978
Campbell, Ramsey, ed. *New Tales of the Cthulhu Mythos*, 1980
Shea, Michael. *The Color out of Time*, 1984
Campbell, Ramsey. *Cold Print*, 1985

Lumley, Brian. Titus Crow
The Burrowers Beneath, 1974
The Transition of Titus Crow, 1975
The Clock of Dreams, 1978
Spawn of the Winds, 1978

In the Moons of Borea, 1979
The Compleat Crow, 1987
McDowell, Michael. Blackwater
The Flood, 1983
The Levee, 1983
The House, 1983
The War, 1983
The Fortune, 1983
Rain, 1983
Rice, Anne. Chronicles of the Vampires
Interview with a Vampire, 1976
The Vampire Lestat, 1985
The Queen of the Damned, 1988
Saberhagen, Fred. Dracula
The Dracula Tape, 1975
The Holmes-Dracula File, 1978
An Old Friend of the Family, 1979
Thorn, 1980
Dominion, 1982
Saxon, Peter. Guardians
The Guardians, 1967
The Curse of Rathlaw, 1968
Through the Dark Curtain, 1968
Dark Ways to Death, 1968
The Killing Bone, 1969
The Haunting of Alan Mais, 1969
The Vampires of Finisterre, 1970
Stallman, Robert. Book of the Beast
The Orphan, 1980
The Captive, 1981
The Beast, 1982
Tremayne, Peter. Dracula
Dracula Unborn, 1977
The Revenge of Dracula, 1978
Dracula, My Love, 1980
Wheatley, Dennis. Duke de Richleau
The Forbidden Territory , 1933
The Devil Rides Out, 1935
The Golden Spaniard, 1938
Three Inquisitive People, 1940
Strange Conflict, 1941
Codeword—Golden Fleece, 1946
The Second Seal, 1950
The Prisoner in the Mask, 1957
Vendetta in Spain, 1961
Dangerous Inheritance, 1965
Gateway to Hell, 1970

Wright, T. M. Children of the Earth
Strange Seed, 1978
Nursery Tale, 1982
The Children of the Island, 1983
Yarbro, Chelsea Quinn. Saint-Germain
Hotel Transylvania, 1978
The Palace, 1979
Blood Games, 1980
Path of the Eclipse, 1981
Tempting Fate, 1982
The Saint-Germain Chronicles, 1983

Series Index

Author Index

Annotations in this index are cited by entry numbers (1-26, 3-216); introductions are cited by page numbers, which are italicized and lack a hyphen. In order to make this index as useful as possible, and keep it to a reasonable length, only substantive references (defined as having some descriptive or critical comment) to authors, editors, or illustrators are included. References are to books by or about authors, editors, or illustrators, with books by the person normally cited first. Author materials mentioned in chapter 12, Library Collections, are indexed. Cross-references from real names to pseudonyms are included.

Certain types of material were not indexed: (1) references to authors with little or no substantive content, e.g., simple mentions of stories in a collection or anthology; (2) mentions of authors in the compare and contrast statements; (3) passing references to authors as subjects, such as in essay collections or in studies which treat a number of authors (such secondary literature is indexed by Hall [6-10] and Tymn and Schlobin [6-11], by Morrison in his introduction to chapter 8, and in the sources whose abbreviations follow About:, as explained in the preface); (4) translators; (5) authors of books listed only in chapter 13; (6) authors of short fiction in collections or anthologies. For the last, consult Bleiler [6-19], Contento [6-7], Schlobin [6-5], and Brown and Contento [6-6], which collectively index the contents of several thousand anthologies and collections.

Arrangement is letter by letter, ignoring spaces.

Title Index

Annotations in this index are cited by entry numbers (1-26, 3-216); introductions are cited by page numbers, which are italicized and lack a hyphen. In order to make this index as useful as possible, and keep it to a reasonable length, only substantive references (defined as having some descriptive or critical comment) to authors, editors, or illustrators are included. References are to books by or about authors, editors, or illustrators, with books by the person normally cited first. Author materials mentioned in chapter 12, Library Collections, are indexed. Cross-references from real names to pseudonyms are included.

Certain types of material were not indexed: (1) references to authors with little or no substantive content, e.g., simple mentions of stories in a collection or anthology; (2) mentions of authors in the compare and contrast statements; (3) passing references to authors as subjects, such as in essay collections or in studies which treat a number of authors (such secondary literature is indexed by Hall [6-10] and Tymn and Schlobin [6-11], by Morrison in his introduction to chapter 8, and in the sources whose abbreviations follow About:, as explained in the preface); (4) translators; (5) authors of books listed only in chapter 13; (6) authors of short fiction in collections or anthologies. For the last, consult Bleiler [6-19], Contento [6-7], Schlobin [6-5], and Brown and Contento [6-6], which collectively index the contents of several thousand anthologies and collections.

Arrangement is letter by letter, ignoring spaces.

Theme Index

For most books annotated in the bibliographies there is a compare or contrast statement which refers to other books with similar themes, structures, narrative devices, etc. This thematic/subject index permits readers to see on a larger scale the recurrent themes in fantasy or horror fiction. It is considerably more specific and detailed than the six rough groupings in *A Reader's Guide to Fantasy* [6-29], or the classified scheme used by Waggoner [6-34] but is far less detailed than the "index of motifs and story types" in Bleiler [6-19], from which this list was partially derived. Other sources consulted include Bleiler's *Checklist* [6-1] and the Magill survey [6-24]. See also the fiction chapters introductory essays for additional discussion of selected themes. Chapter 1 is not indexed here. See the discussion of types of Gothic fiction on pages 8–11.

After selected contributors had reviewed this list for its usefulness and precision, they then considered each annotated novel (collections, anthologies and nonfiction were not indexed unless they were thematically organized). If they judged a book could usefully be indexed/characterized by one to three of the following terms (not all books were so judged), they posted the entry number after the term. The following index represents their collective judgments. In this index only, item numbers are grouped by chapter and abbreviated (e.g., the citation "3-178; 4-30, 97" should be read as "3-178, 4-30, 4-97"). SA = see also.